ARTHUR MILLER

TMT

Christopher Bigsby explores the entirety of Arthur Miller's work, including plays, poetry, fiction and films, in this comprehensive and stimulating study. Drawing on interviews conducted over the last twenty years, on unique rehearsal material and research archives, he paints a compelling picture of how Miller's works were influenced by and created in the light of events of the twentieth and twenty-first centuries. This is an enjoyable insight into a great playwright that will interest both theatregoers and students of modern drama.

CHRISTOPHER BIGSBY is Professor of American Studies at the University of East Anglia and has published more than thirty books covering American theatre, popular culture and British drama, including *Modern American Drama* (Cambridge 1992) and *Contemporary American Playwrights* (Cambridge 1999). He is co-editor, with Don Wilmeth, of *The Cambridge History of American Theatre*, which received the Barnard Hewitt Award for Outstanding Reseach from the American Society for Theatre Research. He is also an award-winning novelist and regular radio and television broadcaster.

ARTHUR MILLER

A Critical Study

CHRISTOPHER BIGSBY

CAMBRIDGE
UNIVERSITY PRESS

PUBLISHED BY THE PRESS SYNDICATE OF THE UNIVERSITY OF CAMBRIDGE
The Pitt Building, Trumpington Street, Cambridge, United Kingdom

CAMBRIDGE UNIVERSITY PRESS
The Edinburgh Building, Cambridge, CB2 2RU, UK
40 West 20th Street, New York, NY 10011–4211, USA
477 Williamstown Road, Port Melbourne, VIC 3207, Australia
Ruiz de Alarcón 13, 28014 Madrid, Spain
Dock House, The Waterfront, Cape Town 8001, South Africa

http://www.cambridge.org

First published 2005

Printed in the United Kingdom at the University Press, Cambridge

Typeface Adobe Minion 10/12 pt.   *System* LATEX 2$_\varepsilon$ [TB]

A catalogue record for this book is available from the British Library

Library of Congress Cataloguing in Publication data
Bigsby, C. W. E.
Arthur Miller: A Critical Study / by Christopher Bigsby.
p.   cm.
Includes bibliographical references and index.
ISBN 0 521 84416 9 – ISBN 0 521 60553 9 (pbk)
1. Miller, Arthur, 1915 – Criticism and interpretation.   I. Title.
PS3525.I5156Z5445   2004
812′.52 – dc22
[B]   2004045813

ISBN 0 521 84416 9 hardback
ISBN 0 521 60553 9 paperback

For Ewan, with love and pride

CONTENTS

Crucible is so hard explore Proctor's religon

ACKNOWLEDGEMENTS

In writing this book I have drawn on introductions which I first wrote for Penguin Books. A version of the chapter on Arthur Miller and the Holocaust (chapter 21) was first delivered as the Morgan Lecture at Dickinson University. The chapter on *Resurrection Blues* is based on a programme note I wrote for the play's world premiere at the Guthrie Theatre. I have also drawn on lectures delivered to the Arthur Miller Society.

No one writes a book in a void. I have benefited from the work of many scholars and friends. The list is long but includes Julia Bolus, Steven R. Centola, Jane Dominik, Stephen Marino, Brenda Murphy and Matthew Roudané. I would also wish to acknowledge the assistance of the staff at the Harry Ransom Center of the University of Texas at Austin and the staff of the University of Michigan libraries.

I would also like to thank the Arts and Humanities Research Board for their assistance.

NOTE ON THE TEXT

Throughout the text references in parenthesis to Arthur Miller's autobiography *Timebends* (London, 1987) appear as *T.* followed by page numbers.

Any unsourced interview material comes from interviews with Arthur Miller by the author over a period of years.

INTRODUCTION

Henrik Ibsen's writing career stretched over forty-seven years, Strindberg's over thirty-seven. Chekhov's lasted twenty years. In 2002, sixty-six years had passed between Arthur Miller's *No Villain*, a university play which won two prizes, and *Resurrection Blues*, voted best new play first produced outside New York. Two years on, in 2004, came *Finishing the Picture*.

Longevity, of course, is no virtue, unless you happen to be a Galapagos turtle. In Miller's case, however, nearly seventy years as a writer had seen a succession of plays that served to define the moral, social and political realities of twentieth- and then twenty-first-century life. At the turn of the millennium, British playwrights, actors, directors, reviewers and critics voted him the most significant playwright of the twentieth century with two of his plays (*Death of a Salesman* and *The Crucible*) in their top ten.

Curiously, he had fallen out of favour in his native America for the previous thirty years. His new plays were not well received, even as his classic plays of the 1940s and 50s were taught in schools and universities and regularly revived. Elsewhere in the world, however, his plays of the 1970s, 80s and 90s found a ready audience. In 1994, *Broken Glass*, his play set at the time of Kristallnacht, was poorly received in New York while winning the Olivier Award, in Britain, as best play of the year.

In part, this is a story of poor productions in America, in part of those drawn to what seemed to them more innovative theatrical figures: European absurdists, the American avant-garde. Wedded to a notion of Miller as an incorrigible realist, an approach laid down early in his career when *All My Sons* was taken as paradigmatic, and when he was attacked by many of those he characterised as Trotskyites, critics failed to acknowledge the radicalism of his theatre. He was regarded by some as deeply unfashionable, at odds with the times. Robert Brustein, Richard Gilman, Philip Rahv, John Simon dismissed his new plays as, in the 1940s, Mary McCarthy, Eric Bentley and Eleanor Clarke had rejected his earlier ones.

His concern with the past and its connection with the present, the basis of a moral logic which tied action to consequence, had always seemed a counter-current to American presumptions. This, after all, was a country which leaned into the future, regarded history, in Henry Ford's words, as bunk and proposed as its central contract with the individual the possibility of beginning again. Miller spoke of the tongue of the past being torn from the throats of American writers. For his part, he felt the pressure of history as something more than a burden to be relinquished, a sepia print transforming lived experience into mere nostalgia. He addressed it not simply because it contained lessons best not disregarded but because we contain the past while private truths reach out into a public world.

For his part, later in his career, he was apt to set his plays in the 1930s, in Europe or South America, as once he had set them in the seventeenth century and in Mexico. He was prone to insist on the individual's responsibility for his or her own actions, and for the state of the culture, even in the 1970s and 80s when the very concept of society, with its mutual interdependencies, was being challenged and self-interest promoted as a virtue. Once he had been drawn to Marxism, seeing in that the political embodiment of his moral beliefs. When that no longer seemed credible, destroyed by those who cloaked themselves in a politics so manifestly at odds with their actions, he was left with beliefs now rooted in nothing more profound than an assertion that individual and society exist in a symbiotic relationship and that the acknowledgement of that fact is central to a moral life.

A Jewish atheist, he felt constrained to reinvent the God in whom he did not believe by invoking a native existentialism. We are, he insisted, what we do and what we do has implications for the social world we inhabit and which in turn is shaped by those who will it into being. It followed that he rejected total-itarianism but also fashionable ideas of the absurd. Humankind, he insisted, was neither the mere product of circumstance, of class, of a history seen as independent of human will, nor a cosmic victim, expression of metaphysical irony. Despite what he saw as the casual games-playing of postmodern theo-rists, nor was he willing to regard individual character as mere construction or authorship as a chimera.

As a consequence, for some he seemed the product of another age who had never matured to understand the futility of human endeavour or the writer's duty to deconstruct his or her art. In Europe, however, where the past is never dead, where history lives on the pulse and totalitarianism has either been centre-stage or standing in the wings awaiting its cue, Miller's seems in every way a modern voice. He is Cato, alive to the possibility of apocalypse, even atheistic Jews being aware of how thin the crust of civilisation can be. But he is also a man who grants integrity to the individual will and imagination, who under-stands the power and limitations of love. He stages the lives of those baffled by an existence whose meaning frequently evades them but whose struggle to understand and prevail is one of the justifications for an art which itself seeks form in seeming chaos.

Miller is Jewish. He was raised in a family that had carried its faith across an ocean, even if the full intensity of that faith diminished under the impact of American pragmatism. His grandfather, once the necessary compromises of business had been set aside (he worked on the Sabbath), became a mainstay of the local synagogue. Miller's parents were less intense in their convictions, adopting new values along (in his father's case) with a new language. They still performed the rituals, respected the traditions, but they were intent on consolidating a new identity which would see them accepted by those who lived their lives beyond the carefully drawn, if invisible, lines which defined their neighbourhood.

As a young boy, Miller felt excluded from such mysteries (writing about his sense of exclusion years later in a short story in which he recaptured the sense of bafflement he felt at alone being granted immunity from religious imperatives), as if he were denied access to necessary truths. Inducted into the faith, he duly mastered the Hebrew necessary for his bar mitzvah at the age of thirteen. This was a rite of passage less elaborate than that performed by his older brother, Kermit, who was required to be fluent in more than one language, a piece of showmanship which had less to do with religion than pride on the part of an upwardly mobile family anxious to underline its new status. He even found himself in a synagogue one afternoon, looking for some secret that might give shape to the swirl of feelings which assailed him, only to be met by the amused smiles of the men he found there, secure in their mysterious faith and disturbing equanimity.

In time, however, other commitments would lead a teenage Miller away from shul. Introduced to Marxism, which saw religion as an opiate, he wondered what would become of the ornate buildings that were a testament to a faith now revealed as factitious and retrogressive and, indeed, as the Depression deepened so congregations did begin to drift away as if something more than an economy was in disarray. When he married he did so outside the faith, though his Catholic first wife no more believed in her religion than he did in his. They were both revolutionaries alert to the collapse of old forms and thrilled to be present at the birth of new ones.

Yet there was more to Judaism than its spiritual core. It spoke its own history, expressed values and attitudes that lived in the blood, having come down through the centuries as so many stories, as a rhythm of confidence and despair. Later, he would declare his commitment to a Jewish culture while renouncing the metaphysical engine that powered it, simultaneously announcing his own self-exile and continued membership in the tribe. In a sense it was his own version of that balancing act Jews had always had to perform as they were simultaneously welcomed and rejected, located themselves as part of a wider culture yet always apart, afraid of the very assimilation which on another level they so desired.

There were those who hid their origins, changed their names (as Miller was himself accused of doing, not least by the FBI), slid into the mainstream by wearing a mask, learning to shape themselves to what they took to be a desirable form. There were others who laid claim to this shape-shifting culture that was America by offering themselves as interpreters, the so-called New York Intellectuals, from Queens and Brooklyn, who set out to explain America to itself and in so doing gave a different sound to the culture. They wrote histories of American literature, became commentators on a changing world, simultaneously evidence of what they described.

By degrees something of the tone of such writers, fiercely and self-advertisingly intelligent, often ironic and humorous, began to seem simply that of modern America. Jewish–American writers became not so much a sub-category as exemplary figures writing out of a sense of insecurity that was by now so general that, paradoxically, they became secure in their role. They spoke of alienation, angst, a crisis of identity, but these were precisely the concerns of those who had emerged from the Depression into an atomic age and who watched as the old certainties seemed to dissolve in an affluent but uncertain age.

Miller, however, was never part of this group and was seldom considered as a Jewish writer. In the many books and university courses which seized on this figure, he was a notable absence. When the New York Intellectuals based themselves in City College in the 1930s, he was up in Michigan, struggling to survive, financially and academically. When he returned he remained in the basement of his family home in Brooklyn or a rented apartment striving to break through into the theatre or churning out radio scripts in order to buy time for what he still believed his real work.

There would, indeed, be those who accused him of wilful defection from a cause he never embraced and even an identity he never denied. Why, they asked, were his self-evidently Jewish characters not acknowledged as such, as though the Jew could not be legitimately proposed as a root for the universal? In large part such questions betoken ignorance of the number of his plays, produced and unproduced, from 1935 to the mid-1990s, which did feature Jewish characters, but beyond that was the implication that he was in flight not only from faith (in truth abandoned by many of the New York Intellectuals) but from his own identity. It is an odd charge to level at the man who wrote *Focus*, one of the first novels about anti-Semitism in America, as it is at the man who, in *After the Fall, Incident at Vichy, Playing for Time* and *Broken Glass* dealt with the Holocaust and its prelude to a degree that no other American playwright has done, and few other playwrights anywhere.

After the war, a curious silence had fallen with respect to an experience that stunned the mind. Those who had lived through the Holocaust at first hand could find no language adequate to express it. It was an experience, it was felt by some, that could only be demeaned by utterance. It was something more than the silence of the grave because it contained a truth about human possibilities which seemed to lead nowhere but such a silence. There was also a sense of shame, undeserved, irrational, that a people could be thought to have conspired in their own extinction as though submitting to a historic fate for which past suffering had suddenly seemed mere prelude.

For Miller, it would be marriage to his third wife, the Magnum photographer Ingeborg Morath, that gave it a concrete reality and hence a legitimate metaphoric force. Together, they visited a concentration camp – she, an Austrian, who as a child and young woman had rebelled against the Nazis but nonetheless felt the burden of genocide; he, Jewish, feeling a connection, always there but never previously so immediate and direct. The themes of his work – betrayal, denial, power – remained the same but were now attached to a history, always known, felt, but now finding dramatic form. As a writer he had always insisted on an organic connection between past and present but here was a past that had resisted understanding. Only when he had written *After the Fall* and *Incident at Vichy* could he write *The Price* in which a Jew is a comic figure and the figure of the survivor as paradigm moves to centre-stage.

Miller himself was born into a wealthy immigrant family. His father, like his mother's parents, came from Poland. America was promise and possibility, liberation from the past. They had journeyed in hope and hope seemed justified. They had worked their way up from a Lower East Side tenement to an eleven-room apartment on the southern tip of Harlem, an apartment that looked out over Central Park. They had a chauffeur-driven car, a Polish maid and a summer cottage on Long Island.

What Henry Luce would later call the American century was well under way. There was even a train called *The Twentieth Century* and those who climbed on board knew that they were doing more than take a train trip. America was rich and getting richer. High above the city, on the underside of clouds, advertisements, projected from the rooftops, boasted of the products of a consumer culture in which consumption seemed a national virtue. If the Jews had believed themselves God's chosen people, against the evidence of centuries of persecution, Americans knew themselves to be chosen, for were they not surrounded by the proof? America was the very image of the modern. The world had begun to dance to its music, to be entranced by the images produced by a film industry which was itself a product of immigrant Jews. The wanderers of the world had found a home.

Then, in October 1929, the foundations began to slip. The clock stopped and the American century went into free fall. And among its many victims was the Miller family. Isadore Miller, who employed around eight hundred people in his women's coat company, had learned the false wisdom of the age. He had invested in the stock market and had borrowed to do so. There was so much more money to be made in stocks and shares than manufacturing that only a fool would choose not to invest. Now someone had thrown a handful of grit in the machine.

The family lost, if not quite everything, then most of what they owned. The car, the maid, the country cottage went, along with Augusta Miller's jewels, sold by her young son Arthur who took them to the pawnbrokers. The eleven-room rented apartment went, too, and they moved across the bridge to Brooklyn. Central Park was exchanged for East Third Street, the vast apartment for a utility home. Family life suddenly became strained. Miller's grandfather moved in with them and the fourteen-year-old found himself sharing a bedroom with a man known contemptuously as 'the lodger' and whose authoritarian ways were the source of further friction. Isadore Miller tried, out of a sense of honour, to pay off his creditors, and to start again, but each year millions more were without work.

In one sense, a young Arthur Miller was unfazed by the move. Brooklyn, still semi-rural, offered a sense of liberation. His main interests were football and track. He could now ride the El to Coney Island for the fishing. But options were closing down. When he graduated from high school none of the family attended the ceremony. Though he was hardly academic, like Biff Loman flunking maths, he had assumed he would move on to university. He even took catalogues home to discuss the options, only now realising that there was no money available. What followed were two years in which he earned money working in an auto-parts company, an experience he would later memorialise in *A Memory of Two Mondays*.

Finally, in 1934, he made his way from Brooklyn to Michigan where the university had agreed to take him on, effectively on probation since his grades would not normally have won him a place. In that first year he dedicated himself to his work and to writing for the *Michigan Daily*, the student newspaper. Though he had little time for the various political groups on campus, he did join the peace movement, signing the so-called Oxford Pledge in which he undertook not to take part in any future war. He had, to be sure, already been converted to Marxism, as a result of a kerbside conversation back in Brooklyn and now sent letters home alternately asking for money and proudly confessing to his new faith in a future to be transformed by radical thought and action. His mother sent the money and waited out what she must have hoped would be a momentary enthusiasm, not least because it would seemingly put her son at odds with her husband, a man who still believed in the system that had betrayed him. A young Arthur Miller, though, had a new faith. He was now consolidated in his beliefs, more especially when, in a distant Spain, the small town of Guernica was bombed by the fascists and when he witnessed at first hand (as a reporter for the *Michigan Daily*) the autoworkers' strike at Flint, Michigan.

He had chosen Michigan in part because of the Hopwood Awards. These offered cash prizes for playwriting and he knew he would need to raise money if he were to complete a degree. According to Miller, in the spring break of his freshman year, he sat down to write his first play, though it was not submitted until the following year (Martin Gottfried, in his biography of Miller, suggests that the play was not written until 1936; for his part Miller is adamant that he wrote it in 1935). It was a work directly modelled on his own family. He knew little about the theatre, uncertain even as to the length of an act. The result was *No Villain*, a play that seems to have shared the Hopwood Award and that convinced him not only that he could write plays but that that was what he wished to do as a career.

In 1937 he won the Hopwood for a second play, *Honors at Dawn*, while in 1938, the year of his graduation, he was runner-up with *The Great Disobedience*.

※

1

The Michigan plays

No Villain, the play Miller recalls writing in the spring of 1935 rather than return to his family home, lays his new Marxist credentials on the table from the very beginning, with an epigraph from Friedrich Engels: 'Now for the first time a class arose which, without in any way participating in production, won for itself the directing role over production as a whole and threw the producers into economic subjection; a class which made itself the indispensable mediator between every two producers and exploited them both.'

No Villain (in subsequent revised versions also known as *They Too Arise* and *The Grass Still Grows*) draws very directly on his family life. It opens in the parlour of a six-room home in 'a suburb of New York City', plainly the Millers' Brooklyn house on East Third Street[1]. The Simons are an immigrant family, once successful but now fallen on hard times. They anxiously await the return of their son, Arnold (in several places referred to as Art, Miller's name), from the University of Michigan.

The father, Abe Simon (Miller's uncle was called Abe), is, like Miller's own father, the energetic but illiterate head of a coat company. Also like Isadore Miller, he had once been a salesman and, like him, is now in financial difficulties, lacking the money even to send his son the bus fare to return from the university. His wife's father, like Miller's grandfather, who had also been in the garment industry, lives with them. He even has the same name as Miller's maternal grandfather – Barnett – though this is changed in subsequent revisions. Both are anti-union.

The other members of the family are Abe's wife Esther, a version of Augusta Miller (like Augusta, described as tall and intelligent, here seen reading a book and, in a subsequent version, *Cosmopolitan* magazine) and Arnold's brother, Ben (in one place in the typescript inadvertently named for Miller's own brother, Kermit, and the same age as Kermit would have been in 1935 when the play was written). Like Kermit Miller, Ben has given up college to work in the family company, while a younger sister, Maxine, is clearly based on Joan Miller. The older characters, in particular, not only deploy a Jewish syntax but, like Miller's parents and grandparents, pepper their speeches with German and Yiddish expressions. Arnold himself, meanwhile, is transparently a self-portrait by Miller, 'over six feet tall, thin and angular', a would-be writer, correspondent for the student newspaper and a Marxist. Like Miller, Arnold has taken a course on abnormal psychology at Michigan.

So, his first play was, to a remarkable degree, a family portrait. The characters were already in place. Their voices already resonated inside his head. Even the ideological disagreements which provide much of the motor force of the play are those regularly rehearsed in the Miller family home.

As with so many later Miller plays, *No Villain* starts as something of a comedy, as the family wait for Arnold, hitch-hiking from Michigan. The father mispronounces words; the grandfather is the butt of humour. By degrees, however, the conflict that will put pressure on the family is revealed. Ben refers to a letter from Arnold which describes the anti-war movement at Michigan, the first suggestion of a radicalism that will manifest itself on his arrival. This, it seems, merely confirms Esther's worries about her son's 'communistic ideas'. After all, he writes for 'that communistic paper', a reference to the *Michigan Daily*.

Ben obligingly explains Marxist principles to his father, who, even more obligingly, listens as he is told that people such as he will no longer own the means of production in a new, socially just America.

The second act opens in the office, factory and showroom of the Simon Coat and Suit Company. On one side of the stage workers operate two rows of eight sewing machines, while a packer folds coats into cardboard boxes. On the other side is the showroom and an office that represents management. The stage, in other words, seems to replicate the economic classes whose competing needs provide its subject.

For the moment work continues, but a strike of shipping clerks threatens the business. Ben sends a packer out with an order, knowing he may be attacked. For Abe, the question is simple: 'If you don't get them they'll get you. You gotta be on one side or the other in this business . . . It's dog eat dog.' The future of the company hangs in the balance as a loan falls due. This is the fourth time, it appears, that Abe Simon (like Miller's father) has had to begin again, but now there seems no way out.

Though one of the judges of the Hopwood Award was to refer to *No Villain* as a 'proletarian play', it is anything but that. The proletariat remain voiceless. They are the figures hunched over machines and are themselves not on strike. The striking shipping clerks remain out of sight. Miller's concern, it turns out, is not so much with the battle between capital and labour, at least in so far as the Simons represent capital, but, as his epigraph from Engels suggests, those who exercise power over both. His subject is the dilemma of the small businessman whose natural enemies are the large companies. *No Villain* is a play about conflicting loyalties, not the self-evident justice of working-class rebellion. Even Abe accepts that his employees are poorly paid. The essential drama lies in the divisions within a family, the competing values of fathers and sons, of brothers, divisions which mirror and model those of society at large.

Arnold has returned from college an idealist, albeit a somewhat self-righteous and priggish one, though there is little evidence that Miller is aware of this. 'The world is different now', he tells his mother, 'it seems to me you strive too much for wealth, and clothes and a car and god knows what . . . Now we've got to change the world.' In the circumstances, Esther's reply is restrained even as it establishes the nature of the conflict, both within and beyond the family: 'it's those books you read . . . those communist books . . . *you* can't be a communist. You don't belong with such a kind of people . . . Arnold you got to realize you're the son of the owner . . . the boss . . . not the working people.' The issue becomes more sharply focused when Abe calls on his son to help him break the strike. As Ben explains, his father's attitude is that 'A boss's son to him is a boss's son.'

This talk of 'bosses' goes back to the kerbside conversation Miller had had with a student at the age of seventeen. There were, he had learned, two classes of people in society, the workers and the bosses. As he later admitted, 'in my family workers had always been a nuisance . . . they were always getting in the way of businessmen trying to make and sell things' (*T.*111). This is the attitude of the father in *No Villain*. He has nothing against the workers beyond the fact that they are preventing him from making a living.

In the middle of this battle for survival, the grandfather dies and in a final scene they gather around the coffin. The bank has now foreclosed on the business. One generation has died, the next is rendered powerless. It is Ben who takes control. He asks the mourners to leave, along with a fellow manufacturer who had proposed that Ben should marry his daughter and thus inherit his business, resolving the problem as an earlier generation of Jewish immigrants would have done. The play ends with Ben defining the moment of change:

> For us it begins, Arny and I . . . For us there begins not work toward a business, but . . . a battle . . . so that this, (covers the scene with an arc motion of his hand) this will never be in our lives . . . Dad, now we not only are working people . . . we *know* we are . . . I couldn't start this thing over again. I've got to build something bigger . . . Something that won't allow this to happen . . . Something that'll change this deeply . . . it's the only way.

The rhetoric is at times overblown, as characters make speeches to one another rather than engage in conversation, but *No Villain* is a surprisingly adept piece of work. If its ideology seems clear enough, Miller is more interested in dramatising the impact of social change than he is with staging an agitprop drama. His focus is on the family, through whom the social conflicts are refracted. They may be the representatives of a class whose day seems to be over but, as in a Chekhov play, they are not so much condemned as presented in all their confusions. There are, indeed, no villains in the play, merely those caught up in a moment of change.

The grandfather, rocking backwards and forwards in prayer, reaches back into another world, his death marking the end of a particular history. The father, his confidence drained by the Depression, is unable to adjust to a world in which family loyalties defer to something else. It had once seemed possible to reconcile the principles of business with the commitments of family life. His dream of the family name being carried forward had seemed wholly in keeping with the dream that had brought the family to America. Now, there are forces at work he cannot understand.

Not the least interesting dimension of *No Villain*, however, lies in the fact that the two brothers, dazzled by a new vision of human solidarity, are themselves caught at a moment of self-doubt, sure of the direction that society must take but unwilling to accept the human price that might be necessary in order to commit themselves to it. The unseen strikers are not presented as working-class heroes. They are described as throwing acid. They rip up the boxes of clothes the company needs so desperately to sell. We know nothing of the details of their case. They never have a human face. Their desperation only exists as a proposition. They are part of the rhetoric deployed by Abe Simon's sons, but never much more than that. The dilemma of the Simon family cuts altogether deeper. Fundamentally decent, struggling with a world so much less dazzling and even comfortable than they had hoped, they try to sustain themselves in the face of forces they barely comprehend.

The play ends with a commitment but without any certainty. Ben's declaration – and it is interesting that the concluding speech is given to him rather than Arnold, Miller's alter ego – is a piece of rhetoric with no roots in experience. It is half prophecy, half unformulated hope. Certainly for this family it is hard to know how its assertions will be translated into action. The new solidarity that it proposes has been forced on it by economic circumstances. There is no sense that Abe and Esther are converts to a newly declared sense of class solidarity. They will get by because they are survivors and not because they will forge a new alliance with the dispossessed. The two sons, meanwhile, are untested. Their vision remains just that. It has no practical consequence. While we are plainly expected to take Ben's stand entirely seriously, its very vagueness introduces an ambiguity which seems Miller's acknowledgement that the move from language to action might not be without its ambivalence.

The judges for the Hopwood Award were not unanimous but finally settled on this play by a freshman student as the joint winner. Alfred Kreymborg submitted his suggested list of winners on 13 May 1936. He placed *No Villain*, entered under the pseudonym 'Beyoum', first among the contestants for Minor Awards, with 'Jay Sebastian' second. It was, he said, 'An excellent modern theme, handled with a tender insight into character'. Alexander Dean placed Miller second to 'Sebastian', as did Edith Isaacs, with the dismissive comment that 'I may add regretfully that all the Minor submissions seem to be quite without indications of talent.'[2] So it was that this play, based squarely on his own family, became his first work and earned him his first prize, a prize which that family was asked to celebrate, and did celebrate, despite the fact that *No Villain* seemingly represented an ideology at odds with their own and offered portraits of the family members which, if largely affectionate, were not without condescension.

It is not surprising that he subsequently decided to expand it. There was enough here to convince him that it could find a place in the professional theatre and for the next five years he revised it with that in mind. As a result, it survives in various forms and, under the title *They Too Arise*, was finally produced, in March 1937, by the Hillel Players in the Lydia Mendelsohn Theatre at Ann Arbor, and, seven months later, in a single performance by the Federal Theatre in Detroit. A subsequent version submitted to the New Plays Bureau in 1937 received an award, while, in 1939, after graduating, he produced yet another version, now called *The Grass Still Grows*, double in length and very different in tone, in hope that it might be accepted by the Federal Theatre, a theatre abruptly closed down by Congress that same year, or by Broadway where it was rejected as too Jewish.

The first revision, *They Too Arise*, carries Miller's address at 122, North Thayer Street, Ann Arbor, where he moved at the beginning of his sophomore year. In this, Arnold becomes the pivotal figure. His is the moral vision. Indeed, before he appears, his brother outlines his likely response to a strike that is already threatening the family business, itself in a perilous state: 'Arnie believes it's perfectly all right for them to strike. He sees nothing wrong in it. He always said the shipping clerks were getting a raw deal and he's right, they are. He thinks they're right and so do I, but I'm too far in with the other side to pull out. If you drag him downtown to scab it'll hurt him . . . it'll do something we won't like.'[3]

To Arnold, his father is not a boss but a pawn of the large companies. 'What do you own?' he asks, 'You own the right to be a club for the men who have millions at stake.' In *No Villain* the battle had been essentially within the family, if nominally between the Simons and the strikers. In *They Too Arise* it is between the large and small companies, a fact underlined by a new character, called Liebowitz, back bent 'from years of work over a sewing machine', who tells a story of being defrauded by the largest manufacturer and then beaten by gangsters for refusing to pay a fifty-dollar kickback on an order.

Arnold's father and brother are prepared to compromise in different ways; he is not. But he is the outsider. He has no intention of joining the business. He has, as his father implies, derived his ideas from books. For him, the world resolves itself into simple terms. When he insists that 'We can live without a business. Ben and I are young. We can work, we'll live', he is substituting language for action. Everything, indeed, about the character makes it plain that he will not abandon his grandstand seat, though it is far from clear that Miller is aware of the moral implications of this.

The family's dilemma is as it was in the earlier play, except that now they are involved with the Manufacturers' Association which plans to hire strike-breakers. The only alternative seems to be for Ben to marry Helen, the daughter of a fellow manufacturer who is anxious to secure a line of succession for his own business. Little more than a reference in *No Villain*, this now becomes a more significant part of the plot. A loveless match, it nonetheless seems to offer the only solution.

From Arnold's point of view the issues seem simple: 'A poor man like you has no business fighting the strike. Your place is fighting the million-dollar corporations who're choking you out . . . you're fighting on the wrong side, don't you understand?' To his father it is equally simple: 'When ya got sons, they help you . . . all you like is your ideas . . . well, this business to me is also an idea.' Here is that conflict between the family and progressive forces that featured in Clifford Odets's *Awake and Sing* and which was to lie at the heart of John Steinbeck's *The Grapes of Wrath* and Miller's own *All My Sons*. For Abe, there is more at stake than a business in that it is the mark of his success, what justified his coming to the country, what defines him and what, through his sons, will ensure that he leaves his mark on the world. And in trying to articulate this he uses an expression that will recur in Miller's work as a virtual refrain: 'I wanna leave ya with . . . a clean name.' It is his limitation that he believes that this can only be secured through 'a healthy business'.

The strike is over money but to the Manufacturers' Association it is essentially about union recognition, a major issue in the late 1930s as Miller discovered on his trip to the autoworkers' strike in Flint in 1937. At a meeting the chairman agrees that a financial concession might be possible but insists that this would be seen as a step towards 'sharing the wealth'. The Association is dominated by the large manufacturers who are anxious to silence dissent. When it is proposed that strike-breakers should be hired, Abe, the small businessman, stands and denounces them, in doing so making a distinction between himself and his college-educated son: 'I will not hire gangsters . . . But it ain't because I'm a . . . college man. I see all the time what's real. I don't think in theories . . . I will not vote for such a thing because . . . I don't think that is the way an honest man does business.'

More significantly, perhaps, he insists that 'it ain't the way for Jewish men to act', and this remark is made in the context of a family now alive to the rise of Hitler. When the grandfather remarks, 'When you're reading the papers it looks like he's getting up in the morning and if he can't find his teeth he kills a Jew', Arnold replies, somewhat curiously, 'He doesn't want anything with the Jews Granpa. When you don't want people to kill you, you get them to kill each other, it's the easiest way.' On the other hand, he acknowledges that 'Anti-Semitism is rising all over.'

At the strike meeting, Ben supports his father, in a speech distinguishing between the large and the small manufacturers: 'I'm convinced that having that much money makes it impossible for you to be kind to anyone but your wife.' By contrast, the small manufacturers, he suggests, understand those who work: 'I'm one of the little ones', he insists, 'and I'm not ready to kill.' The play, in other words, is something more than a conventional strike play. It certainly lacks a stirring victory for an enlightened working class. What is at stake is collusion with power or with what is presented as fate. At home, power is manifested by corporations who offer a temporary alliance, only to turn on their allies when the time seems ripe. Abroad, something similar seems under way, as the Germans move into Danzig and anti-Semitism flourishes.

The irony, however, albeit an irony that would become evident only with time, is that Arnold insists that 'you don't hear anything like that in Russia'. For Arnold, the Soviet Union is a place where 'a young man can be used', and where 'large-scale private property . . . would never be allowed', a direct reflection of a conversation Miller had with his own grandfather. At the time it was the grandfather's belief that the Soviet Union might represent a business opportunity that seemed naive. In retrospect it is Arnold's youthful idealism.

The tension between the generations builds. The grandfather berates his son, goading him to the point at which he physically pushes him aside, thus exacerbating a heart condition. Abe feels alienated from his son, bewildered that he should side with those who are threatening his livelihood. When the grandfather subsequently dies it is as though the family were turning against itself.

For a moment Ben seems willing to go ahead with the arranged marriage that will, ostensibly, redeem them all, but when they discover that the man with whom they would thus ally themselves has actually undermined them by taking an order they needed, even his father will not allow him to make the sacrifice. At last Abe begins to draw the threads of his experiences together and determines to let the business go rather than compromise. As he remarks, 'Only one thing I know . . . This way we got of eating each other . . . it's no way . . . it ain't right! In my life I never wanted to hurt nobody . . . Roth don't wanna hurt nobody . . . Schaft I remember on the East Side . . . why are they like dogs now! Why! That's a bigger story than what kind of coat ya gonna wear next week!'

It is that bigger story that rests at the heart of *They Too Arise*, a story to do with the collapse of a structure of obligation, of relationships that were once something more than business contacts, of a sense of agreed values. And it is that bigger story that Miller was going to tell in play after play.

Here, it is Abe who comes to a final realisation, speaking of himself and his relationship with his sons: 'They ain't gonna go through what I went through in my life for nothing! . . . I wasted my life for what? I'm gonna see to it that they don't waste it like I did trying to get rich!' He has no formula to apply, no redeeming ideology, no plan beyond a commitment to work and to change. As he says, 'A lotta changing we can do . . . a lotta changing.'

The play clearly has its weaknesses. The daughter largely disappears. Helen, the girl Ben is supposed to marry, barely exists. Arnold is altogether too principled, the human price of his ideals never being examined. Characters are at times too inclined to make speeches rather than engage in conversation. But, that aside, what is the more surprising is how assured the work seems. It is tightly plotted, its characters are, with the exceptions noted, fully realised. It moves, with great adroitness, from family comedy to social drama while here, in embryo, is so much that would later define Miller's work.

This is a play about a family but also about a society. It is born out of a concern for the collapse of shared values and the erosion of commonality. It features a man desperate to define his life, to leave his mark, and yet aware of some insufficiency. It engages with the question of power and the necessity to resist it. It acknowledges the seductiveness of colluding in one's fate, of believing that the choice is only between allying oneself with power or accepting the role of victim. It is a play about the need to accept responsibility for one's own life and therefore for the life of the culture, and which of Miller's plays was not going to do that?

The next version of *They Too Arise* turns Arnold into a would-be writer. He also becomes a self-declared communist, explaining that, 'I'm a Communist because I want the people to take the power that comes with ownership away from the little class of capitalists who have it now . . . someday the working class will own what they've built all these years.'[4] His brother is even more specific, explaining that 'Arnie's studying, his thinking, everything he believes in now makes him think a strike is the way for the working people to gain power and bring Socialism to America. He believes it all the way – in his soul almost.'

So he does, it seems, for later he insists to his family that 'We're poor people. We belong with the working class!', plainly not what his parents wish to hear but in this version of the play enough to convince his brother. This kind of rhetoric is largely absent from the earlier versions and is more interesting for the light it throws on Miller's political convictions than for its dramatic force. Arnold, as the ideologically pure voice of the working class, bent on converting his family, is altogether less convincing than Arnold, the somewhat self-righteous but earnest student anxious to uphold his new beliefs while recognising the dilemma of his father and brother.

In this version, the Chairman of the Manufacturers' Association sees the communists as being behind the strike while Ben denounces him and those others in the Association who wish to hire strike-breakers in a way which is indeed reminiscent of the proletarian plays of the era: 'If you spend a dime to scar one kid, if you send one killer out there to crack a single skull, Jesus Christ you'll not only stand for it you'll burn for it! (*They converge on him*) Like rats you'll burn, like rats!'

By now, too, Miller had plainly become more sensitised to the plight of the Jews in Europe and he includes a new speech in which Grandfather observes that 'A Jew can't make a living in Deutschland no more. They're throwing out the Jews from all the jobs. Only they let work a – a hunert pertzent liverwurst.'

There is also a speech, addressed by Arnold to his mother, which in its stress on causality, on moral responsibility, underscores the position Miller was to adopt throughout his career. Indeed its first sentence was to find an echo nearly sixty years later in *Broken Glass*: 'You think that because you close your door in the front of the house then everything that happens outside doesn't have anything to do with you. That's the way you've always been and that's why when something happens you get all excited and you bang your head against the wall; because you don't want to understand causes . . . the time has come when things don't get better unless you make them better.'

In this version, Arnold becomes a more significant figure. Written at a time when Miller's education in Marxism had moved on, when he was more fully politicised than he had been when writing *No Villain*, it offers insight into his thinking, though at cost to the dramatic conviction of a scene in which Abe and Esther do little more than provide a largely mute audience to his elaborate speeches. 'I'm a Communist', he explains,

> because I want the people to take the power that comes with ownership away from the little class of capitalists who have it now . . . you're the people but you won't admit it. You think you're something special. But you're not.
>   You'll either have to make up your mind to get used to being one of the people or you'll rob a bank and become rich. There's no middle way anymore . . . someday the working class will own what they've built all these years.

This is hand-me-down stuff. It is the rhetoric of Odets's *Waiting for Lefty* and a dozen proletarian plays. It is the rhetoric of the age. The Simons, after all, are no more poor people than were the Millers. They are the formerly rich who are now living in straitened circumstances. Abe Simon is a small businessman squeezed, in times of depression, by the large manufacturer but scarcely a friend to the working class let alone a member of it. Within the context of the drama, Arnold can go some way towards convincing his father as, outside the drama, Miller could not convince his own. What he is plainly doing is trying to reconcile his new politics with his old loyalties. He is also justifying his own abandonment of his father's plans for him. What, after all, had the company been for but his sons, what the meaning of his life but building something they could embrace? Abe is Willy Loman in embryo, as he is Isadore Miller, desperate still to pass his dreams on to his son: 'some day . . . I wanna see you on top. You can do it Ben, without me . . . It ain't fair that I should give my life like this and go out with – with nothing.'

In his most elaborate speech Arnold offers an explanation of the capitalist system that resembles nothing so much as the passage in Scott Fitzgerald's *Tender Is the Night* in which the whole world economy seems geared to serving the needs of the rich Nicole Diver, except that in this case that economy exists to frustrate the needs and hopes of Esther Simon:

A man in Chicago gets up in the morning and goes to the Pit – the grain exchange. A man in Chicago a thousand miles away, a place you've never been in and never will be, lifts his finger and suddenly one morning in New York Esther Simon finds that she can't buy her daughter a dress. Why? Because a man in Chicago bought wheat or bought something else on the exchange and raised the price of food in Esther Simon's grocery store. See? . . . Esther never saw the finger, the finger never saw Esther. But it works the same . . . So it must be something else, something very powerful, – a tremendous thing – like an idea. It is an idea, an idea that comes from life – from living people. It's a conviction that if we can take the right of ownership from that little finger in Chicago, then Esther Simon will be able to buy her daughter a new dress. Because the grain is there! The farmer grew that. But by being able to command credit and money, a finger can lift and hold back the grain from the people. And the people will have to pay and pay until that finger drops . . . But how are we going to make it impossible for one man to control the lives of so many people? The best way – the most common sense way is for the people to take that power away.

The analysis is offered by Arnold; the conclusion is drawn by his brother, Ben: 'Did we ever own anything really? What we owned was the great American right to run interference for the big guys.' Now he refuses to close his ears to the 'cry in the street'. The time is coming, he insists, when 'the people are going to take back what's been stolen from them. When it comes I'm holding a gun, not an injunction.'

The introduction of the gun potentially takes the play in another direction, one not prepared for in a work in which resistance is a matter of the spirit rather than a battle on the streets. The play ends with a line, in an earlier version given to Abe but now given to his wife: 'We gotta learn. A lotta things we gotta learn.'

Encomiums to 'the people', announcements of the need to revolt, analyses of the dead hand of capitalism, *They Too Arise* has all the component parts of the conventional left-wing plays of the era. Like Odets, too, and like the Steinbeck of *The Grapes of Wrath*, Miller chooses to make the family the focus of the need for social change. But where Odets has a character announce that 'Marx said it, abolish such families', Miller is too committed to his own family, so transparently his model, to see it as wholly antithetical to change. What he wants is what would be explicit in the title of his first Broadway success, *All My Sons*, a new sense of solidarity. What he offers, too, is a kind of benediction to the failed father he had left behind, a man whose failure, he insists, was a product not of his own insufficiencies but of a system that he barely understands and that has conspired against him as against many.

The weakness of this third version underscores some of the virtues of the first, which remains the best, a version that allows space for ambivalence, for characters who are less prone openly to define their feelings and explain their convictions, less liable to declare their sudden conversion to a new way of interpreting experience and understanding social process. Nonetheless, it was awarded a Theatre Guild Bureau of New Plays Award. The Bureau, organised and directed by Theresa Helburn, created a series of scholarships in the spring of 1936. Miller's play is stamped number 188, presumably indicating the scale of the competition.

This was not the end of the story for the play, however. It exists in one final version, written in New York, following graduation. The script, now called *The Grass Still Grows*,[5] is dated 6 August 1939, and is, as its sub-title declares, 'A Comedy'. It is double the length of the earlier versions and the ideology has now been largely eliminated. There are no more encomiums to the working class and no strike. Arnold is now a newly qualified doctor, arriving from Johns Hopkins University, while his brother Ben is a would-be writer who has just burned his novel because 'the world doesn't need writing to fix it. It needs men like you.' A year or two earlier this would have been an invitation to strike, to acknowledge the self-evident truths of Marxism. No more. The world, it seems, now needs doctors.

At the heart of the play is a series of comic set pieces centring on the question of which brother, if either, will marry Helen Roth, daughter of a rich manu-facturer. In one scene Arnold masquerades as an expert in the garment trade, on the basis of five minutes' training and an unlikely application of his med-ical skills. In another, Ben, supposed to marry Helen, in fact elopes with the company's bookkeeper. The grandfather, meanwhile, is reprieved, no longer dying but operating as a comic character throughout, filling the small house with furniture that reminds him of his earlier days.

The social question is now relegated to a sub-plot. Abe is given a brother who has been reduced to working as a scab for Helen's father. His refusal to continue complements Ben's refusal to trade himself for the company's future. The problem of the threatened company is solved when Abe readily agrees to borrow money from his workers and turn it into a co-operative. The closest Arnold comes to making a rousing speech of the kind that marred the earlier version is when he asks, 'People, People, when the hell are you going to learn that it's entirely up to you! When will you stop this waiting! What are you waiting for!' an echo, perhaps, of *Waiting for Lefty*.

In *The Grass Still Grows* Clifford Odets seems to make way for Phillip Barry. Already, one year on from graduation, the political earnestness has disappeared, despite the fact that Miller remained as much a committed Marxist as ever. What has happened, it seems, is that he is trying to attune himself to a New York theatre no longer showing any interest in left-wing drama. Miller the Marxist is also Miller the theatrical pragmatist. Melodrama has given way to comedy and though some of the dialogue, interestingly particularly that involving Arnold, is stilted and awkward, the scene in which he presents himself as an expert in clothing is written with a wit and energy that would characterise most of

Miller's work in the years ahead and, most immediately, the radio plays to which he would shortly turn his hand.

His second bid for a Hopwood Award came with *Honors at Dawn*,[6] which won the 1937 award, netting him a further $250. Like *No Villain*, this play, too, centres on a strike, this being the most obvious point of conflict between progressive forces and forces of reaction. As in his first work, it features two brothers. One, Harry Zabriski, is an enthusiast for the American way, a believer in the dream. He is the son of a Polish immigrant. His means of access to the culture is to embrace its myths and honour its prejudices. By contrast, his brother Max works with his hands. He is a mechanic. The conflict between them is prompted by a strike for more pay and union recognition by those at the Castle Parts factory. Offered a bribe to turn informer, Max refuses and enrols in the university where his brother is a student and where he hopes such dilemmas will not occur. But in Miller's play, as, later, in *The Great Disobedience*, the influence of money, of corporations, is omnipresent.

The factory owner, it turns out, is a major donor to the university and makes the price of his support the elimination of radicals. When Harry is asked to turn informer and report on radical students and those teaching them, he agrees with some enthusiasm. A professor duly loses his job.

For his part, Max, shocked by this evidence of corruption and betrayal, though resisting the idea that his own brother might be involved, leaves to join up with his former colleagues at the factory. He freely confesses to the gap between himself and those whose company he seeks. He refuses to romanticise their lives, acknowledges their limited horizons and lack of sophistication, but sees them as loyal to one another and aware of the necessities of life. He is not of them but he is with them and eventually dies, a secular martyr, as he gives a rousing speech, having struggled towards an articulateness that had formerly evaded him.

By way of contrast, Miller offers a Polish immigrant, called Smygli, whose command of English is far from perfect. An outsider, his is a different vision of America. A graduate in philosophy of the University of Warsaw, he is now reduced to running a hot-dog stall in his new country. Stripped of his former fluency, placed in a culture whose signs he can only read imperfectly, and unable to communicate with the subtlety he would like, he nonetheless extols an America that has nothing to do with the pursuit of success, material acquisition or a need to patrol the boundaries of thought. He came, he explains, in search of freedom, the very freedom so clearly now in jeopardy. His broken English, which pushes him to the margin of the society he would embrace, is nonetheless more deeply felt, if socially inoperable, than the rhetoric of those who try to justify their bad faith. This is, in a sense, a play that mistrusts its own language, that is doubtful even of the polarities on which it appears to turn.

Max is, by instinct, a man who works with his hands, like those he finds himself among in the factory. Even the Polish immigrant, despite his degree in philosophy, is a farmer. These are people whose identities are involved with what they do. For the factory owner, the university administrator, even the student who gravitates towards power, it is quite otherwise. For them, it seems, betrayal is just another word, like compromise, accommodation, adjustment. To these men it is evidently conceivable to behave in such a way that one's actions are not rooted in the self.

A space opens up between idea and practice, event and consequence, action and responsibility, language and reality. *Honors at Dawn* is in part about what happens when that gap collapses, when word, act, responsibility come into perfect alignment. The sound of that moment is a pistol shot as Max stands up for what he believes and puts the full force of his life behind it.

His brother, by contrast, lacks substance. Dazzled by the dream of success, he is blinded to his failure on a human level. Like Happy in *Death of a Salesman*, he sees people in terms of their utility to his personal plans. A manipulator, he is himself easy to manipulate. There is no counterbalance in his life, no sense of transcendence, no alternative way of viewing himself and the world. He takes himself for what others believe him to be, and his society for what it proclaims it will become.

Max is no ideologist. Unlike the middle-class intellectuals at the university, playing with ideas that fail to sink roots into their own experience, he has no interest in political theory, no sense that he is challenging anything more than immediate injustice. Like so many Miller characters he is most at home when he is working with his hands. If he struggles towards a moment of articulateness, as Arnold Wesker's Beatie would at the end of *Roots*, this is a product of the moment since for the most part he keeps his feelings compacted within himself. In a play in which language can be seen as suspect, his integrity is sealed less by polemic than by his death, a death offered in the name of that very freedom which for much of the play is under assault but which, finally, as the Polish immigrant, Smygli, suggests is the real gift that America potentially has to offer.

Honors at Dawn, whose judges included Susan Glaspell, herself the author of a play in which a university is persuaded to fire a radical professor, is, in many ways a crude work, certainly more so than his first effort. Yet even here it is interesting to observe the emerging playwright, to detect elements that would mark his later career. As in his first play, for example, he uses the tension and the contrast between two brothers to open up a debate that goes beyond the family. Here, too, are characters who, like Willy Loman and Eddie Carbone, find it hard to put into words the passions that direct and deform their lives. The American dream, dazzling, deceiving, is a motivating force, as it would be for Willy Loman. Language is as much a means to deceive, to deny, as to communicate. And, indeed, denial and betrayal, fundamental tropes of Miller's work, are central to *Honors at Dawn*. Max, meanwhile, stumbles towards a moment of commitment and self-definition, as would John Proctor.

This is not to say that it would bear production. It was, in many ways, a five-finger exercise, influenced on the one hand by his reading of proletarian plays and on the other by events beyond the campus, as unions fought for recognition and employers hired spies and informers. Yet there was enough not only to attract the attention of the Hopwood judges but to suggest the direction he might take once the immediate political conflicts subsided and his drama drew less on the energy released by the clash between employer and worker, between competing ideologies, than that generated by the tension between myth and reality, between private needs and public necessities.

His third and last Hopwood play, which came second in that year's competition, owed a great deal to his time spent at the nearby Jackson State Penitentiary, supposedly one of the most progressive in the country. Disturbingly, a friend, Sid Moscowitz, had secured the job of prison psychologist having, like Miller, taken a single course in psychology at Michigan. As such he was responsible for eight thousand prisoners. What struck Miller, apart from the absurdity of his friend's position, which made his clients seem almost sane, was that the majority of prisoners seemed to be serving time for crimes related to the Depression. And though he was drawn less to them than to the more bizarre cases, it was this perception that led to *The Great Disobedience*[7] which was, he insisted, 'the first I ever researched', an attempt to 'get out of myself and use the world as my subject' (*T*.93).

In *They Too Arise*, after all, he had dropped the bucket into the well of his own life, finding in family tensions the root of a wider conflict. Admittedly, in *Honors at Dawn* he did edge out beyond the family, but even here it was through the contrast between two brothers that he sought to get a purchase on a political system still seen in terms of contrasting rhetorics. Now he wanted to step into a more alien environment.

In truth, *The Great Disobedience*, if not quite the 'turgid' piece rejected by the judges, is over-burdened by an ideological conviction that prison is, in a quite literal and identifiable way, a by-product of capitalism. It is a melodrama in which character is seen as a social construct, and the psyche assaulted by the implacable and vindictive agents of industry.

At its centre is Victor Matthews, once a compensation doctor employed by a rubber company. He had become an inconvenience to a company that expected him to offer a professional vindication for its refusal to accept liability for its actions. He is sent to prison ostensibly for carrying out an illegal abortion, a life-saving operation performed on a young woman who is herself a victim of an inequitable society, but in fact because he has become an encumbrance to those in power. His literal imprisonment, and that of so many others, is offered both as a tangible by-product of capitalism and as a metaphor for that loss of freedom experienced by all those required to serve its interests. When the prison guards sell the inmates drugs this, too, is both a literal detail of prison life and an image of a society in which the individual is trapped in a cycle of false needs and artificial satisfactions, in which a potential for revolt is deflected and blunted.

The same company that so casually disposes of an employee who refuses to conform, then arranges that he should be held in solitary confinement, cut off from that potential solidarity which might relieve his suffering and spread an understanding of the system that entraps the prisoners. He is, though, not quite alone. Two former student friends reach out to him. One, Caroline, does so out of love; the other, Dr Karl Mannheim, now the prison psychologist, out of friendship and professional concern. Yet, as in Tennessee Williams's prison play, *Not About Nightingales*, a product of the same year, both are subject to the whim of a vicious Warden.

The focus of the play is essentially on the figure of the psychologist, desperately liberal, anxious to protect prisoners from the consequences of the system under which they suffer. He tries to hold this anarchic world together by introducing his own systems. He fills his room with art, another way of imprinting order on disorder. He gathers evidence of the corrupt system but takes this for action. What he is not willing to do is challenge the system directly. He is, in effect, paralysed. Ostensibly charged with maintaining the mental health of the inmates, though in fact with pacifying them, he edges towards insanity himself, as does Victor, who becomes convinced that Caroline carries a child who will one day challenge the system that has ruined all their lives.

Karl does eventually submit his evidence of drug trafficking in the prison and an enquiry is held which removes the Warden. What it does not do, however, is acknowledge the fact that behind the Warden, and indeed, the whole system of supposed justice, stands the self-same Rubber Company that had secured Victor's imprisonment. Indeed the Warden is replaced by another man also in the pay of the company.

The play ends with a new young psychologist joining the prison staff, just as anxious to moderate the suffering of the prisoners and just as willing, in the end, to make the compromises seemingly required to do anything at all. Yet Miller cannot rest content with such a reductive irony. Karl is thus permitted a speech in which, in effect, he disavows his own profession, which does no more than try to reconcile people to their fate, adjust them to a reality that should be challenged rather than accepted. He calls for a new breed of doctors, by implication less concerned with medicine than revolt (not for nothing was Marxism hostile to psychoanalysis). What the world needs, it seems, is revolutionaries. The liberal is seen as no more than an equivalent of the psychologist, a progressive, assembling evidence as if this were action, offering nostrums, seeking to modify rather than smash an oppressive system.

The prison, meanwhile, is both fact and image. It is the dark flower of society, the mechanism of control for those with power. It is a means of punishing those who find themselves driven to crime by economic need, or who are seen as impediments to progress as defined by those for whom human values take second place to material concerns. It represents the constrictions placed on a genuine freedom, the isolation imposed on individuals who, if allowed to join together, might challenge those whose power derives precisely from their ability to divide. It also, perhaps, stands for those ideas that once seemed to form the basis of American endeavour but which have themselves hardened into dogma.

When Riker, head of the company that has effectively destroyed Victor, Karl and Caroline, announces that 'A man's duty is to go out and get what he wants. An idea like that made this country', he looks to justify his rapacity with the familiar rhetoric of an enabling American myth. American liberal individualism thus collapses into a form of criminality. Forty years later, David Mamet would make a similar point in *American Buffalo*.

The play, however, is overly schematic and melodramatic. Its political analysis is less than convincing, its rhetoric frequently overheated. It does, though, accurately reflect Miller's deepening radicalism, equally evident in *No Villain*. What he had seen in the garment industry in New York, what he knew of the situation in the automobile factories of Detroit, and what he observed in Jackson State Prison convinced him that the war between labour and capital was real enough and that that war would be lost if some kind of solidarity between the dispossessed were not made a reality.

The Great Disobedience had not been designed as a call for prison reform. It was, to his mind, an attack on capitalism itself, which crushed those exposed to its cruelties, and proposed a model of human life for which the prison was an appropriate paradigm. Meanwhile, mental illness was presented as a logical result of the alienation that was itself a product of the capitalist ethos, a displacement from the political and economic realm into the psychosexual.

Together, these first plays reveal a young writer feeling his way not only towards a subject and a usable theatrical language, but a theatre in which private concerns move out into a public space. These are plays which take as their assumption the fact that the theatre is not only a social form but has a social function. He was writing out of his own experience, in the first play remarkably, and occasionally disturbingly so, but his purpose was always to find in the particular the general. They are offered as exemplary works and if they owe rather too much, in theatrical terms, to Odets and, in ideological terms, to a barely digested Marx, they still manage, in their humour and in the dynamics of their characters, to suggest something of the writer who would eventually transcend these early exercises without losing the passion which lies behind them.

— ✳ —

All three Michigan plays were evidence of the political commitment of a man for whom Marxism seemed to hold a key not only to domestic politics and the apparent implosion of capitalism but also to an international situation, in particular the unfolding situation in Spain.

The Spanish Civil War seemed to epitomise a struggle between the forces of reaction and a redemptive communism. Miller, indeed, was himself tempted to go; a friend did travel to what many saw as the principal moral cause of the decade. When that friend died, if anything it reinforced Miller's sense of commitment. It also raised an issue that would concern him in his first Broadway play: why is it that some flourish and others perish? Even in the depths of the Depression there were those who made money, as in the war there would be those who made fortunes while others died.

There is no doubt, however, that his greatest commitment was to his work. He had entered Michigan unsure what he wanted to be. In a sense university represented a protective environment. For four years he was relieved of the problem of looking for work. With the success of No Villain, however, he was convinced he had found his vocation. He was to be a writer. Miller left Michigan in the early summer of 1938 to return to Brooklyn and what he assumed would be a career on Broadway. His confidence was not entirely misplaced. The judges of the Hopwood were themselves drawn from the New York professional theatre and he did receive some response from producers and actors, but nothing came of it.

As yet he had no money and thus had to return to the family home where he worked to revise They Too Arise and The Great Disobedience. He also produced a series of short stories, two of which evidenced a commitment to modernism of a kind that would have surprised subsequent critics. None were published.

There was still, though, the Federal Theatre, a product of Roosevelt's Works Progress Administration. This was designed to give employment to actors, directors, technicians and writers. It had companies across America and it was its Detroit unit that had staged the first professional production of They Too Arise. As Miller explained,

> they created the Living Newspaper which was a journalistic theatre dealing with the big issues of the time: the question of medical care, the agriculture of the United States which was falling apart, we were slaughtering pigs to keep the price of pork up while people were starving in the city. They would tackle these big issues with an editor and numerous writers. It was like a nineteenth-century novelist's view.[8]

It was not what he wished to do but it was a theatre clearly committed to social and political issues and that did appeal, though perhaps less so than the fact that it offered a regular wage and a chance to get on with his own work. As he explained, 'the Division that I was attached to was the Playwriting Division. This was a new idea. People were paid $22.77 a week to go home and write plays. There were thirty or forty writers in New York and I never heard of any of them becoming playwrights but it kept them off the streets.' In fact a friend from Michigan, Norman Rosten, was one of them and he did subsequently write for both radio and theatre, but there was a lifelong competition between the two men which perhaps led to this piece of selective amnesia.

To qualify, it was necessary to be on welfare and since Miller was staying in the family home he would have had difficulty had he and his father not staged a performance for the necessary official. Isadore declared that he would not allow his son in the house, that he no longer shared anything with that son who seemed to believe in nothing, which is to say believed in something so alien as to seem beside the point. For his part, Miller himself had to prove that he was living elsewhere and accordingly persuaded a friend to set aside a room where he was alleged to be living. By good fortune he happened to be there when an inspector came by. The subterfuge worked and he joined the Theatre.

It was a brief appointment in that in 1939 Congress closed it down for alleged (and actual) communist influence, though in fact because of its predilection for staging plays about contemporary events in which Congressmen rarely came out well. In his brief time with the Theatre, however, Miller started work on an epic play about Montezuma and Cortes, a play that he later sent to the Theatre Guild which proceeded to lose it. It had to wait nearly fifty years for its first production.

In 1940, he married Mary Grace Slattery, whom he had met at Michigan and who shared his politics. They had effectively been living together since leaving university and now decided that marriage might have its conveniences. She was a lapsed Catholic, he a lapsed Jew. Nonetheless, he agreed on a Catholic marriage to minimise the resentment of Mary's family. The event nearly descended into farce when the dispensation required for this mixed marriage failed to materialise. In the end the Church relented, but it was an inauspicious beginning. His own family did not attend. Neither family was enthusiastic. Miller's new father-in-law was casually anti-Semitic while his own grandfather threw a clock at Miller's mother, Augusta, when told of the wedding.

The young couple returned from Mary's native Ohio with less than a hundred dollars in the bank. Mary took a job as secretary, supporting her husband for the first years, while he did his best to break into the theatre and the magazine market.

Almost immediately after his marriage, he set out on the Waterman Line merchantman, the SS Copa Copa, in an attempt to research a play and a novel. It was sailing south to New Orleans and then on to South America. He had, he felt, exhausted his own experiences as subject matter and needed to broaden his horizons. He could only afford a single ticket and so married life began with his abandoning his wife in the name of his art. He did work on both projects but could place neither. *The Half Bridge* was a melodramatic story of spies and Nazi agents, with little to be said for it. He followed it later with another wartime play, *Boro Hall Nocturne*, unknown until now. This, too, failed to find a producer but is fascinating, not least because it engages the question of a native anti-Semitism, even in time of war. The novel was a powerful indictment of American racism, influenced, perhaps, by his reading of Richard Wright's *Native Son*, a book which had deeply impressed him. Given that, apart from Tituba in *The Crucible* and a bag lady in *Mr Peters' Connections*, there are no black characters in his plays, it is startling to realise that at the very beginning of his career he chose to place such figures at the centre of a work which, had it been published, would surely have caused a major stir and perhaps taken his career in another direction. Certainly there is ample evidence in those years that racism was a central concern.

✳

2

'The Golden Years', 'The Half-Bridge', 'Boro Hall Nocturne'

The Golden Years, written between 1939 and 1941, about the conquest of Mexico by Cortes and his conquistadors and the overthrow of Montezuma, Emperor of the Aztecs, was Miller's displaced reaction to events in Europe in the late 1930s. Though set in the past, it was his attempt to understand the political and moral paralysis of the Western powers in the face of fascist aggression. Initially written for the Federal Theatre, it was submitted to the Theatre Guild and the Group Theatre in whose hands it languished. When it eventually surfaced it seemed, to Miller, that it no longer fitted the trajectory of his career and was sent, with a pile of other material, to the Harry Ransom Center at the University of Texas as part of a deal that would help him pay off the taxes he owed following the collapse of his marriage to Marilyn Monroe in 1962.

It was a play whose twenty-five speaking parts, and, ideally, a number of non-speaking ones, including 'the whole Aztec Army', would have caused no problems for the Federal Theatre, but made it an unlikely project for any other and, indeed, half a century later it only reached the stage by way of radio and television.

The Golden Years comes as something of a surprise after the earnest politics and sturdy realism of his first plays, though he had tried rewriting *The Great Disobedience* in verse. It is an epic work, suffused with poetry and far removed from the personal life on which he had previously drawn. It is a play whose images are striking, whose language is elevated and whose characters are, to some degree, stylised, being self-conscious performers. It is a play of ritual and ceremony which requires a carefully choreographed staging. Where earlier, like Odets's and many Federal Theatre plays, he had imported into his work something of the energy of the contemporary, now he turned back to the early sixteenth century.

Miller himself was later to comment with some bewilderment on his desertion of realism for metaphor and verse, more especially given the urgency with which he regarded social issues at home and the rise of fascism abroad. The fact is, though, that, as in *The Crucible*, he was looking for an analogy to his own time, staging, as it seemed to him, a drama then being enacted in Europe as the democracies, themselves imperial powers no longer sure of their destiny or confident of their values, were confronted by the brute power and total assurance of Adolf Hitler who announced his absolute right to the future: the Thousand Year Reich.

The Golden Years was, Miller explained, a gesture 'toward a non-existent poetic theatre inspired by Elizabethan models'.[1] In truth, such a model was not quite so non-existent. Maxwell Anderson had combined historical materials and poetic language in a number of his plays, as had T. S. Eliot. Auden and Isherwood also created a number of verse dramas. In 1937 Archibald MacLeish's radio play *The Fall of the City*, starring Orson Welles and broadcast on the Columbia Workshop, had been the first verse play on radio and was itself inspired by the Spanish conquest of Tenochtitlan. It was repeated in 1939, the year Miller began *The Golden Years*. Miller himself has said that it was this play that convinced him that 'radio was made for poetry' and that MacLeish had 'lifted it to a gorgeous level'.[2] In 1939, Norman Rosten also wrote a verse play for radio, *Prometheus in Grenada*, about the execution of Federico Garcia Lorca. Miller himself would write *Juarez*, a verse play for radio.

Radio was one thing, however, and the theatre quite another. *The Golden Years* might have been welcomed by the Federal Theatre but it was, he feared, against the grain of the Broadway theatre he had by now begun to think of as his ultimate destination. It was also, though, the first evidence of an attitude towards language that would later see him reach for a heightened rhetoric and even for dramatic poetry.

The Golden Years is sub-titled 'A New World Tragedy', and is, indeed, epic in its scope, while focusing on the fate of its two protagonists. In one sense it is about imperialist rapacity, as Cortes sets out to strip a country of its assets by murdering its people. In another, it is about a man, Montezuma, who invites his own destruction as he struggles to read the meaning of his life, to discover a destiny beyond that which he has inherited only to find himself mesmerised by the sheer implacability of what confronts him.

Montezuma exists in a world of signs and portents. Aware of his own history of violence, he feels a strange affinity with the invading forces, indeed is tempted to believe that his own significance might be tied to them. He suspects they may represent the promised return of the gods. Who else, after all, would challenge his empire with such confidence? If they are gods then he thereby becomes the apotheosis of his kind, charged with historic significance. And if his life is truly entwined with theirs the golden years of a mythic past will be restored and a golden future assured.

For Cortes, gold represents only wealth and power. It is drained of transcendence, emptied of any significance beyond itself. When he raids an Aztec gravesite he melts down their symbolic golden ornaments into crude ingots, wilfully destroying their history and spiritual beliefs in the name of greed. Their elaborate signs and symbols are dissolved into a mere commodity. Though religion is his agent, it is not his motivation. He looks to live in golden palaces and drink from golden cups. His seduction of a native girl, Marina, who, Christianised, becomes his means of access to alien ways, is an image of his attitude to the beauty he encounters. He is fascinated by her, declares his love for her, and yet thrusts her aside when she stands between him and his objective.

The play begins with an eclipse of the moon. A human sacrifice is necessary if it is to reappear, if the world is to live again. As ever, the future is to be assured with blood. A child is sacrificed to carry a message to the gods as if the death of innocence were something more than the evidence of power, though the spilling of blood makes it impossible to approach the godhead directly. There is thus an ambivalence at the heart of this gesture. It is a moment of national and personal self-doubt.

Montezuma rules over a society that is extensive, a trading empire which is nonetheless crumbling, eroded by inequality, injustice and violence. A world won by the sword no longer seems to validate anything beyond the means it used to come into being. A judge, sentenced for corruption, justifies himself in terms of a culture that appears to serve nothing but its ruling class. And Montezuma's mind is no less clouded with uncertainty. Seemingly implacable, he fears the moral hermeticism of his actions that imply a transcendence in which he no longer fully believes. Body has fallen on body and yet they seem not to have allowed him to climb any higher towards the heavens.

The affinities between Montezuma and Cortes are thus as real as the differences. Both serve an empire. Both are stained with blood. The difference is that Montezuma has lost his certainty. Believing himself the agent of his gods, he sees nothing ahead but repetition or decline and thus, whatever his declared loyalties, has begun to doubt. Cortes is a brigand, not given to self-doubt, who has even broken with the emperor he nominally serves. He retains loyalty not by virtue of tradition but by offering a share in brigandage, a portion of his power. He acts the god; Montezuma aspires to become such. When Marina asks Cortes, who has declared that the Spaniards must present themselves as gods, 'how will you ever break a lie?' he replies, 'When we've conquered, only the truth will reign.'[3] Truth, as ever, bends to power.

The link to Nazi Europe is not difficult to make. Cortes insists he wants nothing more than friendship as Hitler wanted no more, he insisted, than the reuniting of the German peoples, the correction of historic injustices, and then a future golden period albeit, like Montezuma's, stained with atavism. It is his seeming power, his very implacability, which stuns those who try to search out his true motives, understand the root and purpose of his violence.

Cortes's statements of humanity are calculated ('I want nothing here but the brotherhood of man',[4] he insists, while planning murder and theft); Montezuma's are real enough, though generated out of guilt. He has a vision, he explains, of 'another world . . . a world where every door stood wide unbolted in the night, where the single ear of corn grew heavy as a child, and all the brass of war, swords and shields, were melted into rivers and the silver sea'.[5] Yet beneath the differing rhetorics – the blunt prose of the Spaniards, the lyricism of the Aztecs – is a shared brutality, a betrayal of the humanity invoked at the level of language but denied at the level of action. Montezuma has shed more blood than Cortes. Is his self-doubt sufficient to ennoble him or is it a sentimentality, an expression of guilt discharged in words rather than embodied in policy?

Montezuma is paralysed in the face of Cortes because he wishes him to be something he is not, because his own uncertainties render him impotent in the face of such assurance. Thus there comes a moment when Miller tells us in a stage direction that 'the impact of unreasonable, relentless force hits him'.[6] When it does, however, it is already too late. His appeasement, for whatever motives, has invited the destruction that now confronts him. He has been seduced by his own vision of a peace to be won by submission, almost as if he willed the immolation that thereby becomes his fate. As he faces his extinction he declares,

> Let the history tell how an emperor died in search of the golden years. And by no hand but his own. For while his eyes were searching heaven for meanings and signs, a sword was pointing at his breast, and as it caught the light with such brilliant glare, it seemed to hold the sanction of the sun, and he dared not turn the killing blade away. And when the sun was set, and the light was gone, the emperor felt for the face of the god but the steel stood turning in his heart.[7]

The Golden Years is a play that warns against metaphor, even while deploying it. Cortes's power lies in his manipulation of myth and symbol as Montezuma's weakness lies in his refusal to see the world, and his own omissions and commissions for what they are. He retreats into language, the imagery of an exhausted faith, in order to avoid the force of a brute reality. This is a play in which both protagonists themselves deal in a conscious theatricality, staging rituals, ceremonies, elaborate deceits, the one blending into the other.

The relevance of this play to a contemporary situation, as appeasement appropriated the language of idealism and fading empires were mesmerised by the seemingly irresistible, is clear enough. There were, indeed, those who advocated wedding their destinies to that of a new brutalism as if they might thereby reinvigorate flagging national energies. Vichy France was one product of such thought but there were those in all the democracies who flirted with the allure of this new power. Indeed in some senses it was its very crudeness, its lack of sophistication, its brutal directness which appealed. Some members of the British aristocracy, including an abdicated British king and his American wife, were all too happy to fawn on the strutting representatives of the Third Reich as if they could thereby restore to themselves the power they were acutely aware of losing. As German forces moved across Europe, killing and looting, most of the world stood by and watched. Fifty-four years later Miller would write another play, *Broken Glass*, on a similar theme, a play which was rehearsed as once again the world looked on, seemingly paralysed, while Europe slipped towards barbarism, this time in the former Yugoslavia.

Speaking of *The Golden Years* and other of his early plays, especially *The Man Who Had All the Luck*, he has said that, 'An important source of energy in these plays was my fear that in one form or another Fascism, with its intensely organized energies, might well overwhelm the wayward and fixed Democracies.' Both plays, to his mind, were 'struggling against passive acceptance of fate or even of defeat in life, and urge action to control one's fate; both see evil as irrational and aggressive, the good as rational, if inactive and benign'. However, he was struck by what seemed to him to be 'the debility of Americans' grasp of democratic values or their awareness of them' and by the fact that the Depression 'had humbled us, shown us up as helpless before the persistent, ineradicable plague of mass unemployment'.[8]

In other words, he sees these plays both as being historically situated and as establishing a central theme of his work, namely the need of the individual, and through the individual of societies, to reject the idea of his helplessness in the face of what he chooses to see as fate. The role of victim has its attractions in that it relieves of responsibility those who should intervene in their lives, those who should accept their individual and collective responsibility for who they are and what they do. But the role of victim contains and implies its own logic, which is that of a dissolution of the self and of society, sometimes in the most literal of ways.

The Golden Years pictures a man intent above all on giving meaning to his life, on discovering some shape which can retrospectively flood that life with significance. It is a portrait of a man who glimpses an ideal and in the name of that ideal compromises himself and betrays others, a theme which Miller had encountered in his reading of Ibsen and which, like Fitzgerald, he would come to see had a bearing on the utopianism of his own society.

In *The Golden Years* two supposed realities, each founded in myth, collide, as language is seen as an agent equally of the mind and the imagination. Cortes and Montezuma are actor–director–stage managers, setting the stage (Cortes directs his men as to where they should stand, what they should wear, what stage business they should perform; Montezuma self-consciously performs rituals and instructs his followers in their roles), wearing costumes designed to compel belief, offering speeches carefully calculated to sustain their versions of the real. The confident explications of social process to be found in *They Too Arise*, *Honors at Dawn* and *The Great Disobedience*, the unambiguous alignment of character and ideology that had characterised those works, is now abandoned. In its place is a tragedy in which an individual fails the historic moment and sees the collapse of everything that once seemed to define his existence, his sense of history and his place in the metaphysical world.

Cortes, too, has lost in that he has snatched loot at the price of understanding. He has opted for material gain over transcendence. He is what Montezuma was before he realised the insufficiency of wealth and power, but lacks the validation even of a suspect value system. Montezuma, of course, is fatally illusioned. He has sacrificed tens of thousands to a fantasy, a tainted faith, but until now did so out of a misreading of the universe. Now he realises that if the Spaniards are not gods then he is not the acme of historic process and will not be transubstantiated into godhead. His followers abandon him and with him necessarily their belief.

Miller makes of his dying moments, though, less a tragic sealing-off of disorder than a vindication of revolt and a prophecy of the overthrow of tyrants. Dying at the hands of his own people, he declares: 'I was oppression in their eyes. Look on me, Conquistador; in my unmourned face see your face, and in my destiny, the destiny of all oppression.'[9] The speech is not offered ironically. The Aztecs may have been doomed and Spain triumphant, but time would unravel the tapestry of their empire, as it had that of Montezuma. It is, however, in truth, a speech that says more for Miller's sense of the urgencies of his own day than for the likely response even of a dying Montezuma, for whom oppression (though not by that name), and despite Miller's attempts to reinvent him, was a simple fact of history and the logic of faith.

I first read the play at the Harry Ransom Center of the University of Texas at Austin. It seemed to me to merit production but the size of the cast made it a daunting prospect. I suggested that BBC radio might be interested and spoke to the Drama Department. It was. For the production, eventually broadcast in 1987, Miller did no more than 'tidy it up' a little, deleting 'some purple passages'. Reviews of that production were positive, the *Independent* finding Montezuma and Cortes 'mesmeric figures', in Miller's hands. Others described it as 'exciting', 'elegant', 'a baroque piece' with 'excitement and tension'. In many ways, indeed, it benefited from being a radio play, not merely in the sense that sound effects could give substance to its epic qualities but that the individual imagination could give substance and form to the expansive world that Miller invoked. By the same token, the television production which followed suffered from its literalism. While there was a reordering of scenes – as written some were over-extended – it still seemed somewhat static and protracted. Television is not an ideal medium for a work that needs either the expansiveness and invention of the stage or the intimacy of radio drama.

The Golden Years has its faults. The private lives, the ambitions, anxieties of Cortes and Montezuma are revealed in language rather than action. It works by a series of set pieces. It is difficult to give full credence to the figure of Marina, mediating between two worlds and motivated by a love which is, perhaps, not entirely credible, though historically based. On the other hand, here is a new Miller, broadening his canvas, exploring a new style, seeing language as something more than a mechanism, a clear glass through which to see events. Here, too, is a playwright for whom plot is metaphor and private motives a key to public action, a writer for whom past and present are linked by the continuities of human nature, alert to denial and betrayal as defining qualities in personal and social life.

Ironically, the play with which he hoped to address the war most directly, *The Half-Bridge*,[10] was by far his weakest and the one that, despite his research on the SS *Copa Copa*, seemed least authentic. Originally to have been a work about the clandestine establishment of Nazi bases, it turned into a melodrama featuring spies, émigrés, adventurers, Nazis, a wronged woman, a frustrated homosexual. It is written in a language that is not so much heightened as top-heavy and seemed evidence that he had unlearned the lessons he had so recently learned.

At its heart is the figure of Mark Donegal, ambitious without having a clear focus for his ambition, an American pioneer turned Nietzschean superman. He has excelled in a range of activities, from college football to business, but found no satisfaction in any accomplishment. His own country seems to him to have shrunk from its former greatness, lost its sense of vision and purpose. Its enfeeblement seems to justify him in his increasingly amoral drive to fund a life of adventure and excitement.

The play, written between 1940 and 1943, opens on a pier in New Orleans harbour, as Donegal delivers a drugged man into the hands of Dr Luther, a member of the Gestapo. Donegal has smuggled the man from safety in South America on board the *Bangkok Star*, in return for three hundred dollars, two hundred of which he owes to the ship's Captain who, unbeknown to him, is in love with him. This is a somewhat startling sub-plot for a play written at this time and productive of one of the more embarrassing speeches in a play in which Miller shows none of that control of language that would characterise his later work ('You are to me as a white column', he says to the young man he loves, 'an aspiring thing. You are to me as my country before it was defiled'), which rivals Robert Jordan's insistence in *For Whom the Bell Tolls* that he loves Maria as he loves Madrid. Comparing women with countries and major urban conurbations is seldom a wise strategy.

Luther now proposes a further scheme which will apparently involve turning the ship into a raider that will hunt down and sink merchantmen in order to steal their cargo. Somewhat incredibly, Donegal signs on for this since the proceeds will bankroll him for the exploit he plans in Brazil, where a friend has discovered a hidden civilisation, rich in gems. When it is revealed, however, that this plan conceals another, namely the sinking of the *Bangkok Star*, itself owned by the Nazis, and the transfer of the insurance money into party funds, Donegal rebels. He does so not least because by this time he is in love with a young woman, Anna Walden, who desperately needs to secure passage on the ship, in flight, as she believes, from the police. In repelling a would-be rapist she had, as she thinks, killed him and feels unable to stay behind and explain her actions.

The play, in other words, is over-stuffed with plots, each one less credible than the one before. We are asked to believe that the *Bangkok Star*, subject to customs inspection, has been secretly equipped with three eight-inch guns, that port security, in wartime, allows Nazis, fleeing felons and assorted ne'er-do-wells, to wander at will on the dockside and that the idealistic Donegal will hand over fascist victims for small change. The ship, we are told at one stage, is in poor condition, while at another is capable of nineteen-and-a-half knots and can plausibly be proposed as a raider.

Such improbabilities are equally evident in the characters. The Captain is thus not only homosexual but a former U-boat commander and also a drug addict. Dr Luther seems to step out of a Peter Lorre movie. Anna is no more than need personified, an obliging love interest transformed in a single night from desperate woman to sentimental companion as a result of a few drinks in a dockyard bar, her recent experience of men notwithstanding. Donegal transforms from callous egotist to protective hero.

It is not, of course, that melodrama was absent from the American stage of the time. Indeed, quite the contrary. Many thirties playwrights chose to stage the conflict between capital and labour essentially as melodramas energised by violence, morality tales in which progressive forces confronted the forces of reaction. Character was an ideological construct, a product of economic circumstance, idealism or cynicism. Language was frequently no more than rhetoric as the private was infiltrated by public necessities. The war, in turn, seemed to demand a didactic drama, as the theatre enlisted in the battle. Thus, Robert Sherwood's *There Shall Be No Night* (1940) and Lillian Hellman's *Watch on the Rhine* (1940) were hardly restrained in their approach to character or plot while *The Half-Bridge* would not have been out of place as a product of Hollywood. Indeed, despite his aversion to the film industry, it is tempting to see an element of film aesthetics in the chiaroscuro lighting, the plot-driven action (there is considerable waving around of guns), the suitably menacing villains and vulnerable female protagonist, though the over-elaborated speeches seem to root it firmly in the theatre, if a version of theatre against which he would later react.

There is, of course, little point in underscoring the weakness of a play that was never produced. Its chief value lies in what it tells us not only about the faults which he ruthlessly excised from his work but also about themes that would recur.

Mark Donegal is a strange character. He is presented as an achiever, a man who embraces a version of America as a land of possibility. Yet he is also a hangover from the thirties, complaining that 'You gotta crawl to live in this world; crawl to men . . . whose perspiration falls on silk, who eat the bread you make and never know your name.' Yet, if he feels that 'the rich are pigs', the poor seem to him merely 'petty'. He wishes to 'spread myself over a lotta people', to dominate.

At the same time, he regrets the loss of a world in which 'you *belonged*', a phrase Miller might have derived from O'Neill, who does, indeed, seem an influence, though, ironically, the most O'Neill-like passage, one in which he celebrates the sea, anticipates a speech made by Jamie in *Long Day's Journey Into Night*, a play not produced for another decade and a half, though also written at this time: 'the black sea slick as a seal and the engines stroking like a heart under you [where] we'll stand on the bridge drunk in the belly of the night . . . and the cool salt rises to your lips'. There are similar passages in *The Bangkok Star*, the novel which came out of this same trip on the SS *Copa Copa*, where violence is balanced by a striking lyricism.

Like many later Miller characters, Donegal wants to 'feel you're steering your own life, to pull out of the mob'. Yet all sense of adventure and endeavour seems to have disappeared from the world, and particularly from America. Now there is only 'a room with a view', what O'Neill, in *The Iceman Cometh*, was to call a 'grandstand', detached from life.

At times Donegal seems no more than a version of the Nazi, Luther, for whom 'The giants are dead in every land, the little people inherit the earth.' But to Donegal, and in a phrase which is not without its irony after *The Golden Years*, the Germans are 'high school conquistadors'. He is the real thing, ready to 'sail the seas and take . . . what he's got the wit and daring enough to take'. Asked what he thinks of the sailors he will condemn to death if he signs up with the Nazis, he replies, 'They'll go under remembering that right and wrong went out of the world and that'll be their sense.' To challenge 'the way things are' is to invite 'a bullet in the brain'. The future, as it seems to him, is represented by 'the man with the gun . . . We're people . . . more numerous than pins, the cheapest thing in the world!'

Yet, at the same time, and in radical contradiction, he remarks that 'When you take a ship into port at night you know the buoys are going to be in the right place. You know the reefs are marked, the lights haven't been moved. That's . . . civilization.' For him, the Nazis make him 'Feel the plaster falling' around his head, 'dogs dragging children into the streets, a man pulling his daughter into bed', but, by some unexplained paradox, these are the people he is prepared to make his allies. For some reason, too, and before he transforms himself from Nietzschean over-reacher to simple protector of virtue, Anna describes him as the first decent man she has met.

He does, though, change. He comes to understand and confess that 'Everybody suffered so I could swallow the world.' The inspiration for the change comes from Anna, who herself transforms from frightened victim to militant humanist. 'Who should pity us,' she asks, 'if the first thing we're ready to do when there's trouble is give up our lives? All right, the world pushes you to the grave; all right, it's hard to fight death . . . Then the world has got to be changed . . . so we can live, and if you gotta die, then die changing it.' This sounds remarkably like an echo of the concluding line of his first play.

Donegal now has a reason for living and dying. Learning that the Nazis mean to kill him and his friends as soon as the ship is clear of the coast, he plans to put them ashore before sailing. When he is frustrated in this by Dr Luther and his henchmen, a fight ensues in which Anna shoots the SS man. The play ends on a note of triumph. Love, it appears, has done more than conquer evil; it has transformed those previously inclined to embrace what seemed to them to be the implications of an absurdist universe.

The image which gives the play its title derives from Mark's conviction that everyone is born with 'half a bridge sticking out of our hearts, looking for the other half that fits so we can cross over into someone else'. It is, to say the least, an unfortunate image, not made any more plausible when extended from a metaphor for personal relationships to a symbol of universal humanity: 'a bridge is building, a bridge around the world where every man will walk, the Irish with the Jews, and the black with the white, stronger together than any steel'. This is not a rhetoric he would ever use again, though the stress on a common humanity would remain a central and defining mark of his work: that, a distrust of power, and an insistence on the need to accept responsibility for one's actions. Donegal's desire to 'leave a special print on the face of the earth' would likewise be echoed by many later Miller protagonists.

The Half-Bridge is in part a genre piece, an imitative *noir* gesture, and in part a response to the unfolding drama across the Atlantic. The play contains a reference to a concentration camp. We are told that a character has 'been in more trouble than the Jews'. Dr Luther becomes the embodiment of the inhumanity against which Miller wishes to pitch a restored and reinvigorated America. But where does the sexuality of the ship's captain, and former U-boat commander, come in? Why must his concern for Donegal be rooted in homosexual longing rather than a principled commitment? Love, indeed, is simultaneously anodyne and all-powerful in the play. What it is not, in either mode, is believable. This is merely one of the unsatisfactory aspects of a play which heads towards the moment when an all-American girl fights back against the Nazis and, by doing so, triumphs. But that, perhaps, explains the rhetoric, the implausible plot, the polarised characters. This was a wartime play fired with the crude enthusiasms of a writer now anxious to throw his energies into the battle but unable to do so, anxious, also, to write a play that would appeal to a Broadway audience.

Boro Hall Nocturne is a war drama about Nazi saboteurs and those within the country who sympathise with them.[11] Throughout the 1930s Father Coughlin had broadcast anti-Semitic propaganda, often drawing directly on the speeches of Dr Goebbels, while the German–American Bund was powerful enough to prompt the creation of the House Un-American Activities Committee before which Miller would later be called when it was no longer fascism but communism which seemed to pose the greatest threat.

Himself originally a pacifist, Miller had swallowed the Hitler–Stalin pact, despite finding it indigestible. Now he was an enthusiastic supporter of the war and *Boro Hall Nocturne* is an expression of that fact.

It is set in the sector headquarters of the Air Raid Protection Service, at Court Street in a downtown area in Brooklyn. The building is dilapidated and largely unoccupied. The only object of significance is a piano. Plainly air raids do not seem an immediate possibility. Even the man in charge, Mr Goldberg, a piano tuner, is asleep, it being three in the morning.

The play carries no date but seems to have been written in 1942. Transports are leaving the nearby dockyard, where Miller himself worked, to join the Atlantic convoys. The Japanese have reached out across the Pacific. Ironically, though, this store front office is about to become the centre of a drama, or more precisely a melodrama.

Goldberg is relieved by Alexander Kelley, a disaffected musician with little belief in the war. Drafted into the army, he is supposed to report for duty but has decided not to go. He tears up his draft card, refusing any responsibility to others, any duty beyond himself. All that matters to him is his music. The two men are friends, not least because in the depths of the Depression Goldberg had rescued Kelly from destitution. This, indeed, is one of the reasons that Kelley has refused to join the anti-Semitic group which courts him, having seen Jews beaten up.

Into this scene come an unlikely group of people, from a Nazi professor of music turned saboteur, to his sleazy American ally and a group of Italian workers, one of whose homes is destroyed by the attack which is now unleashed the length of the eastern seaboard.

News of the attacks comes over the radio and slowly the professor's cover is blown. He stabs his collaborationist ally and is arrested. The play ends as Kelley tries to patch his draft card together, having learned that there is no separate peace, that what happens in Brooklyn is part of the larger battle for survival.

Boro Hall Nocturne is scarcely a subtle work but these were not subtle times and Broadway, Hollywood and radio were all enrolled in the battle, staging the drama of America's struggle against forces internal and external at a time when there was little to celebrate on the battlefield itself. *Boro Hall Nocturne*, like *The Half-Bridge* (the latter later offered to radio), were a part of the effort not only to rally people to the flag but to recognise that the world was their backyard.

— ✳ —

Now several years out of university, Arthur Miller had little to show. He began to wonder whether he should take a full-time job while trying to write on the side. He even convinced himself that to do so might broaden his experience. So confident of inevitable success when he returned from Michigan, he now felt increasingly depressed. Then a new market began to open up for him: radio.

Radio drama had first come to America in 1935–6. The Columbia Workshop was based on British and German models. By 1940 nearly a third of available air time went to drama (10,000 hours). The normal procedure was for networks to sell time to advertising agencies which produced shows for the sponsors.

'The only way you could make a living', Miller explained, 'was in radio.' His first broadcast play was *Joe, the Motorman*, a work about a rebellious subway driver first transmitted on the *Rudy Vallee Show*. The radio, Miller recalled, 'was purely commercial though there was Norman Cowan's programme on CBS. And he had this Whitmanesque style of chest-beating lyricism, but they were very effective plays. He had a considerable audience and I wrote one play for $100 and they broadcast it. It was *The Pussy Cat and the Expert Plumber Who Was a Man*.'[12]

Before his career as a radio dramatist had really taken off, however, he spent several weeks in Wilmington, North Carolina, on behalf of the Library of Congress. His job was to capture the variety of regional accents and to that end he interviewed a number of local inhabitants, eventually editing the material for a radio programme whose script he finished shortly before Pearl Harbour. The tapes of these interviews still exist and once again reveal his fascination with the racial situation in the south.

He recorded interviews in particular with a group of black workers who had been employed to prepare the new shipyards but who now found themselves excluded from the well-paid craft jobs. Further interviews included those with women, mostly black, seventeen weeks into a strike with a local shirt-manufacturing company. He was especially entranced by the protest songs they had composed and which they sang with a mournful beauty he still recalled sixty years later.

It was radio drama, however, that effectively rescued the family finances. Indeed, he recorded one for the Library of Congress (*Buffalo Bill Disremembered*), just before his trip to North Carolina. Largely improvised, it told the story of Buffalo Bill whose death had been so recent that the programme ended with appeals for anecdotes by those who might have known him.

Working first for NBC's *Cavalcade of America*, and then for CBS's *The Doctor Fights* series, he turned out a succession of plays, some no more than workman-like, others works of some originality and power.

In common with some 75 per cent of the American population Miller had been an isolationist, in his case seeing the war in Europe as the last gasp of the old European empires. For Miller this was complicated by the fact of the Hitler–Stalin pact which, given his Marxist credentials, he found it necessary to accept, no matter how it contradicted everything the Communist Party had previously declared. The pact, he had believed, was a natural consequence of the vacillation of the European powers. Pearl Harbour, however, and the German invasion of the Soviet Union, made the war suddenly a necessary battle against fascism.

He now tried to enlist, only to be rejected because of an old high-school leg injury. The radio plays in part became his contribution to the war effort, focusing as they did on patriotic subjects. As he explained to me in 2003,

> I thought some of them were. I didn't have much illusion that they were vital to the war effort but these things had sizeable audiences for that time. They went into the millions. One was aware that we had a very strong isolationist sentiment in the United States. By the time we entered the war it became a domestic political problem for the Administration and one saw rising in the country real pro-Nazi feelings. So I felt I had to contribute something.

And when that seemed insufficient, he trained as a Fitter and went to work in the Brooklyn Navy Yard, a short walk from his Brooklyn Heights home. This was hard work with unsocial hours, sometimes in the harshest conditions. With his own brother at risk in Europe, he plainly felt the need to do something more than entertain the public with stories of American heroes or those who, unlike himself, were putting their lives at risk.

✳

3

The radio plays

Writing for *Cavalcade of America* largely meant writing to order. In a preface he wrote to a collection of radio plays, he explained, with some irony, the process that lay behind the Du Pont-sponsored series. The particular play that prompted his remarks was a later work, dating from the final year of the war. *Grandpa and the Statue* was designed to celebrate the Statue of Liberty as a symbol of American values and a wartime alliance, but it can stand as a comment on a number of the plays he was required to grind out and his professed attitude to them:

> *Grandpa and the Statue* came out the way it did because I could not bear to do another Statue of Liberty show that would illustrate how friendly we are to France and how it will stand forever as a symbol of a symbol and so on. I believe the government and the Radio Writers' Guild ought to get together and decide on one Statue of Liberty script once and for all, and when the anniversary comes around just do it instead of making every writer knock his brains out trying to get a new idea about it. Everything that needs to be said about it was said by Emma Lazarus anyway.
>   The story behind the script is the same as the story behind most *Cavalcade* scripts, and probably all other radio scripts. The man in the advertising office has a calendar with all the national holidays and celebrations and so on marked on it. I come in and we talk until I get depressed, and then go home and do the script and then try not to think of Washington's birthday coming up. I will not deny though that I had a desire to make people realize that the Statue of Liberty was erected to signify America's former open-door policy. If people get the idea from the show that, Jew, Irish, Italian or what not, we were all welcome here once, that will be a great satisfaction to me.[1]

That last remark is a reminder that this same year would see the publication of *Focus* (originally called *Some Shall Not Sleep*), his novel about American anti-Semitism. It was a reminder, too, that he was not beyond wishing to infiltrate a certain scepticism into these plays, even as he was required to conceal his copies of the *Nation*, the *New Masses* (which was, Alfred Kazin remarked, to the old *Masses* which had thrived from 1911–18, 'what St Francis is to the Inquisition')[2] and *Partisan Review* as he entered the corporate headquarters of the advertising agency that produced the shows, an advertising agency that, sixty years later, would reappear in an early draft of *Resurrection Blues*.

Nonetheless, and despite the ironic tone of his introduction, *Grandpa and the Statue*, starring Charles Laughton and transmitted on 26 March 1945, is an assured and effective piece. Much of it is given over to a gentle comedy about a man who refuses to contribute his dime to build the pedestal on which the statue will be erected. Convinced that it will fall down in the first strong wind, he even refuses to visit it until his grandson urges him to do so. Once there, however, he is persuaded by a veteran of the Philippine War that it does indeed represent his aspirations and by the Emma Lazarus poem at its base that it is a symbol of the welcome that America extends to those in need, of the golden door that it opens to the poor and oppressed.

The play ends as he presses not a dime but a quarter into a crack in the statue. It is true that the encomium to the statue and the America it represents is somewhat trite: 'the statue looks like what we believe . . . big . . . strong . . . holding her light. You just know by looking at her she's got a heart big enough for all the people in the world.' Nonetheless, as a gentle comedy whose ironic tone at times undermines its necessary patriotism it is not without its appeal.

Even in an early work, *Joel Chandler Harris*, he was not beyond celebrating something other than the heroes selected for dramatisation by the company. He has the actor Karl Swenson, as Harris, insist that 'in all my work I have been saying one thing. America has got to remember her roots, the plain people.'[3] His aim, he insists, is for people to find 'comradeship' in his stories, stories which themselves are the result of the fact that 'I listened to the people and I told them what I heard.' A populist stance was not without its utility on a mass medium in wartime but this was a play in which he was also careful to invoke the fact of slavery as the context and inspiration for Harris's Brer Rabbit fables. What Miller was trying to do, he remarked in 2003, was to 'celebrate *American* convictions in a fast-vanishing democracy'.

Later that same year, 1941, Claude Raines starred as John Paul Jones in *Captain Paul*, a play to celebrate Navy Day. Miller, speaking in 2003, recalled the process behind this and other *Cavalcade* plays:

> They would call me in the morning and say they were going to send over a book about John Paul Jones, the guy who started the American Navy. And you had never heard of John Paul Jones and you read the book fast on Monday morning. On Tuesday morning you started writing. I wrote the whole damn thing in a day. I made $250, which was a lot of money.

Set at the time of one war, the Revolutionary War, it is offered as a comment on another: 'America is going to be free . . . There's going to be a war.' But perhaps more of a key to Miller's frame of mind were later works, including *The Battle of the Ovens*, transmitted a year later, in June 1942. Again set at the time of the Revolutionary War, it tells the story of Christopher Ludvig, a 61-year-old Philadelphia baker who lends his skills to the cause and who is offered as 'a symbol of all the thousands who have made our history and who have not been recognized in our history'. He is impelled to join his efforts to those who fight because, like Miller himself, rejected for military service, he wishes 'to do instead of to watch', because 'I feel like a stone in a river that's rushing over me.' 'I can', he insists, 'fight with my own weapons . . . We will fight with our trade.' Miller was doing no less.

Ludvig is partly inspired by his revulsion at war-profiteering, as Chris Keller would be in *All My Sons*. As one such profiteer asks, 'What's a war for except to make money?' The play ends as Washington is reported as declaring 'he would not have won the war unless the bakers and the shoemakers and all the people like us got so mad they could not rest until they won', a theme that would recur in Miller's radio plays which, the biographies aside, do tend to celebrate the working man, the ordinary guy.

In a lengthy statement at the end of *The Battle of the Ovens*, the spokesman for Du Pont, who might have bridled at the notion of war profiteering, was less concerned to underline the virtues of the common people than make a pitch for his company's products:

> It is a far cry from the baker friend in tonight's *Cavalcade* to the problem of supplying a modern mobile armed force with its higher standard of food and service. How would you like to bake bread for a hundred thousand soldiers in one camp? How would you like to bake in the galley of a sub-chaser making knots in a high sea? Some ships of our navy do bake at sea. Others stock up with bakery bread loaves before they leave port.

The problem, it seemed, was the growth of mould. Happily, 'the Du Pont Company is now manufacturing a compound to hold back the growth of mould in loaves of bread . . . This is now being used by the army and, since on the domestic scene bakers are making fewer deliveries to conserve fuel and rubber, they, too, are using this product, part of the nation's food conservation.' Perhaps somewhat alarmingly, the radio audience is informed that 'seventy-five million pounds of butter is now wrapped in paper impregnated with this chemical, as is cheese, some of which is being shipped to England'.

At the end of the show, the star was brought back to underscore a less commercial moral as he remarked that 'the humble baker Christopher Ludvig has innumerable counterparts in real life today. In my own native Denmark among other places thousands of my fellow men are valiantly strug-gling to crush the evils of Nazis that hold them I pray only temporarily in their grasp.'

By far the best of his plays, however, was *Juarez*, a verse drama featuring Orson Welles, which staged the life of the revolutionary Mexican leader whom Miller compared to Lincoln, Miller having a fondnessness for comparing the then current war with events from America's Revolutionary and Civil War past. Welles had been rehearsing another play, whose historical accuracy he was in the process of vociferously challenging, when Miller came in with his type-written script with pencil corrections. It was quickly circulated to the actors and broadcast the following week.

Juarez has a lyrical power that is still impressive today and is a reminder of the extent to which then, and later, Miller was drawn to verse for its concision, its ability to breathe significance into the quotidian. He would, indeed, write a number of his plays wholly or partly in free verse before transcribing them into prose, thereby, as it seemed to him, gaining control over the language, lifting it beyond mere functionalism.

Juarez was a celebration of a revolutionary leader, not perhaps what might have been expected of a play sponsored by Du Pont. Here was something of the poetry that had characterised *The Golden Years*:

> The land is on fire! The sky burns!
> The people lift up like lions,
> Roaring their anger from the coast, from Mazatlan
> And Atoyac, from the towns of the Spaniard
> And the Indian towns! They came from Tehuantepec,
> Durango and the river there, from the Bay of Banderas
> The fishermen with salt on their lips
> As once the fishermen of Marblehead came
> In their boats to crash the Heights of Washington![4]

Miller followed *Juarez* with *Toward a Farther Star*, the story of Amelia Earhart, starring Madelaine Carroll. It was this play that Miller confessed having written to a sceptical fellow shipfitter in the Navy Yard. When he tuned in the man was unimpressed because it was 'all true'.

Though Earhart had died in 1937, the connection with the war was more directly underscored than in his previous biographical plays and, indeed, from now on his plays tended to be contemporary and have a war setting. It was a play that called for an acknowledgement of the role of women and reflected both Miller's own views and the necessities of war. The show begins with an announcer declaring that

> as these words are spoken 22,000 women are piloting civil air patrol planes. Others are ferrying bombers to different places. Thousands of American women are pouring through the gates of factories, shipyards and airplane plants after a hard day's work. Today, we know that there is hardly a job that a woman cannot do. And if there is one woman who proved that fact once and forever it is America's greatest woman flyer.

Miller underscores the moral when he has his central character ask, 'Isn't it time to unlock the kitchen and let women out into the free air?' When the head of an airline refuses to employ her because 'flying isn't a woman's business, just like ship building or rivetting or fighting wars', she replies,

> Try and imagine how much richer it [America] would be if half its popu-
> lation, if all its women, were free to do their part of the world's work. The
> world has been walking on one foot, working with one hand, when it has
> two. Blinding one of its eyes, stifling half its brain. Flying with only one of
> its wings. Do look at the world, Mr Brown, and hold your breath, because
> it's changing. Right now . . . it must be true that a woman can live out her
> personal dream and still be a wife. Women must have the right to lead the
> way once in a while, to search for new things instead of sitting home waiting
> for men to do the work of the world.

It is tempting to feel that the plight of Miller's own mother might have been
in his mind, a woman denied the higher education she craved, able only to
watch as her husband sacrificed the life for which she had yearned. But, then,
Miller's own graduate wife was working as a secretary to enable him to write
this play as well as those with which he still hoped to conquer Broadway. It was
a work, though, which anticipated a change in national priorities. Two years
later, the Office of War Information was involved in establishing a Women in
War programme. In 1940 thirteen million women had been in the industrial
workforce. By 1944 the figure was nineteen million. In 1943, CBS launched a
drama series called *American Women*.

Toward a Further Star, which was transmitted on 2 November 1942, was
followed by *The Eagle's Nest* (28 December 1942), with Paul Muni playing
both the role of Garibaldi and a contemporary Italian fighting against Nazi
oppression, a man 'who embodies the spirit of Garibaldi in modern Italy'.

An unashamed piece of propaganda, it begins with a letter from Garibaldi
written in 1866 and welcoming the support of Americans in his cause:

> The sympathy which comes to me from free men, citizens of a great nation,
> like yourselves, gives me courage for my task in the cause of liberty and
> progress. I regard the American people as the sole arbiter of questions of
> humanity and the universal thraldom of the soul and intellect.

Muni, at last appearing in a Miller play (Miller had courted him earlier), now
plays the role of a narrator: 'So you see, America has the right to speak to Italy.
Tonight the voice of Garibaldi speaks to lovers of liberty everywhere. No Nazi
government will tell this story but we will tell it.'

The play is laced through with rousing references to freedom and the role
of America as paradigm and ally: 'Italians, do you hear this? They're coming
from America to help us!' 'In blood you have written that freedom is possible
for Italians, just as it was possible for the Americans . . . This is your Lexington,
this is your Valley Forge.' Miller was fond of invoking the Revolutionary War,
Abraham Lincoln and any other symbol of American democracy as parallels
to the war in Europe and the Pacific. *The Eagle's Nest*, in which even Walt
Whitman has a walk-on part, was not one of Miller's triumphs. Even Du Pont,

for once, proved incapable of seeing a connection between the play and their own products and ended up celebrating the fact that their nylon was used in parachutes.

Later, even less-convincing plays include *The Story of Canine Joe* (transmitted on 21 August 1944), a dramatised account of the role played by dogs in winning the war: 'Only today', suggests the announcer, 'newspapers all over America carried pictures showing our war dogs helping to run the Nazis out of Normandy'! Du Pont, however, was back on form since it made sulpha drugs usable on both animals and wounded soldiers. Nor was the broadcast without its controversy. Miller had included a reference to dogs biting salesmen. He was told to change the reference since some of the company's products were sold door to door. In the end, after an executive meeting, a mailman was substituted for the salesman.

In March 1945, William Bendix appeared in *Bernadine, I Love You*, in which Red Cross officials solve the marital problems of a parachutist (based on material provided by the Red Cross and followed by an appeal on behalf of that organisation), while in April Edward G. Robinson starred in *The Philippines Never Surrendered* about the role of an American citizen in organising guerilla warfare in the Philippines, a play preceded by an announcement: 'Before we begin, we want to tell you about Du Pont's speedy paint.' Perhaps to balance this, it was somewhat implausibly followed by a declaration of Du Pont's support for the United Nations, since the company was anxious to stress that while it was, indeed, successful in wartime, it was even more so in peace and hence had a vested interest in supporting international efforts in that direction.

Cavalcade of America was not Miller's only outlet. Beyond that, in a now burgeoning radio career, he also contributed to a CBS series called *The Doctor Fights*, which aimed to celebrate the role of the 60,000 doctors serving in the war. The programme was sponsored by Schenley Laboratories, in fact the Schenley Liquor Company, the word liquor, as Howard Blue has pointed out, being unmentionable on radio (though the company did have laboratories and was a specialist in the manufacture of penicillin).

Miller wrote a number of scripts for this series from June 1944 to July 1945. For the most part they were based on actual cases and often concluded with the doctor concerned being interviewed. They pulled few punches, more particularly as the series developed and Miller himself urged greater realism, confronting the problems involved in treating soldiers under fire and the horrifying results of battlefield injuries. Nonetheless, for all its directness, the poet in Miller breaks through from time to time. The series featured Raymond Massey, Robert Montgomery and a number of major stars.

In the third of the series, called *Glider Doctor*, Massey set the scene for a play about glider crews setting off from England into occupied territory:

The moon was round as a barrel head that night; poured her icy light on the English coasts. On the choppy sea England floats like a great moored ship. Along the dark and hidden piersides from Plymouth to the Scottish coast, men stop in the dark to study the moon. In the flared bows of waiting cruisers, doctors lift up equipment for the hundredth inspection, like old women fussing in their shopping bags. Further inland where the concrete carpets of the airports have thrust through woodland, where King Arthur rode, doctors stow plasma in grossly shadowed bombers whose silent motors even now nose toward the wind.[5]

The play concluded with the text of an address by Major General Norman T. Kirk, stressing the reduction in infection rates in the armed forces and a commercial for Schenley Laboratories 'maintaining the health of all of us at home'.

The following week he was responsible for the impressive story of a near disastrous bomber raid on Germany in which the doctor is inducted into the reality of warfare. As the plane goes 'Roaring out of the mouth' of a 'pastel English dawn', one of the crew explains that before joining the airforce he used to watch high-flying aircraft 'like a piece of ice you want to eat'. Now, looking down at the English Channel it seems 'too silver to drown you'. In a play of ironic and often humorous dialogue, with sound effects of machine guns being tested, the explosions of flack and faltering engines, Miller reaches for an affecting poetry and a sense of brotherhood which owes nothing to ideology and everything to a shared experience: 'How quickly the past tense arrives in the air', the narrator observes, as a man dies, but 'Suddenly brotherhood is like a living thing in this plane.'

The bomb-aimer crouches over his bombsight 'like a kid over a gopher hole. And time is a knife turning in your flesh.' Then, the bombs released, the 'plane banks stiffly like an iron gull'. As the action continues, the narrator explains: 'The anatomy of danger is strange, Doctor. You will remember none of this afterward. You will not remember this moment when you sewed the body of the co-pilot to his soul while the plane reeled and bumbled across the channel like a drunken street brawler . . . We remember it for you, and we remember the terrible moment when the world seemed to shut like an eye.' The plane makes its way back to crash-land at its base, the doctor helping the men though, indeed, remembering little of the experience.

The play would still stand up today. Certainly it shows Miller a master of radio drama. What would now seem its false moment is precisely that emphasis on brotherhood which had originally fired his political beliefs and which seemed to find its practical apotheosis in wartime, a solidarity he was hoping would survive the conflict. For a few hours, we are told, the doctor had been 'part and tissue of eight living men'. As the narrator observes, now becoming the doctor he had previously described, 'I was girded to them, I was lost in them and they in me, and losing ourselves we found ourselves. We were brothers there! When will such brotherhood live on the earth! Or – must it always crash when it descends from the air?'[6] *All My Sons* is a breath away.

As with the *Cavalcade of America* programmes, the play was followed by a statement on behalf of the sponsors, which in this case stressed the valuable job being done by military doctors, and, somewhat startlingly for a radio drama programme broadcast into the nation's homes, the effective use of penicillin to treat venereal disease.

Later, Miller would even contribute to American Federation of Labour and Congress of Industrial Organizations radio presentations in support of union rights, in one opposing the Taft-Hartley bill. In the late 1940s a number of radio dramatists would find themselves blacklisted for similar work. It was a fate which, despite being listed in a right-wing publication, Miller escaped.

Though Miller considered most of his radio plays journeyman work, they did provide a means for him to express political and social values that, if in tune with calls for wartime solidarity, were also consonant with his own convictions. Some of that work also has qualities which lift it above bespoke writing. It also had a utility beyond its value as a generator of cash. Working to a deadline, and in a form that encouraged concision, he began to excise those elements that make *The Half-Bridge*, in particular, such awkward reading. He discovered the power of verse, the strength of metaphor, the necessity to engage public issues through the dilemmas of individual characters. There are plays here whose lyricism is compelling and which are highly proficient in their use of the medium.

In his *Theatre Guild of the Air* plays (in which he adapted existing stage plays and novels), he was writing for an hour-long broadcast format, but even this required a rigorous approach to character and plot development. The inessentials had to go. This could put a premium on story, and press character in the direction of caricature, but it also taught him useful lessons in dramatic construction. He learned that time could be collapsed: 'learning how to condense is invaluable. If you can condense a four-hundred-page book into twenty-eight minutes then you might be able to condense your own elaborate fantasies into a time that people would be willing to sit there and listen to. I learned how to condense and to do it gracefully. Radio drama could be a terrific but minor form.'[7]

Speaking in 2003, he remarked that,

> The model is the Book of Genesis. You read about the Creation and in about a page and a half you've got the human race. And that's pretty hot stuff. That is the way to tell a story, and a story that never dies. It is the imprint of a hot iron on the soul. [Writing radio plays] taught me a lot about how to tell a story. Less is better. Why? It's very simple. It's like dreams. Dreams are very brief and some of them you never forget because they are very discrete. Nothing is wasted. No dream has got excessive material. It all counts.[8]

David Mamet has remarked that, 'radio is a great training ground for dramatists. More than any other dramatic medium it teaches the writer to concentrate
on the essentials . . . Working for radio, I learned the way *all* great drama works,
by leaving the *endowment* of characters, place, and especially action to the audience . . . Writing for radio forces you and *teaches* you to stick to . . . the story.'[9] It
is doubtful if Miller would agree that the story is all there is to the theatre, 'the
rest is just packaging', and that this 'is the lesson of radio', but his radio work
did teach him to sweat out the inessentials, to understand that audiences are
quite able to fill those spaces left vacant by a writer because their articulation
would be redundant.

It was his growing reputation as a radio dramatist that now secured him another project. He was contracted to work on a film which would celebrate the life of the ordinary soldier and the work of war correspondent Ernie Pyle, famous for his human-interest approach to reporting. Perhaps astonishingly, Miller had been offered a movie contract immediately on leaving Michigan, and watched as many of his friends took the train to easy money in Hollywood. He refused because he saw his future as lying in the theatre. He signed on now because the project seemed to be something more than the usual melodrama and to offer him another chance to contribute to the national cause. He was set to visiting army bases across the country as part of his research. The film was to be called *The Story of GI Joe.*

He spent some time in Hollywood and eventually discovered that his suspicions had not been ill-founded. He was replaced by other writers and his name does not appear on the credits. He did, however, publish his account of his research for the film and thus *Situation Normal* became his first published book. It is dedicated to his brother, Lieutenant Kermit Miller of the United States Infantry. Miller's work on the film script was money in the bank but it was also clearly something else. It was part of his contribution to the war effort, though, as it turned out, a somewhat curious one.

Situation Normal is a remarkable book, not least because it rapidly becomes clear that the war is marginal to his concerns. What was supposed to be a record of his research for a patriotic film turned into a critique of American values to be published at a time when those values were taken as self-evident. Once again he was determined to denounce American racism as he was to propose a model of society which depended less on myths of material advancement than on principles of mutuality which he believed himself to have found in Marxism.

He travelled in search of men fired by idealism, alert, as he and his classmates at Michigan had been, to the dangers of fascism. He found instead men who understood little of fascism and were concerned only to survive. If they had feelings of loyalty these were not directed to any abstract cause but to one another.

In the letters he received from his brother he read of the idealism which sustained him. As a result, when he himself visited military bases and conducted interviews with soldiers, he looked for evidence of this, for the most part in vain. He was, he confesses, trying to locate 'some basic credo which will explain and justify this war'.[10] It is an odd remark, though for the most part justified by the bafflement he had encountered in Wilmington and encountered again now. For him, fascism had long been the enemy. Indeed, decades later he would confess that in many ways the battle against it had shaped his life.

For those he met as he criss-crossed America, though, it plainly meant little or nothing. Indeed, more than that, he detected, as it seemed to him, a domestic fascism which contradicted the idea that this was a war in which one ideology confronted another. It was a contradiction which puzzled and disturbed him. The paradox, he explained, was that

> still I have to keep remembering that some of the most aggressive-minded officers I have met, men who want to come to grips with the enemy at the earliest possible moment, are men who betray strong traces of home grown Fascist complexes. So many southern officers, strong racists and very reactionary in the deepest sense, are undoubtedly making fine leaders.
>
> (40)

It is hard to believe that this was the kind of material either the Army or Hollywood had been looking for, and indeed the striking dimension of *Situation Normal* is that it is less an account of America at war with Germany and Japan than America at war with itself. This is still the Arthur Miller of the 1930s, interested in social injustice, racism and the battle against internal reactionaries. He clearly regrets that he can find among the men no sense that they are fighting for any cause, confessing that it

> is terrible to me that everything is so personal. I mean that never in any of these calculations about the soldier can I honestly bring in the socio-political context of this war. I can't seem to find men who betray a social responsibility as a reason for doing or not doing anything . . . And yet I can't give up the idea that political and economic beliefs have something to do with how these men react to their training and the idea of fighting.
>
> (44)

The reason for this, he is inclined to believe, is 'the incessant press attacks of those who hate the Belief' (73), an odd remark but seemingly a denunciation of those who see an assault on fascism as tainted with communism. Thus he insists that some may be 'demoralized by this country's non statement of political and moral beliefs' (113).

His own position is clear throughout, particularly with respect to race, the issue that had so engaged him in the novel he had written after his trip on the SS *Copa Copa* and the encounters he had had in North Carolina. It 'will be unfortunate', he insists, 'if we cannot find in the picture a dynamic and integrated place for the Negro' (90). Certainly it seemed to him that the Army itself had not found such a place. 'During the past few weeks', he noted, 'several incidents have occurred when white trainees objected to being instructed by Negroes. I heard an officer say that the Negro cadremen were to be eased out as a consequence' (91). This can hardly have been what the promoters of the film wished to hear.

By way of ironic illustration, he tells the story of the embarrassment caused when it was decided to name the parade ground after the first tankman from the base to die in the war, only for it to emerge that the man had in fact been black. So significant was the incident that he later rewrote it as a short story, though once again one that would never be published.

On a trip to Atlanta he met a Georgia mill-owner. To him, as it seemed to Miller, the 'whole world was visibly falling apart. Negroes were doing mechanical labor. It was a curse and an abomination to him. I could ascertain no reason other than plain fear of their emancipating themselves through learning skills' (98). What he had seen in the military, in other words, was an extension of what was observable in the country. And this is the startling quality of *Situation Normal*. It is not the Army alone that is (in the implied conclusion of the title) 'all fucked up'; it is America.

For its part, the Army uses 'the Negro by and large for menial tasks'. It 'wouldn't do at this time', he insisted, 'to aggravate their justifiable grievances by portraying it naturalistically, it seemed, and yet it simply could not be ignored. I just couldn't see anything hopeful in the situation and I couldn't get myself to lie about it.' It is not clear what force he gives to the word 'naturalistically'. Perhaps it is no more than an indication that he feels inhibited from dwelling on the details of what he has seen. It does, though, suggest an inhibition of which there is very little evidence in a book which effectively challenges America's political leaders, its media and the values of a citizenry wedded to materialism and deeply prejudiced.

Requests to watch 'Negroes drilling or going through training' fell on deaf ears. The idea of them going into combat seemed to prompt derision, though what appears to be a careful publisher adds a footnote listing black service units serving overseas. Miller did, however, find a black lawyer who would speak freely. 'Most white people', he explained,

> don't know it, but there have been a great many outrages against colored soldiers since war was declared. Hardly a month passes without something bad happening . . . All they want is the continuing right to belong to America. The uniform says they do . . . At the same time, though, the uniform highlights all the irony of our position; we are asked to die for a country that literally doesn't always let us live.

> (118)

'I want . . . a man like this' in the picture, Miller insisted, 'I will show how ridiculous is the claim that the races absolutely cannot tolerate each other after prejudice has been instilled' (119). In his outline script, which follows a group of men from their induction through to the eve of D-Day, he indicates that among the throng of soldiers from around the world are 'American Negro troops'. Perhaps it is hardly surprising that in the end he would not write the final script and that his name does not appear on the credits.

The other central theme of the book focuses on a man called Watson who has returned from fighting in the Pacific seemingly impotent. He feels nothing so much as a sense of guilt at being in America while his comrades are dying. He is an apparent idealist faced with one day returning to a society which has no understanding of self-sacrifice, a society divided along lines of class and race. 'Nobody', he insists, 'is a hero if he can still breathe', scarcely an encouraging remark for those facing service overseas, or in a work which had its origins in a desire to boost morale.

What Miller seems chiefly to fear is not the fate of such men in war but their fate when eventually they return to America. In the middle of a book seemingly about men at war he writes about an America apparently bereft of values and in a state of moral decay:

> Riding away from the camp I wondered for the first time whether I ought not to be wandering through St Paul and Kansas City, New York and Los Angeles instead of through the camps. For as far as Watson was concerned it was in America as much as in the island where he fought that his wholeness had been wrecked and his mind distracted. It was not only the Japanese who had shaken his wits. We here did our part in that, and with terrible effect.
>
> (155)

Watson, and others like him, it seemed, would have to return to a divided society. 'Our lifelong boast', Miller says, 'is that we got ahead of the next guy, excluded him' (158). He will be returning to a country with no shared beliefs which cut any deeper than the need to succeed. 'Free enterprise' is a slogan and not a value. What America should be fighting for, he suggests, is what it once stood for: 'We believe all men are equal.' What he sees instead is a 'chaos of the mind' and 'no great social goal' (161). The risk is that Watson, once returned to America, will 'wall himself in from his fellow man . . . live only his own little life and do his own unimportant, unsatisfying job. He must begin again the stale and dreary competition with his fellow men for rewards that now seem colorless' (162).

Situation Normal, supposedly an account of his research for *The Story of GI Joe,* thus stands as a kind of manifesto, as clear a statement as he would ever make of the values he embraced as America went to war, it seemed, oblivious, of the injustices it tolerated at home and of a materialism which did nothing to address the social, moral or spiritual needs of the individual.

Meanwhile, though he continued to make a reputation for himself in radio, Miller was still not succeeding in theatre. Once again he tried his hand at a novel. Though he wrote several drafts it never seemed to work out, not least because there was a darkness to it at odds with the needs of a society at war. He rewrote it as a play and suddenly found it accepted. Six years after leaving Michigan he would at last be seeing one of his works on Broadway. The novel-turned-play was called *The Man Who Had All the Luck*. He could hardly have chosen a more unfortunate title. It was an unequivocal and seemingly unredeemable failure.

Novel and play were inspired by a story told to Miller by his Ohio mother-in-law. It concerned a successful young man who came to believe that he was being defrauded by one of his employees at a service station he owned. The suspicions seem to have been a function of his mental state. Certainly, he shortly thereafter killed himself and was found hanging in a barn. Miller's own cousin, also apparently successful and healthy, suddenly dropped dead on the beach at Coney Island. The two stories, taken together, seemed to Miller to raise questions about the extent to which fate was the operative principle behind human affairs. Why, after all, during the Depression, had some prospered and others failed? In wartime, why was one person killed and another spared? How responsible are we for our own lives and how much the product of pure contingency? Do we inhabit an absurd universe or construct our own fate? Novel and play end differently. The difference is critical.

※

4

'The Man Who Had All the Luck'

The Man Who Had All the Luck, in its novel form, concerns David, a young man in his twenties, talented and successful in everything he does. Setting himself up as a mechanic, he manages to get by on instinct until confronted with a car whose fault he cannot diagnose. He takes it to a specialist garage in a nearby town but accepts the credit for the repairs they effect. As a result he secures a contract to work on the tractors of a neighbouring farmer and from there his business grows. Slowly he adds other ventures, in which he is equally successful. But he is increasingly aware that he is surrounded by those who have failed in life.

One friend, Shory, had lost his legs during the war and as a result feels unworthy of the woman he loves. Another, Amos, is trained by his father to be a baseball pitcher but, despite his talent, fails to be taken on by the major league because his training, directed by his father in the basement of their house, has made him insensitive to other aspects of the game. A third friend, J. B. Fellers, appears to thrive, even having the child that he and his wife had desperately wanted, only inadvertently to kill that child when drunk.

For David, by contrast, everything goes well. He has the child he wanted and succeeds in everything he tries but his very success breeds a deepening paranoia. He awaits the catastrophe he feels must balance his luck, if there is to be true justice in the world. He begins, like the man on whom he was partly based, to inspect the books of the gas station he owns. He prepares himself for what he feels must be the death of his own child, in some kind of perverted trade-off for a life otherwise without blemish. And, finally, he commits suicide, vaguely feeling that he will thereby lift the curse that surely must be on his family.

Perhaps that death is a sign that the novel was still too close to its origins, but perhaps it is also a sign that, to Miller, death raised the odds, gave a deepening significance. He was reaching for the tragic but being snared by the merely pathological. When he came to write the play version he chose a different ending. He also introduced a number of changes, at least one of which would prove of lasting significance.

The Man Who Had All the Luck, as novel, appears to echo aspects of *Situation Normal*, and to anticipate what would become familiar Miller concerns. America, as one of the characters, an Austrian immigrant, remarks, seems to exhibit 'complete chaos! . . . The people are not bound to any *idea*, there is no . . . underlying principle. Is every man for himself, without limitations, without boundaries . . . The only godhead here is every man for himself.'[1] The protagonist, meanwhile, wants to feel a connection between himself and his life. He fears, above all, like so many Miller characters, that he will discover that he has lived to no purpose and that when he dies they will simply change the name on the mailbox.

When the immigrant mechanic observes that, 'A man must see what he makes with his hands; it is not enough to make money . . . he must not lose connection with the things of his hands, the things that he makes', he outlines a dilemma felt by Willy Loman, and expressed by Miller some fifty years later in *The Last Yankee*. Here, too, is the origin of that sense of helplessness that seemed, to Miller no less than to this character, the root of a disabling sense of anomie. Addressing a protagonist bemused by the seeming arbitrariness of experience, the random nature of fortune and justice, this same mechanic, reaching to express himself in an alien language, insists that

> With you is only the same as with millions of people . . . they become like wondering, and afraid like you, afraid because they do not understand or remember where things arise from, they forget the god in their hands, and they look in the sky or in the ground or someplace for the god . . . Of course they become frightened. When one looks and does not find it is frightening.

The play version finds David Beeves's marriage to Hester blocked by her father. A bitter and cynical man, he is abruptly killed off in a traffic accident. The first obstacle to success is thus conveniently removed, that very convenience being a clue to the style of a play which Miller chooses to call 'A Fable'. Its very improbabilities (he buys a gas station and a highway development fortuitously makes it profitable; he invests in mink and survives an accident that wipes out a rival's holdings) are indicators of its status as a moral tale and, indeed, it was the inability of the director to define a style appropriate to this that in part accounted for its failure.

When David is confronted with a fault in a car that defies his skills, he is saved not, as in the novel, by taking it to another garage but by the arrival of an Austrian mechanic. Two elements of the novel are thus tied together while the second obstacle to David's success is removed. And so he emerges as the man who had all the luck, in contrast to those around him, though the sub-plots that had overloaded the novel are now pared away. We learn little, for example, of Shory's previous life, except that he lost his legs in an accident and not as a result of the war. J. B. Fellers does not suffer the death of his child, while the would-be baseball player is integrated into the story when Miller makes him David's brother, a crucial change not only for this play but for his future work.

As he later explained, '*The Man Who Had All the Luck*, through its endless versions, was to move me inch by inch toward my first open awareness of father–son and brother–brother conflict . . . One day, quite suddenly, I saw that Amos and David were brothers and Pat their father. There was a different anguish in the story now, an indescribable new certainty that I could speak from deep within myself, had seen something no one else had ever seen' (*T*.90–1). Only now recognising that two of his university plays had featured brothers, he felt he understood something of the tension which underlaid the play. He, after all, had succeeded in part, he felt, at cost to his father and brother.

Kermit had dropped out of City College to support his family. Miller himself went to university, and though he had struggled at first things had begun to go his way. His brother went to war; he was exempt from military service. His brother had wanted to be a writer; he himself had become one. And now he had a child. Was all this luck, or a reward for effort? Was it a victory of selfishness over selflessness? For a moralist who had mistaken himself for an ideologue, these questions were real enough. And beyond the family, what of an immigrant country which wishes to see itself simultaneously as unaccountably blessed and the product of individual endeavour? Some chose to stay behind; others ventured all. Was this moral purpose or Darwinian logic? In later years he would ask himself what lessons contingency might offer. Potentially, after all, it eroded the idea of purposeful action, private destiny, national purpose. It was evidence of that very absurdity that he set himself to resist. Yet how to justify the notion of willed action, of existential truth, if we wash in and out with the tide, if men and women encounter one another like random particles.

Father–son relationships, those between brothers, suddenly opened up new possibilities that he would deploy in his work for another two decades and more. Within the family unit, he came to feel, are contained alternative possibilities, tensions that are, in some senses, the fragmented parts of a self (spiritual/material, poetic/prosaic, blessed/cursed). The evidence for that seems clear in *Death of a Salesman* and *The Price* where the brothers have a dialectical relationship to one another, albeit one suffused with ambiguities. Father–son relationships, meanwhile, bring past and present together, hopes and fulfilments, or otherwise. They are the locus of anxieties about identity, of contested values, of an ambivalent love, of guilt. In both cases there is a potential conflict that opens up not merely different perceptions of experience but also different interpretations of the private and public world. There is, indeed, an inherent drama in the tension that exists within the family between the desire to stay and to break free which is the basis of much of Miller's early drama. In the context of *The Man Who Had All the Luck*, though, his decision to make David and Amos brothers seems to have rooted the piece in a psychology he could understand and inhabit.

This is a strange play for a self-declared Marxist to write. Whatever else it is doing – and there is at its heart a debate about human agency and the capacity for change – on one level it seems to be concerned with the need of a rich man to justify his riches. To be sure, the central character has luck as well as showing initiative, but that had been the essence of those nineteenth-century primers on the American dream, the Horatio Alger Jr novels. One was even entitled *By Luck and Pluck*. True, Alger heroes were never angst-ridden, a fact which Nathanael West parodies in *A Cool Million*, but they were, like Miller's protagonist, beneficiaries of coincidence and chance. In the end, though, it is not wealth as such that obsesses David Beeves so much as what seems to be the merely arbitrary nature of its acquisition. What Miller is concerned to do in *The Man Who Had All the Luck* is to insist that we are responsible for the world we inhabit and the life we live, and that this is a key to individual action, to a sense of the self. History is shaped by man rather than man by history.

At the heart of the play is a concern with the extent of human freedom. Beyond offering an account of a man's decline into madness, and eventual redemption, it explores the degree to which so many of the characters become complicit in their own irrelevance, the degree to which they collude in the idea of man as victim, as a subject of cosmic ironies. At its centre is the existential conviction, resisted by most of the characters, including David in his madness, that we are the sum of our actions. If not believers in God, a number of them are believers in fate, which is the word they choose to give to their own personal and social paralysis.

As the play develops, David himself is a convert to this faith, looking for some justice, some operative principle in the universe, unable to recognise the connection between action and consequence. Finding no such principle, he comes close to destroying himself, as if his suicide might constitute that balancing justice whose absence has brought him near despair.

It is not hard to see how Miller regarded this as in some ways addressing that political and moral paralysis that he saw infecting Europeans and Americans alike in the face of fascism. To him, such inaction revealed something more than a failure of will, something beyond mere political pragmatism. It was as if belief in the possibility of action had been destroyed, as if the march of fascism across Europe were a natural phenomenon. Beyond that, he seems to have detected a more fundamental defeatism since this is a novel and then a play in which characters, acknowledging the sheer contingency of experience, appear to accept the role of victim, to welcome the sense of vertigo which comes with staring into the depths of a self-generated despair.

At the beginning of the play, David is a man who seizes the day. In the words of his brother, he knows 'how to do'.[2] Others are more quiescent. Thus his father wants success for Amos, having trained him for years, but it is David who finally calls the baseball scout, asking 'can you *just wait for something to happen*?' (124). Shory, in part an echo of the figure of Moe Axelrod in Clifford Odets's *Awake and Sing*, has been made cynical by his wartime experience. For him, 'A man is a jellyfish. The tide goes in and the tide goes out. About what happens to him, a man has very little say' (134).

In years to come, Miller would set his face resolutely against the theatre of the absurd, repelled by the stasis it staged, the ironies which eroded the possibility and purpose of action. The war may have engendered that theatre, along with the *nouveau roman*, with its marginalised figures frozen in space, but the war also bred the necessity for action, for an acceptance of responsibility for history no less than a private life. If he was both an existentialist and a Marxist his model would be the Jean-Paul Sartre of *Existentialism and Humanism*, though he would not read the text until many years later. *The Man Who Had All the Luck* was his attempt to write a philosophical play and not the 'comedy' which a well-meaning Burns Mantle thought it to be in his review of the 1944–5 theatrical season.[3] It was recognised by some critics as a play of ideas but what those ideas might be left them largely baffled.

Gus, in many ways a selfless man, nonetheless insists that 'There is no justice in this world.' This is a view that David resists, if only because not to resist it would bring him to the brink of madness. As he says, 'If one way or another a man don't receive according to what he deserves inside ... well, it's a madhouse' (155). Yet this principle seems not to be operative. So many of those around him fail, and as evidence of this accumulates so he feels a rising tide of hopelessness and despair which transmutes into madness. Like Willy Loman, he buys a life-insurance policy as though the balance he looks for could be secured by trading his life for the future of his family. It is a bargain whose irony escapes him.

Who, after all, is he bargaining with except the God for whose existence he can find no convincing evidence? If we do not exist in God's eye then what is our sanction to exist at all? If God does not exist then all things are possible. It was a question which fascinated both Sartre and Camus and which also concerned Miller, if not his Broadway audience or, perhaps more accurately, the critics who were Broadway's gatekeepers. There is a world of difference between Miller's protagonist and Camus's Caligula, but both of them test out the absurdist proposition that there is not only no moral sanction but no moral system at all. Caligula is a paradigm of Hitler for whom everything was possible. Miller's David Beeves is the democratic Western powers as war approached and also those who saw no purpose in resisting power beyond mere survival. In the novel, David goes to his death, a victim of his own belief in the absurd. In the play he learns a social ethic born out of a private understanding of agency.

At the centre of the opening scene is a car, tangible, the evidence of David's initial grounding in a physical world of work. His identity and social role are invested in the idea that he is literally the maker of his own future but, as doubts begin to intrude (not least because he accepts credit for another person's work), so that meaning starts to dissolve. The focus shifts to his deepening anxieties. His state of mind begins to determine the shape, if not of events, then of his perception of them. The play, in effect, takes an inward track as he filters experience for its meaning, or, increasingly, its perceived lack of meaning. His life, and what he chooses to make of the lives of those around him, is less lived than shaped by himself into an exemplary tale.

He is alienated from his life because he cannot identify the transcendent purpose which he believes alone can charge it with significance. His identity comes close to being destroyed because he chooses to see it in terms of that absent force. Balanced between hope and despair, he fails, for much of the play, to recognise that he holds his own life in his hands and that there are connections – those with wife, child, friends – which contain the essence of the very meaning he has sought in an abstract principle, as Willy Loman would be dazzled by a dream which blinds him to those who value him for himself.

It is Gus who explains what David has lost, in doing so making the most explicit reference to the wider issues involved: 'What a man must have, what a man must believe. That on this earth he is the boss of his own life. Not the leafs in the teacups, not the stars. In Europe I seen already millions of Davids walking around, millions. They gave up to know . . . that they deserve this world' (199). Man is his own God and 'must understand the presence of God in his hands' (200).

In the novel David dies; in the play he lives. He does so because he is finally convinced that his success has been a product of his own hands, just as the failure of some of those around him can be traced to their own culpability. Shory, it turns out, bore responsibility for the loss of his legs, which occurred not on the battlefront but in an accident at a whorehouse. J. B.'s life has never been what he hoped because of his drinking. Amos and his father have narrowed their lives down until they have lost sight of what living might be. Such lives are still in part the product of contingency, but that contingency is not definitional. The play does not end in death. The thunder, representing that arbitrariness, rumbles but, despite his apprehension, he calls out the central existential truth: 'I'm here!' (208).

Writing later, Miller remarked that 'the play's action seemed to demand David's tragic death, but that was intolerable to my rationalist viewpoint. In the early forties', he added, 'such an ending would have seemed to me obscurantist' (*T*.105). But the point was that in the novel it *had* ended with his death. It was a death, however, that seemed to owe rather more to melodrama than tragedy, and in the play version Miller was stepping back from melodrama and tragedy alike. For him,

> A play's action, much like an individual's acts, is more revealing than its speeches, and this play embodied a desperate quest on David's part for an authentication of his identity, a longing for a break in the cosmic silence that alone would bestow a faith in life itself. To put it another way, David has succeeded in piling up treasures that rust, from which his spirit has already fled; it was a paradox that would weave through every play that followed.
>
> (*T*.105)

That last remark is especially interesting, both in its stress on the absences felt so acutely by Miller's characters and in the biblical language. He recounts a conversation with John Anderson, critic for the *Journal-American*, who asked him, in the context of this play, whether he was religious. At the time he found the question absurd yet, of course, the play in many ways focuses on the protagonist's fear of abandonment, his sense that some coherent principle is in abeyance. He wishes to invent the God in which, on one level, he does not believe in order to discover justification, explanation, a sense of justice for which he can find no evidence. He resists the truth, which is resisted by so many of Miller's later protagonists, that he is his own connection, his own God, fully responsible for who he is and what he does.

Paul Unwin's response to the stylistic problems raised by the play, in the Bristol Old Vic production fifty years later, was in part to turn to music, specially composed by Andy Sheppard, and in part to rely on the designs of Sally Crabb, whose productions had included *The Master Builder* and *Our Town*, two plays whose style also moves away from realism and which, in effect, offer themselves as fables. It was, he admitted, a play that 'poses any director some complicated style problems. On the one hand the play is set firmly in the reality of the American midwest, on the other it has a heightened style and events unfold surprisingly.'[4] It was, he insisted, obsessional in the sense of a Strindberg play. It was not a realist work. The coincidences were, to his mind, reminiscent of *Oedipus*. Beyond that, it was a morality tale and David his Everyman.

In talking to Unwin before the production Miller observed that, 'The thing you've got to understand about my plays is that the background is the American dream and the foreground the American nightmare.'[5] And, in one way or another, the characters in *The Man Who Had All the Luck* are dedicated to a dream while the process of the play is to move from dream to nightmare, precisely the transition which offers such a challenge to directors, actors and designers. Meanwhile, like Susan Glaspell's *The Verge*, it also has to move from the comic not to the tragic but the psychotic.

David is the model of that dream, beginning with nothing and rising to success and wealth. He is even, in Willy Loman's term, well liked, before, like Willy, though for wholly different reasons, developing a fevered need to justify his own existence. For Willy, the problem is failure; for David, it is success. He is, indeed, a mirror image of Job, who is stripped of everything in a test of his faith. David is given everything in a test of his. It is not the fallacy, or otherwise, of the dream, however, that compels Miller's attention here, nor its social implications. Despite his remarks, the play is not a critique of the American dream. What it is, in essence, is an ontological argument sharpened by a national myth that validates success and has nothing to say to those who fail according to its definitions.

David feels the need to argue for the existence of God, or immanent justice, on the grounds that without such a concept, without a principle of order in the universe, nothing can have meaning. God, in other words, is created out of need and proved by what at first seems evidence for his existence. But by degrees that evidence seems to disappear, as, it appears to David, sheer chance becomes the only observable mechanism at work in his own life and in that of those around him.

What he is resisting is a purely phenomenological interpretation of experience that strips it of a metaphysical dimension. The idea that things simply happen is intolerable to him, but he is aware that he has not been the sole creator of his own life. Indeed, he slowly ceases to believe that his life is in any way the product of his own actions or that there is an underlying purpose. As far as he can see, some succeed and others fail and there is no reason for it. Having arrived at that conviction he becomes, briefly, an absurdist figure, taking reckless chances, and then a wild-eyed pagan offering to bargain with the God he invokes for no better reason than to justify his sacrifice of himself, as if sacrifice itself might, by some inverse logic, validate such a God.

In the play, as opposed to the novel, David emerges from his trial of the spirit, not yet secure, to be sure, but seemingly convinced that the logic for which he had looked does exist, that people are responsible for their actions, that causality is an operative principle. But the wound is not entirely healed. The thought that anything can happen, at any time, is not purged and the desperate desire for a validating reason not entirely answered by acknowledging his responsibility for his own actions. The arbitrary still exists and, indeed, in invoking the Depression as a presence in the play Miller was doing no more than signal a social, economic and psychological truth of the period.

The collapse of the market was like one of Job's plagues. People lost livelihoods, relationships were attenuated, the future itself seemed suddenly to collapse. And if some people prospered, how much deeper the sense of absurdity and irony. Miller himself has said that, 'Until 1929 I thought things were pretty solid. Specifically, I thought – like most Americans – that somebody was in charge. I didn't know who it was, but it was probably a businessman, and he was a realist, a no-nonsense fellow, practical, honest, responsible. In 1929 he jumped out of a window. It was bewildering.'[6] The Depression was an economic fact but its consequences went beyond social effects. A machine had come apart. Order had dissolved. Something more than a political system had collapsed. The real itself seemed problematic and certainly the sense that meaning inheres in existence. David Beeves believed someone was in charge, not a businessman, to be sure, but someone, until suddenly he could no longer believe this to be true. God, it seemed, had jumped to his death.

Beyond the Depression, however, there was another source for this sense of abandonment, this sudden realisation that anything could happen at any time, that there was no redeeming coherence to experience. The novel version of *The Man Who Had All the Luck* overlapped with the writing of *The Golden Years* and both were in part a response to events far removed from America. The terror that was to strike Sylvia Gellberg, in *Broken Glass*, was prompted by Kristallnacht, in 1938, when Hitler unleashed his Brown Shirts thereby announcing that he no longer recognised a system of law, of moral necessities and human values.

The Miller who wrote these earlier works was, of course, aware of the plight of the Jews in Europe and eventually of the details of the Holocaust. Here, quite suddenly, all the comforting structures were swept away. Rationality, the whole complex of interlocking social, legal and moral obligations, was effectively declared null and void. The Jew was declared a victim whose fate was never again to be in his own hands. He was the ultimate embodiment of human insignificance, ordered to board the train to his own annihilation and invited to pay for the privilege, as if irony would be the last emotion to be felt as hope was sustained until the final clang of the metal door and the hiss of the scattered powder. Souls were sucked from those born with no other fate than to die locked inside their own terror.

Seen in this context, *The Man Who Had All the Luck* seems to reflect that deep sense of abandonment felt by so many, as hope was not only transmuted into its opposite but itself became a component element of absurdity. David Beeves's sense of an arbitrary good fortune is merely the other side of the same coin. His question – 'Why?' – becomes the question of all. It was a question that would not go away, one to which Miller would return in the 1960s as he, and others, began to inspect an event which for two decades had provoked nothing so much as a bewildered silence.

It was against this that Miller pitched his own native existentialism, his belief that man was of necessity his own God, the source of his own identity, obliged to accept responsibility for himself and the society which he joins in shaping. And if suicide might be a logical response to absurdity, renewed commitment was no less logical.

It may be that this fable is too slight to bear the weight of such concerns, that the very systematic nature of the good fortune his protagonist experiences, and the ill fortune experienced by those around him, amounts to the very order whose absence he laments as, arguably, it is in Greek drama. In other words, perhaps there are ironies here not fully explored. Yet at the same time there is something representative, surely, about this figure of a man bewildered by his own experiences, desperate to understand the apparent arbitrariness of his fate.

The Man Who Had All The Luck is, Miller has said, 'trying to weigh how much of our lives is a result of our character and how much is a result of our destiny'. For him, there was 'no possibility . . . to come down on one side or the other'.[7] The question was sparked by the pressure of immediate events, if scarcely limited to them. As he later remarked, in an 'Afterword' to the published edition, '*The Man Who Had All the Luck* tells me that in the midst of the collectivist Thirties I believed it decisive what an individual thinks and does about his life, regardless of overwhelming forces . . . David Beeves arrives as close as he can at a workable, conditional faith in the neutrality of the world's intention toward him.' In that sense he backed off from the severity of Sartrean existentialism which made the individual bear the full burden of responsibility for action and inaction alike. For Miller, contingency could not be denied. What was necessary was to shape it into meaning which is, after all, precisely what he saw the writer as doing.

— ✳ —

The production was a near total failure. Its out-of-town try-out took place in Wilmington, Delaware, headquarters of the Du Pont Company, sponsors of his radio plays. No one, however, seems to have suspected the disaster which lay ahead, though Miller recalls cutting the first act at Philadelphia. It opened, as no play written by a new playwright would today, on Broadway, and closed in the blink of an eye. The reviewers were largely baffled, and though for the most part they let the 29-year-old playwright down gently, even looking forward to his next effort, the notice of closure went up immediately. It ran for four performances, of which Miller could only face one. He had waited so long for his Broadway debut and it had brought him nothing but humiliation. Investors lost their money and he presumed that he had lost his chance. He was approached by a California company willing to stage it but only if he effected certain changes. He refused. But he never entirely gave up on the play and nearly fifty years on it had a successful production in Britain and at the turn of the millennium returned to Broadway, this time as a success, hailed by the very newspapers which had originally rejected it.

That he was not wholly dismayed, back in 1944, was because he still had his radio work. Indeed he was in considerable demand. In the course of writing two novels, even if they remained unpublished, he had also convinced himself that he had another possible outlet. He thus set himself to write what turned out to be *Focus* which oddly, during a war against Nazi Germany, took American anti-Semitism as its subject.

He had lost none of his radicalism since leaving Michigan. Indeed, according to his FBI file he attended Communist Party meetings in the early 1940s. He certainly embraced a number of radical causes. But the fact is that most of his plays would offer a critique of American values in the name of another model of human relationships. If there was a tide running it was likely that he would be swimming against it, even at times when it was unwise to do so. *All My Sons*, written during the war but produced after it, engaged the question of war-profiteering; *Death of a Salesman* offered a critique of the American dream at the very moment Americans were enthusiastically embracing it in a post-war economic boom; his version of Ibsen's *An Enemy of the People* would launch an attack on conformity when conformity was being preached as a virtue, not least by some of those who had once shared his political views; *The Crucible* took him into the eye of the storm. And so it would continue, from *After the Fall* through to *Resurrection Blues*. *Focus* was the first published example of this oppositional stance.

Focus is a remarkable and disturbing book, not least because its social and political concerns exert such a pressure on language, character and plot that at times its author seems to set aside aesthetic issues in favour of other urgencies.

When one of his characters observes that, 'I never saw such Jew hate as there is here. New York is crawling with it',[8] it plainly bears the weight of Miller's own alarm.

Jews and Jewish organisations had been careful during the war to avoid the accusation that they had dragged America into the conflict. There was a disinclination, therefore, to raise one's head above the parapet. Also, at a time of national solidarity they were loath to offer a critique of American social mores. It is the more surprising, therefore, that Miller now chose to address the issue of anti-Semitism in America, and to do so as the battles in Europe continued and reports of the Holocaust began to emerge.

There would, he claimed, be those later who would accuse him of denying his Jewish identity. If he did he certainly chose a strange way to do so in writing a novel which acknowledges the fierce anti-Semitism which had flourished in pre-war America and which polls revealed to be equally virulent in the early 1940s. Admittedly, he chose a narrative strategy which some found disturbing, the central character being a gentile who only appears to be Jewish, but this was in part his point in a novel in which prejudice requires so little validation and moral virtues prove so precarious.

America was still a nation divided, with separate hotels and country clubs for those banned from others which boasted of their 'restricted clientele'. There were still those who thought it safer to pass as what they were not in order to deflect hostility. *Focus* confronted this fact but, beyond that, it carried forward a concern of *The Man Who Had All the Luck* – the extent to which the individual is responsible for his own fate.

However, is there also buried here, in Miller's novel, a critique of Jewish resignation rooted in the process of awaiting a promised messiah, so that not only are Jews, like Willy Loman, 'kind of temporary', awaiting epiphanic meaning, they are, perhaps, persuaded that suffering gains purpose precisely through what has yet to be revealed? If it is a novel in some sense about identity, is it also concerned with the need to relinquish suffering as evidence of obedience to an authority yet to reveal itself? In *Focus* Miller creates a Jew who does not see suffering as part of the logic which makes the messiah the deliverer (from what, after all, but suffering). He acts because not to act is to risk extinction.

At the very least this is a novel which bespeaks a profound anxiety and an acknowledgement, surely, of Miller's own equivocal status as a Jew who is not a Jew, not a practising Jew, and as a person whose seeming immunities are surely provisional. It was not necessary to go to war to understand that civilisation is constructed on a void and that neighbour can become assassin. Beyond that, however, is there at the heart of the book, displaced on to the person of a gentile who comes to accept himself as a Jew, a comment on Jewish self-hatred rooted, George Steiner would insist, in theology? The shadow of Job, after all, falls not only on *The Man Who Had All the Luck*, Job who was required to prove his faith by submitting to suffering. The Old Testament could be implacable. As Steiner has remarked, 'under the weight of the love of this God and His commandments of reciprocity in love, the soul breaks'.[9]

Steiner has described Marxism as 'Judaism grown impatient' (341). Ultimate justice and judgement being endlessly deferred, it proves necessary to enact them in a present vacated of theological content. That had surely been a truth Miller had embraced in the 1930s. It was a truth mocked, however, by the persistence of a visceral hatred which apparently needed little sanction, though in Focus the protagonist is a victim of an avowedly Christian group, not, incredibly, a fiction but a reality of daily life in pre-war and wartime America. Hitler was Catholic as was one of his American followers, Father Coughlan, who broadcast directly into American homes. Hitler was a logical extension of the casual prejudice seemingly structured into life, and not only in Germany, Austria and the former Austro-Hungarian empire. That prejudice was an acknowledged fact of life in the United States.

Focus, though, is not merely a comment on American prejudice. The physical battle against anti-Semitism towards which the novel moves, though it is not, finally, itself the crucial moment of transformation, is a symbol of a deeper resistance for which Miller called, the need to throw one's whole self into the business of living. If it were anything else it would risk becoming a simple plea for reactive violence of the kind he would criticise decades later when discussing Israel's response to Palestinian pleas for justice as much as to Palestinian terror (though he had himself thrilled to the creation of Israel in 1948 and had, indeed, delivered a speech at a public rally to welcome its coming into being).

In a sense there is a reckless optimism about Focus if it is read as a victory of the self coming into existence through an act of resistance, if it is seen as an account of the relative ease with which cruelty may be met and vanquished (though in fact anti-Semitism did quickly decline if not disappear in America in the immediate post-war years). The fact is that the victory at the end of the novel is provisional. The nature of anti-Semitism remains a mystery. The full details of the Holocaust were not yet available and hence the deeply disturbing implications of systematic genocide not yet a part of Miller's consciousness or the subject of debate. For the moment, though, he chose to confront Americans with complicity in the evil to whose defeat the country had supposedly dedicated itself, as he was seemingly willing to charge Jews with acquiescence in what they mistakenly took to be their fate.

※

5

'Focus'

The protagonist of *Focus*, Lawrence Newman, is a quiet man, happy to blend into the background, content to look out on the world from the supposed security of his own privacies. He works for an anti-Semitic company in which his role, in personnel, is to enforce that policy by denying employment to Jews. It is not something he questions but there are few things that he questions. He is a conformist who finds protection, if not meaning, in blending in. His small acts of resistance are so refined as to escape attention by anything but what he takes to be his own exquisitely refined sensibility. He paints his shutters a slightly different shade of green from those of his neighbours, neighbours with whom, for the most part, he abhors to socialise. Indeed, he feels a certain repulsion from personal contact. A single man who lives with his mother, he avoids commitments, accepting prevailing orthodoxies, drifting on the tide of his own disinterest, until suddenly his world begins to collapse and he is forced, literally and symbolically, to see the world anew. He is slowly taken apart and, finally, reconstructed, a new man.

Other races flit across that protagonist's consciousness. They are, though, no more than part of an inchoate city on which some kind of order must be imprinted, and this in a novel in which the city is itself the source of paranoia as people have to endure the forced propinquity of the subway, pressing flesh against alien flesh, and crowds are charged with the potential to transform into mobs. Anonymity is simultaneously sought and feared. In the large offices of the large corporations, people sit in rows, their individualism itself seen as the source of potential inefficiencies.

In the city, different languages and cultures slide over each other, not so much dissolving as withdrawing into themselves. This is a world touched with fear, guilt, the extremes of anxiety. The question is how to survive. Is it by a seemingly reckless act of resistance, or is it by merging oneself into the flux, the moral plasma: the Jewish dilemma throughout the ages? Lawrence Newman finds himself trapped in a nightmare, a Babel Tower of misunderstandings, conflicting languages, clashing values, secret codes and ciphers. He shuttles to and fro through the flying underbelly of New York, reading there subterranean truths which belie the apparent moral stability of the world above his head. He defines himself by what he is not.

To Newman, if Jews, Blacks, Hispanics are the despised and rejected, he is, by the same token, the admired and accepted. This is not, to his mind, evidence of prejudice, merely a description of reality. Thus, while he is happy to buy his newspaper from a Jewish store-owner called Finklestein, who merely serves him, at the same time he hesitates to touch his hand, while happily grasping the handrail of the subway stairs touched by countless numbers of anonymous individuals. He never asks himself why, having simply internalised the values of those around him as if they were no more than a definition of normality. The anti-Jewish graffiti he reads scrawled on the subway station spark a thrill of recognition in him merely because they voice what seems to him an unspoken conviction, a revealed truth shared by all. It is as though he were a member of a secret society of good fellows.

He readily accepts the stereotypes he is offered but, beyond the confines of his office, lacks the will to act, not least because action is at odds with his personality, whose keynote is passivity. The novel, indeed, opens with Newman in his bedroom listening to the screams of a woman being assaulted by a drunken man only yards from his house. He ignores her calls for help, in part from an unwillingness to be involved and in part because the woman appears to be Puerto Rican and such women, he is sure, must be inured to assaults. At the same time he feels an affinity with her drunken assailant who, one of his own, does not confront him with the issue of difference. The tribal connection overrides any other concerns. Here, in a single incident, is the core of the novel. The ethnic thrill, the sense of natural superiority, the desire to remain uninvolved, even social paralysis in the face of violence, are all focused in a scene which already contains the major elements of the novel.

Newman is, anyway, a man with no clear awareness of his own identity, indeed with no clear identity. He is so meticulous about externals because he has no centre. He is self-enclosed, with no great interest in others. His is an isolated sensibility. At work, he has even convinced his employers that they should build him a discrete, though glass-walled, office of his own, separated from those he must supervise. It is an image of his sensibility. He is both present and absent, visible yet withdrawn. Here, he feels momentarily secure, as he does in his own home until his space is invaded by the anarchy he chiefly fears. He is what others make him, deriving his sense of his own significance from sharing the tastes and prejudices of his neighbours.

Lawrence Newman, like Sinclair Lewis's Babbitt, wants nothing so much as to be accepted, conforming to what he takes to be the values, expectations, presumptions of his community. He derives his sense of individualism not only from painting his house shutters a slightly different shade of green, but by hanging them from the side as opposed to the top, as if this were a sufficient mark of distinctiveness. He has no spiritual resources. Religion is no more than a tactical means of accessing a job, a mask behind which to hide one's identity, a mechanism for ensuring one's invisibility, itself the price of success.

He is close kin not only to George Babbit but to Stepan Arkadyevich Oblonsky in *Anna Karenina*, not in his liberalism but in the extent to which he has absorbed the values of those around him:

> Stepan Arkadyevich too read a liberal newspaper, not an extreme one but one advocating the views held by the majority . . . he firmly held those views on all subjects which were held by the majority and by his paper, and he only changed them when the majority changed them – or, more strictly speaking, he did not change them, but they imperceptively changed of themselves within him.
>
> Stepan Arkadyevich had not chosen his political opinions or his views; these political opinions and views had come to him of themselves, just as he did not choose the shapes of his hats or coats, but simply took those that were being worn.[1]

He is what David Reisman, in *The Lonely Crowd*, was to call 'other-directed' and, indeed, Reisman himself incorporates this quotation from *Anna Karenina* in his book.[2]

Meticulous in his habits, Newman lives a constrained life. He is tidy, precise, 'careful', anally retentive. He lives with his aged mother, depending on routine, unwilling to chance an engagement with those he encounters. His real sense of himself derives from his job, and from the insurance company for which he works and whose anti-Semitic policies he is happy and even proud to enforce, less from personal conviction than out of a desire to belong. The world is a given. He feels no obligation to do other than accept it.

Newman's life changes when he makes the mistake of appointing a Jewish secretary. He is no longer able, literally or figuratively, to read his society. His faulty eyesight makes him fail to detect her distinctively Jewish appearance. He is forgiven his mistake on condition that he see an optometrist and thus begins the process whereby he starts to see the world more clearly, in every way, even as the spectacles prescribed ironically give him a Jewish appearance that eventually leads to his resignation from the company, unwilling to accept either the shame of demotion or his supposed association with a group he has been taught to despise.

Before his effective dismissal, though, he refuses employment to a young woman who herself has a Jewish appearance. Ironically, too ironically perhaps, it is she who later secures him a job in a Jewish company and whom he marries, though even this latter step is less one he himself proposes than one he accepts. Passivity pervades the text as it pervades his life – 'he felt a yearning' . . . 'Tears threatened his eyes'[3] – a device Miller perhaps learned from Wright's *Native Son*. He is detached from his own feelings, seemingly incapable of action. Even happiness is too definite a feeling for him to acknowledge: 'Probably, he thought . . . he would start being happy tomorrow' (94).

His first encounter with her, however, had led to a momentary revelation, an insight swiftly suppressed, but one that is the first hint of an understanding that eventually leads to his taking a stand. As he rejects her application, so

> he knew for the first time in his life that . . . [he] was sitting there in the guilt of the fact that the evil nature of the Jews and their numberless deceits, especially their sensuous lust for women – of which fact he had daily proof in the dark folds of their eyes and their swarthy skin – all were reflections of his own desires with which he had invested them. For this moment he knew it and perhaps never again, for in this moment her eyes had made a Jew of him; and his monstrous desire was holding back his denial.

(34)

The moment passes, but he had briefly glimpsed a truth that Ralph Ellison would observe of white attitudes towards black Americans in *Invisible Man*, as a white philanthropist projects onto a black man his own sexual desires, the better to assuage his guilt and secure a vicarious enjoyment of those desires.

Yet the woman to whom he turns himself has no clear existence. Her life is a series of fictions paraded as truths. She is, she says, a singer who had once had a Hollywood screen test and a relationship with an actor. None of this is true. So, what is? It is by no means clear. She is like Ellison's Rinehart, a confidence trickster, a protean figure. She is a series of performances and may or may not be Jewish.

Previously, his neighbours had tried to persuade him to join an anti-Semitic organisation and boycott the Jewish store-owner. Anxious to ingratiate himself, he had complied, even repainting his shutters the same shade of green as the other houses in the street, seeking salvation in conformity. Now, though, the humiliations begin to pile up. He and his wife are turned away by a hotel whose claim to an 'exclusive clientele' is code for its refusal of Jewish customers. His garbage pail, like Finklestein's, is overturned. His neighbours are revealed as members of the Christian Front that has set itself to drive Jews out of the area and out of mainstream public life.

Urged by his wife, who had herself had experience of a similar organisation in California, and, indeed, had lived with a Front leader, he attends one of their meetings, only to find himself turned on and violently expelled as a suspected Jew. From this moment on he begins to change. Having indignantly quoted his British heritage, and the fact that he had worked for 'one of the most anti-Semitic corporations in America', as evidence of his bona fides, he now realises that nothing he does will deflect those who act on the basis of unquestioned prejudice.

The agent of his education is the despised store-owner Finklestein, who confronts him with the irrationality of his own beliefs, the gap between his response to an individual Jew and the generalisations he is happy to embrace. When Newman and his wife are attacked in the streets, it is Finklestein who comes to the rescue and the two of them, back to back, swinging baseball bats, fight off the gang. The novel ends as Newman reports the attack to the police and accepts the designation of Jew, choosing his identity rather than have it created for him.

He becomes a Jew not merely in refusing to dissociate himself from Finklestein but in accepting moral responsibility for a world not of his own making. He, in effect, becomes the persecuted Jew and because he becomes that he also becomes a symbol of the modern American, of modern man. As Leslie Fiedler pointed out in 1957,

> On all levels, in the years since World War II, the Jewish–American writer feels imposed on him the role of being The American, of registering his experience for his compatriots and for the world as The American Experience. Not only for his flirtation with Communism and his disengagement, but his very sense of exclusion, his most intimate awareness of loneliness and flight are demanded of him as public symbols.[4]

It is, as Fiedler hints, an ambiguous role as the Jewish–American writer asserts the particularity of his identity when confronted with either hostility or a homogenising pressure, only to have that identity claimed as paradigmatic in its stress on anomie, dislocation and an existential imperative. A survivors' literature, which turns on a claim to distinctiveness, to the terms of a contract negotiated between the excluded and the excluder, is transformed into evidence of the vitality of a mainstream culture whose virtue lies in an aesthetic openness no matter how at odds with social practice. Ironically, those who wrote out of an awareness of exclusion found themselves assimilated because their observations seemed consonant with anxieties about the self that infected the whole culture.

For Miller, though, writing in 1944–5, such concerns were secondary, though hardly irrelevant. For if Newman is seen as the Jew he comes to accept himself as being, then the debate about his passivity, his failure to act, attaches itself to a larger issue, one that would echo down the corridors of Miller's work. He is concerned not so much with the wisdom as the morality of acquiescence and what it means for the survival of the self. This, indeed, would seem to be the point of a story told by Finklestein in which we learn not only of his family situation but of a fable that his father had told him when he was a child. This story within a story is synechdotal, posing, as it does, the essential dilemma at the heart of the novel.

On a rare visit to the cemetery where his father is buried, and where racists have broken headstones, Finklestein recalls the story, set in that part of Poland from which Miller's own family had come. Here, on a baronial estate, an oppressive overseer had been beaten to death by serfs who knew nothing of their emancipation, declared many years earlier. When other overseers try to revenge themselves, they, too, are killed, at which point the serfs break into the baron's house and steal what they find, including paper money. Since they have never encountered such a thing before, however, they take the banknotes as no more than a series of portraits of the king, which they duly pin to the walls of their shacks.

Anxious to punish his serfs and secure the return of his money, the Baron now approaches Itzik, a Jewish pedlar, and tells him to enter the estate and trade his pots and pans. Itzik, who believes that they have no money, resists, not wanting the barter goods he assumes he will be offered. The Baron insists. Once inside the estate, the pedlar discovers the money and trades his goods for it, but quickly understands the situation he is in. The Baron now has only to instigate a pogrom and he can steal his money back. But Itzik feels powerless in the face of this seeming inevitability. Accordingly, though he is tempted to flee, he accepts this as merely one more indignity to be suffered as Jews have always suffered.

The pogrom duly occurs. His wife is raped and his children spitted like pigs. The Baron reclaims his money, leaving the pedlar bereft and insane. Asked what moral he drew from the story, Finklestein's father replied, 'What it means? It means nothing. What could this Itzik do? Only what he had to do. And what he had to do would end up the way he knew it would end up, and there was nothing else he could do, and there was no other end possible. That's what it means' (131).

This attitude is reflected by an old man Finklestein meets in the graveyard and who points to the broken memorial stones: 'What will be, mister? In America, *noch*.' To Finklestein, his attitude represents that death of hope reflected in his own father's attitude to the story of Itzik. It is an attitude he rejects. To him,

> Itzik should never have allowed himself to accept a role that was not his, a role that the baron had created for him . . . when the pogrom came, as it would have no matter what he did, he could have found the strength to fight. It was the pogrom that was inevitable, but not its outcome. Its outcome only seemed inevitable because that money was in his house . . . That money in his house had weakened him, it was the blindfold they had put upon his face and he had no right to let them put it on him. Without that blindfold he would have been ready to fight; with it he was only ready to die.
>
> (133)

Going home from the cemetery, he says to himself,

> I am entirely innocent . . . I have nothing to hide and nothing to be ashamed of. If there are others who have something to be ashamed of, let them hide and wait for this thing that is happening, let them play the part they have been given and let them wait as if they were actually guilty of wrong. I have nothing to be ashamed of and I will not hide as though there were something stolen in my house.
>
> (133)

He buys baseball bats, determined to fight back, and in so doing redeems Newman.

As the story of Itzik makes plain, the question of Jewish attitudes to their persecution has a long history, but the context of 1945 gave it a particular dimension. Miller was effectively asking whether what had happened in Europe could be replicated in America. Nor was he alone in questioning the extent to which, while victims are not to be blamed for their persecution, a history of abuse, together with a certain fatalism, might have played its role. In a sense, by making Newman a gentile performing the function of the Jew he sidesteps some of the opprobrium which such a suggestion might have attracted. Nonetheless, the issue was a real and painful one.

Writing at the end of the war, the question of the degree to which Jews could be said to have acquiesced in their own destruction came to concern, and even obsess, Bruno Bettelheim. He accused Hitler of depthless villainy, but he accused his fellow Jews of inertia, passivity, a fatalistic collaboration in their own extinction. He even itemised incidents in which, like Itzik, Jews had failed to act because of a desire to protect their investments, material and intangible. It was a pitiless objection, but one, as it seemed to him, rooted in the very historical consciousness that should have been the source of strength. Centuries of persecution and survival had bred a sense if not of immunity then of desperate and tenuous confidence. They had survived, therefore they would survive. But Hitler had brought a new scientistic positivism to bear which itself rested on a recognition of Jewish fatalism. Thus, in April 1942, Hitler reportedly remarked that, 'One must not have mercy on people who are destined by fate to perish.'[5]

What Finklestein asserts, Bettelheim confirms: 'it is never the destiny of a people to be murdered, be they Incas or Indians or Jews'.[6] Given *The Golden Years*, the parallel is an interesting one. The unique feature of the extermination camps, according to Bettelheim, was not that the Germans exterminated millions of people but that millions of people, 'like lemmings marched themselves to their own death'.[7] It is a statement echoed in the seemingly throw-away comment that Miller made before the House Un-American Activities Committee as he sought to distinguish himself from those who had gone unprotestingly into the gas chambers. But what, after all, were they to have done? Something, suggests Bettelheim, anything. It is a desperate assertion but the essence of his refusal of an acquiescence that can only spell ultimate extinction, symbolic or actual.

It is, though, easier to embrace knowledge than to act upon it. Bettelheim speaks of what he calls ghetto thinking: 'to believe that one can ingratiate oneself with a mortal enemy by denying that his lashes sting, to deny one's own degradation in return for a moment's respite, to support one's enemy who will only use his strength the better to destroy one. All this is part of ghetto mentality.'[8] This, of course, is a description of Newman's attitude throughout most of *Focus*. He thinks to protect himself from attack precisely by ingratiating himself, by denying his own degradation, and as such he lends strength to those who would persecute him.

Miller wrote the book before he knew in any detail the reality of the camps, but in essence his concern and his conviction is that expressed by Bettelheim: 'All people, Jews or gentiles . . . who submit to punishment not because of what they have done but because they are who they are, are already dead by their own decision.' He understood, with Simone Weil, that 'the force that does not kill, i.e., that does not kill just yet [that] merely hangs poised and ready over the head of the creature it can kill at any moment, turns a man into a stone, turning a human being into a thing while he is still alive'.[9] This was Lawrence Newman before he was shocked into acting on his own behalf and thereby on behalf of others.

Two years after *Focus*, Saul Bellow published *The Victim* (in fact he had produced two drafts by 1945), in which the dubious educative force is an anti-Semite who, despite his blustering self-justifications, offers an observation that is not without its force:

> Let me explain something to you. It's a Christian idea but I don't see why you shouldn't be able to understand it. 'Repent!' That's John the Baptist coming out of the desert. Change yourself, that's what he's saying, and be another man . . . I understand that doctors are beginning to give their patients electric shocks. They tear all hell out of them, and then they won't trifle. You see, you have to get yourself so that you can't stand to keep on in the old way . . . It takes a long time before you're ready to quit dodging . . . We're mulish; that's why we have to take such a beating. When we can't stand another lick without dying of it, then we change. And some people never do. They stand there until the last lick falls and die like animals.[10]

This, too, was a novel written under a shadow, the same shadow. Newman becomes what his name implies, and what Bellow's Allbee identifies when he says: 'a man can be born again . . . if I'm tired of being this way I can become a new man'.[11] Miller's Newman takes a beating but he, too, determines that he will not die like an animal, that he will quit dodging.

There is at times a gracelessness to the prose of *Focus*, an image that rises too completely into view, an over-explicit scene, almost as if the urgency of the subject subordinated such concerns. Newman is, perhaps, rather too clearly a paradigm, reduced to object by his own reifications, but also by an author who never quite listens to his voice with the attentiveness he would in his plays. Reacting against type, Miller comes close to creating a type, and that is the problem with which he wrestles. He has to make compelling the struggle for self-consciousness and self-definition by a man whose self seems never to have formed. Nonetheless, *Focus* was in many ways an act of courage. He can have had no real hope that this message from the underground would be embraced. He will have known, too, that his fellow Jews would find his fictive strategy suspect and his insistence on resistance accusatory and even dangerous. He, after all, was doing with his novel what his protagonist had done with his baseball bat.

— ✳ —

Focus proved remarkably successful, selling some 90,000 copies. It was his third novel, if the first to be published, and it is tempting to think that he might have considered a future as a novelist rather than a playwright. But in fact he remained as committed to drama as ever. His radio plays were bringing in a considerable income and giving him a visibility he hoped to trade for success in the theatre. It was clear to him, though, that there was little point in creating another fable such as *The Man Who Had All the Luck*, or in hoping to stage a verse drama of the kind to which he had been instinctively drawn.

Even as he had been working on *Focus* he had been sketching out plans for a new play. This time it would be classically constructed. He turned back to Ibsen for inspiration, as he reached out to a story he had heard about from his Ohio in-laws for a subject. *Death of a Salesman* would come quickly. *All My Sons* was a long study. It took two-and-a-half years and underwent many significant changes. He finished working on it at Port Jefferson and sent it to his agent, Kay Brown. Her response was immediate and enthusiastic. He and his wife, together with baby Jane, drove to New York, suffering a puncture on the way which cost them $14, still enough to dent the family finances. Already, though, there was enthusiasm from producers and he was shortly to find himself working with two men he had deeply admired in their days at the Group Theatre – Harold Clurman and Elia Kazan.

It was a wartime play, written during wartime and likely to be produced, so far as he knew, in wartime. In many ways it would pick up issues that had made their way into *Situation Normal*. If he was a long way, now, from the Marxist plays of his college days, he was still interested in offering a critique of a society whose values seemed at odds with his own idealism and the idealism of his brother, still risking his life abroad while others prospered. There is, though, perhaps a shadow of Clifford Odets in a work which, like *Awake and Sing*, would see a tension between the demands of the family and those of society. There is likewise, perhaps, a hint of the philosophy of *The Grapes of Wrath* which offered a similar analysis of the need to transcend the familial in the name of the societal. The very title (not the first he chose) had echoes of 1930s literature.

The writing of *All My Sons* interleaved with his work on the novel and with the radio plays. When eventually it was staged, the war already lay in the past but the issues he raised, relevant in wartime (hence the play's later popularity in Israel where sacrifice and profiteering could come uncomfortably close), proved just as relevant in peacetime. In the end he had written a play which cut deeper than a critique given relevance by social and political events. He had written about fathers and sons, about denial, about the human price not only of moral failure but of an unquestioning idealism blind to human need. He had written a play about the ease with which the individual absolves him- or herself of responsibility even if the price be to indict others.

The play would be denounced by some, both from the right and the left, by the former for its apparent indictment of capitalism, by the latter for its suggestion that the action of a single capitalist was an aberration and not a product of the system. An FBI agent managed to secure a copy of the screenplay for the Hollywood film version of the play, and sent a report to Washington, a report which is laughable in its prejudices but indicative of the changing mood of America. Nonetheless, audiences responded with enthusiasm and most critics embraced the writer whose first appearance had been so disastrous. *All My Sons* established Miller as a major force in the theatre. At last, nine years after leaving Michigan, he had finally stormed Broadway.

Oddly, perhaps, it would leave him ambiguously placed. A play in which a character expresses dismay that idealism should founder on a material imperative brought the former Marxist writer (or perhaps more accurately a writer drawn to Marxism) both financial rewards and fame. On the one hand he could feel nothing but pleasure at a success he had worked so long to achieve. On the other, he remained committed to the values which made the rewards of such success seem suspect. He was certainly seen as suspect by those critics he would later characterise as the Trotskyite left.

✳

6

'All My Sons'

All My Sons concerns a manufacturer of aircraft engines, Joe Keller, who, under pressure of wartime production, allows a batch of faulty cylinder heads to be supplied to the Army Air Force in the knowledge that they may cause catastrophic failure and thus endanger life. He does so rather than risk losing his contract and thus possibly his business, the business he wishes to pass to his sons. In the subsequent court case he denies responsibility, insisting that he had not visited the plant on the day in question and allowing his employee and neighbour, Steve Deever, to take the blame. At the time, Deever's daughter, Ann, had been engaged to the Kellers' son, Larry, himself serving in the Air Force. Following their father's conviction both she and her brother, George, sever all connection with their father, refusing to visit him in prison, or even to write to him. To sustain his own family, Keller sacrifices another.

When Larry, a pilot, goes missing, Kate Keller refuses to acknowledge his death, not least because to do so would be to accept a symbolic connection between her husband's action and her own loss. The play opens as their other son, Chris Keller, invites Ann to stay, intending to propose a marriage which will, effectively, signify public acknowledgement of Larry's death and thus precipitate a crisis for all of them as past and present are brought into immediate confrontation. The action takes place in less than twenty-four hours.

All My Sons is a play in part about the individual's responsibility for his own actions and in part about the obligations he has to his society. The crime at its centre raises in stark form the clash between self-interest and human solidarity. Yet it is a good deal more than this. There are still echoes of the Miller who, in 1941, had sketched out his idea for a character he would never use but who represented a dilemma which would surface in *All My Sons*. This was a man, neither worker nor bourgeois, corrupted by 'opportunity', and there is in the play, and particularly in the early drafts, a conviction that idealism and justice shatter on materialism and corruptions which seem to shadow a desire for success. Joe Keller denies transcendent values. The irony is that his son, who insists upon them, becomes as much a killer as the father to whom he presents his idealistic demands. And if there is an echo here of Ibsen it was a conscious and acknowledged one. For Ibsen, too, committed himself to truth as an absolute value and then, in *The Wild Duck*, wrote a play which dramatised the price of insisting upon it.

All My Sons was born in wartime America but, even this deep into the conflict, there were isolationist forces at work (Miller, himself, had been an isolationist until December 1940, when Germany attacked the Soviet Union) and, to him, Ohio (where the incident on which it is based occurred and where, in an early draft, it is set) typified this feeling. There were, in other words, those who believed in a more limited version of political, social and moral responsibility, those for whom the central priority was looking after one's own. Against this he pitched the idealism he had encountered in the person of Watson when researching *The Story of GI Joe* and that tension is evident in the play, perhaps hardly surprisingly since the writing of the two works overlapped.

In 1944, Miller contemplated the fate of those who would return from the war and re-enter a world whose values would be fundamentally different from those operative in battle. Those prepared to lay down their lives not only for a cause but more directly for one another would find themselves, it seemed to him, back in a society that privileged the individual, that preached the virtues of competition, that substituted the material for the spiritual or saw materialism as an expression of utopian values:

> Many hundreds of thousands of men are going to return from terrible battles, and in some degree they will have shared Watson's feelings of love and identity with their particular comrades and units. And in differing degrees they are going to have to transfer that love to other – civilian – units . . . They walk out of the circle of imperative order, out of the unity of feeling they had known in the Army. They go home.[1]

Like Hemingway's figure in 'Soldier's Home', however, such people are liable to find themselves in an alien world. It is surely this feeling that lies behind *All My Sons* and in particular the character of Chris Keller, back from the war to a family concerned primarily with its own future and the business of making money, a society in which his neighbours, too, seem to have put idealism aside in the name of a post-war pragmatism. The business of America is, indeed, it seems, business.

As Miller said of Watson, the soldier who would soon be returning to civilian life in *Situation Normal*:

> He must lop off at once that onetime feeling of exhilaration he got from the knowledge that whatever the insignificance of his job, it was helping an enormous mass of men toward a great and worthy goal . . . Now he must live unto himself, for his own selfish welfare. Half of him, in a sense, must die, and with it must pass away half the thrill he knew to being alive. He must, in short, become a civilian again. There is a great and deep sense of loss in that.[2]

It is tempting to feel that this is the rhetoric of a man who did not go to war, a writer who projected on to those who did that sense of solidarity and idealism that he himself had experienced in the 1930s. Most soldiers were all too ready to re-enter the competitive race. Yet his conviction that 'Unless Watson's attachment to his family or his wife or his girl is so overwhelming that nothing can distract him from it, he is going to feel the loss of a social unit, a group to which he can give himself, a social goal worth his sacrifice' (33) is undoubtedly reflected in *All My Sons*. It is precisely Chris Keller's sense of betraying his old comrades that makes him feel guilty, a guilt that he is, finally, all too ready to project entirely on to his flawed father. For though the play was seen as a study of a war profiteer, it is equally about the death of the ideal, the failure of society, as it is constituted, to offer the meaning which the individual seeks. 'Watson', he suggests, is alone in American society today . . . because his comrades

> are not with him, the men he loves . . . he is alone and misfitted here . . . because America offers him no great social goal . . . he must live only his own little life and do his own unimportant job when he gets out of the Army. He must begin again the stale and deadly competition with his fellow men for rewards that now seem colorless, even if necessary for his survival.
>
> (36)

Whatever the unifying principle is to be it is not, Miller insists, to be 'free enterprise'.

All My Sons is about a man who places survival above value, self above the group, pragmatism above the ideal, loyalty to family above responsibility to society. It is also, however, about loss, loss of a sense of common humanity.

Miller's failure to secure a production for his densely poetic drama, *The Golden Years*, together with the actual failure in production of *The Man Who Had All the Luck*, whose style eluded directors, critics and audience alike, led him to attempt a more recognisable form. To that end he turned to Ibsen, in part because of his commitment, in his social plays, to realism, but also because 'dramatic characters, and the drama itself, can never hope to attain a maximum degree of consciousness unless they contain a viable unveiling of the contrast between past and present, and an awareness of the process by which the present has become what it is'.[3]

Kate Keller, half desperately moved, half terrified, announces that 'Everything that happened seems to be coming back.'[4] So it does. That, indeed, is the circumstance of the play and its dialectic, as present interrogates the past and the past infiltrates the present. When Chris Keller observes of the family that 'We're like a railroad station waiting for a train that never comes in' (107), he describes a sense of stasis that has drained their lives of meaning, the hopeless hope of which O'Neill spoke and which is exemplified in *The Iceman Cometh*, in which the future is no more than a mirror. They have stopped the clock, stepped out of time into their own self-created fictions. Kate has constructed a myth about her elder son and required the rest of the family to inhabit it, and myth, by definition, is timeless.

In *All My Sons* the clock is started again and as a result the characters are forced to acknowledge the implacability of time and the power of causality. In *Death of a Salesman* Willy Loman was to describe himself as feeling 'kind of temporary'. This is the state in which the Keller family have lived since Larry was reported missing. They have remained in suspended animation, too terrified of the past to acknowledge its authority and hence held in an irony they can only transcend by confronting the demons that so terrify them.

At the beginning of the play, Miller creates an atmosphere of what he calls 'undisturbed normality'.[5] What he was after, he has explained, was to locate an ordinary environment from which extraordinary disaster would spring. Thus it is set in a suburban world in which people are involved in 'cutting the lawn and painting the house and keeping the oil burner running; the petty business of life in the suburbs'.[6]

The first act is designedly slow. It takes place 'beneath a clear landscape in the broad light of a peaceful day'.[7] However, as Miller remarked of Mordecai Gorelick's purposefully ordinary setting, this only 'made the deepening threat of the remainder more frightening' (*T*.134), for into this recognisable domesticity, this Norman Rockwell scene of Sunday morning in an Ohio town, he slowly infiltrates corrosive elements.

There is, we discover, no past that can be confronted with total honesty, no future that does not carry a threat as well as a promise. The characters inhabit a no-man's-land. The primary action that drives the play has already occurred and been buried, apparently, beneath the routines of daily existence. The living are haunted by the dead whom they seek to exorcise with a simple denial of the real. No action any of the characters can take will alter what has happened. What is at stake, though, is truth, responsibility, and what Miller has called the evil of 'unrelatedness'. For in a play in which the principal characters are drawn together by family affiliation, it is the fractures in relationship that most concern him, the limitation of responsibility. The structure of the play, he insisted, was 'to bring a man into the direct path of the consequences he has wrought'.[8]

As in his later work, what seems to have fascinated him is the gap that opens up between action and the interpretation of action, between the self and its idealised projections. These are people who have an image of themselves which, in varying degrees, is at odds with the reality of their lives. Out of that discrepancy comes what elsewhere he would be tempted to call tragedy, but which might equally well be seen as irony, identity being placed at risk by the very strategies which have been devised to sustain it.

When Ibsen discussed the first production of *The Wild Duck* (plainly a primary influence on *All My Sons*) with the director of the Christiana Theatre, he stressed both the 'naturalness and realism' of the play, at the heart of which, nonetheless, was an affecting symbol, and the need for lighting that would reflect 'the basic mood' of each act.[9] Miller's play reveals a similar commitment to realism and a similar symbol, though not with the same centrality and force as the wild duck in the earlier work. He also, perhaps, learned from Ibsen a lighting which reflected the mood.

In the first act the sun shines brightly, as Chris Keller and Ann plan their wedding. In the second act it is twilight, as the mood darkens, while in the third it is two in the morning with the moon casting 'a bluish light' on those whose lives have been drained, suddenly, of colour and purpose alike. Like Ibsen's play, too, it is a combination of the tragic and the comic and brings the flawed idealist into collision with an equally flawed social world, though what in Ibsen's play is a central theme here becomes a largely unexplored dimension of human motivation.

The Keller home is hedged in by poplar trees and has 'a secluded atmosphere', a physical description that develops a metaphoric force as the play unfolds and we learn of the moral isolation of this family, or at least of its patriarch. Miller pointedly tells us the financial value of the seven-room family home (fifteen thousand dollars when it was built in the 1920s), a detail aimed at the designer but also a clue to actors for whom this is to be a house in which money had been a determinant and family a defining term.

Indeed the word 'money' recurs throughout the play, as a kind of counter-point to the idealism generated by the war. Character after character invokes it as a reason for relinquishing ideals or hopes. A next-door neighbour, a doctor, has abandoned medical research, at his wife's insistence, for a more lucrative general practice – 'You wanted money, so I made money' (162). Another neigh-bour becomes financially secure as a result of not serving in the war. Joe Keller, whose wife also stresses money, complains that his son, Chris, 'don't under-stand money', while defending his own actions as no more than a reflection of a more general morality: 'Did they ship a gun or a truck outa Detroit before they got their price? Is that clean? It's dollars and cents, nickels and dimes; war and peace, it's nickels and dimes' (168).

In the garden, meanwhile, are plants 'whose season is gone'. The stump of an apple tree stands down-stage, felled by a storm, its upper trunk, branches still covered with fruit, beside it. Having said that he wished to be 'as untheatrical as possible', and in particular keen to ensure that 'any metaphor, any image, any figure of speech . . . was removed if it even so slightly brought to consciousness the hand of the writer' (128), Miller placed this tree at the heart not only of the stage but of the play, quite as much as Chekhov did the cherry orchard.

Undeniably, a tree fallen in its prime stands as a correlative for a son appar-ently cut down in the war, and is identified as such by the characters, while a storm occurring on the eve of a crisis in family affairs might seem an unneces-sary underscoring of a drama which has its own logic, its own emotional tone, its own internal dynamic. That it does not seem unduly theatrical is precisely because the symbolism is read into it by characters neurotically alert to threat and vigilant for evidence of change.

To be sure, the action takes place in the fall and this could be seen as fore-shadowing that change which is about to come over the Keller household. For Joe Keller, as for the others, after all, the season is about to turn in a play set, as Miller explains, in 'August of our era' (89), and which is, in effect, a story of that era. August, however, also marks the birthdate of the dead son, a reminder of the past that becomes an ironic comment on the present. The fall, then, undoubtedly has symbolic force, as the characters wait for the balance to change, but it is equally an element of that specificity designed to establish the reality of character and event.

Issues present themselves to Joe Keller in an immediate and obvious way. His life is a triumph over disadvantages, a triumph he will not readily allow to slip through his fingers. He is a man for whom survival is a primary necessity, whose ordering of the world has priorities designed to protect him from an extended analysis of consequence. This is a man who has lived through the Depression and knows how fragile a grasp he, or anyone, has on the world. Survival, meanwhile, is not only a matter of maintaining a way of life and a way of being but of insulating oneself from a knowledge of the consequences of one's actions, denying involvement in the world.

Nor is Miller concerned simply with an individual whose values are at odds with those of his society. Joe Keller was not aberrant. In a sense he represented a pragmatism which somehow co-existed with the language and fact of ide-alism in wartime America. As Miller remarked in a 1999 interview, when he wrote the play, 'everybody knew that a lot of hanky-panky was going on . . . a lot of illicit fortunes were being made, a lot of junk was being sold to the armed services, we all knew that. The average person was violating rationing. All the rules were being violated every day but you wanted not to mention it.'[10]

In that sense, if Keller violated fundamental principles of his society he also embodied other values equally observable in a society as dedicated to material achievement as to a utopian vision. As Miller recalled, in his introduction to the *Collected Plays*, *All My Sons* was conceived when the contrast between sacrifice and aggrandizement seemed both sharp and profoundly disturbing: 'when all public voices were announcing the arrival of that great day when industry and labor were one, my personal experience was daily demonstrating that beneath the slogans nothing had changed'. The play was thus 'an unveiling of what I believed everybody knew but nobody publicly said' (134).

Joe Keller's crime is to have sent defective cylinder heads for use in aircraft engines, as it is to have committed perjury in order to defend himself against the consequences of his action. But this is not primarily a play about crime. It is about a man's failure to understand the terms of the social contract. These may not be people whose actions are determined by religious convictions but when Kate Keller observes that 'certain things have to be, and certain things can never be. That's why there's God, so certain things can never happen,' she expresses

Miller's essentially secular conviction that there are certain values whose breach threatens the structure of existence.

Looking back, at the turn of the century, he observed that, 'the justification that Joe Keller makes is that . . . you do what you have to do in order to survive', a defence which is 'always understandable and always unacceptable'. The fact is that audiences 'know pretty well that given the kind of pressure that Joe Keller was under they might have collapsed too, so that people participate in the conflict. They don't stand apart entirely from it because they know they're vulnerable.'[11]

When the play begins, Keller is seen reading the 'wanted' ads in the Sunday newspaper. As he explains, he no longer reads the news section, a news section, we later learn, in which he would have found his own name only a few years before. As his neighbour rightly remarks, 'it's all bad news' (90). Joe and his wife live in fear of bad news, about their son and about the crime they have conspired to deny, the two ineluctably connected in their minds.

Joe Keller is joined by two neighbours, one, Frank Lubey, 'uncertain of himself . . . thirty-two and balding', the other, Jim, a doctor, 'wry, self-controlled . . . but with a wisp of sadness that clings to his self-effacing humour'. Their wives are, respectively, Lydia, a 'robust, laughing girl of twenty-seven', and Sue, 'rounding forty, an overweight woman who fears it'. There is, in these descriptions, more than a hint that this suburban setting contains elements of regret and anxiety that extend beyond the back yard of the Keller household. These neighbours, too, give something more than a social density to *All My Sons*, act as something more than a chorus. They contain in themselves the conflicts at the heart of the play, acknowledging, as they do, a tension between the pragmatic and the ideal, and recognising the compromises that seem an inevitable aspect of daily living.

Marriage itself, it seems, offers an image of such compromises in this Ohio community, a fact that will surely cast its shadow over the proposed relationship between Chris Keller and Ann Deever. The neighbours, too, are hardly unaware of the tendency towards denial as issues which once seemed so urgent and clear begin to seem less so, as ambition and habit blunt the edge of utopian dreams.

The play begins with Chris Keller's admission that he has invited his brother's fiancée, Ann, with the intention of proposing marriage to her. Since his mother still insists that that brother is alive such an action must destroy her fragile faith, for the fact is that, rather than confront her with the truth, both husband and son have remained silent. However, when Chris insists that 'Being dishonest with her. That kind of thing always pays off' (99) this is a statement that foreshadows other dishonesties and other prices that must be paid, as does Joe's reply, 'I ignore what I gotta ignore' (100). Indeed, Chris himself shortly prevaricates in the face of his mother's questioning. And though the focus of the play seems to be on Joe, whose past failings are revealed and whose guilt is affirmed, there is an ambiguity that attaches itself to Chris and which becomes more profound as the play proceeds.

His early statement, for example, that 'I don't know why it is, but every time I reach out for something I want, I have to pull back because other people will suffer. My whole bloody life, time after time after time' (100), seems to lack substance, apart from the immediate issue of his proposed marriage. What, precisely, has he reached for that he has been denied or required to relinquish so that others would not suffer? This is a man, we begin to realise, who sees himself as a martyr, an idealist, yet the suspicion grows that this is an image behind which he hides. Doubts are swallowed up in his self-conscious presentation of himself as an honest man doing nothing more than demand honesty, a self-denier only now able to assert his rights. He presents himself, to himself, as serving truth; truth, however, not only places him at risk but, as we see, becomes a means of directing attention away from himself and his own moral failings.

At the beginning of the play he announces that 'I've been a good son too long, a good sucker. I'm through with it' (102). In what sense has he been a 'good sucker', beyond his failure to confess love to Ann, a love which has not even driven him to see her in five years, and not, surely, solely because of fear of disturbing his mother? He now declares his willingness to leave the family business if necessary, but in fact is anxious to secure the terms on which he can remain, while condescending to it. The business, he explains to the father who has built it, as he knows, in part for him, does not 'inspire' him. But what does? He speaks of having to 'grub for money' (102), as he later talks resentfully of having to join 'the rat race'. He wants, he explains, to build something he can give himself to, quite as though he were still pursuing his metaphor of immolation and sacrifice. Knowing that his father is desperate for him to stay, he threatens to leave. Marriage to Anne, he implies, will secure his loyalty to the business. She becomes his bargaining tool.

Chris feels guilty for his new happiness. In the war he had led men to their deaths. He is a survivor who feels the guilt of the survivor. Beyond that, he can see no connection between the sacrifices of war and the way of life it was supposedly fought to preserve. Wartime camaraderie implies a conception of human relationships and a shared perception of worth that seems to have no correlative in a post-war world concerned with simple materialism, though his own rhetoric seems quickly abandoned: 'Annie . . . I'm going to make a fortune for you!' (122). It is a half-ironic remark but, retrospectively, perhaps, reflects something of his unacknowledged ambiguity as a participant in a tainted company.

Kate Keller, meanwhile, carries the authority in the house, defines its reality. In an earlier version of the text she was in a more dominating position. Her faith in astrology, indeed, a faith that was designed to bolster her desperate belief in her son's survival, generated the play's original title, *The Sign of the*

Archer, the missing son having been born under that sign. Astrology may, as Miller suggests, have given way to psychology, his own flirting with mysticism proving, he thought, one of the problems with earlier plays such as *The Golden Years* and *The Man Who Had All the Luck*, but Kate still remains a powerful figure.

The relationship between father and son may move to the centre of attention but she holds a key to the action. It is her will that has both sustained them and, in a sense, infantilised them since she wishes to deny time, process, causality. For her, nothing must change. Chris must remain unmarried, her husband a charming incompetent, unable to function, since to assume otherwise would be to accept a view of the world that could only destroy her. If Joe Keller uses the family as a justification for his actions, it is equally vital to Kate because beyond it lies nothing but a kind of anarchy, exemplified by the death of a son.

In watching the London production, Miller felt that the emphasis had changed from the father–son relationship, underscored by the title, to Kate:

> The woman has it within herself, quietly and without demonstration, to be a survivor . . . The women are less obsessional. The men are obsessed. The women have to preserve that nest. They're a very conservative force. That production in England really made me think, how I had gotten misled. What had I changed that title to? *All My Sons*. It completely altered the central emphasis of the play . . . It was far more interesting to me.[12]

The Israeli production, likewise, shifted the emphasis as Kate was played by a powerful actress whose leg had been shot off in the attack at the Munich Olympics.

Interestingly, Kate Keller is called Mother not only by Chris and, not entirely incidentally, by her husband, but also by the playwright, her speeches being so indicated in the text. It suggests, perhaps, that Miller, whose stage directions describe her as 'a woman of uncontrolled inspirations and an overwhelming capacity for love' (102), feels close to her and alienated from her husband, who is the only other character in the play not referred to by his first name in the speech indicators. The fact is that the power system in the family changed with Joe Keller's decision to forward the defective parts, and with the criminal case that followed. Kate's knowledge, at whatever level it operates within her, strips him of the authority he once wielded. He cedes his position as head of the house, living in a temporal void enforced by his wife. Her desperate need to deny the possibility of her son's death, understandable in its own terms, also derives from her desire to deny the terrible rhyme between that death and her husband's crime.

That connection is there, long before Ann's revelation in Act 3 that that son had deliberately taken his own life for shame at his father's actions. It is a connection that Kate can continue to deny so long as that son may have survived. If he has not then such meaning as she has constructed will dissolve.

As she says, 'If he's not coming back, then I'll kill myself' (107). Why? Not simply because she will be admitting the death, three years before, of one son, a terrible but hardly unique loss, but because a connection will be made that ties the rest of the family to that loss. The only defence, in her mind, for Joe Keller's action is that it was done in the name of the sons. If one is not returning and the other may defect, then it stands stripped even of this justification. It must be named for what it is. As she says to her husband, 'You above all have got to believe' (108). As a result, she keeps her son's memory polished, like his shoes, which she keeps ready for his return.

That connection is made by Ann. Speaking of her father, who she believes to be responsible for shipping the faulty parts, she says, 'He knowingly shipped out parts that would crash an airplane. And how do we know Larry wasn't one of them?' (117) (admittedly a curious remark since she is carrying a letter from Larry which explains the circumstances of his death). When Keller shows signs of agitation as a result, Kate interrupts to insist, 'He's not dead, so there's no argument' (117).

Joe is an accommodationist. His public denials are matched by his private ones. When Kate asks if Chris has discussed marrying Ann his reply is 'he didn't tell me any more than he told you' (106), though we have just witnessed such a discussion. Having practised private deceits, he seems to have internalised his own denials. Urging Ann to persuade her father to return to the neighbourhood after his imprisonment he says, 'Listen, you do like I did and you'll be all right' (115). The fact is that he is far from all right, but at this stage in the play we are in no position to know this, though already there are sufficient hints to undermine the assurance he displays.

He insists, apparently with conviction, that he had himself deliberately chosen to return and confront his sceptical neighbours:

> none of them believed I was innocent. The story was, I pulled a fast one getting myself exonerated . . . The beast! I was the beast; the guy who sold cracked cylinder heads to the Army Air Force; the guy who made twenty-one P-40s crash in Australia . . . Except I wasn't, and there was a court paper in my pocket to prove I wasn't.
>
> (115)

Yet, of course, he was and knows he was. Is this, then, mere bravado, blatant, calculated lying, or has denial sunk so deep into his being that the real has been reinvented?

The speech ends with his boast that fourteen months later he had 'one of the best shops in the state again, a respected man again; bigger than ever'. Best. Bigger. Respected. The language of material success blots out the language of guilt. It is as though the words themselves define the real, are his defence against self-knowledge. In his own mind he stands doubly vindicated, by the court and by his renewed success.

The 'only way you lick 'em is guts!' he insists, who had, of course, precisely lacked the courage to face the implications of his own actions. He believes, because he has to believe, that there is a space between his actions and the self which those actions define. His observation that 'you play cards with a man you know he can't be a murderer' (116) is less a confident piece of advice than a desperate article of faith for a man seeking the reassurance of normality.

His apparent confidence is easily deflated. A telephone call from Ann's brother, George, combined with her sudden appearance in the house, is enough to put him on the defensive: 'She don't hold nothin' against me, does she? . . . I mean if she was sent here to find out something . . . I mean if they want to open up the case again, for the nuisance value, to hurt us' (124). The call comes from Columbus, where their father is in prison. Suddenly, and with no further prompting, he insists that he wants 'a clean start' for his son, that he wishes him to inherit what he built for him, 'without shame'.

Already the questions begin to accumulate. Why this nervousness, why this insistence on a clean start and absence of shame, if he is not culpable? And why does Miller indicate that his son responds 'a little uneasily' to the inheritance he is offered, and that he is 'a little frightened' when asked to affirm that there is nothing wrong with the money he receives from the company that will one day bear his name?

Ann's father has lost his name, his reputation, in the eyes of the community. Joe defends his by refusing to acknowledge the connection between himself and his actions, while his son tries to sustain his own self-belief by asserting an idealism not without its roots in self-interest. Ann Deever, meanwhile, is to change her name, become Ann Keller, a process that requires certain adjustments and accommodations on her part, her new identity implicating her in the moral values of the family she joins and which by the end of the play she knows to be deeply compromised. The fact is that these are all characters whose motives are mixed, who contain contradictions and who display different levels of consciousness of that fact. They are all characters who insist upon the integrity of their identities when they are in process of denying them.

Miller has said of Joe Keller that he feels justified in his actions because if his business had been threatened he would have had nothing to hand on to his son and 'that would be a fate worse than death because one of his psychological supports is that he is a provider . . . the father of the house . . . the man from whom all power and . . . energy flows'. Nonetheless, 'he does feel guilt about what he has done' but 'at the same time feels that there was no other way for him . . . It's a craze quilt of motivations and contradictions inside of him.'[13]

He would, Miller, suggests, be 'a sociopathic person' if he were wholly insensitive to the social rules he has broken, fully capable of suppressing guilt for his actions, yet at the same time he denies the force of his knowledge. His sensitivity is, hence, both evidence of his guilt and of the survival of a moral conscience.

Interestingly, Miller has also said that he is not criminal. Since he assuredly is, his culpability being slowly exposed, what he seems to mean is that he is not wholly so, that such a word hardly sums up a man who acknowledges a hierarchy of values that places the needs of the family ahead of strangers with whom he feels no organic connection, a man whose denials seem necessary to his survival. But he is not the only person who survives by virtue of suppressing the truth.

Speaking of Kate, Rosemary Harris, who played the part in the London production, said: 'one of the fascinating aspects of playing Kate, is the question of how much she really knows or suspects. It is a very thin line.'[14] Interestingly, in watching the production Miller was convinced that 'Rosemary played it as though she knows it.'[15] For his part, 'Kate knows everything from the time the curtain goes up . . . because she remembers the day it happened.' On the other hand 'her life has consisted of trying to deny what she knows'. The same is true of Chris 'but with him it is buried deeper because it is so intolerable, the idea of his betraying him and his comrades so that he simply will not consider it'.[16]

There is, in other words, a layered consciousness in the play, a sense that each character contains within him or herself a debate about contending values, about competing versions of the moral world and of the real. They are drawn together by love, but that love becomes the source of a certain corruption. It is also not untinged with its opposite. When Chris precipitates the confrontation that is to destroy his father he has, Miller has said, 'to feel a certain, almost vengeance upon his father or he would not be able to do what he does'. It is he, more even than George Deever, who drives the issue to the point of crisis and he has, as Miller suggests, 'to feel resentment and hatred for his father, to some degree' in order to do this.

Indeed, no one in this play is without culpability, without cruelty, without guilt. Kate's obsession with one son's fate makes her act with a callous disregard for the future of the other. Ann and George act in some degree out of guilt for the callousness with which they have treated their father. Even Joe Keller's suicide is, in part, an act of self-justification and 'a counterblow to his wife and son'. Reminding us that the Chinese reportedly hang themselves in the doorways of the people who have offended them, and that many suicides are motivated by a desire to accuse or leave a residue of guilt, Miller sees Joe as laying before the wife and son he had invoked as justification for his actions, their own culpability. Certainly Chris 'would feel a burden of guilt to the end of his life, in part because . . . he really knew . . . that he should not have participated in the business without clearing this up earlier on'.[17]

Joe Keller knows he is guilty but has to preserve the idea of his innocence. Kate knows, on some level, that her son is dead yet has to sustain the idea that he has survived, or deal not only with that calamity but the corrosive truth of her husband's actions. Chris knows, or suspects, on some level, that his father is suppressing the truth but has an agenda of his own that makes him deny it to others and himself and that makes him break his mother's last grasp on hope.

This, then, is in part a play about repression, about the compromises effected by individuals negotiating between private needs and public obligations. Joe is not the only character to substitute the story of his life for his life. They all construct fictions that enable them to justify themselves in their own eyes, as much as in the eyes of others. And this, it seems, is equally true of the neighbours and, beyond them, of a society that generates its own myths about innocence. What we witness is in part a collision of fictions which are mutually destructive, and, hence, their slow erosion, as what has been repressed begins to force its way to the surface.

George Deever is the embodiment of this. He is, Miller insists, the return of the repressed, while acknowledging that 'you can't live without denial', that 'the truth and mankind are cousins not brothers and sisters' and that 'You have to deny something in order to survive.' 'I think', Miller has said, that 'they are all denying something. The difference is that what Joe is denying is a crime.' But if George is a reminder of what is being denied he also represents the innocence of the pre-war world when he was a friend and neighbour to the Kellers. He is, Miller has said, 'the broken promise of the past'.[18]

Such themes, however, are secondary to the principal thrust of the play. As Miller has explained,

> the concept behind it was that Joe Keller was both responsible for and a part of a great web of meaning, of being. He had torn that web; he had ripped his part of the structure that supports life and society . . . that web of meaning, of existence. And a person who violates it in the way he did has done more than kill a few men. He has killed the possibility of a society having any future, any life. He has destroyed the life-force in that society.[19]

The play has a distinctive rhythm as the tension is applied and relaxed, as serious discussion gives way to a deliberately distracting comedy, as truths threaten to break surface only to be momentarily concealed. This rhythm is contained within a larger one as slowly doubts obtrude and lies are stripped away. The first act ends with the news that George is coming directly from the prison, or rather with the slam of a screen door as Joe Keller retreats from what he fears is an impending doom and his wife stares into the future she sees rushing towards her.

In the second act George is nearly persuaded to abandon his mission, seduced in part by a nostalgia provoked by Kate who invites him to suspend his doubts in the name of a past in truth long since compromised. Then, an inadvertent remark strips away the pretence. The act ends with an angry aria from Chris as the truth is finally exposed.

The third act, like the others, begins on a deceptively calm note and then builds to a crescendo as Joe Keller seeks the only absolution available to him by putting a bullet through his head as his wife cries, according to the director of the

Manchester Royal Exchange Theatre production, 'like Clytemnestra sobbing before the temple'.[20] This relaxing and intensifying of the mood constitutes something more than a structuring device, a dynamic plotting of emotional and intellectual tension. It is a rhythm equally apparent in the lives of people who are drawn in opposing directions, torn, as they are, between the demands of the material and the transcendent, in a society which has itself always been a blend of the two.

These are people whose flaws, like those in the cylinder heads supplied by Joe Keller, may have been covered up but still exist. Joe Keller's acceptance of culpability is not the only issue in the play. Meaning is not wholly disclosed nor character as neatly aligned with dramatic function as at times it is in the work of Ibsen – and *The Wild Duck*, for all its virtues, is rather too content to present characters who are, essentially, defined on their first appearance. There is little, for example, to be said for the sanctimonious Gregers Werle, who presents his 'demand of the ideal', beyond his sanctimony. Chris Keller's commitment to idealism, by contrast, is carefully motivated, being rooted in wartime experience and tainted with a self-concern he is unwilling, and perhaps unable, to address. Gregers remains unconcerned by the death he provokes; Chris Keller is broken and left with a residue of guilt that cannot easily be discharged.

By the same token, Joe Keller is more deeply mired in denial, more confused by a world he had taken to be so clear in its necessities, than ever was his counterpart in Ibsen's play. The neighbouring doctor, Relling, in *The Wild Duck*, is there as a humane counterpoint, cynical but clear-headed; the neighbouring doctor in Miller's play is given a history of his own, an ambivalent marriage and an unresolved tension that makes him something more than a marker. And so it continues: Kate, Ann, George are not so many pieces in a jigsaw, fragments of a whole, a completed picture. They are individuals whose motives are deeply ambiguous and whose actions are suspect even to themselves.

This is not a well-made play whose energy is fully discharged with the final pistol shot, whose meaning is wholly revealed in the telling. When, in the final speech, Kate instructs the son, who has just precipitated his own father's death, that he should not 'take it on' himself (171), she is offering him advice wholly at odds with what we have seen in a play in which the necessity to 'take it on' oneself is precisely the point. Why else, finally, did Joe Keller kill himself? Only moments before, his mother had asked Chris: 'Are you trying to kill him?' as the dead son, Larry, had said in a letter, 'if I had him there now I could kill him' (170). The lesson, in other words, has not been learned. The world is not made over and nor are those individuals who acknowledge the issues but themselves remain trapped in contradictory necessities. When Joe cries out 'a man can't be a Jesus in this world!' (169), he hints at a flawed human nature not finally to be resolved by a bullet in the brain. Joe asks of his son that he 'see it human' (118). Chris, desperate to recover a lost idealism, fails to do so, a failure that, in its own way, makes him complicit in the very crime he would condemn and contaminates that idealism.

Miller has never been interested in realism as such. His concern has been with reality. In his own view, 'Realism can conceal reality, perhaps a little easier than any other form.' His own commitment, he suggests, is to 'the poetic, the confluence of various forces in a surprising way; the reversals of man's plans for himself; the role of fate, of myth, in his life; his beliefs in false things, his determination to tell the truth until it hurts'.[21] In *All My Sons* the realism of the style never obscures the reality, though certain truths are confronted and others remain disturbingly unacknowledged. It seems clear that the suburban amnesia, the retreat into routine, the surface equanimities can no longer be maintained. It is as though realism itself can no longer sustain the forces it has delineated with such seeming precision.

All My Sons expresses a familiar 1930s faith in the necessity for human solidarity but the play's true strength comes from the ambivalence that seeps into it. A work that could so easily have resolved itself into a moral melodrama that, in stripping away self-deceit and lies, separating performance from actuality, assumed that the residue was untrammelled truth, becomes instead a drama in which motives remain problematic and the demand of the ideal is as suspect as a life lived with no transcendent purpose. It is, finally, a play whose triumph comes precisely from Miller's own ability to 'see it human', to embody confused values, flawed ambitions, betrayals, denials, profound disillusionments, in characters convincing alike in their needs and self-deceptions.

In other words, there is more to *All My Sons*, and to the characters who act out private dilemmas which are simultaneously public issues, than can be accounted for by casual dismissals of it as 'a well-made play', predictable, shallowly optimistic and content to rest in a simple display of causalities.

On the face of it, Miller's decision to structure the play around the relationship between a father and son implies a historical logic whereby the assumptions of capitalism are challenged, defeated and replaced by a new generation whose values, forged in wartime, are now to be socially and morally operative in peace. Larry died in order to draw a line across a certain historical development. Chris forces Joe to die for much the same thing.

There is, though, no suggestion that Chris will turn his back on business following the death of his father, merely on this particular business. His argument with capitalism seems to dissolve into a generalised assault on a system in which self-interest is the only operative principle and in which, therefore, justice is mocked:

> Do I raise the dead when I put him behind bars? Then what'll I do it for?
> We used to shoot a dog, but honour was real there, you were protecting
> something. But here? This is the land of the great big dogs, you don't love a
> man here, you eat him! That's the principle; the only one we live by – it just
> happened to kill a few people this time, that's all. The world's that way, how
> can I take it out on him? What sense does that make? This is a zoo, a zoo!

(167)

The play may express regret, through several characters, that money has become a primary determinant, but it is money that Chris promises to Ann. What is at stake is a model of human relationships which turns on mutual dependency, mutual responsibility. Ten years earlier Miller would have drawn the political implications of this, and, indeed, did so in his early university plays. Here he seems content with a statement of mutuality, except that this is undercut by the suspect nature of Chris's 'demand of the ideal', as Ibsen called it in *The Wild Duck*.

All My Sons went through several drafts in which plot, characters and themes were subject to radical revision. Miller was uncertain for some time as to where its heart truly lay. The central event remained but he toyed with bringing the convicted man from prison for a confrontation in the Keller house, which itself was to be located distant from the scene of the crime. In these earlier drafts, the whole family, and not just Kate, fail to reconcile themselves to Larry's death. Indeed, Kate is more determined than the rest of them to lay the ghost of her son. Ann and Chris seem not to be planning marriage or even to be romantically attracted to one another while, in the material that survives, the ambiguities of Chris's character move rather closer to the centre. Joe Keller, meanwhile, is, in these early drafts, wealthier and determined to do what he can, short of confession, to expiate his crime.

In an early notebook, we learn that Joe Keller has gone out of his way to employ veterans. 'We're got enough of them in the plant to start another war.' Their number includes an Air Force Lt Colonel: 'He outranks the whole rest of the shipping department', observes Chris, 'Extra flight pay when they go above the fourth floor.' A veteran, indeed a surviving member of Chris's unit, becomes a character in the play, thereby forcing him to recall experiences he would rather forget. It is through him that Chris hears rumours of the Kellers' involvement in supplying damaged cylinder heads. This character, subsequently abandoned, constitutes a living reproach for the betrayal of those who died in the war and for the abandonment of those values that had supposedly necessitated their sacrifices.

The discarded drafts that went to make up *All My Sons* are of considerable interest, throwing light, as they do, on Miller's evolving sense of the characters, on his refinement of the plot and of the process whereby a simple news story became an affecting drama.[22] In an early version, the Keller family had moved from Toledo, where the scandal occurred, to this new town where they hope that nobody will remember or care. The comfortable family home, left as a visual marker in the final version, is here a new acquisition and stands as a sign of the wealth the family has accrued while their sons were at war.

Thus, on returning from the war and discovering what his father's company had done, Chris confesses that

I almost killed Dad . . . The firm had shipped bad heads, that's all that
mattered. And this place – I had a six room house and came back to an
estate. I [had] a tin-roof machine shop and come back to a plant three
blocks square. Even if he'd never seen a jail the word innocent didn't seem
to [occur] at all. I took a hundred and eighty seven beautiful boys into the
line and came out with two.

To this, Ann replies, 'No wonder you feel guilty about Larry.' In other words
here, at this early stage, guilt attaches itself to Chris Keller, as he acknowledges
his unease at what he is becoming.

As he explains, 'I wanted to do something or be something that would make
them immortal.' He wanted to be 'a new man', to 'hold onto the love, the
brotherhood we made there. It was the only good thing we made there and I
didn't want it to die with them. And I hated picturing them, and all the greed
and the cheap chizzling that people have to do in the world. I hated it. . . . I was
against us.' In his army unit he even presented himself as being poor. The guilt,
in other words, predated news that his father had been charged with a crime.

His sense of revulsion, then, was not primarily a product of one criminal
action but of the precipitate loss of moral purpose, the betrayal of the dead
by those with other priorities, people like his father and, more significantly,
himself. He had returned to find himself heir not so much to a company tainted
with corruption as a company, a house, a lifestyle that was a reward for avarice,
a mechanism for turning the death of soldiers into profit.

His father's temporary jailing was the shock that opened his eyes, but his
own guilt went further. It was a product of his failure to become what he had
promised himself he would. He was not a new man nor was this a place for such
and for that reason he says, 'I'll never forgive myself.' Interestingly, however,
just beneath this handwritten speech is a phrase that Miller underlined: 'The
family – live for the family.' It is the one thing, besides Ann, that he sees as left
to him. It is what joins him directly to his father and it is, of course, to be the
justification that Joe advances for his own actions. But his exclusion of Ann
from that note, which was plainly to become the basis for a speech that was
never written, inspires her to reply: 'If your family is the only thing in the world
I had rather . . . all right. It's your family. But it's your family, it's not mine. I
cherish other things more.'

The reference is to Larry but here she goes on to identify precisely the same
contrast between his sacrifice and the enrichment of others that had so appalled
Chris: 'And when he crashed – if he crashed – it made a cash register ring in
certain places...' And one of the 'certain places' is precisely the Keller household.
As she says, 'It's not the money you made. You're simply not mourning him.
You're afraid of him, that's all. Because you sinned against him in your souls!
That's why he won't lay down! For twenty acres of land with a view, for a
four-car garage.'

Plainly Miller's conception of Ann changed. Direct statements to do with the family wealth deferred to a set that becomes a direct expression of it. Chris's guilt, subtly hinted at in the final text, is here specifically and directly addressed. What we are looking at is a writer exploring his characters, testing the thematic balance of his play.

Much of what is to be found in the early manuscripts is stripped away, as revisions slowly expose the core of the drama. Yet at the same time there are traces here that explain attitudes and values that survive but that have an imminent presence. Thus, while Joe Keller was to have announced a million-dollar grant for a memorial park – thus lifting him too clearly and starkly into a world of his own, too remote to act as an image of a more general collapse of values – he was also to have revealed that he had been poor until 1938, recalling that he 'had a dollar change after buying Larry's ice skates'. The reference disappears but the feeling of insecurity does not. The threat of losing everything, that made a morning's lost production seem such a potential tragedy, has an immediate correlative in the Depression decade. What is explicit in the manuscript becomes implicit in the final play.

There is something in the rhetoric of the early manuscripts, though, which suggests that there may be something too absolute in the values that Chris counterposes to those of the world in which he finds himself. For the soldier, he explains, in an echo of *Situation Normal,*

> a man is good according to the severity of his wounds. A man with one leg gone is good. With two legs gone – he is better. And the best of all, the most honored and honorable – the only heroes – are the dead. They're the only heroes, the only ones who are utterly true, without a chance to become petty again, and corrupt and selfish. Only they will not betray what they fought for. They weren't given the chance.

This is a speech which suggests that Chris's guilt lies in something more than his association with a tainted company. Part of the guilt he feels is that of the survivor.

That remains in the final play but the explicit nature of the above speech suggests the extent to which Chris embraces an idealism too implacable to be sustained, an idealism not without its own deflating absurdity. Sacrifice demands a subject worthy of itself, a myth that can validate an ultimate act. But the code of war is too uncompromising to survive the moment. It proposes a standard whose logic is not finally extendable into peacetime. We are, in fact, not far from the Ibsen of *The Wild Duck* where too unyielding an idealism results in death, though this time not of the innocent. But innocence itself can seem deeply suspect in so far as it proposes an impossible standard.

Indeed, even in war, according to these early notes, Chris Keller was unrelentingly severe. We are told that he 'never let a Nazi get away. Other guys would maybe let a Jerry run if he had a mind to. Chris would chase after them. Never think such a quiet guy would be such a killer.' Then, underlined, Miller writes 'Killer Keller we called him.' This disappears from the finished text but, again, a shadow of that unforgiving self survives and he does, of course, indirectly kill. Where other people are inclined to let Joe get away with his crime – including Ann – he will not.

In this early version, Chris's dilemma is closer to the centre of Miller's concern than it would later prove to be while the guilt of the idealist was not a subject, he later confessed, that he had felt ready to deal with. However, *All My Sons* does not end with a pistol shot but with Chris's belated confession of responsibility. He did, in fact, fail, in Joe's words, to 'see it human', not only because an abstract notion of justice proves more important to him than private relationships or compassion, but also because he felt he owed something to those whose death was still on his conscience. In the final version of *All My Sons* it is that idealism which breeds discontent in his doctor neighbour, who feels he should be devoting his talent to research. It is a discontent which threatens his peace of mind and perhaps his marriage.

In an early manuscript his mother tellingly says of him, 'Chris is as neat as a priest' while when Larry came into the house 'it got alive', a contrast which places Chris in opposition to life, though this mother differs significantly from that of the final version, saying, 'It's wrong to cling to the dead. God doesn't like it.' It is the whole family who are tempted not to give Larry up: 'we're not in mourning so much as in waiting. I don't know why.'

In this version the mother does not know the truth of her husband's crime, while the drama seems likely to turn on the arrival of the man convicted in Joe's place, a man whose name – Ekhart – has an Ibsenesque ring about it (Ekdal in *The Wild Duck*, Erhart in *John Gabriel Borkman*): 'Only Chris knows. Play with Mom unaware. Pop arrives with gun. Then Ekhart. Leaving it to Chris to decide who is right.' Of course here, and in the final version, when Chris is convinced of his father's guilt, that guilt necessarily extends to him, since he has been a beneficiary, while if his father could be said to be responsible for Larry's death then so, too, is he – hence the title which Miller tried out in his notes: *But Cain Went Forth*.

The play clearly changed a great deal in subsequent revisions but the early drafts serve to underscore aspects of *All My Sons* which Miller was finally content to leave as trace elements, thematic sub-plots not to be fully developed. Not a single character remains what he or she was in the original drafts. The supposedly well-made play had to be made and the process of its making explains something of the allusive and ambiguous elements, the counter-currents, that make it so much more than a 1930s call for social and moral solidarity or an indictment of a capitalism whose logic runs counter to genuine human needs. Certainly, half a century on from the war that seemingly gave it birth it remained a contemporary play.

As Miller remarked in the mid-1990s:

in these past dozen years . . . *All My Sons* . . . is more and more frequently and widely produced . . . and the reviewers no longer feel obliged to dismiss its structure as not-modern. I have had to wonder whether this is partly due to the number of investigations of official malfeasance in the papers all the time, and the spectacle of men of stature and social influence being brought down practically every week by revelations excavated from the hidden past. From the heights of Wall Street, the Pentagon, the White House, big business, the same lessons seem to fly out at us – the past lives![23]

On the other side of the millennium, in a sell-out production at Britain's Royal National Theatre, it was still winning awards, still inspiring the kind of response it had prompted in a young Harold Pinter who played the role of Chris Keller in repertory, finding in it a play which contrasted with the vapid products of the English theatre.

— ✳ —

All My Sons was an immediate and considerable success. It ran for 328 performances at New York's Coronet Theatre. There was nothing equivocal about
the critical and popular response, aside from some sniping from the communist press, which saw the play as the story of one exceptional capitalist in an
otherwise acceptable system, and from the right-wing press, which saw it as an
attack on American values (it was banned from US bases in Europe). Success,
however, left Miller with a twinge of guilt. He was struck by the fact that every
day money was pouring in without him lifting a hand. It seemed unearned.
He was advised to invest in property, but the idea of becoming a landlord
was repugnant. Had his parents, after all, not spent the 1930s struggling to
pay the mortgage? Had he not been committed to those who were exploited
rather than to those who might be seen to be the exploiters? Indeed, in reaction to his sudden wealth, he sought a manual job at basic pay and did spend
several days assembling box dividers before the pointlessness of it overwhelmed
him.

Miller did, though, attend a number of meetings of the Communist Party,
a fact that would come back to haunt him in the mid-1950s when he was
summoned to appear before the House Un-American Activities Committee.
He also added his name to an increasing number of petitions and appeals, his
new status making him a useful ally for various left-wing causes.

Within two years of the end of the war, however, the Soviet Union had
suddenly become the enemy, even as former Nazis, with desirable skills, were
not only allowed into the country but welcomed as the Cold War got under
way. Miller was a political animal and the fact of his artistic breakthrough did
nothing to diminish his enthusiasms, even as they began to seem decidedly
unfashionable.

Meanwhile, his family life seemed to be thriving. His daughter Jane had been
born in 1944 and now, with his first Broadway success, came a son, Robert.

At the same time, while revelling in his new status, he was not entirely
satisfied with *All My Sons*. By instinct, he was drawn to experiment, despite
the fact that his politics and the nature of his first successful play would lead
critics to characterise him as an incorrigible realist for decades to come. He
now wanted to write a different kind of play, one that would give licence to his
lyrical instincts but one, too, that would break new ground theatrically.

Taken to see Tennessee Williams's *A Streetcar Named Desire* by Elia Kazan, as
Williams had himself seen *All My Sons*, he was struck by the language, poetic,
full-throated. It came as a revelation (as his own play had to Williams) and
seemed to validate his own desire to charge daily life with tragic significance,
to use language as something more than an agent of character or plot.

With his new money he acquired a house in rural Connecticut. He now built
a shed to write in. It had five windows and a door, together with a somewhat

suspect floor. It took him six weeks to construct, the same time, it turned out, that it took him to write his next work, *Death of a Salesman*.

The play's premiere was to prove one of the most significant nights in American theatrical history. In an article in the *New York Times*, to mark its opening, he explained that he was interested in building his drama out of the 'significant commonplaces', though that did not mean that he was intent on creating a naturalistic portrait. He had, he insisted, always been impatient with naturalism. *All My Sons* had paid his debt in that regard. Now he was looking for greater freedom.

Curiously, he explained to his interviewer that he had made a point of working in a factory for a few weeks each year since only those who knew what it was to stand in the same place for eight hours a day could really understand what life was about. In reality, the few days he had spent working for the minimum wage after *All My Sons* was the only time he had undertaken that kind of work since 1934, fifteen years earlier. What he seemed to be doing was expressing a sense of nostalgia for other people's lives, underscoring his connection to those with whom in truth, apart from his carpentry work, he shared little except at the level of ideology.

He was to write an essay on 'Tragedy and the Common Man' not only because he did, indeed, wish to acknowledge that the lives of ordinary people were charged with significance but because he wanted in some way to celebrate their struggle with the given. He had, after all, seen his own father ruined by commitment to a false idea, an American dream rooted not in a Puritan ethic but the belief that he inhabited a country that gifted its citizens rewards which required less work than faith to achieve.

In truth, though still a Marxist, his commitment to the lives of those who seldom had access to power came less from an idea of political and social process than a sympathy for the dreamer betrayed, for those whose lives he knew, not because he had stood for hours in a factory (though he had spent two years in the auto-parts warehouse), but because they had been part of his upbringing. *Death of a Salesman*, he explained, would have less judgement and more pity than *All My Sons*.

In part he was speaking the language of tragedy, in part he was expressing his attitude to characters who here and in his subsequent works sought the meaning of their lives in the struggle to make sense out of what they believed to be their fate. Few of his characters could be said to have brought their lives into alignment with their hopes but out of the struggle to do so was born a significance they seldom understood but which was no less significant for that. Many of them fail to become what they wish themselves to be but the struggle generates something more than mere irony. Attention, Miller insists, must be paid to such people.

✳

7

'Death of a Salesman'

The idea for *Death of a Salesman* had long been in Miller's mind. At seventeen he had written a story called 'In Memoriam', in which a Jewish salesman goes to his death. At university he jotted down some ideas about a man called Willy Loman and then again, immediately after university, wrote a striking stream-of-consciousness story, never published, about a salesman whose hopes have come to nothing and who goes to his death under the wheels of a subway car.

Though he would explain the play's origin by reference to a family member whose extravagant plans for his sons came to nothing, there is a more personal genesis for this play about a believer in the American dream who struggles with a knowledge of his failure. The play is not about Miller's father but one incident had brought home to him what it was to be a believer confronted with daily evidence of his own incapacities. When the family business had collapsed, Isadore Miller struggled to keep his dignity, starting new companies, looking for business. One day he was forced to borrow money for the subway from his son. It was a critical moment in their relationship as it was also a sudden and personal reminder of where America had failed so many of those who believed in the inevitability of success in a country which presented itself as specially blessed.

Even thus reduced in his present circumstances and future hopes, his father had still wanted his son to follow in his footsteps. When a young Arthur Miller explained his plans for college his father regarded this as a betrayal. It was not simply that where he had failed his son might succeed but that in succeeding he would justify that father who had abandoned one country for another on the promise of success. Love, pride, ambition, somehow braided together in that moment. Isadore Miller's identity had become invested in his company and if that had collapsed what was he unless he could see his son go on to do what he had not? It was necessary that his son should stay. For a teenage Arthur Miller it was necessary that he should leave. There was betrayal on both sides and there was love on both sides. Isadore's shamefaced request for money for the subway was evidence of his vulnerability, of a shift in the power relationship between father and son. It was also a reminder, however, that the governing principles of the culture were under strain, that promises had been broken, false values inculcated.

Death of a Salesman is as much about the public as the private world but, to Miller, this is a false distinction. Willy Loman in particular has absorbed the values of his society until they seem part of what he wishes to see as his own definition. His is a salesman, the epitome of a society built on social performance and wedded to the idea of a transforming future. By the same token, however, those who saw this play at the time, and in the over fifty years since that first production, have connected to it less through its comments on a culture wedded to a myth than through characters whose hopes and illusions seem instantly recognisable and archetypal. Willy Loman is a man who wishes his reality to come into line with his hopes, a man desperate to leave his mark on the world through his own endeavours and through those of his children. Though he seems to seek death, what he fears above all is that he will go before he has justified himself in his own eyes and there are few, from New York to Beijing, who do not understand the urgency of that need.

When the play begins, Biff Loman has been summoned home because his mother knows that her husband's life is at risk. He has begun to plan his suicide. Who else but the sons can rescue him? To return, however, is to threaten the peace which Biff has managed to secure for himself on the other side of the anarchy bequeathed by his father. Brought up to expect success, to take what he wants, he has spent time in jail. His brother Happy, meanwhile, has turned into a self-deceiving womaniser who believes in nothing but his own pleasure, getting nowhere but, seemingly like his father, contenting himself with illusions. But there is more to Willy Loman. He is tempted by suicide not because he fails to understand his situation but because he does. It is for that reason that he tracks back through his life in memory, restlessly searching for the moment when he betrayed life or it betrayed him. In that sense it is Willy Loman who constructs much of the play as he returns to a time which had once seemed golden but had, in some way he cannot understand, carried the seeds of his current dismay.

Where he remains illusioned is in his conviction that his death can win what his life cannot. His life insurance will gift his sons the success that has eluded them and him. Meanwhile, by his side is a woman who offers a redemption he is too blind to see. Raised in a world in which appearance mattered more than substance, the world of a salesman in which clothes must be spotless and a smile always on the lips, he fails to recognise something as intangible as her love.

Over the years Miller has offered a number of intriguing interpretations of *Death of a Salesman*. It is about 'the paradoxes of being alive in a technological civilization';[1] it is about 'the alienation brought by technological advance . . . the price we pay for progress'.[2] It is 'a story about violence within the family', about 'the suppression of the individual by placing him below the imperious needs of . . . society'.[3] It is 'a play about a man who kills himself because he isn't liked'.[4] It expresses 'all those feelings of a society falling to pieces which I had',[5] feelings that, to him, are one of the reasons for the play's continuing popularity. But the observation that goes most directly to the heart of the play is contained in a comment made in relation to the production he directed in China in 1983: '*Death of a Salesman*, really, is a love story between a man and his son, and in a crazy way between both of them and America.'[6]

Turn to the notebooks that he kept when writing the play and you find the extent to which the relationship between Willy and his son is central.[7] There are repeated notes about the magnetic force that paradoxically pulls them together and thrusts them apart: 'He is hounded by and is hounding Willy with guilt', he reminds himself; 'Raise the conflict in Biff between wanting NY success and hating Willy. This is the climax'; 'Biff wants to save him, and at the same time to free himself.' He is angry 'at Willy's weakness, helplessness, and at W's love for him'; 'Biff's conflict is that to tell the truth would be to diminish himself in his own eyes. To admit his fault. His confusion, then, is not didactic, or directed to Willy's elucidation or salvation, but toward a surgical break which he knows in his heart W could never accept. His motive, then, is to destroy W, free himself.' The essence of the drama is contained within these tensions. In a brief passage of dialogue, not to appear in the final play, he simultaneously identifies the dilemma of both men and the essence of his dramatic method:

> B: Don't believe the myth – if at first you don't succeed, try try again.
>   Sometimes it's better to walk away.
> W: Just walk away.
> B: Yes.
> W: But if you can't walk away.
> B: Then . . . nobody can help you.

The truth is that neither man can walk away, though Biff will, it seems, do so at the end of the play, stepping out of the drama into a projected, if historically suspect, future. They are wedded to their dreams and they are held together by a complex of emotions they can barely understand, not least because they consist of contrarieties – love/hate, vengeance/redemption, ambition/despair. Father and son are a divided self. Their identities are ineluctably intertwined. For Willy Loman, Biff is his justification and vindication. In refusing to embrace his father's dreams he is, thus, denying him fulfilment, expiation, that sense of identity that comes from passing the torch from generation to generation. For Biff, his father stands between himself and his life. He is the past that has to be transcended, the falsehood that must be rejected, but also the debt that must be discharged.

There is a terrible rhythm to the play as the two men are drawn together and thrust apart, both acting out of a sense of love and yet both aware that the avenue to that love is occluded by guilt, by weaknesses in themselves. The past is the burden they bear in a play in which the past threatens at every moment to break through into an increasingly desperate present. There is a race on, a race for Willy's life and Biff's soul. If they could acknowledge their wrong paths, offer each other the absolution they seek, all might be well, but they cannot. And, for Miller, as he implied in his notebook entry, drama is born out of a situation in which the individual cannot walk away.

Biff and his father see the world differently. When Biff, in lines of dialogue that Miller scrawled in the *Salesman* notebook, announces that his ambition is merely to be happy, Willy replies, 'To enjoy yourself is not ambition. A tramp has that. Ambition is *things*. A man must want *things*! You're lost. You are a lost boy. And I know why now. Because you hate me you turned your back on all your promise. For spite, for spite of me, because I wanted you magnificent.' Elements of this are retained in the final play but Willy's materialism is not so much stated as embodied in his lament over the failure of the consumer goods he has acquired. Beyond that, the irony is that he lacks precisely the 'things' he thought he valued. His dilemma is that of a culture that proposes as a national mission the pursuit of happiness and then confuses this with material possessions, as did the Founding Fathers who debated whether happiness and property were synonymous. No wonder that Linda trumpets the fact that they have repaid their mortgage as if this was in some way the objective towards which their lives had been directed. The fact is that whatever Willy Loman says he is not content with things. He wants, above all, to be well liked, a condition he confuses with success.

Biff and Willy wrestle one another for their existence. Biff is Willy's ace in the hole, his last desperate throw, the proof that he was right, after all, that tomorrow things will change for the better and thus offer a retrospective grace to the past. Willy, meanwhile, is Biff's flawed model, the man who seemed to sanction his hunger for success and popularity, a hunger suddenly stilled by a moment of revelation. Over the years, neither has been able to let go of the other because to do so would be to let go of a dream that, however tainted, still has the glitter of possibility, except that now Biff has begun to understand that there is something wrong, something profoundly inadequate about a vision so at odds with his instincts.

As he says to Willy, in a speech included in the notebook but not the final play, 'You think I'm mad at you because of the woman, don't you. I am, but I'm madder because you bitched up my life, because I can't tear you out of my heart, because I keep trying to do something for you, to succeed for you.' He still feels the need to shine in his father's eyes, though all his instincts now rebel against the notion that the ends justify the means. He, after all, was encouraged as a young man to cut corners, to steal lumber from the nearby building site and basket balls when he wanted to practise. In truth, Miller indicates in his notes, 'Biff is not bright enough to make a businessman. He wants everything too fast.' As he was to have said, 'It took me a long time to understand. When I finished school I was given to understand that if a fella wants it, he'll rise in the firm. I stayed . . . 2 years as shipping clerk and nothing ever happened.'

He returns, now, partly out of a surviving sense of duty towards Willy and partly to resolve his conflict with him, to announce that he has finally broken with the false values offered to him as his inheritance. Two people are fighting for survival, in the sense of sustaining a sense of themselves. Willy desperately needs Biff to embrace him and his dream. As Miller observes in his notebook, he needs the affection and success of his sons 'to destroy his failure'. Biff, by contrast, desperately needs to cut the link between himself and Willy. This is the motor force of the play. There can be only one winner and whoever wins will also have lost. As Miller explained to the actor playing the role in the Beijing production: 'your love for him binds you; but you want it to free you to be your own man'. Willy, however, is unable to offer such grace because 'he would have to turn away from his own values'.[8]

Once returned, though, Biff is enrolled in the conspiracy to save Willy's life. The question which confronts him now is whether that life will be saved by making Willy face up to the reality of his life or by substantiating his illusions. To do the latter, however, would be to work against his own needs. The price of saving Willy may thus, potentially, be the loss of his own freedom and autonomy. Meanwhile the tension underlying this central conflict derives from the fact that, as Miller has said, 'the story of *Salesman* is absurdly simple! It is about a salesman and it's his last day on the earth.'[9]

Part of the plan to save Willy lies in the scheme for Biff and Happy to go into business together. Biff is to return to his former boss and solicit funds. It was never a credible proposition. Indeed it is one more evidence of the unreal world in which the Loman family have taken up residence. It is one more lie to pile on those that have corroded the links between them. And when Biff, at the interview, chooses to steal the pen of the man on whom his future supposedly depends, we have Miller's assurance, in a hand-written note in his notebook, that the thefts he has committed since catching his father in a Boston hotel room with another woman, are, at least subconsciously, indirect acts of vengeance. As he reminds himself, 'It is necessary to (1) Reveal to W that Biff stole to queer himself, and did it to hurt W. (2) And that he did it because of the Woman and all the disillusionment it implied.'

So it is that while humbling himself by soliciting money, in order to give his father the hope he lacks, he simultaneously subverts the action. Beyond that, Miller notes that 'Biff's telling of the theft must suggest the Dream', for the private actions, the personal betrayals, are always to be rooted in a broader truth.

In like manner, the two boys rendezvous with their father in a restaurant only to desert him. Biff, we are told in the notebook, 'left out of guilt, pity, and inability to open himself to W. – Hap out of shame.' The ebb and flow of their affections is an echo of the contradictions that litter Willy's language no less than his behaviour. They are their father's sons and that is the source of their and his dilemma.

Yet for all their abandonment of him, Biff, at least, 'still wants that evidence of W's love. Still does not want to be abandoned by him. And now this is necessary.' He resolves to cut them both free by telling the truth, returning to the house to force a confrontation: 'He has returned here', Miller notes, 'to disillusion W. forever, to set him upon a new path, and thus release himself from responsibility for W. and what he knows is going to happen to him, – or half fears will.' There is, in other words, still a profound ambiguity in his motives. He simultaneously wants to set Willy on a new path, and to absolve himself of responsibility for the death which he now feels is imminent.

However, if by disillusioning his father he will be liberating him to take a new path why does he at the same time see this gesture as freeing himself of culpability for his impending suicide? It is precisely this doubleness of motive, this fluctuating sense of moral duty, this ambiguous commitment to freedom and responsibility that characterises both men. If neither cared for, if neither loved the other there would be no problem. Neither would feel guilt, neither would feel a sense of obligation, a debt that must be discharged. As Biff remarks, in a scene amended in the final version, 'I've got an obligation . . . What's happened to him is my fault. I realized that in the restaurant. I guess that's why I couldn't bear to stay. It's always the same – just when the truth has to be told I run away . . . I don't want anything to happen to him . . . and I know it's me, it's me that's driving him.' As he adds in a note, 'What Biff wants is to be released. But Willy's guilt requires him to help him.' The irony is that when Willy at last acknowledges his son's love for him it merely strengthens his belief that he should bequeath him his dream, speeds him on his way to death: 'Through [Biff's] confession of his having *used* W's betrayal, W sees his basic love, and is resolved to suicide.'

Miller may, in his own words, be 'a confirmed and deliberate radical',[10] but *Death of a Salesman* is not an attack on American values. It is, however, an exploration of the betrayal of those values and the cost of this in human terms. Willy Loman's American dream is drained of transcendence. It is a faith in the supremacy of the material over the spiritual. There is, though, another side to Willy, a side represented by the sense of insufficiency that sends him searching through his memories looking for the origin of failure, looking for expiation. It is a side, too, represented by his son Biff, who has inherited this aspect of his sensibility, as Happy has inherited the other. Biff is drawn to nature, to working with his hands. He has a sense of poetry, an awareness that life means more than the dollars he earns. Willy has that, too. The problem is that he thinks it is irrelevant to the imperatives of his society and hence of his life which, to him, derives its meaning from that society.

Next door, however, in the form of Charley and Bernard, is another version of the dream, a version turning not on self-delusion and an amoral drive for success but on hard work and charity. What Miller attacks, then, is not the

American Dream of Thomas Jefferson and Benjamin Franklin, but the dream as interpreted and pursued by those for whom ambition replaces human need and the trinkets of what Miller called the 'new American Empire in the making' are taken as tokens of true value. When, on the play's opening night, a woman called *Death of a Salesman* a 'time bomb under American capitalism', his response was to hope that it was, 'or at least under the bullshit of capitalism, this pseudo life that thought to touch the clouds by standing on top of a refrigerator, waving a paid-up mortgage at the moon, victorious at last' (*T*.184). But the play goes beyond such particularities.

Charley is described by Miller as 'gruff, ignorant, and peasantlike'.[11] In talking of Howard Smith, who played the part in the first Broadway production, he identifies those qualities common to actor and character alike. He was, he says, 'a hard-headed, realistic, decent man; slightly dense, perhaps, but filled with human worth'.[12] Trying to explain Charley to a somewhat bewildered Chinese actor, when he was directing the play in Beijing in 1983, he suggested that he was motivated in part by his deep affection for Linda, for which his kindness is a kind of sublimation, but beyond that by a kind of envy 'for Willy's imagination, the condiments with which he sprinkles his life as contrasted with the blandness of Charley's more rational existence. Charley', he added, 'can laugh at Willy as a fool, but he is never bored with him.'[13] There is, then, something in Willy Loman, confused, infuriating, resentful, baffled though he is, that nonetheless raises him above the level of those who never question, are undisturbed by dreams of possibility, who rest content with the routines of a life never burnished with a transcendent hope.

In choosing a salesman for his central character Miller was identifying an icon of his society seized on equally by other writers before and since, not least because a salesman always trades in hope, a brighter future. In *The Gilded Age* Mark Twain sees the salesman as a trickster, literally selling America to the gullible. In Theodore Dreiser's *Sister Carrie*, he is a man who values appearance above substance and relies for his sexual success on sustaining that appearance. Sinclair Lewis chose a realtor as the key to his satire of American values as, decades later, John Updike chose a car salesman in his Rabbit Angstrom books. The central figure in Eugene O'Neill's *The Iceman Cometh* is a salesman, as is Stanley Kowalski in Tennessee Williams's *A Streetcar Named Desire* and Rubin Flood in William Inge's *The Dark at the Top of the Stairs*. David Mamet's *Glengarry, Glen Ross* featured real estate salesmen. But what did Hickey sell, in *The Iceman Cometh*? He sold the same thing as Willy Loman, a dream of tomorrow, a world transformed, only to discover that meaning resides somewhere closer to home.

Willy's real creative energy goes into work on his house ('He was a happy man with a batch of cement'). But that is not something he can sell. What, then, does he sell? There were those who thought that a vital question, including Mary McCarthy, Robert Brustein and Rhoda Koenig (for whom his failure to offer this answer was a certain sign of the play's insignificance). But as Miller himself replied, he sells what a salesman always has to sell, himself. As Charley insists, 'The only thing you got in this world is what you can sell.' As a salesman he has got to get by on a smile and a shoeshine. He has to charm. He is a performer, a confidence man who must never lack confidence. His error is to confuse the role he plays with the person he wishes to be. The irony is that he, a salesman, has bought the pitch made to him by his society. He believes that advertisements tell the truth and is baffled when reality fails to match their claims. He believes the promises that America made to itself – that in this greatest country on earth success is an inevitability.

A salesman is a middle man. He is a means serving something beyond himself, an agent whose function is a factor of his own lost freedom. He is involved in transactions and the risk is that such transactions will begin to define his life, that the market which shapes his dreams and that of others, and in which he is implicated, will deprive him of the dignity he seeks and the significance for which he yearns. One of the questions that Miller's play seems to raise is that identified by the writer and salesman Earl Shorris, in his book *A Nation of Salesmen*: 'If America is a nation of salesmen, who are we, each and all of us together, and are we the people and the nation we hoped to be?'[14] For Shorris,

> when the market dictates the imagination and the act, the dream life as well as the day life of men, the true meaning of dignity comes clear. Kant did not pin his ethics on decorum; by *dignity* he meant 'free'. He could not tolerate man as a means, in the grasp of others, even in the grasp of God. He begins with man, with possibility; that is what is meant by freedom . . . The surrender of freedom is the sadness of the age . . . human beings enter into an agreement in which everything exists as part of a transaction. A man is interchangeable with a thing; he no longer determines his own worth; a price can be put on him. Man has lost his humanity.[15]

However, in trying to explain to Ying Ruocheng, who played the part of Willy in the Beijing production, the force of Willy's elegy for the way of life of a salesman, Miller offers an intriguing reading of his sense of the world in which Willy had moved and the meaning of being a salesman:

> Of course, I said, he is romanticizing as he always does, but there is some-thing real underlying his feeling. In the era he is talking about, the buyers for the stores he sold to were either the owners themselves or had held their jobs for many years and knew him. You know there was actually a man called Filene [the Boston department store named in *Salesman*], a man called Gimbel, R. H. Macy – and, for that matter, Louis Chevrolet, Buick, Olds, Ford, Firestone . . . these were actual human beings at one time, and if Willy did not really deal with them in person, their reality was part of his reality, and their beginnings in poverty and their rise in the world were the pantheon that circled his mind. The era of the salesman as mere order-taker whose canned pitch has been made for him on television and who has no options as what to say or charge, this was not yet the case in his time.[16]

The salesman, in the 1920s, was, he insists,

> a vital force in building the trade and commercial network of the country.
> The salesman needed little or no education, but an engaging personality
> and a faith in the inevitability of next week's upswing. Every salesman
> knew some other man who had hit it big, opened his own business, and
> died respected and rich. The myth of the salesman exemplified the open
> ranks of a society where practically overnight a man could leap to the head
> of the line.[17]

Ironically, the closest equivalent he could think of in the present was the
actor who constantly lives in the hope and expectation of sudden fame, after
no more than a year or two of training. Marlon Brando, after all, was a star
at twenty-three. 'Willy believes in just that kind of quick, smashing beginning.
And so his sons are never trained, have no patience with the process of foregoing
and delaying the slaking of whatever thirst is on them at the moment. They are
narcissists.'[18] This is the process that leads Happy into his pointless womanising
and Biff to a prison cell. A deferred future is intolerable; it must be collapsed into
the present. The contemporary equivalent of Willy's desire to be well liked is the
wish to be famous, though not now for anything in particular. Fame is not so
much the spur as the point of living, the substitution of seeming for being.

Death of a Salesman ends with the word 'free'. The irony ricochets back
through the text. Willy Loman, in thrall to the constructed dreams of a country
whose business is business, of a culture whose myths colonise the individual
imagination, reshaping desires to serve a national destiny, becomes no more
than a product, the product he must sell if he is to enter the promised land. He
does, indeed, lose his freedom and his dignity. He can envisage no life outside
the terms of the contract he has signed to subordinate himself to his function.
The death in the play is not that of Willy Loman but of a salesman. His dignity
is, indeed, destroyed as he puts a price on himself, in his encounter with his
employer lowering his salary step by step in an inverse bargaining session ('If
I could take home – well, sixty-five dollars a week . . . fifty dollars . . . forty
dollars'),[19] and this in a play in which dollar sums recur as if they were, indeed,
a measure of a man. 'I'm one dollar an hour',[20] says Biff, 'I'm a dime a dozen,
and so are you!'[21]

Like Faulkner's Joe Christmas in *Light in August*, Willy Loman is a man who
never finds out who he is. He believes that the image he sees reflected in the eyes
of those before whom he performs is real, and, as Timothy B. Spears points out
in *100 Years on the Road*, the metaphor of acting abounds in the literature of
salesmanship. Thus James Knox, in *Salesmanship and Business Efficiency* (1912),
had remarked that a salesman, like an actor, 'speaks the thoughts of other men;
he persuades by his manner of speaking, his manner of acting, and by some
indescribable force of his own personality which he is able to embody forth as
real'.[22]

As a salesman, Willy stages a performance for buyers, for his sons, for the father who deserted him, the brother he admired. Gradually, he loses his audience, first the buyers, then his son, then his boss. He walks on to the stage, no longer confident he can perform the role he believes is synonymous with his self, no longer sure that anyone will care. He lives a temporary life, a life of cars, trains, offices, hotel rooms. The rhythm of his existence is determined by timetables, appointments, sales targets.

Whatever the salesman needs, Willy seems to lack. He is deeply un-self-confident. He fears he is laughed at, that there is something about him that offends. The play is set at a time when America was beginning to boom, when supply had difficulty catching up with demand. Salesmen hardly needed to sell, simply taking orders from those happily escaping from wartime austerity. Yet the year he proudly quotes as his most successful is 1928, twenty years earlier and, not incidentally, the year before the Crash (the year that triumph turned to disaster for Miller's father, Isadore). This is a man who kills his loneliness in a Boston hotel with a woman whose attraction seems to lie less in her sexuality than in the access she can grant to the buyer, the consolation she offers for his sense of failure, a woman herself not without a degree of desperation.

What does she see in him? She, Miller explains, 'is a lonely woman . . . who genuinely likes Willy and his line of gab and his pathos, and so she sees him for dinner perhaps twice a month and they talk and "behave like husband and wife for a night"'. She might, he adds, 'have a similar relationship to a couple of other salesmen from time to time'.[23] Her laughter, which wells up and breaks through Willy's consciousness, is not, then, without a degree of self-mockery as she simultaneously acknowledges Willy's pathos and kills her own loneliness with a man whose humour comes from a deep sense of worthlessness for ever at battle with a desperate need to be acknowledged. It is a scene, however, that turns on what Miller has called an 'hallucinatory surrealism',[24] which had, he felt, got lost in all productions until, in Beijing, he found himself confronted with an actress who came out of an entirely different tradition of acting. This sent him back to the text and the realisation that he and other directors had tried to impose a realistic style on to dialogue that was, he now perceived, patently neither realistic nor a dialogue.

> THE WOMAN: Whyn't you have another drink, honey, and stop being so
> damn self-centred?
> WILLY: I'm so lonely.
> THE WOMAN: You know you ruined me, Willy.[25]

As it now seemed to him, they were not so much talking to each other as 'stating their dream-like, disjointed, and intensely compressed positions'.[26] And, of course, it is the nature of much of Willy's ostensible dialogue in the play that it is in fact a discussion with himself, an externalised account of his internal interrogation. Since he conducts these internal conversations in the presence of others, however, there is a surreal quality to many of the interchanges in a play whose sub-title is 'Certain Private Conversations'. The privacy is that provided by Willy's mind.

Why, though, given his state of mind, given the failure of his sales figures to match the importance of his territory, has the company kept him on, allowed him to represent them until he effectively precipitates his own dismissal? It is not entirely clear. He may, indeed, have once had a genuine relationship with the father of his current employer, but the downward spiral has been underway for some time. It seems that Howard, the former boss's son, has barely noticed him, wrapped up, as he is, in his own concerns, unwilling, it seems, to tackle the issue of an employee who, anyway, has only a few years before retirement. Willy is fired, in the end, not because a hard-nosed employer wants to eat the fruit and throw away the peel but because Willy cannot even sell himself. His pitch to Howard is a disaster.

When Charley says to him, 'The only thing you got in this world is what you can sell. And the funny thing is that you're a salesman, and you don't know that',[27] he simultaneously reveals his own complicity in the reductive processes at work in the culture and the basis of Willy's double failure, as a salesman and as a man who has surrendered freedom and dignity to a fantasy. When Willy replies 'I've always tried to think otherwise', however, it is not a plea for genuine human values but a statement of his belief that 'if a man was impressive, and well liked, that nothing –'. He breaks off, never completing the thought, but this is a significant exchange for if it exposes Willy's faith in appearance, it also reveals the extent to which Charley, deeply humane in his response to Willy, nonetheless subscribes to a reductive view of society and the individual.

Henry James, writing in 1904, had reacted against salesmen as agents of an intrusive commercialism, regarding them as in essence confidence men. He also, though, saw them as 'victims and martyrs, creatures touchingly, tragically doomed' by the business culture they represented but which also left them as solitary figures in the social landscape.[28] There is more than something of this about Willy Loman.

Willy wishes to believe in an identity separate from his actions, a self born out of a desire whose intensity he thought sufficient to bring him into being. He is Willy Loman, he shouts, fearing that that name contains nothing more than its own negation. As Erich Fromm has said, speaking of the dilemma of modern man, there is nothing of which we are more ashamed than of not being ourselves, but our avenue to that self lies through our participation in a cycle of production and consumption. We sell a commodity and become a commodity:

> we feel that we can acquire everything material or immaterial by buying it, and thus things become ours independently of any creative effort of our own in relation to them. In the same way we regard our personal qualities and the result of our efforts as commodities that can be sold for money,

prestige, power . . . Thereby man misses the only satisfaction that can give him real happiness – the experience of the activity of the present moment – and chases after a phantom that leaves him disappointed as soon as he believes he has caught it – the illusory happiness called success.[29]

That had been Willy Loman's fate. Balancing his sense of a life spiralling down, for which his memories of the past are the available evidence, is an equal and opposite belief in a redemptive future. What is missing is the present moment in which alone some consolation is available from those who value him for what he is and not what he might become.

Willy Loman has lost his contact with the natural world, the west of his youth and the tree-lined idyll of his middle age. He can do no more now than sow seeds on barren ground. He has also lost touch with those around him. In that, too, as it seems to Fromm, writing in another book, *The Art of Loving*, he is a representative figure: 'Modern man is alienated from himself, from his fellow men, and from nature. He has been transformed into a commodity, experiences his life forces as an investment which must bring him the maximum profit obtainable under existing market conditions.'[30] Despairing of realising this investment, he turns to the only place he can, his children. As Fromm observes,

> When a person feels that he has not been able to make sense of his own life, he tries to make sense of it in terms of the life of his children. But one is bound to fail within oneself *and* for the children. The former because the problem of existence can be solved by each one only for himself, and not by proxy; the latter because one lacks in the very qualities which one needs to guide the children in their own search for an answer.[31]

When Willy advised Biff not to tell jokes when trying to close a deal with a prospective employer he was, unknowingly, repeating a piece of advice offered at the beginning of the century by George Horace Lorimer in *Letters from a Self-Made Merchant to his Son*. What was conscious on his part, however, was the desire to pass to his son not merely the often contradictory advice he had picked up along the way, but the very values that would drive him to the point of self-destruction. He sees not death but justification, not simply an inheritance to fuel the dream he bequeathed to his son, but the funeral which, like that of Dave Singleman, the old drummer who had in part inspired his life as a salesman, would attract his peers, be the final evidence that he was, indeed, well liked.

There is no crime in *Death of a Salesman* and hence no ultimate culpability (beyond guilt for sexual betrayal), only a baffled man and his sons trying to find their way through a world of images, dazzling dreams and fantasies, in the knowledge that they have failed by the standards they have chosen to believe are fundamental. Willy has, as Biff alone understands, all the wrong dreams but, as Charley observes, they go with the territory. They are the dreams of a salesman reaching for the clouds, smiling desperately in the hope that people will smile back. Needing love and respect he is blind to those who offer it, dedicated as he is to the eternal American quest of a transformed tomorrow. What else can he do, then, but climb back into his car and drive off to a death that at last will bring the reward he has chased so determinedly, a reward that will expiate his sense of guilt, justify his life, and hand on to another generation the burden of belief that has corroded his soul but to which he has clung until the end?

He is engaged in an argument with himself, an exploration of the anxiety that has already come so close to destroying him. He invokes figures from his past to respond to that anxiety, take part in that dialogue. Their voices sound out, contrapuntally or in harmony. This inner orchestra is itself a product and exemplary of his state of mind. From the first flute music through the admonishing tone of Uncle Ben and the reassurances of Linda's voice, he hears the score of his emotional life, listening for the false note, acknowledging the discord, hoping for consonance within the dissonance.

As Miller observes in his notebook, 'It is the combination of guilt (of failure), hate and love – all in conflict that he resolves by "accomplishing" a 20,000 dollar death.' To the end he is a salesman. When he explains his plans to Ben, conjured up precisely to give him licence, to ratify his decision, he is making a sales pitch and since Ben is a figment of his imagination he is, in effect, making the pitch to himself. His death is the bargain on offer. It will solve all his problems. It will not only justify his life, it will also redeem his son. In a line of dialogue from the notebook he has Willy say, 'My boy is a thief – with 20,000 he'll stop it.' But beyond that, also from the notebook, he insists that with 20,000 to his name, 'Nobody will say I didn't accomplish something . . . A little something must be left at the end.'

The insurance policy, now in its period of grace, is, he says, 'the only thing I bought that didn't break'. On the same page on which these lines appear Miller tried out *Period of Grace* as a possible title and, indeed, it is not without its force in a play in which the central character is living on borrowed time in search of grace, forgiveness and benediction.

Miller has explained that the association of his character's last name with the common man – Loman/Low man – was purely coincidental. Yet there is plainly a sense in which Willy does represent if not the average man then one dazzled by a national dream of becoming and possession. He is a man who attaches his life to a myth which proposes a life without limits but who finds himself trapped in a shrinking physical, social and psychological space. As played by Dustin Hoffman, his physical stature suggests someone intimidated and oppressed by the sheer scale of his problems and a world slipping out of his control. As played by Lee J. Cobb or Brian Dennehy, the sight of a large man humbled adds pathos as his physical strength and commanding presence is negated by a helplessness he cannot acknowledge.

Willy Loman's sales trips into the New England territory are ironic versions of a mythic experience in which the frontiersman simultaneously took possession of a country and a selfhood in challenging the physical world and encountering the new. The rhetoric survives: the reality does not. Knocking them dead in Boston is no longer an account of frontier challenges but of commercial success, access to which is controlled not by the threat of the wild but by secretaries to be cajoled, bribed or seduced. The great adventure is now no more than nights spent in seedy hotels and the constant humiliations suffered at the hands of those for whom profit prevails over human relationships. He had failed to go into the literal frontier with his brother, Ben, restrained by his own timidity but also by commitments not without a human legitimacy. By way of substitute, he invests his sales trips with the language of western venturing.

Willy Loman, desperately driving the highways of New York and New England, is at the end of a historical process that once saw men blaze trails into the heart of the unknown and of a utopia that promised a new identity and a new hope. His exhaustion reflects an entropy that infects more than just himself. Biff and Happy are no less bewildered by the loss of energy than their father. Linda's horizons seem never to have extended beyond the domestic limits of a house once located in the heart of the country and now already something of an anachronism in what seems no more than a cloying suburbia.

Charley is apparently at peace with his own limitations and achievements but for all his humanity is more prosaic than Willy, whose glimpses of lost horizons and adherence to flawed promises nonetheless charge his life with significance. As with his father, there is no doubt as to Bernard's success or humanity, a success, moreover, rooted securely in the Puritan ethic whose essence eludes Willy Loman, who believes that he bought into it by virtue of his American identity and by his purchase of consumer goods which seemed conspicuous evidence of his achievement. Bernard's journey to Washington to plead before the Supreme Court may not make him a twentieth-century frontiersman but it does locate him in a tradition which would take him back to Benjamin Franklin and the Founding Fathers rather than Horatio Alger Jr. There is a causality to his success. Nor does it owe anything to his father who prides himself on his hands-off approach to parenthood. At the same time, we never glimpse Bernard's sense of the cause which his upward mobility might serve. An honest and talented striver, he moves onwards with a certain grace and humanity but remains closed to us and therefore an uncertain paradigm of the Dream.

Certainly, Bernard's success seems a mystery to Willy. Why, after all, did Biff not follow a similar path? His gold-helmeted son was to have a golden future but ended up doing no more than steal a gold pen. Biff has spent time in jail, but why would he not when his father encouraged him to regard theft as evidence of initiative and schoolwork as an irrelevance in a society which he believed valued appearance over substance? Getting by on a smile and a shoeshine himself, how could a boy with such good looks and a fortuitous talent for sport fail?

Willy oscillates between awareness and denial. He discounts what he has but has no clear idea what he wants. What would success be for Willy Loman? Would it be to achieve fame as a salesman, like Dave Singleman, still working at eighty but apparently with no life beyond salesmanship, alone in a hotel room, taking orders? Is it to be well liked? Well liked for what? For himself or as a means to an end? He is discontented but unclear as to the real source of his discontent, beyond a troubled sense of guilt with respect to a son he had hoped would resolve his own sense of failure.

In the 1999 production, which began at Chicago's Goodman Theatre before moving to New York, two concentric revolves swung characters and scenes into vision as they were prompted by Willy's memory and imagination. Like the 1996 National Theatre production, which also deployed a revolve, these offered a correlative for Willy's mental process, a Proustian recall triggered by a word, a thought, a gesture. Time, for Willy, is like the sea, advancing and retreating, with concealed currents, disturbing eddies that threaten his equanimity.

The revolves also served suddenly to separate those who a moment before were together, an implied comment on the fragility of the connection between those who seem so close, so dependent on one another for the meanings of their lives. By the same token, the discontinuities within the self stand suddenly exposed. Past, present and projected future co-exist, are pulled apart, and reassemble as Willy tries to fit the jigsaw of his life together in such a way as to offer him the satisfaction or simply consolation he seeks. But the fractures, the disruptions, the sudden disturbing epiphanies slowly edge him towards the logic that will lead him to trade his life for the success he sought but never achieved. It is quite as if that life were indeed a consumer product, subject to the same attrition as had afflicted his car and refrigerator, but which is finally redeemable in one last unimpeachable transaction. In his own mind, at least, he will emerge as the consummate salesman he wished to be. And what greater salesman could there be than one who sold his own life and thereby retrospectively redeemed it, while purging himself of guilt and leaving an inheritance of hope to those whose evident despair has been a dagger pointing at his heart.

Linda Loman's first line, in Robert Falls's 1999 production, was amplified, not because of Broadway's accommodation to the nature of American actor-training, which favours the inward over the projected emotion, but because thereby we enter the play as we do the distorted world of a dream, and the dream is a central trope of the play.

At the end, in the Requiem which Miller regarded as the 'quietly sanctified end of the song',[32] Elizabeth Franz, as Linda Loman, lies on Willy's grave, arms outstretched like a nun prostrating herself before a mystery, and the truth is that, for all her everyday common sense, life does remain a mystery to her. Husband and sons are like strangers whose lives she can never fully grasp. She lacks Willy's flawed vision, the poetry whose rhythm both Willy and Biff hear, though only faintly in a world driven not so much by a dream of avarice as by the idea of striving and becoming. When Biff ran out onto the football field the crowd shouted his name, deafening him to the quieter voice of his own self-doubt. Willy's memories of the business for which he has worked throughout his life is that it had once been a family, connected at a human level. But this is now blotted out by the mechanical sounds of a wire recorder he feels powerless to stop, as he stands in his boss's office while that fantasy of familial loyalty is destroyed with a casual disregard.

Nietzsche saw the modern age as concerned with Becoming rather than Being and in this sense Willy Loman can stand as an exemplary figure. He is never at rest, a traveller for other reasons than his job. He leans into the future – like his own country – as if only in some deferred utopian moment could meaning cohere and the grace of true freedom be born. His is a pending life. He is on hold, waiting to hear the good news of his imminent arrival in the promised land of possibility. He holds his breath in awe of the promise, dying for want of the air he should breathe in a shared present. The irony is that, staring through the windshield towards the future, he increasingly finds himself looking into the rear-view mirror, suddenly struck by the irony that the meaning of his life might exist in the past. It is guilt that draws him back, but the greater irony is that he might, after all, have missed the epiphany for which he has waited an entire life.

Writing to Stephen Marino, in April 1999, apologising for his absence from a conference to be held in Brooklyn where *Salesman* is surely set, he said, 'I did a lot of wandering about in the neighborhood a long time ago, and now there you are talking about the work I was never sure I'd get done. We are forever unknowingly walking over the threads of others' memories, entangling our own with theirs. The transiency is all . . . in America, anyway.'[33] That transiency is a vital element of *Death of a Salesman*, as it would be fifty years later of *Mr Peters' Connections*.

The world is changing. Willy's memories no longer mean anything to his employer. The past seemingly exists to mock him. His horizons have shrunk in almost every respect. He is still waiting for revelation and redemption even as his grasp on the real slackens. The apparent fixities of the social world are revealed as contingent. Yesterday's new technology becomes today's obsolete product. The rural becomes the urban; bright hopes fade into regrets. Yet his memories, specific to himself, are those of a culture attempting to live mythically, to retain the language if not the substance of frontier individualism and a dream of the new.

In that same letter Miller speaks of being discontented, if also secretly envious of, the products of Broadway as he began his career. What they failed to reach, it seemed to him, was 'the spirit'. Their realism was too immediate, too committed to appearance, to exposing the mechanisms but not the essence of human life. 'I recall thinking', he explained,

> that all the important things were between the lines, in the silences, the gestures, the stuff above or below the level of speech. For a while I even thought to study music, which is the art of silences hedged about by sound. Music begins *Salesman*, and not by accident; we are to hear Willy before we see him and before he speaks. He was there in the hollow of the flute, the wind, the air announcing his arrival and his doom.

The music was to express the past which he thought to transcend but to which he and his son Biff are both drawn. It is a problematic past, speaking of his own abandonment and of the betrayal that has so disabled him in his relationship with his son, but it is a past in which father and son can meet in that both value a pre-modern world. Both are most themselves when they work with their hands. At the same time, there is a melancholy to the flute that speaks both to a lost world and to the elegiac mood of a play which concerns a man's last day of life.

Subsequent productions, including the fiftieth anniversary one, abandoned the original music. The latter settled for a jazz-influenced score by Richard Woodbury which, if anything, stressed the modern over the romantic, the urban over the rural. It reflected what disturbed rather than seduced a Willy Loman caught between his own instinctive rhythms and those offered to him by a society on the make, moving on, sweeping the tracks behind it. Nonetheless, the music remained a crucial counterpoint to his mood, a commentary on a man who hears a different drummer but believes his destiny is to keep step with a society resolutely marching towards a promised revelation. For Miller, the music was 'powerful', offering 'a post-romantic view'.

Struck by the play's survival, not only in America but throughout the world (a Japanese actor reportedly played the role for thirty years, finally abandoning it at the age of ninety, only for it to be taken over by his son: a Norwegian audience returned a second night to find out how what they took to be a saga would finally end), Miller confessed that it made him wonder,

> whether we are all forever being hunted, pursued by one or another sloga-nized meaning, one or other packaged view of life and death which in our weakness we surrender to when in the privacy of our midnights what we most long to find is the freedom to be and believe everything. Maybe that is what Willy does, since he is all mood, all feeling, a naked branch of an old tree swaying in the wind. Willy moves with the air and from one moment to the next, one feeling to the next, and in a sense believes everything at once . . . that he is loved, that he is contemptible; that he is lost, that he has conquered; that he is afraid, that nothing frightens him and that everything does, and on and on and on. It may be that he has escaped the categories simply because he is a human, and too self-absorbed to be embarrassed by being one. Whatever else you may say about him, he is unmistakably himself . . . even including the times when he wishes he wasn't.[34]

For Miller, Willy had been in search of his immortal soul. That he chose to look in the wrong place stained his search with irony. It did not, however, invalidate it.

The play ends with a Requiem. Elia Kazan's wife Molly suggested that it could be dispensed with, as she did the character of Ben. Few audiences would agree. We never hear the sound of the car crash. As it speeds off so, Miller instructs, 'the music crashes down in a frenzy of sound, which becomes the soft pulsation of a single cello string'. This, in turn, gives way to a dead march. Leaves begin to appear, as if past and present had collapsed into mythic time. The characters move slowly and in silence.

In the version he first drafted in his notebook, people had turned out in numbers for the funeral. As Linda exclaims, 'Wasn't it wonderful that so many people came?' 'Yeah,' replies Charley, 'he had a lot of friends.' He was, it seems, well liked, after all. He simply 'worried too much about it', because 'he was so small', adds Linda. In truth, as Miller quickly realised, the essence of Willy is that, as he suspected, he has no friends and, outside of his tortured family, was not well liked. In the final version no one has come to his funeral but the family and his next-door neighbours Charley and Bernard. In that sense he is close kin to Jay Gatsby, another believer in the dream, who died alone, who died still believing in the green light of possibility.

In the first draft Biff draws a social conclusion from his father's death: 'He lived to pay his debts . . . Look . . . the whole cemetery is filled with them. All good customers who drove themselves into the dirt trying to buy a character that would fit them.' This disappears in the final version, his exemplary status sufficiently established to render such remarks redundant. What is retained, though in modified form, is Biff's observation that, 'He didn't know who he was . . . He had the wrong dream; it was so [text illegible] for him he had to win it with his life. The pity of it is, that he was happy only on certain Sundays, with a warm sun on his back, and a trowel in his hand, some good wet cement, and something to build. That's who he really was.'

What is also retained is Charley's lament for the salesman, though it appears in the notebook in verse, its opening line, 'A salesman doesn't build anything', offering a counterpoint to Biff's remark, that 'A man who doesn't build anything must be liked.'

The play ends, as it had begun, with the sound of a flute while the leaves dissolve and the surrounding apartment buildings come into sharp focus. Time bends back on itself, a life now complete. Biff is presumably about to light out for the territory, following the sound of the flute. But that rural world was where the first act of betrayal occurred, as it did in the original Eden. Perhaps, as Fitzgerald has Carraway say in *The Great Gatsby*, this had been a story about the west, after all. The west, in this case, is that towards which Biff will go, as it was once the place where Willy's salesman father deserted his family (in pursuit of diamonds in Alaska where, Ben suggests in the notebook: 'Father could make more in a year than most men do in a lifetime'). It was where Uncle Ben began his capitalist enterprise, an enterprise which Willy believed first he and then Biff would match and whose suspect nature would have been underlined in the 1999 production had the Watergate 'plumber' C. Gordon Liddy played the part, a piece of casting seriously considered.

Again in the notebook, we are told that 'Willy both feels deserted by father and worships his "greatness"'. 'All I've got,' he says, 'is my boys.' And there, of course, is the irony for as a note explains, ' . . . the desertion of his sons, loss of their love, with his father's desertion . . . equals proof that he bungled his life'. 'Have flute play', Miller indicates, when Willy puts these pieces together in his mind, the flute that plays at the beginning and then at the end as Willy rides to what he believes to be glory and what Biff alone understands to be nothing more than an empty and dangerous dream.

Willy goes on quests, like some medieval knight, riding forth to justify himself while at the same time his Platonic paradigm for the salesman–warrior is a man in carpet slippers, smoking a cigarette with a telephone in his hand. The maiden in distress in the Boston hotel was, in the notebooks, to have been a hooker but is now a blowsy secretary with a laugh that echoes in his mind and down the years as a reminder of his insignificance. His is a story threaded through with irony.

Death lies at the end of tragedy like the ultimate promise of form. It offers a retrospective grace, flooding contingency with a meaning that can only come from its apparent dissolution. Willy Loman is hardly a tragic hero. He dies with a smile, not relishing an irony or accepting a fate but driving to redemption, as he assumes, deeply self-deceived, bright with the conviction that he has completed the ultimate deal with the Mephistophilis of American utopianism.

Willy Loman dies in the machine that has carried him daily deeper into despair and yet which is the ambiguous symbol of his culture, on the move into the future yet itself always in thrall to entropy. Tragedy is a subjective victory won in the face of an objective defeat. Willy, it seems, is defeated in his very self. There is almost no subjectivity not compromised by internalising the assumptions of the world he believes himself to be seizing, the world he imagines to contain the meaning of his life. When he calls out his name there is no echo because there is no longer any substantial reality to reflect it back to him.

He cannot live in a world not energised by the imagination. He goes gently into the night precisely because his death is drained of the tragic, no matter what Miller may have chosen to believe. He dies in hope. He dies radiant with unexamined optimism, almost an absurd hero finding meaning in his conspiracy with death, purpose in the purposeless. He never does close the gap between what he wishes to be and what he is.

The tragic hero is a thinker dismayed at where thought has taken him, a man betrayed by actions that accomplish nothing but their own undoing, who nonetheless discovers a truth lost somewhere between thought and its realisation. The tragic hero dies in a moment of transcendent truth, all illusion flown. Oedipus learns a terrible truth and stares it in the face. Macbeth understands that he is no more than a man. Lear unbuttons to an unaccommodated man, shedding self-deceit along with kingship. Hamlet, through a play, learns the power of seeming and understands a truth that hastens him to his death. Willy, by contrast, is blinded with the sun of a false epiphany.

Camus said of the absurd man that he was always longing for tomorrow, where everything in him ought to reject it. Willy thought time his friend until he was suddenly aware of it as an enemy. Camus spoke of the fact that no code of ethics and no effort are justifiable *a priori* in the face of the cruel mathematics that command the human condition. Willy is aware of that mathematics.

At the end of the century, in a play that would look back through the century, Mr Peters (in *Mr Peters' Connections*, Miller's 1998 play) would confront that same disturbing human economy, watching the meaning he had spent a lifetime constructing unwind itself, no more than a series of images unspooling in the face of a gathering night. Willy Loman sees those same pictures, replays them trying to detect the logic that has brought him to this moment of bewilderment.

So long as the mind keeps silent in 'the motionless world of its hopes', Camus remarked, nostalgia could seemingly offer a secure foundation. But with its first move, he warned, this world would crack and tumble. Willy's world has done no less. The memories that flood his mind, far from offering the reassuring structure of nostalgia, underscore the irony which increasingly disables him as he recalls, and re-experiences, 'the feelings and joys of his great moment, decades ago, when through Biff he felt he was within inches of some fabled victory over life's ignominious leveling'.[35]

For Samuel Beckett's 'Let's go. (*they do not move*)', Miller offers, 'The trouble is he's lazy', 'There's one thing about Biff – he's not lazy.' Willy is caught in contradictions because the world fails to come into line with his desires and because there is an irony in welcoming a future that in fact conceals the truth of dissolution and finality. It is that tension which is the source of an absurdity that he attempts to resist by succumbing to it, dying while still denying the finality of death. Even in the face of death, he insists, there is still a tomorrow. In part that is the tomorrow of the American dream, of a culture that instructs its citizens to pursue happiness, as if it were a destination and not a condition, but in part it is final evidence of that absurdity which is a product of a refusal to acknowledge the fundamental condition of existence and the need to discover meaning as though it would become apparent in some final revelation.

What Willy Loman finally seeks is not success but immortality. He wishes to pass something more than an inheritance to his sons. He wants to live in and through them, which is why he offers a death with such equanimity. It is Biff's declaration of love, as Willy interprets it, that enables and justifies his decision to trade his life for an insurance policy. But what he has insured/ensured is, he believes, precisely that life will continue.

For Miguel de Unamuno (referring, as Miller is prone to do, to the figure of Cain), man is prepared to sacrifice not only his life but his happiness for the sake of his name. Is it pride, he asks himself, which drives the desire for immortality, to leave an 'ineradicable name'? No, he replies, it is a terror of extinction, just as it is a fear of poverty that drives a poor man to seek for money. Willy Loman had striven for success because of his fear of failure. He dies for the sake of his name – the name he shouts out in desperation – for fear of leaving no trace of his having existed. He wants to live in the divine memory. And since the world he inhabits seems to offer no transcendence, no consoling God, he tries to write his name in flesh. The irony is that his sons are bequeathed absurdity.

This is not to say that Miller is somehow a version of Beckett. He, himself, after all, would resist such a suggestion. But where in his essays he saw a contrast between himself and a playwright who seemed to him so different, perhaps there is, after all, a point of contact as well as contrast. Beckett's ironies are puritanically severe, though their expression contradicts that severity. Beckett lifts his characters out of a social environment, isolates them in a featureless world, for the most part strips them of a past unless that be the echoing repetition of *Krapp's Last Tape*. Miller, on the other hand, creates dense social worlds, characters whose choices are real and who are capable of decisions which define them. Nonetheless, in Willy Loman he comes close to creating an absurd hero whose very hope is the source of his absurdity. It is Biff's understanding of this, however, that deflects the absurd logic.

Where, then, does that leave us with respect to Willy Loman who Miller wished to see as a tragic hero? Perhaps the best summary was that which he offered to a group of Chinese actors struggling with an alien play about a dying salesmen. They were, he felt, still acting and not being. The key, he explained to them, was indeed, love, that between a man and his son and between both of them and the culture which they embraced and from which they urgently needed to separate themselves. But there was something else, too,

> not admiration, necessarily, but a kind of visceral recognition that in his fumbling and often ridiculous way he is trying to lift up a belief in immense human possibilities. People can't stand him, often, they flee from him, but they miss him when he isn't there. Perhaps it is that he hasn't a cynical bone in his body, he is a walking believer, the bearer of a flame whose going-out would leave us flat, with merely what the past has given us. He is forever signaling to a future that he cannot describe and will not live to see, but he is in love with all the same.[36]

For Miller, the ironies at the heart of the absurd are simply too implacable. This, after all, was a play written out of pity. Willy Loman's faith in human possibilities has taken wholly the wrong form but Miller was himself not ready to surrender his own faith in a redemptive future even if, like Biff, he increasingly defined it in terms of a past in which the individual had not yet been alienated from the products of his labour, from the natural world and from those others who constituted a functioning community dependent on a mutuality of needs and satisfactions.

Death of a Salesman is, as Tyrone Guthrie understood, a long poem by Willy Loman. For much of the play it is he who hears the voices, shapes the rhythms, creates the rhymes. He turns experience into metaphor, bringing together discrete moments to forge new meanings which then dissolve. When he dies we leave his consciousness for a stripped-down stage and people whose words are baffled approximations for the man whose world we have seen from the inside.

There is, as Miller has said, a space between the Requiem and the play. It was not only Molly Kazan but also some directors who thought it should be cut. But to Miller it is crucial as a moment when the contradictions are stilled, the false hopes laid aside, and we no longer see the world through the eyes of a man who never knew who he was, or what he might be, apart from the flickering images projected by a society at risk of subsuming the spiritual in the material. And though Happy rededicates himself to Willy's false dreams, his is a voice that now lacks social resonance. Biff, alone, draws the necessary conclusions from the death of a man he loved but from whom he had to separate himself, Biff the man who 'returned for Willy's blessing without which he cannot find himself as a man', a fact which was unplanned by Miller, but, as he once remarked, 'there it is'.

Writing to a director in 1975, Miller explained his sense of this moment:

> The people are in the mood of that kind of death-shock which moves us to what one might call an emblematic feeling – one wants to utter something to leave in the grave, a summing up.
>
> So they are not quite talking to one another. Yet the death has drawn them together, each in his own separate relation to the dead man.
>
> There is nothing overwrought or self-conscious or pompous about such a thing, it is as common as a funeral, and there is no reason to fear self-consciousness. We hire clergymen to say a few words. Silence seems inhuman at such moments. Here they are their own clergymen, that's all.
>
> They should stand in a group. There is no viable image now; instead there is a kind of timorousness. There is no reason to be afraid of it. Before rehearsals Kazan feared this scene too but when he saw the piling up of feeling in the last twenty minutes he ceased disputing its validity. It says something we want to hear, it sends Willy off and somehow helps us to believe everything all over again.[37]

Willy Loman's last ride takes him out of time and into myth, where he will be immune to decay. The future, to which he had looked for resolution, but that so tormented him, will now be dissolved. His family and neighbours gather together at the end, suddenly freed, no longer projections of his troubled mind, as if surrendered by him as a final act of grace. They now walk forth released from their roles, like actors whose pretence is at last laid aside, liberated from the story in which they have been contained.

The man who feared he meant so little and whose ending is attended by so few, was, we see, central after all. Why else do these people feel a sense of loss, regret and, in Linda's case, desolation? Tomorrow she will live in an empty house. The mortgage will have been paid but no longer will there be the smell of shaving soap or the sound of a man talking to himself as if arguing the case for his own existence. That very emptiness is a measure of the man. He failed his family. He was guilty of betrayal and subsisted on denial. Yet he was the centre of their world. Linda has the key to the play at the very beginning. She has found the evidence that he intends to kill himself. Her battle is now lost. The irony is that Willy believed that his was won.

'We're free . . . We're free', cries Linda, as the hard towers of modernity rise up and the stage is slowly shrouded in darkness. The silence that invariably seems to follow this moment in the theatre – a silence that disturbed Miller when the play was first staged and he waited to judge the nature and extent of the applause – is surely an expression of the audience's unwillingness to break the moment, to step out of the unresolved tension with which they have been confronted as a man slips away from life mourned only by those who lacked the power to stop him. Ironically, it is, finally, the absence of Willy Loman that is the measure of the man. There may be only this handful of mourners at his grave but the audience is added to that number. The play edges towards silence with only the flute music now audible, as the surrounding apartment buildings come into sharp focus. America's past and present are thus brought together, as they had been in Willy's mind, a reminder of utopian dreams lost somewhere in their materialisation. Like Fitzgerald's Gatsby, Willy 'believed in the green light, the orgastic future that year by year recedes before us. It eluded us then, but that's no matter – tomorrow we will run faster, stretch our arms further . . . And one fine morning – So we beat on, boats against the current, borne back ceaselessly into the past.'[38]

Willy Loman's vision of the future, too, lay behind him, as it does for a country that weds the idea of progress to a myth of innocence and endlessly renewed beginnings. To see life as destiny is a form of nostalgia and that is Willy's plight. He seemingly yearns for tomorrow but is repelled by all evidence of the modern – high-rise apartments, wire recorders – which lie outside his control. The problem is that the future holds the certainty of dissolution. The lesson is to hand. His refrigerator, his car, are disassembling themselves before his eyes and so, he knows, is he.

Only the past can shape the future as he wishes. Only the past is uninfected with decay. His destiny is thus contained in the flute music with which he entered the world, his world and that of the play. He is drawn back to that day when his son, an extension of himself, climbed some ultimate mountain to perfection in a ball game that shines golden in his mythic memory.

On rereading the play in 1958, Miller noted that while Biff confessed that he was nothing, Willy insisted on his name. 'I like Willy better', Miller observed. Biff, it seemed to him, had settled for failure. Willy set his face against it.

It is a curious comment for the fact is that Biff only thought himself a failure when accepting his father's measure of meaning. Released from a corrosive fantasy he reclaims an identity rooted in the real. Willy insists on his name but is blind to the fact that he has drained it of individuation. Yet there is, indeed, something about Willy Loman that is compelling, something that justifies Miller's retrospective embrace of this failed man inhabiting an unreal world. He may dream the wrong dreams and fail to understand the redemption he is offered by those who care more for him than he appears to care for them, but he retains the capacity for wonder.

In an article Miller wrote a year after the play's opening, he anticipated that a time would come 'when they will look back at us astonished that we saw something holy in the competition for the means of existence'. He had not, it seems, forgotten the language at least of the pre-war years, but the real force of the play lay elsewhere. The 'tragedy of Willy Loman', he said, derived from the fact that he gave his life, or sold it, in order to justify the waste of it. 'It is', he said,

> the tragedy of a man who did believe that he alone was not meeting the qualifications laid down for mankind by those clean-shaven frontiersmen who inhabit the peaks of broadcasting and advertising offices. From those forests of canned goods high up near the sky, he heard the thundering command to succeed as it ricocheted down the newspaper-lined canyons of his city, heard not a human voice, but a wind of a voice to which no human can reply in kind, except to stare in the mirror of failure.[39]

In 1992, Miller wondered why he was still capable of being reduced to tears by this drama of an aging salesman with the wrong dreams when 'he is such a damned fool'. But in the end what audiences responded to then as now was not a damned fool but the portrait of a man desperate to make sense of his life while aware of his failure to do so. What compelled was the drama of a man blind to the love of those who watched dismayed as he sacrificed himself to an idea, the false promise of a golden future.

8

Arthur Miller: time-traveller

In an article published in *Harper's Magazine*, in March 1999, Arthur Miller insists that 'there is no such thing as "reality" in any theatrical exhibition that can properly be called a play. The reason for this is that stage time is not, and cannot be, street time. In street time, Willy Loman's story would take sixty-two years to play out instead of two and a half hours . . . with the very act of condensation the artificial enters even as the first of its lines is being written.'[1]

Time and reality, then, are intimately related, while to enter a theatre is to acknowledge that we enter a time warp in which the normal laws of physics no longer apply. Time flows at a speed determined by the author. The price of entry into this world is that we experience a temporal anomaly in which past and present may co-exist within a factitious moment. And few writers have been as interested in time, and its various ramifications, as Arthur Miller – time, that is, as history, time as memory, time as a component of identity, as productive of guilt, nostalgia, hope, psychological and social imperatives. Even his concern with shaping language, with moulding speech into distinctive rhythms, is an aspect of his concern with time for, as Sam Shepard has remarked, 'rhythm is the delineation of time in space'.[2]

In his preface to *Salesman at Fifty*, Arthur Miller says, 'As far as I know, nobody has figured out time. Not chronological time, of course – that's merely what the calendar tells – but real time, the kind that baffles the human mind.'[3] The remark is made in the context of his amazement at the passage of fifty years since writing his classic play, but it goes a good deal deeper than that in so far as time is a recurring concern, device, paradox, metaphysic in his work: the mechanism of causality, the source of reproach, irony, metaphor. In a country where eyes are resolutely fixed on tomorrow, on the green light across the bay, he insists on the authority of a past which can be denied only at the price of true identity and the moral self. And in some sense Miller has worked against the American grain.

The American writer, he insisted, behaves as though 'the tongue had been cut from the past, leaving him alone to begin from the beginning, from the Creation and from the first naming of things seen for the first time . . . It is as though they were fatherless men abandoned by a past that they in turn reject.' (T, 114–15). It was Ralph Waldo Emerson who insisted that, 'Time and space are but physiological colors which the eye makes', and who asked, 'Whence . . . this worship of the past?' It was he who insisted that '. . . history is an impertinence and an injury, if it be anything more than a cheerful apologue or parable of my being and becoming'.[4] And the central American project, as Willy Loman well knew, was precisely about the connection between being and becoming, the necessity to deny the past in the name of his and his culture's manifest destiny to colonise the future, a process which it is assumed will gift the individual and the country a true identity.

As Jonathan Morse observes, in his book on the language of memory, *Word by Word*, when President Bush was asked before his 1989 inaugural to comment on his campaign rhetoric of the previous year he replied, 'That's history. That doesn't mean a thing anymore.'[5] It was a very American statement, fully in line with Hester Prynne's pronouncement that 'Let us not look back . . . The past is gone! Wherefore should we linger upon it now'[6]? History, in other words, leaves no residue. It is used up. It exists only to be invalidated by time.

The myth of American society is that the journey to America was a journey back through time towards innocence, a world free of history and ultimately, of course, of time, a movement which logically washed the individual free of responsibility and hence a utopianism stained at source. It was a journey into myth.

To Miller, on the contrary, history makes authentic demands and provides a spine to mere events. As he has said, 'chaos was life lived oblivious of history'.[7] But this was not history as a fast-receding present. T. S. Eliot spoke of 'the historical sense . . . a perception, not only of the pastness of the past, but of its presence'.[8] That is Miller's historical sense. Interestingly, Eliot made that remark in the context of his essay on 'Tradition and the Individual Talent'. In that essay he insisted that:

> the historical sense compels a man to write not merely with his own gen-
> eration in his bones, but with a feeling that the whole of the literature of
> Europe from Homer and within it the whole of the literature of his coun-
> try has a simultaneous existence and composes a simultaneous order. This
> historical sense, which is a sense of the timeless as well as the temporal
> together, is what makes a writer traditional. And it is at the same time
> what makes a writer most acutely conscious of his place in time, of his own
> contemporaneity.
>
> (38)

It is in that sense, and perhaps that sense alone, that Miller, who sees the Greek theatre as at one with his own, who has spoken of his acute sense of the contemporary but also his sense of the timeless as well as the temporal, of simultaneity, is traditional. He is traditional, in other words, in Eliot's sense of a writer with an awareness of the presence of history.

For Eliot, the past must live 'not merely [in] the present, but the present moment of the past . . . conscious, not of what is dead, but of what is already living' (44). Explaining further what he meant, Eliot observed that 'the difference between the present and the past is that the conscious present is an awareness of the past in a way and to an extent which the past's awareness of itself cannot show' (39). It is a remark that is simultaneously banal and, in the context of a consideration of Miller and time, a useful reminder of the sense in which history operates in Miller's work. It is not only that the present interrogates the past for a meaning which only becomes apparent with the passage of time, but that the present already contains the past whose shape and form it tries to measure.

Miller has never written a play set in the past if it has not served the presence of that past. He is not, in other words, a historical dramatist in the sense that Gore Vidal is a historical novelist. With William Faulkner's Gavin Stevens, he insists that 'the past is never dead. It's not even past.'[9] It is a truth that Willy Loman knows all too well, while desperately denying it. L. P. Hartley's The Go-Between famously begins, 'The past is a foreign country: they do things differently there.'[10] For Arthur Miller, the past is far from a foreign country. They do things in much the same way and that is its utility. In Miller's work the significant fact is not the difference between past and present but the continuity, the causal, moral connection, the concurrence of what was with what is.

John Fowles called a collection of his essays Wormholes. At a time when more people speak Klingon than Esperanto, there is perhaps no need to explain that. It refers to the 'hypothetical interconnection between widely separated regions of space–time'.[11] So that it is possible, virtually instantaneously, to move from one space–time to another. It is essentially what Miller implies in the title of his autobiography Timebends. It is the mechanism behind Death of a Salesman, After the Fall, 'Clara', The Ride Down Mount Morgan, Mr Peters' Connections and Timebends itself, all of which fold time together, bring past and present into immediate contact. And the assumption behind that is that meaning is a product of such interactions, that the parallel universes of 'now' and 'then', once brought into contact, generate significance, speak to one another in the language of memory.

Wormholes are not theoretical interconnections. They exist. We can already move instantly to another space–time. The mechanism for that journey is, in one sense, the theatre itself, and, in another sense, memory. Different times and places are brought together in an instant and theatre, with its power to transform space and time, becomes itself a paradigm. In Salesman the two – theatre and memory – come together as the play recapitulates not only the processes of memory but also the processes of art, as Willy Loman constructs a past, trying to find form in contingency, a logic in mere event, a character and an identity in incidents and social relationships; a connection, in short, with his own life.

In effect he is the author of much of Death of a Salesman, as Tom is the author of Tennessee Williams's The Glass Menagerie, in that he constructs the text out of the memories he chooses to recall and in part remake. To a degree he writes the script and performs himself quite as if it were indeed a play and he an actor, albeit one who has lost the attention of his audience. He is like John Osborne's Archie Rice in *The Entertainer*: he has lived on beyond the moment when his particular skills can command attention – and for an actor attention must be paid. In the same way, Miller constructs Willy Loman as a fictional marker in his own desire to make sense of a culture, to render up a coherent personal and public meaning.

Willy does bear the marks of the past. He reaches back, in memory and language, to the days of the frontier, and Miller has said that 'it was part of his nature, to me, that he sprang from people who were wandering in the mountains'.[12] But he also, in his occasional linguistic formality, aspires to what Miller calls 'a more elegant past, a time "finer" than theirs,' that offers a dignity he feels he lacks. Thus Miller draws attention to Willy's remark that he had 'been remiss', not a Brooklyn locution, and not, incidentally, a Jewish locution. He is, indeed, in Miller's telling phrase, 'light years away from [the] religion or community [that] might have fostered Jewish identity'.[13]

He is, in other words, stranded in time and space and stripped of an identity that could only have come from acknowledging the authority of the past and the necessities of the present rather than the seductive light of a golden future. He is, Miller suggests, instead, 'on the sidewalk side of the glass looking through at a well-lighted place',[14] He is mesmerised, separated from the reality of his own being, as he stares at a life he can envisage but not reach, a world that exists, tantalisingly, on the other side of a transparent membrane, a future he can see but cannot reach. And perhaps it is worth recalling that the phrase 'a well-lighted place' has echoes of Hemingway's short story about a suicidal old man kept alive by a comforting and consoling vision.

But when does this play, written both by Miller and, in part, at least at the level of narrative assumption, by Willy Loman, take place? What is its time? What Miller has said of 'Elegy for a Lady' he could have said of *Salesman*, and, incidentally of *Mr Peters*, but also, in a sense, of many of his plays. It takes place, he has said, 'in the space between the mind and what it imagines'.[15] Indeed, asked when *Salesman* was set he replied, 'all I can tell you is that I think it is suspended outside of chronological time'.

One of its titles, as we have noted, was to have been *A Period of Grace*, a reference to that anomalous period in which the time of an insurance policy has expired but it continues, temporally, with no temporal referent. Just how much this play is 'suspended outside of chronological time', however, can be told from the notebook he kept while writing the play. In this he writes of Willy, 'he is fired, or the Depression hits'.[16] The Depression? But this play is seemingly set in 1948. Yet there is, in fact, something of the Depression about Willy's fear of losing his job, though, in fact, at the age of sixty-three, he is only two years from retirement and the mortgage is about to be paid off.

The play, Miller confesses, 'is a bit like a dream. In a dream you are in two places at the same time and *Salesman* is in two places at the same time.'[17] The wormhole. He could almost be talking about *Mr Peters' Connections*, which is equally suspended in time, 'a bit like a dream' and which, as its title implies, concerns a man's attempts to trace the connections which could be said to give some kind of coherence to his life, connections that he seeks through memory, different moments in time brought together in a moment outside of time.

But, then, time, to Miller, is an agent of connectiveness, a clue to the hidden code of experience, that connectiveness which generates social, individual and moral coherence. Those connections across time are the essence of coherences in individual lives but they are also a primary motive and method in Miller's work. He bends time in the belief, for example, that history does, indeed, have lessons to offer. When Cortes confronts Montezuma, in *The Golden Years*, the space–time continuum is breached in a number of ways. Indeed, when the play opens the threat is of an end to time as the sun goes into eclipse, an eclipse which Montezuma and his followers believe may mark the apocalypse and which does, in fact, foreshadow the eclipse of an entire culture which is about to suffer as time runs out on their civilisation.

Beyond that, not merely do two different times, two different histories, two different modes of being come together in a moment which is both in time and outside of time, which is to say within a myth, but an arc of electricity shorts across time and space, through the wormhole linking sixteenth-century Mexico to twentieth-century Europe. In that sense, though in a different way, we are once again 'in two places at the same time'.

Miller wrote of Montezuma's paralysis in the face of the implacable power of Cortes because, at the end of the 1930s, he saw the same thing as the Western powers appeared transfixed by the sheer fact of Adolf Hitler. The same kinetic energy surges through the wormhole from 1692 to 1953 in *The Crucible*, while the mere title of *The American Clock* should alert us to the significance of time in a play in which, as he has told us, he went 'in search of those feelings that once ruled our lives and were stolen from us by time'.

The American Clock was in part inspired by Studs Terkel's *Hard Times*, described by Terkel as 'a memory book'.[18] In a note he insisted that it was 'a book about Time as well as *a* time' (vi). It was a book about Time in the sense that it was a collection of testimonies by what he called 'an improvised battalion of survivors' (3), testimonies in which the passage of time had transformed fact into memory. As he warned, 'in their remembrances are their truths' (3), and memory has a problematic relationship to truth. Memory is, after all, not a time capsule, suddenly revealing a fragment of the true past. The story of *a* time is thus subject to the alchemical force of passing time, memory being selective, bearing the impress of a transformed self. Time, in other words, is intensely subjective. As Miller has said, 'memory inevitably romanticizes, pressing reality to recede like pain' (*T*. 179). That is true of Studs Terkel's respondents, as it is of Willy Loman, whom Miller has identified as a romantic.

But again, *The American Clock*, written in the late 1970s, opened a wormhole on to another time, the 1930s, beginning, though, with a glimpse at the 20s when time appeared to have no meaning. In that earlier decade Americans had believed that 'for them the clock would never strike midnight, the dance and the music could never stop'. In 1929 the clock struck, and reality returned and it was to remind people of that reality, of the fact that we live in time that he wrote the play at the end of the 1970s because

it seemed to me that we had completely lost any historical sense. We continually seem to devour or wipe out the past. Consequently there is always a grasping for some kind of handhold on reality . . . I think we just do not give a damn about what happened. It is mildly interesting. Occasionally you see an old car and think, oh, that's the way they used to make cars . . . But any old idea, any old way of life is of no conceivable use . . . So I thought it would be interesting to paint a canvas of life thirty or forty years ago.

Why? Because, as he said, 'this [the 1930s] is when there was such a thing as necessity', and in the 1970s this truth of the 1930s seemed to have been forgotten. The two things, therefore, had to be brought together. The 1930s had to appear through the swirling spiral of the wormhole.

And that same wormhole effect, that same bringing together of different times, was true across a whole range of his plays. *A Memory of Two Mondays*, for example, is set in what Miller calls 'bygone days', clearly, from internal references, the 1930s when he, like his characters, worked in an auto-parts warehouse, but it is a play for the 1950s. As he explained,

what it is saying to the mid-1950s, which the mid-1950s chose not to hear, was that this was the bedrock. While we were busy doing this boom there were a lot of people in warehouses who were condemned, as though to death, by an economic system from which there was no recourse for them, and that they were what you might call important people. They were not supposed to exist, so it was news from the nether world . . . Of course, nobody could be less interested in such events in the mid-fifties when the tail-fins were going on to cars, television was roaring up, Eisenhower was in heaven, and all was well with the world.

Thus memory, his memory, becomes an agency of moral and social value as the 1930s and the 1950s are momentarily linked, the 1930s boldly going through the wormhole to encounter the 1950s.

The same logic, he has suggested, applied to *Incident at Vichy*, set in Vichy France but about 'today', and to *Broken Glass*, set in 1938 but written at a time of revivified fascism and ethnic rivalries. And the link between widely separated regions of space–time is evident in other ways in that play as Sylvia Gellburg feels a sudden, inexplicable and paralysing link with events in another place, Europe, while from another time come memories which offer a further explanation for her physical paralysis.

But of course memory, as Studs Terkel warned, is not an objective truth. It is deformed, reshaped, decontextualised, prised free of its temporal location. Past events, actions, emotions are recalibrated, retuned. They are dissected in search of some meaning that is less imminent than revealed by the polarised light of passing time and present need. And that is true of *Salesman*, a play which, as he has said, is 'full of the concrete evidences of living in this country but . . . is also suspended over all that. It transcends all that.'

Memory is important in a number of ways to Miller. I once started to research Miller's family in Poland, only to realise that the Nazis not only killed the Jews, they systematically destroyed the archives which registered their individual and collective histories. They wished, in other words, to annihilate memory and identity as, in seeking later to destroy the evidence of their crimes, they sought to deny responsibility for their actions. They conspired against history. They killed time. No wonder, then, that memory, identity, moral responsibility, denial, betrayal, became central themes of Miller's work or that time, folding back on itself, becomes a distinguishing tactic of his drama. Memory is not a device, for Miller. It is a moral responsibility. As he has said, 'I think the job of an artist is to remind people of what they have chosen to forget.'

In *Playing for Time*, adapted from Fania Fenelon's book,[19] the protagonist exists in a world in which time is effectively suspended as she is lifted out of normality and relocated in a world in which causality itself seems inoperative. Here she plays for time, in the sense that she plays to stay alive, she buys time by playing in the orchestra of the concentration camp to which she is sent. The time signature of the music constitutes the alternative rhythm by which she lives. She becomes a Scheherazade, with music rather than words being the mechanism of survival. Sheherazade tells stories in order not to be murdered and story is a device for resisting death, for denying mortality, as, of course, it is for all writers who seek to win some final victory over time by the act of writing. They construct an alternative universe immune, like Keats's Grecian urn, to the depredations of time, if not to the ironies generated by the contrast between art and the human agency that creates it.

Yet, for Fenelon, as for Miller, the memory of that time is crucial, and hence both in turn lay that time before this one, bring it through the wormhole so that, in the theatre, we see that other time, so that these ghosts from the past breathe our air as, for a moment, we breathe theirs and hence acknowledge, at least within the factitious present of the theatre, our co-presence and hence immediate affininity. Time and space collapse into a singularity. That singularity is the play.

Time haunts Willy Loman. The memory of what was collides with a knowledge of what is. He is supremely conscious of what G. J. Whitrow, first President of the International Society for the Study of Time, called the thermodynamic arrow of time, characterised by a tendency towards disorder. For Willy, yesterday's open country has become today's oppressive urban reality. Yesterday's dreams have deferred to today's disillusionment. Then the family would climb into the car to ride to Ebbets Field and glory; now he prepares to ride to his death alone. Yesterday's bright hopes can now be carried in two battered suitcases. They contain his life. Then, the world was charged with energy and he at its heart, the hero of his own story. Now, entropy rules. Once-new machines are in a state of collapse. A golden boy has become a disillusioned man as Willy, once the principal in his own life and the centre of attention, now finds himself pressed to the margin, leaching energy.

Unable to change his present he reimagines the past which becomes simultaneously pregnant with possibility and the prelude to despair. In the past the season is always spring, with elm trees in leaf and lilacs in bloom. But this was the time when lilacs last in the dooryard bloomed. Something has died, in Willy Loman and the society he believes himself to serve. In the present, grass will no longer grow. Seeds fall on barren ground. The elm trees have been cut down to make room for apartment houses.

Bewildered by such spiralling decline, by the eclipse of youthful dreams, struck by the irony which is underscored by the now permeable membrane between past and present, he retreats not so much into a real past as a past charged with nostalgia. Like F. Scott Fitzgerald's Gatsby, he is a romantic, unaware of the collateral damage that results from his pursuit of a dream, from the unworthiness of the god to which he has dedicated his life and to which he, too, will finally sacrifice himself.

But the very happiness he invokes in his created past serves to underscore the gap between such images and his own sense of insufficiency and despair. He summons into existence a brother who is an embodiment of his own needs and ambitions, who will retrospectively validate past decisions no less than his present plan to ride to glory, but whose very existence is, in his own mind, a measure of his failure. He gradually loses control of the past as he has of the present, darker memories beginning to seep through. And where is Willy all this time, his mind flooded with memories of the past, his eyes still bright with visions of a possible future? He feels 'kind of temporary'; in other words he feels effectively outside of time, caught between a suspect past and an ever-receding future.

Time is the needle that sews the sampler that is *Death of a Salesman*, and time does strange things in that play as in the first minutes we leap, via the sound of a flute, from the late nineteenth century to the 1940s and then the 1920s; but that is because Willy Loman is a time-traveller. Past and future are as substantial as the present within which, nonetheless, they are both compacted. In one sense the events of the play take place over a period of twenty-four hours. In another sense, as Miller suggested, they take place over some two-and-a-half hours. In yet another sense the time period is nearly sixty years.

But Miller has also talked of the 'social time' of the play and of its 'psychic time', in other words, the social setting, with its assumptions about private morality and public actions, and the special time created by the tumble of memories which form an interference pattern with Willy's daily life. Time is curiously plastic and multi-layered in *Salesman*, a fact which sets directors and designers significant challenges. And the effect of clashing time scales is to breed irony, expose causality, dissolve identity, imply responsibility, reveal emotional and spiritual debility, social change, psychological process.

As Miller has said, 'I wanted a way of presenting [time] so that it became the fiber of the play.'[20] Perhaps not so much the fibre as the fibre optics, as light from one time and place suddenly floods into another. He wanted, in particular, to turn the diachronic into the synchronic, cutting down through time 'like a cake'. And, indeed, past and present do exist within the same moment in this play. Why? Because 'everything we are is at every moment alive in us' (*T.* 131).

His aim, then, was to capture 'the mind's simultaneity', to enable Willy Loman 'to see present through past and past through present' (*T.* 131). Although Ibsen is thought of as an influence behind *All My Sons* rather than *Salesman*, what Miller saw in Ibsen is equally applicable to this story of an aging salesman caught in a time warp, re-experiencing the past not as memory but as present fact. In Ibsen, Miller has said, 'past and present were drawn in to a single continuity' so that as a consequence 'a secret moral order was . . . limned', an order in which 'present dilemma was simply the face that the past had left visible'. For Miller, indeed, 'a play without a past is a mere shadow of a play'.[21]

There are other kinds of time in *Death of a Salesman*. Willy Loman is mesmerised by a national myth embodied in the person of his brother Ben, who went into the jungle and came out rich. But, as Frank Kermode has said, 'myths take place in a quite different order of time'. The only way to gain access to them 'is by ritual re-enactment. But here and now, in *hoc tempore* [in this time], we are certain only of the dismal linearity of time.'[22] That is the special dilemma of Willy Loman, as myth comes into conflict with the quotidian. He desperately wishes to re-enact the rituals which will revalidate the myth, the myth which operates in a quite different order of time, but is trapped in the desperate logic of linearity. He engages in ritual actions – setting out on the road to his future, sowing seeds for a fruitful tomorrow – but these are gestures without meaning, without consequence. He summons Ben as evidence of the myth, but linear time, for this 63-year-old man, will not relent.

The link between myth and language is metaphor. It is Willy Loman's fate, therefore, to be trapped in a metaphor, that of a tantalising dream, the American dream for which identity, meaning, epiphany are a product of tomorrow.

Then there is another kind of time that Miller sees as bearing on this play about a salesman who travels in the belief that a journey implies a destination, who shadows his pioneer father who headed west before the frontier was closed, selling what he made. This has to do with making as well as selling, the time measured by how long it takes to write a play or make a piece of furniture. Willy's father made the flutes he sold. Willy is alienated from the products of his labour. He has nothing more to sell than himself. For Miller, the break between making and selling 'has terrible consequences'. As he has said,

> there are so many elements in things that a man or woman makes that you never even think about. The whole question of time is different. A man who is, say, a good carpenter will look at a job and immediately has got to think how long this is going to take . . . it is congealed time and what the machine has done is, in effect, to destroy that element of the human mind for a lot of people. They no longer respect the time that is in objects . . . human time. They lose contact with reality, which is also the question of the rolling away of your life, in terms of its minutes and seconds and hours. It is terribly important.

To make something, then, is to retain a grasp on the real, to maintain a sense of 'human time' and hence of 'mortality' and thus ultimate values. Willy Loman has lost that. He no longer makes things, though we are told that he was never so much himself as when he did, briefly, do so. But now he inhabits a world in which such things no longer seem to have true significance. Human time, the time locked up in a piece of furniture or a front stoop, has deferred to something else. Now, time is measured by how long it takes a refrigerator belt to fail or a car to break down or a salesman to sell a product that is so detached from him that he never refers to it.

This concern is there, too, in *The Last Yankee*, in which a wife upbraids her carpenter–husband for not putting his skills at the service of success. But he is a craftsman. There is time invested in the work he does, as there is in the life of a man or woman. And there is a line to be traced from there to *Mr Peters' Connections*, for Miller has said that once people have lost touch with the human time embodied in the objects they make, they, in turn, 'get disembodied' – like Mr Peters – and lose contact with reality. And once the connection between making and doing has gone, once a fundamental awareness of that congealed human time has disappeared, what is left appears to be no more than passing time or, more significantly, killing time.

Instead of living our lives, we are, Miller suggests, now 'living other people's lives', and the mechanism for that is television, which, he laments, in this country, 'is all night and all day'. For Mr Peters, his is a country that has lost the plot, its subject. It is no longer Willy Loman who feels 'kind of temporary' but the whole culture, as buildings are torn down and rebuilt, businesses disappear, history itself becomes disposable (an echo here of the lament in *The Price* that now everything is disposable), and, on television, programme succeeds programme with no logic, inner coherence or connection with individual lives.

In *Death of a Salesman* the failing machines have their parallel in a failing man. Willy's boss, Howard, no longer recognises the human time locked up in this aging salesman, a man who enters his office to insist on the moral authority of the past, on a contract once made, an obligation once acknowledged. But

Howard's values are those of business. He is a man for whom time is money, who has no time for the man who has served the company for most of his life and has little time left. Ultimately, of course, Willy's only means of stopping time is to stop himself, as, in *A View from the Bridge*, Eddie Carbone, who had tried to stop the biological clock by denying his niece's sexual maturity in order to deny the reality of his own sexual feelings towards her, can finally only retain his own innocence by stopping the clock of his own life.

The past, actual, distorted, reinvented, is crucial to Miller's work. It is hard to think of a Miller play in which it does not rest heavily on the present. It is fundamental to his belief in causality and moral responsibility. His repeated reminder that his plays – like those of classical Greece and Ibsen – are about the chickens coming home to roost merely underscores a truth evident from *The Golden Years* through to *Mr Peters' Connections*.

The denial of which so many of his characters are guilty is in essence a denial of the past and of its secrets. And since the denial of the past is necessarily a denial of the self, of an identity that is a product of the past, no wonder his characters tend to shout out their names when they are in process of denying the identity with which they like to believe they have invested those names. A denial of the past is, in effect, a denial of identity and of reality.

Yet the past is not hard-edged, verifiable, agreed. As a character says in *The Creation of the World and Other Business*, the past is always changing. It is a field of contention. And since memory exists not in the past but the present, there is a temporal distortion as that past is made to serve current needs. As Miller has said of Willy Loman, his 'attitude to the past is always romantic . . . his brain embellishes everything. For Charley, what is real is real.' That is, perhaps, Charley's redemption and his limitation.

For Willy, past and future alike are golden. Only the present throws back no glow. It is that fact which simultaneously corrupts his present with irony and suggests a longing for transcendence and transformation that distinguishes him from Charley's realism, a realism whose limitation is signalled by his reply to Willy's accusation that he never took an interest in his son, Bernard: 'My salvation is that I never took an interest in anything.'[23] Willy has a passionate interest, fired by a disturbing amalgam of hope, need, guilt and love, by a desire to understand why his life is as it is. Willy has the writer's desire to charge the world with significance.

In *The Price*, too, a play in which the past has an objective correlative in the form of a roomful of furniture, differing versions of the past become the arena in which two brothers seek to justify their lives. In *Some Kind of Love Story* the past is deeply problematic. Two people locate themselves within competing narratives, while desperate for some connection, perhaps no longer between one and another but between themselves and their lives, between themselves and the real. And implicit in the question of memory is the question of reality. Without memory reality is literally deracinated, a series of gestures, events, feelings with no precursors, no cause, no form, no structure of meaning. But the reality of memories is itself, as we have seen, suspect. The past, then, is not secure in these plays. Things happen – betrayals of one kind or another – but the meaning of these things, the motives that generated them, is less so.

There are few Miller characters for whom the past is unambiguous. It contains too many secrets, the seeds of too much guilt. All wish to declare their innocence, but how can that innocence be assured if the past is granted true authority? They want to exist outside of time but, as Miller insists in *The Creation of the World and Other Business*, we exist, in the words of another play, after the Fall. It was, after all, the Fall of man that started the clock of history, that started the biological clock which numbered our days, that introduced time and with it causality and death.

Memory and consciousness are directly related. To understand a life you have to understand in what it has consisted. For William James, in *The Principles of Psychology*, that primary memory is to be distinguished from what he called secondary memory – 'the rearward portion of the present space of time'.[24] The past is not the trailing edge of the present: but it is part of our present. We contain it. And that is why Quentin, in *After the Fall*, insists that the past is holy, for there is a price to be paid for denying it. It is a price paid by Joe Keller, by Willy Loman and, arguably, by the culture of which they are defining symbols. In Miller's plays we are taken back to that past through the wormhole which is memory, which is history, but which is also the theatre itself, surely the supreme time-machine with the power to transport us to that space between the mind and what it imagines, that space within which Miller's plays, indeed arguably all plays, have their being.

— ✳ —

The success of *Death of a Salesman* (it won the Pulitzer Prize, which Miller claims never to have received) was phenomenal with all but the so-called Non-Communist Left, for whom Miller seemed an unregenerate Stalinist. His continued commitment to Marxism and, as became apparent at the Waldorf Conference for World Peace in which he participated in 1949, to the Soviet Union, made him deeply suspect. There was thus a tendency to see him as attacking capitalist society. Others, further to the left, attacked him for his portrait of moral capitalists in the figures of Charley and his successful lawyer son. Such assaults were reminders of the fact that in Cold War America artists now found themselves inspected for their politics. *Death of a Salesman* was, in a sense, an unassailable success, hailed as a landmark in the American theatre. At the same time, however, for some critics it was seen as ideologically suspect.

All My Sons, as we have noted, had already been banned from US military bases in Europe as playing too directly into the hands of America's enemies. *Death of a Salesman* was now picketed by the American Legion, an organisation of veterans seemingly at odds with the First Amendment. When a film version was made, with Frederic March as Willy Loman – a version intensely disliked by Miller, who has also suggested that the film version of *All My Sons* would benefit from burning – a short film was shot insisting on the vital significance of salesmanship and its attractiveness as a profession. The latter, thanks to a threatened law-suit by Miller, was never distributed but the fact that a movie studio stood ready to sabotage its own film says a great deal about the growing hysteria in America.

The black list was already a part of American life (a number of actors having been summoned before the House Un-American Activities Committee in 1947 and the industry promising not to employ known communists). Two actors who suffered from this – Frederic March and Florence Edridge – now approached him and asked him to write an adaptation of Ibsen's *An Enemy of the People*, a play in part about what de Tocqueville had called the tyranny of the majority. The play opened a few weeks after *Salesman* finished its Broadway run. It closed after thirty-six performances.

Miller saw it as posing the question of whether the rights of political minorities should be set aside in times of crisis. In Ibsen's play the issue is not immediately one of politics, there being a convergence of the political parties against the maverick individual, but there seems little doubt that for Miller the heart of the play lay in the pressure brought to bear on those unwilling to embrace current orthodoxies. Miller's fear was that under pressure America would willingly sacrifice its liberal principles. The reception of *An Enemy of the People* and, later, *The Crucible*, suggests that he was not far wrong.

Committed Ibsenites have treated the text with circumspection and even some disdain[25] and certainly Miller saw the play as addressing immediate priorities. For Benjamin Nelson, in his study of Miller, the playwright's misreadings of Ibsen were 'devastating', as he presented a polemical comedy as a tragedy.[26] In fact, Miller was not insensitive to the ironic comedy of a man so convinced of his own rectitude that he expresses contempt even for those in whose name he supposedly acts. Dr Stockmann, the protagonist, is self-righteous, blind to familial and social obligations. That he is also correct in his analysis is what generates the ambiguity which in part is what fascinates Miller. Stockmann speaks truths that others would deny and as a result is made a pariah. Indeed, as interesting is the shift in Miller's attitude towards the mass of ordinary people or, more accurately, the common people as a mass. In *Focus* they had become the raw material for reactionary mobs and in Ibsen's play they become the basis of a mindless conformity. Miller felt the pressure of that conformity.

If Dr Stockmann, in Ibsen's play, had been an equivocal figure, in his assertion of the moral superiority of the individual in what he takes to be his idealism, he remains equivocal in Miller's version. However, the choice of this play at this time was assuredly a sign that Miller was ready to challenge those who would if not silence then marginalise him, even as he was aware of the ironies which attached themselves to a man such as himself whose political loyalties had indeed been misplaced. Nonetheless, he watched appalled as America seemingly abandoned the very freedoms it purported to be defending.

For Nelson, Miller misses the ironies of Ibsen's play, the comical self-righteousness of its protagonist. It is hard to agree, though the circumstances of its production made the joke more difficult to appreciate. But in both versions Stockmann is both right and wrong, frequently a defining characteristic of Miller's characters as they simultaneously announce and subvert their own identities. *An Enemy of the People* plainly lacks the human force of *All My Sons* and *Death of a Salesman*. The characters exist to serve an idea. They are part of a dialectic. But so, too, they were for Henrik Ibsen in a play in which idea dominates character.

✳

9

'An Enemy of the People'

An Enemy of the People was unusual among Ibsen's plays. It was written quickly, being staged within a year of *Ghosts*, whose negative reviews in part explained its mood. It is an angry play, and one in which the idealism of its central character is presented without quite so many of the unfolding ambiguities and ironies as attach themselves to *The Wild Duck*, for example, and which Miller echoed in *All My Sons*. Like *Ghosts* it is about corruption, but the corruption here is to the body politic, to a venal business world, a tainted media and a vacillating and self-serving liberalism for which compromise and moderation are the fundamental tenets. In other words it is a play with multiple targets.

To be sure, the central character, Dr Stockmann, has flaws of his own. He suffers from pride, arrogance and a belief in the moral and social primacy of the intellectual. These, however, are elements that Ibsen presents but does not explore, and that Miller would not choose to elaborate.

An Enemy of the People concerns a small Norwegian community about to break out of its torpor and provincialism thanks to a newly developed spa, the inspiration of Dr Stockmann, whose work has revealed the special properties of its waters. His brother, the Mayor, part of the syndicate operating the baths, is one of the city elders to benefit. Now, however, Stockmann has evidence that the water harbours potentially dangerous organisms and believes that his discoveries will be honoured by a community that can only be delighted to be warned in time. All that is required is that the existing system of pipes should be relocated on higher ground, albeit at considerable expense.

The result is predictable, though not predicted by him since his scientific insight does not extend to an understanding of human nature. The revelations threaten temporary ruin and though at first radical and reformist elements in the town seem pleased to embrace and, indeed, publish his ideas, when the Mayor proposes to raise funds for the new work by public taxation they withdraw, though not without offering to support Stockmann, whom others see as a troublemaker, so long as he will undertake to finance them. When Stockmann is denied the right to present or publish his work he calls a public meeting, but this is taken over by his enemies, more especially his brother, and he is branded an enemy of the people. He subsequently loses his house and, effectively, his profession. His children are threatened and he is tempted

138

to leave for America, finally deciding to stay and resist the tyranny of the majority.

An Enemy of the People is driven by a fierce energy. It is almost as reckless in its catholicity of targets as the figure at its centre. Ibsen's characters here are a deal too obliging in their willingness to reveal their motives, expose their political corruptions and discharge the meaning of their lives. Subtlety and ambiguity take second place to a drama designed to celebrate the resistant spirit and castigate the forces of reaction, whether of the left or right. There were also aspects of the play that caused unease at the time and which disturbed Miller as he prepared his text from the literal translation provided by the play's Scandinavian producer, Lars Nordenson, who, in turn, had a copy of the director's script from the original production.

Dr Stockmann believes that his superior intellect grants him special status and even seems to hint at a Darwinian basis for this. This is a man, too, who seems to have something of a Christ complex, gathering together a group of twelve disciples at the end, ready to convert the world to the centrality of the truth. It is true that Ibsen seems alert to the self-deception built into such a stance but the circumstances of the plot, and the exigencies of the play, mean that this is no more than a gesture towards that ambivalence that would characterise so many of his other plays in which the demand of the ideal is asserted in the face of its cost in terms of individual lives.

Here, the family suffer but, as in *All My Sons*, to place family before a more general humanity would be plainly retrograde. Thus, to Miller, Ibsen seemed to be echoing a sentiment that he himself had found first in Marxism and then, perhaps, in a more native liberalism. For the fact is that de Tocqueville had spoken of the tyranny of the majority in *Democracy in America* and Miller has spoken of de Toqueville's perception that Americans 'don't want to be set aside from the mob', that 'people will adopt a mask in order to be like everybody else',[1] while Thoreau had debated the role of the individual when faced with democratic decisions in conflict with moral principles.

Confronted with those aspects of the play that most disturbed him, Miller reminded himself that he, too, had claimed a certain privileged status if not for the intellectual per se, then at least for the artist. Ibsen had spoken elsewhere of moving the boundary posts. Miller's metaphor was different: the artist was 'point man into the unknown' (*T*.324). As to Ibsen's Darwinism, his stress on the aristocracy of revolutionary thinkers, Miller was reminded by Robert Lewis, who had conducted hurried research at the Theatre Collection of the New York Public Library, that the playwright had disavowed this before a trade union meeting, insisting on the avant-garde's right to advance new ideas rather than claim democratic legitimacy.

In fact Ibsen's speech to the working men of Trondheim, following an exile of eleven years, was a mixture of political regret and self-justification:

> My experience has shown me that the most indispensable individual rights
> are not as yet safeguarded as I believed I might hope and expect under the
> new form of government. A ruling majority does not grant the individual
> either liberty of faith or liberty of expression beyond an arbitrarily fixed
> limit . . . I fear that it will be beyond the power of our *present* democracy to
> solve these problems. An element of *nobility* must enter into our political
> life, our administration, our representation, and our press.
>
> Of course I am not thinking of the nobility of *birth*, nor that of *wealth*,
> nor that of *knowledge*, neither that of *ability* or intelligence. But I think of
> the nobility of *character*, of the nobility of will and mind. That alone can
> make us free.[2]

That nobility he hoped to find in two groups who had not as yet been harmed
by party pressure: women and working men. An animus against party, present in
Ibsen's original, does not play as strong a role in Miller's version, while neither
find room for women and working men as the source of nobility, though
Peter Stockmann's villainy is underlined in Ibsen's version by his persistent
denigration of what he calls the 'peasant class'. For Miller, the play became
essentially a work about 'the holy right, to resist the pressure to conform'
(*T*.324).

For an increasingly embattled Miller this was the key element of a play which
Ibsen, interestingly, was unsure whether to call a comedy or a tragedy, and,
indeed, tragedy and low comedy attach themselves to Dr Stockmann, alternately
idealistic and self-promoting, honest and bombastic. The humour drops away,
though, as Stockmann's unpopular views strip him of his livelihood, a fate
increasingly facing those in fifties America who were touched by the palsied
hand of the House Un-American Activities Committee.

Nor was Miller unaware of the risks involved in staging this play which could
only serve to 'move the lot of us closer to the bull's-eye of the Red hunters'
target' (*T*.323). But for a man flushed with two Broadway successes such a
challenge was not unwelcome. It was somewhat ironic, however, that having
turned his back on what he regarded as the Greco-Ibsen element in his work
after *All My Sons*, he now returned to Broadway with an Ibsen play presented
in a straightforwardly realist manner, thereby further exacerbating a tendency
in American criticism thereafter to regard him as essentially a realist.

In contemporary terms, Stockmann is a whistle-blower, a truth-teller who
pays the price of exposing corruption. But he is something more than this in
that he is an evangelist for the truth and there is a sense, not fully explored, in
which he welcomes the persecution that he suffers as a consequence, truth and
messianism becoming closely related. Arrayed against him are party politicians,
small businessmen, liberal reformers, self-identified radicals and a press that
serves its own purposes before those of a public presented as easily swayed by
appeals to self-interest. The target is thus as much hypocrisy and social coercion
as the power of conformity. It is certainly tempting to feel that Miller might

have felt something of Ibsen's sense of betrayal by those who seemingly shared his own beliefs but were now found wanting.

In a letter written in the context of the critical response to *Ghosts*, Ibsen identified as 'the most cowardly' the 'so-called liberals' because they were 'in downright bodily fear that they should not be able to clear themselves of the suspicion of being in any kind of agreement with me'.[3] It was ironically those who characterised themselves as liberals who were anxious to distinguish their own liberalism from Miller's and who accordingly treated his drama with suspicion.

In Ibsen's hands Dr Stockmann is frequently a ranter, given to extreme statements and an inflated rhetoric. Entering the offices of the supposedly radical newspaper he declares that he will 'smite them to the earth. I will crush them, level all their entrenchments to the ground before the eyes of all right thinking men.'[4] Miller not only omits the speech but drains his language of its hyperbole, its God-like tone.

When, in Ibsen's play, Stockmann is finally allowed to address the public meeting he has called, he is, somewhat unbelievably, permitted to speak at length, attacking all sections of his society in extreme language and developing his Darwinian thesis:

> The masses are nothing but the raw material that must be fashioned into the people. Is it not so with all other living creatures on earth? How great the difference between a cultivated and an uncultivated breed of animals! . . . Don't you believe that the brain of a poodle has developed quite differently from that of a mongrel? Yes, you may depend upon that! It is educated poodles like this that jugglers train to perform the most extraordinary tricks. A common peasant-cur could never learn anything of the sort – not if he tried till Doomsday . . . we are animals . . . there is a terrible difference between men-poodles and men-mongrels.[5]

In one sense this speech is designed to expose Stockmann's own patrician sensibility, as he attacks 'the vulgar herd', using essentially the same language as his brother, but Ibsen was himself drawn to Darwinism, while in his speech to the working men of Trondheim trying to make a distinction between a nobility of character, will and mind rather than of birth. Miller strips this out, normalising Stockmann's language, shortening his intervention and making him sound altogether more balanced. Out, therefore, goes Stockmann's insistence that 'It doesn't matter if a lying community is ruined! It must be levelled to the ground, I say! All men who live upon lies must be exterminated like vermin! . . . I say, from the bottom of my heart: Perish the country! Perish all its people!'[6] Miller retains only the last phrase from this speech. He wants a saner spokesman for the non-conformist, someone whose resistance to the majority has a moral base.

Thus, he removes, too, Stockmann's insistence that ideals should only last for seventeen or eighteen years. Into the speech went more familiar

images: 'Was the majority right when they stood by while Christ was crucified', Miller's Stockmann asks, 'Was the majority right when they refused to
believe that the earth moved round the sun, and let Galileo be driven to his
knees like a dog? It takes fifty years for the majority to be right. The majority
is never right until it *does* right.'[7] Miller's Stockmann is still carried away by
his own rhetoric, still a flawed spokesman for the ideal, but no longer quite as
manic, quite as insensitive, as Ibsen's.

What Miller did find in Ibsen's play that chimed with a central concern of his
own was the individual's regard for the integrity of his name. Thus Morton Kiil,
Stockmann's father-in-law, who buys up the stock of the ruined baths, insists,
in Ibsen's version, that 'I stand for my good name . . . I will live and die a clean
man.'[8] As in so many of Miller's plays, however, the association of identity with
innocence is a suspect one, for here Kiil is seeking to deny his own responsibility
for the tainting of the water as a consequence of his mismanagement of his own
tannery, whose effluent is the cause of the problem.

For Miller, then, the relevance of the play to America lay in its concern with
the pressure to conform. He spoke, he assumed, to those who, like him, felt
threatened by the atmosphere of political intimidation. But for Robert Brustein,
writing some fifteen years later, Miller had 'bowdlerized' the play. The 'antisocial elements of the play are called "fascistic", and cut; its apocalyptic quality is
tempered with moderateness and reason; and its posture of defiant individualism, is watered down into a plea for the protection of minority groups'.[9] As
a statement it is a mixture of half truths. It is true that the young Norwegian
producer had expressed alarm at his own country's drift to the right and that
this was echoed by Miller's own experience of America. The fascism, though,
if it could be said to exist, lay not so much in the self-serving majority as in
Stockmann himself, a messianic leader in his own eyes, and preaching the
supremacy of his own breed over mongrels.

It is true, too, that the American playwright moderates what Brustein sees
as an 'apocalyptic' quality in the original, but what he sees as apocalyptic
could more accurately be characterised as evidence of Ibsen's anger, and even
contempt, which has the effect of making Stockmann seem little more than
deranged at times, effectively destroying his own arguments to such a degree
that the playwright subsequently found it necessary to clarify what he had
meant.

Perhaps this is why Brustein characterises the original play as simultaneously
'an inferior work of art'[10] and a direct expression of Ibsen's beliefs, unmediated
by the characters in whose mouths he places those beliefs, itself a criticism
of a playwright who he earlier praises for resisting precisely this tendency.
In fact, Miller tries to rectify some of the more egregious elements of the
play, particularly softening the contempt which Stockmann expresses for the
ordinary people, indeed for almost everyone. The cuts have nothing to do

with removing the antisocial elements in the play. What went were mainly over-extended and repetitive statements, usually by Stockmann himself. Had there been more of a space between Ibsen and his central character it would have been tempting to see this as another of his portraits of an arrogant and self-serving idealist, but there is nothing to suggest that this is how he saw him, though the level of bombast alone might seem to hint at this.

Brustein thus wishes at the same time to see this as a suspect play and one whose depths must be defended against Miller's changes, modest though they are. His final observation is that Miller 'proceeds to lop off its more radical limbs', quoting as evidence for this the change of a single line. What in Ibsen's text reads 'the strongest man upon earth is he who stands most alone',[11] becomes, in Miller's, 'You are fighting for the truth, and that's why you're alone. And that makes you strong – you're the strongest people in the world . . . And the strong must learn to be lonely.'[12] There is a difference. In Ibsen's play the statement seems further evidence of Stockmann's megalomania. He has just announced that his wife is 'mad' for thinking he will be driven out of the town and declared that he is 'one of the strongest men upon earth'. He announces that he will set himself up as a teacher, calling for a 'few specimens' of 'good-for-nothings' on whom he can experiment. In Miller's version the statement is that of the defiant non-conformist insisting on the truth.

The original play ends as his father-in-law capers around shouting 'Hurrah!' while his daughter looks, trustingly and adoringly, up at Stockmann as he focuses not on the truth, the plight of his family or that of his society, but on himself. Miller's play, by contrast, ends with Stockmann protecting his family, as stones come through the window, and including them in his future plans. The contemptuous remarks about conducting educational experiments with a few specimens of good-for-nothings are removed. In the radical stakes, Miller hardly comes off the worse.

The fact is that in many ways Miller improves on the original. Stockmann becomes a more credible figure. While still unaware of his own faults, he is no longer a blind Darwinian, no longer so contemptuous of those he seeks to lead. His bombast is moderated. The uncertain tone of Ibsen's play is adjusted and its social ethic sharpened. Ibsen wrote it when he felt personally persecuted, when he regarded himself as being an artist in a hopelessly vulgar environment, a victim of an unholy alliance of forces. In Miller's hands the play becomes more of a social document.

He himself was not as yet in the eye of the storm and perhaps that gave him the perspective to see beyond the immediate anger to the underlying principles that did, indeed, apply to a society already sliding not merely into reaction but also a coercive conformity. He does shift the emphasis, as he alters Ibsen's five-act structure to a three-act one. At the public meeting he has the Mayor offer a reason for stifling freedom of speech which is not in the original and perhaps says more for America in the 1950s than Norway in the 1880s, though it is a natural extension of Peter Stockmann's sense of values as being subordinate to immediate needs:

> we are a democratic country . . . God knows, in ordinary times, I'd agree with anybody's right to say anything. But these are not ordinary times. Nations have crises and so do towns. There are ruins of nations and there are ruins of towns all over the world, and they are wrecked by people who in the guise of reform and pleading for justice . . . broke down all authority and left only revolution and chaos . . . I believe there is a line that must be drawn, and if a man decides to cross that line, we the people must finally take him by the collar and declare, 'You cannot say that.'

However, America is also a point of reference in Ibsen's play and though Miller was attacked for incorporating a line, taken to be ironic, in which Stockmann refers to a planned escape to America where, 'in a big country like that, the spirit must be bigger',[13] in fact the ironies are far deeper in the original. Here Stockmann, having confessed that there are 'plebeians' everywhere, and having identified the central problem as lying with the party system, remarks that 'perhaps that's no better in the free west either; there, too, the compact majority thrives, and enlightened public opinion and all the other devil's trash flourishes. But you see the conditions are on a wider scale there than here; they may lynch you, but they don't torture you; they don't put the screw on a free soul there as they do at home here. And then, if need be, you can live apart.'[14] The irony reflects back on Stockmann, the antisocial and arrogant isolate, and outwards to an America in which lynching is sanctioned alongside a rhetoric of freedom. If anything, Miller, far from adding an egregious and superfluous comment on America, mitigates Ibsen's implied critique.

— ✳ —

An Enemy of the People opened at the Broadhurst Theatre on Broadway on 28 December 1950, directed by Robert Lewis. It had an abbreviated run. These were not good days for a play which appeared to suggest that freedom of speech was under pressure and that the mass of people were happy to conform to the views of demagogic politicians, however true that seemed to be.

Politically, though, Miller had changed. His appearance at the Waldorf Conference in 1949 had been his last public show of solidarity with the Soviet Union. Attendance at this conference was taken by many as a mark of loyalty to communism and *Life* magazine obligingly published photographs of those it suggested supped with the devil. One of the photographs was of Miller. By the time of *An Enemy of the People*, however, he had already moved on. Finally, even he was ready to acknowledge the villainy of Stalin. What he was not ready to do was submit to the reactionary mood of the country. In 1947, the House Un-American Activities Committee had summoned Hollywood actors to Washington in an investigation of their communist affiliations. This had seen the start of blacklisting which extended to a number of Miller's friends, both in radio and the theatre. The issue, then, was no longer one of political ideology but of a defence of American rights and values. The issue, as *An Enemy of the People* suggested, was a new coercive orthodoxy.

For his part, however, he was ready to start what seemed a new career as a screenwriter. At the turn of the year 1950–1 he travelled with his director Elia Kazan to the west coast. They were taking with them a screenplay called *The Hook* which they hoped to sell to Hollywood. Set on the Brooklyn waterfront, it was concerned with a man's struggle against the corrupt unions which control the docks. Kazan, as director of the film version of *A Streetcar Named Desire*, was a hot property. Miller was a Pulitzer Prize winner. Nonetheless, the script was rejected, in part at the behest of the FBI, when Miller refused to compromise by making the gangsters into communists. He returned to New York but not before encountering someone who would change his life: Marilyn Monroe. For the moment, though, he put film and Monroe out of mind.

In 1952 the director of *Death of a Salesman*, Elia Kazan, was summoned by the House Un-American Activities Committee and though in a first hearing he refused to name colleagues who had attended Party meetings when, for some eighteen months he had been a member, he asked to be seen again and now offered those names.

Miller, never a member of the Party, was not among their number but knew that Kazan would happily have offered him up had he been so. It was a crisis in their relationship. On the eve of the hearing, Kazan telephoned him and the two met at Kazan's Connecticut home. Their accounts differ but it became clear that their relationship, professional and personal, was at an end, at least for a while. In fact, twelve years later the two men would once again collaborate on a production but for now the rift seemed permanent.

Kazan had called Miller on the eve of the latter's trip to Salem, Massachusetts, where he was to research his new play. Miller had known of the story of the Salem witches since college days. Only now, though, did he see its immediate relevance to the times through which he was himself living. As he returned from Salem so he heard news reports on the radio of the names Kazan had offered. It seemed more urgent than ever to get his play written and produced. It opened the following year.

✳

10

'The Crucible'

Salem in 1692 was in turmoil. The Royal Charter had been revoked. Original land titles had been cancelled and others not yet secured. Neighbour accordingly looked on neighbour with some suspicion for fear their land might be reassigned. It was also a community riven with schisms which centred on the person of the Reverend Parris, whose materialism and self-concern was more than many could stomach, including a landowner and innkeeper called John Proctor.

As Miller observed in his notebook: 'It is Shakespearean. Parties and counter-parties. There must be a counter-party. Proctor and others.'[1] John Proctor quickly emerged as the centre of the story Miller wished to tell, though not of the trials where he was one among many. But to Miller, as he wrote in the notebook: '*It has got to be basically Proctor's story.* The important thing – the process whereby a man, feeling guilt for A, sees himself as guilty of B and thus belies himself – accommodates his credo to believe in what he knows is not true.' Before this could become a tragedy for the community it had to be a tragedy for an individual: 'A difficulty. This hanging must be "tragic" – i.e. must [be] result of an opportunity not grasped when it should have been, due to "flaw."'

That flaw, as so often in ▓▓▓▓▓▓ work, was to be sexual, not least because there seemed a sexual flavour to the language of those who confessed to possession by the Devil and who were accused of dancing naked, in a community in which both dancing and nakedness were themselves seen as signs of corruption. But that hardly seemed possible when Abigail Williams and John Proctor, who were to become the central characters in his drama, were eleven and sixty respectively. Accordingly, at Miller's bidding she becomes seventeen and he thirty-five and so they begin to move towards one another, the gap narrowing until a sexual flame is lit.

Where the girls were, in the historical record, reported as dancing in the woods, Miller has them dancing naked, in part, as he explained, to make it easier for the audience to relate the Puritans' horror at such a thing to their own. But in part he made the change in order to introduce the sexual motif at the very beginning of a play in which sexuality is both the source of Proctor's disabling guilt and, in some way, at the heart both of the hysteria of the accusing girls and of the frisson that made witchcraft simultaneously an abomination and a seductive idea.

Elizabeth Proctor, who had managed an inn, now becomes a solitary farmer's wife, cut off from communion not only with her errant husband, who has strayed from her side, but also in some degree from the society of Salem, a woman whose sexual coldness is both a motivating force in her husband's sin and a quality that lifts her above the frenzy of bad faith which surrounds and eventually engulfs her.

Other changes are made. Giles Corey, a cantankerous old man who carelessly damns his wife by commenting on her fondness for books, was not killed, pressed to death by stones, until 19 September, a month after Proctor's death. Miller brings that death forward so that it can prove exemplary. By the same token John Hale's growing conversion to scepticism did not come to its climax with Proctor's death but only later when his own wife was accused. The event is advanced in order to keep Proctor as the focus.

At the same time the playwright resisted another aspect of the story that would have damaged the parallel to fifties America, though it would have struck a chord with those in many other countries who were later to seize on *The Crucible* as an account of their own situation. For the fact is that John Proctor's son was tortured. As Proctor wrote in a Petition: 'My son William Proctor, when he was examin'd, because he would not confess that he was Guilty, when he was Innocent, they tied him Neck and Heels till the Blood gushed out of his Nose.' The effect on the play of including this detail would have been to transform Proctor's motivation and diminish the significance of the sexual guilt that disables him.

Historically, John Proctor did not immediately intervene on learning of the trials and does not do so in the play. The historical account offers no explanation. In the notebooks Miller searched for one: 'Proctor – guilt stays his hand (against what action?)' The guilt derives from his adultery; the action becomes his decision to expose Abigail.

In his original plan Miller toyed with making Proctor a leader of the anti-Parris faction, who backtracks on that role and equivocates in his dealings with Hale. He entertained, too, the notion that Proctor should half wish his wife dead. He abandoned both ideas. If Proctor emerges as a leader it is inadvertently as he fights to defend the wife he has wronged and whose life he has placed in jeopardy because of his affair with Abigail.

What is at stake in *The Crucible* is the survival of Salem, which is to say the survival of a sense of community. On a literal level the village ceased to operate. The trials took precedence over all other activities. They took the farmer from his field and his wife from the milk shed. In an early draft of the screenplay for the film version Miller has the camera observe the depredations of the countryside: unharvested crops, untended animals, houses in disrepair. But, more fundamentally than this, Miller is concerned with the breaking of that social contract which binds a community together, as love and mutual respect bind individuals.

What took him to Salem was not, finally, an obsession with McCarthyism nor even a concern with a bizarre and, at the time, obscure historical incident, but a fascination with 'the most common experience of humanity, the shifts of interest that turned loving husbands and wives into stony enemies, loving parents into indifferent supervisors or even exploiters of their children . . . what they called the breaking of charity with one another'. There was evidence for all of these in seventeenth-century Salem but, as Miller implies, the breaking of charity was scarcely restricted to a small New England settlement in a time distant from our own. For him the parallel between Salem in 1692 and America in 1953 was clear:

> people were being torn apart, their loyalty to one another crushed and . . . common human decency was going down the drain. It's indescribable, really, because you'd get the feeling that nothing was going to be sacred any more. The situations were so exact it was quite amazing. The ritual was the same. What they were demanding of Proctor was that he expose this conspiracy of witches whose aim was to bring down the rule of the Church, of Christianity. If he gave them a couple of names he could go home. And if he didn't he was going to hang for it. It was quite the same excepting we weren't hanged, but the ritual was exactly the same. You told them anyone you knew had been a left-winger or a Communist and you went home. But I wasn't going to do that.[2]

Neither was John Proctor.

One dictionary definition of a crucible is that it is a place of extreme heat, 'a severe test'. John Proctor and those others summoned before a court in Salem discovered the meaning of that. Yet such tests, less formal, less judicial, less public, are the small change of daily life. Betrayal, denial, rash judgement, self-justification, are remote neither in time nor place.

The Crucible, then, is not merely concerned with reanimating history or implying contemporary analogies for past crimes. It is Arthur Miller's most frequently produced play not because it addresses affairs of state nor even because it offers us the tragic sight of a man who dies to save his conception of himself and the world, but because audiences understand all too well that the breaking of charity is no less a contemporary fact because it is presented in the context of a re-examined history.

There is, then, more than one mystery here. Beyond the question of witchcraft lies the more fundamental question of a human nature for which betrayal seems an ever-present possibility. *The Crucible* reminds us how fragile is our grasp on those shared values that are the foundation of any society. It is a play written not only at a time when America seemed to sanction the abandonment of the normal decencies and legalities of civilised life but in the shadow of a still greater darkness, for the Holocaust was in Miller's mind, as it had been in the mind of Marion Starkey, whose book on the trials had stirred his imagination.[3]

What replaces this sense of natural community in *The Crucible*, as perhaps in Nazi Germany (a parallel of which he was conscious) and, on a different scale, fifties America, is a sense of participating in a ritual, of conformity to a ruling orthodoxy and hence a shared hostility to those who threaten it. The purity of one's religious principles is confirmed by collaborating, at least by proxy, in the punishment of those who reject them. Racial identity is reinforced by eliminating those who might 'contaminate' it, as one's Americanness is underscored by the identification of those who could be said to be Un-American. In the film version of his play, Miller, free now to expand and deepen the social context of the drama, chooses, in an early draft, to emphasise this illusory sense of community: 'The CROWD's urging rises to angry crescendo. HANGMAN pulls a crude lever and the trap drops and the two fall. THE CROWD is delirious with joyful, gratifying unity.'

If it was Alexis de Tocqueville who identified the pressure towards conformity even in the early years of the Republic, it was a pressure acknowledged equally by Hawthorne, Melville, Emerson and Thoreau. When Sinclair Lewis's Babbitt abandons his momentary rebellion to return to his conformist society he is described as being 'almost tearful with joy'. Miller's alarm, then, is not his alone, nor his sense of the potentially tyrannical power of shared myths which appear to offer absolution to those who accept them. If his faith in individual conscience as a corrective is also not unique, it was, perhaps, harder to sustain in the second half of a century which had seen collective myths exercising a coercive power, in America and Europe.

Beyond anything else, *The Crucible* is a study in power and the mechanisms by which power is sustained, challenged and lost. Perhaps that is one reason why, as Miller has noted, productions of the play seem to precede and follow revolutions and why what can be seen as a revolt of the young against the old should, on the play's production in Communist China, have been seen as a comment on the Cultural Revolution of the 1960s in which the young Red Guards humiliated, tortured and even killed those who had previously been in authority over them: parents, teachers, members of the cultural elite.

On the one hand stands the Church, which provides the defining language within which all social, political and moral debate is conducted. On the other stand those usually deprived of power – the black slave Tituba and the young children – who suddenly gain access to an authority as absolute as that which had previously subordinated them. Those ignored by history become its motor force. Those socially marginalised move to the very centre of social action. Those whose opinions and perceptions carried neither personal nor political weight suddenly acquire an authority so absolute that they come to feel they can challenge even the representatives of the state. Tituba has a power she has never known in her life.

To be a young girl in Salem was to have no role but obedience, no function but unquestioning faith, no freedom except a willingness to submit to those with power over their lives. Sexuality was proscribed, the imagination distrusted, emotions focused solely on the stirring of the spirit. Rebellion, when it came, was thus likely to take as its target firstly those with least access to power, then those for whom virtue alone was insufficient protection. Next would come those who were themselves regarded as politically vulnerable and finally those who possessed real power. Predictably it was at this final stage that the conspiracy collapsed, just as Senator McCarthy was to thrive on those who possessed no real purchase on the political system and to lose his credibility when he chose to challenge the US Army. The first three witches named were a slave, a labourer's wife, who had become little more than a tramp, and a woman who had absented herself from church and reportedly lived in sin.

The Crucible is a play about the seductive nature of power and for pubescent girls that seductiveness is perhaps not unconnected with a confused sexuality. These were people who chose not to enquire into their own motives. They submitted to the irrational with a kind of perverse pleasure, a pleasure not entirely drained of sexual content. They dealt, after all, with exposure, with stripping souls bear, with provoking and hearing confessions of an erotic forthrightness which no other occasion or circumstance would permit. The judges saw young women cry out in a kind of orgasmic ecstasy. They witnessed men and women of position, intelligence and property rendered into their power by the confessions of those who recalled abuses and assaults revealed to them only in a religiously and therapeutically charged atmosphere.

These were the 'recovered memories' of Puritan New England and the irrational nature of the accusations, their sexual frisson, the lack of any proof beyond 'spectral evidence' (the dreams and visions of the accusers) was a part of their attraction. When Mary Warren accuses Elizabeth Proctor she says, 'I never knew it before . . . and all at once I remembered everything she done to me!'[4] In our own time we are not so remote from this phenomenon as to render it wholly strange. Men and women with no previous memory of assaults, which were apparently barbaric and even demonic, suddenly recall such abuse, more especially when assisted to do so by therapists, social workers or religionists who offer themselves as experts in the spectral world of suppressed memories. Such abuse, recalled in later life, is impossible to verify but the accusations alone have sufficed to destroy entire families. To deny reality to such abuse is itself seen as a dangerous perversion, just as to deny witchcraft was seen as diabolic in Puritan New England.

Did the young girls in Salem, then, see no witches? Were they motivated solely by self-concern or, in Abigail's case, a blend of vengeance and desire? *The Crucible* is not concerned to arbitrate. Tituba plainly does dabble in the black arts, while Mrs Putnam is quite prepared to do so. Abigail seems a more straightforward case. Jealous of Elizabeth Proctor, she sees a way of removing her and marrying John. In the original version of Miller's screenplay, however, in a scene subsequently cut, Abigail does have a vision of Elizabeth's spirit visiting her in her bedroom:

> Int. Night Abigail bedroom
> *She is asleep in bed. She stirs, then suddenly sits up and sees, seated in a nearby chair, a* WOMAN *with her back to her.* ABIGAIL *slides out of bed and approaches the woman, comes around to see her face – it is* ELIZABETH PROCTOR.
> ABIGAIL Elizabeth? I am with God! In Jesus name begone back to Hell!
> ELIZABETH'S FACE *is transformed into that of a* HAWK, *its beak opening.* ABIGAIL *steps back in terror.*[5]

Whatever her motives, she plainly sees this phantom even though it is conjured not from the Devil but from guilt and desire, which in Puritan New England were anyway seen as synonymous. In the early screen version Proctor is described as 'Certain now that she's mad'. This takes us beyond the portrait we are offered by the play where she is presented as more clearly calculating, but the essential point is not the nature of her motivation nor even the substantiality or otherwise of witches, but the nature of the real and the manner in which it is determined. Proctor and the others find themselves in court because they deny a reality to which others subscribe and in which, whatever their motives, they in part believe, until, slowly, scepticism begins to infect them with the virus of another reality.

Six months after the play had opened, when Miller restaged it prior to a national tour (the New York run ended on 11 July), he interpolated a new scene to be added to the second act. The *Playbill* for 1 June lists it as Act 1, scene 1. However, since Act 1 was then nominated as the Prologue it appeared in the acting edition as Act 2, scene 2. It features an encounter between Proctor and Abigail, the night before his wife is to appear in court. They meet in the forest, that antinomian world, the place where the whole drama had begun and where the play was originally to have opened had construction costs not led to the elimination of the scene.

Proctor comes to save the life of his wife. He warns Abigail what he intends to do. He has, he explains, documentary proof that she knew that the poppet discovered in their house had no connection with Elizabeth. For her part, Abigail, dressed, significantly, in a nightgown, still hopes that their relationship will flare up again. Why else, after all, has he thrown pebbles against her bedroom window? Most significantly, however, this Abigail has convinced herself that she does indeed do the Lord's work. Accused by Proctor of hypocrisy, she defends herself and it seems not without some inner conviction.

As in the deleted film scenes, she appears to have an imperfect grasp on reality. Her outrage that the victims should be permitted to pray seems genuine enough. She is, we are told, 'Astonished, outraged'. Equally clear, however, is her state of mind. As Proctor talks to her, a stage direction indicates that he sees 'her madness now'. He feels 'uneasiness, as though before an unearthly thing', detects 'a wildness in her'.[6] She looks at him as if he were out of his mind, as he warns her that he will confess to adultery if necessary, but the real fear is that she is out of hers. He accuses her of being a 'murderous bitch!' but she responds by accusing him of hypocrisy, the real terror being that she seems to believe it.

The additional scene does throw light on their relationship. Miller also uses it to underscore the extent to which Abigail has gained notoriety and a kind of sexual allure which accompanies her fame. However, it blunts the force of the court scene and, like the rejected film scenes, risks turning Abigail into a pathological case, less evil than herself deluded.

It is the essence of power that it accrues to those with the ability to determine the nature of the real. They authorise the language, the grammar, the vocabulary within which others must live their lives. As Miller observed in his notebook: 'Very important. To say "There be no witches" is to invite charge of trying to conceal the conspiracy and to discredit the highest authorities who alone can save the community!' Proctor and his wife try to step outside the authorised text. They will acknowledge only those things of which they have immediate knowledge. 'I have wondered if there be witches in the world', observes John Proctor incautiously, adding, 'I have no knowledge of it', as his wife, too, insists that 'I cannot believe it' (66). When Proctor asserts his right to freedom of thought and speech – 'I may speak my heart, I think' – he is reminded that this had been the sin of the Quakers and Quakers, of course, had learned the limits of free speech and faith at the end of a hangman's noose on Boston Common.

There is a court which John and Elizabeth Proctor fear. It is one, moreover, which, if it has no power to sentence them to death, does nonetheless command their lives. As Proctor says to his wife: 'I come into a court when I come into this house!' Elizabeth, significantly, replies: 'The magistrate sits in your heart that judges you' (55). Court and magistrate are simply synonyms for guilt. The challenge for John Proctor is to transform guilt into conscience and hence into responsibility. Guilt renders him powerless, as it had Willy Loman in *Death of a Salesman*; individual conscience restores personal integrity and identity and places him at the centre of social action.

Despite the suspicions of his judges, though, Proctor does not offer himself as social rebel. If he seeks to overthrow the court it is, apparently, for one reason only: to save his wife. But behind that there is another motive: to save not himself but his sense of himself. In common with so many other Miller protagonists he is forced to ask the meaning of his own life. As Tom Wilkinson, who played the part of Proctor in a National Theatre production, has said, 'it is rare for people to be asked the question which puts them squarely in front of themselves'.[7] But that is the question which is asked of John Proctor and which, incidentally, was asked of Miller in writing the play and later in appearing before the House Un-American Activities Committee.

Jean-Paul Sartre objected to the French production of the play, which opened at the Théâtre Sarah Bernhardt on 16 December 1954, translated by Marcel Aymée. For Sartre, the play was essentially a battle for possession of the land between the old and the new settlers. He thus found the ending as smacking of what he called a 'disconcerting idealism'.[8] Proctor's death, and the death of his fellow accused, would 'have had meaning if they were shown as an act of revolt based in social conflict'. He blamed the production in which, he said, the social conflict had become 'incomprehensible' and the death of Proctor 'a purely ethical attitude, not like a free act which he commits to unleash the shame, effectively to deny his position, like the only thing he can still do'. The result was that the play became 'insipid' and 'castrated' because 'the political ideas and social bases of the witch-hunt phenomenon do not appear clearly here'.[9]

The argument is presented as though it were a debate with the translator but actually he is arguing with the original text, which he approaches as a Marxist and finds unsatisfactory precisely because it lacks a Marxist perspective. The fact is that Miller did not see the witch-hunts as emerging from a battle between old and new money, there being precious little new money in a colony quite as young. There were, to be sure, arguments over property, and such arguments often lay not too far below the surface as complainants came forward to point the finger, but this is not where the essence of the play lies. Miller is, indeed, careful to expose these to the audience. But, in a time of flux, property rights had been thrown into some disarray and authority was uncertain.

Power, certainly, is an issue in *The Crucible* but it is not in the hands of the rich landowners. It is in the hands of young girls who contest the order of the world. It is in the hands of those offered a sudden sanction for their fears and prejudices. Indeed, it begins to contaminate the agencies and procedures of the state and hence of God's order. It is not, then, the politics of the affair that is Miller's primary concern but precisely Proctor's free act, his ethical attitude. He does not die for the landless, for social justice, but for his sense of himself. It is, strangely, given Sartre's engagement with the play, an existential act and, as Sartre was to say, and as Miller certainly believed, individual decisions do have social consequences. That is the connection between the private world, in which a man decides whether to sign his signature to a lie, and the public world, in which conformity is demanded in the name of an ideal. Sartre, however, looked for some more tangible and external evidence of the social dynamics he assumed to lie beneath the events in Salem.

It is not that Miller wished to focus on the dilemma of a single man. Quite the contrary. In fact in an article to mark the 1958 Off-Broadway production, which was to run for 653 performances and, incidentally, to employ a narrator called 'The Reader' to set the scenes and convey the historical background, he expressed his regret at the narrowing focus of much drama. He now believed, he said, that it was no longer possible to contain the truth of the human situation 'within a single man's guts'. The documentation of 'man's loneliness', he insisted, 'is not in and of itself ultimate wisdom'.[10]

In *The Crucible*, he explained, he wished to explore the tension between a man's actions and his concept of himself, and the question of whether conscience is an organic part of the human sensibility. He wished to examine the consequences of the handing over of that conscience to others. Aware of the degree to which conscience may be a social construct, as of the degree to which public forms and procedures are a product of willed choices, he set himself to stage the dilemma of the individual who comes to acknowledge a responsibility beyond the self.

Proctor begins the play as a man who believes it possible to remain aloof. The betrayal that obsesses him is born out of a private action and instils a private guilt. He debates with himself as history gathers momentum. He finally steps into the courtroom to defend something more than his threatened wife and dies for an idea of community no less than of personal integrity. Asked to concede a lie – not simply the lie of his own supposed actions but the lie of the state which seeks to define the real and consolidate an abstract authority – he declines. It is simultaneously a private and a public act and it is this that Sartre seemed not to understand or, if understand, accept.

When, later, Sartre wrote his own adaptation of the play for a film version, *Les Sorcières de Salem*, he injected those very qualities he found lacking, concluding not with the sound of drums rattling 'like bones in the morning air', but with the beginnings of revolt. Miller was not amused.

Nor was this the end of Miller's argument with Sartre. In a discussion of Judge Danforth, he confessed he should have made him more irremediably evil. Danforth, he explained, was something more than an arbiter of the law in this frontier community. He was the rule-bearer. He patrolled the boundary. He, in Miller's phrase, 'is man's limit'. He stands between men and knowledge. Sartre, as it seemed to Miller, 'reduced him to an almost economic policeman'.[11] Sartre's Danforth never comes to the point at which he realises that he has appropriated his faith to serve the interests of the state and consolidate his own power. Miller conceded that he had himself been remiss in this respect, failing clearly to demarcate the moment at which, knowing, finally, the deceptions being practised, Danforth nonetheless decides to proceed. This, as he suggests, is the obverse of Proctor's final decision that he cannot sign his name to a lie. Danforth can. Sartre's version, however, lacks even the ambivalent awareness that is a mark of Miller's text.

To Miller, therefore, Sartre's conception 'lacks a moral dimension' because it precludes 'a certain aspect of will'.[12] In his version, Danforth remains the same throughout. Lacking self-awareness, he never confronts and rejects the possibility of being other than he is. He is implacable, but the nature of that implacability is different. There is no kinetic morality, no momentary doubt and therefore no decision. He is a representative of unyielding power but his evil is less conscious, seemingly, than a product of historic process. He is a member of a ruling elite, of an unquestioning ideology. He is, in other words, a significant marker in the kind of drama that Sartre preferred to construct from *The Crucible* rather than the figure Miller created, whatever the playwright's subsequent regrets at his failure to sharpen the issues at stake.

Not that Marcel Aymée, translator–adapter of the first French production, seems to have been any more in tune with Miller's intentions. Having offered something of a travesty of the plot, complete with historical inaccuracies, he observes that 'the sympathy of the American spectator belongs to the seducer' because he is a rugged pioneer and one of a breed of 'New England plowmen who carry in their Puritan round heads the shining promises of the age of skyscrapers and the atom bomb'. The farmer, he concluded, 'is an indisputable hero from the outset. He has only to step on a Broadway stage. It's as if he were wrapped in a Star-Spangled Banner, and the public, its heart swollen with tenderness and pride, eat him up.' This, he suggests, is inadmissible for a Frenchman. No doubt it would be, but the interpretation has a certain ring to it, as does his further suggestion that Abigail is presented as 'little more than a little slut come to sully the glorious dawn of the USA'.[13]

Such, of course, is liable to be the fate of writers who offer their work for translation, as cultural values do not so much clash as annihilate one another. So, with John Proctor cast as the wilful seducer, nonetheless perversely embraced by the American psyche, Abigail becomes the ruined girl to be celebrated by the French translator. Aymée then asks, not unreasonably perhaps, why, in his remorse for his sin, Proctor assumes so little responsibility for the girl he has ruined. For, as Aymée insists, 'he shows no regrets regarding his gravest shortcoming, that of having led astray a little soul who had been entrusted to him', an orphan, to boot, he points out. After all, 'In the eyes of the American today, a Puritan family in Massachusetts in 1690 [sic] is one of those good biblical families in which the master of the house exercises prudent thrift in conjugal patience by screwing the servant girls with God's permission.' This delightful travesty has the virtue of misreading the play, theology and social history simultaneously and within a single sentence. To Aymée, John Proctor is a 'petticoat-rumpler' who 'dreams only of restoring peace in his household'.

So, where Sartre sought to redress the political balance of the play, Aymée set himself to rebalance the scales between seducer and seducee: 'It seemed to me necessary', he explained, to bring the pair of lovers back into balance, that is, to blacken the victim and give her a Machiavellianism that she does not have in the Arthur Miller play, in which, in order to save her life and in the sway of group hysteria, she is led to unleash a witch hunt. I wanted to give her full consciousness of the evil in her. Doubtless, in doing that, I greatly falsified the author, and I sincerely regret it.[14]

The regret did not, however, extend much further than resisting too complete a falsification. 'I am far from taking all the liberties with his text that seemed desirable to me', he insisted, as if this were sufficient by way of moral virtue to purge such alterations as he did make. He would, however, he insisted, abjure from any further adaptations. He did not. In 1958 he adapted *A View from the Bridge*.

Miller seems to have written *The Crucible* in a kind of white heat. The enthusiasm and speed with which he went to Salem underlines the urgency with which he regarded the project, as did his later comment, on returning from Salem, that he felt a kind of social responsibility to see it through to production. His achievement was to control and contain that anger without denying it. Linguistically, he achieved that by writing the play, in part, first in verse. Dramatically, he accomplished it by using the structured formality of the court hearings, albeit hearings penetrated by the partly hysterical, partly calculated interventions of the accusing girls.

Much of the achievement of *The Crucible* lies in his creation of a language that makes the seventeenth century both distant and close, that enables his characters to discover within the limiting vocabulary and grammar of faith-turned-dogma a means to express their own lives. For British dramatist John Arden, who first encountered the play at a time when his own attempts at historical writing had, in his own words, proved 'embarrassingly bad', it 'showed me how it could be done'. In particular, 'it was not just the monosyllabic Anglo-Saxon strength of the words chosen so much as the rhythms that impregnated the speeches', that and 'the *sounds* of the seventeenth century, not tediously imitated, but . . . imaginatively reconstructed to shake hands with the sounds and speech patterns of the twentieth'.[15] The language of *The Crucible* is not authentic, in the sense of reproducing archaisms or reconstructing a seventeenth-century lexis. It is authentic in that it makes fully believable the words of those who speak out of a different time and place but whose human dilemmas are recognisably our own.

Proctor and his judges were articulate people, even if they were fluent in different languages: he, in that of a common-sense practicality, they in that of a bureaucratic theocracy. He believed what he saw and finally accepted responsibility for his actions. They believed in a shadow world in which visions were substantial and the observable world no more than a delusion, seeing themselves as the agents of an abstract justice and hence freed of personal responsibility. These figures speak to each other across an unbridgeable divide and that gulf is the flaw which fractures their community.

But there is never any sense that those involved in this social and psychological dance of death are rhetoricians, pushing words forward in place of emotions. There may have come a time when the judges ceased defending the faith and began defending themselves, but there is a passion behind their calculation, albeit the passion of those who sacrifice humanity for what they see as an ideal. In that they hardly differ from any other zealot whose hold on the truth depends on a belief that truth must be singular.

These are people, Miller has insisted, who 'regarded themselves as holders of a light. If this light were extinguished, they believed, the world would end.' The effect of this, however, was that if 'you have an ideology which feels itself so pure, it implies an extreme view of the world. Because they are white, opposition is completely black.'

This was the world of Puritan New England but it was also the world of 1950s America and, beyond that, a defining characteristic, perhaps, of the human psyche. 'We have come to a time', he insisted, 'when it seems there must be two sides, and we look back to an ideal state of being, when there was no conflict. Our idea is that conflict can be wiped out of the world. But until man arrives at a point where he realizes that conflict is the essence of life, he will end up knocking himself out.' The crucible is designed to drive out impurities, but impurities are definitional. At the same time a messianic impulse is potentially deadly. What gave a special force to the world of Salem was that he was dealing with people who were very conscious of their ideology, 'special people' who 'could voice the things that were buried deep in them'.[16]

The Crucible is both an intense psychological drama and a play of epic proportions. Its cast is larger than that of almost any of Miller's plays until *The American Clock* (1980) because this is a drama about an entire community betrayed by a Dionysian surrender to the irrational. Some scenes, therefore, people the stage with characters. It is also, however, a play about the redemption of an individual and through the individual of a society. Some scenes, therefore, show the individual confronted by little more than his own conscience. That oscillation between the public and the private is a part of the structural pattern of the play.

It is a play in which language is a weapon but it is also a physical play, never more so than in Richard Eyre's 2002 Broadway production in which actors sweated in the heat of the day and Proctor, the farmer, enters from the fields and throws water on himself. These are people who seize one another in anger, hope, despair as if they could shake the truth free. Imprisonment leaves Proctor scarred and wrecked. The set itself becomes an actor as an attic room becomes a vaulting courtroom reaching up into an indefinite space, wooden beams swinging ominously up and then down again to compress those committed to jail, their options run out. The play ends, in this production, as abstract shapes seemingly fixed to vertical beams cascade down while Proctor goes to his death, the force which held this community together collapses and we hear the sound of a society crack apart.

Miller was not unaware of the danger of offering the public such a play in 1953 and thereby writing himself into the wilderness, politically and personally. Three years later, he knew that his refusal to name names would be to invite charges of being unpatriotic. Indeed, appearing before the House Un-American Activities Committee he was stung into insisting on his patriotism while defending his right to challenge the direction of American policy and thought.

In the end, though, the House Un-American Activities Committee lost all credibility, the Red Scare passed, and if the accusers did not stand in a church, as Anne Putnam did in 1706, and listen as the minister read out her public apology and confession ('as I was the instrument of accusing Goodwife Nurse and her two sisters, I desire to lie in the dust and be humbled for it . . . I desire to . . . earnestly beg forgiveness of all those unto whom I have given just cause of sorrow and offence, whose relations were taken away and accused'),[17] they quickly lost their power and influence.

Today, compilers of programme notes feel as great a need to explain the history of Senator McCarthy and the House Un-American Activities Committee as they do the events of seventeenth-century Salem. In fact, the play's success now owes little to the political and social context in which it was written. It stands, instead, as a study of the debilitating nature of guilt, the seductions of power, the flawed nature of the individual and of the society to which the individual owes allegiance. It stands as a testimony to the ease with which we betray those very values essential to our survival but also to the courage with which some men and women can challenge what seems to be a ruling orthodoxy.

In Salem, Massachusetts, there was to be a single text, a single language, a single reality. Authority invoked demons from whose grasp it offered to liberate its citizens if they would only surrender their consciences to others and acquiesce in the silencing of those who appeared to threaten order. But The Crucible is full of other texts. At great danger to themselves men and women put their names to depositions, signed testimonials, wrote appeals. There was, it appeared, another language, less absolute, more compassionate. There were those who proposed a reality which differed from that offered to them by the state nor would these signatories deny themselves by denying their fellow citizens. There have been many more such since the 1690s, many more, too, since the 1950s, who have done no less. But The Crucible is not to be taken as merely a celebration of the resister, of the individual who refuses incorporation, for John Proctor had denied himself and others long before Tituba and a group of young girls ventured into the forest which fringed the village of Salem.

Like so many of Miller's other plays it is a study of a man who wishes, above all, to believe that he has invested his life with meaning, but cannot do so if he betrays himself through betraying others. It is the study of a society which believes in its unique virtues and seeks to sustain that dream of perfection by denying all possibility of its imperfection. Evil can only be external, for theirs is a City on a Hill. John Proctor's flaw is his failure, until the last moment, to distinguish guilt from responsibility. America's flaw is to believe that it is at the same time both guilty and without flaw.

In 1991, at Salem, Arthur Miller unveiled the winning design for a monument to those who had died. It was dedicated the following year by the Nobel laureate Elie Wiesel, thus forging a connection, no matter how fragile or disproportionate, between those who died in Salem in 1692 and those in Europe, in the 1940s, who had been victims of irrationality solemnised as rational process. Speaking of the dead of Salem, Miller said that he had written of them out of 'a strong desire to raise them out of historic dust'.[18] Wiesel had done likewise for the Jews of the camps.

Three hundred years had passed. The final act, it seemed, had been concluded. However, not only do witches still die, in more than one country in the world, but groundless accusations are still granted credence, hysteria still claims its victims, persecution still masquerades as virtue and prejudice as piety. Nor has the need to resist coercive myths, or to assert moral truths, passed with such a final act of absolution. The witchfinder is ever vigilant and who would not rather direct his attention to others than stand, in the heat of the day, and challenge his authority?

Writing more than forty-five years after *The Crucible*, Miller explained that part of the attraction of the play for him lay in the chance it offered for him to write in a new language, 'one that would require new muscles'.[19] One of the interests in reading the notebooks he kept at the time he was writing the play, indeed, is to see him tensing those muscles, not only choosing the story he wishes to tell, forging the historical record into a dramatic shape, but exploring a language that can simultaneously convey the linguistic rhythms of the age and the heightened prose of a work accommodating itself to a tragic sensibility.

He was responding to a phenomenon which, in the seventeenth century and the contemporary world alike, was not only 'paralyzing a whole generation' but was 'drying up the habits of trust and toleration in public discourse'.[20] Language, indeed, was in part the battleground. God and the Devil, capitalism and communism, constituted the ideological site for a conflict in essence about power but also, therefore, about which legitimising language would prevail. Within America, it was not a true debate since in neither time frame were there any who spoke out either for evil or a diabolic communism. Victory was to be declared over those whose cunning made them foreswear themselves or invoke ambiguity at a time of absolutes. Yet those who exercised power felt insecure in their possession of it.

The victory of righteousness in seventeenth-century Massachusetts seemed threatened by internal and external powers while, in the twentieth century, the Soviet possession of nuclear weapons and the 'loss' of China to communism made the United States seem physically vulnerable and ideologically insecure. To be an un-American was to move outside a set of presumptions about national values and also outside of a language. Suddenly, the issue was loyalty. In whose book had you signed your name, God's or the Devil's? And the signing of names became an iconic gesture, again in both periods. If *The Crucible* is full of petitions, warrants, confessions, then before the House Un-American Activities Committee individuals were confronted with their signatures on petitions, Party membership forms, published articles, invoked now as evidence of collusive and public subversion. Miller himself, during his own appearance before the Committee, was repeatedly asked to confirm his signature, the listing of his name on declarations, statements, calls for social justice.

Nor was this only a product of the right. Miller has spoken of the linguistic contortions exercised by left-wing critics desperate to follow a shifting Party line and consequently exchanging one language for another as a work was hailed as progressive one week only to be condemned as reactionary the next, or vice versa. Language was unstable. It was no longer a precise agent of communication, fully transitive. It was a weapon, blunt, coercive, and frequently opaque. It was like a spell, pronounced over those who appeared the source of threat. Open discourse gave way to slogans, jargon, a pseudo-scientific mock precision.

His sense of being trapped in an Escher drawing perfectly reflected the paradox of a Puritan state or modern American society in which confession of guilt resulted in absolution while declarations of innocence were seen as the ultimate proof of guilt. His sense of inhabiting an art form, a metaphor, a system of signs whose meanings were the province of a select priesthood, simultaneously left him with a profound sense of unreality and a determination to capture that feeling in an art of his own, equally arbitrary but a means of laying bare the mechanisms of unreality.

Informing was presented as a duty in the 1950s, professors on students, students on professors, as neighbour was encouraged to inform on neighbour in seventeenth-century Salem. What both societies felt in the face of such sanctioned betrayal was a form of impotence. It was a world in which 'the outrageous had so suddenly become the norm'. And impotence, or, more precisely, paralysis, became a familiar Miller trope as he witnessed and dramatised individuals and societies seemingly in thrall to the idea of their own powerlessness. Proctor stays his hand when he should have intervened but learns that there is no separate peace. The price of living is involvement. His sense of guilt with respect to Abigail momentarily freezes his will to act, as guilt clouds the mind of a number of Miller's other protagonists. The problem, as he saw it, was that 'we had grown detached from any hard reality I knew about. It had become a world of symbols, gestures, loaded symbolic words, and of rites and of rituals.' What was at stake was ideas, by their nature invisible, and a supposed conspiracy aimed at the overthrow of established powers. His problem, as he saw it, was how to 'deal with this mirage world'.[21]

At issue, after all, was not simply a vision of the moral world but a definition of reality in a culture in which those in power sanctioned belief in spirits, embraced a paranoid version of social behaviour. The real was what such people held it to be. In one sense, then, the fictions of art were to be pitched against those of the state as, in another sense, history was to be invoked to redress the balance, though a history seen not from the perspective of those who presumed themselves its primary agencies.

For Miller, one of the curiosities of the Committee hearings was that few if any of the accused chose to stand their ground and defend their supposed faith, instead deploying legalities and appeals to constitutional guarantees. There was, in other words, an absence at the heart of the whole affair. The irony in Salem, in 1692, centred on another absence, that of the witches whom an investigating body sought and was obliged to identify in order to justify its own actions. Indeed, with every new victim it became necessary for its members to announce their belief with ever greater assurance or confront not only responsibility for injustice but a vision of the world that would leave them adrift, with no moral structure to embrace save one which would leave them profoundly culpable.

In the end, he said, the more he worked on *The Crucible* the less concerned he became with analogy, despite the cogency of such: 'More than a political metaphor, more than a moral tale, *The Crucible*, as it developed for me over the period of more than a year, became the awesome evidence of the power of the human imagination inflamed, the poetry of suggestion, and finally the tragedy of heroic resistance to a society possessed to the point of ruin.'[22] The choice of words is instructive. It is as if he saw in the events that took place in Salem the elaboration of a human drama that seemed already to have shaped itself into theatre because it drew on the same resources. The witch trials were produced, performed, staged because it is the essence of life seen under pressure to take on the appearance and substance of art. How else to engage it, then, except through the homeopathic agency of the theatre?

What drew him finally, though, as he researched his drama, was less the parallel between the investigation of supposed conspiracies than the rituals developed, rituals by which confession was seen as validating accusation, betrayal was seen as the route to redemption while proof lay in reiterated suspicion rather than in anything so banal as concrete and testable fact. The accusation was that the witches, the communists, the fellow-travellers, had chosen to inhabit another narrative, to perform roles in an alternative drama.

The existence of godless communists necessitated and justified the existence of those who identified, exposed and punished them. So, too, in Puritan

New England, with a neat piece of inverted logic, the existence of investigators implied the existence of those they were appointed to investigate.

It is not that Miller himself was free of illusion, or that self-righteous vigour that comes with certainty no matter how shallow the soil in which it sinks its roots. Perhaps something of the force of *The Crucible*, indeed, comes less from the cant of his own subsequent accusers – not, in truth, like many of those who set themselves to track down modern witches, genuine ideologues – than from his own youthful dedication to the fantasies of a Marxism that required no evidence, no reliable witnesses, to validate its assumptions.

His own rejection of those who failed to endorse the orthodoxies of his new faith was no less peremptory, surely, than that of those Puritan judges who believed they saw evidence of unbelief or association with the forces of darkness. In retrospect, his own commitment to Soviet ideals which turned out to be no more than cover for rapacity and ambition could not have seemed so remote from the delusions embraced with such evident enthusiasm by Puritans and fifties conservatives alike.

At stake, he realised, was a language, so easily accommodated to the purposes of power, whether in seventeenth-century Salem or 1950s Washington. In both periods people were ensnared with words, forced to present themselves and interpret their actions in terms of an idiolect precisely designed to create a new ontological matrix. McCarthy's America found itself not only at the interface of two ideologies, with their supporting linguistic systems, but at a moment in American history when New Deal politics, and the utopianism of thirties and wartime America, shattered on the ambition of those who rode a new conservatism, as it did on the paranoia they fostered.

It was the very insecurity of authority that made it implacable, as though it could stabilise a disturbingly fluid world by fiat. Language was policed, inspected for its hidden subversion, revealing nuances. The word 'socialist', Miller recalls, was less a word describing a particular ideology than a marker for the foreign and the menacing.

To speak of 'right' or 'justice', to lay claim to freedom of speech or assembly was to identify yourself as a non-player in the American game, a dissenter from that aggressive conformity that passed for patriotism. Why, after all, would you need to lay claim to American freedoms if you were not using them to conceal subversion? What was needed was confession and there was, as Miller has suggested, a religious tone to the period. Confession was required; absolution was available. The thing was to be in a state of grace. Sinners who repented were welcomed to the fold, especially if, as in seventeenth-century Salem, they traded in a few fellow sinners. In both cases, confession plus informing was the formula for personal security. By the same token, the sanction of excommunication was available, excommunication from the true church that is America. No wonder Miller felt convinced of the authenticity of the parallel between fifties America and the Salem of 1692.

There was, and seemingly not incidentally, the same distrust of intellectuals in both periods. One of the Salem accusers – like so many of them, young girls – denounced an older woman because she was seen to read books. Giles Corey directed a similar accusation at his wife, with fatal results. Only the Bible and the authorised texts of witch-finders are legitimate. McCarthy, himself scarcely an intellectual, made a point of going after and humiliating Ivy Leaguers, New Dealers, writers and teachers. Books were, indeed, banned. A deputation visited American embassies around the world, weeding out subversive publications, including Miller's, while American intelligence agencies were doing their best to infiltrate and influence the cultural and intellectual lives of their allies, secretly funding foundations, student organisations and publications.

In the end, *The Crucible* is perhaps about the tendency – never fully resisted – to condemn difference. We are, after all, constantly reminded – from Salem to the former Yugoslavia – that neighbour can swiftly turn informer, betrayer, accuser and even assassin. When the Stasi files were opened in Germany, after the fall of the Berlin Wall, husbands were found to have informed on wives and vice versa. In the pages that fluttered down from the looted building were the devastating truths of lifelong betrayals. The same was true in Rumania. In 1690s Salem, Sarah Good was doomed when her three-year-old daughter claimed that her mother had three familiars – 'three birds, one black, one yellow, and that these birds hurt the children and afflicted persons' – while her husband confessed that he thought her a witch.[23]

It is as much that mystery as any that Miller's play explores. As he explained, writing in 1999,

> Salem village, that pious devout settlement at the very edge of white civi-lization, had taught me – three centuries before the Russo-American rivalry and the issues that it raised – that a kind of built-in pestilence was nestled in the human mind, a fatality forever awaiting the right conditions for its always unique, forever unprecedented outbreak of alarm, suspicion and murder. And to people wherever the play is performed on any of the five continents, there is always a certain amazement that the same terror that had happened to them had happened before to others. [24]

He has observed that there are times when he wishes he had chosen to write an absurd comedy rather than *The Crucible*, this being closer to his sense of a world in which rational principles were in abeyance. Indeed, he recalls the fate of two young men from Boston who were arrested when they responded to one of the more egregious idiocies of the Salem trial by laughing. These two figures, indeed, appear in an early draft of the film script in a scene subsequently deleted.

In the notebooks Miller tried out a number of possible titles for his play: *The Devil's Handyman*, *The Spectral Experience*, *That Invisible World*, *The Easiest Room in Hell*, *Delusion*. He even copyrighted an earlier version under the title

Those Familiar Spirits, which has unfortunate overtones of Noel Coward. In the end, however, *The Crucible* had the advantage of applying to all the characters, not excluding John Proctor, and the society itself. For this is a play about a testing time, about a moment, repeated throughout history, in which the true metal of individuals, and the society they have collaborated in creating, is finally exposed.

That few people seemed to know what a crucible might be was less important when the play opened than the cold alarm he felt move through the audience as they began to sense that they were becoming confederate with an attack on the ruling political orthodoxy. A securely remote historical work had transmuted in front of their eyes and confronted them with the passions of their own times. Half a century later, *The Crucible* still has the power to disturb. It may have been generated by a particular alignment of circumstances, but the dilemma at its heart, its concern with betrayal, self-interest, power, a coercive language, personal and public responsibility, abusive authority, injustice, corrosive myths, remains of central significance, as does its awareness of the individual's struggle to locate and define him or herself in the face of forces that seem to leave so little space for a moral being.

In 1703 the General Court of Massachusetts ruled spectral evidence inadmissible. In 1704 the Reverend Michael Wigglesworth wrote to Increase Mather suggesting that the failure to atone for the killing of the innocent meant that it was necessary for those who had been 'actors' in that calamity to acknowledge their guilt. The word was a telling one. For all Puritan hostility to theatre, few were as aware of life as drama. Miller, then, was not the first to recognise the nature of the inner procedures and central trope of that time. In his study of the witch-hunts, Charles Upham, in 1867, remarked of the young girls who brought so many to their deaths that they were better actors than were to be seen in the theatre and clearly there was a drama played out in Salem that was liable to fire the imagination of a playwright.

When, in 1706, Ann Putnam, still living in Salem Village, and now fourteen years older than the young girl who had named twenty-six people as witches, stood as the Reverend Green read her confession, it was less than a fulsome apology. She was, she insists, 'deluded by Satan'. Senator Joseph McCarthy, however, made no such an apology. He, after all, was deluded by nobody and nothing but his own inadequacies and ambition, a self-authenticated witch-hunter in search of significance. For Arthur Miller, such responsibility lay at the heart of *The Crucible*. John Proctor found himself at the intersecting point of private and public meaning. His decision, in fact and fiction, to confront those who offered him life at the price of capitulation played its role in ending the witch-hunt of 1692, as it simultaneously demonstrated the ability of the individual to challenge power and the language with which it seeks to legitimate itself.

In October 1710, the General Court finally agreed to reverse the convictions and attainders of a number of those who had suffered. Among these was John Proctor, now eighteen years dead. John Hale, meanwhile, stricken with guilt at having collaborated with the general frenzy, declared that the disaster had been a product of 'the darkness of that day' when 'we walked in the clouds, and could not see our way'.[25] The darkness, he implied, had now lifted. The evidence for that, however, as the centuries have passed and other witch-hunts, other acts of betrayal, have been committed, has been far from conclusive. The innocent are still destroyed by those who seek their own immunity or self-interest, by those so certain of their own convictions that they make others the proof of their righteousness, evidence of a faith that requires sacrifices to legitimate its central tenets. How else can you be sure that you live in the City on the Hill unless you can look down on those who thus confirm your own elevation?

In writing *The Crucible*, Miller saw himself as resisting what seemed to him to be a reductive tendency in modern playwriting and modern thought. As he remarked, 'Today's writers describe man's helplessness and eventual defeat.' In Salem, he conceded, 'you have the story of a defeat because these people were destroyed, and this makes it real to us today because we believe in defeat'. However, he insisted, these were people who 'understood at the same time what was happening to them. They knew why they struggled . . . they did not die helplessly.'[26] It was, he said, 'the moral size of these people' that drew him. They did not 'whimper'. In terms reminiscent of William Faulkner's Nobel Prize address, he insisted that 'we should be tired by now of merely documenting the defeat of man. This play', he asserted, 'is a step toward an assertion of a positive kind of value in contemporary plays.'[27]

Somewhat surprisingly, he chose to suggest that since 1920 American drama had been 'a steady, year-by-year documentation of the frustration of man', asserting that 'I do not believe in this . . . this is not our fate.' He was thinking, perhaps, of O'Neill but also of those writers who had chosen to document the oppressive details of social life. 'It is not enough', he insisted, 'to tell what is happening; the newspapers do that.'[28] Even so, his observation that 'in our drama the man with convictions has in the past been a figure of comic fun' seems curiously at odds with a decade of committed drama in which the man with convictions had been the central protagonist of plays which presumed the immediate possibility of transforming society. Meanwhile, his assertion that 'he fits in our drama more now' and that he was 'trying to find a way, a form, a method of depicting people who do think' was a statement of intent which, beyond *The Crucible*, would not find its fulfilment until *After the Fall*.

Miller has always had an aversion to films. For him, they are incorrigibly trivial, favouring action over ideas and language. The role of the writer in the cinema is that of a hired man who does not own the product of his labour and who is subordinate to those who wield the real power: producer, director, actor. It is a world in which spectacle can replace thought, a world of Dolby Surround Sound, hugely magnified images, a made object, unyielding, unchanging. The theatre, by contrast, deals in danger and vulnerability. Actor confronts audience, words become a primary means of communication. The adaptation of play to film seemed to him necessarily a reductive process, one which rarely benefits either medium.

With *The Crucible*, however, he was forced to revise a number of these assumptions. Suddenly, it became possible to constitute the community of Salem more directly. He recalled his research, four decades earlier, in which the testimonies of those involved had 'created a marvellously varied tapestry of that seventeenth-century America still in the earliest stages of defining itself', and found that 'once I had begun thinking about it as a film it became obvious that I had in fact always seen it as a flow of images which had had to be evoked through language for the stage'.[29]

What was previously reported could now be shown, from the sexually charged scene in the forest, as repressions are momentarily abandoned, the disciplined code of the community secretly rejected, to the physical location of that community, clinging to the edge of the continent and slowly subordinating the land to human will in the service of divine intent. Suddenly the wild anarchy of the meeting house, breaking through the carapace of rational process, could be presented in its disturbing reality, as itself a product of a deepening hysteria rooted in private no less than public anxieties and fears.

The fact remained, however, that *The Crucible* was made from language, that much of the notebook he kept when writing it is concerned with capturing a tone, with creating what he has called 'a kind of sculpted language',[30] generating precise rhythms. These, to some degree, would have to take second place to images if it was not to become 'a static photographed play', which was all too often the fate of adapted works.

The script, he has explained, was rejected by at least a dozen directors before it fell into the hands of Nicholas Hytner, whose background at the Royal Shakespeare Company gave him a sympathy both for Miller's dedication to language and the challenge of creating a film based, as he understood, on that 'insistence on the inseparable link between communal chaos and personal trauma'[31] which lies at the heart of *The Crucible* and, indeed, most of Miller's work. Hytner felt, he has explained, 'the ancient stirrings of pity and terror'[32] as he read the screenplay, itself an indication that the director of Shakespearean tragedy registered Miller's intention in a work that had originally been crafted as a modern tragedy. Hytner's account of his approach to the making of *The Crucible* is, in fact, and unsurprisingly, a highly intelligent analysis of the play as well as of the screenplay that emerged in the course of filming.

For him, the essence of theatre is that, in film terms, it 'operates in permanent medium shot', while a film can 'contain a whole society and move in close enough to see into a girl's heart'. In truth, so can a play which, after all, its conventions once accepted, can have a fluidity and shifting perspective capable of matching that of a film. For Hytner, however, the energy that comes from cutting between shots, 'so that the violence of the mob becomes both the consequence and the source of pain and confusion behind the eyes of the girl in the close-up',[33] is different in kind from that produced in the theatre. The cascade of images, each one causally plausible, becomes a correlative for that seemingly unstoppable momentum created out of 'individual betrayals' and 'collective panic'. Certainly one of the achievements of the film version lies in this pulsing between private and public, cause and effect.

What it was not was a work that required the historical context of the 1950s to appreciate. The parallels were closer to hand and Hytner, and those involved, felt their pressure as they prepared to shoot the film: 'it spoke directly about the bigotry of religious fundamentalists across the globe, about communities torn apart by accusations of child abuse, about the rigid intellectual orthodoxies of college campuses'.[34] Nonetheless, as Hytner recognised, its power as paradigm depended on the very specificity of location, the details of a life simultaneously lived symbolically, and with a tangible facticity.

He was also concerned to capture another aspect of the play and, incidentally, one of Miller's own thematic concerns throughout his career. Salem was a utopia whose own utopian presumptions opened the way for corruption. In Hytner's words, 'The light gives birth to the dark.'[35] This, after all, was to be a new Eden and it became necessary to patrol its boundaries to prevent evil entering and to extirpate it should it appear. Violence, in other words, was imminent, a kinetic force ready to discharge itself in action. The location of his Salem, then, with the sea to one side and the forest to another, was to create a kind of *cordon sanitaire*. In both directions lay risks: the religious corruptions they had fled in Europe and the antinomian world of the frontier. That double threat left the community and the human heart open for the Devil's work. Hytner, accordingly, chose an idyllic setting, a paradise on the edge of the ocean whose equivocal location, whose tenuous hold on the continent, was in part an explanation for the hysteria which could fan from a spark to a fire.

In fact, as Hytner acknowledges, Salem is more than a mile inland, a harbour town, but for his purposes he wanted the sea in vision, as a reminder of their exposed location, of the world from which they had fled. In particular, he wanted to play the final scene here, on the edge of a continent, to dramatise the fact that the fate of a continent, as well as that of a single man, was at stake. In this he had Miller's support, as he did in his requests for amendments to the script that would adjust to new possibilities and new visual ideas, though much of the original dialogue remained. Interestingly, every one of the scenes quoted earlier from the original screenplay was excised as part of this process.

The first two acts, as Hytner has explained, were substantially revised. The camera was able to move swiftly around the community with news of

Betty's sickness, not merely thereby establishing the extent of the town and its interconnecting relationships, but recreating the process whereby stories, rumours, insinuations, accusations were to move around the same social space, gathering momentum as they went, heightening tension, creating an emotional vortex. This swirl of movement, meanwhile, was to be played against the static, withdrawn, contained world of John Proctor whose 'passivity is matched by the camera's'.[36]

This is that paralysis that lies at the heart of *The Golden Years* and *Broken Glass*, a failure of will that is ultimately a failure of morality and individual responsibility. Through guilt, Proctor hesitates to involve himself and thereby becomes culpable. Not to act, therefore, is to become guilty. Not to speak is to become complicit, which is perhaps why *The Crucible* exists, why Miller did not withdraw from so public a confrontation with powers whose authority was growing daily.

For Hytner, the camera was to be an agent, an active player, static when observing moral stasis, swooping down as an embodiment of imagined evils, racing through the town as time accelerates and emotions run ahead of thought. It observes and participates in the sensuality of the opening sequence. This is no longer a report of the young girls' dancing in the forest but their actual and hesitant performance, their shedding of inhibitions and, indeed, clothes, their playful abandonment of repressions which anticipates the more lethal aban-donment of repressions that follows and which makes the girls offer evidence of supposed depravities that will lead to the execution of their elders. Miller had, in fact, anticipated such a scene in his early notebook in which, in free-verse form, he has Abigail seek a genuine potion to render Proctor into her hands:

> O Tituba. I can't wait.
> I am of age, my blood, my blood.
> My blood is thrashing in my hips,
> My skin revels at every breeze
> I never sleep but dreams come itching
> Up my back like little cats
> With silky tails! You promised
> When I came of age you'd work a charm
> No man can break outside my love
>
> Then let's pretend; let's believe
> I do, but that he never touches me
> Like some I've heard don't touch a wife
> But once a year. My husband's there,
> Tituba, inside that tree. Now what
> Shall I do to bring him out?
> What shall I do to turn his face to me?

Miller's original film script had begun with a collage of shots, including fishermen returning with their catch, a blacksmith shoeing a horse, two men sawing a log, a house being raised, its beams tennoned and pegged, a man squaring a log with an axe, the normality, in other words, to be disturbed by the events that will follow. This segues into a further series of shots which introduce some of the principal characters, from the Putnams to Martha and Giles Corey to the Proctors. These scenes were to have their parallel at the end of the film as we see the fields in a state of decay and revisit fishermen, blacksmith and sawyer in order to register the general collapse of social order provoked by the witch-hunters. Looters are at large. This framing was abandoned in favour of entering the film through the young girls who leave their houses for the rendezvous in the forest which will provoke what follows, and leaving it through the climactic death of John Proctor.

The film ends with the intoning of the Lord's Prayer by one of those about to be hanged, a supposedly impossible feat for witches. In fact, when the historical John Proctor was killed, Sheriff Corwin hurried to his home and, in a reminder of the suspect motives of the witch-finders, illegally seized his property:

> The sheriff come to his house and seized all the goods, provisions, and cattle that he could come at, and sold some of the cattle at half price, and killed others, and put them up for the West Indies; threw out the beer out of a barrel, and carried away the barrel; emptied a pot of broth, and took away the pot, and left nothing in the house for the support of the children.[37]

It was one last cruel action, one last evidence of tainted motives, of the fact that a campaign to defend the good requires its defining victims.

John Proctor was not the only one to lose his life and his property, but in Miller's hands he became the crucial figure. It was, after all, as he had reminded himself in his notebook that it should be, 'basically Proctor's story.' There is, indeed, a causal link between his affair with Abigail and the death of his neighbours. Her revels in the forest were her attempt to lure him back into a relationship to which he had once committed himself. His sense of guilt does stay his hand when he might have intervened. In an early version of the film script, as Abigail visits Proctor in his prison cell to urge him to escape with her, and the Rev Hale tries to salve his own conscience by convincing him to confess to untruth, Miller indicates that 'PROCTOR looks into HALE's eyes and understands his guilt. Now he looks to this 'whore', who bears the same message as the Minister. The guilt is now upon all of them, and it creates a kind of communion for this moment.' 'A strange matter, isn't it' he says, 'that you . . . and she . . . and I . . . be all of us guilty?'

For the first time in his career, Miller was happy with the film version of one of his plays. Perhaps, in part, this was because his son Robert was its producer, and anxious to protect his father's work. But it was also because in Hytner he found someone, trained in theatre, with a respect for language but who brought to the production a strong sense of how film could be used to relate the private to the public. It seemed to him that film could add depth to certain aspects of the drama and the camera move through the community whose tragedy this ultimately was. The film also had one other long-lasting effect. It was while it was being shot that Miller's daughter Rebecca met Daniel Day Lewis whom she was to marry. In 1953, though, this lay well over forty years in the future.

— ✳ —

Predictably, *The Crucible* sparked controversy. There were a number of respectful reviews but once again he was attacked by the Non-Communist Left who, like Elia Kazan, rejected what they saw as the false analogy at its heart. There had, they insisted, been no witches but there were communists. Hence there was no parallel. Miller pointed out that to declare witches non-existent, in seventeenth-century Salem, or in much of Christendom, would have been dangerous to say the least. That, indeed, had been part of the evidence adduced against the Proctors in his play. But beyond that it was the procedures practised in both 1692 and the 1950s which interested him, the coercive power of the state, its rallying of a popular support based on fear. Even the 'spectral evidence' accepted by the Puritan Court had its parallel in the vague 'evidence' offered by Senator McCarthy as he held up blank sheets of paper asserting them to contain the names of known communists.

The play, however, which had only a modest run in 1953, has outlived the circumstances of its first production and gone on to be Miller's most produced play, reinterpreted by every generation and in every country to address the particularities of new injustices.

Meanwhile, back in mid-century America, and as if to validate the idea of a hostile state happy to sacrifice the individual in the name of ideology, Miller now found himself stripped of his American passport when invited to attend the Belgian premiere of *The Crucible*. He was to be punished for having once been a supporter of causes and ideas not merely out of fashion but dangerously perverse. He had, indeed, supped with the Devil and now was to pay the price. When he was commissioned to write a film on juvenile delinquency, pressure from the House Un-American Activities Committee, supported by a series of hostile newspaper stories in the *World-Telegram* and the *Journal-American*, led to his firing.

He returned to the theatre in 1955 when he was approached by Martin Ritt, who was then appearing in Clifford Odets's *The Flowering Peach*. He asked Miller whether he had any one-act plays that might be performed by the company on Sunday evenings. Miller had nothing to hand but wrote *A Memory of Two Mondays*. Like Tennessee Williams, he had spent time working for a large company, in Miller's case Chadick-Delamater's auto parts warehouse. Neither was inclined to romanticise his contact with the working man but both went on to write plays which drew on that experience. In Williams's case, *Stairs to the Roof* was a somewhat surreal comedy. In Miller's, *A Memory of Two Mondays* was a largely, though not wholly, realist account of lives which seemed anything but fulfilled. Williams wrote only a few years after his experience as a would-be poet trapped in a prosaic routine. The play itself was an early effort by a playwright yet to make his mark. Miller was looking back twenty years on a world he had escaped but which others had not.

It seemed to Ritt, and the company's producer, Robert Whitehead, that *A Memory of Two Mondays* was too short on its own. Miller was asked to write a curtain-raiser. He picked up an idea he had been tracing out for some time, a play which until then had defeated him. Now, though, he realised that it would work well as a one-act. That curtain-raiser turned out to be *A View from the Bridge*.

He had first heard the story while working at the Brooklyn Navy Yard and had tried to work it out both as a story and a play but they had come to nothing. Something of the atmosphere of the docks had gone into *The Hook* but that, too, had proved abortive. Now asked for a one-act play he realised that the shorter form solved a number of the problems he had been having and wrote it quickly.

Meanwhile, the Odets play had come to an end before they could mount the productions so that when the double bill opened it was no longer as a Sunday evening attraction but a full production at a Broadway theatre.

✳

11

'A Memory of Two Mondays'

A Memory of Two Mondays, dismissed by one critic as 'uninterruptedly bad' and another as a 'pedestrian chronicle', is a play which Miller insisted was written with much affection. The result was neither pedestrian nor warm-hearted. Most of the characters are stunned into spiritual immobility, passing the time as the seasons change. Set in what is plainly the Chadick-Delamater warehouse on Sixty-third Street and Tenth Avenue where he had worked, and where Lincoln Center would one day be built, it presents a collective portrait of those he had known as he waited out time before going to the University of Michigan. In effect, his life had been on hold. The difference was that he would be moving on. This was a means to an end. For those whose lives he observed it seems to have become both means and end.

Those who work in the warehouse plainly have private lives but we see nothing of them, only receive reports, mostly hinting at private pain, an existence which generates little beyond despair and frustrated dreams. These are hidden behind stories of drunken evenings and nights on the town which leave little beyond the taste of irony. These lives seem to have no more content than the dull routines of a workaday life which simulate the cohesiveness of community.

A Memory of Two Mondays may have started out to capture the lives of ordinary people but at its heart is a sense of dismay at those he would once have been inclined to celebrate as the source of political energy. Instead the prevailing mood is one of entropy. Marriages are in disrepair; alcohol substitutes for something lost along the way. Death is in the wings.

Their days begin and end with subway rides, as they travel not so much in hope or expectation as resignation. They share a fate and very little else. They are capable of unity, if only to resist the power of their employer, but that solidarity is momentary. When Bert (an echo of Miller's diminutive, 'Art') leaves at the end of the play they hardly notice, as they had hardly noticed when Miller himself had left. Years later, on a whim, Miller himself returned to be met by a blank face. There was no friendly greeting. He had hardly scratched the surface of their lives.

The play, as the title suggests, takes place over two days, separated by time and by the seasons. In the first it is summer; in the second winter, a progression which contains a more fundamental regression. The workers duly arrive for work, bringing with them fragmentary stories of a life outside. They are, though, desperate people even if, for the most part, they seem unaware of the depths of their desperation or, if aware, unable to address it. The play is a mural, each character sketched lightly, characterised by particular traits. This is a pointillist piece, a memory play in which individual moments are assembled to form a picture.

Those working here include a drunk, a man with a deaf wife, a womaniser, along with young women looking forward to dates or discussing clothes. An Irishman, Kenneth, has a sense of poetry about him but this slides towards prose as the play proceeds. They do, indeed, change in the course of the play but collectively merely shuffle the possibilities, a drunk becoming sober, and a sober man drunk.

This is Miller's version of *The Iceman Cometh*, as his characters settle for fantasies or deaden themselves to the circularities of their lives. There is no sense here, as there would be in David Mamet's *Glengarry, Glen Ross*, of an unforgiving capitalist system setting them against one another. They are simply waiting out their lives. What they do in this place has no meaning. They are not, like Mamet's characters, animated by the stories they tell, redeemed by performance, nor, like O'Neill's, numbed into unconsciousness. They are, however, adrift in time. One Monday is much like another. We are closer here, indeed, to the Beckett of *Waiting for Godot*.

The play begins with what seems like a parody of a naturalistic play as an extensive stage direction describes in some detail what we do not see: 'The front of the loft where we cannot see, filled with office machinery, records, the telephone switchboard, and the counter where customers may come who do not order by letter or phone.' This seems to be David Belasco, lovingly creating a detailed reality against which to locate people who gain reality from their setting. But in fact absence is a ruling principle in the play. Something has been evacuated from lives whose rhythms derive from the metronome of mere routine.

In fact this is not a naturalistic play. There are moments when prose gives way to free verse. The seasons change with a wave of the hand. Bert, whose memories these are, stands back from time to time and becomes a commentator, an observer, delivering verse monologues from a time never defined.

The play, we are told, in the opening stage direction, is seen 'with two separate visions'. The warehouse is dirty and unmanageably chaotic' but it is also 'romantic'. It is a workplace but also a retreat. It is located precisely. Internal references make it plain that this is the year Miller went to work at Chadick-Delamater. We are deep in the Depression. One of the characters buys a pair of second-hand shoes for a quarter from a man in the park. They stay in these jobs in part because they desperately hope they are secure at a time when others have nothing. But this is not offered as a period piece. Time means nothing here, except that its depredations are visible.

On the one hand are young women – one described as 'blankly pretty' – on the other are one man of sixty-eight and another in his mid-seventies who is 'troubled'. Age seems to have brought nothing but a sharper sense of betrayal, not so much by the system as by fate. Speaking later, Miller would confess that something of the mood of the play was generated by a time when indeed people seemed to have little control over their lives. The Depression had come from nowhere, with no one clear as to its origins or its solution. A job won one day could be lost the next. Reaching back, it is that mood he captures. Bert confesses that he cannot understand why he escapes and the others do not, almost as if Miller were still worrying at the dilemma highlighted in *The Man Who Had All the Luck*.

The dust of the warehouse, filming everything in grey, suggests something of those who work in it, as the accretions of time dull the outline of their hopes and ambitions. The extent of those ambitions is a five-dollar rise, or a car they can ill-afford and which offers them no more satisfaction than the relationships they contract. Across the street, once the grime has been removed from the windows, is a whorehouse, an echo of the warehouse in which they have traded desire for hard cash.

At the same time, he bleeds out of the play the bitterness that might have formed part of it. Miller had been the only Jew ever to be employed by the company and was made aware of his difference by those he found himself among, especially the manager. There is none of that here. It is a play of some pity and a certain bafflement. He escaped. They did not. That he returns there in memory, however, suggests that he did not himself entirely escape. He still feels it necessary to track back through the years to understand the lesson he was offered, even if it is not quite the lesson he assumed at the time, as he turned his back on those others who saw no stars projected from the rooftops and settled for what they could grasp rather than what they could reach.

As the title suggests, this is a memory play. It is what its protagonist chooses to recall as it is what Miller himself makes, twenty years on, of those years of labour that would win his way to university and take him away from family obligations. This is no *Lower Depths*, no glimpse into an underclass. In the play, if not in life, these characters stand centre-stage.

Is there an element of condescension? Perhaps. His role as author, his protagonist's as narrator–observer, suggests not merely a sense of distance but also an element of judgement. In granting a retrospective order to lives which seemingly lack one, beyond the specious pattern gifted by habit, he simultaneously grants and rescinds meaning. For the most part they seem not to be fully conscious of the lives they live. Disappointments, betrayals and occasional celebrations (always, seemingly, tinged with a certain desperation), pile up without shaping themselves into anything as definite as purpose or direction. They are waiting out their existence. For some, the end is distant; for others it is close. It makes little difference. The protagonist alone, it seems, will walk away, lay claim to a freedom which is neither imagined nor embraced by those who journey to and fro each day but never really arrive, having no destination beyond this place which stores automobile parts, many from vehicles no longer manufactured, piled in dusty boxes against a resurrection which seldom comes.

A Memory of Two Mondays is a particular favourite of Miller's. Perhaps this is because it reaches back in his life to a moment when he was poised to move forward, to set his feet on the path that would lead a young man, who read Dostoevsky on the subway train to work, towards ultimate success as a writer. But I suspect there is another reason, to do with the deceptive simplicity of a play which creates a collective portrait of a group of people waiting out time in a society itself in a state of suspended animation. He is not nostalgic either for those on whom he based his portraits or for that moment. He was always in transit, passing through and on. Yet there is a respect for these people living uninspected lives of quiet desperation, as there is a pride in finding a form and a language to invest those lives with a significance in the theatre which he suggests they lacked in a world whose reality had seemed so oppressive.

Could he have written this play twenty years earlier when, like Williams's *Stairs to the Roof*, it would have been rooted in more recent experience? Perhaps. Certainly the style of the piece suggests that he was trying to write in a mode which in part reflected the period, even as it recalled his fascination, then and later, with suffusing realism with a sense of the poetic. The passage of time, however, has lent it something more than an impression of distance and detachment. The irony of the stasis which typifies his characters is deepened precisely by knowledge that there was another who was not so infected. It is a character study but it is also a coda to a time when mere survival had seemed a virtue.

12

'A View from the Bridge'

A View from the Bridge concerns a longshoreman living in an Italian community in Red Hook, an area adjoining Brooklyn Heights, Miller's home for many years. It was a world he knew. Eddie's is, as Miller has said, a dangerous occupation and it has bred a certain masculine bravado. Passion is a language, a way of life. It is what has consolidated this community and what has the power to break it apart. The longshoremen's union has been infiltrated by organised crime, which effectively controls hiring and firing and protects illegal immigrants, of whom there are many, taking a percentage of their wages. In other words, this is not a world in which the law prevails. It is a community governed by codes and one in which one's masculinity is an essential component of one's work. It is these codes, and this masculinity, that provide the axes against which Eddie plots his life.

Conventionally religious, with no ambition to do more than get by from day to day and be respected by his family and workmates, Eddie agrees to provide refuge for his wife's two cousins, Marco and Rudolpho, illegal immigrants from Italy. Having, in his own eyes, succeeded in realising the American dream himself, he understands what drives them and takes pride in allowing them in his home. When we enter the play, however, there is already a tension that as yet owes nothing to the strangers who are about to disturb his apparent equanimity.

His niece, Catherine, for whom he had assumed responsibility on the death of his wife's sister, is on the verge of womanhood, already anxious to enter a new life. His wife, Beatrice, seems disturbed by his reluctance to let her go. The dilemma is a familiar one but there is an undercurrent that quickly forces its way to the surface as the audience begins to see that Eddie's affections are not purely avuncular, though he himself is unable or unwilling to see his feelings as anything more than familial love.

The arrival of an attractive young foreigner, therefore, particularly one charged with added glamour because of the secrecy that necessarily surrounds him, raises the temperature. With a potential, if unacknowledged, rival in the house, Eddie is confronted with a dilemma he can barely acknowledge, let alone resolve. At stake is his sense of himself, no less than the fate of a young woman whose innocence he would preserve, if only as a means of preserving his own. Whether literal or not, it is the fierce undertow of incest that forges a link with tragedy, the sign, as it is, of an ultimate disorder, as moral and spiritual anarchy press the individual beyond the boundaries of the tribe.

Eddie Carbone is a victim, but he is not crushed by modernity, by a social system at odds with his needs. His is not a fragile sensibility, inadequate to survive in a world governed by money and pursuing a dream of becoming. He is not someone committed to moving on, lighting out for the territory ahead of the rest, one step ahead of a civilisation that declares his irrelevance. Nor is his an argument with America. He is a victim of a desire which simultaneously exalts him precisely because it is implacable, because it is pursued with total recklessness, because it takes him outside the moral universe where he stands, Lear-like, abandoned. Unlike Lear, though, whose conception of love is also faulty, he never comes to see with his blind eyes because to see would be to annihilate that sense of his own integrity without which existence itself would be drained of meaning.

Eddie is an expression of those impulses usually and necessarily repressed in the name of an ordered social life. Yet even he is constrained. Feeling never makes its way into action in terms of the relationship that has become so central to him. In his own mind he is never more than a protective father-figure, willing to lay down his life to protect innocence – his own and therefore his niece's. But, in her case, such innocence is unnatural, encysting her in a protective membrane. In a sense his abstention from sexual relations with his wife is less simply a product of his transference of affection to Catherine than it is a denial of the logic that leads from childhood to maturity, that earths the relationship between the sexes in a physicality that he knows, subconsciously, he can never attain with his niece.

A View from the Bridge was originally a one-act play in part because he consciously wished to find a contemporary equivalent to Greek drama, which also unfolded within a single act. Its action was to form a single arc, 'like an arrow shot from the bow', and not, as he explained, like *Death of a Salesman*, designed to 'suck tons of water like a whale' since the Greeks 'never thought that art could be a crap-shoot'.[1]

As a result the play was to be stripped down, with every action attached to the thematic structure, like a muscle to the bone. There was, anyway, no moment, as it seemed to him, for the curtain to fall. In another sense, he had told all he knew, all that was relevant to a man who had reduced his life to a single, intense point of light with everything else in the shadows. It was not that there was no material for a longer play. He, himself, listed issues raised but not pursued. There is, most strikingly, no past. What were the circumstances that led to Catherine being raised in this house? We are told of a promise made on her mother's death, but nothing more. When did Eddie Carbone's obsession begin and what are its roots? There is no back story. There is a past in this play but it is not Eddie's. It is a mythic past, a past of elemental feelings and ancient

taboos carried forward by the subconscious as much as by traditions forged in
a distant Italy.

We enter this drama when it is already under way and that, in a sense, is where
its energy is generated. For Miller, writing at the time of its first production,
'as many times as I have been led backward into Eddie's life, "deeper" into the
subjective forces that made him what he evidently is, a counter-impulse drew
me back. It was a sense of form, the shape of this work which I saw first sparely,
as one sees a naked mast at sea, or a barren cliff.'[2] When a character entered,
'he proceeded directly to serve the catastrophe'.[3]

The two illegal immigrants who arrive at Eddie's door are concrete expressions of the nemesis he fears without acknowledging. They are the demands
of the tribe, two messengers from another place and another time. They precipitate that clash between unexpressed need and social responsibility which,
in his case, can only result in catastrophe. Each person in this drama is driven
by what Miller has called an 'autonomic egocentricity', itself a kind of 'iron-
bound purity'. In other words, they are governed by their own motives, pursuing their objectives with a single-minded intensity generated by a necessity
almost beyond questioning. But the weaving together of those individual needs
amounted to what he regarded as 'almost the work of a fate',[4] composed, as it
is, of objective and subjective forces while retaining, finally, a sense of mystery,
despite Alfieri's observation that Eddie was a man who allowed himself to be
wholly known.

The original play differed in a number of respects from the two-act version
which he wrote for the subsequent London production, under Peter Brook. In
the initial production, the set was to be stripped of everything not immediately
essential. The room was to do no more than contain the acting area. At its back
was to be an opaque wall-like form. Down-stage were 'columnar shapes' ending
in air. When Alfieri appears he does so to welcome the audience to the theatre
and his opening speech, and many of the speeches that follow, is in free verse.
In other words, the theatrical nature of the play is underscored and through the
verse its connection with what in a stage direction he calls the 'ancient element'
of the story.

His conception of the play, as performed at the Coronet Theatre in
New York, was that it should be spare, almost skeletal, and that 'normal
naturalistic acting techniques had to be modified. Excessive and arbitrary
gestures were eliminated' as the set was 'shorn of every adornment'.[5] The
problem, as he subsequently saw it, was that neither the director nor actors
had any experience of this and that the style they were reaching for evaded
them.

In this first version, the action, of necessity, moves faster but what is implied
in the two-act version is, at times, more explicit in the one-act one. Thus, when
Catherine and Rudolpho are left alone in the apartment there is no doubt that
they are to make love, Catherine taking the initiative. Eddie kisses his niece on

the lips not in this scene but at the end of the play where the stage direction indicates that he does so 'like a lover' and 'out of his madness', while insisting, none too ambiguously, 'it's me, ain't it? You know it's me!'[6] He dies grasping Catherine and with her name on his lips. In the later version he dies in Beatrice's arms and with her name on his lips, as if in the final seconds he had, perhaps, finally rediscovered himself and his true loyalty.

The play fell into a single act because Miller saw the characters purely in terms of their actions and the light they cast on the dilemma of Eddie Carbone. He was primarily interested in the reasons for which a man 'will endanger and risk and lose his very life'.[7] The ending was to be implicit at the beginning so that audiences would be held less by the suspense of an unfolding plot than by the unwinding of an inevitability. It was, he said, not to be the 'what' that compelled but the 'how' and, beyond that, the 'why'.

For Michael Gambon, who played Eddie Carbone in a National Theatre production of the two-act version of the play, acting in *A View from the Bridge* was 'rather like being on a high speed train – a terrific sense of forward movement, with the world outside being a blur through the window . . . Sometimes, when a sharp bend was coming up, we would shout: "Hold it! Slow down or we'll come off the rails."'[8] It was not a question of speed, or the pace of the production, but of the fact that the play is carefully honed so that each action leads to the next, with no redundancy.

Miller wanted, he insisted, 'to reveal the method nakedly to everybody so that from the beginning of the play we are to know that this man can't make it, yet might reveal himself somehow in his struggle'.[9] The forward movement, as Gambon suggested, was to be relentless. There are no scenes that do not advance the action and whether Eddie is on-stage or not, and he is for much of the play, none that do not in some way or another focus on this man. His conflict, though, is not so much with the person who he increasingly perceives as a threat, as with himself. It is with a passion he cannot allow himself to see for what it is, and with a code for which he has absolute respect but which he must break if the logic of his passion is to be pursued to its ultimate conclusion, if he is to be able to sustain his sense of self-respect even at the moment of the dissolution of that self.

Still thinking in terms of modern tragedy, he saw the Greek sense of fate as giving way to an obsessional idea. In *Death of a Salesman* it was Willy Loman's desire to be well liked, to succeed in a material world that had little connection to his inner life. In the case of Eddie Carbone it is the love he holds for his niece, a love that will not speak its name. But whereas Greek tragedy ended by reaffirming the existence of a cosmology, of a structure to existence that might precipitate disaster but which equally affirmed an underlying order, modern tragedy appeared to have no such consolation to offer. And yet, he insisted on the felt need for such order, a need which ultimately Eddie, at least subconsciously, sacrifices himself to sustain.

The first production, while receiving some positive and perceptive reviews, was, in Miller's view, a failure. In part, it seemed to him, this was because the actors found it difficult to enter the language, convincingly to establish the particular milieu, the sound, the texture of a community that was to provide something more than the setting, something beyond a backdrop for a private drama. The British director Peter Brook, however, had another explanation. Miller had, he thought, been too ruthless in paring the action down. The play was too sharply focused on the figure of Eddie at the expense of the two women, whose relationship to him was so crucial. It was also at the cost of establishing the community, the breach of whose values was to turn private betrayal into public scandal.

At Brook's urging, therefore, and despite the cogent reasons he had advanced for the one-act form, Miller rewrote the play, expanding it to two acts and giving more space and hence substance to Beatrice and Catherine: 'I could see on the stage that I could give those actors more meat, and let the structure take care of itself a little bit. I relaxed the play in the sense of allowing it to have its colors.'[10] What he did not do was extend the play backwards in time. The two-act version still enters the action at the same point. It still leaves a sense of mystery as the characters enact a personal drama whose roots lie in feelings none of them can speak aloud or fully understand. We learn no more of Eddie's past or when or why his life took what Miller sees as its tragic course.

The text is now transposed into prose. References to Eddie and Beatrice's children are stripped out, further isolating them in the moment and in the intensity of their relationship. With no children of their own, Catherine becomes more of a surrogate child while Beatrice faces life wholly without consolation at the end. Extra scenes are introduced that expand on the relationship between Eddie and Catherine, Eddie and Beatrice and Beatrice and Catherine. We learn more of the characters, their relationships and their motivations.

As Miller explained, he now felt able to include elements of what he called simple human motivation previously excluded, specifically Beatrice's viewpoint and her dilemma in relation to her husband. This, he suggests, accounts for almost all the added material. It is not quite so, though what does come into sharper focus is the precise nature of Eddie's dilemma. His response to his niece is sexualised precisely because we now learn of his sexual alienation from his wife, two truths that are connected in his mind because he refuses to see Catherine as herself the object of his sexual need. He reads her behaviour, her actions, purely in terms of his own sublimated and displaced desires.

Yet for all the additions, Miller was still intent to create a play that would strip the action to its essentials. Indeed, as he explained in his autobiography, 'the play's main significance for me lay in its unpeeling of process itself, the implacability of a structure in life. For around me I felt a wasting vagrancy of mind and spirit, the tree of life turning into a wandering vine' (*T*.355). Beat literature, then much in vogue, seemed to Miller to produce texts that appeared to spin out of themselves, to be generated moment by moment. They had no more form, no more sense of direction, than the road that the protagonist frequently followed. Such works simply flowed, like the paper rolls on which Kerouac wrote. These were improvised lives, soaking up experience, surrendering to chance. But, for Miller, here and later in his career, there were necessities, there were urgencies that would become visible once the surface had been sand-blasted away.

The first change comes in the opening stage direction which is more elaborate in the one-act version in which we are told that, 'Like the play, the set is stripped of everything but its essential elements.'[11] Where in the later version we are told that the focus is on 'a worker's flat, clean, sparse, homely',[12] in the one-act version the emphasis is on abstraction. There are the same table, chairs, rocker and phonograph, required by the action, but otherwise he calls for 'a free form designed to contain the acting space required, and that is all'.

He then specifies that the intention 'is to make concrete the ancient element of this tale through the unmitigated forms of the commonest life of the big-city present, the one playing against the other to form a new world on the stage'. This note disappears from the two-act version, not least, perhaps, because it smacks a little of O'Neill's impossible stage directions. He also dispenses with the metatheatrical gesture with which he originally began the play, having Alfieri wish the audience good evening and welcome them to the theatre.

The next change comes in the conversation between Eddie and Catherine at the beginning of the play. This is now expanded, the banter between them slowly exposing her hopes for a new life and his anxieties, unfocused as yet but tangible. Where the first version pushed forward with the plot, now Miller establishes character and something of the ambiguous relationship between uncle and niece. Catherine's possible job as a secretary is absent from the first version and a key fact at the beginning of the second, as Eddie struggles against the idea that she may leave him.

Towards the end of the second act Miller adds a scene between Beatrice and Catherine in which the older woman tries to explain, obliquely, what is going on, urging her niece not to appear in front of Eddie in her underwear and to give up the intimacies appropriate to childhood. She implicitly confesses to a rivalry for Eddie's affections.

Later, there is an additional speech in which Catherine explains her feelings for Eddie in a way that suggests that she, too, is capable of sublimation. 'If I was a wife', she remarks, 'I would make a man happy instead of going at him all the time. I can tell a block away when he's blue in his mind and just wants to talk to somebody quiet and nice . . . I can tell when he's hungry and wants a beer before he even says anything.'[13] She seems to be precisely setting her own feelings up against Beatrice's.

In the later version Beatrice confronts Eddie with the true nature of his feelings: 'You want somethin' else, Eddie, and you can never have her!' When

he replies, 'That's what you think of me – that I would have such thoughts',[14]
he acknowledges a possibility, even as he rejects it. In the one-act play such an
idea could never make its way into speech.

The final change affects Alfieri's last speech, of which only one sentence is
the same. What follows are the two speeches, the first from the one-act version:

> Most of the time we settle for half,
>   And I like it better.
> And yet, when the tide is right
> And the green smell of the sea
> Floats in through my window,
> The waves of this bay
> Are the waves of Syracusa,
> And I see a face that suddenly seems carved;
> The eyes look like tunnels
> Leading back toward some ancestral beach
> Where all of us once lived.
>
> And I wonder at those times
> How much of all of us
> Really lives there yet,
> And when we will truly have moved on,
> On and away from that dark place,
> That world that has fallen to stones?
>
> This is the end of the story. Good night.[15]

The end of the two-act version differs radically:

> Most of the time now we settle for half and I like it better. But the truth
> is holy, and even as I know how wrong he was, and his death useless, I
> tremble, for I confess that something perversely pure calls to me from his
> memory – not purely good, but himself purely, for he allowed himself to be
> wholly known and for that I think I will love him more than all my sensible
> clients. And yet, it is better to settle for half, it must be! And so I mourn
> him – I admit it – with a certain . . . alarm.[16]

In the first version, he is plainly seeking to establish the universal significance
of these events in Red Hook, to stress the continuity of human nature, the extent
to which we have been watching a mythic re-enactment. One city becomes
another; past and present are connected by a single arc of action. If there are
also suggestions of a reversionary impulse, he seems to acknowledge that there
remains a level on which the primitive is structured into lives lived on more than
a conscious level. Eddie Carbone's passions are themselves the bridge between
past and present, a link to an earlier period of development. The dark place
exists in the early stages of human existence and survives in the psyche, in the
subconscious, the id.

In the second version, that concern with a surviving primitive instinct defers to something else. Eddie now emerges as a kind of hero, an Ahab following his obsession to the grave. Not for him a Starbuck-like commitment to domestic values. He treads the edge and breaches boundaries. He is a believer in his own suspect integrity to the end. Like Gatsby and, indeed, Ahab, he sees life only through a single window and pays the price for an obsession that nonetheless lifts him above the banality of routine and the safety that comes from compromising with passion. Did he allow himself to be fully known? Not in his own mind, surely. His actions, though, speak what he cannot.

It is clear, surely, that Eddie Carbone was not simply Miller's attempt to understand the informer, to offer a counterblast to Kazan's *On the Waterfront* in which the protagonist's decision to inform is presented as a necessary social and moral act, a justification, thereby, of its director's similar decision and, as it happens, that of its screenwriter, Budd Schulberg, and actor, Lee J. Cobb. Eddie does not inform out of weakness but out of the intensity of his need. He offers none of the rationalisations heard before the House Un-American Activities Committee. Indeed, to explain himself would be to risk betraying what he wishes above all to uphold. He believes himself loyal to something far more fundamental than the rules of his tribe. So sacred is it that he cannot approach it, define it, acknowledge it. He cannot stare into the bright light of his own passion, merely accept its consequence in order to protect its integrity. In dying, he shows that there are values inscribed in the structure of feelings as well as thought.

Eddie Carbone goes to his death to protect his sense of himself. He has to believe that his motives were pure. He informed against Rodolpho because he had convinced himself that it was the only way to protect Catherine. He seeks retrospectively to give her back her innocence, to turn the clock back by removing the man to whom she had lost it. Catherine must remain a child because in doing so his feelings are purged of any sexual component. Her short skirts are to him what Caddy's perfume was to Benjy in *The Sound and the Fury*, a sign that she is changing, becoming sexualised, consciously or unconsciously appealing to others. Caddy's brother, Quentin, also noticed the change and tried desperately to stop the clock, ultimately stopping himself as the only remaining way to ensure her continued innocence. Eddie does much the same. If she is innocent then so is he and he need never consider what his feelings might be called.

When she sleeps with Rudolpho that error must be denied, as Gatsby demands that Daisy Buchanan deny her love for her husband, as Carraway attempts to rub out the obscenities he finds inscribed on the steps of his mansion. Like Gatsby, Eddie believes that it is possible to go back, to reinvent innocence. Both men pay the price for that illusion. But in their illusions they both move the boundary posts, pressing beyond the accepted limits. For Alfieri, a lawyer – detached, an observer, adept at the business of compromise and negotiation – there is an attraction in a man who will not settle for the small change of daily life, not accept that there are frontiers to possibility, limits to passion.

When Miller came to write the two-act version for its British premiere, then, it was not simply a matter of expanding certain roles or locating the action more securely within a social milieu, though lower pay scales enabled Brook to hire actors to constitute the neighbourhood within which Eddie lives and whose values he abrogates, the community whose respect he needs and forfeits, finally, in favour of something he can barely understand and certainly not explain or confess. In New York, the neighbourhood was represented by four actors. In Britain, Eddie's interior dilemma was resonated by a denser social world constituted on stage by some twenty actors who represented the normality for which he yearns but which he must sacrifice. They were a physical expression of the moral judgement he invited, a measure of the sacrifice he made. At the same time, Miller admired the British actors' ability to manage the transition from naturalism into 'the larger-than-life attitude which the play demanded . . . without the self-conscious awkwardness, the uncertain stylishness which hounds many actors without classical training'.[17]

The denser social environment seemed to legitimise the realistic detail that now began to invade the text. A Christmas tree was added (the play, ironically, takes place in part in the season of good will), while make-up became more realistic, something avoided in the New York production that, like so many other Miller Broadway productions, seemed to have had difficulty in arriving at an appropriate style. The characters themselves now seemed to have a greater social weight, indeed a greater realism, even though in the context of a play reaching towards myth.

Meanwhile, Miller himself had changed, as had his sense of the play's gravitational centre. As he explained, 'I had originally designed it as bare as a telegram, its story in the foreground, its appeal essentially to the mind's awe at its amazing concatenations. But I thought differently now, that it could move people with pity for the protagonist and even identification with him, a man who does so many unworthy things. Perhaps', he added, 'in the nearly two years since writing it, I had learned to suspend judgement somewhat and to cease holding myself apart from the ranks of driven men – and not as a matter of principle but for real' (T.412). Certainly, he had now come to understand more completely what it was to be drawn to a younger woman, to feel a passion whose force he had been hesitant to admit even to himself and which had finally swept him away. Marilyn had re-entered his life.

Eddie Carbone is a protagonist who compels attention not for his actions, which tear up something more than the social contract, but for his uncompromising desire to remake the world to suit what seem to him to be human necessities. Fatally illusioned, he inhabits a paradox he can never hope to resolve, becoming, thereby, something more than a victim as he refuses to surrender what seems to him to be a vivifying passion, and pays the ultimate price for sustaining his flawed faith to the very end.

In a world in which 'we settle for half', Eddie Carbone is a man who can do no less than demand that the world become what he needs it to be. Between writing the two versions of the play Miller had grown to feel a greater kinship with a man he should have shunned but was now inclined to embrace as someone whose compulsions, betrayals, glimpses of sublimity he recognised in himself (his affair with Marilyn Monroe, eleven years younger than him and once no more than a fantasy, was now real enough). If Eddie seems to act out of the same self-interest as those who named names in *The Crucible* or at the hearings of the House Un-American Activities Committee, this is an illusion. He serves less himself than the integrity of his passion, no matter how little he understands it for what it is. He serves less himself than the idea of Catherine's innocence, somehow detached from the person of the young woman eager to grow up and embrace life.

There was, Miller has said, something Greek about the situation, as fate constructed tragedy out of human passion, as a breach opened up not only in the community but in the very notion of order, a breach inevitably to be closed by death, and Eddie's death is the fixed point towards which the action moves, though in the original story, as recounted to Miller, the man had been hounded from the neighbourhood. 'In ancient times', he later remarked, 'he would have gone out into the mountains, vanished amongst the wild beasts.'[18] For Miller, the more interesting question was: what would have happened if he had stayed where he was and been forced to confront what he had done, to face the community whose values he has betrayed? How could he have hoped to sustain an idea of himself so much at odds with his actions? As ever in Miller's plays, the real question is what happens when it is impossible to walk away.

In the British production, that community was given greater force in so far as the tenement wall opened to reveal a basement apartment and a tracery of fire escapes running across buildings in the background. On those fire escapes Peter Brook placed Eddie's neighbours, the audience before whom he stages his life, the jury of his peers who will pass their judgement on him. These became the chorus which otherwise would be represented solely by the figure of Alfieri. In the 1999 opera based on the play, once again a chorus was specified. For Miller, the opening up of the three-story tenement building was 'awesome', opening the mind 'to the size of the mythic story' (*T*.431).

When the curtain rises, then, we see a tenement building, its skeletal front laying bare what lies within, as the action of the play will lay bare the passions of the characters who inhabit it. But on this same stage, and in full view, is a desk which is to represent a lawyer's office (and lawyers and policemen abound in Miller's work as he debates the nature of justice, legal and moral), together with a telephone booth, the future that is a present possibility, the possibility that will become a reproach. Indeed, those two elements of the set represent past and future perfect, an event that will have happened before the play is done.

Stairs lead up to the Carbone apartment and beyond to the next floor, while a street runs upstage, providing a physical link with the social world against which the drama will unfold and through which it will resonate. A foghorn blows, much as it does in *Long Day's Journey Into Night*, and perhaps in part for much the same reason, as this small portion of a city is isolated for a moment and a warning sounds.

This is the community which exists in the shadow of the Brooklyn Bridge. The narrator's view 'is the view from the Bridge, or, rather, he is looking at it all both from the point of view of American civilisation and that ancient one that is really down there'.[19] It is a play that unfolds in a particular time and space but there is more than one perspective being deployed and, implicitly, more than one time and space. Brooklyn's Italian community has its own conventions but Marco and Rudolpho are products of a more implacable code. They bring the air of Italy with them. Meanwhile, the narrator offers us a longer perspective which takes us back to Carthage, Rome and the theatre of ancient Greece.

A View from the Bridge is a narrated work. Like *Our Town* and *The Glass Menagerie*, it is summoned into being by a man able to look back on the events and see them entire. Alfieri places the frame, deciding where the story begins and ends and what, therefore, that story is. His narration is in the present, the action in a factitious past, factitious because lifted out of time, with no past and no future. The tense is the present but the action has already been completed. Alfieri knows what went before and what comes after but chooses not to tell us. What happened to Catherine and Rudolpho? What of Beatrice, like Linda Loman left to lament a man whose mystery she could never finally penetrate? These are simply not the story he has chosen to tell.

For his part, Alfieri is far from being a successful lawyer. He deals in the small change of human life on the margins of the city. His function has less to do with justice than with facilitating the minor adjustments necessary to social life. The law is there to offer some kind of order, though hardly an adequate compensation for the vicissitudes of life lived on the edge. And there are times, as he knows, when the law has nothing to say because the breach in experience is too profound to be filled. This story is one such and it serves to remind him of his own paralysis in the face of passions and necessities that the law has no power to address. He is an observer because there is no other role he can adopt. He is a witness, struggling to make sense of what he has seen. He tells the story of a man as powerless as himself, in thrall to passions that are elemental and beyond the reach of reason and statute.

The play begins not with the central action but with two longshoremen pitching coins in the street, a game of chance, a reminder of the community which creates the context for what is to follow. It is Alfieri, though, who sets the drama moving, summons it into being and offers an explication of sorts.

He sees in the desperate and uncomprehending actions of one man an echo of other times and other places, thereby conferring significance on the actions of a marginalised man. He understands what Eddie Carbone cannot. He sees in the events he recalls something more than an anecdote. To him it is a myth, a fable. The immediate, the physical, the real are absorbed for him, and hence for us, into something whose significance extends beyond mere fact. As a lawyer, he deals in justice but there is another kind of justice here, for Eddie Carbone will commit no crime, indeed quite the opposite since, from the point of view of the law, he does no more than his civic duty. What he will do is breach more fundamental contracts.

The action begins as Eddie returns from a day's work to be confronted by Catherine, anxious to have his blessing for her decision to work as a stenographer. Immediately tensions begin to manifest themselves. He is, the stage directions tell us, 'strangely nervous . . . somehow sickened' at the news, and when he is persuaded to agree it is with 'a sense of her childhood, her babyhood, and the years'. The lesson he would teach her is 'don't trust nobody',[20] because, as he explains, 'most people ain't people', while 'the less you trust, the less you be sorry'. So far this seems little more than the warning of an anxious guardian, alert to the danger facing a young woman as she moves out into the wider world. Ironically, though, it could stand as a warning against himself and perhaps unconsciously it is so offered, as in Paula Vogel's *How I Learned to Drive* the male protagonist warns his niece against what he plans.

In the same way, the advice he gives to Catherine and Beatrice, when he warns them against mentioning their cousins – 'if you said it you knew it, if you didn't say it you didn't know it' (23) – applies equally to himself. So long as his feelings never make their way into language he can deny them to others and to himself. It is, perhaps, in part why he is sparing of language because 'you can quicker get back a million dollars that was stole than a word that you gave away' (24). Indeed this is precisely the conviction that enables him to function. For a man with an imperfect grasp of words, language has an almost magical power. Thus, when he calls Catherine 'Madonna' it is almost as though the word offered its own protection, for him no less than for her.

At first, Eddie seems genuinely like a father, reluctantly waving a daughter on her way, awkwardly acknowledging that she has grown beyond her need for him, and thereby revealing a love that never had to be spoken because implied in the nature of the relationship. He reveals 'a knowing fear', but this seems, at first, a product of nothing more than the sudden vulnerability that comes from awareness that he is no longer a necessary part of her life. She is eager to move on. He is anxious to hold on to her. Which parent has not known such ambivalence, except that in his case it slowly becomes clear that the love is of a different kind and the feelings more profoundly ambivalent.

It is a play in which the battles are fought indirectly. Catherine's growing independence is signalled by her short skirts and high heels, both contested by Eddie for whom they are signs of her sexual maturity. Rudolpho's song (he sings 'Paper Doll') is interrupted by Eddie who recognises and challenges a rival, while offering a plausible, but not wholly convincing reason for silencing him (people may hear and betray him). A boxing match becomes cover for a genuine hostility. A parlour game involving the lifting of a chair becomes a threat and a warning, no less powerful for being expressed by some other means than words. Every action is charged with meaning. The growing tension is acknowledged less through language than through gestures which in this context of desperate reticence become the way in which it is possible to speak the unspoken, to articulate feelings. Thus when Catherine spoons sugar into Marco's coffee this is simultaneously a piece of harmless flirtation and a gesture of defiance aimed at Eddie whose face is 'puffed with trouble'.

Eddie is bewildered, 'a lost boy' (40), but Rudolpho's arrival merely accelerates a dilemma that has been coming towards him with the inevitability of time. Her innocence is about to end, and with it his. He no longer has a real relationship with Beatrice and cannot have one with Catherine. He is caught and can see no solution because he cannot accept the nature of the problem. When he kisses his niece on the lips, a shock registers with characters and audience alike. He has crossed a line whose very existence he could not acknowledge and at that moment a process begins to play itself out as the man who was paralysed by contradictory emotions is provoked into an action that will precipitate a crisis.

Catherine, too, though, is poised. She has come to the end of one stage of her life and is about to launch on another. She, too, has her regrets; she, too, has been blind to the reality of her transition from childhood to adulthood, unaware of the consequences of the changes she is going through. And she, too, is momentarily outside of time. Like a ball thrown into the air which, at its apogee, is momentarily stationary, she is suspended in a world seemingly with no consequences. She wanders around in her underwear in front of Eddie with no sense that it might have any significance because she is still, in her own mind, a child.

This changes when Beatrice, herself acting out of mixed motives, confronts her with the reality of her situation, albeit obliquely, as afraid to name her fear as any of the characters. Thus, when she says, 'It's wonderful for a whole family to love each other, but you're a grown woman and you're in the same house as a grown man . . . You're a woman . . . and now the time came when you said goodbye' (44), we are told that Catherine 'turns with some fear, with a discovery . . . as though a familiar world had shattered' (44–5). And so it has. Something breaks and it is at this moment that Eddie makes his first visit to Alfieri who recognises that he is suffering from 'a passion that had moved into his body like a stranger' (45). And that, of course, is the problem in that he is alienated from his own feelings, unable to recognise the truth of his life.

He finds himself arguing contrary theses. Thus Rudolpho is simultaneously a sexual threat to his niece and a homosexual.

Of all the characters, it is Alfieri who comes closest to confronting Eddie with the truth of his feelings: 'every man's got somebody that he loves, heh? But sometimes... there's too much. You know? There's too much, and it goes where it mustn't... there is too much love for the daughter, there is too much love for the niece. Do you understand what I am saying to you?' Eddie does not because he cannot. When Alfieri says 'She wants to get married, Eddie. She can't marry you, can she?' Eddie replies, 'I don't know what the hell you're talking about' (49). Nor, on a conscious level, does he but when he responds 'furiously', the very fury hints at a level of awareness, a sense that Alfieri's insinuation strikes a chord somewhere in a man who had come to have his motives affirmed and his judgement confirmed but who has achieved nothing but an implied accusation.

In the house, all conversations carry overtones. Eddie's statements tend to be accusations, challenges, expressions of resentment. Beatrice responds in kind. The tension is tangible yet, for the most part, is expressed indirectly. They all have a vested interest in heading off the crisis that is in the air and yet they all engage in actions which threaten to precipitate it. Rudolpho and Catherine dance together. Eddie seeks to stop them. Unable to articulate his true feelings and hence discharge his frustration and anger directly, he twists his newspaper into a tight roll and then tears it in two. The tension momentarily broken, he devises a new way to expose what he takes to be Rudolpho's effeminacy, offering to teach him to box, anxious to humiliate him in the eyes of Catherine but, in doing so revealing how little he understands the young woman whose love he needs and seeks. He succeeds only in driving them together as once again they dance.

The meaning of this incident is not lost on Marco, taciturn, anxious not to offend, but sensitive to slights on his honour and that of his family. The first act, accordingly, ends with that moment of pause for which he had searched in vain in the earlier version as Marco challenges Eddie to lift a chair by one leg. It is, apparently, no more than a game but, in the unspoken contest for power being enacted in this tenement apartment beneath Brooklyn Bridge, it is a direct challenge to Eddie's authority. Thus, when Eddie fails and Marco lifts the chair high over Eddie's head, the dancing stops and everyone watches a moment in which, without benefit of words, we and they identify those who are to be the true antagonists of this drama. Marco, we are told, '*is face to face with* EDDIE, *a strained tension gripping his eyes and jaw, his neck stiff, the chair raised like a weapon over* EDDIE'*s head*'. He thus '*transforms what might appear to be a glare of warning into a smile of triumph, and* EDDIE'*s grin vanishes as he absorbs his look*' (58).

The second act opens on 23 December, but this is not a festive house. Catherine and Rudolpho are alone. She brings her fears and suspicions to him, suspicions planted there by Eddie. He has warned her that this illegal immigrant is feigning love only as a means of gaining citizenship. Nor, as Miller has admitted, is his an unreasonable suspicion. Within weeks of Rudolpho's arrival in the house, marriage is being openly discussed. How, after all, could anyone responsible for her well-being favour marriage to someone liable to immediate arrest, whose declared love of America, and what it has to offer, might be greater than his affection for the woman who may be no more than a passport to inclusion in this dream?

When Miller was asked whether it was Catherine or America Rudolpho loved, he replied,

> I suppose a little of both. She's a lovely girl and he is crazy about her. But it is also an opportunity to get his roots started in this country. Purposely, I think, we are left to wonder about that. The question is whether Eddie has a good case against Rudolpho, and I think he does, given the desperation of people in Italy at the time. People do this all the time . . . simply to get the passport . . . so he has got a good case.[21]

But Eddie's avuncular role clashes with a deeper need that renders his ostensible concern merely ironic. This is an inverted world in which concern masks self-interest and the informer serves the law. Eddie Carbone visits Alfieri in search of a justice that is no more than his name for a sanction that will rationalise his suspicions.

In seeking to stop time, Eddie is resisting the natural order of things. There is never a suggestion that he would act on his quasi-incestuous feelings for Catherine. He wants to do no more than lock his niece and himself within a myth, a story, where they will be immune to the intrusion of others, the depredations of time. His sexual withdrawal from Beatrice is of a piece with his desire to sustain an innocence that must be recoverable.

Catherine's love for Eddie, meanwhile, has turned to fear as she detects something in him she cannot name. She, too, is aware of a sense of loss. She is balanced between two commitments but this is the moment at which loss turns into something else as she and Rudolpho make love, and this in a Catholic community where such a step, at such a time, was charged with significance. When Eddie returns from the docks, drunk, he sees first the paper pattern that Catherine had laid on the table (echoes of 'Paper Doll') as an indicator of a special occasion, and then Catherine and Rudolpho emerge from the bedroom, her dress evidently in disarray. When he demands that Rudolpho should leave, however, it is Catherine who moves to do so and when she announces, minutes after losing her innocence, that 'I'm not gonna be a baby any more!' (64), Eddie kisses her directly on the mouth.

It is a defining moment, though hardly less so than what follows. Eddie pinions Rudolpho's arms and kisses him, too, on the mouth. The first kiss is a territorial claim, an assertion of proprietary rights. Though he loves his niece this is a kiss that has nothing to do with love and everything to do with possession. The second kiss is a gesture of humiliation, as if, thereby, he offered evidence for his claims of Rudolpho's homosexuality. 'You see?' he says to Catherine, as though he had demonstrated something, confirmed something more than his physical superiority.

For him, these are two spontaneous actions with no ambivalence. That they are revelatory of something more than ownership and contempt would not, and cannot, occur to him. It is as though he had finally demonstrated, with absolute clarity, the truth of what he had been implicitly and explicitly claiming. Catherine is his; Rudolpho is a sexually ambivalent interloper with neither the right nor the power to challenge his authority. It is the moment, though, when he enters a territory from which there is no escape. They are definitive actions that destroy the very thing he was so anxious to protect. He stands naked, believing himself to be clothed in righteous indignation. Thinking himself to be doing no more than exposing a self-evident truth, he has in fact exposed something about himself that he will die rather than acknowledge for what it is. For a man whose command of language is imperfect, for whom language, indeed, is seemingly disconnected from his feelings or at risk of betraying what he wishes to deny, action seems to have a clarity of line that allows no space for misunderstanding.

There is now a break in more than time. We learn nothing of the immediate consequences of Eddie's actions, see nothing of the crisis which ensues. Miller foregoes an opportunity to dramatise Eddie's encounter with his wife, the revelation to others of what has occurred. We learn that a marriage that was mooted has now been agreed. It is as though the needle had been nudged forward on the phonograph. We have moved on but learn almost nothing of what has happened in the interim. Indeed we are told that the house is now characterised by silence – 'Marco don't say much . . . Nobody's talkin' much in the house' (66).

When we next encounter Eddie, the victory has already turned to defeat and a baffled man consults Alfieri. Catherine has now declared that she is to marry Rudolpho who has not left the apartment. Eddie exists in a deepening silence. He steps out of that silence into a more profound one as a telephone booth lights up, 'a faint, lonely blue' (67), and he drops a dime to report his cousins to the Immigration Bureau.

His action is entirely legal, indeed, in one sense no more than his civic duty. But though Alfieri remarks that 'the law is nature. The law is only a word for what has a right to happen', he adds that, 'when the law is wrong it's because it's unnatural' (66). Informing, in this context, is legal but breaches more fundamental codes. And here, of course, is the connection with the political environment in which this play was written just as Eddie's attraction to a younger woman had its immediate parallel in Miller's life. He was, he has confessed of himself, 'in a swift current' in which 'there was no stopping or handhold', a description that could equally apply to Eddie Carbone, drawn to

Catherine as the source of truth and yet vaguely aware that he is being pulled into a vortex from which there is no escape (*T*.359–60). Miller felt much the same with respect to Marilyn Monroe.

He has since said that his memory of the play's poor first reception, a memory only partly justified (and elsewhere ascribed to the impossibility of communicating its images of privation and desperation to a 'booming and increasingly self-satisfied country') (*T*.397), was 'because something in me was disowning the play even as its opening approached' (*T*.356). Wanting his marriage to continue but unable to turn aside from Marilyn, he was at war with himself in much the same way as Eddie, unable to reconcile his feelings with his sense of right action.

Miller has spoken of the irony of rehearsing a play so close, in many respects, to his own life, even while remote in setting, character and language: 'How to get up on the stage and describe to Van [Heflin] the sensation of being swept away, of inviting the will's oblivion and dreading it? . . . How could one walk toward the very thing one was fleeing from?' (*T*.370). And that, of course, is Eddie's dilemma. He feels himself caught in an inevitability, engaged by a passion he can no more accept for what it is than name it, and drawn towards a solution that solves nothing but his sense of guilt and his distorted sense of honour as he seemingly struggles to protect Catherine while actually protecting himself from knowledge of his own motives. Betrayal awaits on all levels. He dies because he will not compromise. To him, Catherine offers a sense of harmony, a natural order, an alliance against unmeaning. When she is threatened, as he sees it, her virtue compromised, he does no more than seek to set things right. The irony is that he puts his own integrity at risk in order to affirm that integrity; he threatens order in the name of order. He is the anarchy he fears.

When Eddie has informed on his cousins he returns to his apartment, insisting 'I want my respect!' (68), having just surrendered it. The Christmas decorations are being packed away. The celebration is over, along with much else. The marriage is imminent, but so, too, is the arrival of the immigration officials and when they appear the connection is made by everyone. They shrink away from him. Like so many other Miller protagonists he can only call out, 'I want my name!' (82), aware that he has drained that name of any meaning, betrayed not only others but himself. Only now does Beatrice confront him with his desire for Catherine, an accusation that shocks not only him but his niece as well. For the fact is that neither was prepared to acknowledge the strength of the feeling that had held them together, nor are they now as Marco's arrival rushes the action to its completion, a completion played out in front of the community.

Alfieri's final speech, sealing off the drama, concentrates not on the betrayal at its heart but a transcendent quality that he sees in Eddie Carbone: 'even as I know how wrong he was, and his death useless, I tremble, for I confess that something perversely pure calls to me from his memory – not purely good, but himself purely, for he allowed himself to be wholly known' (85). It is a curious epitaph if only because Eddie worked so hard not to be known for what he was, nor even to confront himself in his complex simplicity. Denial builds on denial. He denies his feelings for Catherine, his reasons for withdrawing from Beatrice and his responsibility for the arrest of his cousins.

For Miller, though, 'he is not facing it and he's facing it. The way it should be played is that by denying it verbally he is confessing it actually. He does know and experience the full truth by the end of the play.'[22] His redemption lies in his total commitment to love: 'it may be a perverse love, but it is love. It gets twisted and corrupted . . . but it is there.'[23] In the end Eddie dies to confirm the code he has breached and affirm the love that has become the centre of his life.

Eddie Carbone's tragedy is born out of the misalignment of his deep personal needs and an implacable code to which he is committed but which he is drawn to deny. This is the fracture in his universe, a flaw in himself, to be sure, but equally in an experience in which access to meaning seems denied. Beside him, Rudolpho, with his naive faith in the American Dream, dazzled by the material world, caught up in a romance in part his own making but in part the product of a culture blandly optimistic, seems shallow. Eddie moves in water too deep for him but he chances all. That is his tragedy; it is also what lifts him above compromise, a concern with a normative existence.

Marco's eyes are fixed on getting by from day to day, and beyond that on living by an outmoded code, unforgiving and self-perpetuating. For Catherine, life crystallises around the first man she encounters as she sees in him a realisation of her frustrated dreams. For Beatrice, the overwhelming need is to return to the status quo ante. For Eddie alone the stakes are higher as he places his life behind a need he can never confide even to himself.

Hamlet dies as much to preserve a sense of himself as to act out a necessary revenge. Eddie dies to preserve his sense of himself and his vision of Catherine. Now the unspoken need never be spoken and hence, in Eddie's view of things, never was. Now he need never see evidence of Catherine's coming of age, the formalities that confirm the loss of her innocence. He dies for his name, for her innocence. On some level, too, perhaps, he dies in order to restore the sense of order which his own actions have threatened but whose authority, at some level, he still concedes. This is that sense of order that Miller had detected in the play, that structure of meaning no longer a product of cosmology but of the necessary rules of the tribe, without which Eddie knows there is only the merest anarchy. Eddie dies to restore the order he has breached twice over, once in his unacknowledged feelings for Catherine and once in his betrayal of his cousins, but his passion, his struggle with himself, his misdirected sense of dignity and honour lift him above the banality of his times.

He is, as Miller has suggested, fighting for his survival. When he makes the telephone call he is acknowledging the supremacy of his needs over his obligations; he is destroying the competition. There is another Eddie Carbone who could have 'gone to the wedding, congratulated everybody and sat there drying up, frustrated in self-denial'.[24] Eddie is not that man. He is, Miller accepts, a fanatic but so, too, he insists, was Hamlet, so, too, are all tragic heroes. He reveals himself not to himself but to those who watch.

Eddie Carbone is not only acting, he is re-enacting. It is precisely his passion that forges a link with others undone by a passion that elevates even as it destroys. He disturbs the ordered way of life and must be expelled, but his feelings have an unequivocal profundity that marks the outer boundary of passion, the extreme edge that others fear precisely because it threatens the dissolution of the self no less than of society. He exists in and through his passions which thereby become the same thing as his existence. He dies, like Willy Loman, for his immortality, for an integrity, compromised beyond his ability to know, which will invest his life with the meaning he believed his passion alone could confer. Both men trade their lives for their significance.

Eddie Carbone steps outside morality because morality maps the known world. He ventures beyond, into a place where nothing is named, driven not by anything as simple as necessity but by a desire which itself exists beyond words. He steps, too, outside of time into a world of myth, isolating himself from the corrupting comfort of community and domesticity. For Miller,

> He is not a very nice fellow but I think humanity is enlarged by knowing this man and what he did more than if he were a careful little fellow who didn't go over the edge like that. There is also, in a perverse way, something fascinating about somebody who pursues his obsession, right down to the end. That's the engine of that play. The idea of a man fulfilling his destiny is absolutely compelling . . . What I was after was that the audience could achieve self-knowledge . . . It is this understanding that gives us importance, gives a human being importance, gives someone who is watching it the feeling that life is not just a lot of chaotic impulses pushing us this way, pushing us that way, most of them unfulfilled.[25]

Ours is not a tragic age. For Hemingway, the very idea of tragedy had died along with those who had perished in the trenches of the First World War. Death was too promiscuous, the individual too powerless to sustain the idea of human will in contention with destiny. He might see grace under pressure as the nearest equivalent, and in the enthusiasm of his commitment to Spain create a Christ-like tragic hero in *For Whom the Bell Tolls*, but it was his early work, stripped of sentimentality (its mannered ironies aside), that seemed a true mark of the times. The systematised slaughter which ran like a tarnished thread through the twentieth century, deploying the science and technology that was to have liberated to destroy, left nothing but the residue of irony. The absurd seemed a natural product of the concentration camps as bureaucratised slaughter underlined the truth of lives lived astride the grave. There was a purity, it seemed, to such despair elevated to philosophy.

Miller, though, resists the absurd as compounding human suffering, as invoking an antinomian existence in which values are subverted by irony. The function of art, he insists, is not to sanction a view of man as victim but to constitute a resistant force. He has always been drawn to the tragic, at first attempting to recuperate it by way of a verse drama set in the sixteenth century: *The Golden Years*. In a sense, as he recognised, there was an element of evasion about this. What primarily interested him, in part because it seemingly brought his politics into alignment with his aesthetics, was the idea of accommodating the tragic mode to the quotidian. As *All My Sons* and *Death of a Salesman* both suggest, he was powerfully influenced by Aristotle and an admirer of the Greek theatre which precisely seemed to forge a connection between immediate political and social concerns and the nature of the human condition. What he wished to do was create modern tragedies, which acknowledged the irrelevance of social rank as alone dignifying private lives. To his mind, Ibsen, Strindberg and Chekhov had pointed the way, creating bourgeois tragedies which registered a shifting social and political world. He wanted to go one stage further, finding in the common man a tragic sensibility, and not merely created a series of plays which exemplified this conviction but wrote a number of essays in which he elaborated his ideas. Indeed, in Arthur Miller the American theatre found its most prolific essayist and a man fiercely committed to resisting what seemed to him as capitulation to ideas of man as victim – of history, an absurd universe, a failure of nerve.

13

Tragedy

In turning to tragedy Miller was remembering the lessons he had learned back in Michigan when he had studied a Greek theatre for which the tragic and the political were closely allied. Athenian tragedy, as Paul Cartledge observes,[1] was in a straightforward and broad sense political, and here was the segue between Miller's student social dramas of the 1930s and the 'tragedies' of the 1940s and 50s. The writer of tragedies was a civics teacher. Greek theatre had offered a drama of ideas able, as Cartledge suggests, to challenge social norms.

Miller also seems to have responded to a Hegelian sense of the tragic, which refracted its seemingly irremediable determinism in the direction of a social ethic, of active characters fully responsible for their actions. Here was an existential twist that managed, it seemed, to accommodate social concern to a personal ethic. For Hegel, 'To genuine *tragic* action it is essential that the principle of *individual* freedom and independence, or at least that of self-determination, the will to find in the self the free cause and source of the personal act and its consequences, should already have been aroused.'[2] This individual, though, could be seen as in some way containing the social tensions of the culture and hence be at least tangentially related to the Marxism that had yet entirely to leave Miller's bloodstream.

As a practical playwright, rather than an academic critic, he discovered that he had 'unwittingly entered an arena of near-theological devoutness which I had not known existed'.[3] He was not, though, ready to retreat. Acknowledging that he lived in an ironic age, he suspected that tragedy now seemed to many to be anachronistic because the rituals of grief had become eroded while the dignity and centrality of the self had been undermined. In a century that had experienced the carnage of two wars and the literal and symbol reductiveness of the Holocaust, a century 'spendthrift . . . with human lives', the tragic proposal seemed, perhaps, 'simply presumptuous – this making so much out of one death when we know it is meaningless'.[4]

It is a point that would be made by others, including the critic George Steiner for whom the Holocaust, in particular, seemed to threaten not only our view of the self but also the inner structure of art, its implicit claim to resist rather than collaborate with moral anarchy. But, more than that, what Steiner chose to call 'absolute tragedy' was itself a rarity since the theatre seemed to demand something other than a stripped-down, naked confrontation with ultimate truths. It had, at its heart, a compromise with the familiar, with the

hybrid nature of experience, which saw the tragic infiltrated with the comic as
if the sheer rigour of absolute tragedy was too much to bear. Thus, Steiner has
observed that:

> in the theatre, more probably than in any other representational mode,
> likeness, credibility, the underlying gravitational force of the reality prin-
> ciple, are persistent. As they are in the Homeric epics, which are the font
> of drama. Niobe has seen her ten children slain. Her grief makes stones
> weep. But as it ebbs, she takes nourishment. Homer insists on this. It is
> an interposition of daylit truth central also to Shakespeare. The organic is
> tragi-comic in its very essence. The absolutely tragic is, therefore, not only
> insupportable to human sensibility: it is false to life.[5]

Seen thus, if tragedy draws us towards the absolute, theatre exerts a counter-
force which pulls in the direction of the immediate, the tangible solidities and
emotional necessities of the known. The gods may set the terms of existence but
existence itself must be rooted in the quotidian, not merely if we are to recognise
the human relevance of what we see but if the tension between immediate and
ultimate meaning is to be felt. There is, in other words a compromise at the
heart of the tragic which invites us to turn defeat into victory, despair into an
accommodated norm: Hamlet gives way to Fortinbras. The pressure is released
at the play's end, intensity diminished, itself offering an ironic restitution of
meaning, but a meaning in some ways attenuated.

There is already, at the end of a tragic drama, a kind of shocked nostalgia for a time of pure passion, a sun too bright to be stared at for more
than the briefest moment, too dark to be contemplated without coming to
the edge of oblivion. Disorder, chaos, generate energy and implosive unmeaning at the same time. Order restored offers salvation but no more than the
dull echo of a human potential, all kinetic energy now discharged. We are
drawn to Eddie Carbone, in *A View from the Bridge*, as we are to Oedipus or
Lear, because of the absolute nature of his commitment. When he and they die
that pure energy is dissipated. When Ahab dies, sounding the ocean depths,
the narrator of *Moby-Dick* returns to the vapid shallows of the domestic life
described by Starbuck, an accommodated man who prefers safety to chancing
his soul.

It is a compromise, of course, at the heart of the artistic enterprise itself, an
irony from which Beckett sought release in vain. For the very form of the drama
constitutes a containing order. It is what invokes a nostalgia for pure anarchy,
for the Dionysian with which theatre flirts but to which, whether its god or
not, it never ultimately submits. It is the dubious redemption which, within
the work, lies only in the last moments, in the codas which begin the business
of sealing off this glimpse of total human commitment in the presence of pure
feeling and a relentless pursuit of life's meaning, even if death is the key to the
cipher.

For Steiner, a century of death camps and killing fields, of dispossessions and imminent nuclear extinction, demanded or recalled a bleaker model: *King Lear* by way of Beckett. He acknowledged the unlikelihood of a renaissance of tragic drama since 'the scale of modern violence and desolation is resistant to aesthetic form', while our sensibilities are numbed by the 'routine of shock pre-packaged, sanitized by the mass media and the false authenticity of the immediate'.[6] The urgencies of immediate time, in other words, which simultaneously detach us from an awareness of the continuum and make us impatient with an art that demands contemplation to expose its inner dynamic, preclude attempts to expose the inner core of meaning. Perhaps, he suggests, the only true response in such a context is the 'inchoate scream out of the blackened mouth'.[7] The Jew thrust into a gas chamber and thence the oven is denied access to tragedy no less than to life. That scream, or the silence with which it ends, is the only true representation and expression of our plight.

These are, perhaps, elements in Miller's sense of the tragic (though I doubt he would readily confess as much), for the tragic and the absurd are not as far separated as he would perhaps like. It was Schopenhauer through whom, in part, Eugene O'Neill, another admirer of the Greeks, approached tragedy and it was Schopenhauer who said that 'Only the dull, optimistic, Protestant–Rationalistic or peculiarly Jewish view of life will make the demand for poetical justice and find satisfaction in it. The true sense of tragedy is the deeper insight, that it is not his own individual sins that the hero atones for, but original sin, i.e. the crime of existence.'[8]

While Miller has repeatedly asserted his resistance to aspects of absurdism, insisting that life can escape the irony which death injects into it, he, too, has been repeatedly drawn to the question of original sin, or at least the Fall, and hence to an ambivalent view of the responsibility which on a social and moral level he wishes to assert. He would not endorse Schopenhauer's belief that tragedy is concerned with 'the unspeakable pain, the wail of humanity, the triumph of evil, the scornful mastery of chance, the irretrievable fall of the just and the innocent',[9] but he was increasingly disturbed by what lessons the Holocaust might offer to a world intent on denying not only the moral but the metaphysical questions it raised.

To Miller, tragedy was a means of injecting meaning into experience. It was a way to resist an absurdity whose force he nonetheless concedes. As he said of *King Lear*, it was essentially form which redeemed a threatening anarchy, the pointlessness of suffering.

He accepts that the stakes are high and acknowledges as much by bringing so many of his characters to the moment of death, from *The Golden Years* through the original version of *The Man Who Had All the Luck* and all his plays until and including *A View from the Bridge* (*A Memory of Two Mondays* aside) and then, perhaps, again in *Broken Glass*, though the ending is equivocal. The question is, what meaning can be snatched for the self in the face of the dissolution of the self?

For Nietzsche, what enabled the individual to confront his death without being turned to stone was a Dionysian life-force and one aspect of that will to life is art. As he argued, 'The truth once seen, man is aware everywhere of the ghastly absurdity of existence . . . Then, in this supreme jeopardy of the will, art, that sorceress expert in healing, approaches him; only she can turn his fits of nausea into imaginations with which it is possible to live.'[10] For Miller, though, there is something beyond this minimalist, Beckettian defence. There is still a shadow of his Marxism in a version of tragedy that turns on the death of the old and the birth of the new.

Miller acknowledged the pull of the absurd while resisting its implacability, noting, in particular, that the power and attraction of classical tragedy still commanded the attention of audiences. What had changed in the contemporary world, it seemed to him, was respect for and acknowledgement of grief, an embarrassment in the face of suffering. It may be, he suggested, that 'we have lost the art of tragedy for want of a certain level of self-respect, finally, and are in disgrace with ourselves'.[11] That last phrase is a recognisably Miller formulation, as he implicitly draws from tragedy the notion that it deals with the need for the individual to retrieve his good opinion of himself, that the tragic hero is willing to lay down his life to sustain a vision of himself sometimes profoundly at odds with his former actions. Tragedy, he insisted, 'is the consequence of a man's total compulsion to evaluate himself justly'.[12]

Steiner, too, acknowledges that the tragic, or at least the structure of the tragic form, has exerted a powerful purchase on the dramatic mind in the twentieth century, though often, as he suggests, in a recursive form. The Greek theatre has repeatedly been invoked as model by – and he lists them – Hauptman, Eliot, O'Neill, Sartre, Gide, Cocteau. For the performance theatres of the 1960s the myths at the heart of the tragic were refashioned as celebratory rites, their improvisatory thrust, their distrust of the inauthenticity and yet pedagogic force of performance deflecting attention from the tragic to the rectifiable problems of social and political life. Tragedy, or the hollow shell of its forms, thus remained at the centre of attention, but stripped of its rigour.

For Raymond Williams, what had changed was that hero had become victim. Thus, where what he chose to call liberal tragedy had at its centre, 'a man at the height of his powers and the limits of his strength, at once aspiring and being defeated, releasing and being destroyed by his own energies',[13] he now saw drama as drifting towards a representation of that man no longer resistant to cruelties because identifying with them. Miller he saw as 'a late revival of liberal tragedy'. What distinguished him, in his mind, from many of his contemporaries, was 'the retained consciousness of a false society',[14] in other words the trace elements of his socialism.

Liberal tragedy, Williams explained, places at its heart 'the self against the self. Guilt, that is to say, has become internal and personal, just as aspiration was internal and personal', though such a stance leads towards the eventual breakdown of liberalism as we enter 'the self-enclosed, guilty and isolated world; the time of man as his own victim'.[15]

Miller, from Williams's perspective, treads the edge, acknowledging the need for radically revised social values and yet presenting us with a series of victims: 'it is still seen as a false and alterable society, but merely to live in it, now, is enough to become its victim'. Translating this into terms of *Death of a Salesman* he says this:

> Willy Loman . . . has become, in effect, a commodity which like other commodities will at a certain point be discarded by the laws of the economy. He brings tragedy down on himself, not by opposing the lie, but by living it. Ironically, the form of his aspiration is . . . the form of his defeat, but now for no liberating end; simply to get by, to see himself and his sons all right . . . a new consciousness is then shaped: that of the victim who has no living way out, but who can try, in death, to affirm his lost identity and lost will.[16]

This seems simultaneously perceptive and misleading. The ideology of the critic and the writer seem not quite to have come into alignment. It is true that Willy Loman complains at his status as commodity but much in the play resists this reading. He provokes his own dismissal, is supported by a man whose humanity is not necessarily divorced from his working within the rules of the economy and whose son exemplifies the possibility of combining achievement with understanding. It is not the capitalist reality but national myths that command Willy's imagination and which he believes legitimately demand his submission. His sons do not steal because property is theft but because they have been taught by their father that human worth can be expressed through status and possessions and by their uncle that they should never fight fair with a stranger. That is not what Charley and Bernard believe or practise.

Williams contrasts *Death of a Salesman* and *A View from the Bridge* with *The Crucible*. Where Proctor becomes 'virtually . . . the liberal martyr', though 'characteristically complicated by [his] personal guilt', in the other two plays 'the wider implication is absent. It is not now the martyr but the victim; the disconnected individual. In Willy Loman's death the disconnection confirmed a general fact about the society; in Eddie Carbone's death, Miller has moved further back, and the death of the victim illustrates a total condition.'[17]

Again, this is an interesting mixture of perception and slight waywardness. His comment about Proctor's 'martyrdom' being characteristically complicated by personal guilt is an aside never picked up, despite the fact that it suggests one way in which Miller seeks always to find the public as rooted in the private, breaches in the social contract having a common source to breaches in private ones. His observation that 'the wider implication' is absent from *Death of a Salesman* and *A View from the Bridge* is contradicted by his own remark that Willy's death confirmed a general fact about society and that Eddie 'betrays the human connection by which he has lived . . . to the inhuman and alien society'. Which inhuman and alien society, one is bound to ask? Apart from Eddie's unexpressed and unacknowledged desire (though he is not, as Williams suggests, driven towards 'both incest and homosexuality'),[18] society seems organic and thriving, a genuine community largely uninfected by alienation. Marco and Rudolpho essentially share Willy Loman's dream, and describe it in lyrical terms. The difference is that they are willing to sweat to achieve it, unless Rudopho's motives are as suspect as Eddie not unreasonably supposes them to be.

The fact is that Williams's own sympathies – liberal deepening to Marxist – lead him to locate Miller's drama on the cusp of a dramatic and social change which is not quite that which Miller himself envisages. Take this comment on *A View from the Bridge*:

> . . . isolated contemporary man, wanting no more than to be himself, fails even in this and transfers significance to his name and his death. To preserve one's life, as things are, is 'to settle for half', as Miller puts it at the end of *A View from the Bridge*. And if this is so, in a false society which the individual alone cannot change, then the original liberal impulse, of complete self-fulfilment, becomes inevitably tragic. The self that wills and desires, destroys the self that lives, yet the rejection of will and desire is also tragedy: a corroding insignificance, as the self is cut down.[19]

The only problem is that Miller does not present society as false and resistant to transformation. Indeed, the very essence of his public stance, in a life lived publicly, is that the individual can make a difference, hence the causes to which he has lent his name, hence his insistence that history is a product and not an implacable force.

Miller's choice of a tragic model seems to have been entirely deliberate. If it was recursive it was so because it contained and expressed values threatened, on the one hand, by a bland materialism, drained of transcendence, and, on the other, by the sheer enormity of the Holocaust. In *After the Fall* he acknowledges the bleakness of a world dominated by a concentration-camp tower, seemingly evacuated of God. But essentially he feels the need to reinvent values so precipitately challenged. He reaches for tragedy precisely to reinvest individual guilt with social force, to offer as paradigm not the disabled psyche, still less man as victim of cosmic ironies, but a self charged with acknowledging the logic which ties past event to current consequence and private action to public significance. He writes of broken connections that must be mended and a mechanism with which to achieve this is to restore a theatrical form whose continuity had itself been threatened.

His rejection of Beckett was a conscious refusal of the absurd, in which causality was denied or ironised and time no more than a recurrent pattern. He refuses equally absolute tragedy and the annihilation of tragedy by the reduction of the self to simple victim, Williams's remarks notwithstanding. He resists indifference, a moral agnosticism, a despair transcended only by slapstick figures who respond to the cosmic joke by themselves becoming expressions of it. His own humour is entirely different. Like Shakespeare's, his tragedies, if such they are, are tragi-comedies. Their focus, however, is to be on the lives of those who seem to exist on the margins of history and society alike, insignificant except in the universal significance of their passions.

Nor was Miller as out of step as he suspected he might be in writing an essay on 'Tragedy and the Common Man'. He was, for example, entirely in tune with the work of a man equally fascinated with the sense of guilt that Raymond Williams had stressed and equally disturbed by the implications of the Holocaust. Karl Jaspers survived the war, living in Germany, and immediately thereafter published a book called *The Question of Guilt*, which assailed his fellow Germans and denied them the absolution of ignorance or non-complicity, as individuals no less than as members of society, a position which Miller shared. It was this same man who turned to the question of tragedy, democratising the concept precisely in response to what he saw as the arrogant elitism that had been invoked to justify a derogation of responsibility towards those declared historically irrelevant, the atavistic celebration of the hero, invoked to validate barbarism.

In such a context tragedy becomes no more than a hand-maiden to those who alone are granted historical substance, philosophical and moral significance. As Jaspers observed in *Tragedy Is Not Enough*,

> tragedy becomes the privilege of the exalted few – all others must be content to be wiped out indifferently in disaster. Tragedy then becomes a characteristic not of man, but of a human aristocracy. As the code of privilege, this philosophy gives us comfort by pandering to our self-esteem . . . Misery – hopeless, meanly, heart-rending, destitute and helpless misery – cries out for help. But the reality of this misery without greatness is pushed aside as unworthy of notice by minds that are blind with exaltation.[20]

This, to him, seemed no more than another version of nihilism, the violence associated with tragedy seeming to charge with significance what was in effect a conspiracy with deconstructive forces. Equally abhorrent was sheer apathetic surrender, 'a mere pinpoint of self-assertion'[21] substituting for an active acknowledgement of responsibility. All of this would have been readily embraced by Miller.

For Miller himself, 'the tragic feeling is evoked in us when we are in the presence of a character who is ready to lay down his life, if need be, to secure one thing – his sense of personal dignity'. The fear is 'of being torn away from our chosen image of what and who we are in this world'.[22] Thus, Hamlet is driven not simply by a desire for revenge, by a need to put things right, but by a need to close the gap between his sense of himself as a man of action and resolution and his growing conviction that he is in fact a man seemingly content to discharge his energy into language and equivocation, calculated wit and a too-conscious irony. Joe Keller, Willy Loman, John Proctor, Eddie Carbone all die to sustain a notion of themselves which otherwise must be deeply compromised. All, consciously or unconsciously, are aware of the space that has opened up between what they are and what they would be. They die to close that space.

There is a sense, though, in which Raymond Williams is perhaps right when he detects a surviving radical impulse in Miller's tragic vision in that he sees the destruction of the hero as positing an evil in society, and hence as being revelatory of a moral law, as values contest. And that contest he sees as indicative of a 'thrust for freedom', a 'revolutionary questioning of the stable environment',[23] though he insists that that is not to say that it must preach revolution. He does, however, see tragedy as asserting 'the perfectability of man',[24] the struggle between the given and the possible which lies at the heart of the tragic enterprise having, thereby, perhaps a social no less than a philosophical implication. Certainly tragedy has always constituted a contended site where the limits of freedom and determinism are debated. It exists within that tension.

For Miller, it also exists within another tension. Commenting on the erosion of a tragic vision, he blames it on the pull of the psychological and the sociological in contemporary writing. As he says, 'if all our miseries, our indignities, are born and bred within our minds, then all action, let alone the heroic action, is obviously impossible'. By the same token, 'if society alone is responsible for the cramping of our lives, then the protagonist must needs be so pure and faultless as to deny his validity as a character'.

Death of a Salesman plainly exists within the tension between these two views. Its claim to tragic status lies in part in Miller's belief that in the tragic view 'the need of man to wholly realize himself is the only fixed star', the necessity 'to throw all he has into the contest, the battle to secure his rightful place in his world',[25] to claim 'his whole due as a personality', a struggle which 'must be total and without reservation'.[26] And in this contest the possibility, if not the reality, of victory must be present. Where the potential for such a victory does not exist the result is pathos, 'the mode for the pessimist'. The pathetic, he suggests, 'is achieved when the protagonist is, by virtue of his witlessness, his insensitivity or the very air he gives off, incapable of grappling with a much superior force'.[27]

The question this provokes is what are we to make of Willy Loman? He, after all, commits himself without reservation to securing what he sees as his rightful place in the world, and his whole due as a personality, but he perceives that world inadequately and allows his personality to be so completely infiltrated by the values of that world that he does not so much contest it as seek incorporation. He mistakes the structure and values of his society for a true ontology. To be sure, he is incapable of grappling with a much superior force, the force of a myth which has commanded his imagination and shaped his actions. But when audiences cry during the Requiem, do they respond to a man who had all the wrong dreams, destroyed by a system that barely acknowledges his existence, or do they thrill to a man who has thrown his whole self behind his need to believe in the authenticity and meaning of his life?

We encounter Miller's protagonists in the moment of collapse, when they acknowledge the unravelling of their lives, when the hidden is revealed not to others but to a self at risk of disintegration. But, as Jaspers remarked, 'breakdown and failure reveal the true nature of things. In failure, life's reality is not lost; on the contrary, here it makes itself truly and decisively felt.' Montezuma, in *The Golden Years*, and John Proctor, in *The Crucible*, confront such a failure, finding transcendence through that knowledge. In Jaspers's words, such a process 'is a movement toward man's proper essence, which he comes to know as his own in the presence of his doom'.[28]

There is plainly a level at which Willy Loman and Eddie Carbone are aware of the 'true nature of things', but they are willing to lay down their lives in order to sustain an unreality, to prevent that knowledge becoming definitional. Theirs is an act of denial but one which they are prepared to substantiate with their lives. Neither has that unconditional will to truth, of which Jaspers speaks, but they evidence that sense of guilt which he saw as crucial. 'Tragedy', he insisted, 'becomes self-conscious by understanding the fate of its characters as the consequence of guilt, and as the inner working out of guilt itself. Destruction is the atonement of guilt.'[29] Neither man would acknowledge this, but what is Willy Loman doing but atoning for his life? What is Eddie Carbone's death but a consequence of a guilt which would destroy him were he to acknowledge it directly?

As Miller confessed, these are common men. Their struggles seem far removed from the dilemmas of those whose actions resonate as a consequence of the power they possess or challenge. But, again as Jaspers suggests, 'that man is not God is the cause of his smallness and undoing. But that he can carry his human possibilities to their extreme and can be undone by them with his eyes open – that is his greatness.' The tragic hero 'is shipwrecked by the consistency with which he meets some unconditional demand, real or supposed'.[30] It is not a question of rank. The greatness lies elsewhere than in social status.

Willy Loman's eyes are not fully open, and that is, perhaps, what deflects the tragic arc. In the case of Eddie Carbone, Miller states that he is 'obeying an ancient law which predates the laws we know'. *A View from the Bridge* was, he insisted, 'an attempt to look at informants informing as a tragic act, as an act which finally is unavoidable'.[31] Eddie acts on a compulsion no less absolute and no more remediable than the heroes of Greek drama. Indeed, the arbitrary placing of Catherine in his household, and the arrival of Eddie and Rudolpho like some nemesis, is the beginning of a drama whose classical echoes are deliberately amplified by the narrator–chorus. Eddie breaks a fundamental law not through a sexual act, which is resisted in fact and imagination, but by breaking the bonds of the clan, itself an objectification of the anarchy he comes to represent (incest being a symbolic marker of the anarchic for Freud).

All Miller's protagonists in these early plays, then, contain and express a tension within the culture between private needs and public forms. These have their social and political representations, but at their heart is the question of how the individual is to sustain a sense of himself when infected with guilt and assailed by doubt. The deaths to which they separately go are the price they pay to assuage that guilt, to deny that doubt.

Some, like Willy Loman and Eddie Carbone, die to preserve the meaning with which they wish to invest their lives, a meaning which, objectively, is forfeit but which, subjectively, is not without its inner coherence, at least to themselves. They have, indeed, had the wrong dreams and the wrong desires, and pay the price for having done so, but they have thrown their lives behind the only self they feel they can embrace. To do otherwise would be retrospectively to unmake themselves.

Others, like Montezuma and Joe Keller, stand aghast, all illusion stripped away, aware, suddenly, of a truth which their death serves to underscore. John Proctor, meanwhile, breathes meaning back into a life from which it had been all but evacuated, purging himself at last of guilt and redeeming not only himself but his society by reinstating truth as an unforgiving but ennobling marrow to existence. None, however, was prepared to compromise, finally. Death draws a line across the ledger. None has settled for half, even if what some have settled for is to perform rather than be themselves, actors in a world whose reality is more than they can bear.

In the end it hardly matters whether these plays are seen as tragedies or not. Their meaning is not dependent on conforming to categories or embodying principles laid down by theorists, even, retrospectively, by Miller himself. What does matter, beyond the fact of the plays themselves, their inner dynamic and tangible reality, is Miller's desire to insist that they address not only the plight of individuals but the status of meaning itself.

When he talks of tragedy he is asserting the significance of the lives he stages, the survival of the individual, committed to the integrity of his name, in a world in which so much has been done to deny the integral self and the persistence of identity. He is also acknowledging the continued existence of a society with its legitimate demands as well as corrosive myths, and which he sees as an aggregation of those thinking, feeling individuals, rather than an abstract and threatening force. In deploying the vocabulary of tragedy he is trying to reinvent a language purged alike of despair and irony. He is endeavouring to reach back beyond that breach in experience which leaves the modern world standing aghast at the edge of the pit in which a generation buried its hopes and humanity.

In an essay on 'The Nature of Tragedy', published in 1949, Miller sought to arrive at a definition, while acknowledging the dubious enterprise of trying to stabilise a form which he insisted was always in flux. You are witnessing tragedy, he suggested 'when the characters before you are wholly and intensely realized' while the story in which they are involved, 'is such as to force their complete personalities to be brought to bear upon the problem, to the degree that you are able to understand not only why they are ending in sadness, but how they might have avoided their end'. Tragedy, he insisted, 'arises when we are in the presence of a man who has missed accomplishing his joy. But the joy must be there, the promise of the right way of life . . . Otherwise pathos reigns, and an endless, meaningless, and essentially untrue picture of man is created – man wholly lost in a universe which by its very nature is too hostile to be mastered.'[32]

Willy Loman is only in part the victim of his time and place. There was another path he might have trodden. He is adrift (Linda's banal image of a boat looking for port is not wholly inappropriate), but there are suggestions that he might have rooted his life in meaning. Such meaning has not been evacuated. The realisation, though, lies with the audience not the character. In part this was because Miller had determined that the characters, and Willy in particular, should never go beyond their intellectual and emotional capacity. The consequence, he explained, was that 'unlike standard tragedy, where you have the right . . . to make self-aware statements . . . I never let them become aware of the play they are in.'[33] Willy's problem is in some senses that the door to self-awareness is almost closed. His sense of insufficiency is what drives the play, indeed, in a sense, what brings it into being, since it is constituted in large part by his attempt to retrieve meaning from mere experience. Yet to confront it directly would, in his own mind, be to disestablish the identity he has so laboriously created.

Eddie Carbone, likewise, is denied access to his feelings, as to the language with which he might express and hence confront them. Yet he dies for something, if not for what he or others imagine. He dies because to live would risk that suppressed knowledge breaking through to the surface, not knowledge of his betrayal of his cousins to the immigration service, but the reason for that betrayal. Early in the play we are told of a man, banished from his community for a similar offence. Eddie cannot re-enact such a penance since to leave would be to abandon Catherine, which would be death of another kind. The irony is, therefore, that to stay or to leave would be to lose the person he loves but cannot confess to loving, even to himself. Death is thus the only way he can resolve the dilemma, hold on to an idea of himself as one whose motives sprang from a love thus sanctified if never articulated.

At the moment of his death John Proctor recovers what he was at risk of losing: the love of his wife, the respect of his community, his name. The man who had withdrawn from his marriage and his society alike is brought back to both in an action he resists, Christ-like, but to which he knowingly succumbs. A connection is recovered and asserted not only between an individual life and private and public experience, but between that life and a human meaning that transcends the particularities of time and place.

Willy Loman drives off into the Empyrean, fatally illusioned, but totally committed because defined now, as he believes, by a gesture that has finally marked the true worth of his life. Can a tragic hero die fatally illusioned? It depends, perhaps, on the nature of the knowledge that you grant a Lear who is winnowed and stripped bare but still stands amazed by the undoing of life, as if true understanding can do no more than numb the mind. Can a salesman, mocked by buyers, whose life has been marked with failure and whose language has been infiltrated by the values of the society he is so desperate to embrace, aspire to the stature of tragic hero, as Montezuma, last leader of his people, presumably could? The debate, perhaps, has less to do with this man from Brooklyn, whose heroic quests and epic journeys have taken him no further than New England, than it does with our sense of the connection between private experience and ultimate meaning, with the survival of a sense of human worth which transcends questions of social role.

In a way the debate was particular to a historical moment in which the theatre was posing itself a question about the utility and relevance of past forms. T. S. Eliot and Christopher Fry were exploring verse drama. Greek theatre reappeared in modern guise in adaptations or as model, acknowledged or unacknowledged. Meanwhile, evidence of the systematic cruelties and profound inhumanities of the concentration camps prompted a re-examination of the status of the self, of human nature and of the supposedly humanising nature of art, though many of the works which responded to that re-examination post-dated Miller's early essays on tragedy. Camus's *The Myth of Sisyphus*, written in the early forties, appeared in translation in 1955, Beckett's *Waiting for Godot* appeared in French in 1953, the year of *The Crucible*, but not in English until 1955, the year of *A View from the Bridge*.

Miller seems to have moved away from a concern with the tragic with his plays of the sixties, with *After the Fall*, *Incident at Vichy* and *The Price*. These are works in which a tragic potential is deflected, in which dramatic logic leads in the direction of redemption (*After the Fall*), sacrifice (*Incident at Vichy*) and survival (*The Price*). And when, later, he did write a play, *Broken Glass*, which might seem to bear more directly on his earlier concerns, there was little evidence that he or his critics saw any particular benefit in debating its status as tragic drama, though here, surely, was a work in which the central character reaches a moment of self-understanding in the last minutes of his life, in a play in which the subject is nothing less than the meaning of unmeaning.

Confronted with the reality of Nazi inhumanity (more profound for the audience than the central character since they possess a knowledge in part denied to him), and with his own cruelties and self-denials, the protagonist acknowledges such only in the face of death, an acknowledgement, however, which is enough, perhaps, though only perhaps, not only to grant him absolution, to transform guilt into an uncontested responsibility, but also to reaffirm that there is another avenue than capitulation, another interpretation of suffering and despair. As in classical tragedies, there is a survivor, in this case his wife, Sylvia, who is released to act in a world made more explicable and responsive as a result of a death which is simultaneously an expression of absurdity and a resistant force.

The fact is that discussion of tragedy throws as much light on Miller's state of mind and the state of the culture, on post-war debates about the meaning of human life and the function and integrity of the self, as it does on individual plays. Yet, even so, it shows how quickly he responded to the intellectual and moral no less than the social and psychological issues of his day. Acknowledging that a wound had opened up in human experience he sought neither to cauterise it nor to deny its existence, but to people it.

'It may be the Holocaust clinched the case for reducing personality to a laughable affectation', he observed, adding, 'I am inclined to believe this to be so . . . Scale – implictly defeated us, broke confidence in our claims to being irrevocably in the camp of what was once securely called humanity, and left us with absurdity as the defining human essence.'[34] But if that is so, his drama was designed to resist the logic. To his mind, indeed, theatre itself was a means of reducing the scale, focusing not on the totalising and potentially paralysing fact of a seemingly implacable history, but the struggle by individuals to secure themselves against time and the threat of annihilation.

He was not content to regard that individual as the residue of process and the product and expression of absurdity. Such an individual existed in time, with a history that he must acknowledge and reclaim and with obligations which extend beyond the self. That web of time and causality, that acceptance of the connective tissue linking individual to individual and the self to society, that commitment to redeem a meaning not so much lost as abandoned, he chose to call tragedy.

— ✳ —

The double bill of *A View from the Bridge* and *A Memory of Two Mondays* ran for 149 performances, 80 per cent fewer than for *Death of a Salesman*. For some, *A View from the Bridge* was primarily an attempt to engage the issue of informing and hence part of his argument with Elia Kazan. Miller rejected the idea as reductive. The idea of the play, after all, had been in his head for fifteen years. There is even a reference to it in the notebook he kept while working on *Salesman*.[35]

Much closer to his mind, in truth, was the question of illicit love, of a man in thrall to passions he cannot contain. Even as he was attending rehearsals he was conducting an affair with Marilyn Monroe and had to walk past a life-size cut-out of her in a nearby movie theatre, skirt billowing around her, an image from the Billy Wilder film, *Some Like It Hot*.

His own marriage was in a state of collapse, and had been for a number of years. Monroe was effect rather than cause. Nonetheless, his life was suddenly in turmoil and he has confessed to giving less attention to the double-bill at the Coronet Theatre than he should have done. In retrospect, he was content neither with the acting nor the direction, but his mind was elsewhere.

In 1956 he was summoned before the House Un-American Activities Committee, supposedly because of an enquiry into the misuse of passports but in fact, it seems, because the Committee was increasingly desperate for the kind of publicity that Miller (now divorced) and Monroe could lend to it. While answering questions about his past, he refused to name those with whom he had attended Communist Party meetings. As a result he was cited for Contempt of Congress and potentially faced a year in prison together with a fine.

In the course of the hearings he announced his impending marriage to Monroe, who had been staying at his lawyer's house in Washington, and the marriage duly followed; or, rather, two marriages: one civil and one Jewish. Within two weeks they were on their way to England where she was to star, with Laurence Olivier, in a film of Terrence Rattigan's *The Sleeping Prince* (renamed *The Prince and the Showgirl* for the film version, the first film by the newly established Marilyn Monroe Productions). He, meanwhile, worked with Peter Brook on the British production of the new two-act version of *A View from the Bridge*.

Both saw the marriage as addressing their separate needs. They believed, in particular, that both could continue their careers in a mutually supportive environment. It proved to be an illusion. She was in a more desperate psychological state than he had realised, needing not only prescription drugs to keep her going but also an unquestioning love which required him to intervene on her behalf in disputes with directors, studios and her fellow actors.

For his part, what he wanted was the privacy to write, but being married to Marilyn Monroe was not a quick route to privacy. He had always distrusted Hollywood; now, through his wife, he found himself indirectly married to it, acting as an intermediary for Monroe and even, briefly, becoming a script doctor. There were to be happy times in their brief (though in fact her longest) marriage, but the tensions between them grew. Nor was she to have the children she wished for, suffering two miscarriages.

In was after one of these, and in an attempt to console her, that Miller adapted one of his short stories, 'The Misfits', in an attempt to create a part worthy of the dramatic talent he believed her to have. It was to be a gift. The producer, Frank Taylor, was a friend, the director, John Huston, a man who had helped her earlier in her career. Even the cast was one she admired, in particular Clarke Gable, whom, as a child, she had regarded as her fantasy father. In other words, every effort was made to create an unthreatening environment in which she could work. But when shooting began in Nevada, in 1960, she began to fall apart, as did her marriage.

As was by now her habit, she failed to appear on set until late in the day, often communicating via Paula Strasberg, whose husband Lee was the head of the Actors' Studio where Monroe had worked in New York. Strasberg was widely detested by those working on the film, as she had been by Olivier when she had performed the same role in England. She certainly did nothing to help Monroe's decline. Monroe was now heavily dependent on drugs and the effects were beginning to show on the daily rushes. The studio considered closing the film down but instead agreed to her hospitalisation for a week. In 2004, Miller was to dramatise these events in a play called *Finishing the Picture*.

She did finish the picture and it proved an affecting work. The film ends with her reconciled to the older man to whom she is drawn. In reality, when the picture wrapped she and Miller went their separate ways and she quickly acquired a Mexican divorce. *The Misfits*, however, for all the problems involved in its making, remains an impressive piece of work and a reminder of why people were prepared to tolerate the behaviour of a star who for all her problems could still compel attention, acting out on screen a vulnerability that was real enough.

※

14

'The Misfits'

'The Misfits' first appeared as a story, published in 1957, its title not entirely inappropriate for a man so recently declared Un-American and sentenced to prison for Contempt of Congress. Inspired by Miller's brief stay in Reno where he had gone for divorce proceedings, it tells the story of a group of men who like to think of themselves as cowboys, though to finance their time in the wilderness beyond the city line they have to work. The closest they get to living the life they seem to value is occasional forays in search of wild horses or the rodeos in which, from time to time, one of them displays skills for the most part no longer relevant to a society that has seemingly lost touch with its past and the values it embodied.

Into this world comes a vibrant young woman, Roslyn, her own life in a state of disarray but with the power to energise those around her. In the short story, she remains off-stage, a product of peripheral vision. Yet she is hardly irrelevant. She becomes the catalyst, a source of moral and spiritual reproach as well as of a vivifying energy.

In the film version, she moves to the centre, becoming the outsider who forces the men to reinspect their lives, to see themselves and what they do stripped now of the mythologies with which they have chosen to protect themselves. In their own minds they are free spirits, uncontaminated by modernity, external to the demeaning imperatives of a material world. They are men alone, avoiding emotional commitments as a threat to their independence. Aware that the world is changing, they nonetheless cling to the belief that they are the natural inheritors of a national story of male freedom, but the open range has become the rodeo arena and the cowboy a performer on an empty stage. As John Huston remarked, 'This movie is about a world in change. There was meaning in our lives before World War , but we have lost meaning now. Now the cowboy rides pickup trucks and a rodeo rider is an actor of sorts.'[1]

These are figures who move through and within a space no longer undefined and unlimited. They celebrate their freedom while at every moment offering evidence that they are contained and constrained. They buy what they believe to be their freedom by brief and deeply resented periods working for wages, but that freedom has been drained of meaning. The void is not external but internal. They are empty, and unclear as to how they may address that emptiness. One of them, Guido, had begun to build a house, out beyond the town, but abandoned it when his wife died. It was planned for a life he can no longer live. It stands unfinished and seems an image of lives that are equally unfinished. The incomplete doorway, blank windows staring out into a wilderness, decaying materials, are a correlative for this group of men who cling to an idea whose moment has passed.

In some senses, Guido seems the most vulnerable of them all. He had been dismayed by the death of his wife and protects her memory, or seemingly so. He sees no point in completing the house he was building for her. Yet he is also capable of invoking that memory in his desire for Roslyn. As John Huston observed, 'Guido is probably the most complex character in this film, a bit of a hypocrite. He changes tune. None of the others would. He'd become an animal lover if he could have the girl. He has made his compromises.' As Eli Wallach remarked, 'At the very moment he speaks of his wife he is wooing the girl . . . Guido is a man wrapped up in himself . . . Just about right for a woman who stands behind him one hundred percent, and is as uncomplaining as a tree.'[2]

Guido's real feelings for his wife are exposed when Roslyn asks him why he had never danced with her. Theirs had plainly never been the relationship he chooses to present it as being. He never danced with her in fact or in spirit. Now, he loses out almost immediately to Gay, an aging cowboy clinging to a world already slipping from his grasp, as he appropriates this new woman who seems miraculously to enter his life. Guido knows that for Gay women are merely momentary consolations, distractions. For him, they are potentially something more, if also, essentially, something less, as they do no more than serve his own ego. Nonetheless, when Roslyn asks the men to light a fire in the previously unused fireplace, for a moment the house seems to be the planned home and they to have a purpose once again.

This is a world leaching energy. Guido's aircraft – used to locate and drive the few remaining wild horses – is severely in need of repair, in constant threat of breakdown. The men are scarcely different. They sustain themselves with a rhetoric now evacuated of real content as they implicitly recall a world to which they no longer have real access. They live parodistically, supporting one another in the fantasies they mutually inhabit, fantasies linked to a past in which meaning is presumed once to have existed.

Yet at some level they know they are in a descending spiral. Their hunt for wild horses is conducted from an aircraft and a truck. For all their attempt to appropriate the western myth at the level of language, their actions are already a mockery of that myth. They have broken the code they imagine themselves to be sustaining. The machine is in the garden. Their rights over nature do not derive from their participating in it. They stem from the fact that they are part of the process they despise, a process that begins with an aircraft and a truck and ends with the dogfood can for which the wild horses are destined. Their reward for participation is a fee which they are anxious to distinguish from wages as though they were independent of the procedure they serve, as if they were, indeed, principals and not mere agents. In truth, they are part of a capitalist imperium, possessing the natural world as it governs the lives of these men without women.

They make little money from their ventures and have to suppress their own sense of disgust at what they do and feel. They betray the wild animals and that wild part of themselves they wish to preserve. There is a kinship between the men and animals that they are forced to deny in order to sustain an idea of themselves as free beings engaged in a worthy contest. Yet, in effect, they are killing themselves as well.

Nor are the horses any less misfits than the men who hunt them. They are also the last of a dying breed. Their freedom is contingent, liable to be revoked at any moment. Their natural fears are turned against them. Like the men who hunt them, they cling together in a small group, as if that gave them some protection against what threatens them. In the end it is what makes them more vulnerable.

At one level, this group of men know they are playing a losing game, that the open spaces are closing and that the coherence they seek is draining from their lives. It is evident in the mantra they repeat about the danger of working for wages; it is there in the rhetoric of freedom counterpoised to the reality of their existence. In their own minds, however, they can still act with integrity, perform exemplary, even archetypal roles, having a place in some master-story. Yet they cannot help but be aware that their lives are deeply compromised. They rely on one another not simply to capture the wild horses but to sustain their image of themselves as free souls, defining themselves in terms of their relationship to a nature they wish to believe is resistant to contamination and co-option.

The problem is that space has become place. A timeless world is now subject to mechanical rhythms. There is an ecological and biological clock ticking. They, the wild horses, and the environment they inhabit, are at the end of the line. There are already tracks into the wilderness that will become roads. This is a story about America no less than this scattering of people on what was once the frontier, simultaneously the heart of a vivifying and defining nature and the leading edge of American civilisation. It is a contradiction that defined much of nineteenth-century American literature, from Cooper to Twain, as it was the contradiction at the heart of an American enterprise that celebrated a New Eden and proposed progress as a national destiny.

However, Roslyn seems suddenly to have charged them with possibility. Guido and Gay, the latter being the heart of the story, abandon the town for the country, as though she could, indeed, revivify them and it. But there is an air of the temporary about them, as if they were staving off an already inevitable ending. The myth to which they commit themselves is seemingly the guarantee of continuity and continuance but they are plainly in a literal and spiritual cul de sac.

Reno itself is a place of bars, divorce lawyers, people passing through, disrupted lives, a cityscape as unpeopled in its way as the land that surrounds it. It is a last stop, a place where dreams founder and relationships end. This America is uncommunal, with no access to its own myths, no sense of purpose or direction. Men and women are drawn together and thrust apart. The city's two principal businesses are divorce and gambling, the former evidence of a gamble that failed to pay off.

When he subsequently published *The Misfits* at book length, in 1961, it was, he insisted, written in an unfamiliar form, 'neither novel, play, nor screenplay'. Conceived as a film and devised 'for the purpose of telling the camera what to see and the actors what they are to say', it nonetheless expanded on the abbreviated, 'telegraphic, diagrammatic' manner of screenplay-writing in order to explore more completely 'the nuances of character and place'.[3] The result, he believed, was a 'mixed form'.

At times the speech is set out like dialogue in the film script from which it derived, yet at the same time it sinks its roots into a more fictive soil:

> Guido: 'Oh, hello! How'd you make out?'
> Roslyn, shyly: 'O.K. It's all over.'
> He nods, uncertain how to proceed, and beckons Gay over, partly as a relief
>   from his tension.
> 'Like you to meet a friend of mine. This is Gay Langland. Mrs Taber . . .'
> Gay, realizing she is the one: 'Oh! How-de-do.'
> Guido, of Isabelle: 'And this is . . .'
> 'Isabelle Stears.' To Roslyn . . .
>
> (24)

The narrative voice becomes the instructional plural of camera direction – 'We can see through our windshield almost to the end of Main Street, a dozen blocks away' (9). That voice is disinterested, observing without commentary, except through interpretative juxtapositions. Thus, a 'sedate' bank and 'elegant' women's clothing store are seen next to a store with the word 'Craps' on its window. Other signs – 'Horse Betting', 'Casino' – are alongside one for 'Wedding Rings'. Characters drift across what is, in effect, a camera eye, only to disappear, not so much aspects of the plot as the backdrop to lives as yet not in vision.

We hear, too, the voice of a central character before we see him. We are led into the story through the passing figures, each of whom contributes to the sense of a town whose proud claim is to be the biggest little city in the world. Thus, of a woman who asks directions of the still invisible driver, we are told, 'There is a rural pathos in her eyes, an uprooted quality in the intense mistrust with which she walks' (10). Thin, with an ill-fitting dress, a baby and a suitcase, she asks the way to the courthouse which in this town can only mean divorce and, indeed, a moment later we are told that a sign reads 'Divorce Actions One Flight Up'. This is a city of lost souls in a country of lost visions. When they were shooting the film Miller and the cast gravitated to Virginia City nearby, a ghost town recalling a time of lost dreams.

The car continues through daylight streets on which neon signs nonetheless continue to shine and along which figures move with 'the preoccupied air of the disconnected' (10). Inside the stores, shoppers pause to pull the levers of slot-machines with little hope of reward. From the car radio, meanwhile, comes jazz, interrupted by commercials for coffee and sleeping pills, the stimulants and depressives that define the parameters of those who live in a place that proudly declares itself the divorce capital of the world, a title wrested from Las Vegas.

The car finally comes to a halt in a decayed suburban area and only now does the first of the five characters at the centre of the story come into view. Guido, about forty, working for a Reno garage, seems, we are told, a university sophisticate at one moment and 'a man in the usual industrial haze' (12) the next, though in truth there is little evidence of the former. Before the first words are exchanged Miller thus creates a portrait of a small town, surrounded by 'a stateful of sand and mountains', that seems to have no reason for existing beyond its utility as a centre for gambling and divorce. He describes a society with the air of the temporary.

The town has a statue, facing the divorce court, commemorating the pioneer families that once passed this way. As the story develops so the symbolic force of this becomes apparent, the ironic gap between frontier values and modern reality generating the irony that contains and defines the lives of those who act out the rituals and lay claim to the myths of a world that has gone. Around the statue, meanwhile, sit derelicts and old men, watching strangers on their way to end relationships they once thought the source of meaning and hope. Sometimes, Miller suggests, young couples are to be seen looking through their wedding photographs, unaware of the significance of the divorce court across the street, versions of Beckett's characters born astride the grave.

Guido has arrived to appraise a new Cadillac convertible, 'banged up all around', whose battery is drained, a vehicle that shares something with those we encounter. Isabelle, the woman he now meets, bears similar scars. She is described as kind, sentimental, 'with an amused untidiness that approaches an air of wreckage and a misspent intelligence' (13), a woman who has been a witness at twenty-seven divorce actions. The men also carry the marks of their encounter with the world. By contrast, though, Roslyn, who appears framed in the window of the rooming house, is a 'golden girl . . . in perfectly good order', though with 'a certain stilled inwardness' (15).

Roslyn's case against her husband, though not one that can be adequately expressed in the legal jargon she struggles to learn, is that he was simply 'not there'. There is an absence at the heart of their relationship, an absence echoed in the lives of those she now encounters, as in the literal and psychic territory they inhabit.

This is the place, then, where people come to acknowledge failure and regain a freedom that already carries the weight of defeat. For Gay, the bruised and disoriented women who come to Reno are a kind of natural prey, though not in a destructive sense. They are his way of killing a loneliness he will not acknowledge. They look for something redemptive and lasting, he for a temporary alliance, a way of filling a void to which he will not confess. He admires those women who understand the nature of the contract he offers, but it is a contract that underlines the incomplete, evanescent nature of relationships that are no more than evidence of his lack of commitment to anything but his own self-image as a free soul.

It is a life based on betrayal and defeat, of himself no less than of others. The wild in him has been defeated as much as it is in the horses he hunts and which are dragged to a halt by car tyres at the other end of ropes strung round their necks. The cowboys, too, are dragged to a halt not only by their broken lives and personal histories, but also by the weight of modern society which reaches out to them, even here where they like to believe they are free souls defining themselves through their relationship to nature.

Gay is forty-nine, his life on the turn. He seems in some respects to be suspended in time and space. He lapses into moments in which he is 'simply not here and not now' (21). Relationships are deliberately distant. We encounter him first as he says goodbye to a woman who is looking for love and permanence, but her function, for him, is to be a 'good sport', which is to say leave without regret and without demands. Towards Guido, meanwhile, he has 'a business friendliness, but there is no business'. He does not 'expect very much' and 'has no desire to lead' (21). His time horizon is seldom more than two weeks. Life, for him, 'is a pageant with no head and no tail'. He has no home beyond the perimeter of his own self. He has no guile, because his commitments do not bite deep enough. Neither do his minor betrayals. Like the others, he seems to seek no more than 'a path through the shapeless day', but when Roslyn enters that day it suddenly acquires a shape.

He sees himself reflected in her eyes and what he sees enlivens and disturbs him in equal proportions, for she is a woman who refuses to dissemble. Hers is an emotional world. She encounters other people at the level of need, registers their pain, their sense of abandonment. She craves, acknowledges and offers tenderness and as a result is vulnerable even as she recognises the vulnerability of other people. She is a catalyst.

For Huston, Gay is the 'modern hero' who has 'faced the responsibilities of manhood', but 'there is an element of absurdity' about him and his companions 'in that what they're doing is pointless, if not ugly. Their accomplishment is subjective.'[4] For Miller, 'Most of us are looking for a place to hide and watch it all go by. But one of Gay Langland's great mottoes is "I'll teach you how to live."'[5] He is able to hold on to his illusions, if not his convictions, because of the world in which he moves.

As Miller remarks, 'The freedom that Nevada offers is the opposite of selling your existence for the rewards and punishments of a so-called civilized existence, in which you can have everything but yourself . . . The cowboy was never a part of civilization. He is a natural man, wandering all over the state.'[6] The cowboy, moreover,

> had no need to prove himself through violence . . . The Hemingway guys have to find some physical proof of their existence. In my character this proof is carried within himself. The reason he takes her out there to the mustangs is that's his trade. He fears he's losing her. He asserts his identity. He wants to call up his powers. When he's doing his work he feels most himself. He wants her to see the power within himself. Probably the best way of summarizing it is that the balance of disaster and hope in life is finally struck by both these people.[7]

The hope, ironically, lies in his willingness finally to lay his powers, his magic, aside, like some latter-day Prospero, not least because he, too, comes to understand that that magic has actually served to isolate him from the organic world of change and growth. For her part, Roslyn, too, must change. It is, as Miller insists, the end of flight, 'when she comes to see that the violence in man, which is the violence in all of us, can exist side by side with love'.[8] Until this point, she, and the man she has travelled west to divorce, had been content to live 'the half-sincere existence which leaves people basically concealed from one another and half alive'.

To Miller, 'It's a disaster. We're no longer real. We're becoming shallow people . . . What this picture is trying to do', he insisted, 'is awaken us to ourselves.'[9] When at the end of the film Gay captures the stallion only to cut it loose it is, Miller suggests, 'his last totally free act'. But on the other side of that act is another kind of freedom as he prepares to commit himself to a woman who is herself at the end of a journey of understanding.

After a series of plays in which his central character died, Miller insisted that 'the documentation of defeat' was no longer on his agenda because 'man always squeaks through'.[10] But the balance was a delicate one and the ending rewritten several times. Meanwhile, it took Gay the full length of the film to reach the level of understanding that Miller finally felt necessary.

For most of their lives, Guido and Gay have been in recoil from complexity. They want to simplify their lives. Commitment, after all, carries the risk of entrapment and it is that which they think they escape in opting for the open spaces beyond the town. But the frontier has long since closed, the contrast between nature and civilisation collapsed. Guido's aircraft can now encircle the open land as the vehicles on which they travel cut tracks across a once trackless waste. Even Guido's half-finished house is a bridgehead for the domesticity they imagine themselves to be escaping. Not merely have they lit out for the territory ahead of the rest, they are the contamination they fear, and, as in the western, the woman is both desired and resisted, a symbol alike of consolation and entrapment. Gay fears the very domestication that may be his ambiguous redemption as Roslyn fears a wildness that encompasses cruelty as well as freedom.

Nor were the ironies attaching themselves to the story only a product of the script. When it was filmed, each of the principal actors was at the end of things in the most literal of ways. Gable was weeks away from his death. Montgomery Clift, who played Guido and Gay's fellow hunter, was physically and mentally injured, while Monroe, for whom this was also a last film, was acting out a divorce on screen as her marriage fell apart off screen. Failure, however, was already written into the text. Though it appears to end on a note of assonance and hope, the failure of this seems implicit in everything we have seen of these desperate people struggling to handle the fact of decline.

But, for Miller, no matter how slender the hope, how fragile the relationship between Rosyln and Gay, there remained a tenuous possibility. As he explained at the time of filming, 'For a long time now I've wanted to make something of existence. It's tragic – after all, we all die here – but there's something in between. Gay and Roslyn will die, but they can face it with dignity. They can do right, and not be like jerks. It may not sound much but it's taken a lot to get me to that point.'[11] The release of the horses, at Roslyn's insistence, may seem to humiliate Gay but in fact it frees him, too. Their new alliance may be fragile but there is a commitment neither had felt free to make before.

For Roslyn, life has been defined by absence and withdrawal. Her parents had abandoned her for months at a time. The house, where they all gather together, is as 'alone as a stranded boat' (130), and seems an apt image of those who arrive there, having driven from town. To Roslyn, it is 'like an unrealized longing', and that, indeed, is its function. It is possibility, once abandoned, and now brought to life again.

Gay is transformed. He and Roslyn settle down together and he sets himself to prepare the garden as if he will be there to see the results of his labour, as if the future had suddenly been reinvented and his temporal horizon extended beyond two weeks. Yet there is still a gulf between him and Roslyn who is, unsurprisingly, like the woman in Miller's short story 'Please Don't Kill Anything', since she, too, was based on Monroe. When Gay moves to defend this new garden by killing the rabbits that threaten it, it is as if he has brought violence into the heart of their new domesticity, as if she were at risk from something in a man who has previously shown her only gentleness and concern.

Roslyn feels a growing horror at the fate of the wild animals they are capturing, animals once caught for riding but now, she eventually learns, for dog food. Their beauty is as easily reducible as her own. Her new respect for Gay does battle with her deeper instincts. Having been hurt herself, she cannot bear to think of pain coming to the animals they hunt. At stake on the one hand is the pride of the men and on the other the fate of the vulnerable.

When Gay takes a shotgun to a rabbit Roslyn tries to stop him because 'it's alive', recognising a kinship with the vulnerable animal, a fact underlined by Guido's comment that she has 'the gift of life'. For the moment, though, Gay and Roslyn appear to have found a refuge. The house is transformed. It has the feeling of a shelter, though a shelter that provides an incomplete protection. As Guido suggests, they are all looking 'for a place to hide and watch it all go by' (56). This might be that place. It was where he himself had worked when he was 'still ambitious' (55), but, as with the others, his future now lies behind him.

For Gay, there is the memory of a marriage that went wrong. He admits to having two children, who he sees a couple of times a year, and a former wife, who had betrayed him with one of his best friends, a fact which taught him that 'nothin's it. Not forever' (50). We also learn something of Roslyn's past as she opens a cupboard to reveal photographs of herself in fishnet tights outside a second-class nightclub in which, it appears, she was a nude dancer (a shadow of Monroe's past). Hopes have degraded into regrets.

In an effort to break their mood they set off for a rodeo, on the way picking up Perce Howland, a bucking horse rider in his late twenties, 'a resident of nowhere, who sleeps most often in his clothes' (59), and bears the marks of his profession. They wait as he makes a call home from a payphone, a one-sided conversation that nonetheless communicates the distance between himself and his family (a scene which Montgomery Clift managed in a single take). There is, it appears, betrayed love in his life, too, a betrayal that has set him on the move like those he now joins. His father, we later learn, had died and his new stepfather offered him wages to work the land which should have been his. His mother had chosen a stranger over her son, leaving him what he now is, a wanderer, another misfit.

The drive to the rodeo takes them through alkali waste, sterile and empty. Nature, it seems, is no resource. As they approach Dayton we are offered a description of the river valley, coated with white gypsum, and the mountains 'like dumps of slag the colour of soot . . . There is no tree, no bush, no pool of water.' The land is acid-stained. It is 'absolute' (64) in its ugliness. This is a town with no police and no law. Violence is in the air, a sense of absurdity. When Roslyn says that it is 'Like in the movies' (65), she is not wrong for this is a place in which the cowboys model themselves on the images they have seen on the screen. Stephen Crane's 'The Blue Hotel' and Nathanael West's *The Day of the Locust* are not far away.

Miller offers an impressionistic account of a town of mingled privacies and clogged crowds, a place of simmering insanity, surreal and disturbing. In the bar, two juke-boxes and a television compete in a 'paralysing noise' (68). Roslyn finds herself playing with a child's paddle bat (in a scene added to the film when Miller saw his wife demonstrating her skill with this toy) as Perce takes bets on the number of times she can hit the ball. She nearly gives the money away when accosted by an old woman ostensibly collecting for church funds, responding to her mad appeals to give to 'the only one that loves you in your lonely desert' (71).

At the rodeo, Roslyn reacts to the suffering of the animals as much as to the danger confronting the men, perhaps because the suffering is sexual, the strap looped around the horses' testicles inducing the bucking. In the rodeo, though, the men are cut off from her. She cannot understand what drives them or why they accept the pain. Miller's description in part provides the answer in the sheer momentum of the event, its power to suck fractions of time, fragments of experience, into a narrative that echoes the timeless logic which forces the characters on, sheer intensity substituting for the kind of meaning for which Roslyn searches.

The account of the rodeo is impressive not only for the Hemingwayesque descriptions of fact and action, productive rather than descriptive of emotion, but also for its subtle staging of the relationship between the three men and between Roslyn's concern for the tortured animals and alarm at Perce's injuries. Beyond the battle of man and beast is another, just as elemental, as men are torn between their commitment to one another and their desire for the woman who has suddenly charged their lives with an ambiguous meaning.

At the centre, then, is a damaged woman, wanting to believe in the reality of love, adrift in a world that never holds still long enough for her to make sense of it. Afraid of change, she is frightened, too, that she seems to inhabit a place quite alien to those around her: 'It's like you scream and there's nothing coming out of your mouth, and everybody's going around, "Hello, how are you, what a nice day", and it's all great – and you're dying!' (83).

When Perce, still partly in shock and bewildered by the effects of an injection, makes a play for her, she says, 'I don't know where I belong' (86), a statement that Perce echoes but which any of them might have endorsed, as they might her conviction that 'Maybe all there really is is what happens next, just the next thing, and you're not supposed to remember anyone's promises' (88).

The truth of that becomes apparent when Gay's son and daughter arrive but immediately desert him in a bar before he can introduce them to Roslyn. For a moment, as he stands on the hood of a car and calls for them, it is possible to detect what drove them from him as it is what attracts them back. The only continuity in this world of broken people and shattered relationships seems to be provided by the figure of an Indian who moves stoically and silently through the action, merging into the countryside, always alone even when he finds himself in the middle of a crowd.

As they drive back from the rodeo, so Guido seems to drift into a strange frame of mind. Despite Roslyn's protests, he accelerates to ninety miles an hour, recalling his relationship with his wife, not quite as perfect, it seems, as he had implied: 'We're all blind bombardiers', he says, 'we kill people we never even saw ... droppin' a bomb is like tellin' a lie – makes everything so quiet afterwards. Pretty soon you don't hear anything, don't see anything. Not even your wife' (91–2).

There is more to this broken man than his graceless gestures at seduction. 'How do you get across to somebody', he asks, 'I don't *know* anybody. Will you give me a little time?' (92). But time is running out on all of them. When they arrive back at the house he can do no more than walk away into the darkness before trying to hammer sheathing board on to the unfinished house as though reclaiming it as his own. The evening winds down, the implications of the day slowly catching up with them. Roslyn, in particular, has seen a glimpse of Gay's anger that leaves her, suddenly, alone again. There are unresolved tensions in the air.

For Gay, they will be resolved the following day, when the hunt for the horses begins, though Perce's reaction has already implied the absurdity of the venture. For him, rounding up a thousand horses would make some sense, but hardly the fifteen Guido has located. In the end, the fifteen will become five. Their quest has effectively become absurd. For Roslyn, though, it has become worse than that. Hypersensitive as she is to suffering, her belated discovery that the wild horses are to die leaves her distraught.

On the trail, Gay's horse begins to shake, aware, according to Guido, that if other animals are to die, its life is threatened. Shortly afterwards Roslyn, newly aware of the purpose of the hunt, herself begins to shake, and for much the same reason. For her, there is no distinction between the wild horses and herself. She feels the threat and Gay is its origin.

For Gay himself, the world has turned around. He hunts because 'up here I'm my own man'. In his mind he has not changed. He is still enacting not only a primal ritual but a national myth. The world has changed; he has remained constant:

> 'When I started, they used a lot of them I caught. There was mustang blood pullin' all the ploughs in the West; they couldn't have settled here without somebody caught mustangs for them. It . . . it just got changed around, see? I'm doin' the same thing I ever did. It's just that they . . . they changed it around . . . It was a good thing to do . . . it was a man's work.'
>
> (100–1)

It is not a man's work now, in its means no less than its end, but it is what he does, and that is as far as his logic extends. In his mind the world must be what it was. Guido, in staring at the stars, had remarked that their light perhaps came from worlds which no longer existed, '"In other words, we can only see what something was, never what it is now."' (98). That would seem to be true of Gay and, in a sense, of all of them. The light from their past is what floods their lives, though they are aware that something has died, that the grace they had sought has been withdrawn somewhere along the line. They are trying to live with the fact of that withdrawal.

Gay's aria continues as he recognises Roslyn's sense of betrayal, suggesting, in his own defence, that the compromises into which he has been forced are merely those pressed upon everyone by the processes of living.

> Maybe we're all the same . . . We start out doin' something, meaning no harm, something that's naturally in us to do. And somewhere down the line it gets changed around into something bad. Like dancin' in a night club. You started out just wanting to dance, didn't you. And little by little it turns out that people ain't interested in how good you dance, they're gawkin' at you with something altogether different in their minds. And they turn it sour, don't they? . . . I could've looked down my nose at you, too – just a kid showin' herself off in night clubs for so much a night. But I took my hat off to you. Because I know the difference . . . This . . . this is how I dance, Roslyn. And if they made somethin' else out of it, well . . . I can't run the world any more than you could. I hunt those horses to keep myself free.
>
> (102)

As they hunt down the horses so the tension rises until, with the animals trussed up, Roslyn finally cracks. Gay is on the point of freeing them as a gesture of his affection for her when she offers to buy them from him, a gesture he interprets as an insult. The tensions between them, meanwhile, seem to release the other men to make their own approaches to what they had grudgingly accepted as his woman. She rejects them but Perce releases the animals. Gay then recaptures the stallion, re-establishing his pride, pitching himself not so much against the animal as against the forces that threaten to overwhelm him.

For Guido, the moral of these events is that 'we don't need nobody in this world' (138). Gay himself, however, now makes his peace, acknowledging, at last, his own complicity: '"God damn them all! They changed it. Changed it all around. They smeared it all over with blood, turned it into shit and money just like everything else . . . It's just like ropin' a dream now."' He accepts the need to find 'some other way to know you're alive . . . if they got another way, any more' (138–9).

For a moment, everything is in the balance but finally they make their way back to one another. To her question, 'What is there that stays?' (140), the answer seems to be the relationship between two people, damaged, bewildered, but together in their sense of the possibility of renewal. When she asks, 'How do you find your way back in the dark?' (141), the question is not simply about how Gay navigates across the featureless desert in the night. It is query about how he and she will rediscover what they had thought lost.

The potential sentimentality of the ending is vitiated by the raw pain they have separately and mutually suffered, and by their awareness of the doors that have finally closed in their lives. It is also contained and controlled by a language that is spare to the point of the poetic. If the story is itself a metaphor it also works by a series of metaphors, each unelaborated, working in and through characters who see their connection to one another and the natural world in terms of simple necessities that remain unexamined until a final confrontation brings them face to face with the failed utopias that are their lives.

In an earlier ending Gay was to have been defeated by the mustang and left lying on the lake bed. The crucial difference between the two endings lies in the fact that in the final version he is never broken. He simply lays his life before the woman he loves. At the same time, Clark Gable, though pleased with the revised ending, believed that 'if this place was full of horses, he'd go right on catching them at the end of the picture . . . He only quits because of his love for the girl, which is a hell of a fine reason . . . He was in hopes she would see his side of it, but all she sees is the cruelty.'[12] Now he has to 'find another way to be alive'.[13]

Nonetheless, in a letter to Miller in December 1960, following Gable's death, Eve Arnold, the Magnum photographer, recalled a conversation with the actor in which Gable had insisted that not a word of his part should be changed. It was, he remarked, all in the script.

— ✳ —

In the nine-year silence between *A View from the Bridge* and *After the Fall* Miller finished nothing but *The Misfits*. There are a number of pieces from this period but nothing that was pressed through to completion. Nor had he been as active politically and socially as he had been before. The Contempt of Congress conviction, however, had been quashed and America was manifestly changing. He had watched the Kennedy–Nixon debates on television when he was in Nevada and the subsequent election seemed to mark something of a transformation in the country. Indeed, he found himself invited to the White House for the inauguration. What he had seen as a repressive period seemed to be over. Suddenly intellectuals, writers, artists seemed welcome in Washington, though he joked that it seemed to be strange to be going there without a lawyer.

His personal life also took a turn for the better. He had met a young woman on the set of *The Misfits* and though this had been no more than a casual encounter, back in New York they were drawn to one another. With two failed marriages behind him, however, he hesitated to commit himself again, as did Inge Morath who had a failed marriage of her own.

Inge had suffered in the war. Born and raised in Austria, she had refused to join the Nazi Party and was required to do compulsory war work in Berlin (in fact a requirement for most people of her age), walking free, finally, as allied bombs fell on the city. In shock and despair, she had set out to walk to her native Salzburg, on her way climbing on to a bridge with suicide in mind. She survived and in time became a photographer with the Magnum picture agency.

Now married to Miller, in 1962 she took him to Mauthausen concentration camp, confronting her own demons there. She had suffered under the Nazis but still felt guilty. Miller had witnessed events in Europe from a distance. Now he was brought face to face with the evidence of wartime depravity. It would leave its mark on his plays.

In part to work out his complex feelings he began to write a play which would address his own anxieties and locate them in the context of a history littered with human betrayals. At the heart of the play was clearly the figure of Marilyn Monroe, while the protagonist was equally clearly himself. *After the Fall*, though he was inclined to deny it at the time, was a confessional but also an attempt to understand the past in an effort to justify the future.

While he was writing, Monroe died of an overdose. During rehearsals President Kennedy was assassinated. Things seemed to be falling apart.

The play was staged by the new Lincoln Center company, designed as a national repertory theatre, though never in fact to fulfil that function. The building was as yet incomplete but a temporary building was constructed and *After the Fall* inaugurated it. The play reunited Miller with Elia Kazan. This was the first time the two men had worked together since Kazan's appearance before the House Un-American Activities Committee in 1952. Ironically, Kazan was a character in the play he now proceeded to direct.

✳

15

'After the Fall'

After the Fall seems to be Miller's attempt to draw together a number of threads in his own life, the life of his society and a post-war world still haunted, nearly twenty years on, by the implications of the Holocaust. It is a play which equally acknowledges the superfluity of evil, which was the black gift of the Nazis, the wilful surrender of private conscience in the face of public coercion, evidenced by the witch-hunts of the fifties, and the insidious and corrupting banality of private betrayals.

At its heart is Quentin, on the verge of his third marriage and unsure how he can commit himself having failed twice before. The betrayals of those earlier relationships seem to disqualify him from such a commitment. Accordingly, he searches back in his mind in an attempt to understand the nature and extent of his failure. But what is true on a personal level is true, too, on a social, political and moral level. He has lived through the witch-hunts of the 1950s, in which betrayal was proposed as a national virtue, and become more conscious than once he had been of that most profound of human failings: the Holocaust. The play is thus concerned not merely with Quentin's struggle to justify moving on, but with the need to make sense of what seems a deeply flawed humanity.

Betrayed human commitments, at whatever level, are, he insists, evidence of something factored into human behaviour. And yet there is no nostalgia for innocence here: 'It's quite the opposite to me, I think.' Miller has said that

> the basic thrust of the play is that the enemy is innocence . . . That is, until you give up your innocence, you are very open to crime . . . The problem with crime is that those who commit it cannot conceive themselves as the ones who committed the crime. In one way or another we are all victims, one man of his family, another man of society . . . and if that's going to be the limitation of the vision then we are really finished because everybody can justify anything on the basis that he is only paying back the world for what it did to him. If there is an enemy, so to speak, of man, it's the idea of innocence.[1]

The challenge was to find a form which could draw together seemingly diverse elements. In the end that form is a product of its method as memories crowd into the mind of Quentin, the central character. Sometimes these are no more than recovered words or phrases, seemingly dislocated, shaken free of context. At other times they take the form of an image or even an unwinding narrative performed in what appears to be real time, except that there is no real time beyond that moment in which these memories crowd together in a single consciousness, slowly forming a moral mosaic.

Meaning resides in the individual fragments, in the juxtapositions and in the accumulating logic of layered moments, words, actions. This is a kaleidoscope in which the protagonist and, beyond him, the playwright, discovers the patterns, the stories that will emerge with each shake of the hand. If music is form without content, *After the Fall* is a play in which content generates form.

After the Fall, like *Death of a Salesman*, takes place inside the head of its protagonist, a man who admits to being a stranger to his own life, to having lived an unexamined life. Now, bewildered by a sense of moral failure, debilitated by a stultifying guilt, he is afraid to move forward. The future is 'like a vase that must never be dropped'.[2] The reason for his paralysis lies in the necessity to undertake an honest evaluation of the past. Much the same is true of a society which is equally characterised by denial. As he confesses, 'we conspired to violate the past, and the past is holy and its horrors are holiest of all!'[3] *After the Fall* is Miller's attempt to stare into the heart of darkness. The repressed returns in a play in which memories become the evidence on which the central character draws as he acts as judge in a trial in which not only he but mankind stands accused.

After the Fall, Miller explained, was to be 'a way of looking at man and his human nature as the only source of the violence which has come closer and closer to destroying the race'. As he confessed, he was no longer concerned to 'look towards social or political ideas as the creators of violence, but into the nature of the human being himself'. Not fascism as such, then, viewed as an aberration to be explained by reference to socio-political pressures, or even the pathology of those who developed its ethos. Not reactionary demagoguery, with its callous disregard of individual lives; nor even the small change of daily life, with its casual betrayals and broken compacts, but man himself. The 'common denominator', it now seemed to him was 'the human being'. That, in turn, led him back to the Bible, the ur-story of paradise lost. The Fall constituted a primal choice. It was the moment that the concept of the self was born, along with a sense of guilt and the reality of death. And from that came the logic of Cain's equally primal act. From the sense of self derives a drive to survive, an urge for primacy.

In writing an introduction to the version of *After the Fall* that appeared in the *Saturday Evening Post*, Miller outlined his sense of human history as a battle between the imperial self, the urge to 'express without limit one's unbridled inner compulsion, in this case to murder', and the attempt to 'pacify the destructive impulses of man, to express his wishes for greatness, for wealth, for accomplishment, for love, but without turning law and peace into chaos.'[4] For him, *After the Fall* was about how that pacification is to be attained.

Quentin enters the play oppressed by his sense that neither his own life nor the world makes any sense. A successful man, his success seems without meaning, precisely because it is detached from any deeper meaning. He is living in a world without transcendence. At the heart of everything, as it seems to him, is nothing more meaningful than his own egotism. Others have failed, indeed everybody in the play, with the possible exception of the redemptive figure that is Holga, has failed, but he feels unable to apportion blame so aware is he that he himself is a hollow man. It is the fact of Holga, however, a woman he loves, that makes him aware that he has a choice; how to survive without subjecting the world to his will, how to acknowledge the pull of absurdity and yet assert the survival of values? To Miller, such a choice requires self-knowledge. Hence the form of the play, which is that of a confessional (even if the priest in whose ear he whispers is himself, the God to whom he speaks is the tortured self), a trial (even if he be both penitent and judge), a psychoanalytic session in which he is patient and analyst alike.

The central impulse, Miller suggests, is, like Cain's, to deny responsibility, to absolve oneself, yet within the terms of the biblical story there can be no innocence. As he observes, there is no way of sticking the apple back on the tree. Quentin yearns for that innocence, but when did it exist? He pushes back beyond the failure of his second marriage, beyond the failure of his first, back beyond the political persecutions of the 1950s and the genocide of the 1940s. He reaches towards childhood, only to discover, in retrospect, that betrayal and cruelty, self-regard and a casual use of power, equally typified that moment. The remembered unity never really existed. Paradise, Miller observes, 'keeps slipping back and back'. We are born with needs which we regard as taking precedence over others'.

Here, then, as it seems to him, is the origin not only of private but also public cruelties. His assertion of that causal link, however, is not without its problems and that is apparent in the language of his summary of the play's central theme. 'Always, and from the beginning, the panorama of human beings raising up in him and in each other the temptation of the final solution to the problem of being a self at all – the solution of obliterating whatever stands in the way, thus destroying what is loved as well.'[5] The phrase 'the final solution' is not used innocently, and while critics at the time were distracted by autobiography the greater problem, potentially, lies in a homogenising of guilt. We are all flawed, all ready to subordinate others to ourselves, so that the concentration-camp guard and his victims hold hands in depravity and the cruel words of husband to wife seem to be seen as having an equivalence with mass murder.

Merely to state the objection is to suggest that Miller would hardly wish to sustain such an idea. He does, quite deliberately, suggest that those guilty of genocide *were* close kin to those who suffered and that it was not impossible to conceive circumstances in which the roles might be reversed, that, in fact, this is a central and painful truth of these events. But he makes a distinction between those who, like Camus's Caligula, live out the logic of a perceived absurdity and those who pitch against it a meaning whose contingency is redeemed by its humanity. The essence is for the individual to acknowledge his murderous instincts but 'forever guard against his own complicity with Cain'.

It is, he confesses, a play written 'at the edge of the abyss', which is where Quentin, and, indeed, mankind finds himself. It is a play in which he struggles to find an answer to the absurdists as much as it is an attempt to understand the murderous instincts which his protagonist struggles to acknowledge and yet to resist. It is a play which borrows the form of a psychoanalysis but which also borrows from Freud. The model of murderous impulses, an anarchic id and dominating superego necessarily restrained, was one entirely familiar from his work.

After the Fall is a play full of accusations, threaded through with a sense of potentially debilitating guilt. It takes place within the mind of a man momentarily stunned by a sudden awareness of his complicity with a world he thought he had the right to judge, only to discover the roots of faithlessness, cruelty and denial in himself. No longer defending his own innocence he allows others to voice their accusations, while understanding that their own cruelties stem from the same desire to stand justified, to deny blame and responsibility. Fearful that he has been in the service of nothing more than success, aware of the fragility of his moral commitments, he becomes defence and prosecuting attorney, presenting the evidence of his own failures, his own moral dubiety, but also the failures of a culture and a world in which some fundamental principles seem no longer operative. For private cruelties have their public counterparts, a fact he learns when he meets Holga, a woman who takes him to a concentration camp.

The apparently contingent, he realises, conceals a human nature capable equally of love and cruelty, compassion and disregard: 'One day the house smells of fresh bread – the next of smoke and blood. One day you faint because the gardener cut his finger off, within a week you're climbing over the corpses of children bombed in a subway.'[6] This, in short, is a world seen after the Fall. But such a perception may open up the passage to something more than remorse, something more than guilt. For the double heritage of the Fall was, of course, death and knowledge.

In an entry in one of his notebooks, dated 27 January 1958, Miller commented on 'The insufficiency of guilt as a basis for morality'. *After the Fall* is, essentially, concerned with the need to overcome that sense of paralysis, evidenced in a number of his plays, which comes when guilt becomes merely an occluding fact, intransitive, untranslatable into action. In fact the play, though it tumbles with incident and seemingly moves back and forth in time, occurs within that stasis until, in the final moment, the protagonist, Quentin, discovers reason to move on.

After the Fall is a play in which Miller seeks, no doubt for profoundly important personal and psychological reasons, but also, clearly because he thought the passage of time had made it possible to explore the implications of recent history, to find some justification for continuing. And since the play itself marked his return to the theatre it should hardly be a surprise to discover that such a reason is advanced or that its central thrust should be a move towards redemption.

Indeed, when the cast assembled for the first read-through, one in which Miller himself chose to read the whole play through to them, he announced that 'This is a happy play, the happiest work I've ever written.'[7] For a play dominated by a concentration-camp tower, in which the cruelties of the House Un-American Activities Committee led to the suicide of one of its victims, and in which friends prove false and marriages collapse, this must have seemed a strange remark. The happiness, however, plainly comes from the reconciliation with private and public history towards which it moves.

And there were a number of personal reconciliations in play. The involvement of Elia Kazan as director meant the healing of a breach that had opened up when Kazan appeared as a friendly witness before the House Un-American Activities Committee. Miller's return to the theatre was another significant act of reconciliation after a period in which he felt that the American public would have no interest in what he wished to say. Beyond that, the play, and despite Miller's denials at the time, was clearly an attempt to come to terms with two failed marriages of his own before, like Quentin, embarking on another, that with the woman to whom the play was dedicated and whom he had married in 1962.

The achievement of the play, however, lies less in the fact that this is a *drame à clef*, than in the fact that Miller searches in the personal for the roots of the social. To him, the larger concerns of the moral world are not matters of abstract debate but a product of human responses most easily understood when traced to their origin in the individual. The honesty of the play lies in the fact that he offers his own life as evidence. And if, in the years immediately following its first production, he wearily rejected those who saw it as little more than a public act of self-justification, this was because too many critics were prone to ignore the exemplary nature of the experiences he dramatised, too obsessed with the image of Marilyn Monroe. Few chose to concern themselves with the wider concerns of a play which attempted to explore the nature of innocence and guilt, of betrayal and denial, of a history seemingly too implacable to absorb or too recent to understand.

Here, after all, was a work which acknowledged the guilt of the survivor and attempted to discover the basis on which life might continue; here was a play in which a disturbing logic was traced which connected the death of love in personal relationships, and a more general and profoundly disturbing collapse of human obligations and connectiveness. To him, the play 'seemed neither more nor less autobiographical' than anything else he had written for the stage (*T*.521). In one sense that is true enough. To review his plays is, repeatedly, to discover the extent to which they draw on family relationships, moral dilemmas, psychological conflicts which have their source, or their correlatives, in his own life. At the same time there are works in which those submerged autobiographical elements break surface. *After the Fall* and *The American Clock* (together with *No Villain* on which it draws) are two such plays. The question is not whether, or the extent to which, such elements exist as how they function. The key problem was how to integrate this material. As he explained,

> I began to search for a form that would unearth the dynamics of denial itself, which seemed to me the massive lie of our time – while America, as I could not yet know, was preparing to fight a war in Vietnam and methodically deny it was a war and proceed to deny the men who fought the war the simple dignity of soldiers. I saw American culture, the most unfettered on earth, as the culture of denial; even the drug, in expanding the mind, denied that it was destroying the mind, and the new freedom of sexuality denied that it was dissolving the compassionate self-restraint that made any human relationship conceivable over time.
>
> (*T*.520–1)

Camus's novel *The Fall* provided both a form – the confessional – and a philosophical foil, as the play engages with that novel on a number of levels. In *The Fall*, Clamence is a successful Parisian barrister who appears to himself and others a model of decency. A chain of incidents, though, serves to disturb his assurance and sends him, 'a judge-penitent', on a downward spiral. His story is a monologue apparently delivered to a stranger.

The book carries an epigraph from Lermontov which, in part, reads, '*A Hero of Our Times*, gentlemen, is in fact a portrait but not of an individual; it is the aggregate of the vices of a whole generation in their fullest expression.' Much the same might be said of the barrister–attorney Quentin, whose own address to the stranger who is simultaneously the audience and himself – 'judge–penitent' – slowly reveals his exemplary function. Nor is the other part of the Lermontov quotation without its relevance: 'some were dreadfully insulted, and quite seriously, to have held up as a model such an immoral character as *A Hero of Our Time*: others shrewdly noticed that the author had portrayed himself and his acquaintances'.

The problem for Clamence is that the only link he can discover between himself and others lies through guilt. He is an attorney in more than profession. He deals in accusation and punishment. He is incapable of true love though anxious to escape from a suffocating egotism. He accuses himself of indifference, having watched, paralysed, as a young woman committed suicide by throwing herself into the river from a bridge, itself evidence of that egotism (a scene with a special resonance for Miller given Inge Morath's putative suicide in the last days of the war, in her case restrained by a passing stranger). Many of these elements are present in Miller's play, though he himself saw *After the Fall*, as its title suggests, as in part a riposte to Camus.

'*The Fall*', he suggested, 'ended too soon, before the worst of the pain began' (*T*.484). He wrote that comment more than twenty years beyond *After the Fall*, so that, perhaps, though he offers it as part of his initial reaction to Camus's book, it is more properly seen as a description of the process whereby his own play engaged the novel. Certainly, the issues he identifies are those that he chose to dramatise, while his discussion of the novel in his autobiography elides, in a fascinating way, with his account of Marilyn Monroe.

Perhaps, though, this was no more than the starting point and not the destination of a play whose concerns went far beyond the public act of confession and exorcism it was so widely regarded as being. The truth of this lay in the success of the play many years later with audiences unschooled in the details of his personal life but acutely attuned to the wider issues it addressed.

Meanwhile, it is perhaps worth recalling the, admittedly suspect, observations of Clamence in *The Fall* when he says that 'I have ceased to like anything but confessions, and authors of confessions write especially to avoid confessing, to tell nothing of what they know. When they claim to get to the painful admissions, you have to watch out, for they are about to dress the corpse.'[8] The consciously callous language aside, it is worth reminding ourselves that in a play in which the central character is both accused and judge, in which the subjective nature of truth is staged and explored, in which the desire for innocence is seen as deeply problematic, confession itself, as in Camus's novel, may be a strategy rather than a truth.

Camus's novel is an extended monologue in which Jean-Baptiste Clamence seems to address a stranger, apparently offering his services as a barrister but in effect making a confession. He lives in the Jewish quarter of Amsterdam, on the site of 'one of the greatest crimes in human history', since it was from here that seventy-five thousand Jews were 'deported or assassinated' (10). He, himself, had flirted with the idea of joining the resistance during the war but had not done so. Indeed, when confronted with an individual loss of life, when the young woman plunged into the Seine, he had proved equally indifferent. His life, it appears, is dominated by self-love, which seems to lie behind all actions, even those in which he appears most charitable: 'That's the way man is ... He has two faces: he can't love without self-love' (26–7). Tragedy, meanwhile, is no more than a 'little transcendence', an 'aperitif'.

He has become, as it seems to him, little more than an actor, simulating concern, easily bewitched by his own sentimentalities. At the centre of his being, meanwhile, 'I, I, I is the refrain of my whole life and it could be heard in everything I said.' His apparent acts of charity are born of 'pure condescension' and 'in utter freedom' (37).

These are all elements that Miller explores, through the person of Quentin, in a play that takes place in what Camus, in another context, calls a 'negative landscape . . . nothingness made visible' (54). For Clamence, the Holland he describes is a kind of 'flabby hell', a world without human beings, except as he summons them to mind, a colourless space. He has, he explains, no friends but 'accomplices,' whose number has expanded to contain 'the whole human race' (55). And here, too, is a connection with Miller's play in which there are 'no walls or substantial boundaries' (1). Clamence refers to a 'pile of ashes', a 'grey dyke' as Miller identifies, for his set, something 'neolithic, a lava-like, supple geography' with 'pits and hollows', a world with 'no color', distinguished by 'the greyness of its landscape' (1). It is against this background that Quentin will summon up those who have themselves been accomplices in his life as he will also contemplate a wider complicity in the crimes of the Holocaust.

In *The Fall*, Clamence comes to feel that those he has known have 'lined up as on the judge's bench' (58), to judge him, not least because 'People hasten to judge in order not to be judged themselves', since the idea 'that comes most naturally to a man, as if from his very nature, is the idea of his innocence'. And this becomes a key element in Miller's play as he explores the corrosive power of the wish to absolve oneself of all guilt and responsibility. Thus Clamence's observation, that 'We are all exceptional cases. We all want to appeal against something! Each of us insists on being innocent at all costs, even if he has to accuse the whole human race and heaven itself' (60), has a direct echo in Miller's play, in which the desire to claim innocence becomes the heart of corruption.

Clamence contemplates the possibility that 'we should like, at the same time, to cease being guilty and yet not to make the effort of cleansing ourselves. Not enough cynicism and not enough virtue' (62). The result, he suggests, is that, like Dante's 'neutral' angels, we exist, as a consequence, in limbo. And there is a sense in which both Camus's novel and Miller's play take place in just such a limbo, Quentin forced to a radical re-examination of his motives and actions, poised, in moral hesitation, unsure of the extent of his guilt, unclear as to the possibility of renewed action. When Clamence announces 'I used to declare my loyalty and I don't believe there is a single person I loved that I didn't eventually betray' (63), it finds an immediate echo in Quentin's growing awareness that he, too, while celebrating loyalty, has been repeatedly guilty of betrayal.

For Clamence, however, such betrayal extends to Christ, who must bear the guilt of the slaughter of the innocents. His comment, 'who would have believed that crime consists less in making others die than in not dying oneself' (83), is directly mirrored in Quentin's observation of the concentration camps that there is no one who would not rather have indirectly sanctioned such deaths rather than dying there himself. The guilt of the survivor, indeed, is a central theme of Miller's play. Yet, for Clamence, there may be a virtue in survival. Recognising the universality of betrayal, at all levels – 'one can wage war in this world, ape love, torture one's fellow-man, or merely say evil of one's neighbour while knitting' – he insists that 'in certain cases carrying on, merely continuing, is superhuman' (84). In his own case the observation is made suspect by its context, but in some senses it is the grace for which Quentin is looking.

In a world in which 'there is no father left, no rule left' (99), Clamence sees men as refusing the freedom they are thus offered precisely because the cost is too great. While looking to declare themselves innocent, they willingly accept their guilt if this is the price to be paid for reinventing a lost order. Having been released, they choose slavery, not least because it offers the semblance of communality. And he, Clamence, becomes the agent for in offering his confession he provokes confession in others, holds the mirror up to them: 'imperceptibly I pass from the "I" to the "we" . . . we are in the soup together . . . I provoke you into judging yourself and this relieves me of that much of the burden' (103).

In his case this is a cynical strategy that releases him to indulge himself, invested now with the sense of superiority he might otherwise have lost. In becoming an exemplary figure he has restored his sense of supremacy. Indeed, we finally discover that the person he has been addressing is none other than himself, so that his conversation has been nothing more than an elaborate and hermetic self-justification.

Miller, though, reaches back into this novel and drains it of much of its irony and all its cynicism. In *After the Fall* it is entirely possible that Quentin's conversation is also, essentially, with himself, but it is not designed to be hermetic, nor is his exemplary status merely another means of restoring a sense of superiority over his fate. He is a judge-penitent, and is not free of suspect motives, yet his self-accusations are not the play-acting that Clamence confesses his own to be. He is committed to the necessity of surviving but not to facilitating the indulgence that Clamence favours. *After the Fall* is an exploration of guilt and responsibility. It is confessional but here confession is an avenue to truth, a journey towards at least a limited grace. *The Fall* left Miller dissatisfied, because

> it seemed to say that after glimpsing the awful truth of one's own culpability, all one could do was to abjure judgement altogether. But was it enough to cease judging others? Indeed, was it really possible to live without discriminating between good and bad? In our eagerness to accept the fecund contradictions of life, were we no longer to feel moral disgust? And if we were to lay no more judgements, to what could we appeal from the hand of the murderer?
>
> (T.520)

At the beginning of the play Quentin is a kind of dangling man (and not the first in Miller's work), like Saul Bellow's character poised in hesitation. He had, he explains, abandoned his job some three or four months before, following the death of Maggie, a name which as yet means nothing to us except that in uttering her name he effectively animates a memory made concrete in the form of Maggie herself who 'stirs' on the platform above him. And this is to become the method of the play as characters, conversations, places materialise in his mind, which is the site of this drama. The effect, Miller suggested, was to be 'the struggling, flitting, instantaneousness of a kind questing over its own surfaces and into its depths' (11).

Stripped of those ideas and values which once motivated and justified him – 'Socialism once, then love,' (25) – Quentin is surviving without purpose and living without meaning. Once, he had felt the world threatened by injustices he had been born to correct, a Manichean world in which to live was to battle for a self-evident right. Once, history, or an agreed set of values, might have served to render some verdict on his life, a verdict that would have condemned or justified but at least offered a structure of meaning. Now he feels that 'the bench' is 'empty' (13).

A visit to a concentration camp reinforces this idea. So absolute a denial of transcendence, or even of a common humanity, leaves him aghast, his own lack of faith merely rendering him powerless before the rational processes and irrational faith of those who constructed such temples to death, since 'Believers built this, maybe that's the fright – and I, without belief, stand here disarmed' (25). And though he confesses to having rediscovered love, his history of failure and betrayal, resonated on a public level, seems to earn him no right to it.

The play, in effect, is his attempt to discover a reason to go on, to embrace his newly discovered love, and therefore faith, in the face of this private and public history of failure. He thus scans the past in order to accuse so that, at the end, he can perhaps absolve, and not himself alone. As a consequence, he seeks to discover and reveal the connections between his own betrayals and those which seem, to him, to have threatened meaning itself, for only then will redemption be a possibility.

Beyond the personal failures lie two facts which seem to threaten any conception of order, any notion of shared values: the concentration camp and the House Un-American Activities Committee. And if these seem disproportionate in their substance and their effects, as is the connection between them and the private denials and betrayals that he recapitulates and re-experiences, then a central function of the play is to establish those links. For behind the play is a conception of history that proposes it as a product of human actions and not a force of nature defying understanding and unrelated to the quotidian.

The concentration-camp tower looms over the stage and, therefore, over Quentin's consciousness. It constitutes the context within which he struggles to understand the entropic nature of his experience. It stands as an expression of an absolute denial of human connectiveness. It is an image of human abandonment and the nullification of values whose echoes he hears in his own life and that of his nation, for the assumption of the play, and the justification for its method, lies in the belief, expressed by Quentin, that 'Everything is one thing' (42). Thus, when he speaks of the isolation he feels when offering to defend a friend, Lou, summoned to appear before the House Un-American Activities Committee, he could equally be talking of a truth discovered at the camp: 'It's like some unseen web of connexion between people is simply not there. And I always relied on it, somehow; I never quite believed that people could be so easily disposed of' (47).

The truth towards which Quentin makes his way is that the camp does not stand as some alternative reality, some caesura in human affairs, but that it is of a piece with entirely recognisable human characteristics:

> This is not some crazy aberration of human nature to me. I can easily see the perfectly normal contractors and their cigars, the carpenters, plumbers, sitting at their ease over lunch pails; I can see them laying the pipes to run the blood out of this mansion; good fathers, devoted sons, grateful that someone else will die, not they, and how can one understand that if one is innocent? If somewhere in one's soul there is no accomplice – of that joy, that joy, that joy when a burden dies . . . and leaves you safe?
>
> (65–6)

Quentin is taken to the camp, in memory, by Holga, a German woman who herself refuses to deny this past, as Miller had been taken to Mauthausen by Inge Morath who, he explained, 'kept sifting through a past with which she wished to make peace' (*T*.523). Holga offers herself as translator, insisting that this place must be sustained in human memory precisely as evidence of that flawed nature that must be embraced and transcended rather than erased.

It is a place that offers a contemporary truth that cannot, finally, be relegated to another time and place, because, in Quentin's mind, and in that of society at large, it is implacable. Its insights threaten our notion of human relationships and what we once thought a contract which could be abrogated only at the cost of meaning itself. But it also haunts us because on some level we understand, if not the enormity, then the desire to declare others guilty in order to sustain the idea of our own innocence. We understand, too, those who built this place while abstracting themselves from the implications of their actions, secure in their exclusion from those singled out to die as if they had earned their immunity.

It is in this sense that not to have died is to incur guilt, the guilt of the survivor. It becomes necessary to justify one's existence precisely because it was not ended here. For Quentin, the camp is remote, seemingly unconnected with a life lived on another continent, at another time. What he comes to discover is that there is more than an analogy here for the betrayals and cruelties of personal and social life, more than a metaphor. The camps may lie at one end of the spectrum, deep in the ultraviolet, but the spectrum itself is entirely recognisable and what he comes to understand is how far along that spectrum he has lived his life.

However, in terms of Quentin, Holga, who is his guide to this underworld of human consciousness, represents not only this shadow of a profound inhumanity but the hope of a new beginning that he is afraid to embrace precisely because his knowledge of repeated failure leaves him stunned: 'how do you dare make promises again?' (42) he asks. For much of the play, in other words, he cannot do as she has done: accept imperfection and renew commitment. He clings to an idea of innocence which is no more than a name for self-interest and denial, failing, perhaps in a particularly American way, to acknowledge a flawed human nature and the danger of a utopian ideal. She, a European, who has stared into the heart of darkness, has a dream, that of an idiot child who must be embraced. It takes Quentin the whole play to arrive at the same insight.

In *After the Fall*, the camp becomes the site for a debate about innocence and guilt. Quentin feels and is an accomplice. He is aware that no one who did not die in this place can ever be innocent again. Yet he also begins to understand that the desire for innocence may itself be an expression of a desire for non-involvement, for a spurious and self-centred freedom from responsibility, for egotism disguised as concern. As Quentin asks himself, 'is it altogether good to be not guilty for what another does?' (39) as Camus's Clamence had observed that it was not enough to accuse oneself in order to clear oneself.

There can seem something portentously solemn about Quentin's philo-sophical journey and the language with which he expresses it. It was certainly something that Kazan felt as, in another sense, did Jason Robards who, report-edly, saw the role as pivotal without being dramatically compelling. The action turns around him as if he were no more than the axle that drives the wheel of the play. The text abounds in question marks as Quentin tries to understand his life, to synthesise his experiences. The play may recapitulate the processes of the human mind but Quentin is required to distil the meaning of each scene, to become a critic analysing his own text. That synthesis can occur in his mind rather than in that of an audience.

In his earlier plays Miller had often dealt with characters incapable, for one reason or another, of analysing or expressing their situation. The audience was placed in the position of judge. Here, Quentin is the judge as he is also the penitent. He arrogates to himself responsibility for discovering and elucidating meaning. With Quentin, Miller chooses for his protagonist a man who deals in words, whose job, as a lawyer, is to analyse and deploy evidence either to defend or prosecute.

Yet that is precisely Quentin's dilemma. The linguistic probing is both an expression of his search for truth and of his evasion of it. He is a lawyer, used both to defending and prosecuting. He is the accuser and the accused and language is the agency of his being. Professionally, he works through questions, each one designed to build a case, uncover a truth. And, as with any lawyer, that truth lies in the past which must be explored for the light it throws on present justice. In that sense he necessarily exists in his past, unable, as yet, to claim a future.

If the camp constitutes one evidence of betrayal, the Committee repre-sents another. It summons before it those whose past commitments must now be disavowed as the price of membership of a community to be defined by exclusion. Confession can transform Un-Americans into Americans, provided they offer the names of others who can in turn be offered salvation or condemned.

Quentin, as a lawyer, is one of many figures associated with the law to appear in Miller's plays, debating, as they do, questions of justice, morality, the acknowledged and unacknowledged codes of society. He undertakes Lou's defence, at personal cost to himself as his own law firm tries to distance itself from controversy. He is freed of the burden, however, when his client commits suicide. His feeling of relief is offered by Miller as a measure both of his grudging courage and, simultaneously, of the instinctive ease with which we contemplate the suffering, and even death, of others, the more especially since it offers a seeming security to ourselves. It confers a spurious innocence, others bearing the burden we feared might fall on us.

The play seems to enter another phase when Maggie appears which, effectively, is not until the second act. Plainly a portrait of Monroe, it is hardly disguised by Miller making her a singer. Indeed, in a treatment for a proposed screenplay even that subterfuge is abandoned as she becomes an actress. Maggie is a version of Lorraine, a figure confessedly based on Monroe, from an abortive play about the atomic bomb. The play came to nothing; the character survived.

This time the accusation that Quentin levels at himself is that he felt less love for her than a kind of power, an almost Christ-like desire to rescue and redeem. Acknowledging that she was 'a beautiful piece, trying to take herself seriously' (78), he sets himself to 'transform somebody, to save' (102), only to acknowledge that 'whoever goes to save another person with the lie of limitless love throws a shadow on the face of God' (113). Through her relationship with Quentin, Maggie hopes to be granted a seriousness previously denied her, while he looks for some sensual release, liberation from judgements and convention. And here, once again, it is hard not to recall Miller's own comments about his relationship with Monroe and the collapse of his first marriage, a state of crisis mirrored in *After the Fall*. This crisis was both emotional and artistic, a time when his life was 'havoc, seizures of expansive love and despairing hate, of sudden hope and quick reversals of defeat' (*T.*327). As he explained, years later, in his autobiography:

> I knew in my depths that I wanted to disarm myself before the sources of my art, which were not in wife alone nor in family alone but, again, in the sensuousness of a female blessing . . . In some diminished sense it was sexual hunger, but one that had much to do with truthfulness to myself and my nature and even, by extension, to the people who came to my plays . . . By now, even after only those few hours with Marilyn, she had taken on an immanence in my imagination, the vitality of a force one does not understand but that seems on the verge of lighting up a vast surrounding plain of darkness. I was struggling to keep my marriage and family together and at the same time to understand why I felt I had lost a

sort of sanction that I had seemed to possess since earliest childhood . . .
I needed the benediction of something or someone, but all about me was
mere mortality.

(*T*.327)

This coincided with what he called the 'weird games going on under the
House Un-American Activities Committee pressure' (328), so that the lacing
together of private dilemmas and public issues was not merely a product of
Miller's artistic strategy but a fact of his immediate experience.

Maggie's appeal, paradoxically, is that she was not 'defending anything,
upholding anything, or accusing – she was just *there*, like a tree or a cat' (62).
Yet, as the play continues, so that supposed simplicity disappears. Her own egotism emerges and love dissolves. Like Monroe, she begins to flirt with suicide.
Quentin declines responsibility for her life and even finds himself, if not wishing
that that life should end, then at least refusing to intervene when intervention
might save that life.

These, then, are some of the component parts of *After the Fall*, a play in which
Miller, and despite what he said at the time when he denied the autobiographical
thrust of the play, explores his own life, as well as the life of his times, in order
to confront what he sees as a failure of humanity. As a scientist will experiment
upon himself, so he takes his own experiences as the test case, not least because
he sees the self as lying at the heart of the problem. 'In whose name', Quentin
asks himself, 'do you ever turn your back but in your own?' And if that is so
then what are we to make of love, which seems to fail repeatedly: 'No, not love;
I loved them all, all! And gave willingly to fortune and to death that I might
live' (119).

So, we are confronted with petty betrayals between parents and children,
failed relationships between husbands and wives, and, beyond these, the breaking of faith required by an investigating committee and, more fundamentally,
the profound denial of human solidarity and mutuality in the camps. Against
all these he pitches nothing more than the acknowledgement that we are flawed
and must live with the flaw. Holga represents redemption not because she offers
love, whose fallibility we have seen demonstrated, but because she represents
acceptance without capitulation, because she stands for a hope made more
tensile by a knowledge of terror.

As Quentin asks,

> – is that exactly why she hopes, because she knows? What burning cities
> taught her and the death of love taught me: that we are very dangerous! . . .
> Is the knowing all? To know, and even happily, that we meet unblessed; not
> in some garden of waxed fruit and painted trees, that lie of Eden, but after,
> after the Fall, after many deaths . . . the wish to kill is never killed, but with
> some gift of courage one may look into its face when it appears, and with a
> stroke of love – as to an idiot in the house – forgive it; again and again . . .
> for ever?

(120)

Quentin leaves the stage with the whispering of 'his people' in his ears. He has not purged them. Their continued existence, indeed, is the evidence for what he has learned. He carries his failures with him, embraces them, but moves ahead. What else, after all, is there to do except remain paralysed by the knowledge of failure?

In Camus's novel, Clamence arrives at the point at which he observes that 'I realized once and for all that I was not cured, that I was still cornered and that I had to make do with it as best I could. Ended the glorious life but ended also the frenzy and the convulsions. I had to submit and admit my guilt. I have to live in the little-ease' (80), this last being the name of a prison cell in which it is impossible either to stand or lie. Quentin, too, recognises that he is not cured, that he also has to live as best he may, but his mood is now changed. He is free, not of his responsibility but of his guilt.

Clamence's liberation is of a wholly different kind. 'I continue', he explains, 'to love myself and to make use of others. Only, the confession of my crimes allows me to begin again lighter in heart and to take a double enjoyment first of my nature and secondly of a charming repentence' (104).

Quentin survives on something more substantial than the thin gruel of irony. The democracy of guilt holds no attraction for him. He finds in Holga the figure of his redemption, acknowledging the past and the insights of others but committing to the future. He is no longer a victim of history, his own or the world's, but prepared to live with a knowledge of freedom and the uses to which a flawed humanity will put it.

Arthur Miller re-entered the theatre he had left, embraced the director he had regarded as betraying the values they had once shared, wrote a play, his next play, in which selfless love is presented as a possibility, and married Inge Morath, living happily with her for the next forty years. That is not, perhaps, what the play is about but it is, perhaps, what it facilitated and celebrated. In *After the Fall* he struggled to discover the basis on which life could be lived in a world in which no one could regard themselves as innocent and no one could regard innocence as desirable.

Perhaps the best account of *After the Fall* is one that Miller outlined in a treatment that he wrote for a proposed film.[9] Though it differs in certain regards from the stage play, the essentials remain in place and his comments there are worth quoting at length. Fundamentally, he explains, the story 'must follow the unravelling of Quentin's self-illusions, his descent into despair and his ultimate grasp on certain values for himself and society'. The various elements – his legal practice, psychological life and life with Maggie – were to be 'strands of one rope, analogues of each other'.

He begins, Miller explains, as a man 'nagged by a sense of inauthenticity', who, when menaced by the rising tide of intolerance, feels the need to understand his own relationship to the world. Politically, he begins with a feeling of solidarity with those on the left, people whose beliefs in some sense make them better than those who threaten them. He is nostalgic for a time of perfect order analogous with childhood, when there seemed a simple harmony between himself and his parents.

In both cases such relationships seemed unconditional, as did that between his first wife and himself. Given this assumed state of grace, he believed that 'a person cannot be disposed of when he fails to live up to some part of the assumptions which his partner has about him and which he had about himself'.

But this Eden comes to an end. Parents betray their children, as his wife and he effectively disposed of one another when 'pride, repressed hostility and intolerance' broke their compact. The embattled left-wingers, meanwhile, betrayed one another when placed under pressure, revealing, thereby, the 'emptiness and sentimentality' which had anyway long since replaced shared convictions.

Each had had a personal reason for joining the Party, 'but they all shared the need for some human connection, a human solidarity transcending self-interest'. Now they have changed, have careers to defend. Only one, Mickey in the stage version, sees that there is a power-conflict and acknowledges that he is victimised because he lacks precisely that. However, Miller goes a step further in the screenplay, though there is a speech in the play in which Quentin acknowledges the sentiment. There is, Miller explains, 'neither an ethic involved nor a morality – if the tables were turned he would show little mercy himself'.

The principal dilemma for Quentin is that he knows what he is against but not what he is for: 'What new arrangement, between human beings, and between the state and human beings, are they suffering to bring about?' He prepares to do battle without knowing quite what he is fighting for beyond an ideal now so thoroughly compromised as to have lost all shape and conviction.

Maggie appears to stand in contrast to all this. She seems to have no hidden motives. She acknowledges her past and accepts the present, responding to him because he appears to find more in her than have others. To her, he offers the chance of transcending the past, redeeming her and, in the play, there is a moment when he is conscious of playing a Christ-like role. She is not judgemental and seems to have an immediate rapport with the downtrodden. In other words, her position emotionally is what his position had been intellectually. For him, it was politics; for her, it is intuitive empathy. His radicalism had existed in and through language; hers is instinctive. This is idealism felt on the pulse and her sexuality is an extension of that. She gives without expecting anything in return. For a moment at least he is reborn as a hero in his own eyes. For a moment, the different parts of his life seem reconciled.

What follows in the screenplay takes the story much closer to Marilyn Monroe than the play. Indeed, it recapitulates their joint history with some precision. Nonetheless, there is much common ground between play and film. Slowly, she begins to make demands. She becomes the principal, he the agent.

If he had formerly possessed the power, as potential healer and redeemer, she now regains it as she uses him to challenge those who she believes have failed her. Love begins to turn to resentment.

In the screenplay, she is an actress who fails to turn up on the set, as Monroe had failed to do. Here, too, he is to be called before the Committee as in the play he is not. In the play he is even relieved of the duty of defending his client when that client commits suicide. Now, when he is summoned, he confesses to fear, a fear that she despises. But what is he supposed to defend? 'These are not early Christians dying with a sublime vision in their eyes; they are caught people, one or two still refusing to recognize what has really occurred in Russia, living in a time gone-by.' One of their number, surely, was Miller himself.

Recognising that fear, Maggie sees his authority crumble and since he was the source of her new sense of self-worth, contempt contaminates her own self-image and self-destruction follows. She, who had been abandoned as a child, sees herself abandoned once again. The old paranoia flares. Quentin, meanwhile, acknowledges the recurrence of a pattern, as husband and wife grow cold, sexually remote and hostile.

In a state of desperation, he abandons his defence of the leftists only to be subpoenaed himself, and we are closer still to Miller's own situation, all pretence of a space between himself and his protagonist surely abandoned. He is summoned by the Committee, he knows, because of his publicity value as Maggie's husband. He is visited by an emissary from the studio urging him to co-operate, as he and Monroe were in fact visited.

As with his first wife he blurts out a truth that he thought might restore them to bedrock, only to discover that truth can kill. She will accept no guilt and no responsibility. She is a victim again, innocent, and her attempts at suicide a reinforcement of this conviction. But, as in the play, he recognises the murderer in himself, the desire for another to die in order to affirm his own innocence, his own freedom from the past, from responsibility.

He appears before the Committee and, like Miller, refuses to name names. 'He sees', Miller observes,

> and says, that the country must not do this; that we are too capable of destroying one another whatever our social opinions and moral justifications. And that is what the law is for – to stake out the bounds of tolerance through which the state must not venture nor Power be permitted to break, or we are left, man against man, unguarded from ourselves. He knows it is hopeless to try to move the Committee, and speaks without ring, almost as though it were an address to his life, to his own experience.

This is partly the speech Miller made before the Committee and in part, perhaps, the speech he wished that he had made.

As he leaves the building so young protestors fight police outside, 'precursors of the present youth rebellion', calling for 'a world without hypocrisy', a 'world full of truth where people might be human again'. It is an odd and, it seems, inauthentic moment as 'Quentin says that the world won't come through some resolution passed; it is far harder than they can know to live honestly. And that it is the only fight worth fighting. He agrees to help them if he can.' This is the Miller who did, indeed, go on to help the anti-Vietnam War movement, who did stand side by side with students. It takes the film, however, in a totally different direction from *After the Fall*, offering what seems a sentimentality.

The screenplay ends with Quentin seeing Maggie emerge from a hotel into the spotlights, her maid behind her with a barely concealed cup of whisky. She smiles to the crowd, stumbles and is assisted by her escort. She climbs into a limousine and is driven past him, head flung back 'and her eyes closed as though she had died', Quentin watches the limousine pass and walks away.

The screenplay is fascinating in a number of ways. On the one hand, it offers insights into Miller's sense of the play's emerging themes. On the other, it abandons fundamental elements of the play. Out goes the concentration camp and out goes the figure of Holga, and though the parents are mentioned they seem not to have the role they do in the play. For all the attacks on the autobiographical dimensions of *After the Fall*, in revising it for a possible Hollywood version Miller has intensified those dimensions. Maggie becomes a film star. Quentin is called before the Committee and invites Contempt of Congress by refusing to name names.

Most striking of all the changes, however, beyond the fact that Maggie dies symbolically but not actually, are the removal of references to the Holocaust and to his third wife. Quentin's redemption no longer lies in a woman who carried her own historical burden but with joining his strength to that of an emerging generation. Where, in the play, his relationship with Holga had encouraged him to accept his life and live with the burden and responsibility, in the film script redemption seems to come rather more easily.

There were no crowds of students protesting against the House Un-American Activities Committee. It is as though Miller wished to ally himself, or at least his protagonist, with a new idealism. Thereby, of course, he potentially recreated that search for idealistic solidarity which had set him up for disillusionment in the first place. A generation on and the radical activists of the 1960s became, in too many cases, the reactionaries of the 1980s. For the moment, though, it was as if that sense of unity, whose loss is in part the subject of *After the Fall*, could be reclaimed on the streets of Washington with an ahistoric gesture making them rebels, too, against the red baiters of the 1950s.

The screenplay becomes an essentially American story, about domestic reaction and an American icon. What is lost, but is present in the play, is the sense that betrayal, a lust for power, a flawed sensibility are human characteristics. What is missing is the blank stare into the darkness from which Holga had emerged, a darkness which, nonetheless, she illuminated precisely because she had been tempted to succumb but had chosen to live, not in denial of the past but in its acceptance. She had dreamed of giving birth to an idiot child, the child that was her life and the life of many, and learning to kiss and embrace it for what it was. Her American counterpart, Maggie, had and represented a different dream, one that denied the past and insisted on an innocence perpetually reborn, an America creed.

For Camus's Clamence, 'we cannot assert the innocence of anyone, whereas we can state with certainty the guilt of all' (81), and 'since we are all judges, we are all guilty before one another' (86). To a degree, Miller would agree with this, except in so far as he sees guilt as intransitive, self-referring, consoling, when he is interested in responsibility. The danger he risks, in *After the Fall*, in placing side by side familial treacheries and the death of millions, is that he thereby implies a moral equivalence. That is not, though, finally, what he means. That we are none of us without sin does not destroy the basis of morality. It can, however, open the door to understanding, enable us to understand how 'One day the house smells of fresh bread – the next of smoke and blood' (21–2), the extent to which we are not merely close kin to killers but contain the potential to become what he affects to abhor.

— ✳ —

After the Fall was a *succès de scandale*. Popular with audiences, it was castigated by a number of critics, while Miller was accused by some of bad taste. With Monroe recently dead, it was seen as his attempt to exculpate himself. The situation was not improved when he disingenuously affected to see no auto-biographical dimension to the play. Though later there would be those who objected to his use of the concentration camp as a point of reference and a metaphor, most attention focused on his portrait of a woman whom people imagined themselves to know. There was much heated debate but little attempt to come to terms with the play itself.

The critics aside, however, the production proved such a success that Miller was asked if he would write another. After nine years of silence as far as the theatre was concerned, he thus produced two plays within a year. Nor had these been waiting in his drawer. They were reactions to immediate events, even if the second play was set in the past.

For *Incident at Vichy* he turned back to the Holocaust. Not only had he visited Mauthausen, but in 1964 he and his wife attended the Auschwitz trials in Frankfurt. These had involved concentration-camp guards, twenty years after the war, called to answer for their crimes. It was as though the world had stood still for two decades, unable to grasp what had happened. Now, witnesses struggled to remember and the accused defended themselves on the grounds that they had done no more than obey orders. A number had thrived in post-war Germany and there was a feeling that this unearthing of the past was far from welcome. For those trying to penetrate the mystery of Nazi depravity there seemed little on offer besides these figures denying responsibility for their actions and for a past which seemed not merely distant but irrelevant.

Victim and oppressor alike, it seemed to be implied, had been powerless before forces not susceptible of analysis and impervious to investigation. Miller wrote an account of the trials for the New York press but it was not enough. The result was a play set in that past which raised questions about the nature and extent of freedom and which was written out of a conviction that past and present are linked by something more than causality.

✳

16

'Incident at Vichy'

In some senses *Incident at Vichy* was a companion piece to *After the Fall*, though this time without the personal dimension and focusing on an aspect of the Holocaust, a subject in Miller's mind because of his visit to Mauthausen and his attendance at the war-crimes trial in Frankfurt. Nor was he the only playwright to have been stirred by those trials in that the German dramatist Peter Weiss, whose *Marat/Sade* was one of the most striking productions of 1964, went on to write *The Investigation*, an essentially documentary play concerned primarily with detailing the guilt of the accused rather than, as in Miller's case, exploring the psychology of those chosen as victims.

In contrast to *After the Fall*, the concentration camp does not appear in *Incident at Vichy*. It is an immanent fact, a product of peripheral vision. Its existence creates the logic that determines the action which we observe and the surreal procedures which transform a man into a victim and his companions into collaborators. For, as Miller remarked, in a newspaper article written after his visit to Frankfurt, 'the question in the Frankfurt courtroom spreads out beyond the defendants and spirals around the world and into the hearts of everyman. It is his own complicity with murder, even the murders he did not commit with his own hands. The murders, however, from which he profited if only by having survived.'[1] And there is the bridge between *After the Fall* and *Incident at Vichy*. They both address the guilt and responsibility of the survivor.

Miller has identified the origin of the play as lying in a story he had heard from a psychoanalyst friend, Dr Rudolph Loewenstein, who had hidden from the Nazis in Vichy France. A Jewish analyst had been detained and taken to a police station where he found others waiting. He had false papers. Each in turn was called in. Some did not return through the door at the end of the corridor. Others did, free to go on with their lives. He was saved through the intervention of a stranger.

The inspiration for one of the characters lay in a friend of Inge Morath's, Prince Josef von Schwarzenberg, an Austrian who had refused to co-operate with the Nazis and spent the war doing menial work in France. He seemed to Miller an image not only of a resistant spirit but also of cultural integrity, sustaining his own aesthetic and moral code in the face of a brutal and vulgar power. It was ten years before the story shaped itself into a play.

The link with *After the Fall* lay not only in the moral implications of survival but in his expressed desire 'to locate in the human species a counterforce to the randomness of victimization', a force which, in a curious phrase, he regretted could 'only be moral', (T26). *After the Fall* had, after all, engaged the question of victims, in terms of the concentration camp and the investigating Committee, but also the notion of self-created victims, in the form of Maggie and, indeed, in one way or another, of all the characters. If the former play had, in part, been inspired by a contemplation of Camus's *The Fall*, and the failure of its protagonist to go to the rescue of a suicide, his new play was to explore the idea of a selfless act. It was, he explained, to be 'a counterpoint to many happenings around me in this past decade' [2]

In *After the Fall* characters act out of self-interest and self-concern. In *Incident at Vichy* he created a character capable of overcoming this hermeticism and thereby eroding the idea of himself as simple victim. As Miller remarked, speaking in the context of *After the Fall* but with direct relevance to his new play, 'In one way or another we are all victims, one man of his family, another man of society . . . and if that's going to be the limitation of the vision then we are really finished because everybody can justify anything on the basis that he is only paying back the world for what it did to him. If there is an enemy . . . of man, it's the idea of innocence.'[3]

This is a play in which Miller acknowledges the impossibility of understanding something as absolute and irrational as the Holocaust. Each of the characters advances a theory which collapses of its own weight, offers an analysis which proves inadequate to the point of irony. And while his own play is directed at locating the source of resistance, a transcendent act which denies the premise on which the Holocaust is based – that there is no human contract to be honoured – he also acknowledges the degree to which art is itself, if not contaminated, then easily accommodated by a power which subordinates everything to its own arbitrary necessities. The play, in other words, like the transcendent gesture towards which it moves, is no more than an act of faith, a single coin to be tossed on the scales of history.

The play was originally described as taking place in a police station but Miller changed it to the vaguer, and somehow more ominous, 'place of detention', in Vichy France, 1942. At the rear of the stage is what appears to be an office, separated from the foreground by grimy window panes. In front of this room is a long bench, itself in an empty area whose normal use is indeterminate. There are two doors; one leads into the private room, the other out on to the street. These are the two options whose meaning slowly becomes apparent.

For the moment, though, there is, perhaps, something Beckettian about the minimalism of this staging, as there is about a situation in which people wait, trying to infuse their waiting with rational purpose, trying to understand why they are summoned, in the midst of life, in order, as they slowly comprehend, to be handed over to death. This is *Waiting for Godot* in which the arrival of Godot will deconstruct not create meaning, though the irony, perhaps, seems much the same. *Incident at Vichy* is *Waiting for Godot* with man as his own Godot.

For most of the play, it is as much about waiting as Beckett's play. Some hidden meaning is about to be revealed. However absurd the nature of that meaning, it is the reality within which they are obliged to live. As the gathered characters wait, so they try out several comforting scenarios, convince themselves of their unique immunity, talk not only to fill the silence but because language might imply a compact which will prove their ultimate protection. This is the mood of such an exchange as the following:

> . . . it can never be a lesson, it can never have a meaning. And that is why it
> will be repeated again and again forever.
> Because it cannot be shared?
> Yes. Because it cannot be shared. It is total absolute waste.[4]

But this is Miller, not Beckett, and the ironies that follow are balanced, if not vitiated, by the possibility, and indeed the reality, of wilful action. Miller cannot rest in such a tension. Not to rebel against the absurd is to succumb to it, to compound it. It must be possible to resist and in resisting discover the values which seem to have been evacuated from the world. The gesture, when it comes, is arbitrary; hence its shock value. To some, though, the risk is that its very arbitrariness is itself evidence of the absurd. If all things are possible, why not gratuitous good as much as gratuitous bad? Such an act does not reinvent the moral world; it merely underlines the nature of its contingency.

And this is the risk he runs in both *After the Fall* and *Incident at Vichy*. Genocide and utter selflessness can seem no more than two sides of the same coin if they are the products not of a moral system but a profoundly ambivalent human nature, capable of oscillating wildly between extremes without explanation beyond the fact that it is capable of doing so. One critic accused him of creating a medieval morality play in which characters are effectively no more than abstractions: 'The Supercilious Actor, the Deceived Autocrat, the Communist Worker whose Faith is in History, the Old Jew etc.'[5]

As the lights rise we discover six men and a boy of fifteen 'frozen there', Miller explains in a stage note, 'like members of a small orchestra at the moment before they begin to play'. This is a telling image given the subject of the later *Playing for Time*, which deals with the orchestra of prisoners at Auschwitz–Birkenau. There is something, too, of a realist painting about characters whose attitudes, we are told, are 'expressive of their personalities', and, indeed, as the lights rise so 'their positions flow out of the frieze' (245).

The play's director, Harold Clurman, on first reading the text, planned thirty seconds of silence in which the characters were to seem fixed, like figures in a memorial tablet commemorating the dead. Their very frozen poses were to be emblems of the waiting that defined them as they were of what he called their '"frozen" psychological postures.' He abandoned the gesture when he found that the inadequate lighting of the American National Theatre and Academy theatre in Washington Square meant that the gesture would have been liable to misunderstanding. He needed the stylised nature of the gesture to be immediately apparent. The second frozen moment, though, was retained. This was 'a long wait of anxiety' on the part of those 'in a hell of expectancy, uneasiness, bewilderment, wonder',[6] a metonymic thirty seconds which compresses, embodies and presages the 'action' of a play that has virtually no action in the sense of movement.

Yet while acknowledging the difficulty of such non-naturalistic moments, Miller noted approvingly that Boris Aronson's set was 'almost mythic' (*T*.540), and the play does, indeed, balance between the real and the metaphoric. One of the prisoners, himself an artist, tellingly remarks that in a world in which the irrational rules people still seemingly look for realistic paintings. For him, realism is placed under pressure precisely by the irrational, the arbitrary, and his comments might be seen as applying to Miller's play.

It has the appearance of realism. These characters have pasts, and fragments of those pasts are exposed. But in the reified situation in which they find themselves, such pasts are without meaning. They are lifted out of a conventional world of social function and personal identities. They are lifted, indeed, out of time. Their future is suddenly attenuated. They are no more than figures in a myth, waiting for the end, reduced already, and before the ultimate decision is made, to fixed attitudes or values. The complexities of their lives are rendered down by their circumstances until they risk becoming no more than their fears, their defining anxieties. What, after all, would a realistic play look like that was designed to capture the unreal?

This is not a world in which some are free and others are not, though some of the prisoners will, in time, be released while those who guard them, and will seemingly decide their fate, presume their own autonomy. In fact they are all subject to the same fiat. All exist within a universe in which the real is defined by a power which lies beyond the walls of this place where they act out their ritual. There is a script to be followed.

This is not a place that admits of ambivalence. We are in the anteroom to hell, in limbo, where people are gathered together to learn their fate, a fate against which there appears to be no appeal. This very circumstance places the apparent realism of the play under pressure. Characters make explicit what they would normally suppress, or desperately suppress what is patently the case, conforming in some senses to their representative functions. To Miller, the play was, in that respect at least, in the tradition of Molière, in which characters oblige by explaining themselves.

Alongside Molière, however, surely stands Kafka, for here again, as in *The Trial*, are the accused, desperate to know the crime of which they are guilty, even if it should only be the crime of living. In a world which, against the accumulating evidence, they still feel to be rational, they look for reason and meaning where there is none but the logic of nightmare. Those gathered in this place have one question which obliterates others, the primary question: Why? We, the audience, already know. We stare back at this place through history and know the depths of the irony which these characters can only suspect. That gap between their knowledge and ours generates not the drama itself but the judgements we make of the judgements they make. They fear their fate. We know it. That is the nature of the burden we bear, unable as we are to deflect a process which others once permitted to take its course, as if it were indeed inevitable. Yet we are not insulated from the dilemma that the play poses. It is a challenge delivered in one time to be taken up or ignored in another.

Different in their backgrounds, religions, social circumstances, attitudes, they are briefly homogenised by their situation. Those who interrogate them simulate rational enquiry but reason has already been imprisoned. Some will live, their characters broken open by this challenge to their values; some will die. But the taxonomy here, in this place of detention, is no more than the arbitrary order of an antinomian world. It is not susceptible of interrogation by the questing mind or the moral conscience.

Those gathered in this anonymous space have, we slowly discover, been arrested, seemingly arbitrarily, to undergo a process which at first they hardly comprehend beyond the fact that some will survive it and others not. There is, indeed, something consciously representative about them. They constitute different ideologies, ethnic backgrounds, classes, attitudes. In other words there is a confessed artifice about the construction of this group, even as they have a metaphoric force. They are, if not a ship of fools, then at least a representation of those who were indeed vacuumed up by the disinterested bureaucracy which administered genocide, but also of the possible responses to such an arbitrary fate.

There is, indeed, something of Kafka here, as punishment is presumed, by an inverted logic, to imply guilt, and guilt in turn to suggest the need to enter a plea of innocence, even at a cost to others. But Miller is unwilling to leave such a logic in place. However, if he did, indeed, wish to offer a counter-force to the randomness of victimisation, the problem lay in the fact that the sacrifice, which was to constitute the essence of that counter-force, and that once had been a commonplace of committed literature in the 1930s, is here to be explored in the context of a more profound assault on the self.

He was concerned not only with the implacable reality of the Holocaust but also with the literature of the absurd that had seemingly been born out of its ashes. Nonetheless, he has insisted that his primary motive for writing the play is that 'the time comes when somebody has to decide to sacrifice himself . . . the play comes down to that, the step from guilt to responsibility and action'.[7] The question behind this work and others was whether 'a work simply exploits chaos or strives to resist it for survival's sake' (T.498).

Incident at Vichy is about more than the survival of one man, as a result of the sacrifice made by another; it is about the survival of an idea of mutuality precisely when it was being denied with such absolute authority. Such literal sacrifices were, of course, made and, indeed, one such lay at the heart of the story that inspired this play. The problem was to make it dramatically believable, to understand not simply the mechanism of sacrifice but the state of mind, the secular faith, that made it credible and gave it metaphoric force precisely because it had psychological and moral plausibility.

These are, Miller insisted, to be 'flesh-and-blood people, each with a subterranean life' of their own, 'but they are also symbolic in the bearing they have on ourselves and our time'.[8] And that last point is a crucial one in that Miller was writing this play in 1964. It is not offered as a historical work, though, for Miller, the Holocaust had been a turning point. The Nazis had transformed a people into seeming collaborators in the destruction of their own autonomy. Beyond the annihilation of a race, they had annihilated an idea of human connectiveness and this was the tainted inheritance they had passed on, along with the literal and symbolic victory of the machine over human nature. As Miller said, 'There is unquestionably a contradiction between an efficient technological machine and the flowering of human nature, of the human personality. It's for that reason that I'm interested in the Nazi machine, the Nazi mechanism.'[9] The play, he insisted, might have been set twenty years before but it 'is about tomorrow morning. There is a difference', he suggested, 'between the occasion of the play and what it's about.'[10]

Those thus gathered together in this place include an old Jew, a gypsy, a businessman, an electrician, a painter, an actor, a doctor and a prince. They have nothing in common except their circumstance and in most cases their Jewish identity. In charge is a German major, uneasy about the task handed to him (but not to the point of risking his own future), along with a German professor. The latter is not unlike the witch-finders of *The Crucible* ('Science is not capricious . . . my degree is in racial anthropology' (271)), charged this time to detect Jews, gypsies, those assigned to death by the bureaucracy he serves. The prisoners have been enthusiastically arrested by members of the Vichy French police. One by one they are now summoned into an office from which they emerge either with a pass to freedom or a slip of paper effectively signifying death.

Bayard, the communist electrician, attempts to make sense of the fascism that menaces him by seeing it as a product of monopoly capitalism: 'You should try to think of why things happen', he insists, 'It helps to know the meaning of one's suffering' (248). Clurman, in thinking of his costume, suggested that it should be 'typical of the French worker' and 'have some of the "stiffness" of armor'.[11] His background, his commitments, his sturdy ideology is, Bayard thinks, his protection. The problem of this suffering, however, is that it has no meaning, that being the essence of a Holocaust whose implacable contingency is a mirror of the absurd.

Marchand, a businessman, secures immunity but not for the reason he believes, nor even because he shares something of the human contempt exhibited by their captors. He is simply not Jewish. The values that secure his release have nothing to do with the code which he believes still operative in the world. He is not saved or condemned because of what he has done, because of his importance or lack of it, but simply because he is not who they seek.

Two of the number are already condemned, and known to be such by the others and by the audience: a gypsy and an old Jew. They are, in effect, self-evidently what they are. They are what the others struggle not to be. They are those from whom they wish to distance themselves. Plans for escape never extend to these two. They are the standard by which they expect to be measured and they are, in effect, therefore, what must be denied. To Clurman, the Jew is a chorus and his behaviour a 'spiritual pantomime' (78). He prays, he waits, he despairs, he pleads. His gestures and attitudes are to offer an unconscious commentary on what is said around him. The gypsy, by contrast, inured to arrest, believes he will sit this one out as he has sat others out.

While menaced, they struggle to make sense of what is happening in terms of their own experience, of logic, of history, finding consolation in rumour or, in some cases, in what they would hesitate to call their innocence. Von Berg, the Austrian aristocrat whose self-sacrifice will be the defining action of the play, confesses to finding it impossible to understand how 'people with respect for art' can 'go about hounding Jews', admitting, finally, that 'Art is perhaps no defense against this' (260). In a play in which the characters are gathered together like members of an orchestra, awaiting the response of their German 'audience', this has a special significance, as, of course, it does to the play itself. For while Von Berg is an amateur musician, Monceau is an actor who attests to the sensitivity of German theatrical audiences.

In other words, *Incident at Vichy* itself is subject to a subversive irony since the supposed humanising qualities of drama had proved no more effective than the music which the Nazis affected to love while performing what Himmler called their 'difficult work', in stamping out the Jewish race. The order of art could no more, finally, make sense of contingency than could political ideology or moral codes. And that leaves Miller himself ambiguously placed, offering a play whose moral force is so easily vitiated by power or, worse still, accommodated to it.

The advice of the released businessman is 'not to look like a victim' (263), as if this were merely a business of appearance, of performance, and, indeed, the actor takes this to heart, desperately wishing to believe that by reinventing himself he can secure immunity. But his theatre is finally no defence, any more, perhaps, than is Miller's. For these people did not will themselves to be victims, nor is the playwright suggesting that they have permitted themselves to collude in their destruction. They do decide not to rush the guard in an effort to escape, but the Major informs them that such an escape was always impossible since there are further guards beyond the one they can see. In other words, for most of them there is no exit.

Perhaps the key speech of the play, the one that reaches out from 1942 towards the present and the future, and which, for Miller, provided the reason for writing the play in the mid-1960s, is that given to the Austrian Prince. His detachment, his apparent immunity, seems to give him, if not wisdom, then a kind of contingent insight. He, alone, for much of the play, is not blinded by terror but simply by unexamined prejudices presenting themselves as opinions. It is he who advances the familiar concern with moral paralysis which recurs in Miller's work from *The Golden Years* to *Broken Glass*, and who explores that tribalism which Miller had seen at work in American society and, beyond it, in a world at war with itself. It is he who recognises the nihilism that Miller himself saw as increasingly commanding the imagination of the intellectual and the nature of the modern world, a nihilism born out of a celebration of unmeaning, a systematisation of despair.

Incident at Vichy could so easily be a version of Camus's *Caligula*, in which the Roman emperor lives out the logic of the absurd, were it not for the fact that, as a Jew, Miller knew who the first victims would be in a dulling of the moral self. Confronted with the fact of the Holocaust, Von Berg attempts to explain the inexplicable, beginning with the paradox that is at the root of its power, and this is a speech so crucial that it is worth quoting at length. Asked why he chooses to believe in a fact apparently so incomprehensible and extreme, he replies:

> Because it *is* so inconceivably vile. That is their power. To do the inconceivable; it paralyzes the rest of us. But if that is its purpose it is not the cause . . . They do these things not because they are German but because they are nothing. It is the hallmark of the age – the less you exist the more important it is to make a clear impression. I can see them discussing it as a kind of . . . truthfulness. After all, what *is* self-restraint but hypocrisy? If you despise Jews the most honest thing is to burn them up . . . They are poets, they are striving for a new nobility, the nobility of the totally vulgar. I believe in this fire; it would prove for all time that they exist, yes, and that they were sincere. You must not calculate these people with some nineteenth-century arithmetic of loss and gain. Their motives are musical, and people are merely the sounds they play. And in my opinion, win or lose this war, they have pointed the way to the future. What one used to conceive a human being to be will have no room on this earth.
>
> (269–70)

He ends by urging them to attempt escape, as though they would, thereby, resist the truth of his own analysis, as though he, alone, could sit in the grandstand and offer advice to those confronted with a choice which is no choice at all. The ultimate logic of his position, however, is that there is no immunity and that paralysis can only be resisted by action. He, after all, has a choice which the others do not have (the released businessman recognising no solidarity and thus becoming complicit with the forces he believes himself to have escaped).

The reference to 'musical motives' and people as 'sounds' played by those who conduct their lives, picks up Miller's reference to the characters gathered here being like members of a small orchestra about to play. The question raised by Von Berg's speech, however, is how can a dissonant sound break into such a terrible harmony of death. He also, later, recalls an orchestra he had supported in Austria, destroyed when the Nazis arrested its oboist. They had listened to him play before arresting him: 'The instrument lay on the lawn like a dead bone . . . they took him. It is as though they wished to take him at exactly the moment he was most beautiful . . . I tell you nothing any longer is forbidden' (275–6). Once again we are back in the world of *Caligula*.

The most articulate of the group is Leduc (and we are given only the last names, the ranks or the functions of all the characters). He has no monopoly of wisdom, assailed, as he is, by the same fears, the same despair as those others assembled in this place where they are to appear before a judge, accused of the crime of existence. Yet he recognises the danger of seeking to accommodate what is happening to a model of experience which turns on logic or rationality. The process may be logically conducted but it is engendered by, and depends for its success upon, an atavistic fiat. The Nazis, he insists, rely upon their victims to 'project our own reasonable ideas into their heads . . . They rely on our own logic to immobilize ourselves' (275). They rely, too, on a passivity born out of disbelief and despair. And they instil a desire to declare innocence as if there were a legitimacy to the accusation seemingly levelled at them.

But, as Miller had implied in *After the Fall*, the price of innocence may be the guilt of others. As the actor Monceau observes, 'The Russians condemn the middle class, the English have condemned the Indians, Africans, and anybody else they could lay their hands on . . . every nation has condemned somebody because of his race, including the Americans and what they do to Negroes. The vast majority of mankind is condemned because of its race' (278–9). Most significantly of all, however, as Leduc confesses, 'Each man has his Jew; it is the other. And the Jews have their Jews' (288). That this speech has echoes in both *Playing for Time* and *Broken Glass* underscores how central it is to Miller's beliefs.

When the German Major momentarily confides his own incomprehension of the process in which he is required to participate, Leduc refuses to offer him the absolution he seemingly seeks, inviting him to kill himself, preferably along with others of his kind. The Major responds by asking him if he would refuse release if the price were simply that the others should be condemned. The question hangs in the air as Leduc acknowledges the force of the self-interest to which he is appealing and thereby, perhaps, the truth of the Major's observation that 'There are no persons any more ... There will never be persons again' (280).

Pressed back against the wall of his own inauthenticity, Leduc expresses his anger that he should have been born 'before the day when man had accepted his own nature; that he is *not* reasonable, that he is full of murder, that his ideals are the little tax he pays for the right to hate and kill with a clear conscience' (287). He is angry, in other words, at his failure to recognise that we exist after the Fall. At the end of the play the Major's hypothetical question will become actual.

In effect, Leduc then confronts Von Berg with the same question, the same challenge, with which the Major had presented him. Will he acknowledge his complicity, for without that 'there is nothing and will be nothing' (288). At first Von Berg resists, for what can he have to do with the anarchy that has undone his world? But he then realises that knowledge is not enough. When Leduc insists that 'It's not your guilt I want, it's your responsibility' (289), he expresses not only a fundamental of Miller's own credo but a challenge to act. Given a free pass to leave, Von Berg hands it to Leduc who, in relief and with some horror, accepts the pass and his life. The play ends, however, not on this act of sacrifice, nor even on the incomprehension of the Major whose defence of his own passivity thus lies exposed, but on the arrival of further detainees. The process continues.

A central fear behind the Holocaust is that expressed by Leduc. It is that the suffering is pointless and that as such it can have no redeeming meaning. It 'cannot be shared' and is 'total, absolute waste' and hence 'will be repeated again and again forever' (285), much as George Orwell had presented a vision of the future as a boot stamping on the human face for ever. The problem is to acknowledge the nature of that suffering and the idleness of attempts to offer explanations, rational accounts, while insisting that it is not a template for the future.

This is not a play that insists on the uniqueness of the event. Indeed, its raison d'etre rests on Miller's recognition that the incubus lies within everyone. What he is concerned to do here, as in *After the Fall*, is to acknowledge this fact and identify the possibility of a resistant spirit, even in the face of continual defeat. When the Old Jew is taken away, a pillow he is carrying explodes into feathers which fill the air. In the end Von Berg's gesture is merely one feather in the scales but, to Miller, the one feather is evidence of a possibility not yet extinguished, as guilt is, indeed, transmuted into responsibility. It is a private action which has public significance, as Von Berg transforms himself and thereby his circumstances.

This one character, socially detached, placed under pressure, redefines himself and thereby human possibility. His action cuts a tangent to the logic of a world in which meaningful sacrifice has supposedly been a primary victim of the new dispensation which relieves everyone of responsibility for themselves and other people: 'Who knows', Miller asked in an interview in 1980, 'but that the world will be saved by the most unlikely personality . . . at the last moment?'[12]

Von Berg responds with an arbitrary action. He is, in a sense, testing a proposition. If it is possible to harden your heart to stone, is the opposite also possible? Is selflessness, sacrifice, love possible? Yet it comes, surely, from the same source. It is an irrational, instinctive action. If all things are possible then why not murder; but if all things are possible then why not love? In a context in which there is no choice, he chooses. In a world of pseudo-science, he conducts an experiment with his own sensibility. He becomes the embodiment of refusal in a context in which so many were later to defend themselves against accusations of genocide by insisting that they could not refuse. What they meant, Miller suggests, was that they were unwilling to pay the possible, even probable, price of refusal.

What, then, are we to make of his gesture? After all, fascism, too, called for martyrs, spoke of sacrifice. Erich Fromm, in *The Fear of Freedom*, acknowledges as much, conceding that 'Fascism proclaims self-sacrifice as the highest virtue and impresses many people with its idealistic character.' However, he insists that there 'are two entirely different types of sacrifice. It is one of the tragic facts of life that the demands of our physical self and the aims of our mental self can conflict; that actually we may have to sacrifice our physical self in order to assert the integrity of our physical self.' That sacrifice, he insists,

> will never lose its tragic quality . . . Such sacrifice is fundamentally different from the sacrifice which Fascism preaches. There, sacrifice is not the highest price man may pay to assert his self, but is an aim in itself. This masochistic sacrifice sees the fulfilment of life in its very negation, in the annihilation of the self . . . and its utter submission to a higher power . . . True sacrifice presupposes an uncompromising wish for spiritual integrity. The sacrifice of those who have lost it covers up their moral bankruptcy.[13]

The Prince's sacrifice carries the force of the Talmudic statement that whosoever saves a single life it is as if he had saved the whole world; whosover destroys a single life it is as if he had destroyed the whole world. The gesture is plainly not, to Miller, to be self-referring and self-justifying but an assertion that the process of redemption must begin somewhere.

Incident at Vichy, he has insisted, is not 'about nazism', in the sense that it is a historical work concerned only to address a historical phenomenon.[14] It is about 'us now', with 'our individual relationships with injustice and violence'. It is, he has said, about 'the people in Queens refusing to call the police while a woman was being stabbed to death on the street outside their windows', and those delinquent boys he had once studied for a film script in the early 1950s and whose distortions of character sprang 'from a common want of human solidarity'. Indeed, the selfless act which gifted a man his life would, he insisted, come to mind 'whenever I felt the seemingly implacable tide of human drift and the withering of will in myself and others'.[15]

In his mind the plight of the Jews in Europe and that of the African–American was the same, not because of any comparability in their fate (though the number killed during slavery was immense, if unknown, and a product of capitalism and greed wedded to human disregard and sadism rather than fascist ideology), but because their treatment required the acquiescence of so many who thereby became complicit.

'How many of us', he asked, 'have looked into ourselves for even a grain' of the cause of the violence around us? Compromise with evil, he suggests, leads to moral atrophy. Is it, he asks, 'too much to say that those who do not suffer injustice have a vested interest in injustice?'[16] How far do we consent to the ill-treatment of others if it gives us greater assurance as to our own safety and immunity?

The play is not about a hero who is free of this incubus but about a man who is shocked to discover that he is not, that his own equanimity has been bought at too great a cost. Here, in this place, at this time, a general feeling of distant sympathy has no meaning. Confronted directly and immediately with the physical embodiment of his generalised guilt, he is forced to confront not the other but himself. He now has to transmute guilt into responsibility and responsibility into action.

On his mind, Miller confessed, were not only the victims of Nazi atrocities but also those who had died in the south working for the Civil Rights movement. But it was not only the plight of black Americans he had in mind. In 1965, he was also thinking of Vietnam and the photographs he had seen of the torturing of Viet Cong prisoners. The Vietnamese, he pointed out, were wearing 'United States equipment, are paid by us, and could not torture without us. There is', he suggested, 'no way around this – the prisoner crying out in agony is our prisoner.'[17] The play's theme, he suggested, is not 'Am I my brother's keeper?' but 'Am I my own keeper?'

Miller often returns to the biblical figure of Cain and he does so both in his account of the Frankfurt trials and in his essay on *Incident at Vichy*. In the former, he asks, 'If man can murder his fellows, not in passion but calmly . . . can any civilization be called safe from the ravages of what lies waiting in the heart of man?'[18] In the latter, he suggests that Cain comes at the beginning of the Bible precisely because 'the sight of his own crimes is the highest agony a man can know and the hardest to relate himself to'.[19] We do, he reminds us, exist after the Fall. It is necessary to reconcile ourselves to that fact instead of parading a specious innocence.

Miller also hints at another dimension of the play when he says that 'death, when it takes those we have loved, always hands us a pass. From this transaction with the earth the living take this survivor's reproach . . . the debt . . . which we owe for living, the debt to the wronged'.[20] The frisson which comes from the fact of survival is coded with feelings we hesitate to decipher. Someone dies: we live. Along with grief and regret is there not a shadow of something more than relief in this fact?

The play was not without its critics. For Leslie Epstein its fault lay precisely in its failure to acknowledge the specificity of the crime and of those responsible. It would, he predicted, be popular in Germany: 'A free wallow, with no exact indictments drawn up'.[21] Miller might not be wrong in suggesting that everyone is guilty; his fault was to fail to distinguish degrees of guilt. There was simply no equivalence between a generalised tendency towards crime, an acceptance that everyone has their Jew, including Jews, and throwing 'millions of people into ovens'. To suppose no difference is, he suggests, 'moral nihilism'. To suggest, as Miller's psychiatrist does, that all gentiles hate Jews, 'is not a judgement, it is a shrug' (172). Epstein then invokes Karl Jaspers's *The Question of German Guilt* on the danger of generalised accusations: 'The categorical judgment of a people is always unjust. It presupposes a false substantialization and results in the debasement of the human being as an individual . . . To pronounce a group criminally, morally or metaphysically guilty is an error akin to the laziness and arrogance of average, uncritical thinking.' Miller, he suggests, has written a morality play, an *Everyman*, but one which settles for sentimentality: 'Unable to judge men, Miller offers his handkerchief' (173).

Interestingly, Epstein acknowledges that 'the world has been in a state of shock for twenty years', unable, by implication, even to address the subject of the Holocaust, and certainly *After the Fall* and *Incident at Vichy* are among the first plays to engage it. The tone of his essay, even its anger, however, seems to derive largely from his belief in the special status of the Holocaust and the need for indictments which do not detract from it. He does not want to be told that we live after the Fall, that we all contain the potential to be killers, or at least to ally ourselves with them provided only that we remain secure. He wants, it seems, analysis, names, the specifics of this particular cataclysm.

His comment on *Vichy* as a morality play is interesting, not least because he assumes that this can hardly have been what Miller intended. The characters fall short of the realism towards which he assumes the author aspired. Yet in many ways this surely is a morality play for a post-Christian society. The characters are to be real in terms of their physical presence, their histories (invoked as explanation, validation, justification), but they are also to be symbolic. They are representative men for whom redemption is a desperate hope which comes, if it comes at all, not from a forgiving God but a human gesture born out of that very desperation. It is an absurd drama deflected by a gesture whose quixotic nature is a gauge of how tenuous is the resistance to absurdity.

The fact is that this is not a play simply about the Holocaust. It is a play in which he stages the drama of those who seek to understand their vulnerability, a vulnerability against which there seems no appeal. We know, of course, as they do not, the full details of their fate, the perverse logic which governs their selection, the falseness of their hope, the arbitrariness which will lead most to die and some to survive. But that knowledge is not theirs nor does it retrospectively gift the situation a redeeming logic. They, and we, look for a reason, as though, once discovered, an order would manifest itself, a coherence that made this profound crime comprehensible and isolable in the very particularity for which Epstein calls. After all, there has, does there not, to be an explanation, a reason that will pull these events into a familiar world governed by logic.

The rise of Hitler can be documented, explained, in terms of economic and political dynamics. The mind from which genocide emerged as policy, however, is more difficult to confront and certainly for those obliged to stare its consequences in the face, unfathomable. Indeed it was precisely the attempt to bring reason to bear or, failing that, simply a desperate faith rooted in ideology or religion, which was the source of the disabling irony of which many have written. It is precisely because the mind stops, stunned, in the face of surreal evil that Miller's play takes the form it does.

The final act is desperate. It is little more than the bet that something survives, that some light can escape this black hole. It is a morality play but God does not reach out, though many waited for Him to do so and died still hoping. Man reaches out. It is a suspect gesture and it is its suspect nature that is a measure of the desperation of Miller's gamble on behalf of mankind.

There have been more fragile bases for hope. Consider Edward Bond's *Saved* or *Lear*. Consider, indeed, Christ, God-as-man resisting the fate that would change the fate of others, before submitting. Consider the thief crucified along-side Him and transforming himself at the moment of his death. And there is, of course, an ambiguity in the ending of *Incident at Vichy*. After all, in saving another the Prince saves his conception of himself. It is a gesture not entirely purged of the self-concern which provides a sub-text to the play.

There were, of course, guilty men and women. There was a ruling orthodoxy which made this hell possible. There was a technological proficiency whose ingenuities can be traced to their origins. And, of course, indictments were made, trials held, some few of those responsible made to pay the price as though, in current jargon, that would create closure. But there was and is no closure precisely because there is an anterior question, the one which in part Miller probes. It is the same question that Dostoevsky raised in *The Brothers Karamazov*, the book that Miller had read as a young man. Here, he observed that man is by nature a despot and loves to be a torturer. Still more, perhaps, it engages the question raised by Raskalnikov in *Crime and Punishment*, with its portrait of a killer testing the limits of human possibility.

Epstein fears, and it is a genuine enough concern, that the notion of a gen-eralised human flaw may take us outside the moral world altogether. What all suffer, what all commit, cannot be condemned, merely accepted as the mark of humanity, the mark, in Miller's work, of Cain. Guilt, Epstein suggests, in

Incident at Vichy, is presented as classless. The aristocracy acquiesce while the working class 'adore Hitler' (267). It is also nationless: 'Strange; if I did not know that some of them in there were French, I'd have said they laugh like Germans.' It is also without race: 'I have never analyzed a gentile who did not have, somewhere hidden in his mind, a dislike if not a hatred for the Jews' (287). Guilt, in other words, or, more cogently, responsibility, is a defining characteristic not of those who conceived, planned and executed genocide, but of all. How, then, issue indictments against those whose hands were genuinely stained with blood?

But Miller does not argue for an equivalence, though the rise of Hitler did indeed involve an alliance of those who might otherwise be assumed to be natural enemies. Genocide is not vitiated by indicating that all possess the potential to kill, an instinct for self-protection that makes us willing collaborators in evil if only by refusing to act, by choosing non-involvement. His problem in *Incident at Vichy* is surely not in making extremes of cruelty plausible but in making an act of seemingly pure selflessness seem not only believable but something more than quixotic.

He does this, surely, by rooting the Prince's gesture in his own psychology so that his potential sacrifice itself stems from his own desire for redemption, his own recognition of collaboration when he had imagined himself innocent of such. Hence Miller's remark that the play's central theme is 'Am I my own keeper?' rather than 'Am I my brother's keeper?' itself, of course, Cain's reply when asked where his brother might be, the brother he had killed to secure his own future.

It is also surely worth remarking that though this play was born out of a renewed concern for events now more than two decades behind him, it is also a work concerned with metaphysics as well as politics and morality. The overtones of Kafka and Beckett are a reminder that this is a play in which the characters debate the arbitrariness of death. Like Kafka's protagonist from *The Trial*, they wish to declare their affront at news that they are condemned. Like him, they plead that some mistake must have been made, that they are uniquely innocent. As Camus observes in *The Fall*,

> The idea that comes most naturally to man, as if from his very nature, is the idea of his innocence. From this point of view, we are all like that little Frenchman at Buchenwald who insisted on registering a complaint with the clerk, himself a prisoner, who was recording his arrival. A complaint? The clerk and his comrades laughed: 'Useless old man. You don't lodge complaints here.' 'But you see, sir,' said the little Frenchman, 'my case is exceptional. I am innocent!'[22]

The people gathered in this French place of detention wish to plead their innocence, no matter the fate of those others who stare into the same darkness as themselves. Some are momentarily reprieved; others face a more immediate fate. And though the death of others is a reminder of our own there is still, Miller suggests, a sense of relief at having survived another day, another month, another year. To have survived, he insists, both in the context of the Holocaust and of a more general experience, is to have incurred a certain burden, a certain guilt, which derives precisely from an awareness of complicity with the very forces one fears the most. As Camus observes in *The Fall*, 'Each of us insists on being innocent at all costs, even if he has to accuse the whole human race and heaven itself.'[23]

This is a play in which the characters, for the most part, barely move. In blocking it, Clurman remarked of them that they 'stand up when it is impossible to remain seated'.[24] As in a Beckett play, all action seems rendered pointless or ironic by the fundamental situation. Language becomes circular, self-evidently drained of meaning. These people can do nothing but wait, their fate effectively already determined, absurd victims of an absurd system.

For Camus, however, the 'end of the movement of absurdity, of rebellion . . . is compassion . . . that is to say, in the last analysis, love',[25] and this is the path Miller takes. In one way it was to become the piety of 1960s America, but here the price of the compassionate gesture is so high as to purge it of sentimentality. The Prince's final gesture is one of love. Greater love hath no man than this. Of course, the absurdity is not thereby annihilated. It is, however, rendered irrelevant.

But why, some critics, particularly Jewish critics, wished to know, present Jews who are so compliant in their fate? Why place on stage Jews who fail to draw on their faith, Jews, seemingly, without a future because they are presented as without a past, merely objects of attention. Seen thus, the play becomes a recapitulation of the processes it would present. But, painful though it may be, it was that paralysis, that refusal to believe in the seemingly unbelievable, that conviction that there were depths which no one would plumb that was, indeed, the reason that so few even of those who could escape chose to do so.

In this play, it is objected, there is an open door, with apparently only one guard. Why did they not storm their way out? After all, they were not to know that there were more guards outside. But this is surely the point. Quite apart from the near-certainty of them being caught, more significantly they somehow believed both that the rumours could not be true and that they themselves might yet explain why they, uniquely, should not, could not be included. And the fact is that millions did go to their deaths, carrying with them their belongings, money for a supposed new life and, beyond everything, hope, irrational, baseless, frighteningly ironic hope. It is not Miller's play that is false to history in this regard but those who wish that the past could be redeemed at least within the bounds of the stage.

To mix metaphysics with an enquiry into the roots of the Holocaust, however, is, to some, to enter dangerous territory not because this should be seen as a world of heroes and saints, with the only obligation being to distinguish one from the other, but because to use it as metaphor, as Miller determinedly does, seems in some sense to reduce the pressure, diminish its significance. To Miller, though, it opens the door to more disturbing questions precisely because they are not limited to an event in Europe, distant in time and place. To speak of the Civil Rights movement, however, to some seemed disproportionate. Even Vietnam, with its atrocities, belonged in another world. And when he offered an altogether more mundane example, the gulf seemed to open a little wider.

Having remarked on our capacity for collaboration with the evil we condemn he offers, as an example, a real-estate developer dedicated, 'with the logic of his own calling', to 'clearing' a scenically wooded area in order to build a parking lot. 'It's the real-estate man's business to develop', he suggests,

> and that's the only logic that applies for him. Whether the development has a damaging effect on the esthetics of the countryside, whether it will incon-venience as many people as it is theoretically designed to convenience, does not concern him. This is true of every other pursuit and profession, each dominated by its own logic, totally unconcerned with any overall judgement of values, any sense of complicity or willingness to assume responsibility.[26]

Doubtless what is in his mind is those companies who designed the gas chambers, who manufactured the ovens, who supplied the gas, who devised the logistical support, who timetabled the trains without which the deaths of millions would have been, if not impossible, then conducted with less efficiency. The problem is that in trying to root a principle in what must seem a reductive example he ran the risk of appearing to trivialise the very event which is the basis for his metaphor.

Epstein, however, was not the only critic. For Philip Rahv, *After the Fall* had been 'pretentious and defensive'. There was virtually nothing good to be said about it. He found it 'more pitiable than ingratiating'.[27] *Incident at Vichy*, by contrast, was more impressive, albeit suffering from the author's ideological ambition and frequent sententiousness of language. However, since the article in which he addressed the play was called 'Arthur Miller and the Fallacy of Profundity', these were the least of his objections. What he primarily resisted was the play's ending, in which the Prince offers his free pass to the otherwise doomed Jewish psychoanalyst. He found the selflessness of the gesture at odds with Miller's presentation of a deeply flawed human nature, a mere *coup de théâtre*, detached from dramatic logic and unrelated to the character of a man who now willingly sacrifices his life for a total stranger.

His own explanation is that Miller, in common with many ex-Marxists (of whom Rahv was one), had 'been looking for "profundities" to cover their new nakedness. As a result, Miller, in *Incident at Vichy*, prefers', he suggested, 'to replace analysis of historical forces with moralistic gestures. Attempts to understand Nazis either in terms of individual psychology or a generalized human nature results in nothing more than mystification.' For Rahv, Nazism contained no mystery. It was a replay of other mass slaughters, this time facilitated by technology, and openly signalled by Hitler in *Mein Kampf*.

The interesting question was how the Nazis had come to power without being required to fight for it: 'only by examining the latter question', he suggested, 'can some useful lessons for the future be drawn' (387). The fault, he insisted, lay with big business, the military, the communists, the social democrats and the intellectuals, the latter, like Miller, he implies, 'instead of thinking and acting politically, were engaged as usual in misinterpreting life and history with their seductive abstractions and profundities' (386).

In other words, Miller was writing altogether the wrong play, though, unlike Epstein, Rahv did feel that the Holocaust was best related to other acts of genocide and that it could be explained by the guilt of virtually all sections of German society. Thus *Incident At Vichy*, it seemed, acted as the focus for long-delayed discussions of the Holocaust itself, discussions in which the play seems often to have been set on one side.

Nonetheless, Rahv did have a more specific complaint. He takes exception to the comment by the Austrian Prince who observes that 'Many times I used to ask my friends: To be a good German why must you despise everything that is not German? Until I realized the answer. They do those things not because they are Germans but because they are nothing. It is the hallmark of the age – the less you exist the more important it is to make a clear impression.' Rahv characterises this as having a 'modish existentialist ring'. What it does not do, he insists, is explain the German contempt for other nations. Such a contempt, he suggests, is far from mysterious: 'It is a willed contempt functionally serving as the rationalization, politically and culturally, of their urge to exterminate other peoples in order to make *Lebensraum* for themselves' (388).

Why mystify ourselves, he asks, with 'the metaphysics of nothingness' when the explanation is so much simpler? Suddenly the answer is revealed. The Nazis set out to liquidate the Jews so that they would have more territory! Aside from the fact that this makes no kind of geo-political sense, and ignores what is known both of the psychology of Hitler and the social programme he believed himself to be following, such remarks do not come close to understanding what Miller is attempting in the play, though he is not wrong in his detection of an existential ring.

It was Erich Fromm, writing in 1942, who observed that 'In our opinion none of these explanations [for Fascism] which emphasize political and economic factors to the exclusion of psychological ones – or vice versa – is correct.'[28] What interested him was precisely the paralysis that seemed to typify all parts of German society, the swift collapse of resistance and of the will, a resignation that he also detected in democratic countries.

As to the question of German contempt for others being rooted in a sense of their own insignificance, Fromm is far closer to Miller than Rahv. The attitude in Nazi Germany was that 'the individual is nothing and does not count. The individual should accept this personal insignificance, dissolving himself in the higher power, and then feel proud in participating in the strength and glory of this higher power' (200). In *Mein Kampf*, Hitler had explained that 'Idealism alone leads men to voluntary acknowledgement of the privilege of force and strength and thus makes them become a dust particle of that order which forms and shapes the entire universe' (201). Out of that sense of nothingness is born association with power, the sole source of meaning.

As Hitler further explained, in relation to the huge rallies which he thought the best agents of power (and this is worth recalling in relation to *Focus*, in which just such a Nazi rally occurs): 'The mass meeting is necessary if only for the reason that in it the individual, who in becoming an adherent of a new movement feels lonely and is easily seized with the fear of being alone, receives for the first time the pictures of a greater community' (193). How else will this new power, born out of powerlessness, express itself in the Nazi world-view than by exerting itself over others? As Fromm suggests, 'While Hitler and his bureaucracy enjoy the power over the German masses, these masses themselves are taught to enjoy power over other nations and to be driven by the passion for domination of the world' (195).

Part of the problem of Rahv's remarks, and, indeed, Epstein's, is that he picks an argument with the expressed views of characters as if they were consistent at all times with Miller's own. In particular, he regrets their failure to offer a historico-political analysis. His objection, in other words, is to the interpretative strategy of characters, themselves baffled by a plight which they can barely understand and confronted with a terror that is, at first, not much more than the subject of rumour.

In like manner, Rahv objects when the Jewish psychoanalyst offers the observation that 'Jew' is only the name we give to the stranger, to that agony we cannot ourselves feel, that death which we look on with cold abstraction. Each man, the psychoanalyst suggests, has his Jew, even the Jews (389), the observation that equally irritated Epstein. Once again, though, he conflates author and character. Hence, on the basis of a character's response, he observes that he is not impressed 'by Miller's reaction to anti-Semitism' (389).

People are drawn to anti-Semitism, Rahv informs us, because Jews appear too 'pushy' and 'too prosperous', on the one hand, and 'helpless on the other'. If Miller is merely saying that everyone looks down on somebody else this is 'the merest cliché'. That, of course, is not what Miller or the character is saying. What the psychoanalyst is saying is that there is an assumed discontinuity to human experience, an exclusivity to the tribe which depends on the excluded for definition. It is not a question of looking down on others but of assuming there is no continuity of feeling, no commonality of needs and desires, and, ultimately, no absolute right even to exist.

In like manner, Rahv objects to the statement that 'It's not your guilt I want, it's your responsibility' (389) (in this case character and author do agree), insisting that guilt is essential to a stirred conscience. This, however, is patently not what either character or author is saying. Miller wishes to distinguish a passive, self-referring sentiment, complete in itself, from an active discharge of duty.

Robert Brustein, whose vendetta against major American dramatists contin- ued (he also attacked O'Neill, Williams and early Albee), described *Incident at Vichy* as exhibiting 'noisy virtue and moral flatulence'. It was, he said, 'a moral dray horse about to be melted down for glue . . . tedious, glum, and badly written'.[29] It looked back, he suggested, to the 1930s and the moral melodra- mas of Robert Sherwood, while possibly borrowing from Max Frisch's *Andorra* and Rolf Hochhuth's *The Deputy* or, in terms of its theme, Hannah Arendt's *Eichmann in Jerusalem*. Like Rahv, he accuses Miller of mock profundity (as he accused Paddy Chayevsky of 'middle seriousness'), and like Epstein of letting the Germans off the hook by proposing a generalised guilt by which 'If every- body is guilty, then nobody is guilty, and the extermination of six million can be attributed to the universality of human evil' (261).

In an earlier review, interestingly, Brustein had praised Arendt's book as revealing how Germans had been 'inured to totalitarianism through the cor- ruption of language' (82), as though language, and its distortions, rather than a flawed humanity, should be standing in the dock. He also objected to the play's static nature, to the casting, and the 'slack New York tonalites' of the actors, that 'we have come to think of as the Lincoln Center style' (262). Since there had only been two productions by the Repertory Theatre to that date, *Incident at Vichy* and *After the Fall*, with different directors and actors, the comment was effectively one aimed at Miller. Beyond that, his attack extended to Elia Kazan, for his pleasure in producing two hits, not, evidently, what Lincoln Center was to be about, and to the Board of the new theatre which was indeed, as he suggests, in process of replacing Robert Whitehead as director since it had belatedly discovered that repertory theatre was inevitably a deficit operation.

Part of the explanation for Brustein's dismissal of Miller, along with other home-grown talents, was his respect for the European and, to some degree, American avant-garde. Thus, while praising Beckett, Ionesco (with reserva- tions) and Genet (together with a slightly older avant-garde represented by Brecht, Pirandello and Camus), though dismissing Pinter's *The Caretaker* as the work of an 'abstract technician' (183), he treats with great circumspection new works by Miller and Williams and revivals of O'Neill.

Beyond that, however, Brustein's argument with *Incident at Vichy* turns partly, at least, on the question of the Holocaust. Disturbed by a play that seems to absorb German responsibility into a flawed humanity, he is less inclined than other critics to ask for a precise account of the political processes which underlaid mass murder, still less for an identification of those responsible. Indeed, in 1963, in his review of Frisch's *Andorra*, he spent as much time describing his notions of German guilt and responsibility as he did reviewing the play. The Germans, he explained, had 'gotten away with mass murder' (187). His point was rather different.

The trial of Adolf Eichmann, he insisted, was a travesty in its suggestion that moral depravity could be laid at the door of a named individual rather than 'an entire nation'. He quotes Brecht's widow, Helene Weigel, as remarking that 'I know my dear Germans. They would do this again. Tomorrow' (187–8). Meanwhile, 'the Germans exhibit their guilt with as much national pride as their Volkswagens' (188). When he accuses *Incident at Vichy* of being Miller's 'new entry in the Guilt Sweepstakes' (259), therefore, he seems to suggest that far from levelling an indictment it is pandering to German masochism, offering an implicit route to absolution.

While resistant to the notion of a shared human guilt, he seems happy to accept, and indeed, to propose, the notion of German guilt. The irony is that Miller shared this conviction. The fact is, though, that *Incident at Vichy* is more subtle than this, even while deploying the symbolic roles which Brustein identifies and Miller sees as part of his design.

The 'scientist' is no more than a functionary, carrying out the orders of the state, as so many doctors did, indeed, lend their skills to the state. The Major, however, is more complex, acutely aware of the moral issues, contemptuous of those he serves, and yet collaborating, finally, simultaneously an agent and a victim of the state, not, it seems, because he is German but because he lacks the courage to resist.

It is simply not true to say, as does Brustein, that only 'one character has an option on the Truth' (260), in a play in which truth itself – the truth of motive, of character, of moral being – is problematic. Nor is it true to say that the 'single discovery to approach a dramatic revelation' is that 'the Austrian has a Nazi cousin!' (260) in a play in which the characters struggle to make sense of their situation, of their fate, of their relationships to one another.

Like Rahv, he suggests that while the characters have private lives they exist for their symbolic roles. This, however, was precisely what Miller had had in mind. He insisted that the characters in his play were flesh-and-blood people, each with a subterranean life of his own, but that they were also symbolic in the bearing they had on ourselves and our time. It is, of course, precisely that projection into the future that had disturbed Epstein.

Later, other critics would question historical details. How far, in Vichy France, would this situation have arisen in precisely this way? To what extent would a Jew have considered leaving France before the war was even under way? On the other hand, Howard Taubman insisted that the play returned the American theatre to greatness. True or not, this first Arthur Miller play to be set in Europe brought audiences face to face with an issue that no other American playwright had chosen to confront. In doing so, however, he trusted that he would be seen as revealing something more than a fascination with history, remote in time and space. The incident at its centre had occurred in Vichy France. Its relevance, he insisted, extended into a troubled present, not least because he was concerned with a human trait that had found its exemplar and archetype in Cain.

— ✳ —

It is tempting to see Miller's marriage to Inge Morath as marking a new commitment to internationalism. She had emerged from a devastated Europe and brought with her a European sensibility. She travelled as part of her job and Miller, who had seldom left the country before, now frequently accompanied her. He was in Paris in 1965, when he was approached to become President of International PEN, the writers' organisation. Anxious to open a dialogue with those in eastern Europe, in particular, he agreed. Thereafter, he travelled widely in his new capacity and worked for the release of imprisoned writers.

From 1965, too, he threw himself into the Vietnam protest movement, attending teach-ins (including one of the first at his alma mater, the University of Michigan) and marches, even flying to Paris in an attempt to negotiate with the Viet Cong. If he had withdrawn from the political arena during his years with Monroe, he now threw himself into it with enthusiasm and commitment.

In 1968 he worked for the election of Senator Eugene McCarthy, the anti-war candidate, making speeches on his behalf and writing articles for the press. America, meanwhile, was undergoing convulsions, with the assassination of Martin Luther King, which led to America's cities burning, and Senator Robert Kennedy, who seemed on the point of taking over as the principal anti-war candidate.

Miller attended the 1968 National Democratic Convention as a delegate from the state of Connecticut and thus watched as Mayor Richard Daley unleashed his police on the protestors who had gathered there. Inside the convention hall, meanwhile, delegates elected Hubert Humphrey, Vice-President to Lyndon Johnson, who had withdrawn from the race in the name of a national unity for which there appeared little evidence.

It was in that year, too, that Miller staged his most successful play for two decades, *The Price*. For all his political activities, however, it seemed to have little to say about the issues of the day: Vietnam, civil rights, civil unrest. At a time when the avant-garde productions of Off- and Off-Off-Broadway seized the imagination of critics, if not always the general public, this play seemed conventional. He appeared concerned with the residue of another age. To Miller, though, *The Price* engaged with the present precisely because it acknowledged the past. It was, indeed, concerned with the price to be paid for ignoring the past and denying its pressure on the present.

✳

17

'The Price'

At a time when the American theatre was turning its back on what it dismissed as 'well-made plays', staging works that were not designed to transcend the moment, Arthur Miller created a drama that was not only 'well made' in its own right but took as a central metaphor a roomful of antique furniture which was itself well crafted and redolent of another time. When society was engaged with immediate political issues, he seemed to be concerned with yesterday's demands upon the present. If the theatre was intent on deconstructing character, plot and language, he was committed to asserting their centrality. At a time when the irrational was seen as a primary resource against a seemingly dangerous rationality, a soulless technology and perverted science, he chose to stress and deploy a rational analysis, to see morality as rooted in causality.

Yet the fact is that *The Price*, written in 1967 and produced in 1968, was offered as a response to the moment. If it was a reaction against the bleak metaphysics of the absurd and the neo-romanticism of theatre groups which deified feeling over thought, pitched the body against the machine and stressed improvisation as the correlative of a natural existentialism, it was also a work with a politics of its own. This politics, he insisted, bore directly on those political events which some accused him of side-stepping. *The Price* was of and about 1968 just as it was of and about the 1930s, and despite the fashionable enthusiasm for the work of the Living Theatre, the Performance Group and the Open Theatre, this play does indeed seem to have struck a nerve.

Behind the play, Miller suggested, indeed behind almost any play of his, were 'more or less secret responses to other works of the time',[1] evident either by imitation or rejection of 'the dominating forms of the hour' (60). In this case what he was reacting against was those absurdist-influenced plays with which younger American playwrights were experimenting, and a performance theatre which celebrated the moment. It was not that he found no enjoyment in the new theatre. Indeed such plays and performances seemed to him to have the virtue of 'moving us closer to dreams and for dreams', he added, 'I have nothing but respect' (61). What such work did not seem, to him, to do was confront the implications of Vietnam.

In truth, the theatre was not quite as unresponsive to Vietnam as he suggests but it did seem to be more interested in myth than history. Indeed, since disavowal of the authority of the past was fast becoming the new orthodoxy, resistance to causalities seemed especially strong. And what was true in terms of social continuity and historical process seemed equally true of private lives. Nineteen-sixties romanticism proposed a new self, liberated from convention, suspicious of rationality and resistant to historic imperatives. As Miller observed, 'the very idea of an operating continuity between past and present in any human behaviour was *démodé* (62) and irrelevant. The present moment was apotheosised, by the new theatre no less than by those who declared theirs to be a new age uniquely aware of its singularity.

Miller, though, was acutely conscious that in Vietnam 'we are fighting the past' (62), while denying its substance and force. Nationalism as a motive for the war, first against the French and then the Americans, disappeared in the paranoid vision of world communism, historic enmities supposedly forgotten in the search for world domination. The domino theory, which was applied to Southeast Asia and proposed country after country falling to Marxist dictatorships, could equally be said to apply to the political assumptions of an America in which 1950s convictions toppled forward into the 1960s and 70s and justified the overthrow of democracies and the maintaining of deeply corrupt and oppressive dictatorships, provided only that they purported to oppose the menace of creeping communism.

Vietnam, as writers and film-makers swiftly appreciated, was a surreal world often experienced by troops high on drugs, cheap sex and licensed killing. It was a world in which body-counts were validated by severed ears, as Native American deaths had once been confirmed by scalps (and the parallel was acknowledged by film-makers), villages were liberated by napalm and the perpetrators of massacres either went unpunished or were protected from the full consequences of their actions. Helicopter gunships raked the fields, chemicals rained from the skies and b-52s carpet-bombed the forests as if this were, indeed, as Frances Ford Coppola suggested with *Apocalypse Now*, an updated version of Joseph Conrad's *Heart of Darkness*.

As Miller later remarked, some fifty-eight thousand Americans and unknown numbers of Vietnamese died 'to support a myth' (62). They died with no clear idea as to how the war had come about. Reason itself seemed to be a war casualty and when it was over it was, for a while at least, wiped from the national consciousness, along with awareness of its causes. In the end, more medals were awarded for the 1983 invasion of Grenada (which effectively has no army, navy or air force) than for the whole Vietnamese conflict.

There is, however, as Miller notes, no mention of the war in *The Price*. His target was not the war itself but the power of denial. He wrote it, he explained, 'out of a need to reconfirm the power of the past, the veritable seedbed of current reality, and in that way to possibly reaffirm cause and effect in an insane world' (63). He offered, in other words, a metaphor for a process equally corrosive on a national and personal level. To do so, he created characters who looked back almost forty years, to another moment when history caught up with America – the Depression. This, too, had been the origin of a trauma with the power to deform private and public life, generate denials, self-deceits, a mythology with the power to shape social and individual life. The decision once again to create a dialectic between past and present is an assertion about his sense of history, his conception of the moral world and of the formation of the self.

The Price brings together two brothers who meet to dispose of their father's assets but who, in doing so, are forced to re-examine their relationships with that father and one another. Their lives have taken divergent paths. They have each created myths out of a past which they have reshaped to serve current needs. At stake is their sense of themselves, as they seek to justify what they have become, explaining their perceived success and failure in terms of past actions, and their sense of the world they inhabit. Resentment, accusations of betrayal, exploitation and denial, make their confrontation simultaneously painful and strangely therapeutic. This is an act of exorcism.

These are people who have paid a price for errors of commission and omission. They are brothers, and as such reach out to one another even as they accuse. They are two sides of a single sensibility, rather as Biff and Happy had been in *Death of a Salesman*. Their struggle for reconciliation with one another is equally a struggle for reconciliation with themselves and with a past whose truths must be acknowledged if they are to survive. That past contains a social no less than a personal trauma and it has always seemed to Miller that the Depression, which shaped both brothers, had left unfinished business.

It was itself a time of confusion when a particular version of America seemed to have been betrayed, when public no less than private values appeared compromised. Just as the 1950s would see the American right attempt to exact vengeance on the very New Deal liberals whose essentially socialist policies had apparently redeemed a Republic in crisis, so that same anti-communist hysteria would feed a myth which dictated political values in the 1960s and beyond. Vietnam, in other words, could be traced back to the 1950s, which in turn could be seen as a response to the 1930s.

The Price was a play not without its personal resonance for Miller. While insisting that the characters were not based on the relationship between himself and his brother Kermit, nonetheless he has observed that 'the magnetic underlying situation was deep in my bones' (*T*.13). And, indeed, as we have seen, his first play, *No Villain*, based squarely on his own family, like *The Price* had portrayed two brothers, one of whom grudgingly stays with the family firm while the other feels the necessity to break away, driven by ambition. Miller's father, meanwhile, after various attempts to relaunch his failed business, had, as in *The Price*, allowed himself to be supported by his eldest son. The Miller family, like the Franz family, had employed a chauffeur, owned an expensive apartment and lost the family firm in a matter of months. Any attempt to shoehorn biography into the play, however, beyond 'the magnetic underlying situation', would be if not mistaken then a distraction. What interests him here is a divided human nature and a society resistant to understanding the present in terms of the past.

The first word of the stage direction of *The Price* is 'Today'. The first props that we see speak of yesterday: a radio from the 1920s, old newspapers, a wind-up Victrola. Between those two time periods is an electrical arc of meaning. The building in which the play is set is about to be demolished, the furniture piled in its dimly lit attic about to be dispersed. The past, in short, is to be eliminated, denied. It is no longer relevant. The meaning compacted into the clutter of tables, chairs, sculling oars, fencing foils, is on the verge of being deconstructed. There is, Miller explains, 'a weight of time' upon the 'bulging fronts and curving chests marshalled against the walls'.[2]

The room is dense with the accumulated residue of a world about to be swept away. This is the record of another time, laid down like geological strata. It is the assembled furniture of ten rooms, the evidence of a family that had once been solidly established and well off. The harp, the chandeliers, the carved serving table, not only come from a past which seems remote and irrelevant, but hint at a secure and comfortable existence undone by death and something more. For we slowly learn that this house, once so expansive, boasting armoires, book cases, multiple couches and settees, had begun to change its function as the patriarch of the family was slowly displaced to the upper floor, a room was let out to boarders and the family retreated to the loft.

Contemplating this furniture the characters are 'caught by the impact of time' (9), as what once had seemed so fixed and certain has lost its function, as the taste of another generation is rejected by the present. The set for *The Price* is not merely the setting for what is to follow; it is the physical evidence of personal histories. The furniture becomes the site and subject of their arguments but also the embodiment of their memories. It is a metaphor, at once solidly real and symbolic. Reminiscent of the *mise en scène* for a realist drama, it dissolves the real, becoming instead the currency of their exchanges, an expression of what oppresses them, their means of access to a past not so much forgotten as reinvented.

Yet, if memories give access to meaning, they may also be a wall piled up brick by brick, or in this case, chair by chair, precisely to block off access to meaning and to that past where perhaps it resides. For memories may be no more than constructions, reality reconstituted to serve current needs, the mechanics of denial and self-justification. And so they become for much of this play. *The Price* is a memory play in that it is centrally concerned with how we use memory, with a willed amnesia, with the process whereby the past is transformed into a usable myth. This, we soon learn, is effectively what these characters have done as they meet after many years.

The father of the two men who now come together to settle the estate has died sixteen years before. Theirs has been a long-deferred confrontation. When they meet they proceed to fence with one another but their weapons are not foils but competing memories. Coming together to share out the remains of their father's estate, they discover how little they share, not least the histories which might be assumed to be their common property. They have been bequeathed something more than a roomful of furniture. The past is unfinished business and this the occasion for concluding it.

Into this world of frozen memories, lit only by the uncertain light of daylight filtering through windows grimed over with dirt (itself a product of passing time), comes a policeman, Victor, who wanders around with a kind of measured solemnity as if in the presence of the dead. In part he is, since this is the accumulated history of a life, that of his now dead father and hence of himself. He looks at his watch 'waiting for time to pass' (5) but time is effectively suspended here. He removes his gunbelt, momentarily laying aside his present role, though perhaps hinting at an incipient if unstated violence, and plucks the string of a harp. As with the flute music which opens *Death of a Salesman*, the sound takes us back to another time.

He picks up a fencing foil and snaps it in the air, his gaze, we are told by Miller, being 'held by memory', as if some membrane were being dissolved, as if his muscles somehow held that memory in their very tissues. He cranks the handle of the phonograph and places a record on the turntable. The sound – a 'laughing record' by Gallagher and Shean – also comes from another age and when he inevitably joins in the infectious laughter he weds past to present, time being momentarily annihilated. And time is central to this play, as to all of Miller's dramas. For his is a world of causalities, of moral consequences, of responsibilities.

In a society in which denial of the past is a tenet of its myths, in which the demolition of buildings, the sweeping away of the old, is a function and an image of its claim to modernity, he is a resistant force. It is not that Miller sentimentalises the past. His is not a theatre of nostalgia. He stresses the past because it is deeply implicated in the present, because memory is a present fact with present consequences, and because, as he has so often said, the chickens come home to roost. Present realities are not free-floating, improvised into existence as if they had no roots, no origins, no cause. They are the result of decisions taken or not taken, actions denied or acknowledged, commitments made or broken.

The play, then, opens with laughter, a recognisable strategy of Miller's drama. His work frequently moves from a comic scene, often a two-hander, into more serious concerns as if both to ease the audience into more disturbing territory and to move us from the personal to the public.

Victor is now joined by his wife Esther, and immediately the air thickens with tension. He smells alcohol on her breath, as James Tyrone had detected the signs of addiction in Mary (in O'Neill's *Long Day's Journey Into Night*). She is, evidently, an alcoholic, on edge, dispossessed. When she learns of her husband's soiled jacket she is 'seriously disconsolate'. Her reactions seem disproportionate.

She is sensitive about his job and has stored up memories of slights and social embarrassments which come from a career which clearly disappoints her. She suffers an 'unrelenting moodiness'. There is 'despair in her voice'. She has no job of her own and wanders the streets, restlessly. Their son has left home. The last consolation has gone so that, as she confesses, 'I don't know who I am' (18).

For his part, Victor is approaching fifty, eligible for retirement from the force and playing with the idea of retraining for another career, the purposeful career he had plainly always hoped might lift him out of the banality of the one to which he has never reconciled himself. Like Willy Loman, he has been living a temporary life, convincing himself that retirement will at last render some kind of meaning for his life. As Esther insists, 'everything was always temporary with us. It's like we never were anything, we were always about-to-be' (18), a defining condition of a culture whose central myth is of becoming: the American Dream. When he picks up the fencing foil his wife asks him, 'Can you still do it?' (24). The reference is to fencing but some other capacity has leached away from him that was once there when he last held the blade in a college team that beat Princeton. He is, seemingly, impotent in the face of what he assumes to be his fate.

If Victor has something of Willy about him, Esther seems at first the opposite of Linda Loman. Looking back over their lives, she says that 'if I demanded more it would have helped you more' (18). It is he, and not she, who had valued security, as it was she and not he who had dreams of fortunes to be made. However, in a pattern typical of *The Price* (and, indeed *Death of a Salesman*) assertion is followed by retraction, claim succeeded by counter-claim. Thus Victor reminds her that both of them had been frightened of a repetition of the Depression and hence had, in the end, clung to the security which was the other side of the coin to the feeling of entrapment that so alarmed them.

Victor hesitates to retire precisely because he feels that he will thereby effectively be drawing a line across the ledger, forced to draw up a final balance sheet in which profit and loss will be calculated in terms of his life. His achievement, his identity, the meaning of his life stand exposed and he will have to acknowledge what he has made of himself: nothing. As he says to his wife, 'I look at my life and the whole thing is incomprehensible to me. I know all the reasons and all the reasons and all the reasons, and it ends up – nothing' (23). He stands on the edge of retirement, unable to decide whether to recommit himself to life. In a word reminiscent of many other Miller plays, she accuses him of being 'paralysed'. And like those other plays *The Price* is in essence about the cause of such paralysis and the necessity to end it by confronting the past.

Victor and Esther are mutually disappointed but they are still together and we are told that their relationship is 'quite balanced'. But the balance is one of disappointment and disillusionment. Esther once wrote poetry as her husband once looked forward to a career in science. Both dreams have faded. We are certainly made aware that money is a problem. The stain on his suit is a blow because the cleaning bill will have to be paid. Her own purchase of a suit has to be defended as a thrifty and wise economy.

Victor is proud of their son but his pride takes an odd and revealing form: 'nobody's ever going to take that guy' (47). The implication is that he himself has been taken, has allowed himself to become a victim. He recognises his wife's concern with money but is determined not 'to lay down' his life for it (a tension echoed in *The Last Yankee*). In a world of winners and losers he knows that he is in the latter category, but consoles himself that he has acted out of moral principal. The play explores that conviction, as it does the notion of the self-created victim.

Into this situation comes a true survivor, Gregory Solomon, a retired second-hand furniture-dealer, picked from an out-of-date edition of the yellow pages, whom they inadvertently resurrect. Against their earnest anguish he pitches a resilient humour. He represents another time, his experience taking him back beyond the Depression that has so seared their own lives. He seems at first little more than a cheerful pragmatist, a vaudevillian charming his way through life. But his past, too, contains truths he has had to address. His Jewish identity, meanwhile, gives survival another dimension.

Gregory Solomon, like the furniture, seems a remnant of the past, himself showing signs of age and depredation. His hat is dusty, his topcoat shapeless, his tie frayed, his collar tab curled up, his waistcoat wrinkled, his trousers baggy, his leather portfolio wrung out. He coughs as he enters, breathes heavily and leans on a cane. At the age of nearly ninety he had been ready for the end, retiring from his job, unwilling to undertake anything that might take more than a year or so. But this man is still resilient, straight-backed, elegant. A one-time acrobat, he has not lost his sense of physical and moral balance. An immigrant from Russia, he still remains committed to a faith in possibility.

He is a man who has 'struggled in six different countries,' who 'nearly got killed a couple times', and whose daughter committed suicide, but he remains what he ever was, a 'fighter', holding on and never letting go. He is the epitome of the resistant spirit, though even he had withdrawn from the fight, retiring since a foreshortened time seemed to render his efforts merely ironic. The putative sale is thus a challenge to him no less than to those who have returned to this brownstone house, nearing the end of its life, to confront the past and in doing so determine their future. Gregory Solomon is tempted back into the life he had thought nearly ended and in being so becomes emblematic.

He is aware, as on some level are Victor and his his brother Walter, that this is something more than a meeting to dispose of furniture. His remark that 'you cannot talk reality with used furniture' (33) is not merely a delaying tactic, as he nerves himself to step back into a life from which he had withdrawn. It is an acknowledgement that reality is a matter of interpretation, as is memory. As he says, 'the price of used furniture is nothing but a viewpoint' (38). Its value is not innate. It is the worth ascribed to it as circumstances and needs change.

And if a man is no more a piece of furniture than he is, in Willy's telling phrase, a piece of fruit, the meaning of his life is a matter of perspective. Thus Solomon, defending the idea of his marrying at the age of seventy-five, insists that 'it's the same like secondhand furniture . . . the whole thing is a viewpoint' (43). Tempted to withdraw from the sale, as from life, Solomon decides to opt for life: 'I'm going to buy it! . . . I'll have to live, that's all' (42).

His commitment, however, is already implicit in his life, which consists of repeated failures, in business and life – he has been married four times and was wiped out by the depressions of 1898, 1904, 1923 and 1932. It is implicit in his humour, which is his way of dealing with pain and anxiety. To him, the idea that Victor's father had simply collapsed in the face of the Depression is unthinkable: 'to lay down like *that* . . .' (45). To Victor, his defeat came precisely from his faith in the system, a faith which Solomon never fully embraced, acknowledging failure, the sudden collapse of hope, as part of an older rhythm. As Victor remarks, 'you're different. He believed in it . . . The system, the whole thing. He thought it was his fault' (45). For Solomon, though, it is not a question of a naive faith being shattered by events, leaving nothing but despair and apathy, but of the necessity to renew faith in knowledge of its fragility. In that he is close to Quentin in *After the Fall*. In Solomon's words, 'it's not that you can't believe nothing, that's so hard – it's that you still got to believe it. *That's* hard' (37).

That, essentially, is the dilemma equally facing Victor. He, too, had had a dream of success which he has struggled to keep alive over the years. His college career had been abandoned, he tells himself, so that he could look after his father. The police force, in which he has done anything but excel – being posted away from the action and making nineteen arrests in twenty-eight years – was to be a temporary expedient, a way-station on the road to a temporarily deferred success. Now he seems like his father. His energy has leached away. The dream is no more than a fantasy, kept alive by his wife at times to neutralise her own despair and at times as a weapon to turn against the husband she loves, but who seems to have betrayed them both. As he says, 'you plan too much, you end up with nothing' (46).

Now he determines to rely on his brother, as his father had once seemingly relied on him. And his mechanism is the same as his father's: guilt. His father had used his apparent dependency as a principal weapon; Victor now deploys the same device believing, as he does, that his brother's success had in effect been built on his own failure. He had, after all, abandoned a college career to look after his father while his brother had gone on to a successful career as a surgeon. That brother, Walter, now appears, after several years.

Victor has summoned him partly out of a feeling that the two of them should dispose of their father's property together, and share the proceeds, and partly because he wishes to confront him with the past and ask for help in creating a new career. Beyond that, he seems to want confirmation that the decision which had closed down his options had been the right one.

We are told in a stage direction that Walter's 'interest is avid, and his energy immense' (58). He is divorced, but this seems to leave him with a 'naive excitement'. He is the achiever, as his brother is a failure, but as the encounter develops so we learn that he has suffered a breakdown and been away from his work for three years. He has returned, it seems, with a new social conscience, now devoting half his time to public health. He has disposed of his opulent apartment and moved into a more modest one. He has withdrawn from the stock market and insists that 'I'm alive. For the first time' (81). He has come, indeed, less to dispose of his father's furniture than because he has a sense of mission. He wishes to explain himself and his feelings, to become reconciled with the brother who apparently has so little to show for a life of service.

Walter is a man who believes he has experienced and survived a crisis. He has come to a life-changing realisation. As he confesses, 'You start out wanting to be the best, and there's no question that you need a certain fanaticism . . . Until you've eliminated everything extraneous . . . including people . . . You become a kind of instrument . . . that cuts money out of people, or fame out of the world' (82). In search of power, he has become its agent. Human feeling, he has come to believe, has taken second place in his life. He now recognises and acknowledges the price he has paid for the 'daily fear you call ambition and cautiousness, and piling up the money' (83).

The irony is that he has come to this conclusion as a result of misreading his brother's life. He imagines Victor's decision to sacrifice his life for a father who needed no help to be a decision to opt for 'a real life'. In fact, we slowly learn, it was no more nor less than a concession to fantasy built out of fear, a fear that he feels still relevant, as a policeman and citizen: 'We're a goddamned army holding this city down and when it blows again you'll be thankful for a roof over your head!' (10).

In his own case, Walter has come to feel that pride and competitiveness has undermined his utility as a surgeon, that, and a sudden acknowledgement of the sense of the vertiginous nature of experience, that fear of falling and shock at collapse that his father had felt. He, too, now knows what it is to feel meaning dissipate. He has ended up in 'a swamp of success and bankbooks' (84) as Victor has ended in a civil-service job whose sudden ending leaves him with a sense of threat rather than possibility.

In search of expiation, in an effort to exorcise his demons, he now offers Walter a job, a cavalier gesture which not merely ignores his brother's lack of qualifications but which he feels sufficient to neutralise three decades of misunderstandings. From his point of view, Victor has made himself a victim, feeling oddly comfortable with the role. Convincing himself that he has sacrificed himself for the good of his father, in fact he had knowingly chosen not to chance himself in the world. He had asked his brother for five hundred dollars to help him finish college, a request which Walter had refused because he knew that their father had ample resources of his own and hence had no need of the sacrifices his son seemed determined to make. The evidence for this lies in the very furniture which now confronts them and whose price they are debating. Here is the solid proof that Victor chose to ignore.

Victor finally acknowledges this seemingly suppressed knowledge but insists that he understands why his father had denied the four thousand dollars he had hidden away. 'One day you're head of the house, at the head of the table, and suddenly you're shit. Overnight . . . It's not that you don't love somebody, it's that you've got to survive . . . We do what we have to do. What else are we talking about here?' (107). What we are talking about, it transpires, is what such survival might amount to. Victor insists that he acted out of simple humanity, out of a desire to hold up a crumbling house: 'You're brought up to believe in one another . . . I wanted to . . . stop it from falling apart' (108). To Walter, though, this is to sentimentalise. They were, he insists, not brought up to believe in one another but to succeed, hence his father's greater respect for his surgeon son.

'What was unbearable', he insists, 'is not that it all fell apart, it was that there was never anything there' (107). In a speech reminiscent of *After the Fall*, which similarly recalls the Depression, he remembers their mother almost literally throwing his father's life in his face, unable to comfort him in his need. The problem, he insists, is 'not that there was no mercy in the world . . . It's that there was no love in this house' (109). As a result, he no longer looks for evidence of betrayal, because there was nothing of value to betray and that was the root of their separate failures in life.

Walter's new faith is that 'we invent ourselves . . . to wipe out what we know' (110). Victor's life has not been an upholding of principle but a denial of reality. His father had not been a will-less victim but a frightened man prepared to sacrifice his son to shore up his sense of a disintegrating world. Walter has not been a selfless surgeon but a man intent on winning fame and success by ignoring the reality of individual pain and need. By failing to address the reality of the past they have become its true victims. Victor and Walter, apparent failure/apparent success, ineffectual moralist/competent achiever are not so different, after all. As Walter observes, 'we're like two halves of the same guy. As though we can't quite move ahead – alone' (110). Reconciliation is not quite achieved within the play, but illusions have been stripped away. The past now stands exposed. It ends with Solomon playing the laughing record, no longer intimidated by the task he has accepted so late in life, no longer giving up, accepting that new beginnings are always a possibility.

Miller has insisted on the sense of balance at which he was aiming in *The Price*. The fluctuating sympathies of the audience are a response not merely to revelations about a past that has become a field of contention, but to the necessities which drive the two brothers. This is not a play about a selfless man confronted with a selfish one. It is not even primarily about the limits of loyalty, the extent and nature of guilt, the acknowledgement of error and the search for forgiveness or simple understanding, though all of these become part of a larger argument. Nor is it only concerned with denial and betrayal, though both are as significant here as they are in other Miller plays. That larger argument seems to turn in part on those human qualities required if the race is to survive or even advance.

Victor's self-deceiving acquiescence, his willingness to embrace the role of victim, is balanced by a vision of mutuality which, if compromised by self-deceit and hedged around by fear, is nonetheless the embodiment of values which can be abandoned only at too great a price. By the same token, Walter's pride, arrogance, self-serving ambition are balanced by an aggressive drive without which history would lack a dynamic and progress be no more than simple rhetoric. Even his ability to change, to reorder his priorities, is evidence of an adaptability without which past, present and future would be coincident.

Talking in 1980, Miller spelled out the differences between the two brothers. Walter, he suggested, 'is the one who invents new procedures because he is not bound by any reverence for what exists; he's perfectly selfish and temperamental and idiosyncratic. Whether it be in physics or automobile engineering or business, those types add something new to the way the world goes . . . And the other brother is a terrific husband and father.'[3] Well, not such a terrific husband, in fact, since his wife is an alcoholic deeply frustrated precisely by his lack of drive, by his refusal to act. What Victor does represent is a desire for order, a need to contain the incipient chaos of the world. He is a policeman who patrols the narrow borders of experience, accepting and, as we learn in the course of the play, even inventing obligations of a kind which give meaning to an otherwise arbitrary world. On the other hand, he is concerned for his wife but can never take the necessary steps to address her deepening despair. And this is a mark of *The Price* as Miller swings the sympathy of the audience first one way and then the other.

As he has said:

> I didn't want to let the audience off the hook. They're very comfortable in the second act of that play. They say, 'Ah, this poor nice policeman: how he was screwed by that rich neurotic jerk.' Everybody hates surgeons anyway . . . Well, it turns out at a certain point he had something to do with his fate. It's marvelous once the audience can discover that . . . the satisfaction is the perception of the tension . . . it is not solved, and life isn't. It can't be solved. It's a play without any candy.[4]

On the one hand, he suggests, lie 'dutifulness and self-sacrifice', on the other 'the more aggressive nature'. The irony with which he plays is that the selfish man may have more to contribute.[5]

The real achievement, though, lies in the fact that neither of those polarities is quite what it appears. Victor's selflessness conceals a deeper selfishness; Walter's egotism leads him in the direction of a new idealism. To Miller *The Price* was in part concerned with

> what it takes to be a person who refuses to be swept away and seduced by the values of the society. It is in one sense the price of integrity. In other words the policeman has refused to adopt the sex and success motives of the society. He has walled himself up against them and has kept a perverse integrity as a result of that but you see what he pays for that. Still, he is saner than Walter, with a hold on reality. So basically what is involved in the forefront of the play is the question of the deformations that both viewpoints take in this society.[6]

Both men change in the course of the play, not least because they are obliged to acknowledge their inner contradictions. That there is no ultimate reconciliation, however, that neither entirely abandons his contrastive and distinguishing characteristics for some bland and compromising middle ground, is indicative of Miller's conviction that neither is wholly right or wholly wrong. Some tension is not only inevitable but desirable. As he explains in his production note,

> A fine balance of sympathy should be maintained in the playing of the roles of Victor and Walter. The actor playing Walter must not regard his attempts to win back Victor's friendship as mere manipulation. From entrance to exit, Walter is attempting to put into action what he has learned about himself, and sympathy will be evoked for him in proportion to the openness, the depth of need, the intimations of suffering with which the role is played.
>
> The admonition goes beyond the question of theatrics to the theme of the play. As the world now operates, the qualities of both brothers are necessary to it; surely their respective psychologies and moral values conflict at the heart of the social dilemma. The production must therefore withhold judgement in favor of presenting both men in all their humanity and from their own viewpoints. Actually, each has merely proved to the other what the other has known but dare not face. At the end, demanding of one another what was forfeited to time, each is left touching the structure of his life.

That last phrase, of course, could apply to any of Miller's plays. That is, indeed, the dramatic logic which lies behind them, as does the distinction between what is known and what is faced. But not the least interesting part of these remarks lies in Miller's observation that the qualities of both brothers are necessary to the world as it 'now operates'. Perhaps it is possible to detect in those two words a sense of regret that things are not otherwise, a wistful nostalgia for a time when he might have regarded the social dynamic less ambiguously.

The fact is, though, that *The Price* is not only about the price paid by two siblings who so wilfully misread their own and one another's lives, it is also about the public world. They are drawn to the past because it is there that the fissure opened, there that the process of denial began. They meet in the present but the past is literally and metaphorically piled up between them, both in the form of the furniture and the memories over which they contend. And what is true of them is true, too, of the society they inhabit.

This is the 1960s, a period in which the theatrical slogan, derived from Antonin Artaud, was 'No more masterpieces', as if the past not only had no authority but should have no authority. This was a time when, in the arts, the spontaneously created event, the improvised moment, the co-presence, in the present, of actor and audience generated epiphanies. Mainstream politics was no less anxious to deny the past. The passage of civil-rights and voter-rights legislation was assumed to have sealed off historic injustice. The dream was now of tomorrow. National energy was redirected into space. And when American cities burned, and a distant war began to be costed in terms of body counts, there was little inclination to probe the origins of such discord, to see this as the price to be paid for a history which had been too easily transmuted into myth.

The furniture in the Franz household is an embarrassment. It no longer fits in the present. Its very solidities seem to deny the possibility of changing taste, to invoke the ethos of a time when private and public values were not merely a matter of pragmatics. The house, however, is to be swept aside, a link with the past broken. For Miller, this is emblematic and *The Price* an assertion of continuities, a moral logic, a causal connection seemingly denied by the culture. Solomon, reinfused with a desire to live, never forgets the suicide of his daughter. It is a pain, indeed, which must be acknowledged if he is to find a justification for his own tenacious commitment to life. A similar acceptance of painful past truths seems, to Miller, the minimum price to pay for a society which calls for sacrifices in the name of principles rooted in an unexamined past.

Writing on the occasion of a Broadway revival of the play, in 1999, he insisted that it 'grew out of a need to reconfirm the power of the past, the seedbed of current reality, and the way to possibly reaffirm cause and effect in an insane world'. While it did not 'utter the word Vietnam, it speaks to a spirit of unearthing the real that seemed to have very nearly gone from our lives'.[7]

It was, thus, not a play at odds with the moment, whose dramatic concerns were at a tangent to those of a society then confronting disorder at home and a ruinous war abroad. It was a work written precisely in response to the Vietnam War and the theatrical avant-garde. He had, he declared, been concerned to 'confront and confound both'.

> [A]s the dying continued in Vietnam with no adequate resistance to it in the country, the theater, so it seemed to me, risked trivialization by failing to confront the bleeding, at least in a way that could reach most people . . . one had to feel the absence – not only in theater but everywhere – of any interest in what had surely given birth to Vietnam, namely its roots in the past.

Indeed, the very idea of an operating continuity between past and present in any human behavior was démodé and close to a laughably old-fashioned irrelevancy. My impression, in fact, was that playwrights were either uninterested in or incapable of presenting antecedent material altogether. Like the movies, plays seemed to exist entirely in the now; characters had either no past or none that could somehow be directing present actions. It was as though the culture had decreed amnesia as the ultimate mark of reality.

(297)

The Vietnam War was acknowledged as an immediate political reality, demanding a response from politicians and artists alike. What it was not seen as being was a consequence of historic processes. To him it was a product equally of American history and American myths, the denial of which was an article of faith.

As the corpses piled up, it became cruelly impolite if not unpatriotic to suggest the obvious, that we were fighting the past; our rigid anti-Communist theology, born of another time two decades earlier, made it a sin to consider Vietnamese Reds as nationalists rather than Moscow's and Beijing's yapping dogs. We were fighting in a state of forgetfulness, quite as though we had not aborted a national election in Vietnam and divided the country into separate halves when it became clear that Ho Chi Minh would be the overwhelming favorite for the presidency. This was the reality on the ground, but unfortunately it had to be recalled in order to matter. And so 50,000 Americans [in fact 58,000], not to mention millions of Vietnamese, paid with their lives to support a myth and a bellicose denial.[8]

In the response of the young to the Vietnam war, as the decade advanced, he saw, he explained, a curious echo of the Spanish Civil War. He had once before seen political engagement followed by disillusionment, once before seen external issues distract from an acknowledgement of complicity at the level of private failures of morality, a pervasive self-concern. Once again, he remarked, 'we were looking almost completely outside ourselves for salvation from ourselves; in the absolutely right and necessary rebellion was only a speck of room for worrying about personal ethics and our own egotism' (T.542). It was a typical observation in that here, as elsewhere, he was concerned to insist that public issues do not exist on another plane, that they are not detached from private values.

Beyond that, repetition was a primary theme of a play in which two men who come together to redeem the past proceed to re-enact it. As he remarked, 'Despite my wishes I could not tamper with something the play and life seemed to be telling me: that we were doomed to perpetuate our illusions because truth was too costly to face' (T.542). The laughter with which the play concludes echoes the laughter with which it had almost begun, thus underscoring this sense of repetition. Now, as then, that laughter contains an element of nostalgia. But it is charged with something else as well. For as Solomon laughs and the lights fade to black we have learned something of the characters' capacity to betray themselves and others, we have learned of Solomon's dead daughter and the ease with which the past can be denied. There is, to Miller, a brutal quality to the laughter as well as a suggestion of 'acceptance rather than denial of the deforming betrayals of time' (*T*.542).

The gap between the two brothers has not closed; the past, momentarily brought into contact and juxtaposition with the present, is about to be relegated to oblivion. But there is a residue. Something has been acknowledged, something has survived. The ironies are plain but in the person of Solomon so, too, are the possibilities, limited but real.

For Miller, Solomon is a key figure. He is, he has said, 'the force of life with all its madness and its poetry'.[9] He has failed in a series of marriages and is haunted by the death of his daughter. These are ineluctable and inexplicable facts. Yet such facts do not defeat him, turn him into a victim of his own incapacities. As Miller has said of *The Price*, there is

> an aspect of the cruelty of human existence in it, which is accepted by the play as well as by the character of Solomon. And, in effect, there is no solution to this problem which stands there finally like a fact of nature and not a problem at all. The play is a cul-de-sac for me: it simply lays out the forces that exist, and probably must exist. I don't know the solution excepting that Solomon takes joy in the dilemma, a joy that is not at all cynical.[10]

And what of the women? They do in many ways seem victims: Solomon's daughter and former wives (one of whom he has forgotten, a reminder that he, too, is self-concerned), Walter's wife, sacrificed to his career, Esther, driven to drink by the failure of her life to come into alignment with her expectations. There is no doubt that the male characters occupy centre-stage, the women suffering the consequences of their moral confusions. Esther, to be sure, has collaborated in her own irrelevance, simultaneously blaming her husband for his lack of ambition and drive while colluding in the fear which has blunted such. But she takes her lead from a man whose self-delusions are of a piece with his sense of decency, his desire for a world at moral attention.

As elsewhere in his work, however, this represents the balance of power within the marriages of those shaped by the values of the 1930s, 40s and 50s. In *Broken Glass* Sylvia would painfully work her way towards a sense of autonomy but it is clear that such was at odds with conventions, in America and elsewhere. To be sure, Walter's and Solomon's marriages have ended in divorce, though we learn nothing of the fate of the women concerned. Esther's dilemma is that she still loves a man whose actions she despises. She is stunned into paralysis by her own inner contradictions, as is the man who simultaneously frustrates her needs. The question at the end of the play is whether paralysis has now been cured. After all, Solomon, on the verge of his nineties, is pulled back into life, hearing in the laughter which concludes the play something more than mere irony.

— ✳ —

The success of *The Price*, in 1968, was to prove a highpoint. For the next thirty years Miller would find himself increasingly marginalised and disparaged in the United States, even while being celebrated as the author of classic plays now several decades in the past. Europe in general, and Britain in particular, would remain committed to the idea of him as a living playwright engaging immediate issues, but in America his was regarded by many as a voice from the past. Play after play failed, only to be enthusiastically staged elsewhere in the world.

Attention switched to the experiments of Off- and Off-Off-Broadway or the products of the European avant-garde. New playwrights emerged, first Sam Shepard and then David Mamet and later August Wilson and a range of women writers belatedly laying claim to the stage. Audiences were fragmenting along lines of race, gender, sexual preference. The audience that Miller had once addressed, believing it to be representative of the country at large, was being reconstituted to reflect a new sense of pluralism. In radio and television, broadcasting was giving way to narrow casting. Niche publications began to emerge serving discrete audiences. And the theatre felt the impact of this. Broadway, meanwhile, with its high prices tended to become home to tourists, businessmen and bus tours. It was certainly not an originator of drama, preferring work that had been tested in regional theatres or across the Atlantic in a Britain which retained its cultural allure.

Miller, meanwhile, somewhat perversely it seemed to some, chose to offer a play set in the biblical Eden, another set in eastern Europe and another in the 1930s. To a number of influential critics and reviewers this appeared evidence that he had lost his sure grasp on the moment. *The Creation of the World And Other Business* in particular was dismissed as little more than a self-indulgence, as if it could have no relevance to a war still being fought on a distant continent, as if its humour could have nothing to say to a generation beginning to retreat from the barricades of the 1960s. The dominant metaphors of the theatre were now derived from isolating diseases or constricting conditions, whether they might be blindness, deafness, aphasia, cancer. There was, it seemed, a move from the public to the private.

To Miller, of course, the past – a mythic no less than a historical past – contained the clue to what interested him. The American predilection for severing past from present had always seemed to him evidence of a particularly dangerous commitment to an idea of national innocence and personal denial. It was precisely the idea of a flawed mankind that had led him in the direction of tragedy, precisely the conviction that past and present form not only a causal chain but a moral logic that had always sent his characters searching into their own past in an attempt to understand the tensions which unmake them, and beyond them their culture.

The figure of Cain recurs. *All My Sons* was to have carried the name and hence the mark of Cain. For Miller, therefore, *The Creation of the World and Other Business* was not time out from the serious business of playwriting, a *jeu d'esprit*; it was a morality play doing what morality plays do. That is to say, it was designed to explore the story of man's Fall into life and hence moral ambiguity. It was an attempt to trace to its origins the instinct alike to question and to kill.

*

18

'The Creation of the World and Other Business'

In an essay on the Book of Genesis, Miller commented on the origin of *The Creation of the World and Other Business*. 'I think the occasion for this play', he explained, 'was the revolts of the Sixties, oddly enough. I was struck, even troubled by, a kind of echo of the Thirties, a time when I had come of age . . . I couldn't help wondering, at that high tide of idealism and outrage, how they would manage their inevitable, if at the time unmentionable, disillusionment. The Fall had to follow the Creation.' The story of Genesis 'appeared to me as myth generated by strictly human dilemmas that no human logic was able to rationalize. It became the story of how man created God, but a god and a cosmology that so beautifully answered to human needs that he ended up being worshipped.'[1]

The play, in which the metaphor behind *After the Fall* is explored, was, then, as he explained, in part prompted by events in Southeast Asia, even if the setting was the Garden of Eden and its characters included God and Lucifer along with Adam, Eve, Cain and Abel. The war, and its prosecution, once again raised fundamental questions about human nature. The events of the Second World War had not stunned the civilised world into a horror of violence. Vietnam was merely the latest evidence of a seemingly unending taste for resolving differences by conflict. Behind the daily details of distant battles Miller saw imperfect man ready in the name of an ideal to betray that ideal.

This had been proposed as a Century of Progress (the slogan of the Chicago Exposition in 1933) and yet human kind had discovered ever more inventive ways to destroy itself. It was always, seemingly, preparing for another war.

> Somewhere. Sometime. We tried it in Viet Nam. Killed a couple of million there, I guess. Or whatever it was. And now building up those armaments to a point where there'll be no going back . . . But there's only one decision that could be made and that's man's decision. He's got to make the choice – live or die and God is just there to give him the means.[2]

In *The Creation of the World and other Business* Miller set out to trace this impulse to its origin, tracking back to the first murder and, beyond that, the expulsion from Eden. It was to be a fable which explored human nature. That, no doubt, is why it was originally called a 'catastrophic comedy'. The story of the Fall is the story of the moment mankind chose freedom and, along with it, death, the price to be paid for that freedom. In stepping outside of Eden, man assumed responsibility for a nature no longer entirely given. As Miller has explained, 'what the play is probing is whether there is in the human condition a force which makes man's capacity for high, low, good and bad, right and wrong inevitable' (251).

In a way, that had been what had interested him about tragedy, the extent to which destiny and freedom weave themselves together, along with the conflicting elements which create and define the human being. Here, he turns it into a comedy which veers from farce to morality tale. The familiar story, it seems, is familiar because it touches on a recognisable human paradox: freedom and death are related, progress seems ineluctably wedded to moral regression.

The Creation of the World and Other Business was, Miller explained, a 'wry' comedy but with an underlying earnestness. The 'other business' of the title was 'the business of becoming human' (280). It was a work, he confessed, that contained echoes of his other plays. It was, he half-jokingly explained, a family play. It was certainly a play about brothers – Cain and Abel – and it was concerned with betrayal, denial, guilt, responsibility, virtually the full palette of colours available in a Miller play.

His affection for the play is underlined by the fact that he subsequently collaborated in a musical version called *Up From Paradise*. Indeed, the original was to have had songs by Stanley Silverman, though this idea was abandoned. *Up From Paradise* was staged at Ann Arbor in 1974. Neither version, however, prompted much in the way of positive reviews.

The play opens as Adam gives names to the animals, for the most part familiar names but occasionally absurdly wayward. Adam, unsurprisingly, emerges as naive and none too bright. The tree of knowledge, after all, remains untouched. Eve, by contrast, immediately asks the primary question: 'Why?' It is this question which leads simultaneously to disaster (her eating of the apple and subsequent expulsion from Eden) and to progress. It is, after all, a question which should not be asked in Eden where perfection is assumed.

Somehow, discontent had already infiltrated utopia and discontent, as Melville had suggested in *Typee*, is simultaneously the root of violence and the spur to advancement. The very concept of innocence presupposes an alternative and though Eve evinces only the first stirrings of curiosity the Fall will bring with it a sudden consciousness of the meaning of innocence and hence the certainty of guilt. How else can innocence define itself and, as Miller had suggested in *After the Fall*, in order to lay claim to innocence it is necessary to insist on the guilt of others; already the origins of conflict are seeded.

The Fall, Miller has explained, 'is the fall from the arms of God, the right to live, to eat, to be conscious that there exists all the world. It's the fall from unconscious existence and from the pleasant and unconscious slavery of childhood . . . the threat of freedom, of having to make choices instead of having them made for you' (354). In other words, the Fall is not only a story of origins; it is an account of a process recapitulated by each individual who moves from the Eden of childhood and discovers his or her capacity to act on the world. Innocence is the state of unconsciousness, unawareness. The 'fall' into adulthood gifts a different kind of freedom, aware, liberating, burdensome, responsible.

Innocence is thus not a desirable state, merely a pre-conscious one. There is no morality in Eden because there is no choice nor even an awareness of alternatives. This is why Lucifer becomes an ambivalent liberating force, tainting the world with an evil which introduces an alternative possibility. In Eden, there is no death. There is thus no possibility of murder. There is no envy, no desire for power. Without sin, there is no virtue. Men and women meet less as lovers than companions. Power, being ceded to God, has no meaning. Freedom undoes such absences. Suddenly there are opposites: one seeks supremacy over another, brothers are in contention, the absence of authority breeds the desire for authority and tomorrow differs from today and hence ambition is born. The paradox lies in the fact that love does not drive out hate. These possibilities co-exist.

The irony is that Lucifer urges indifference while Cain's crime is one of passion. He is competing for the love of God, baffled by what seems the arbitrariness which favours one brother over another. As Miller remarked,

> The play turned out – rather unexpectedly for me – to prove love, as opposed to Luciferian indifference, the driving force of Genesis. And the force, as well, driving the need of God's moral adjudication; He may not exist in Heaven but he surely does in the mind of man, if not as a ruling power then one to bargain with. I began thinking about the play as a casting of light upon the rule of myths that seem so heaven-borne but spring from man's commonest needs, and are his inventions.[3]

The Fall is both fortunate and the source of a primal curse acted out by Cain, who exercises his choice by choosing evil. It is the Fall, after all, which sets the motor of history running, human imperfection carrying it forward. God's grip is loosened and mankind attains an autonomy which is simultaneously blessing and curse. The play ends with Adam acknowledging that 'we are all that's left responsible!' a truth reiterated by Miller in most of his plays, and by a cry for 'Mercy', though now less from God than one another. God has banished man and man has banished God.

Miller has said that the play 'proves there is no possible rational ground for any hope whatsoever – And that's wonderful. There's nothing to do but go on living as happily as possible.'[4] Life, in other words, is existential and not absurd. Adam and Eve and their progeny are condemned to be free. If they kill it is because they choose to do so, having the capacity and will. But they have the choice and must bear the burden of exercising that choice.

Transcendence, for Miller – though he keeps a Bible in his studio and claims to reread the Old Testament (the New proving more difficult) – is not a matter of a god but of a quality to life and living which justifies itself. Perhaps unsurprisingly, he relates this to creativity. 'I think', he has explained,

> there is a destiny beyond the bread and butter, but it consists for me in creativity. I think there is a spirit that can be killed in a society and in an individual that, for want of better words, is the life of the spirit, the creative spirit. This is holy, and it takes great effort, a kind of prayer, to keep it alive and to nurture it. Without it, we might as well not be around. Life becomes simply a series of objects and chance relationships, and it gets pretty desiccated.[5]

Art, for him, is indeed his religion but it also stands for a quality to life without which there would seem little purpose in mere existence. It is also menaced by that anarchic spirit which draws the human race ever closer to spiritual no less than literal extinction. *The Creation of the World and Other Business* is thus both a contemplation of human depravity and a celebration of creativity.

'At the end of the day', he has said, 'it seems hardly to matter whether God came from man or man from God; an appeal to an ultimate sanction above and beyond our wits' end is part of the essence of our human nature, an ultimate yes or no hangs above our heads, there and not there. If there is a hostile force in all this, it is indifference, the sealing up of the heart.' Cain, to Miller, 'has filled out the definition of the real nature of man',[6] which is to be both active and dangerous, in need of love and capable of denying its authority.

The production was not a happy one. It ran for only twenty performances. Its director, Harold Clurman, was fired during previews in Boston and two of the cast were replaced before the opening. According to Mark Lamos, who played Abel, the final act was rewritten fourteen times. He remembers Miller slapping the floor of the set, saying 'This is the best goddamned play I've ever written. It's better than *Salesman!*'[7] It is not. Nor did its rewriting as a musical make it so.

What it does reveal is a man concerned to track back beyond the social, the political and the psychological to the metaphysical and to do so with a sense of irony. Vietnam may have provided some of the stimulus to write it but *The Creation of the World and Other Business* became something more than a lament over human failure. Beneath the sense of abandonment, which leaves Adam pleading for mercy, is a sense of man as his own god, capable himself of creating what was not there before.

In *Resurrection Blues* God would seemingly re-enter human experience in the person of a suspect Christ. His rejection, though, would prove less a gesture of resilience and independence and more a sign of corruption, a refusal of an implied ideal that no one has a vested interest in sustaining. Being human, it seems, is a complex fate not least because it is not a fate, except in its biological necessities. The paradox is that life, in its complexities, is a gift of Lucifer, who challenged Edenic stasis. Man fell into freedom, the freedom whose contradictions Miller chooses to explore in his plays, contradictions which are in some way definitional.

— ✳ —

Inge Morath had long been fascinated with Russia and it was her enthusiasm as much as Miller's involvement in PEN which led to a series of visits there. In 1969, this resulted in a book – *In Russia* – one of several joint works which husband and wife produced. This was the country which thirty years earlier he had admired as a progressive force, a bastion against fascism and anti-Semitism. Now he went there in part to challenge its practices, particularly with respect to those writers who wished to lay claim to proscribed freedoms.

It was a society which professed as much contempt for the past as his own society yet, as Morath's photographs show, one in which that past remained a powerful influence in terms of its buildings, its reverence for writers from another age, and in its social rituals. It was Russian literature that had first stirred Miller's interest in writing and he and his wife went in search of writers' houses, the actual settings of their fictions as if actuality would still bear the impress of their imaginations.

His own plays, he discovered, were treated with a certain cavalier carelessness, and, moreover, after the publication in 1969 of *In Russia* they were not produced at all, as exception was taken by a minor functionary to what she believed to be an unflattering photograph of herself. Miller and his wife would return in later years but it was in part his experiences there in the 1960s, and a visit to Czechoslovakia not long after the Soviet invasion, that would lead to *The Archbishop's Ceiling* (1977), the second of his plays to be set in Europe.

At home, the debacle of the Democratic Convention of 1968 had revealed the Party as being in disarray. The result was a Republican victory and the return of Richard Nixon, a figure Miller had held in contempt since his days on the House Un-American Activities Committee. The Vietnam War continued, as did Miller's opposition to it. In preparation for the next election, Richard Nixon then became involved in what came to be known as the Watergate scandal, approving a break-in at the Democratic national headquarters in the Watergate building in Washington. Miller tried his hand at a play about it but abandoned the project after a few pages. In the ensuing investigation it became apparent that Nixon had systematically bugged his own office, though he was not unique in doing so. In later years it would be revealed that both Presidents Kennedy and Johnson had done the same before him. The techniques of east European communism, it seemed, were hardly alien to those seemingly committed to the values of Western democracy.

✳

19

'The Archbishop's Ceiling'

When the Berlin Wall came down, in 1989, crowds invaded the headquarters of the secret police, the Stasi, and threw files down stairwells and out into the street, a blizzard of reports by informants. Down floated words – true, false – that had reshaped lives, the language of a paranoid state like some vast, encompassing novel. This, rather than Party headquarters or the site of an ersatz parliament, was the centre of a power that had not merely held the people in thrall but determined the nature of reality, the form of human relationships, the context within which citizens lived their lives.

This place was, in a sense, a repository of truths, half-truths and lies which defined the limits of possibility for individuals and for the state. Later, when the euphoria had subsided, those same documents were gathered up, the mosaic of shredded papers glued together, to discover the extent of the betrayals embodied in an archive of calumny. The result was profoundly disturbing. Friend had spied on friend, husband on wife; dissidents were exposed as agents, foreign academics as accomplices. For nearly forty-five years East Germany, and beyond that, plainly, the other countries of the Eastern bloc, had been turned into a theatre in which people masqueraded as what they were not, played out roles assigned to them, spoke dialogue handed to them by those who thereby became the authors of their lives.

The personal, social, political and metaphysical implications were incalculable, for not the least of the ironies was the fact that dissembling had become a national habit, indeed a civic duty, and hence the reality sought by the investigators became ever less available. The whole state became a Borgesian library, catalogued, systematised and unreal.

The existence of this archive, and the shape-shifting science of informing, was the basis of power but, in a factitious state, power itself must be suspect. Indeed, in a world in which citizens are required to signify their loyalty to a system which oppresses them, even the normal signs of acquiescence must be deemed at the very least ambivalent. In a context in which power seeks to justify itself in terms of the will of a people it profoundly distrusts, it detaches itself from the ideology in which it seeks to find justification and ends up serving nothing but itself. The fact of betrayal, meanwhile, dissolves the solidarity in whose name power is exercised.

Twenty years earlier, just a year after Soviet tanks had rolled into the country and suppressed the Prague Spring, Miller visited Czechoslovakia. In Prague he met the playwrights Vaclav Havel, later to be the country's President, and Pavel Kohout, later forced into exile in Austria. It was a revelation in a number of respects. Firstly, he had not previously realised how much Prague was essentially one of the great European cities, rather than looking east for its models and significance. It was what Vienna might have been had the Soviets not unaccountably decided to withdraw from it. In other words, it was a familiar environment made unfamiliar by the evidences of revolt and suppression. Buildings, indeed, still bore-bullet marks from the invasion by a supposedly friendly power intent on suppressing counter-revolution, saving it from a freedom it so recklessly claimed, language, as ever, being a mechanism and a victim of power.

Secondly, his visit reminded him of the circumstances in which writers were forced to operate. As he and the two fellow playwrights dined, a car waited outside as a signal of continuous surveillance. The very openness was a gesture of contempt in a society in which, like Puritan New England, everything was a sign to be decoded, everything was seen and known by the eye of God or the state. Yet the meaning of the code itself was deeply problematic.

Speaking of the Czech intellectuals with whom he had talked in 1969, he observed that, 'With Soviet soldiers occupying their city, they were under the gun, yet they were not entirely able to dismiss the possibility that the invasion was to some degree the result of self-delusion on the part of the Soviet party, a sign of its incapacity to recognize realities which its a priori theories denied existed.'[1] In other words, had the invading forces been responding to a fiction of their own construction and accommodated the world to that fiction?

In 1975, Miller received a New Year's card from a Czech writer. In it husband and wife, he dressed in dark jacket, with crisp white shirt, polka-dot bow-tie and hat, she in flowered top, dark skirt and floppy hat, stand up to their waists in water with, between them, a dog emerging from a lifebelt. By now used to reading Czechoslovakia as a text, he extrapolated what seemed to him to be the coded meanings behind the surreal image, normalising it as a wholly rational response to a society which was itself little more than a surreal gesture.

The writer, one of 152 such forbidden to publish within the borders of the Czech Republic or have their plays presented on its stages, had officially been declared to have emigrated, while manifestly still there. His decision cheerfully to stand up to his waist in water while fully clothed was of a piece with such curious logic. He was, officially, non-existent, having just sufficient reality to warrant his expulsion but not quite sufficient actually to be expelled. His plays were published and performed abroad, where he supposedly resided, not here, where he actually did and where he was not permitted inside a theatre. Once again, standing in water hardly lifted him out of Czech reality. Had he endorsed the 1968 invasion by Soviet forces, of course, he would have become real again. His words could then be spoken aloud, but only if he was prepared to lie.

Miller published his satirical piece in 1975 in *Esquire Magazine*. In that same year he published another, this time in *Harper's*. It was called 'The Limited Hang-Out: the Dialogues of Richard Nixon as a Drama of the Antihero'.[2] In this he contemplated the situation of the President of the United States who had bugged his own office and then proceeded to discuss with his aides ways in which they might evade the law and circumvent the Constitution he was sworn to uphold. This was not Miller's attempt to balance his critique of the East with one of the West. It was that both instances staged modern reality as a surreal drama, a piece of theatre whose humour is only subverted by its human consequences.

Nixon, besides, for the most part, forgetting the presence of the microphones, dealt with his dilemma by creating a figure called the President, representing something called the Presidency, entirely separate from the low-level crook angling for a get-out-of-jail-free card from his fellow players. Here was a man who was prepared to set up an investigation into events already known to him with the intention of such an investigation exonerating him by a series of yet-to-be-invented finesses.

The word 'innocence' thus becomes freighted with ambiguity, as a second-order language co-exists with the first-order language which it contradicts but with which it must be brought into convenient alignment. Words spoken here must no more be spoken in public than in the Czech Republic. This is a closed theatre, intended to have no public, except that here, as there, a spool of magnetic tape slowly turns, the ultimate power behind mere appearance. In his article, Miller effectively reviews this performance as, indeed, a play in which the characters, believing, even wishing themselves to be participating in a tragedy, have an increasing conviction that they are performing in a farce. Integrity and authenticity are roles to be adopted and discarded, depending on the presumed audience.

At the heart, in both countries, is a moral question about power, but the questions proliferate as the real seems to become attenuated and language to bend and distort. And since this dialogue is not merely with those who may or may not be listening but with the self, the question becomes both metaphysical and ontological. How may we know ourselves if we speak to our own minds and in doing so allow ourselves latitude? How, within a rush of performances, may we reach out and touch the world and hence confirm our own existence? It was from these fragments that Miller constructed *The Archbishop's Ceiling*, whose theme he characterised as 'what the soul does under the impact of immense power, how it makes accommodations and how it transcends power'.[3]

Nor was Miller unaware of his own limitations in trying to 'read' another culture. When he came to write the play set in this environment, he even included an American writer who admits his inability to hear 'the overtones', who confesses that 'it's unreal to me',[4] as though he thereby acknowledged the problematic nature of the task he had set himself. The gesture is perhaps Miller's way of confessing the difficulty that he himself faced in creating a work which is informed by his own reading of a society whose inner processes depend on inhabiting rather than merely observing it.

Miller, himself, of course, was scarcely unused to the idea of surveillance, which existed far closer to home than central Europe, and later requested his FBI dossier under the Freedom of Information Act. Much of it was blacked out, forcing him to reconstruct the whole from the remaining fragments so that it became a form of fiction, as doubtless it was already, constructed by paranoid sensibilities trained in over-interpretation. It was evident, however, that he had, as he suspected, been watched by agents of the state. He had, unknown to himself, performed for the benefit of an invisible audience.

American repressions might have differed significantly from those deployed in the Soviet satellite states, nonetheless a number of writers, actors and directors had been blacklisted, and hence denied work, as a result of information derived from informants and their own refusal to renounce former loyalties. In eastern Europe, the threat to freedom was more obvious, as was the threat to a sense of the real, for how do those who expect to be watched, who assume the existence of concealed microphones, behave? In a world of informers who can speak the truth and in a world without truth, what could be said to be real?

His own country, meanwhile, offered a parallel in more than the existence of FBI files. In the 1950s informing was encouraged as evidence of one's loyalty. In a visit to his alma mater, the University of Michigan, he discovered that staff and students had been enrolled to report on one another. The bugging of public buildings and private residences by agents of state security, meanwhile, was, in a Cold War world, seen as a necessary measure. Embassies and hotels were regularly fitted with microphones as the protagonist's apartment had been in George Orwell's *Nineteen Eighty-Four*, a satire on Soviet villainies whose film version was effectively underwritten by the CIA.

In 1974 this process seemed to reach its acme when the President of the United States chose to turn the centre of government into a form of theatre with himself as the leading actor. Sometimes he remembered the existence of the hidden microphones and sometimes he forgot; sometimes, in other words, he was a conscious and sometimes an unconscious actor. In 2001, Miller would deliver the Thomas Jefferson Lecture for the National Endowment for the Arts. In this, he spoke of the politician as actor, valuing performance above truth, no longer able, indeed, to distinguish one from the other.

But this was also a time when the performing self became a central trope, and not merely in the context of theatre or literature. For the sociologist, the psychologist, the self was seen as a series of performances, constructions, elaborations. For the deconstructionist, meanwhile, the self became a suspect notion. The connection between sign and signifier was seen as unstable while language itself was exposed for the fallacies inherent in a word-centred conception of reality. By this token, history became suspect and reality itself a naive notion, as perhaps it had always been in a country which dedicated itself to belief in a national dream, the dream before which Willy Loman laid down his life.

Beneath the apparent certainties of the Cold War world, then, in which two systems, ideologically defined, historically situated, confronted one another, was a deepening sense of unreality, as politics became melodrama and private lives were invaded by uncertainty. In the play that he wrote to capture something of this mood the word 'reality' becomes deeply suspect. Realpolitik, after all, seemed a branch of fantasy at a time when the enveloping Cold War tactic of both sides carried the acronym of MAD (Mutually Assured Destruction). Ronald Reagan's Star Wars system (properly Strategic Defence Initiative), already on the horizon, derived its name from a Hollywood fable of the conflict between forces of light and dark, a moral melodrama so deeply ingrained in the national psyche that in 2003 President George Bush could speak unproblematically of an 'axis of evil' and know that his words would be understood and applauded in a country so sure of its own role in an international morality play.

For Arthur Miller, always inclined, like Thoreau, to 'front' a fact, to insist on respect for a tangible and recoverable past, these complexities became increasingly fascinating and, at the end of the seventies he wrote *The Archbishop's Ceiling* to engage them. It is a play which, like many of his others, is essentially concerned with power, its nature, its necessities, its mechanisms. It is about personal power, in terms of relationships, ambitions, psychological authority. It is also about public power. In both senses it is inevitably also about the nature of the real in that power accretes to itself the right to define and elaborate reality. This is true whether it be at the level of contested memories, that is to say, history, or the codes, conventions, ideological assumptions which define the parameters of daily life.

Nor is this only a matter of political commissars, for when one of the characters claims, ironically, that *Vogue* magazine is 'the truth', the irony does not bite so very deep in that it, too, is part of a system which offers to define the world in a country in which the media do more than mediate, in which, indeed, they are a source of power and a mechanism for describing the real. For Willy Loman, after all, the advertisements have a kind of social sanction, helping to define the world in which he wished to believe he existed, and validating a life dedicated to a dream.

The Archbishop's Ceiling is set in 'a capital in eastern Europe' (in fact, Prague), and in a building which is something more than a location and an environment. Indeed the description of the *mise en scène* requires two pages. It takes place in the former residence of the Archbishop, itself, then, once the centre of power. The room, Miller pointedly tells us, 'has weight and power' (89) though its contents, by contrast, are 'chaotic and sensuous'. The decoration is baroque, dramatic. The room, like that of Elia Ehrenberg, whom Miller and his wife had visited in Russia and whose relationship to power was deeply problematic, is full of unhung paintings, carved armchairs, Bauhaus furniture, a collection of art objects and furniture from several decades. It has what he calls 'layers of chaos' and that will prove symbolic of the layered chaos which infects a palace once the very definition of order, purpose and meaning. This is plainly the home of a person of power and influence, though someone who brings to it a sense of improvisation, a careless relish for art and the physical.

When John Shrapnel, who appeared in a British production of the play, went to what became the Czech Republic he met Vaclav Havel, by now President, and was taken by him to a building which he believed had provided the inspiration for Miller's play. As Shrapnel has explained, he found himself 'in an apartment which had belonged to the Czech painter Alphonse Mucha, stacked with art objects, settees, piano, unhung paintings and bits of Bauhaus'.[5] Whether this was the model, or not, Miller derived from it something more than an authenticity of setting. He also added a crucial detail.

Not evident to the eye, though quickly alluded to, is the fact that there may or may not be microphones concealed in the room. There may, it seems, be an audience to what ensues beyond the cherubim which stare down from the baroque ceiling. These characters in *The Archbishop's Ceiling* thus exist, if no longer in God's eye, then possibly in that of forces to whom knowledge is a form of power and whose hidden presence is as much a curb to deviant behaviour as a deity had once been. Indeed, before any words are exchanged, Adrian, an American writer, is seen searching the room for evidence of what he assumes must be there. 'Is it always like a performance?' he asks, 'Like we're quoting ourselves?' (108).

When Miller and his wife visited Russia in the mid-1960s, he observed that

> There is an almost universal conviction that all hotel rooms are tapped, as well as many apartments. Visitors sometimes arrive with paper and pencil communicating by writing while they carry on banter directed toward the bug, or at home play loud Beethoven passages while discussing anything of importance . . . One sits down to discuss some ordinary matter, and the host turns on a loud rock-and-roll number . . . Pretty soon, though, a sort of surrealistic mood develops.[6]

Following a conversation with two writers, he noted that 'once they had left my hotel room I looked around at the walls and up at the ceiling where the bug must be hidden, wondering if both these men had really been addressing it all along rather than me alone, rather than the issues, which perhaps they understood quite as well as anyone'.[7] He assumed the existence of the bug and hence reinterprets their conversation as theatre. He has no evidence for it, however. Neither do the characters in his play.

We never learn the truth or otherwise of the assumption that the ceiling may be bugged, but the ambiguity is crucial to what follows. It is the more surprising, therefore, that Miller, in the name of clarification, allowed himself to be persuaded to resolve this ambivalence for the first American production, thus undermining a crucial element of the drama. As a consequence it had a curious production history.

In 1983, in Miller's studio in Connecticut, I asked him what had become of *The Archbishop's Ceiling*, a copy of which he had sent me several years before. 'It didn't do any business', he replied, reaching into a filing cabinet and handing me the typescript. As we talked so I thumbed through it and gradually realised that it differed significantly from the version I knew. In particular, the ambiguity about the microphones seemed to have gone, and there were a number of other changes. It was markedly inferior to the original, which had never been published. I asked whether he would be willing to publish the original version.

Miller felt that the American production of *The Archbishop's Ceiling* had suffered from an emphasis on realism. As it happened I had just completed a report on the problems of translating academic books, a problem so intractable that a colleague and I put the Escher drawing of a hand drawing a hand on the front. It seemed to me that Escher drawings might prove apt for both *The Archbishop's Ceiling* and two one-act plays then called *Two by A.M.* but which I suggested might helpfully be retitled *Two-Way Mirror*, readers, directors and actors thus entering the texts by way of impossible drawings. As a result, the covers of both British editions now carry those illustrations. Following publication of the original text, *The Archbishop's Ceiling* was produced in England, by the Bristol Old Vic and the Royal Shakespeare Company, as it was in America and, eventually, eastern Europe.

The play centres around the fate of a writer, Sigmund, under pressure to leave for the West. To Miller, he is the most unreconcilable and the most talented of the writers who gather together with profoundly different motives. He has, Miller suggests, 'no permanent allegiance except to the love of creating art'.[8] He is 'choking with rage and love' and has a degree of cynicism, bitterness and contempt for others. In short, he is 'most alive', a fact which in itself would 'fuel his refusal' to accept the contempt with which the state seems content to treat him.

The representatives of the state imagine that compromise is a possibility because they think they are dealing only with a man. The fact is that they are dealing with an idea, which is altogether a different matter. The state wishes to believe in the predictable. Pressure must secure results and if it does not then the solution is simply to increase the pressure. In Sigmund, and the art which he, an imperfect man, nonetheless wishes to defend, they are up against a principle of improvisation. But the state, too, can deal in uncertainty and ambiguity, hence the microphones which may or may not be concealed in the ceiling. The very doubt has a subversive quality. To take a stand against what may not be there is to tread the boundary of paranoia. To doubt one's friends is to doubt oneself. Only the work retains its integrity. Well, then, remove the work.

The latest intimidation, indeed, takes the form of the theft of the typescript of his new novel. That pressure, though, comes not only from the state, inconvenienced by his statements to the foreign press, but also from those who seem his friends: Adrian, an American author, who also has motives of his own, Marcus, influential but unfathomable, and Maya, a compromised writer nonetheless drawn to Sigmund's moral stance and national significance. *The Archbishop's Ceiling* stages a debate about power, the nature of reality, the responsibility of the writer.

The play takes place in a single room. The hermeticism is an aspect of the drama as the characters come together on what is, in effect, a stage with, if there are indeed concealed microphones, another audience than that gathered to see the play.

Adrian, who has been at a conference in Paris, flies in to visit the friends who, unbeknown to them, have become characters in his new novel. He hopes, too, it transpires, to pick up, if only momentarily, his relationship with Maya, his one-time lover and lover, too, to the writer whose home this is. Adrian is a successful writer, momentarily stalled on his novel, who has used his reputation to speak out on behalf of dissident authors, but whose motives, perhaps, are not entirely selfless.

For all his professed doubts about his ability to read the text of this alien society, meanwhile, Adrian displays an arrogant assurance. In fact, dogmatic in his judgements, he is confident in his abilities to improvise a response to the crisis in which he now finds himself, as Sigmund, its leading writer, is pressured into leaving the country, not least by the theft of his manuscript. Presenting himself as using his success to serve the cause of his friends, Adrian is, it increasingly seems, using his friends to serve his own success, transforming them into fiction, their suffering into his art.

And here, plainly, is a familiar dilemma not merely for this particular character. Miller himself, after all, has, from his very first play, drawn not only on his own life but the lives of those around him. It scarcely needed the attacks on *After the Fall* to alert him to the ethical implications of doing so. And, indeed, one of the sub-texts of *The Archbishop's Ceiling* is a concern for the relationship between art and the world it purports to engage.

The Archbishop's palace is occupied if not owned by Marcus, a magus figure, a master manipulator who performs his legerdemain, his particular magic, by the skills with which he manipulates his own persona and the lives of those who come within his power. This is the site of his magic, a place of hidden meanings, of transformations and entrapments. Whether that magic is white or black is precisely the source of his power, in that he lives in the heart of ambiguity. It is this that enables him to survive and flourish, and perhaps to save or condemn. He is the master of the revels, the tempter and perhaps the source of redemption. He surfs the wave of his own inauthenticity and yet it is never entirely clear whether his reputation as a kind of Proteus may not be a disguise for values he can only hold by apparently disavowing them.

He is, seemingly, successful, both at home and abroad, having the imprimatur of the state, though, following his imprisonment, his place in the national heart has been taken by Sigmund, now effectively the conscience of the nation. Once the founder-editor of the country's leading magazine, he has made his accommodations and as he has done so his talent seems to have deserted him. This room is now, it appears, his fiction, the place where his imagination can operate. He travels freely in part because he is willing, to an extent, to act as an apologist for the state which grants him this contingent freedom. Indeed, he argues that it is fantasy to challenge those in power, who simply acknowledge the reality of the country's strategic situation and are, anyway, considerably more liberal than those they have replaced.

He tries, accordingly, to convince Sigmund to acquiesce: Sigmund who, he has learned, is to be charged with slandering the state following protest letters he has sent to foreign newspapers and the United Nations. He argues that a show trial can only endanger everyone and force the system back to its former repressiveness. For Marcus, who has suffered prolonged imprisonment in the past, the present repressions seem more tolerable. He offers to use his contacts to secure return of the stolen manuscript, though at the price of Sigmund agreeing to exile.

Yet Marcus is no more what he appears than anyone. He had, in the past, himself been an exile, even serving in the American Army for three years. Trying to emigrate to America after the war he found himself deported as a suspected spy, only to be arrested for the same offence on his return to his own country. In such an environment, the real becomes deeply ambiguous. An attractive young Danish woman whom he brings back with him from his travels, a woman who speaks hardly any of the language, wanders through the action, like some drunk in a western brawl scene, oblivious to what is going on, simultaneously an indication of the difficulty of understanding another culture and a sign of Marcus's willingness to use other people for his own ends, a mark of his dubious morality.

Is he, then, a friend to the state, lying to serve a higher cause, or is he a friend to a writer whose talent he respects and who he wishes to protect even against himself? And who, anyway, knows his own motives, can act as an impartial judge of his own actions? When Adrian says of Marcus and Maya that 'they lie a lot' (116) Sigmund agrees, but in the context of this house, and the society it reflects, what is said is not necessarily what is meant. Language is designed less for those who hear it than for those who might overhear it. This is a house of mirrors in which the real is necessarily distorted. It is, as several of the characters confess, a theatre in which people perform lives whose substance they are afraid to reveal. It is a house of lies, where lies are used both to enforce and to escape power. It is Sigmund, with his broken English, who says to the American author,

> We . . . believe we can escaping power – by telling lies. For this reason, I think you have difficulty to write about us. You cannot imagine how fantastically we lie . . . but perhaps it is not exactly lying because we do not expect to deceive anymore; the professor lies to the student, the student lies to the professor – but each knows the other is lying. We must lie, it is our only freedom . . . we know we cannot win but it gives us the feeling of hope. Is like a serious play, which no one really believes but the technique is admirable. Our country is now a theatre, where no one is permitted to walk out, and everyone is obliged to applaud.
>
>   (155)

In theatre, he explains, he believes in everything but is convinced by nothing. And there, of course, is potentially the lament of the playwright, of Arthur Miller, that the arbitrary truths of art may be wholly convincing in their own terms and within their own immediate context, but seem unrelated and inapplicable to the world beyond. For the fact is that Sigmund's lament stresses not only the inauthenticity of the country in which he is trapped, the room in which he finds himself and where he must perform to a possibly hidden audience, but also the inauthenticity of art, lies not meant to deceive, indeed lies which are an expression of freedom.

The state may invent its own version of history, its own definition of the real, but Sigmund is praised by Maya because he 'creates our memories' (160), a statement offered as praise but which recalls the contingent nature of art. The lies of fiction may differ in kind and intent but they are lies nonetheless. When Marcus asks of Adrian, 'To whom am I talking . . . the *New York Times*, or your novel, or you?' (157), he identifies another way in which the real fractures into pieces. The same words used in a journalistic polemic, in fiction or a supposedly private conversation change their function and meaning. The common currency of language is not so common, after all. And Miller was conscious, too, of the extent to which his own work had drawn on the lives of others, the degree to which he was an eavesdropper using other people for his own ends.

The Archbishop's Ceiling is in part an exploration of such ambiguities. Indeed, Adrian suggests that the reason for his fascination with this country is his sense that it is where history is an operative concept and where ambiguity is acknowledged to be functional. Speaking if not for America then for his own generation, he observes that 'History came at us like a rumour. We were never really there', and that ambiguity 'is always clearer in somebody else's country' (153).

Sigmund, meanwhile, is under pressure to leave the country and thus relieve the state of an embarrassment. It is to this end that agents seize the only copy of his new novel, five years in the making. Marcus implies that he may be in a position to help, not least through his contact with a female government minister, a woman of no literary talent but whose books are praised by those who think it prudent to admire someone whose works are seen in the flattering light of her own power. Yet none of these characters is quite what they appear. Indeed, a primary concern of the play is the problematic nature of the truth in such circumstances, a disturbing ambivalence in private and public affairs.

Sigmund, may, as Maya suggests, have captured the essence of his country but his responses to his own circumstances are baffled and inept. The crude blackmail of suicide, which he considers threatening, seems to him a plausible tactic to deploy, though this is difficult to relate to the sophistication that he brings to his writing. But, then, intellectual acumen and artistic accomplishment are hardly incompatible with a lack of common sense. This, after all, is a man who creates only a single copy of a novel it has taken him five years to write, and then reveals its hiding place to a foreigner over a dinner monitored by agents of the state, almost as if he sought the martyrdom they threaten. Which is the reality of Sigmund – subtle reader of his culture or political illiterate and social naïf, cultural symbol of resistance or victim of others' machinations and his sense of his own cultural and political importance?

He, too, after all, is the source of power, in a play in part about the nature and mechanisms of power, a fact recognised by those who wish to drive him out. The irony is that it is a power that is in large part a product of the system that oppresses him. Once in exile, as he and they accept, that power will dissipate. The fate of Solzenitsyn offers a powerful example of just this process. Those in possession of political power create their own nemesis. But those whose cultural power comes from the act of resistance lose that power when the other element of the dialectic is removed.

Maya, meanwhile, has compromised with power and, it seems, become its agent, while at the same time remaining a fierce defender of the values which she thereby undermines. Herself a dramatist, she has abandoned the stage and settled for a trivial programme on the radio. Imagining herself now unpolitical, she seems not to realise the politics implied in her action. On a personal level, she has distributed her sexual favours with the liberality of one who can see no principle that would deny this, as if it were possible to retreat to the merely personal. But in such a context there is no truly personal, as Orwell had suggested in *Nineteen Eighty-Four*. Indeed, it is implied that sexual relationships, facilitated, perhaps, by Marcus and Maya, in this very room, may have been used to compromise their fellow writers. Sex itself, in other words, is another source of power.

In a society without justice, with laws which, if not corrupt in their nature, are corrupted by the means employed to enforce them, without the mutuality of trust, what survives beyond the fact of power? This is a power, moreover, which has the added virtue of invisibility, for where can it lie if its legitimacy supposedly rests with the very people it betrays? This is a country in which the law-breakers are the law and in which power takes unlikely forms. As Adrian

observes, they are 'living in a world of antonyms' (107) in which words mean
the opposite of what they appear to mean. It is, perhaps, this that makes the
writer such a crucial figure, charged as he is with purging the language of the
tribe. Yet the writer is merely another variety of liar whose fictions are justified
because they offer thereby a different kind of truth.

When Maya remarks that 'some truths will not change, and certain people,
for all our sakes, are appointed never to forget them', recalling the Jewish saying,
'If I forget thee, O Jerusalem, may I cut off my hand' (128), it seems to echo
Miller's own conviction. Yet, in the context of this play, in which language is
suspect, motives unknowable, character a product of performance, the real
problematic, history a construct of ideology and power, even the memory of
truths is uncertain. And if the writer is to be the means to access that truth how
can he abstract himself from this context of relativity? As Adrian observes of his
own attempts: 'here I'm laying out motives, characterisations, secret impulses –
the whole psychological chess game – when the truth is I'm not sure anymore
that I believe in psychology. That anything we think really determines what
we're going to do. Or even what we feel' (95).

His own wife's depression, whose origin was mysterious and whose consequences thus seemed arbitrary, was cured by a pill, as though feelings, and
beyond them a sense of the real, were no more than a product of chemistry.
As he observes, where does that leave the writer if tragedy can be resolved with
pharmaceuticals? She is saved from suicide and once again engages with her
career: 'She knows neither more nor less about herself now than when she was
trying to die. The interior landscape has not changed. What has changed is her
reaction to power. Before she feared it, now she enjoys it. Before she fled from
it, now she enjoys it. She got plugged in' (96).

What is lost is, perhaps, the knowledge that comes from suffering but since
knowledge is a form of power why not short-cut the process? Where, after all,
is the virtue in suffering? A pill offers reconciliation with the status quo and
the rewards that go to those ready to concede the legitimacy of the given. Here,
it seems to him, a similar reward is on offer to those who concede that power
lies with the state. Personal and political compromise are the equivalent of the
pill. Despair is a product of discontent. Access to power, to being plugged in,
to being part of the real, lies in conceding that the real is what it is claimed to
be by those with the power to define it.

Yet the writer is not immune to this virus and it is very tempting to hear
an element of confession, by Miller, in Maya's observation that 'writers . . . all
write books condemning people who wish to be successful and praised, who
desire some power in life. But I have never met one writer who did not wish to
be praised, and successful . . . and even powerful. Why do they condemn others
who wish the same for themselves?' (97).

The Archbishop's Ceiling is not simply a study of a remote culture; it is as
much a recognition of fundamental needs and failures as his other plays. Once

again, betrayal and denial are presented as simple facts of experience. And once again at the centre of betrayal and denial lies the self, declaring its own innocence at the price of others. Adrian uses his friends to further his career, both by transforming them into fiction and by using his concern for their plight to consolidate his liberal reputation. Marcus secures his own immunity by working with those who do not extend that immunity to others. Maya becomes a licensed entertainer by abandoning her political values and possibly collaborating with Marcus. Even Sigmund, it is suggested, uses others in his fiction and is prepared to dissemble to achieve his ends.

As Marcus points out, when Sigmund is not allowed to leave he is indignant; when he is pressured to leave he is morally affronted. Maya, meanwhile, confronts him with another painful possibility. Perhaps, she suggests, he resists leaving for America because

> you will not have them in America to hate! And if you cannot hate you cannot write and you will not be Sigmund anymore, but another lousy refugee ordering his chicken soup in broken English – and where is the profit in that? They are your theme, your life, your partner in this dance that cannot stop, or you will die of silence.

It is a cogent analysis, and reminiscent of Sartre's insistence that the rebel is in part defined by that against which he rebels, in part derives his significance from the act of rebellion. Her further observation that 'They are in you . . . And if you stay . . . it is also for your profit . . . as it is for ours to tell you to go. Who can speak for himself alone?' (175) is no less telling and Sigmund has no response.

Her last remark is reminiscent of Miller's aphorism, with respect to the relationship between the individual and society, that the fish is in the water and the water is in the fish. There is no clear distinction between the private and the public world, no individual gesture that does not have moral or logical connections with the social and the political. Indeed, Marcus is given a speech which, at first glance, appears a restatement of Miller's conviction when he asks 'When was a man ever conceivable apart from society?' (159). His further remarks, however, that 'The collective giveth and the collective taketh away – beyond that . . . was never anything but a sentimental metaphor; a god which now is simply a form of art', moves him away from the notion of man as a social animal as he embraces a reductive ethic.

At the heart of this play is a concern with a world in which the link between God and man has been severed. The Archbishop's residence has lost its function. The art once designed to be expressive of that link, created to celebrate God's power, is now, that power removed, no more than art. It is drained of its transcendence. The question is, as Adrian puts it, 'Whether it matters anymore, what anyone feels . . . about anything. Whether we're not just some sort of . . . filament that only lights up when it's plugged into whatever power there is'

(159). Once men sought meaning in a deity, now they look elsewhere for the source of their significance: to ideology, to material success, to dominance in personal relationships.

Free, they choose to submit once again, believing meaning to lie outside themselves. Just as once, to exist in God's eye was thereby to gain significance, now, perversely, the possibility of hidden microphones implies the existence of a power which gifts significance again. The greater terror, after all, is perhaps that we live and die unnoticed, that there is no audience to our lives, that we are wholly responsible for what we are. It is in this sense that this is an existential play.

But in *The Archbishop's Ceiling* the construction of the self is problematic. As Miller has explained, 'We're all impersonators in a way. We are all impersonating something, including ourselves . . . Everybody feels he is really playing. We have all become actors. The actor becomes the most significant figure, culturally speaking. He's doing professionally what we are all doing as amateurs.' The question, therefore, becomes 'what is the irreducible in man, in the human being. Is there something irreducible or are we totally adaptable, totally and completely adaptable?'[9] The answer: 'One often thinks so.'

In such a context the question of reality itself moves to the fore and, indeed, Miller has said that 'it's not a social play . . . It's really a play about reality.'[10] As the director of the Royal Shakespeare production, Nick Hamm, remarked of the rehearsal process: 'What we found most difficult to work out was who was speaking the truth at any moment. The play', he added, 'became a tangled web of possibilities. The normal process an actor goes through in exploring motive, reason and character – truth, was complicated by the simple fact that what anyone says in the play may be being listened to with a tape recorder.'[11]

If Miller is thought of as a writer with a simple and clear moral vision, for whom history is both ineluctable and sharply defined and reality tangible and fully revealed, *The Archbishop's Ceiling* is a reminder that this is not so and was not so in *Death of a Salesman, The Crucible, A View from the Bridge, The Price* or *After the Fall*. His characters have always had to find their way through their lives uncertain as to their own motives, unclear as to the nature and imperatives of their society, unsure where meaning may reside. Memory and desire are braided together in a way which makes both suspect as the source of the coherence they seek, while identity, a defining and defined self, is the raft they cling to, unsure as to its integrity even as they rely upon it.

So, they seek to reason with unreason, deploy a language ready to betray them at every turn, rest their hope on a future which is no more than an expression of unexamined needs. The struggle is not to locate a truth self-evident in its clarity, to acknowledge a reality momentarily obscured by misprision or wilful denial. It is to create the values by which to live. It is to accept responsibility for one's actions and to recognise the logic, moral no less than social, which ties the individual to a common humanity. It is to summon into being the meaning once sought in the external world. The Archbishop's palace is no longer home to a prince of the Church, privy to a hidden metaphysical truth. It is occupied by men and women for whom truth is a construct and who propose a meaning they alone can command.

Miller has confessed to becoming more interested in the nature of reality and how it is constituted as his career has developed and in that sense, perhaps, *The Archbishop's Ceiling* does stand as a pivotal play. The issues that it raises, however, have never been absent from his work from the moment in *The Golden Years* when Montezuma and Cortes debated the nature of the world and its meaning, finding the answer in God or Mammon and being deceived in both regards, through the dream reality of Willy Loman to the factitious truths of the Puritan judges in *The Crucible.*

And what of art, once seen as expressive of an immanent meaning? What can it serve, once its transcendental function no longer seems relevant? In a play full of writers we are offered several possibilities, from Maya's anodyne entertainments, Adrian's possibly self-serving commercial successes, to an art designed to serve the state or to challenge it. Art, in other words, does not reside in some other sphere, uncontaminated, unmarked by the world in which it exists or the individuals who give it life. It is shot through with the same ambiguities that infect all other aspects of experience.

It is an act of communication. It offers itself to the world. Yet whether it does so in good or bad faith it can never free itself of ambivalence. But ambivalence implies a tension, a tension which itself may hint at a truth worth acknowledging if not finally embracing. For Miller's point is not that everything is relative, that there are no values worth embracing, that the world is no more than a series of distorting mirrors (despite the title of a later work). Rather, he is concerned to identify the degree of difficulty, the genuine effort required to elaborate meaning out of mere event, to find a purpose beyond simple survival, to reinvent transcendence in a world in which the human spirit seems subservient to private ambition and public subversion.

If Sigmund was indeed based on Vaclav Havel, as Havel himself believed, the rebel against the state became the state; the writer laid aside his writing to become a politician. This was, of course, a victory but the meaning of that victory, on a personal and public level, was perhaps not quite as clear as it appears. State repression ended. Barriers of all kinds were lowered. But with this went the significance of the writer, the centrality of theatre and even a certain cohesiveness not only in the state, which itself quickly fragmented, but in lives which now began to reorient themselves in terms of new imperatives having to do with international capitalism and its products. The most popular television channel became one transmitting pornography. The fantasies of the communist state were exchanged for the fantasies of a capitalist state. The microphones may or may not have disappeared (they are certainly still in place in America) but here, as elsewhere, individuals still perform their lives, act out their roles and ask themselves what the meaning of their lives might be.

For Miller, with the passage of time it was possible to see that this was not a play about the East alone for

> we are all secretly talking to power, to the bugged ceilings of the mind, whether knowingly or not in the West; even unconsciously we had foregone the notion of a person totally free of deforming obeisances to power or shibboleth. It was more and more difficult to imagine in the last quarter of a century the naked selfness of a free human being speaking with no acknowledged interest except his own truth.
>
> (T.573)

The bugged ceilings of the mind, it turns out, have greater longevity and a more ominous significance than those of the state, so uncertain in its certainties as to create a theatre within which to stage its own betrayals.

— ✳ —

The Archbishop's Ceiling was staged not in New York but at the Kennedy Center in Washington. Plans for a New York opening were shelved. The changes in the text did not serve the play and it was received with some bafflement.

It was followed in 1978 by a television production of *Fame*, a brief work about the insubstantial nature of reputation. It was not well received. In that same year Miller travelled to Brussels for a production of *The Crucible*, twenty-five years after he had been denied a passport for its French-language premiere, an event he commemorated by losing his then current passport.

Later that year, he and his wife went to China, a visit marked by the publication, in 1979, of their joint book, *Chinese Encounters*. The year also saw a successful revival of *The Price*, followed by a film adaptation of Fania Fenelon's moving account of her time in Auschwitz–Birkenau. *Playing for Time*, made for CBS television, stirred considerable controversy when Vanessa Redgrave (an outspoken supporter of the Palestinian cause) was cast in the role of Fenelon. Fenelon herself, under five foot in height, also objected to being played by the six-foot-tall Redgrave. Miller received a number of accusing letters, not only with respect to Regrave's appearance but also with regard to what were seen as distortions of historical detail. He was, as he well knew, entering dangerous territory. In the end, however, the film proved popular and Miller subsequently adapted it for the stage.

✳

20

'Playing for Time'

In 1943, Fania Fenelon, a cabaret singer in Paris who worked for the Resistance, was arrested and taken to Auschwitz–Birkenau. Her life was saved when she was enrolled in an orchestra whose job was in part to entertain the camp personnel and in part to provide the background music to genocide. She and her fellow musicians played as prisoners marched off to work or filed towards the gas chambers. They had to suffer not only the rigours of the camp but also the contempt of some of their fellow prisoners as they survived while others did not. But survival carries its own weight and its own obligations. Fania Fenelon rebuilt her life but eventually felt the need to bear witness to those events in wartime Europe and in 1977, over thirty years later, published her account of this time.[1]

This was the book that Arthur Miller was asked to dramatise for a television film that was to star Vanessa Redgrave. In some ways he had the advantage of showing aspects of what Fenelon could only describe, but in place of testimony he could only offer drama, impersonation, a semblance of the real. For the authenticity of the first person, in the film version he could only present the seeming authenticity of setting and a simulation of emotions once felt on the pulse.

In the play version, which eventually followed, he had the advantage of the present-tense reality of theatre, the confrontation of audience and performer in which there is no mediating camera, in which the conjoined experience of the women, which Fenelon expresses when she insists that it is the group of women and not herself alone who recall, who validate, finds its correlative in ensemble playing. The 'orchestra' of the women, selected against by the close-up in the film, remains a present fact for the theatre audience whose attention is free to encompass more than the speaker and the individual to whom the speech is directed.

Miller's screenplay for *Playing for Time* remains close to the original, though scenes are sometimes transposed, events elided and, curiously, Clara, whom Fania befriends on the train, and whose character remains essentially the same, becomes Marianne. Time is necessarily collapsed. Thus Dr Mengele, who arrived after Fania had been in the camp for some time, is shown receiving the transport on which Fania is travelling. Fania is also shown in a work detail as Miller attempts to pull into the film something of the reality of the daily drudgery which she herself escaped.

After the preface, which details the rendezvous of the women thirty years on, Fenelon's book begins at the end of her experience in the camps, before jumping back to the beginning of her time in Auschwitz and the period she had spent in Drancy prison before being taken to Auschwitz. It begins, in other words, by creating a sense of vertigo. The film keeps a stricter chronology. It opens in a Parisian café as Fania Fenelon plays the piano and sings for German troops and their French girlfriends. She is playing for the conquerors. The women she meets later in the camps are thus not the only collaborators. Music, performance, her own talents are already compromised but the stakes are less high than they will later be. An invisible sense of irony seems enough, perhaps, to protect her from the implications of that compromise. A moment later, though, and the civility is stripped away. We are inside the freight-car of a transport heading, unbeknown as yet to its occupants, to the camps. The Drancy experiences are excised.

'The ordinariness of the types is emphasized', Miller instructs, but lest the word 'types' should seem reductive he adds, 'but above that their individuation.'[2] This, of course, is the essence of Fenelon's book and his screenplay. The Holocaust was precisely designed to obliterate such individuation. A memoir is what it says. It is the invocation of a resistant memory to deny such reductivism.

Fania is dressed in a fur coat and hat. She carries an elegant valise, has food and water with her. All of these are stripped away. The orderly, if cramped, transport quickly becomes a scene of degradation, foreshadowing what is to follow as it did in fact. The doors are rolled open and the 'selection' begins. As in the book, many climb into the backs of trucks, leaving Fania and Marianne to walk, inadvertently saved from their fate. Miller indicates that 'the camera memorializes the faces' (13). Not, then, a crowd: individuals. This, indeed, is a defining quality of Miller's script.

Thus, when later Fania is offered boots, necessarily those of a woman consigned to the gas chamber, Miller indicates that the camera 'either vivifies this boot, gives it the life of its deceased owner – or actually fills it with a leg, and we see the pair of boots on living legs . . . perhaps walking on a city street' (31). If Fania Fenelon's book was written out of a desire to memorialise, then Miller's film script was born out of a similar impulse and seeks to find a filmic method of resisting the reductivism which was both method and intent to the Nazis.

When we first see the orchestra rehearsing, the camera introduces us to each of the main supporting characters in turn, Miller offering brief portraits. In a note he insists that,

> From time to time, one or more of the secondary characters will emerge on the foreground of this story in order to keep alive and vivid the sense that the 'background group' is made of individuals. If this film is to approach

even an indication of the vastness of the human disaster involved, the minor
characters will have to be kept dramatically alive even in shots where they
are only seen and don't have any lines.

(33)

The shift in their fate follows the shift in their direction, as the moral world
is about to turn around, a fact reflected in Miller's choice to include in the
railway wagon a boy scout with a compass, who reassures them first that they
are travelling south and then alerts them to the fact that they are moving east.

As the train comes to a halt, the film script calls for cuts from the freight-car
doors rolling open, to the debarkation area, with its spectral lights and kapos,
to people loading cases like bizarre porters, to Fania on the platform, to a close
up of Dr Mengele watching those disembarking. This in turn cuts to SS guards
pushing people into line, as dogs snarl, barely under control. Mengele gestures
to the right or left, the people parting from one another, one group climbing
into trucks marked with a red cross. The first words spoken by Fania, as they
await their fate (perhaps a faint echo of Willy Loman's, 'It's all right. I came
home'), are 'It's going to be all right – you see? – the Red Cross is here' (12). It
is, as is evident to the viewer, anything but all right. What speaks is less reason
than hope, the source of the irony that becomes definitional.

The swift cutting turns space into time, relates individual to group, confronts
victim with persecutor in a montage which establishes the new reality into which
they are born as they are disgorged from the doors of the wagons.

Inside the camp they are confronted with a group of Polish women prisoners,
'hefty, coarse, peasant types' (15), themselves commanded by an SS woman
described by Miller as 'brutal' and 'stupid'. Fania's coat is taken away, along
with her shoes and all the signs of her social position and individuality. Her
hair is cut and her arm tattooed with a number. On a table is a jumble of
toys, including the boy scout's compass. The script largely follows the book,
except that the boy scout and the compass are Miller's invention. Here events
are compressed.

In a brief invented scene Fania is knocked to the ground for insisting that
she is French rather than 'Jew-crap'. In Fenelon's book the obscenity is not
accompanied by a slap. That is metaphorical. Explaining her sudden realisation
of her situation, Fania describes the images that surround her as striking her
'full in the face like a slap' (20). In terms of film, the metaphor becomes literal.
And it is the literalness of film that is both its advantage and its drawback. Thus
we see Fania and others labouring, digging ditches, dragging stones. We see
women drop with exhaustion. The sheer facticity is underlined. At the same time
it remains an external view. Thoughts must be spoken or translated into action.

An essentially realistic form, it creates a tension between the authenticity of
the events and the artifice of performance. Yet the sight of a 'Beckstein grand,
shiny, beautiful', contrasted with the gaunt and shaven-headed musicians, has

a surreal force that Fenelon's description alone cannot. Likewise the shot of her hands, 'crusted with filth, nails broken', playing this piano, offers a contrast which Fenelon describes in her book but which here, as two dislocated experiences are brought together, creates a metaphor of genuine and disturbing power. Film, then, has its own access to the metaphorical. It also has the power, visually, to present two experiences simultaneously. Thus, when Dr Mengele is listening to Fania singing his face is superimposed on hers and then we see him 'with finger raised, directing deportees emerging from a freight car to right and left, death or life. *Flames reflect orange light on his face*' (41).

The effect is simultaneously to underscore the degree to which he dominates Fania's mind and controls her fate, and the nature of the irony with which the women are forced to live, namely their knowledge that survival depends upon the appreciation of their art by a man who is also the agent of death to others. Mengele is both people and that is a double mystery which lies behind the Holocaust: that art was not a protection but a collaborator and that those responsible for killing were human beings, capable both of unspeakable cruelty and subtle emotions.

Two other incidents underscore this in Miller's script. As Fania sounds a chord on the piano, shots ring out and someone screams. She plays the chord again. She has accommodated and so has art. She gets up and walks through the hut, only to find her friend prostituting herself for food. Not only does she continue with the orchestra; she accepts part of that same food. A beautiful violin solo, played by the conductor of the orchestra, which momentarily seems to link the different nationalities and religions, is abruptly halted as the kapos crash into the room and divide Aryans from Jews. Art is no defence, only, it seems, a momentary cessation of danger.

As in *Incident at Vichy* there are those whose ideology or faith offers both explanation and, to them at least, the possibility of redemption. Hélène is a communist, who determines to see the triumph of her creed. Esther lives in hope of seeing a Jewish state in Palestine. It seems likely that both die in a final liquidation, though this is never confirmed.

Beyond the room in which the half-starved women play, others are being tortured and killed. The musicians, by contrast, are offered limited privileges. Thus a mother, desperate for a child torn from her arms, is dragged off even as concern is expressed that Fania's voice may be harmed by the cold. It is not merely that the members of the orchestra are offered the possibility of survival while others are casually killed, but that there is a connection between their survival and the death of others. As the Commandant explains of their music, 'it is a consolation that feeds the spirit. It strengthens us for this difficult work of ours' (56).

This is an irony that Fenelon finds all but disabling. Aware that they will be tolerated only as long as their skills are required, they endeavour to please those who murder. And lest they are inclined to deny their complicity, Marianne, in the play version, desperate to justify her own actions, reminds them that 'if anybody's not sure you're on the side of the executioners, you ought to go out and ask any prisoner in this camp, and they'll be happy to tell you' (77).

One by one sustaining elements are stripped away. The young couple who have survived, and whose love for one another has kept alive the notion of normality and human values, are hanged. The leader of the orchestra, whose courage and will has given them a necessary discipline and unity, is murdered. Slowly, Fenelon is educated in the truths that make her experience doubly disturbing, chief among which is the fact that those responsible for the slaughter are close kin.

Of the brutal chief of the women's section she observes, 'She's beautiful and human. What disgusts me is that a woman so beautiful can do what she is doing. We are the same species. And that is what is so hopeless about this whole thing . . . She *is* human . . . Like you. And me' (62). This is the truth that resonated through both *After the Fall* and *Incident at Vichy*. For, to Miller, the lesson of the camps lay precisely in the fact that those who killed were not part of some alien breed but extreme expressions of a flawed human nature. It is not that he believes in an equality of guilt.

Nonetheless, denial and betrayal, two key themes of his work, are fundamental human traits which simply find their purest expression in the camps. They are survival mechanisms for the prisoners, and policy for those who determine their fate. Plainly there is a scale to guilt. Private betrayals magnified to political strategy can pull down the sky. But imperfection is etched on the human soul and the Holocaust serves to magnify that flaw.

Fenelon and the others, meanwhile, arbitrarily chosen for their Jewish identity, are invited, by guards and prisoners alike, to embrace that identity as defining them. Fenelon resists. She is, she insists, 'a woman, not a tribe!' (53). When she sews the yellow star back on her clothes, therefore, having earlier removed it, insisting that she was only half-Jewish and should therefore wear only half a star, she does so as a sign of solidarity with those around her and not because she accepts it as defining her. In the context of an American playwright it is hard not to recall the moment Hester Prynne chooses to sew the scarlet letter 'A' back on to her dress, claiming as a badge of honour what was offered to her as a sign of contempt.

Behind this, perhaps, lies the dangerous irony pointed out by George Steiner in his *Portage to San Cristobal of A.H.* (1979) in which Adolf Hitler (surviving, in this fiction, beyond the war) argues that he was merely taking seriously the Jewish claim to a unique status and hence a unique fate. But this was not something that Miller chose to address here, or elsewhere, beyond his evident resistance to a tribalism that he plainly sees as the source of a desire for innocence that can only leave the rest of the world condemned.

Innocence is not enough. The Nazis regard themselves as innocent, as do those whose failure to intervene, now or earlier, made the Holocaust possible.

In Miller's text, rather than Fanelon's, Fania remarks to a fellow musician, a non-Jewish Pole who had worked for the Resistance, that the ones 'who are destroying us . . . only feel innocent . . . I almost pity a person like you more than us. You will survive, and everyone around you will be innocent, from one end of Europe to the other' (100). This is the Miller who, in *After the Fall,* had said that to preserve our innocence we kill most easily. Innocence implies guilt and a lack of responsibility. In a world seen after the Fall it implies a level of denial.

Thus, again in a passage that is Miller's own addition, Fania remarks that 'we may be innocent, but we have changed. I mean we know a little something about the human race that we didn't know before. And it's not good news.' Asked how she could regard the Nazis as human, she replies, 'Then what are they?' (124).

The lesson, the disturbing and potentially annihilating lesson, is precisely that they are human and that thus there is connective tissue between victim and persecutor. It is not that this destroys a crucial distinction between those who murder and those who are their victims, but that there is within human beings the potential for this most profound of betrayals and necessity forces a recognition of this. The victims are not saints but necessary sinners. Those who were to walk or be carried from the camps did so in large part because they inhabited what Primo Levi called the grey zone, a world of compromises, small and large, which added guilt to suffering.

To underscore this, Miller expands the role of a man called Shmuel. An electrician, he is one of the only male prisoners who has access to the hut where the women are kept. Shmuel appears in Fenelon's text but his role is here extended and sharpened. Miller describes him as 'perhaps deranged, perhaps extraordinarily wise' (46). He makes brief appearances, sometimes offering news of the outside world, but essentially operating as a goad and a conscience.

He urges Fania to survive and to witness, whispering to her as though he were in her head. 'Don't . . . Turn away,' he instructs, 'You have to look and see everything, so you can tell him when it is over' (55). The 'him', it appears, is God. Shmuel appears repeatedly, with his mantra of 'Live', and 'Look', underscoring both the cruelties around them but also her own role, the irony that infects her. Thus, when Paulette, the cellist, discharges herself from the hospital despite suffering from typhoid because she has been told that all the patients are to be gassed after the concert for which they are rehearsing, Shmuel appears and wordlessly gestures with his eyes. Fania looks at Paulette and the orchestra, at Alma, conducting 'full of joyful tension, pride, waving her arms, snapping her head in the rhythm and humming the tune loudly, oblivious to everything else' (92), and at her own work on the orchestrations. She had been 'shielding her eyes' when Shmuel appeared, eyes 'opened extra wide'. As the camera cuts between these, so Fania and the viewer become acutely aware of the oblivion they seek, their denial as they prepare 'to play for the doomed' (92).

The necessity for memory, embodied in the figure of a man balanced between wisdom and madness, involves not merely recording the evil of those who command their lives and deaths but also the memory of their own compromises, their own collaboration, the extremities to which they have allowed themselves to be pressed in order to survive. Marianne may literally prostitute herself in order to survive but they, too, trade not just their talent but their moral scruples to live. Their ambiguous redemption is that they do so in order to witness. Fania's consolation, and that of others, is that if they entertain in order to survive, the stories they will one day tell will do something more than shape an accusation. They may serve as a warning, which itself could offer a key to survival for a human race which prefers denial.

Similarly, and in a way that is familiar from his own comments over the years, Miller stresses the similarities rather than the discrepancies between the prisoners, laying more stress on this than does Fenelon: 'I'm sick of the Zionists-and-the-Marxists; the Jews-and-the-Gentiles; the Easterners-and-the-Westerners; the Germans-and-the-non-Germans; the French-and-the-non-French . . . I am a woman' (78). One lesson the camps do offer is that ideology and difference are deadly, that there is an irreducible identity which stands apart from exclusionary definitions which turn on the supremacy, the moral superiority, the innocence of one race, religion, nationality, tribe.

In *Broken Glass*, Harry Hyman offers an ironic version of this when he says that '*Everybody's* persecuted. The poor by the rich, the rich by the poor, the black by the white, the white by the black, the men by the women, the women by the men, the Catholics by the Protestants, the Protestants by the Catholics – and of course all of them by the Jews.'[3]

Hitler, too, saw himself as the victim of a conspiracy, hence his own conspiracy against the Jews. The incubus, in other words, exists in a flawed humanity. Miller does not observe this in order to absolve the Germans; indeed his own suspicion of German reunification derived from a fear that that lesson might not have been learned. But, as in the comments he gives to Fania Fenelon in *Playing for Time*, he looks beyond the immediate circumstances in which she found herself.

If art can be collaborative, it can also be accusatory. When the uniformed Frau Mandel rescues a child from its mother only to sacrifice it later, as a sign of her loyalty, Fenelon describes her entering the hut and ordering the duet from *Madame Butterfly*. We are told no more than this. In Miller's hands it becomes a subtle scene in which acquiescence gives way to accusation, the poignant music becomes a weapon.

The duet between Butterfly and Suzuki finds the former, abandoned, holding her baby and awaiting the return of the man who has betrayed and abandoned her. The lyrics bear directly on Mandel's state of mind as Butterfly sings to her child: '*Sweet thou art sleeping, cradled in my heart . . . Safe in God's keeping, while I must weep apart. Around thy head the moon beams dart . . . Sleep my beloved.*' Mandel revels in the false sentiment, arrogating to herself the very role of mother for which she has shown contempt. She wallows in the human emotions she has consciously denied through her role in the camp, and through her destruction of the child.

Fania, 'nearly insensible' (130), is forced to collude in this charade, this parade of bad faith, but as she does so begins to reveal her contempt. As Mandel stares up at her so Fania *'takes on a challenging, protesting tone'* (131), until the duet is interrupted by the sound of bombers overhead and explosions. Later, Miller has Mandel re-enter in search of the child's hat (in fact, of course, the hat of a child who had already been gassed when it was allotted to this latest victim). Her false emotion is contrasted to that of Etalena, a Roumanian violinist, who has just witnessed her two sisters and father on their way to their deaths.

The scene in which the orchestra play for those in the hospital who are about to die, not only combines occasions which, in Fenelon's book, were different, but is laced with an irony that is of Miller's making. Thus, when they play *The Blue Danube* the prisoners begin to hum and are permitted this potentially subversive act of solidarity. This is then followed by their playing of a 'laughing polka', which, in the book, follows the murder of the orchestra's conductor, and does not occur on the occasion of the concert in the hospital. Miller, however, derives an additional irony as the orchestra members are forced to humiliate themselves and mock both their own and the patients' situation, for it is during this piece that the latter are slowly led out by the kapos to be gassed. For Fania, Miller indicates, this is 'the ultimate agony' (134).

The concluding section of the film shows the 'orchestra' taken away from the camp by train. Marianne is now made kapo and beats Fania to the ground. The friend of the opening scenes has become the victimiser. The women are gathered together, awaiting their deaths, when Shmuel reappears, as he does not in Fenelon's account, transfigured now into a messianic figure: 'The light behind him contrasts with the murk within the building and he seems to blaze in an unearthly luminescence. He is staring in a sublime silence, as he lifts his arms in a wordless gesture of deliverance, his eyes filled with miracle' (145). Behind him, a British soldier appears. They are delivered. Fania sings the Marseillaise.

The film ends, as Fenelon's book had begun, with the reunion of survivors of the orchestra. It ends as they grasp hands across the table, the tattooed numbers visible on their wrists. The concluding direction is something more than a camera instruction, underscoring, as it does, the central theme of survival and continuance which drove Fania Fenelon and her fellow captives and which drives the film: 'The camera draws away, and, following the waiter as he crosses the restaurant, we resume the normality of life and the irony of it; and now we are outside on the avenue, the bustle of contemporary traffic; and quick close shots of passers-by, the life that continues and continues . . .' (150).

In 1985, Miller produced a play version of *Playing for Time*. For the most part it followed the film script, though with minor transpositions of characters and events. The principal innovation in this two-act version was to make Fania a narrator, an active recaller of a traumatic past. In his production notes Miller suggested that there should be no set and that the few changes in locale should be made in full view of the audience, with only light changes to shift the audience's attention. Indeed, he suggested the possibility of playing the whole work under an unchanged set of lights. There was, he indicated, no need to naturalise changes of costume or scene. Everything, he thought, could be done in full view 'and should be since the play, in one sense, is a demonstration, a quality that need in no way be disguised'.[4]

It is as if by openly displaying the theatricality of the piece, by, for the most part, dispensing with scenery and playing it under unchanging lights, he were purging it of deception. He was stripping away the normal processes of an art of simulation and confronting, if not the experience itself, then a version not contaminated by the legerdemain of aesthetics. The framing narrator thus becomes part of this process of distancing, of alienation. The play is the story she tells. She is the survivor and these her memories and the acknowledgement of theatricality part of a bargain with the audience whereby they understand the status of what they see. It is simultaneously presented as truth and as a representation of truth.

The open admission of the theatrical component thus becomes part of that bargain whereby the lies of art themselves become suspect and simple narration or framed dramatic enactment an attempt to abjure the manipulative power of the stage. When the women are shorn of their hair, for example, they merely remove their wigs to reveal the bald-caps they already wear. The effect is to underline the fact that this is, in Miller's words, a 'demonstration'. But it is also, I suspect, to ritualise actions and there is, of course, another history than that recounted here, the history of theatre.

The stripping of Lear to the unaccommodated man is as much a part of our common imagery as the shaven-headed inmates of the concentration camp or those others whose hair would be shorn after the war as a mark of their collaboration. The terrible reminder of *Playing for Time* is that there are many kinds of collaboration, from Marianne's prostitution, to the orchestra who collaborate to live. The theatrical and the real are not easily untangled precisely because they inhabit one another and this, after all, is a story about those who were themselves performers, necessarily suppressing their true selves to survive.

The paradox is that while these events happened, and the figure of Fania Fenelon is offered as a mark of their authenticity, the process of shaping these events (first by her in her own book and then by Miller, in the form of a television film and a play), inevitably displaces them from one realm into another. Book, film, play, come at a price. They are available for review. They solicit praise or applause. Living people become characters performed by actors who deploy learned skills to persuade us that they are not what they are. Contingency assumes coherent form; ethics defer to or are expressed through aesthetics. Meanwhile, it is the nature of memory, of editorial selection, of juxtaposition, to create rather than simply to recall.

Plays work through and generate metaphor and metaphors are themselves constructions. At one moment, in the play version, Miller forgets his admonitions about lighting and indicates of Pauline, a member of the orchestra, that 'She is lit like a Dutch painting, although in rags' (34). She is turned into a metaphor as two time frames, two conditions of being, are brought together. She is, in short, aestheticised as suffering is briefly recreated as art. The distance between the lighting effect and her appearance generates an irony that slides into pathos as she plays, the sound of her music being described as 'lonely'. A moment later, the light 'spreads' and we become aware of two other members of the orchestra, desperately and incompetently practising on accordions.

The contrast between Pauline, who plays a Bach chaconne on a cello, and Liesle and Greta, who play on instruments as inappropriate as themselves, is itself a calculated drama. At the same moment it literally reproduces the circumstances of the camp and generates a surreal image which reflects the consolations and desperations of the musicians, at once separate from one another and incongruously brought together.

There is no true documentary theatre, if by that we mean an unmediated presentation of history. Fania Fenelon, in her book, wished to bear witness, to deploy memory as a tool and even a weapon. Yet hers is not, and could hardly have been, a daily diary. From the continuum, she selects moments that carry the force of the whole, which are exemplary. She recalls incidents of crisis, revelatory events, ironic moments. From the whole orchestra she chooses, of necessity but also for a definable purpose, a limited number of those who played, those who lived and died. She chooses, in part, because they represent different approaches to their dilemma, different categories of prisoner, different religions, nationalities. Miller, for his part, builds up some characters and eliminates others, also for his reasons, having to do in part with dramatic structure but also his own thematic concerns.

The power of the piece, of course, comes in part from the reality to which it has a metonymic relationship. Fenelon's claim is that of Primo Levi. She was there. She suffered. The irony of her situation, however, was that in her own soul she felt she did not suffer enough. She did not die as others died. But there was also a space between her and those prisoners for whom she played and who went not to their immediate death but to soul-destroying labour. She had privileges, limited but real, and ultimately life-saving. Then there was the space she was determined to maintain, namely that between her and those for whom she performed and whom she despised, as at some level she despised herself for performing for them.

Her redemption lay in the fact that while she sustained herself with the thought that, if released, she would kill a Polish woman, she did not, and by the fact that she never came to hate the music she was forced to play or the language of the oppressor. She was redeemed, finally, by living her life and by writing the book which preserved the memory of those who had suffered alongside her. For Miller, at one level this was a commission quickly and easily completed. At another, it was a further stage in his own exploration of an experience that seemed to pose a central question about human nature, about betrayal, about the struggle to survive, about the relationship between the individual and the group. The orchestra, in which each person relied on the other, was something more than a mechanism of survival. It was an image of that mutuality which lies both at the heart of Miller's social philosophy and at the centre of the theatrical enterprise.

Fenelon's reason for revisiting such a painful past is, in a sense, Miller's, and hence ours. How can an event that seemed to annihilate meaning yet be made to render up meaning? What is the connection between the particularities of the camp and the specifics of a human nature that made it possible? How permeable is the membrane between then and now? For Miller, the play was neither generated by nor expressive of a merely historical interest. It bore on the present because the same principles were in play.

Playing for Time could almost be a Beckett title. The woman (Alma) who asks Fania to accept a 'little hope' is killed; the woman (Hélène) who insists that there is still hope does so because she looks forward to a time when Europe will be dominated by communism. Fania, meanwhile, can only 'hope . . . it ends soon for all of us', an ambiguous enough statement when death alone seems the likely end. For Miller, though, such ironies are not a complete account. It is not a play that seeks to extend guilt beyond the perpetrators, but it is a play that seeks to extend responsibility, and such a responsibility is rooted in an acknowledgement that we share not simply the plight of the victims but also the potential to be the perpetrators, if only by silent acquiescence.

After the Fall, Incident at Vichy and *Playing For Time*, taken together, form a kind of triptych. Thus, for Miller, it was not the autobiographical elements of *After the Fall* that lay at the heart of the play but 'that watershed of our history', the Holocaust. It is a telling phrase, for clearly he does feel not that human nature changed, as Virginia Woolf once only half-jokingly proposed it had in 1910, but that our perception of it did. Of *Incident at Vichy* he has remarked that at its core he sees 'the anomie and paralysis before the knowledge of mass destruction'. *Playing for Time*, in his view, 'completes the theme'.[5]

The reason for revisiting this past, however, lay, Miller insists, in his conviction that in the post-war world 'the same questions haunt us'.[6] Those questions, then, were scarcely born out of, or restricted to, the rationally conducted, irrational genocide of the Second World War. In *The Creation of the World and Other Business*, he had tried to track them to their origin. They did, however, find their starkest form as, under extreme pressure, his characters, like those who in reality trod that vertiginous path from a supposedly civilised existence, are made to confront ultimate truths about themselves and about human possibilities. It is as though time were reversed and mankind moved backwards towards origins. Social facades are stripped away. Denials and suppressions, the very mechanisms of civilisation according to Freud, are exposed as simply that.

These plays differ in style. In *After the Fall* the pressure on the central character is such that his world seems to splinter and fragment. Quentin's self-imposed task, indeed, is to discover some inner coherence that can make real what seem to him no more than random memories and events. At the same time there is in him that which would resist such coherence because of the truth with which it may confront him, the very truth which is disabling him.

In *Incident at Vichy*, the characters are reduced by their circumstances to something less than they would be. They resist incorporation in a plot whose single coherence threatens their existence but thereby find themselves forced to deny the solidarity which might be the source of meaning. The play has the surface appearance of realism. We are offered glimpses of their social lives. But in this place, at this time, these become irrelevant and the presumptions of realism in some way mocked. There is a reductive process at work and the integrity of the play requires that that bleed into the style. The specifics of setting are removed. We learn nothing of the inner lives of several of the characters to whom we, like their judges, respond purely viscerally, thereby drawn into the moral maelstrom ourselves. Of others, we learn only what breaks surface as their anxieties force inner concerns briefly into sight and consciousness. This, then, is a realism in which the defining qualities of realism are sandblasted away.

In *Playing for Time* the characters reduce their lives to what is necessary for survival. Their past histories have no relevance. There is no future they dare plot beyond the moment or beyond fantasies disconnected from their daily experience. The play begins with a collage of people, pressed together in a boxcar. They act out their lives in a series of mimes: students read novels, intellectuals play chess, a boy scout ties knots, the chic distance themselves as far as they can, appearing bored. Within minutes these poses are broken down as the deprivations of the journey lead them to relieve themselves in public. As they move forwards in time towards their unknown destination, so they move backwards in time towards a pre-civilised existence. On arrival they are stripped of their clothes, as though they were reborn, totally vulnerable, amidst the unwelcoming desolation, and, within a short time, they are stripped of their lives. Time is, indeed, reversing itself. The surviving characters then enter a limbo similar to that in which the characters in *Incident at Vichy* were required to await their fate.

Miller has said of these plays that their metaphorical preoccupations may be disguised for some by a design that asks for a realistic recognition of events and characters on the surface of a highly condensed interior life but the word 'realism', for him, is plainly elastic. He does, he confesses, want life 'to seem like this'. But the condensed interior lives that he refers to are a consequence of the pressure placed on the characters by their circumstances. These are not 'well-rounded characters' because they are characters reduced to their essentials and the attenuation of their lives is an expression of their circumstances. The plays, in other words, bear the impress of their subject as the characters bear the impress of their situation.

With all social and ethical systems in abeyance, Miller wishes both to deny and embrace the consolation of form. At the heart of these works is sheer contingency, a fiat shaped out of anarchy become dictat. It follows that the stylistic correlative will reflect this fact. The characters search for reason at the heart of unreason and find none. There is no consoling shape, not even that of a wilful absurdity. So their lives do break apart, shatter along the lines of least resistance. Yet at the same time, as Fania Fenelon desperately needs to believe, art itself, if co-opted by those same forces of anarchy, if deeply compromised is still a pathway to transcendence. It is the ambiguity on which her life turns. Its justification lies in the fact that she acknowledges the enormity which it struggles to balance.

Desperate not to look at what lies beyond the window, to settle for an art untouched by the surrounding circumstances of its creation, she nonetheless does look, for how else can she be a witness and later summon this world into being, the evidence for which is the memoir that became a film and in turn a play. The justification for art, then, is that it is presented in full awareness that no one, not its creators, not its audiences, is free of the incubus of the anarchy against which it pitches itself. This is the tension out of which these plays come.

21

The shearing point

The Israeli writer, Joshua Sobol, in planning a play about the Holocaust, came across a slogan from the Wilna ghetto in Lithuania, in which over fifty thousand of the seventy thousand Jews were massacred. It read: 'There can be no theatre in a graveyard.'

The Holocaust stands as an intimidating and disabling fact. For the writer, its sheer implacability is a challenge. The disproportion between event and its representation, between fact and the meaning of fact, leaves nothing but the stain of irony, a taste in the mouth that can find no equivalent beyond itself. Even for those who survived it, the Holocaust defied expression, understanding, belief. One of only two survivors of the Chelmo extermination camp returned to the place where he had once been forced to feed the crematorium ovens and tried to describe what he had experienced, what he had seen, for Claude Lanzmann's film *Shoah*. 'There were', he said, 'two ovens and afterwards the bodies were thrown into those ovens, and the flames reached to the sky. It was terrible.' Beyond that he could hardly go. As he said, 'No one can describe it. No one can recreate what happened here. Impossible. And no one can understand it. Even I, here, now . . . I can't believe I'm here. No, I just can't believe it.'[1]

For George Steiner, the world of Auschwitz lies 'outside the normative syntax of human communication'.[2] For Hannah Arendt it is inexpressible because it stands outside of life and death. And if it can be spoken, can it be heard? For Lionel Trilling it challenges even the most mordant of satirists: 'The simple eye of the camera shows us, at Belsen and Buchenwald, horrors that quite surpass Swift's power . . . before what we know the mind stops . . . The activity of mind fails before the incommunicability of man's suffering.'[3] In the face of the Holocaust it is tempting to say that the only legitimate response is a respectful silence and, as Samuel Beckett reminded us, 'speech is a desecration of silence',[4] and 'nothing is more real than nothing'.

And there is a case for silence in the face of enormity since not merely may the disproportion between word and fact breed distracting ironies but the mere act of allowing it to enter language at all is to risk normalising it, to grant it the legitimacy of utterance. Thus, for Primo Levi, who experienced the camps, the paradox lay in the fact that, as he explained, the 'true witnesses' of the Holocaust were not those who, like himself, wrote their memoirs, but those who returned mute in that their silence tells a truth that words cannot.

During the war, however, Thomas Mann asked, 'should a writer, made responsible through his habitual use of language, remain silent, quite silent, in the face of all the irreparable evil which has been committed daily, and is being committed in my country, against body, soul and spirit, against justice and truth, against men and man?'[5] The question was rhetorical. His refusal of silence grew out of a desperate attempt to deflect history. For he knew, with Lear, that nothing comes of nothing.

Those who advocated silence after the war did so for different reasons – out of respect and reverence, and perhaps also because the sky had already fallen. Even memoirs could seem suspect. As Levi remarked of his own work, 'An apology is in order. This very book is drenched in memory . . . Thus it draws from a suspect source.'[6] The solution, perhaps, is to consider its effects in the way it is possible to detect an invisible planet by the distorting effect it has on the orbit of another. The Holocaust, in other words, can be best known through the distorting effect it has on history, language, character, religion, literature.

But there are other problems in addressing the Holocaust in literature, for art offers the grace of order and coherence in a way which may be a denial of the moral anarchy, the willed destructiveness of the Holocaust. To lift the Holocaust into art is, perhaps, to give retrospective purpose, to offer the sanction, the sanctification of form, aesthetic pleasure, even a nullifying and ahistoric sense of dignity where the mark of the Holocaust was precisely the lack of such. We seize on Anne Frank and Oscar Schindler because they have names among the nameless, because the story of the first stops short of the camp gates, though we know that those gates eventually closed behind her (indeed Fania Fenelon was to encounter her), while the story of the other is about the one man who acted and not the million who did not, about the rescued few and not the condemned many.

Theodore Adorno also suggested another source of unease when he said that 'the so-called artistic representation of naked bodily pain . . . of victims felled by rifle butts, contains, however remote, the potential of wringing pleasure from it'.[7] Beyond that, but potentially allied to it, it may be the source of a free emotional ride, a sentimentality in the Yeatsian sense of an unearned emotion. In other words, writers can incorporate an emotional charge into their work by evoking the horrors of the camp, as William Styron did in Sophie's Choice.

Yet for Hans Magnus Enzensberger, to refuse to apply the transfiguring power of art is to become complicit with the forces art can challenge. Then, there is the need for witness. Elie Wiesel, who experienced the camps directly, has said that 'If someone else could have written my stories I would not have written them. I have written them in order to testify. My role is the role of witness . . . Not to tell, or to tell another story, is . . . to commit perjury.'[8]

To remain silent is implicitly to tell another story, a false story, a story of our time and our nature that omits a central truth. While Bruno Bettelheim has acknowledged the paradox – 'Those who have not lived through the experience will never know; those who have will never tell; not really, not completely' – he has also insisted that, 'if we remain silent, then we perform exactly as the Nazis wanted: behave as if it never did happen'.[9] It is not that nothing comes of nothing but precisely that something does come of it.

And there was another necessity, one recognised by Arthur Miller, but here expressed again by Elie Wiesel: 'we must invent reason: we must create beauty out of nothingness'.[10] There is a story by Wiesel, called *The Town Beyond the Wall*, in which the protagonist is locked in a cell with an idiot boy. He tries to redeem the pointlessness by endeavouring to teach him human responses. It is a hopeless task but he continues because, with God evidently dead, he 'resumes the creation of the world from the void'. For Beckett, such a story would have been the basis for cosmic irony. For Wiesel, as for Miller, it underlines the necessity to reinvent if not God then the sense of moral responsibility which is perhaps another name for that God. And interestingly Miller uses a similar image in *After the Fall* when he talks of the necessity to take one's life in one's arms, like an idiot child.

Why was Miller so concerned with the idea of resuscitating tragedy in the late 1940s and 50s? Perhaps because tragedy was assumed to have died with the six million and he wished to resurrect it because tragedy invests death with meaning and, if death, then life.

It is too easy to be transfixed by the camps, mesmerised, imaginatively paralysed by them, to see in their existence the signs of apocalypse and eschatology. Miller set his face against this and so did a fellow Jewish writer, Saul Bellow. As his pseudonymous protagonist remarks in *Herzog*, 'We must get it out of our head that this is a doomed time, that we are waiting for the end . . . Things are grim enough without these shivery games . . . We love apocalypse too much.'[11] As Martin Buber said, 'The task of the genuine prophet was not to predict but to confront man with the alternatives of decision.'[12] For Bellow and Miller alike this was equally the function of the writer.

Miller was not in the camps. He saw from a distance. But if there was a terrible price to be paid for being there, there was also a price for not being so. George Steiner has confessed to feeling 'maimed for not having been at the roll call'. That may sound like mere posturing. Who, after all, would wish to claim the privilege of being present at the apocalypse? But the guilt of the survivor is real enough and it lies at the heart of *After the Fall*, as perhaps it is shadowed in *The Man Who Had All the Luck*, about a man who is destabilised by the fact that he seems to be immune to the disasters suffered by others, as Miller was immune to the disasters of the camps.

Camus's protagonist in *The Fall* contemplates the notion that Christ must have felt the guilt of the survivor: 'he must have heard of a certain Massacre of the Innocents. The children of Judea massacred while his parents were taking him to a safe place – why did they die if not because of him? Those blood-splattered soldiers, those infants cut in two filled him with horror . . . I am sure he could not forget this . . . who would have believed that crime consists less in making others die than in not dying oneself.'[13]

The sheer power of the Holocaust is such that Tony Kushner has spoken of resenting its particularity, its resistance to being used as metaphor, as if its status were such that it had set a standard of evil by comparison with which all other evils would appear insignificant. Thus, he has set himself to use it promiscuously, to undermine its unique status, relating it, in particular, to the plague of AIDS, and the political and moral disregard it prompted.

Miller, too, has acknowledged the difficulty of confronting the implacable. As he has said, 'regardless of what one wrote or read, to so much as contemplate the systematic gassing of small children was to feel a cold hand clapped to one's mouth, and one understood to some small degree why the Germans could not think about it'. Yet mere testimony was not enough. As he insisted, 'important though it might be to memorialize the Holocaust lest it fade away, its in-built causation remained largely unexplored terrain for most people, who continued their fear of tribes and persuasions other than own like something sacred' (T. 526). And that is the essence of the Holocaust for Miller. There was a human mechanism at work.

The Holocaust was not a brute fact free of causation, with no antecedent, no continuing relevance, inexorable, intractable, an expression of the absurd. Indeed to regard it as such was to succumb to its inner dynamic, to accept and promulgate a passivity which became complicit with the forces at work. For Miller, history is not an abstract force, a juggernaut crushing the bones of humanity. It is a human product, with its own mechanisms. In his Nobel Prize acceptance speech, Albert Camus remarked that 'the writer's function is not without its arduous duties. By definition, he cannot serve today those who make history; he must serve those who are subjected to it.'[14] But Miller sees everyone as the maker of history in an existential sense, while not denying that there are those whose lack of power makes them victims of power. Nonetheless there is something consoling in the role of victim and it is for that reason that he insists that no one is without responsibility for their lives and in some degree for the world to which they submit as if to some irremediable force.

Nor was history simply an expression of an irony rooted in the human condition. Beckett's 'We give birth astride the grave' may have had a terrible relevance in camps where that was quite literally the truth, but it was a fact which (both in its enactment and its subsequent denial) exposed a flawed humanity that could not be addressed as simply a by-product, a logical extension of cosmic absurdity. So it was that Miller found himself at odds with certain aspects of European literature.

It is not hard to identify the extent to which the European theatre and novel bore the marks of the war. Plot, character and language came under extreme pressure. The marginalisation of the human figure in the *nouveau roman* was once described by Robbe-Grillet as simple realism, an expression of what he saw in wartime France. Beckett's characters, lifted out of time, isolated in anonymous spaces, disappearing into the ground, reduced to disembodied upper torsos, mouths, employing a parodistic and intransitive language were perhaps no more than markers for a world that could sustain no other art. For Miller, however, such gestures compounded the damage already done to the self. He wished to insist on causality where the absurdists, to his mind, believed that such rational and moral connections had been snapped, like an arm across someone's knee. Beckett's characters are lifted out of causality, except in the sense that human needs and responses breed vulnerability. For them, survival depends upon the elimination of human responses.

For Miller, that is not possible. Character is marked by something more than irony. It is a product of willed choice. Evil does not exist as a free-floating signifier. That is a sentimentality, shorthand for the apparent opacity of certain extremes. For him, all human flaws, as all human graces, begin somewhere. They begin in the self, which, psychopathology aside, is the product of choice, in an egotism that must be transcended if there is to be salvation. And the theatre, literature, is intimately involved in such transcendence.

Beckett's characters are exiles, stranded in a featureless setting. They are products of the passive voice, victims of recurrence, habit which annihilates time, at least as a generator of meaning. Miller's characters are grounded in time and place. There are ironies – Willy Loman sowing seeds in his barren backyard by flashlight, Eddie Carbone insisting on his honour while in process of sacrificing it – but these ironies are the product of their personal failure to acknowledge the nature of their experience.

For Miller, the camps do not summon the blank face of atrocity to mind, a perverse force of nature. It is not the obscene workings of an efficient machine that strikes him, still less the remoteness of this world. It is its familiarity. It is the broken human contract, the personal betrayal, the denial of responsibility. Having attended the Frankfurt trials he returned to America and, as he explained, 'began to feel committed to the new play [*After the Fall*], possibly because of its theme – the paradox of denial'. This seemed to him 'so eminently the theme of Germany', but equally 'Germany's idealistically denied brutality' which was 'emblematic of the human dilemma in our time'. The play, he explained, was 'about how we – nations and individuals – destroy ourselves by denying that this is precisely what we are doing'(*T.* 527).

The Holocaust was not a secret. In December 1942, Edward R. Murrow, broadcasting from London, talked of the 'extermination' camps. In 1944, the War Refugee Board published a report about Auschwitz which the Office of War Information's Elmer Davis tried to suppress fearing that nobody would believe the scale of the deaths it reported and that this might damage the agency.

The fact is that a silence fell, a silence which had a number of causes. It was to be some twenty years before the Holocaust found its way into literature on any scale, and when it did Arthur Miller's would prove a central voice. In fact, throughout his career, in stories and plays, published and unpublished, he would create Jewish characters and engage with the implications of a Jewish identity though feeling no obligation to do so, no burden he was bound to carry.

During the war there had been a hesitation by Jewish writers and those in the media to stress the plight of the Jews. That was true of NBC, whose President was Jewish, as it was of the *New York Times*, whose Jewish publisher Arthur Salzberger had tolerated those anti-Semitic advertisements which reserved jobs for Christians or referred, coyly, to a 'restricted clientele'. It was these advertisements which a young Arthur Miller had scanned when looking for a jobs in the 1930s. The emphasis, once the war was under way, was to be on winning, not on the plight of the Jews. There was a desire not to make waves, not to antagonise those already inclined to see the war as in part a product of Jewish influence in the media and Washington. In the words of a familiar Jewish joke, ironic, dense with a cold historical awareness, 'What is anti-Semitism? Being against Jews more than is necessary.' However, in a radio play on Pastor Niemoller, Miller, despite the fact that he was working for an anti-Semitic sponsor, was one of the few radio dramatists to insist on including a reference to the Jews. In April 1943, he has his narrator remark that 'Out over the American land . . . under the sign of the cross and under the six pointed star of Israel, men and women of good will are reaffirming . . . the right of every man to worship after the manner of his believing. But in Nazi Germany this right no longer exists.'[15]

Asked to identify the trace elements of the Holocaust in his work he has stressed his continuing concern with characters and cultures which deny the substance of their experience: 'the whole idea of someone unable to awaken to reality', he has said, 'is implicit in the Holocaust', in the Jews who could not believe the evidence of their senses, and the Germans 'who were transfixed' by a dream, a self-image which rationalised and sanctioned such slaughter, what he calls 'the sleep of reason from which one cannot be awakened'. He has, he insists, seen the germ of this in America, in witch-hunts of various kinds throughout its history, a disease to which it has not fully submitted because its heterogeneity leads to what he ironically calls 'an uneven development of irrationality at any one moment'.[16]

Only in *Playing for Time* does Miller look directly at the camps. For the most part it is a question of peripheral vision, as if a small mark had been etched on the lens of the eye so that it becomes impossible to see anything that is not marked by awareness of this imperfection.

There is, of course, a danger in that and Bruno Bettelheim has spelled it out:

> As the subject became popularized, so it ceased to be sacrosanct, or rather was stripped of its mystery. People lost their awe. The Holocaust became a literary 'free for all', the no-man's-land of modern writing . . . Novelists

made free use of it in their work, scholars used it to prove their theories. In doing so they cheapened the Holocaust; they drained it of its substance . . . Suddenly everybody began calling himself a survivor. Having compared Harlem to the Warsaw ghetto and Vietnam to Auschwitz . . . some who spent the war . . . in a fancy apartment in Manhattan, now claim that they too have survived the Holocaust, probably by proxy.[17]

In other words, the Holocaust is unique and of itself and not available as paradigm or metaphor. No one who was not there could claim to be a survivor. In that sense he might be said to be at odds with the Arthur Miller who wrote *Incident at Vichy*, which, as we have seen, though dealing with an act of self-sacrifice, was described by Miller as relating to other, more contemporary situations. 'It concerns the question of insight – of seeing in oneself the capacity for collaboration with the evil one condemns. It's a question – that exists for all of us – what, for example, is the responsibility of each of us for allowing the slums of Harlem to exist?'[18]

For some, the jump from the final solution to the slums of Harlem would seem too great to contemplate. But his point is not that America treats African–Americans as Germany treated the Jews. It is that certain human characteristics remain constant, characteristics to do with the ease with which we contemplate the suffering of others, become complicit, subtly or otherwise, in the evil we would condemn, place our own survival, or even simply comfort, before that of others, refuse the implied human contract which links us to others, fail imaginatively to place ourselves in the position of others, as the central character in *Incident at Vichy* does in the most literal of ways, like the protagonist of *Focus*, assuming the identity and hence the fate of a Jew.

And do those who survived not feel guilty if not simply because of the fact of their survival then because of their unvoiced relief that others and not they died there? But Miller goes further than this. He has said:

> I have always felt that concentration camps, though they're a phenomenon of totalitarian states, are also the logical conclusion of contemporary life. If you complain of people being shot down in the streets, of the absence of communication or social responsibility, of the rise of everyday violence which people have become accustomed to, and the dehumanisation of feelings, then the ultimate development on an organized social level is the concentration camp . . . In this play [*After the Fall*] the question is, what is there between people that is indestructible? The concentration camp is the final expression of human separateness and its ultimate consequence. It is organized abandonment.[19]

The Jews were the primary victims of that human separateness but even the Jews have their Jews. As the Jewish detective in his one-act play *Clara* remarks: 'That day in 1945 . . . When they first showed those pictures of the piles of bones . . . The bulldozers pushing them into those trenches, those arms and legs sticking up? That day I was born again . . . and I'll never let myself forget it. "Do it to them before they can do it to you. Period".' Asked what he believes in he says: 'Greed and race . . . that secret little tingle you get when your own kind comes out ahead. The black for the black, and the white for the white. Gentile for Gentile and the Jew for the Jew. Greed and race . . . and you'll never go wrong.'[20] This was the other legacy of the camps. If they were an expression of atavism, tribalism, a deep Manichean impulse then, potentially, they confirmed rather than denied the legitimacy of a reactive separatism, a countervailing hardening of the heart, a consolidating of racial identity and ethnic primacy: 'Do it to them before they can do it to you.' The residue of that is not hard to see.

Cynthia Ozick, who has herself written a Holocaust play – *Blue Light* – has said that, 'I refuse to write a play that reduces the Holocaust to an image or myth.'[21] By contrast, and while insisting on its unique status, Bruno Bettelheim himself acknowledges the paradigmatic nature of the Holocaust, like Miller seeing in it an expression of a broken human contract. Thus, despite his comment on its sanctity, its mystery, he, too, sees its relationship to more fundamental failures in human thought and action. And, indeed, the great risk of seeing the Holocaust as a mystery is that its human mechanisms are ignored, its roots in human behaviour obscured. Thus, he has said:

> That we ought to care for one another, that with our concern we ought to counteract the death-like and death-provoking desperation that there is nobody who cares for one, has been taught since the beginning of time. But in each generation, one event more than any other makes this lesson especially pertinent, giving it a character specific to that age. For this century I believe this event is the extermination of the European Jews in the gas chambers.'[22]

For him, the reason for its special relevance lay in the fact that it was enabled by a totalitarian mass society obsessed with a pseudo-scientific delusion. For Miller, whose imagination has also been constantly drawn to this event, its relevance lies elsewhere, not in the nature of the society – totalitarian regimes historically being the norm rather than the exception – nor in a pseudo-scientific delusion which he had seen operating in seventeenth-century Salem and was to see again in the recovered-memory theories of the late twentieth century (and which he was to denounce), but in the operation of entirely familiar human traits taken to an ultimate extreme. For here he found tribalism, betrayal, denial, the victory of idea over value, a specious belief in innocence, the breaking of charity, the denial of a common humanity, all of which could be traced to their origin in the self.

'In whose name', his protagonist asks in *After the Fall*, 'do you ever turn your back – but in your own? . . . No man lives who would not rather be the sole survivor of this place than all its finest victims.'[23] When Quentin remarks that 'I have cooperated with my persecutors' (121), this is less a comment on

Jewish passivity, though for Bettelheim that remained a constant theme, than an acknowledgement that the world that oppresses him must to some degree at least be his own construction.

In part that is why Miller wrote *Incident at Vichy*, to show that action was possible, that, offered a specious absolution, at the price of denying the human contract, one could refuse collaboration. And what was true in Vichy France or Nazi Germany was equally true in the private lives of all who together constitute the moral world and are the motor force of history.

It is also why, years later, he returned to the persecution of the Jews in *Broken Glass*, a play set in 1938 at the time of Kristallnacht but first performed as shells landed on Sarajevo and mass murder and so-called ethnic cleansing became realities once again as the world stood by, paralysed. And as in *The Golden Years*, what strikes him, in both thirties Germany and nineties Yugoslavia, is the paralysis which people feel in the face of such events, that and a sense of remoteness that makes it seem that such events have no connection with the daily experience of those who are, in these cases, neither Jewish nor Muslim.

But the paralysis has another cause. It is provoked by the notion of an evil that seems in some way independent of human volition. It is almost a natural force or perhaps an aspect of the human psyche that is unchallengeable because always present, coincident, as it appears to be, with our human fate, which is to live and to die. Is the notion of death itself, after all, any less arbitrary, cruel and absurd than these reminders of that fact? Such moments in history create a sense of giddiness as we stare not only back into our own past as a species but forward into our own shared fate.

The answer Miller gives throughout his work is that with God dead, who but man can create the values by which he must then live? Thus, he says of Quentin in *After the Fall*: 'He sees through the course of his life that unless by an act of will he . . . creates good faith and behaves with good faith, it will never exist. He has got to will it into existence. Otherwise, we're serving death.' The play, Miller explains, 'is trying to recreate through one man an ethic on the basis of his observations of its violation.'

It is not, then, that Miller denies a history of betrayal, egotism, cruelty and moral stasis. As he has said, 'I see perfectly well that we all harbour in ourselves the destruction of each other. We all harbour in ourselves these murderous desires. We all harbour in ourselves this breach of faith.' But he adds these crucial words: 'I can't accept that as his last word. Why? Because if I do accept it as his last word, life has no reason for me.'

Thus, *After the Fall* ends with Quentin embracing his life like an idiot child, knowing that joy is also a reality and choosing life over death, 'aware', as Miller says, 'that this struggle will never end',[24] *Broken Glass* ends with Sylvia seemingly recovering from her paralysis, ready likewise to be an actor in her own drama. Maggie, in *After the Fall*, by contrast, dies, finally, because she is a slave to the idea of being victimised, while the play's title indicates the realisation, so vital to Miller's drama, that the Fall is the threat of freedom, of having to make choices.

The play in which he chooses to enter through the gates of the death camps is *Playing for Time*, which concerns the defeats and the triumphs of the human spirit in the camps. It stages the compromises, the resistances, the despair of those who did what was necessary to survive while struggling to keep alive a sense of themselves that made survival worthwhile. But buried in the play is a disturbing question, a question that has equally fascinated and haunted George Steiner. Dr Mengele, and those whose cruelty knew no bounds, kept Fania Fenelon and her fellow musicians alive because they played music and the killers of men, women and children were lovers of music.

The question, then, the potentially destabilising and even annihilating question, is not merely how could killers love culture, but was culture powerless in the face of power and, if powerless, its handmaiden? If that is true then writing itself becomes deeply suspect and its claims to privileged insight and transcendent values void.

Then again, if literature has survived should it not bear the marks of that time? Should its syntax not be fractured, its prose dislocated, its characters seared and blasted? But in Miller's work all these do survive. At most he offers an affecting symbol – Sylvia's paralysis in *Broken Glass*, the metonymic concentration-camp tower in *After the Fall*. Yet in some sense, this is the point. Miller is precisely insisting that he will not embrace this apocalypticism, that he will not submit to the ironies which so readily suggest themselves. His concept of character, his sense of language, his faith in moral responsibility turn on the need to accept the causalities which underlie the blank face of evil. Damage was indeed done but it is the writer's responsibility to purify the language, to restore that very sense of identity, of character as a product of lived experience, which the camps sought to destroy.

Arthur Miller is a Jewish writer and that gives his work a particular edge. As he has said, 'My feeling is that when you sell nihilism . . . you are creating the grounds for nihilistic destruction, and the first one to get it is the Jew.' The Jew, he has said, 'is always the one . . . who stands at the crack of civilization, in geology it's called the shearing point'. But, as he has also said, 'the roots of my aversion may be Jewish, but my concern is for the country as a whole'.[25] And not, of course, the country alone, for Miller's plays address the human plight.

Fifty and more years ago the concentration camp was the shearing point, the place where civilisation began to crack and the abyss appeared, the place where we were reminded that death has dominion over us. The ground has moved before and it will again but civilisation is as much a product of human will as is its threatened destruction. Bertolt Brecht, a very different playwright from Miller, once recalled seeing a picture of Tokyo destroyed by an earthquake. Most of the picture showed a scene of devastation but a few buildings remained. The caption underneath read: 'Steel stood'. Miller does not deny the devastation but he chooses to focus on the steel that stands, the steel in the characters who struggle to resist their own capacity for destruction. And for Miller the theatre, his theatre, has a role to play in this, and the writer a particular responsibility.

The slogan which Joshua Sobol saw painted on the wall of the Wilna ghetto read: 'There can be no theatre in a graveyard.' The remarkable thing, though, was that even here, on the edge of death, in this antechamber to the Holocaust, there *was* a theatre. It was founded in January 1942, and gave over a hundred performances before the ghetto was liquidated on 23 September 1943. Poetry, art, theatre, may not have saved a single Jew, but it evidently remained necessary, even to those about to die. It was a testimony to the power of creation at the very moment of destruction. Joshua Sobel wrote his play. Arthur Miller wrote his.

Miller has said that: 'what I got out of reports of the Holocaust was that memory was being destroyed forever'. But,

> if one looks at it from a distance, the Holocaust, dreadful and terrible and significant as it was, was only one part of a wider phenomenon. Count the people who have been killed in wars this century . . . Think of the memory that has gone. I often times think of that . . . Maybe there were six people among the tens of millions who could have saved the world . . . some philosopher who could have illuminated the whole universe . . . Maybe one's function, a writer's function, in part anyway, is to remember, to be the rememberer.

In a country in which history is 'like a fever that you pass through',[26] he insists on the central significance of a past whose truths we conspire in denying only at our peril. He does so because those truths are part of a reality that we must confront if our individual and collective lives are to render up a meaning we can embrace. In speaking of the audiences that have come to see his plays over the years, in so many different countries, he has said, 'I like to believe that the feeling that they have is that man is worth something. That you care about him that much is a miracle, I mean considering the numbers of ourselves that we have destroyed in the last century. I think art imputes value to human beings.'[27]

Miller's art has imputed value to human beings while acknowledging the terrible betrayals of which they are capable. He is a rememberer and, as Martin Buber once reminded us, 'to remember is to live'.[28]

— ✳ —

Playing for Time, despite the controversy which raged around it, proved highly successful and the stage version opened at the Studio Theatre in Washington in 1985.

It had taken him very little time to write the film adaptation but he had another major project in 1980, though one also set in the past. *The American Clock* would take him back to the 1930s and incorporate material from the first play he had written one spring vacation at the University of Michigan.

Inspired in part by Studs Terkel's interviews with those who had suffered through the Depression, it was offered to a new generation for whom this must seem little more than a historical footnote. To Miller, though, the past holds lessons not to be ignored. The prevailing mood in late seventies and early eighties America was one which seemed to sanction self-concern and self-interest. What had been called the 'me-decade' was giving way to a time when greed was offered as a value and social responsibility seen as aberrant to the American way. Miller was determined to remind people of a time when such assumptions had run full tilt into economic realities which had brought many close to destitution. He was telling his own story but he was also telling America's story. This was to be a personal play but it was also to be an epic play and therein lay the challenge to writer and director alike.

✳

22

'The American Clock'

Miller entered the 1980s with a play that looked back to the 1930s, to the era of the Depression and to his own first work, *No Villain*. He began work on it in the early 1970s but it was first produced at the Spoleto Festival's Dockside Theatre in Charleston, South Carolina, on 24 May 1980. It came to the Biltmore Theatre in New York on 20 November of the same year. It was not well received, or, rather, as Miller somewhat bitterly lamented, it closed after a few days, despite playing to nearly full houses, because the producer ran out of money to advertise its existence.

In 1984 it opened at the Mark Taper Forum, in a revised version and then, in 1986, at the National Theatre in London, where it was not only a considerable success but also found the style that had evaded its first American directors. Perhaps, too, the changed political situation (Thatcher was in power in England; Reagan in America) gave an edge to a play that recalled the fragility of the social world. In a decade in which Thatcher memorably insisted that there was no such thing as society, Miller chose both to celebrate a sense of shared experience and to recall the necessity for bedrock values, though not without an awareness of the problematics of summoning up a past reinvented by memory.

However, Thatcher's view was not so remote from that which had prevailed in America until the New Deal. As Miller recalled, in the context of a discussion of *The American Clock* with Studs Terkel, in 1980,

> people, in order to believe they were real Americans, believed they were responsible for their own fate . . . Remember, America had hardly participated in contemporary society. We had no Social Security at that time, no unemployment compensation, hardly any income tax. The average American could live and die without getting next to a government form . . . He had no personal connection with the government, so that he could deduce 'society' had the slightest effect on him. Today, since the New Deal, the relationship of the individual to society is altogether different.[1]

In a sense, the Depression marked the emergence of a new consciousness in America and it is that process that lies behind *The American Clock*, as the stories of scattered individuals begin to create the portrait of a country discovering the falsity of old paradigms. The individual, with no obligation beyond self-definition, no longer seemed credible in the context of economic collapse. It was the moment that America entered history, its former immunity finally

nullified. The consequence was a new sense of interdependence as those previously separated by space, class, race, found themselves confronted by forces
not susceptible to American nostrums to do with individual destiny and the
inevitability of progress.

Miller followed Terkel in listening to, and capturing, the voices of those
who experienced the Depression (as he himself had done for the Library of
Congress in 1941). In a kind of psychological and social equivalent of Roosevelt's
Works Progress Administration's Writers' Project, which created a state-by-state
Baedeker guide to America, he set himself to tell some of the overlapping stories
that constituted the master story of a culture caught in a moment of crisis. And
among those to whom he gave a voice was his own family, ghosts from a far
away time.

This is not, however, his *Long Day's Journey Into Night*, tense with the need
for retrospective forgiveness, born out of a desire to confront himself in re-
experiencing an unexamined past. It is, though, his acknowledgement of a pain
he was once too young to recognise for what it was, of a wound whose nature
only became fully apparent with time. There are ghosts in this play but they
return not to haunt but to explain, to speak their lives, to witness.

The fact of the Depression, of course, is not news but, fifty years on, the
sharp edge of the truths it exposed have dulled. Personal suffering and national
trauma have become the stuff of history, so much data on the turning pages of a
book. Miller, indeed, began his play in the middle of a boom, though evidence
of something else would not be too long in coming. He did not, he insisted,
'have a prophecy of doom' in mind, though the sight of a steadily rising market
left him with a faint feeling of alarm. He wished, he has said, to 'show how it
was and where we had come from . . . to give some sense of life as we lived it
when the clock was ticking every day'.[2]

Miller, like Terkel, sets himself to reanimate that world and if there is, perhaps,
an element of reconciliation with several generations of his own family, and
with his own former self – so confident once, in its analysis of the world,
so unforgiving of those who represented what he had once seen as defunct
values – then this is part of a larger negotiation with a time whose necessities
are not, perhaps, as remote from the present as they might seem.

The American Clock is history as a show, complete with tap dancing and
popular songs. It is a work whose own energies can seem at odds with the
entropic realities it recalls. We remember that era, of course, in drab, through
the black-and-white photographs of Walker Evans, quite as though that were the
only aesthetic for a time in which all colour had been bleached out by suffering
and neglect. Fixed in the mind is John Ford's version of *The Grapes of Wrath*, in
which gaunt characters found themselves inhabiting a monochrome country
lacking in charity. We have come to feel, indeed, that black and white is the sign
of authenticity and that, Hollywood aside, with its deliberately distracting whirl
of dancing figures, music and conspicuous wealth, the truth of that period is

best addressed through a kind of Puritan restraint. Miller offers another version of that time, catching the cadences of hope and despair, animating a past only inert because we view it as completed, sealed off from the present.

There is a dynamic to the characters as there is to a dramatic structure that leaps, through memory, from time to time, place to place. If it is a vaudeville, there is, perhaps, an element of John Osborne's *The Entertainer*, in which a failing music-hall entertainer performed in a faded theatre which represented the culture beyond its doors, an empire in a state of collapse. Certainly the mainspring of American society seemed to have broken. But Miller's portrait is not that of a society fading into historic irrelevance, but of one baffled by the failure of old models and unclear what might yet replace them.

And though the same unspoken ironies await his characters as had awaited Steinbeck's, in that the Depression would be ended by war and then by post-war boom (though many, including Miller, had expected a return to deprivation), a truth had been exposed about human affairs, about the supposed fixities of American life, which, to Miller, has never lost its relevance. As he was to say of his country, in the late 1990s, 'I don't think it ever got over the Depression because I don't think there is any real basic confidence in the economy. I think that there is a certain lingering expectation somewhere in the back of the brain that the whole thing can sink without a trace at a moment's notice.'[3] It is that conviction that gave birth to *The American Clock*.

When the stock market crashed Miller, unsurprisingly, at the age of fourteen, had felt immune. With a canny sense of impending disaster he had withdrawn his twelve dollars' savings from the bank and bought a second-hand bicycle, just one day before the Bank of the United States closed its doors. Personal and public experience seemed satisfyingly remote from one another. A week later, the bike was stolen and he rejoined the rest of humanity. The lesson was a salutary one: there is no immunity. His own family's decline offered daily evidence that there was no separate peace.

By the time of *The American Clock*'s London production, in 1986, the Depression was back in style, at least with Hollywood. Gaunt faces, calico dresses and the distant horizons of heartland America once again appeared on American cinema screens. Genuine social concern and a yearning for shared values had been so thoroughly evacuated from American public policy and rhetoric that the past was invoked to restore a lost balance. As America rediscovered the soup kitchen and rural bankruptcy, the relevance of a drab and painful decade, which nonetheless generated a sense of genuine community, seemed increasingly apparent. Now, however, the black-and-white images of *The Grapes of Wrath* or Walker Evans's still photographs had given way to full-colour wistfulness; a hard-grained immediacy had been exchanged for a richly textured sentimentality.

The American Clock predated most of those retro movies and did not share the then-current vogue for giving the past a patina of nostalgia, though in turning to his own past he was celebrating a private world that had slipped away from him, as well as a period that had the rough grain of reality. For him, it was above all a brutal decade which offered some brutal lessons. 'There's a romance going on about the Depression', he suggested,

> a conviction that because everyone was broke they were kinder to one another because they understood that everyone was in this together. Well, all I can remember was that I wanted to go to school [university] outside of New York because I thought that they were cutting each other's throats. There was idealism. There was radicalism. This gave a loftiness to some of the sentiments. But, underneath, it was murder. The structure of the world shook. What could you believe in?[4]

There is something almost Calvinist in his diagnosis of the period. The 1930s were the pay-off for the 1920s. The Jazz Age was to be expiated by the Depression, and the significance of the Depression is underlined in the first lines of *The American Clock*. It was a moment of national trauma and he saw something of the same mood around as the seventies moved into the eighties. Looking back at those earlier decades, he observed that

> America had been on some kind of obscene trip, looking to get rich at any cost right through the Twenties, at any cost to the spirit, and had elevated into power the men who could most easily lead that kind of a quest. And that aggrandizement is what led to the disaster of '29 and the Crash. They were sharks leading not only the economy but the spiritual side of the country. And there's a bit of that today, not only here but all over the world. There's never been a more materialistic moment since I've been around.[5]

And though these parallels are not pressed in *The American Clock* they were the context in which he turned back to a decade whose significance has never left him. They were also keenly felt by a man who lives in a small New England township and shares something of that area's stern moral vision, which charges the individual with full responsibility for his actions and sees all members of the community as responsible to one another and for one another. The town meeting is a reality in Roxbury; it is also a metaphor.

At a time when the word 'morality' was being highjacked by the right, he, like Thoreau, saw and sees no necessary connection between what is moral and what is subscribed to by the majority. De Tocqueville was right, he insisted, 'in this country there's a tyranny of the majority. People want to go with the crowd. It's what's wrong with the society; it's what's wrong with the theatre.' Those who accused him of un-Americanness could hardly have been wider of the mark. He is almost Jeffersonian in his insistence on the individual's moral responsibility for the state of his society. He even shows something of Jefferson's faith in the significance of specifically rural values. Speaking in his Roxbury home he explained: 'I have a lust for the country. There's still a functioning democracy there. People still meet and make decisions. You get an atmosphere in which an individual still counts for something. It's harder to tell a fool in the city. Out here you count for something.'[6]

Yet if *The American Clock* is, in one sense, an attempt to turn back 'the American clock . . . in search of those feelings that once ruled our lives and were stolen from us by time',[7] if it is a reminder of bedrock realities, it was written by a man who was now distant from the self-confident and perhaps self-righteous young man who had written his first plays in the depths of the Depression. Thus, if it was offered as a 'mural', an epic account, *The American Clock* was also to be a 'vaudeville', in which history would be staged as a series of acts, performances. His own family history was recuperated, a series of fragments shaken into form by a character looking back on his own past and that of others in a search for moral and social coherence.

But the world to which he seeks to give shape and meaning is in a state of collapse, flying apart under the impact of economic pressures. Private loyalties, national myths, social imperatives are in a state of dissolution. How to make sense of this crisis of being, more especially looking back, as he is, through time, with its power to distort, through the agency of memory, itself subject to deforming necessities?

As he has said, 'I've become more interested in what is real . . . the mystery of time. I could reduce the history of cultures to how they deal with time, memory, self-formation. We're all impersonators. We're all impersonating even ourselves. We've all become actors.'[8] *The American Clock* is Arthur Miller's attempt, fifty years on, to understand himself no less than the world in which he grew up and which, at the time, seemed merely contingent.

With the Depression the gods had spoken. Some kind of judgement had been made. Reality had changed and a hidden principle had revealed itself: 'It transformed the world from one in which there was an authority of some kind to one in which you were convinced that there was no one there, that there was no one running the store.'[9]

After the 1920s, a decade of hucksterism in which reality was defined by pieces of paper (share certificates, bonds, and paper money), suddenly you could hear the sound of America breaking apart. And Miller, at least in memory, as a 65-year-old playwright, creating a 50-year-old narrator, in turn recuperating an adolescent self, heard that sound as clearly as anyone, certainly as clearly as that poet of decline, F. Scott Fitzgerald. The thirties brought if not reality then necessity.

Writing four decades after the events he stages, and after the 1960s in which, once again, the real seemed to be held at arm's length, and in the middle of the seventies, which seemed totally self-absorbed, he felt the need to assert certain truths. His play identifies the potency of fictions celebrated as realities; it announces the breaking of a spurious authority. But while offering to capture the mood of a nation at a critical historical moment, it is, perhaps, at its most vital when it comes closest to Miller's own life, when memory is reshaped as image.

In part this is a public drama, which recreates a world of failed financiers, ruined businessmen and bankrupt farmers, a tapestry of social decline, the animation of defeat. But it is also Miller's personal odyssey in time as he travels back to his youth, pulling into some kind of shape events that had once seemed merely contingent. So, the long-ago stolen bicycle is transformed from social fact to social symbol. Worries about college tuition, once immediate and practical for the young Miller, whose hopes of Cornell and Ivy League education foundered on the reality of changes in family life he could, at first, barely comprehend, are now seen in the context of a national experience in which personal dilemmas render up a public meaning. And to sharpen the personal dimension, in the original American production the character that is a portrait of his own mother was actually played by his sister, herself an actress of some considerable reputation. Joan Copeland, indeed, recalls searching through her mother's sheet music for use in the show, while seated at her mother's piano.

In a sense, this personal dimension, as Miller enters his own play as a character and his sister performs her own mother, serves to underscore the performatic nature of experience to which Miller alluded. The playwright thus restages his life as he restages history. Both are reinterpreted for their dramatic coherence. Retrospect redeems the contingent, reasserts a lost order. There was a point, it appears, in seeming randomness. The stolen bicycle becomes charged with significance. A dispossessed farmer, whose life had lost its meaning, has that meaning restored in the context of dramatic hindsight.

If there is a didactic intent, as the past is summoned as witness before the court of the present, that past has to be given the grace of form. At the same time, though, life as art, life as performance, potentially deflects ethics into aesthetics. The struggle is to sustain a sense of rooted values in the context of constructed selves and history seen as overlapping stories.

The play opens with a stage direction that indicates the breadth of his intent. The few pieces of furniture required are to be carried on by the actors, who thereby might appear in part to construct the play in which they are to appear. They exist, however, within the memory and imagination of the central character, Lee, a version of the playwright himself.

The audience is to have 'an impression of a surrounding vastness ... as though the whole country were really the setting, even as the intimacy of certain scenes is provided for. The background can be sky, clouds, space itself, or an impression of the United States' geography.'[10] The space, then, is simultaneously that of the mind that recalls and that of the country which it summons into being. It is also the space in which theatre is presented, the bare stage to be filled by the actions which constitute the meaning. The theatre director Richard Eyre has said that 'Plays are about the spaces in between the spoken word, as much as about speech itself; about how people react as much as they react. The playwright has to balance revelation against concealment, has to animate character through action rather than description.'[11]

Miller's stage, in *The American Clock*, offers a *bricolage*, a mosaic, a series of disparate actions whose connections are no less real for being unvoiced. At one moment the space expands to encompass events happening half a continent away; at the next it narrows to explore the private drama of a family in Brooklyn coming to terms with the death of dreams. Time, similarly, expands and contracts. Language, meanwhile, as Eyre suggests, is as much concerned with concealment as revelation, as characters struggle to hold painful truths at bay. When the stock market begins to collapse there are those who believe that rhetoric alone will stem the tide. If the boom had been unreal then perhaps the crash was much the same. The central character 'waited . . . for the dream to come back', like everybody else. After all, for a decade 'they believed in the most important thing of all – that nothing is real! That if it was Monday and you wanted it to be Friday, and enough people could be made to believe it *was* Friday – then by God it was Friday!' (10). This, after all, is not a play about cynics but about believers who suddenly lost their faith and with it their sense of themselves. Speaking at the end of the 1990s, Miller remarked that,

> When I was doing *The American Clock* I did some research, just to remind myself of what it was like. So I went back through the New York Public Library and got out some issues of the *New York Times* of those weeks and months. In one article, a news story on the front page, a couple of reporters had gone out and interviewed people; they estimated that about a hundred and fifty thousand people in New York City who, a year before, had had good jobs, now were not only unemployed . . . but considered they would never work again because of the psychological trauma that was the impact of the Depression. See, it was not just the money. This is what is important about it. It is the illusion. These people were profoundly believers in the American dream and, when they stopped working, the day the money stopped, their identity was gone. They did not know who the hell they were.[12]

The play, then, deals with individuals whose lives had been drained of purpose and direction, living in a country that suffers from a similar condition. The two stories, the interconnecting crises, are braided together, much as John Dos Passos created his *USA* by interleaving fiction, documentary, biography. Here, an actual speech by Roosevelt is sandwiched between a fictional account of a southern sheriff trading with a black cook and a dramatised version of Miller's actual family. In the same way different rhetorics are pitched against one another, the self-conscious polemic of the politician, the assured simplicities of Marxist dialectics, the hysterical tone of a woman on the verge of collapse, the desperate pleading of the poor and destitute. Miller tries to capture the sound of an America negotiating between despair and hope, no longer confident of its own voice, its own discourse of progress.

And in a play punctuated by music, played by an increasingly desperate Rose, on a piano eventually to be taken from her, Miller provides not only a visual representation of a catastrophe which extends to all classes and races, across the country, but the dissonance that lies behind false harmonies. The sentimental songs, like the mantras of politicians, are so much whistling in the dark.

Yet there is an underlying harmony. It is precisely that created by Miller himself as he insists on identifying those connections that survive America's broken promises, connections glimpsed in individual gestures (a young woman feeds a starving man with milk from a baby's bottle, surely an implied reference to the final scene in *The Grapes of Wrath*; poor and rich side by side in a relief office). If there is something of the vaudeville about the structure of *The American Clock*, which works by a series of fragmented scenes, then, there is also, perhaps, something of a folk opera about it as well, as voices are blended in a work in which melodrama is a product of character placed under extreme pressure.

The American Clock is a diorama painted on the memory but why, except for the renewed relevance, the sudden urgency of recall? For Lee Baum, narrator and participant, the past is not some distant country but a warning. His first speech is an echo of Miller's own frequently expressed belief that there have only been two truly national disasters, 'Not the first or second World Wars, Vietnam or even the Revolution. Only the Civil War and the Great Depression touched nearly everyone wherever they lived and whatever their social class.' And the reason for contemplating the latter? 'Personally, I believe that deep down we are still afraid that suddenly, without warning, it may all fall apart again. And that this fear, in ways we are rarely conscious of, still underlies every . . .' (5). He breaks off as another figure enters the stage, but we have been offered the key.

He and we look back on the past through the Vietnam War, through renewed economic uncertainty, through decades of insecurity born out of geopolitics no less than of personal experiences of dissolution. For here is a man in his fifties who contemplates his younger self, looking to revisit a moment when the world tilted suddenly on its axis and all that was certain became suddenly unsure.

He is joined by Arthur Robertson, a man now in his seventies, a corporate leader, who had thirty years before heard the first tremor of the approaching quake and withdrawn from the stock market and the banks. A sceptic then, he is now himself a believer: 'I don't think that kind of collapse is really possible again' (5). Nonetheless, he is ready to 'get out' if necessary, acknowledging Lee's sense that 'there is a deep fear that the whole thing can cave in and that nothing is really under control' (6). Why else does the play exist? Why else do these two men look back to a past that they now enter?

That past is, in a detailed way, Arthur Miller's. Indeed, in many ways this seems to be a play in which he comes to terms with his own ghosts, seeks to understand his own early self, the family he loved but with whom he was in contention. The man who had been called before the House Un-American Activities Committee and disavowed his early faith, though not his friends, now revisits the past in which his political loyalties had been forged. *The American Clock* is an exploration of a society at the moment of crack-up but the route into that world is through autobiography.

Lee Baum is Miller, child of a rich family, employing a maid and a chauffeur, whose father has borrowed to invest in the stock market. The most upsetting evidence of change for the teenager, as once for Miller, is that his mother suddenly bobs her hair. Then, the Crash suddenly sends them from their eleven-room Manhattan apartment out to Brooklyn, where their relatives live and where their horizons rapidly shrink. Space closes down. Lee shares a bedroom with his grandfather, who feels he no longer has room to store his clothes.

Even the countryside, that was then Brooklyn, begins to shrink as apartment houses close in, an image, of course, familiar from *Death of a Salesman*. The expansive future is suddenly foreshortened. College plans collapse. Lee begins to consider a career working with his hands, as did Miller. He is sent, as Miller was sent, to the pawnbrokers, carrying his mother's jewels in a paper bag. And that mother, Rose, who once had a scholarship to university but was forced into marriage, who once lived a life of ease and now performs unaccustomed housework, is plainly Miller's own.

We see her, as Miller observed his own mother, wrestle with the fact of her husband's failure, guilty at what she sees as a betrayal of her son's hopes, playing cards to make pin money and stave off the hysteria which constantly threatens. Fifty years on Miller retraces his steps in an effort not only to understand the times that made him and the country what it became, but to understand those whose lives were either closed to him or, as a young man wrapped up in his own needs and ambitions, ignored as his new-found radicalism found him at odds with those whose love for him had seemed, for a while, beside the point.

If Rose is clearly offered as a portrait of his mother, then Moe, named for an uncle, is a portrait of his father, whose own decline had, paradoxically, ceded authority to a son whose judgements had more to do with his sense of revolutionary change than private anguish. Moe, like Isadore, had come over from Europe as a child, and became a success only to lose it all, in part, Rose, like Augusta Miller, insists because he felt obliged to support a number of his relatives. He is now right-wing and baffled as his world collapses minute by minute.

Meanwhile, somewhere in the distance, another threat begins, as news of the rise of Hitler impinges on this Jewish family, the grandfather's response being exactly that of Miller's as he watches amazed at the collapse of civility in a country he regards as the epitome of culture.

The poor turn up on their doorstep, as Miller has described them doing on his own. Indeed he has talked of the family suspecting that some secret sign must be chalked on the wall or sidewalk to guide them there. When Lee's bicycle is stolen he says, in retrospect, 'I guess that's when I knew there was a system' (28), or if not a system then a logic that defied understanding but which drew everyone into its heart.

In *The American Clock* Miller replays in detail his actual visit to the relief office with his father, in which the two were required to act out mutual hostility in order to convince the official that he was not living at home and could thus qualify for relief and hence the Works Progress Administration programme. Lee describes his presence, as a reporter, at the sit-down strike at the Ford plant in Fort Michigan, which Miller himself had covered for the *Michigan Daily*. His grandfather, like Miller's own, calls for the cancelling of elections, having swung from opposition to Roosevelt to the suggestion that he might be made king. And, again like Miller's own grandfather, he suggests that Lee should go to Russia, the new land of opportunity.

It is as though Miller has chosen to lay the grid of his personal life over the social history of the time, finding in his own experience a map to the country that is the past, a country, moreover, in which the fixed points seemed to have been erased. Richard Eyre, preparing to direct *King Lear*, and feeling somewhat intimidated, sought advice from Peter Brook.' It seemed unapproachable, he said, until you start to think about it as a play about a family. Oh yes of course, I said. There's a Persian proverb: the way in is through the front door, why is it that no one uses it? Exactly, said Peter – who had probably coined the proverb in the first place' (22).

Forty-five years earlier the family had been Miller's way into the Depression and so it is here. It is the front door through which he chooses to enter an experience which can seem opaque and distant if it is presented as no more than an animated history, a collage of public scenes. The Baum family is the prism through which he chooses to view a national trauma. But, as he insisted, 'I've attempted a play about more than just a family, about forces bigger than simply overheard voices in the dark. It's the story of the United States talking to itself.'[13]

Miller's interest was in part a formal one. As he has remarked, he was 'fascinated by the idea of having an objective view of society and running through it, as a counter-motif, the story of a family'.[14] Speaking to Studs Terkel, he elaborated his schema for the play:

> There's an attempt here to do two things at the same time, which is the nature of a mural. Rivera's and Sequieros's in Mexico are prime examples. Large Renaissance paintings are in that order. When you look close at any face, it may turn out to be a real person's. When you step away, you see the whole pattern, the grand movement. It's fundamentally a picture of many

people interacting with each other and with the heavens. I don't care for a theater that is absolutely personal and has no resonance beyond that.'[15]

The central challenge was to 'unify the two elements, objective and subjective, epic and psychological',[16] reflecting his sense that the Depression gave birth for the first time to a new sense of common consciousness and to this end his revisions consisted in part of moving the scenes around to arrive at the right sense of balance.

The next scene takes us into a speakeasy as financiers calculate the extent and speed of their ruin and discuss the suicide of one of their number, plunging down literally, as they do figuratively, from the heights to which they have aspired. From there, by way of the Baum family home, we are in the midwest, as an auctioneer, backed by a judge and deputies, seeks to dispose of the assets of a farmer whose loans have been called in by the banks, only to be faced by open revolt.

This momentary victory, however, is dissolved in the next scene as the farmer, now starving, presents himself at the Baum family front door in search of food. The producer of food now begs for it in a society in which everything is reversed. As Lee observes, 'fellows with advanced degrees were out on the block throwing footballs around all day', while Robertson notes that it was the American Banking Association that 'asked the new Administration to nationalise the banks' (38).

Miller reaches back to his 1930s play *No Villain* for another element of his plot, as Lee's aunt tries to persuade her son to marry the daughter of a neighbour and thus relieve them all of their financial worries. In that early play, elaborated through several versions, the incident became a central theme. Here it is no more than a quotation. But this incident, too, went back not simply to an earlier play but an earlier experience. *The American Clock* is as close to an autobiographical play as Miller has written.

When he introduces a scene in which the father is forced to borrow money from his son for the subway fare, this comes not merely from the story he wrote at the age of seventeen, or that which he wrote on leaving university in 1938, about a suicidal salesman, but from his own experience. He has certainly spoken movingly of his sense that under the pressure of the Depression his father had lost his authority in the house:

> My mother was smart enough to understand that it was not his doing; but the frustration was so great that she could not help blaming him anyway. She blamed him and pitied him at the same time. It is one thing when everything is going great, and both people are feeling absolutely secure . . . But when suddenly they do not know from one week to the next where the money is going to come from, the recrimination begins and a loss of respect, loss of mutual toleration.[17]

This dissolution is both the subject and the method of a play whose stylistic fragmentations reproduce its own subject. It is a broken narrative in which private and public seem juxtaposed, except that each is so thoroughly infiltrated with the other that the distinction cannot hold. Private lives – sex, marriage, family relationships – all bear the impress of public events, as public events are expressions of private needs. There is no private space not invaded by the realities of social entropy, no social space that is not a projection of personal anguish. Rhetoric alone seems impervious to human necessities quite as if language had magical powers of denial. For the National Theatre production, in 1986, Miller had produced a new text, or, rather, an older one, for the truth is that, as with *The Archbishop's Ceiling*, he had been persuaded to modify his first version. As he has explained,

> I felt the happy sadness of knowing that my original impulse had been correct . . . but as had happened more than once before, in the American production I had not had the luck to fall in with people sufficiently at ease with psychopolitical themes to set them in a theatrical style, a challenge more often tackled in the British theatre. I had described the play as a 'mural' of American society . . . but the very word *society* is death on Broadway, and . . . I had hopelessly given way and reshaped a play for what I had come to think of as the Frightened Theatre . . . I had felt despairingly alone then and was persuaded to personalize what should have been allowed its original epic impulse, its concentration on the collapse of a society.
>
> (*T*.586–7)

He, perhaps, goes a step too far in this explanation in that the strength of the play lies precisely in its intercutting between, its interfolding of, the personal and the epic. In particular, Miller introduced the figure of the President-elect of General Electric who rebels, suddenly, because he cannot face the idea of America changing from a country of firms, independent businesses, to one of giant corporations. The character embodies a process but is also splendidly individualistic, perhaps hardly surprisingly so since he had a real-life model, a near-neighbour of Miller's. Played by a tap-dancing David Schofield, he became a high point of a production which also featured a jazz band, which was filled with music and whose finale had been changed.

Its director, Peter Wood, had been so nervous about this last change that he had still not had the nerve to tell the playwright as he entered the theatre. The new ending recapitulated the ensuing history that linked the Depression to the mid1980s and was greatly liked by Miller. In Peter Woods's production there was more music than in the original. The action was choreographed, narrative turned into action, actors doubled and trebled, thereby forging further links between those from different backgrounds united, briefly, by their situation.

These are all characters transformed by the shock of the Depression. Their identities have been eroded, their social roles abandoned. The past and future seem to breed nothing but irony. They are nervous, fretful, hysterical, doggedly determined. In the context of a play that reaches towards the epic, they are simplified in the sense that a Dickens character can sound a single note in a social symphony. Such simplification, though, is itself a product of trauma. They are hungry. Everything else is winnowed out. They are terrified of debt. They trade their past, their former beliefs, their hopes for the necessities of the moment. They are in survival mode. Denial, desperate hope, cynicism, anger, an unfocused sense of loss, stand in place of ambiguity and complexity. Time has run out. Everything is urgent. The clock is ticking.

There is something of the thirties about the structure of the play, an Odets-style family drama embedded in a social play which offers cameo portraits of an America in which the lives of the rich and the poor momentarily coincide. And it is a play which, for all its images of privation, its staging of the gaps which open up between those normally united by family ties or social obligations, still reflects something of the idealism and even optimism of the period. Miller deliberately chooses to conclude it with the same upbeat ending characteristic of the period.

It is a play that seems to offer some kind of benediction in its suggestion that, ultimately, the crisis returned America to itself, Roosevelt becoming a genuine agency of the general will. But, then, as Miller has said, it is ultimately about those who survived, albeit changed by a new knowledge. The story is, after all, told by a survivor, by the industrialist who withdrew from the unreality of the market but, more importantly, by Lee, the alter ego of the playwright himself. Miller is the survivor and this his testimony to a vitality not sapped by the Depression, to the possibility of learning from the past.

The disjunction between what he called 'a smiling and extroverted style' (*T*.588) and the subject matter of decline and loss did create ironies, but he wished to leave his audiences, 'along with the textures of a massive social and human tragedy, a renewed awareness of the American's improvisational strength, his almost subliminal faith that things can and must be made to work out. In a word, the feel of the energy of a democracy. But the question of ultimate survival must remain hanging unanswered in the air' (*T*. 588).

It is interesting to place that testimony to his faith in America alongside his similar statement before the House Un-American Activities Committee, which, at the time, had seemed forced, a product of the near intolerable pressure placed on him. The fact is, though, that Miller has always written out of a commitment to American values. It is the distortion of those values, their betrayal, that has concerned him. Joe Keller defends himself by reference to his sense of the necessities of business, what he sees as the legitimate demands of the family, two foundations, as it seems to him, of the American way. He is forgetful of a more fundamental human contract and national idealism which he thereby denies. Willy Loman has 'the wrong dream', but by definition there is a right one. So, too, with character after character. Miller's plays are never restricted to America in their implications but he is himself a true believer in national principles which he may see abrogated but in which he places his own faith. The play, after all, is called *The American Clock*.

America's momentum had seemed unstoppable. Its investment in the future was such that its myths were always of becoming, of amelioration, of unambiguous progress. Then the clock stopped and with that came the more important knowledge that it could stop. As Miller has said, 'there is a clock running on all civilisations. There is a beginning and an end. What is the hour? That is the question.'[18] The job of the artist, he has said, is to remind people of this question and what they would rather forget. *The American Clock* was written in the 1970s, when President Carter was, in Miller's view, offering empty assurances, and first performed in Reagan's America, which seemed willing to tolerate and re-enact the conditions of the Depression. Like all Miller's apparently historical plays, it was provoked by his conviction that it spoke not simply of the past but to the present.

The National Theatre's production seemed to him finally to have given his play its full theatrical life: 'I at last heard the right kind of straightforward epic expressiveness, joyful and celebratory rather than abashed and veiled . . . In this antic yet thematically precise spirit, accompanied by some forty songs out of the period, the show managed to convey the *seriousness* of the disaster that the Great Depression was, and at the same time its human heart.'[19] To him, the style of the production had 'fused emotion and conscious awareness, overt intention and subjective feeling', which had been his intent when he first sat down to write it.

It was, indeed, a memorable production that seemed to capture precisely that blend of the personal and the social, the despairing and the redemptive, which, for Miller, was the essence of a period in which America came face to face with the collapse of its utopian principles and began the task of accommodating itself to the fact of its loss of some fundamental immunity.

— ✳ —

Miller had begun work on *The American Clock* in the early 1970s. Its failure was one of many blows he suffered in the last three decades of the century. The following year he travelled to Paris where two of his plays (*A View from the Bridge* and *Incident at Vichy*) were running, and then to Venezuela, a trip which, along with his visit to Colombia in 1982, would eventually make its way into *Resurrection Blues*. He was also at work on *The Ride Down Mount Morgan* which would not be finished for another decade. Whatever his problem with new works, however, his older plays continued to be produced – *All My Sons* in London and *A View from the Bridge* at the Long Wharf in New Haven. It was at this time, too, that Dustin Hoffman signed up for the production of *Death of a Salesman* that would follow in 1984.

In 1982 he took part in an anti-nuclear march and began working on a novella set in Haiti that would eventually appear in 2004. He also wrote a play in support of Vaclav Havel, called *The Havel Deal*, a satirical piece in which a communist functionary proposes the arbitrary arrest of Western writers (including Miller) to balance the number of those under arrest in Czechoslovakia.

Also in 1982, he agreed to direct two of his own one-act plays at the Long Wharf Theatre. These went under the unprepossessing title *Two by A.M.* and featured Christine Lahti and Charles Cioffi. The production was successful with audiences but again not with the critics. Two later one-acts, *Danger: Memory!* scarcely fared any better. Later produced in England, however, they were enthusiastically received.

✳

23

The one-act plays: 'Two-Way Mirror' and 'Danger: Memory!'

Miller opened *Two by A.M.* at the Long Wharf Theatre in New Haven in 1982. It was less than a triumph. For its British publication I proposed *Two-Way Mirror*, to reflect, if that is the right word, the fluctuating realities within the plays, the change of perspective as a two-way mirror, with a simple alteration of lighting, turns from clear glass to mirror, from a view of the other to a view of the self. The plays, which can be performed separately or, if together, in any order (at the Young Vic they alternated), showed the extent to which the problematic nature of the real had moved to the centre of his concern. Consider the note that he wrote for the published version of *Elegy for a Lady*, one part of the diptych which is *Two-Way Mirror*:

> It isn't always clear exactly where one stands in psychic space when grief passes up through the body into the mind. To be at once the observer and observed is a split awareness that most people know; but what of the grieved-for stranger, the other who is 'not-me'? – Doesn't it sometimes seem as though he or she is not merely outside oneself but also within and seeing outward through one's own eyes at the same time that he or she is being seen?
>   There is an anguish, based on desire impossible to realize, that is so unrequited, and therefore so intense, that it tends to fuse all people into one person in a so-to-speak spectral unity, a personification which seems to reflect and clarify these longings and may even reply to them when in the ordinary world of 'I' and 'You' they cannot even be spoken aloud. Nor is this really so strange when one recalls how much of each of us is imagined by the other, how we create one another even as we actually speak and actually touch.[1]

This, to say the least, is not the sturdy realist pictured by so many. The prose style of the above remarks itself reflects something of the complexities to be found in a printed text only eighteen pages long.

Elegy for a Lady, like its companion piece *Some Kind of Love Story*, features only two characters. It takes place in what appears to be a boutique, though this is suggested only by a sweater draped over a bust, a necklace over another, 'a garter on an upturned plastic thigh, a watch on an upturned arm, a knitted cap and muffler on a plastic head' (3). The store 'consists of its elements without the walls, the fragments seeming to be suspended in space' (3). The fragmented body parts, meanwhile, are to be echoed in characters who seem to exist only through the passions that dominate them. This is as much an interior as an exterior landscape. In the background, meanwhile, coming and going, is music that has what Miller calls 'a fine, distant fragility, a simple theme, repeated – like unresolved grief', though the loss that is grieved for is by no means clear.

The man 'appears' in a beam of light, almost as though the light summons him into being; a woman is 'discovered', motionless, in 'passive thought', as though waiting to be animated, waiting for a story to claim her. The man announces that he wishes to buy something for a dying woman, a statement that seems more problematic, along with his apparent certainties, as the play proceeeds. She, apparently, is to die by the end of the month, but it soon transpires that he infers this from nothing more than the fact that she anticipates a 'big day' (15). Thus, his assurance that she is to have an operation for cancer in ten days is withdrawn under her questioning as he confesses that her tumour was benign and was removed a year before. Something is surely dying, but not necessarily the woman.

He is a married man and older than the supposedly dying woman, who has just turned thirty. Yet there is a vagueness in his descriptions that seems at odds with the apparent intensity of his emotions. Neither he nor she, it appears, can remember whether they have known one another for two or three years. Indeed, she is characterised by a number of negatives.

She cannot remember; she cannot stay on any subject for long; she is not religious. In the process of summoning her to mind he dissolves her identity as he suspects she may wish him 'to disappear' (6). Indeed, he admits that neither has told anyone of the existence of the other. She will not answer the phone. She will not see him. She retreats from him. She is never home. By the same token, in trying to decide what gift he can give her he rejects every suggestion; so, not spring flowers, not cut flowers, not a plant, not a book, not a kerchief, not a bandanna, not a scarf, not a negligée, not anything, indeed, so definite that it will have a restrictive meaning: 'every single thing makes some kind of statement that is simply ... not right' (8). Indeed, 'absolutely nothing is right' (8). He wants something that 'doesn't necessarily *say* anything' (11).

The negatives pile up until the absent woman is defined more by what she is not than what she is. If she even momentarily begins to assume a definable characteristic, to assume a coherent outline, that is immediately negated and she is deconstructed: she shows 'a really cool nerve right up to the moment she flies to pieces' (12). Ironically, he insists that they never talk of 'negative things', but nonetheless contemplates the possibility that 'the whole thing really doesn't amount to anything very much' (11). Indeed, if they are joined by anything it is their mutual 'uncommitment' (17).

The absent woman is, at thirty, at her apogee, able to stare down on her youth and her dying at the same time. Dying, therefore, is introduced less as present fact than as present apprehension of future inevitability. If the woman is dying, then, so are we all. The grief may be for her future rather than her present and, if for her future, then for his too. For him, looking round the store, everything suggests the end, his end as well as hers. Does she, in fact, exist? For when he observes that 'these things are usually a case of loving yourself and wanting someone else to confirm it' (14), he is, perhaps, describing the process whereby he has called the absent woman and, perhaps, the Proprietress (now surely merged with her) into existence in order to still his own fears, strengthen his own threatened ego.

She does, it seems, have a counterpart in that the Proprietress is 'just about her age' (9). The woman only liked to be seen when she was well dressed, as the Proprietress is described as appearing, 'wearing a white silk blouse and a light beige skirt and high heeled shoes' (3). When talk is of cancer she presses her own abdomen and says, unprompted by any detail from him, that 'the thought of disfigurement is terrible' (10). When he describes the woman as having a throaty, almost vulgar laugh, slapping her thigh like a hick comedian, the Proprietress bursts into just such laughter and slaps her own thigh. The woman is described as being successful; so, too, is the Proprietress. He seemingly intuits the Proprietress's desire for children on the basis of no apparent evidence, quite as if he already knew her. Indeed, in what is perhaps a slip of the tongue, he refers to her as 'dear', as she similarly claims a sudden intimacy: 'I never condemn anyone; you know that' (18). How should he 'know that' unless they are intimately involved with one another? 'You were one of her friends', the Proprietress suggests, before, a moment later, projecting that interpretation onto the woman she supposedly does not know: 'why not believe her – you were . . . simply one of her friends' (19).

Is she, then, the woman he describes, as she begins, passionately, to represent a woman of whom she supposedly knows nothing, and as they assume a sudden intimacy in their conversation? Certainly, Miller instructs, 'she embraces him, her body pressed to his, an immense longing in it and a sense of a last embrace . . . presses his face to hers, they kiss . . . With a new cry of farewell' (20). The play ends with the man finally selecting a present, a watch on a gold chain, and placing it around the neck of the Proprietress. 'You never said her name', she remarks, to which he replies, 'You never said yours', and 'On each of their faces a grin spreads – of deep familiarity.'

This, it appears, has been a game. Two intimates meet as strangers. By externalising their fears they reconcile themselves, seal the rifts between them. Two separate selves come together and part, having touched a truth that once eluded them. And yet, is it necessarily that clear? Could it not be that both women are merely the objectification of his thoughts? For the play ends as the lights begin to lower, the man moving away from the setting and staring ahead. Woman and boutique both go dark and vanish before he strolls away alone, quite as if their existence is of a second order, as if they had been summoned and were now dismissed, having served whatever psychic needs that justified their coming into his mind. Or was he, perhaps, the personification of her need, an imaginative projection encountered in a place defined by memory and desire?

Miller's note, quoted above, indicates some of the ambiguity with which he wished to flood the text, as he speaks of a doubleness of vision, of being simultaneously within and without, of the self and the other potentially occupying the same space. But this is not entirely new to his work.

There is a sense, for example, in *Death of a Salesman*, *After the Fall* and *The American Clock*, that the characters are projections of a central sensibility, embodiments of guilt, fear, anxieties that earth themselves through memory. The real comes to us through a mediating imagination. But, then, as Miller suggests, this is how we do in fact apprehend the world. We inhabit a post-Heisenberg universe in which the act of observation is acknowledged to transform the thing observed. Others, in what we like to call real life, surely exist in plays of their own devising, obligingly enacting supporting roles, fortifying or challenging our psyches, in part to order. They enter and exit the stage of our minds, their lines and actions to be interpreted in terms of our own necessities. And when they leave us they cease, for a while, to exist, to be summoned, in memory, and on cue, when we have need of justification, consolation, confirmation of our own existence.

As Miller suggests, the very act of communication invents the object of that communication. *Elegy for a Lady* is thus a paradigm of a familiar process. It is simultaneously a celebration of the imagination and a confession of its limits. It is also, perhaps, offered as a portrait of the writer who invents a world whose existence is contingent, who summons forth characters only to reliquish them again. There is, clearly, a metatheatrical dimension to *Elegy for a Lady* as a character is animated by the stage lights and leaves the stage as they fade again.

For Miller, the play takes place 'in the space between the mind and what it imagines'.[2] He might have said the same of *Salesman* or *After the Fall*, and, indeed, did. It takes place outside of time. Its location is the mind. Of its companion piece, *Some Kind of Love Story*, he remarked that 'it concerns the question of how we believe truth, how one is forced by circumstance to believe what you are only sure is not too easily demonstrated as false'.[3]

Some Kind of Love Story takes us through the same mirror for, as Miller has suggested, in 'both the unreal is an agony to be striven against and, at the same time, accepted as life's condition'.[4] This time he presents what appears to be a genre piece, and the film subsequently based on it, *Everybody Wins*, intensifies this sense. The play centres on two characters, Tom O'Toole, a detective investigating a crime, and Angela, a woman who may or may not hold the key to that investigation. A third character, Angela's husband, remains unseen in the kitchenette, 'lip-readin' his racin' form' (25).

In other words we appear to be moving in the world of crime fiction, in which evidence, logical deduction, rational process will triumph over anarchy.

The process of the play, we can reasonably expect, will be coterminous with the gradual revelation of the reality of the event at its centre, an event slowly reconstituted by Socratic dialogue. The frustration of this expectation, the drip-by-drip corrosion of a sense of the real, is what makes this a fit companion to a play from which it otherwise differs, in style, in language and in tone.

The action takes place in Angela's bedroom, garishly decorated, the bed itself being in what Miller calls Grand Rapids Baroque style. The floor is covered with discarded clothes. Angela herself sits, barely visible, on the bed as Tom enters, wearing the narrow-brimmed hat and raincoat of the genre detective. Though the play takes place in the present, he seems like a quotation from another era. His first question, 'Are we decent?' (25), has an irony which casts a shadow forward over the play, for at stake is both the question of the decency, or otherwise, of the society beyond this bedroom in an American city, and the decency of the relationship between two people brought together by something more than the need to resolve the mystery of a crime.

The fact is that Tom and Angela have been lovers, though both are married. Their marriages are fragile. Angela is beaten by her husband while Tom confesses to talk of separation. Their affair seems over. They are, ostensibly, brought together only because she may have the information he needs. The air of flirtation between them is, hence, ambiguous. Is he drawn to her because of the case or is the case the excuse to be drawn to her? Does she withhold the information for fear or to retain her grasp on him?

He tries to build his case from fragments, to infer the whole from the part. But the real is not only elusive, it is various, for Angela, based on an actual figure from a crime case in which Miller was momentarily involved, exhibits multiple personalities, suddenly transforming herself before falling into a sleep. She is Angela, once involved with the Mob, then Leontine, 'a house whore. Horrendous vulgarity' (35), then Emily, an eight-year-old girl, and then Renata. Under pressure, her character fragments. But, then, as Tom remarks, 'sometimes you got to go to crazy people for the facts, though . . . maybe facts are what's making them crazy' (36–7).

What is making her crazy at the moment is that she feels she is being followed by police cruisers. At first Tom assumes this is no more than illusion, a device to hold his attention or a projection of her fear. But at the end he, too, sees them. There is, then, a reality and little by little Angela reveals the truth of the crime he has been investigating for so long, a truth she has always known but refused to tell. This is in part to protect someone else, in part for fear of losing the man who seeks a truth which is not the one to which she wishes he would commit himself.

At stake is the fate of Felix Epstein, who has spent five years in prison for a crime he did not commit. Slowly she explains what happened. A drugs dealer had been murdered by one of his confederates, a crime concealed because prosecutor and police were involved. Felix was no more than a convenient scapegoat. Angela has the proof in the form of letters but still refuses to reveal them. The story must continue. She is Scheherazade keeping herself alive by spinning the story. She and Tom must meet again.

The point of *Some Kind of Love Story* does not lie in the solution to a crime. It is in fact not genre fiction. It is a debate about the nature of the real and how that reality is perceived, constructed, used. Miller is, perhaps, making a social, even a political point. Thus Tom observes that 'somewhere way upstream the corruption is poisoning the water and making us all a little crazy' (63). That is to say, we all inhabit a world in which the real is carefully deformed to serve other interests than our own. John Proctor was the citizen of a culture in which witches were declared real, as Miller was of a society that declared him Un-American for exercising his American rights.

Beyond that, though, is the question of reality itself. For Tom, the time has come to 'stop looking for some red tag that says "Real" on it . . . If it's real for me then that's the last question I can ask, right?' (62). Right or wrong, he seems to be acknowledging the extent to which the subjective operates as a governing principle. Angela contains different personalities, but so, surely, do those who do not obligingly precipitate them out quite so readily. There is a truth to the crime, a reality. A man did die. Someone killed him. But the meaning of those events depends upon the lives of those who claim their relevance. For Angela and Tom it is one story inside another story. For five years the events of a tawdry murder have been transformed into something else, a relationship itself part real and part fantasy. As Miller has said, 'In both plays the objective world grows dim and distant as reality seems to consist wholly or partly of what the characters' needs require it to be, leaving them with the anguish of having to make decisions that they know are based on illusion and the power of desire' (*T*.590).

Some Kind of Love Story, radically rewritten, was later made into a film, *Everybody Wins* (eventually renamed *Almost Everybody Wins* on publication in the fifth volume of Methuen's collection of his works). In the original screenplay something of the subtlety of the original remained: certainly, Angela's unstable personality. However, in the hands of Hollywood it slid, seemingly inevitably, towards an unambiguous realism. Such ambiguity as survived was presented as no more than a function of character or misread experience. As Miller observed, 'In the course of production Angela's character lost its various personas and her fantastic quality and she ended up merely a terrified woman who dares not reveal what she knows about a frightful murder.'[5]

Miller has always been deeply suspicious of Hollywood, a stance only modified by the effective version of *The Crucible*. The primary reason seems to lie in its relegation of language to a subordinate role, in a literalism that bleeds the energy out of metaphor. Words give way to images which carry the authority of the real. While insisting that the distinction is not necessarily one of quality but of 'aesthetic feeling, of timbre and tissue',[6] he plainly does see screenwriting as a second-order activity, stripping him not merely of control (the writer's function being primary in the theatre and subordinate in the world of film) but of the tools of his craft.

The writer necessarily becomes self-effacing, and if he had any doubts in that direction Miller was reminded of it by his role in the production hierarchy. The script became a 'libretto for camera'. It was 'an equivalent to the words in a cartoon balloon or the titles sometimes given photographs or paintings' (vii). This is hardly the comment of a man neutral as to the cinema. The script may indicate its own juxtapositions, its own narrative flow, but the cinematographer, the director, the editor finally determine how a story is to be told and hence what that story is.

Interestingly, this single one-act drama, when published, first as play and then as screenplay, prompted, by way of introductions, first an essay on the nature of realism and then one on the nature of film language. It is as though it crystallised a number of Miller's concerns, though there was a considerable gulf between script, film and publication. The sensitivity about realism came from his frustration at so persistently being seen as a realistic playwright, a term whose ambiguities he, anyway, wished to explode. He was, in his own mind, an essentially poetic, deeply metaphoric writer who had found himself in a theatre resistant to such, particularly on Broadway, which he continued to think of as his natural home, despite its many deficiencies.

The attraction of film lies in the images it projects, images whose sheer size dominate the imagination, relieved thereby of its function. Each image replaces that which went before as though narrative momentum were itself a value, as if plot, indeed, had primacy. The actor, by consequence of sheer dimension and the primacy of action, becomes iconic. In effect, Miller says of the impact of the actor on the screenwriter, he 'has eaten him' (viii), hardly the comment of someone agnostic about the distinction between theatre and film. There could not, he suggests, be an O'Neill in the cinema, nor, he implies, a Miller. In some sense, indeed, he suspects that film is thought of as being at its best, its purest, when stripped of language, in favour of images that can tell a story, progress a plot, delineate a character with no more than a gesture or a sequence of actions. As he remarks, 'no Shakespeare play would last more than an hour' if the same principle were applied.

The function of language in the movies, he suggests, is to justify the silences that are their main business, hence the relative failure of most novelists and playwrights paid to lend their reputations but not, it often transpired, their talents to scripts whose special signature was precisely what was likely to be stripped away. Dialogue is 'the musculature of the gestalt, the combination of images whose interactions create meaning' (x). The reason for the supremacy of the image lies in film's replication of the dream, a point made elsewhere by David Mamet, and the dream is an expression of the preliterate, the primitive. It is, in essence, passive and this is, in part, why Miller has always tended to regard the cinema as less demanding and hence, ultimately, less rewarding than the theatre.

In the theatre we are, in part, the constructors of the reality we engage, and it is in that sense that *Elegy for a Lady* recapitulates the processes of theatre. That it is also oddly dream-like, almost painterly in its composition, its language curiously oblique, suggests that the opposition Miller proposes is far from absolute. For the theatre, too, is concerned with images; it works by and through metaphor. The difference, perhaps, is that in film the images are likely to be less paradoxical, mystery being consigned more to plot and character revelation. In the theatre, they are less concerned to drive the action than to deepen our apprehension of a meaning which does not render itself up completely.

When in *Everybody Wins*[7] Angela remarks that, 'Everything in the world is suggestion . . . like one step away from a dream', there is an immediate context, to do with her attempt to give up smoking, but it is tempting to feel there is rather more to it, in that, as in *Some Kind of Love Story*, she is hinting at the extent to which the mechanisms of the real are elusive. Indeed, Miller corrects his earlier remark in suggesting that 'film is even more primitive than a dream if we consider how far more densely packed with ambiguity and insoluble mystery dreams are' (xii). In that sense, then, his own work in the theatre is perhaps more susceptible to analysis in terms of dream than the cinema. After all, memory has affinity with dreams and memory is so often the site of his drama. Indeed, two one-act plays, also written in the 1980s, were to be performed under the title *Danger: Memory!*

In the cinema, he suggests, the writer is an inconvenient reminder of the first cause, the initial order which exists only to be creatively abandoned in favour of the spontaneous revelations of actors, director, editor. He has power only in the sense that he creates a first draft, that he legitimises that explosion of industry in which money is mixed with craft skills, technology and salesmanship to project two-dimensional images onto a screen in return for cash. As far as film is concerned, the 'often agonizing stylistic effort that writing normally demands is obviated' (xiii). It demands a kind of rigour, in terms of a relentless reduction to story, relationships, thematic consistency, but it is, to his mind, a form of shorthand, an indication to actors of what is to be conveyed perhaps by no more than a gesture, an expression. Conceding that this may require a condensation that seems akin to the skills of a poet, he nonetheless sees the role of the screenwriter as being a member of the orchestra rather than the virtuoso soloist.

In some ways, of course, this suspicion of the cinema is a reflection of the complaint made by most writers hired by Hollywood. From being the centre of creativity they find themselves at best marginalised and frequently dismissed. But it goes beyond this. His comments perhaps bear less on the cinema, indeed, than his conception of theatre. For him, the co-operation there is not only that with actors and director but, crucially, with the audience, an audience that must be implicated in the experiences of those they observe. And that seems to have become more important to him with time. In play after play he has explored the processes by which his characters construct the reality to which they then submit themselves. Such characters frequently feel temporary, with only a tenuous grasp on the identity which they nonetheless wish to affirm. They are at odds with the essence of their own beliefs, trying to reconstitute themselves through a fretful search of their memories or through relationships that are problematic and, indeed, aspects of their uncertainty.

In *Elegy for a Lady* he in part mocks and in part mimics the audience's desire for clarity, for a real that will manifest itself with casual efficiency and directness. In *Some Kind of Love Story* the very rationality implied in the unravelling of a crime leaves us, the audience, the more aware of what has yet to be unravelled. Character proves protean, plot something more than a moment-by-moment move towards revelation. We do, perhaps, learn who committed the crime but other, greater, mysteries remain, mysteries about human behaviour, about the capacity of language to seduce, ensnare, deceive, reveal, about the forces that attract to one another those who seek what they cannot confess, even to themselves, that they are seeking.

When Miller began his career, he dealt in certainties. Character and plot were means to an end, agencies of social, political, economic cirumstance. Language was designed to explain, to analyse, to exhaust its meanings, resolve itself in action. That disappeared quickly. Not only did his work open up to ambiguity but he became increasingly fascinated by the means by which we invent not only ourselves but others, by a past that is not fixed in time and space but invoked by need and deformed by memory. He was not concerned to dissolve fact or deny history. Personal and social responsibility still turned on a belief in causality. He was not ready to dissolve the world into competing fictions. But he was committed to a view of the world that turned on an awareness that we are the constructors of something more than our fate, that our motives are sometimes beyond our understanding and our identities in a state of flux, responding to shifting needs, pressures, awarenesses. Angela's multiple person-alities in *Some Kind of Love Story* are not so remote as they might seem from the multiple personalities of Willy Loman, father, husband, salesman, lover, dreamer.

Four years on from *Two-Way Mirror*, in 1986, at the Mitzi E. Newhouse Theatre at Lincoln Center, he presented two more plays that turn on the uncertainty of the real and the suspect nature of memory. Significantly entitled *Danger: Memory!* they explore the uses to which we put the past, the sometimes fluid, sometimes occluded nature of memory. They are both, he explained, 'about trying not to remember. Memory is the danger.'[8]

The first, *I Can't Remember Anything*, was inspired by two neighbours of Miller's, she a great-niece of Henry James and he Sandy Calder, the son of the sculptor responsible for the arch in Washington Square and a painter and sculptor himself, whose work was to be seen in the Miller home. They recalled another time, were seldom entirely serious, yet were somehow tenacious and enduring. Miller insisted that 'I love those two people in the first play.'[9]

In *I Can't Remember Anything*, an ageing man and woman meet in the 'living room-kitchen' of a country house which itself shows signs of decline. On the wall are a few line drawings of dead friends and a number of dusty landscapes. It speaks of another time, while the man, Leo, is dressed in clothes that are as worn-out as the man who wears them. He is joined by a woman whose name is a female version of his own, Leonora, almost as if they were two sides of the same personality. Leonora speaks with an accent that also hints of another time and place. Her New England speech is overlaid, we are told, with a European aristocratic colouration.

These two are clearly accustomed to one another, to their vulnerabilities, their incapacities, their habits. It is Leonora's birthday, though it is not an occasion they celebrate, her steady consumption of alcohol being only one sign of a sadness buried beneath routine. Married for forty-five years before the death of her husband, she is twelve years older than Leo. She feels stranded, with no future to look forward to and no past that she cares to recall since to do so would be to remind herself of the irony of her life: 'why can't you just admit that it's all nothing? . . . our lives, the whole damn thing', she asks Leo. He reads the newspaper, as if his connection to the world were worth maintaining. She does no more than shuttle painfully from her own house to his. She is a Beckettian figure who has wandered into a Miller play. 'I *think* I remember something, but then I wonder if I just imagined it. My whole life seems imaginary.'[10] She is doing no more than kill time before time kills her.

To her, Leo seems absurd, wilfully closing his eyes to present decline, in himself and in society. 'This country,' she insists, 'is being ruined by greed and mendacity and narrow-minded ignorance, and you go right on thinking there is hope somewhere. And yet you really don't . . . but you refuse to admit that you have lost your hope.' (24) For her part, she refuses to recall the past, a happiness which only serves to render her present absurd. Her forgetfulness is part real and part willed.

Leo, once a teacher, maintains a purchase on life, seeking no transcendent purpose beyond existence itself, aware of his friend's pain but not capitulating to it, indeed quietly offering such consolation as he can. He arranges to leave his organs to the local hospital, allowing himself to think beyond the fact of his death, which he refuses to see as an absolute ending breeding nothing but absurdity. Despite herself, Leonora is drawn into a dance, putting a record on the phonograph sent to her by her son, albeit in a package in which he also announces his impending divorce. In effect they move back into the past from which she has been so intent on distancing herself and in that past are fully alive again. She leaves after thanking him for celebrating their birthday, another hint, perhaps, that these two people, representing, as they do, apparently opposing approaches to life, have more in common than at first appears.

For all her seeming misanthropy, they generate meaning out of one another's presence, offering consolation even in their arguments, watching over one another. If there is an elegiac tone it is because, beneath the confusions, the wilful refusals to recall, the apparent loss of coherence, dignity and purpose, is a resilience that recalls a time before decay and decline came to seem the determining qualities of experience.

Once again, as with *Two-Way Mirror*, the companion piece to this elegiac play is a detective story. In *Clara*, a young woman is dead and her father struggles to answer questions put to him by a detective. In a state of shock, he is unable to comprehend what has happened, is resistant to thinking of his daughter in the past tense or even acknowledging her death. But beneath the immediate trauma lies a guilt which provides another motive for denial. And though as the play progresses concealed truths are exposed, there is more to this work than the revelation of past events and hidden motives.

Under questioning, Albert Kroll slowly recalls seemingly irrelevant facts about his own life. In the army, he explains, he had once served in a black unit and saved a number of his men from a lynch mob, a fact that, in the retelling, made him seem a hero in his daughter's eyes (incidentally a real event which Miller records elsewhere). She, in turn, had fought for the underdog, bringing home as her fiancé a Puerto Rican man who had served time in prison for violence, a man whom, covertly, her father favours in contrast to the woman he suspects of being her lesbian lover.

Kroll is also Chairman of the Zoning Board, in which job he has supported the building of cheap houses which will allow the influx of the poor and the black, those, in fact, who might be presumed to bring with them the virus of violence. It is plainly his daughter's Puerto Rican lover who killed her, though it takes the whole of the play for Kroll to bring his name to mind. He cannot, at first, accept it because his whole life seems to have laid the foundation for the murder. It is his own name he protects, rather than that of the killer. In effect her life has been sacrificed to uphold views he no longer holds and a self that is no longer what he had represented it to be.

But the violence which seemingly shocks him is far closer to home than he will admit, since it transpires that he has connections with a crime family. The one-time hero, whose former self we hear when a record is played in the background, a record of a choir, has now become something he would rather not acknowledge. The story of his valour is now contained within another story.

The play works obliquely. The crime at its heart is not the one that has left a young woman dead or the one a detective investigates. That detective, meanwhile, offers a disturbing and curious parallel to Kroll. He is Jewish and has had to struggle with the same racism that Kroll had engaged. His son is dead, 'shot dead by propaganda that he had some kind of debt to pay' (59), a

propaganda that he had himself failed to deny. He understands Kroll not because
he is different from him but because he is so much the same. 'I failed him', he
says of his son, 'I failed to simplify the way it was simplified for me. I took the
Sergeant's exam three times; I know I got perfect grades three times, but I was
one of the Kikes, and they gave me my stripes out of sheer embarrassment. I was
on a par with an Arab bucking for Sergeant in the Israeli police department'
(59–60).

Yet there is something strange about the parallel in that not only has the
detective lost a child, a fact which Kroll seemingly intuits, but Kroll also recalls
a friend who seems to merge into the man who now confronts him: 'I mixed
you up with Bert, but you're almost the spitting image, even the way you sit
with your legs crossed. And the same kind of attitude' (30). Indeed, like Bert,
the detective has even lost toes from his left foot, again a fact of which Kroll
seems instinctively aware.

Beyond that, Kroll sees his daughter, not only dead – slides appear of her
dead body as, in another room, a photographer records the crime scene – but as
a figure who moves through the scene, sometimes silently, sometimes speaking,
as memories assume concrete form. It is a play in which time becomes plastic,
in which the past explodes into the present with such force that it leaves Kroll
numb, unable fully to articulate, face to face with his own former self as with
the daughter he has loved and lost.

In one sense what we are watching is the power of shock to transform the
world, of trauma to reorder the sensibility. But, beyond that, Miller seems
to suggest that motives, identity, perception are more fluid than they appear,
more subject to immediate necessities, as the past is re-edited and the present
filtered of suspect information. Kroll's character is not static. It is a series of
contending selves which has the appearance of order and coherence but is, in
truth, fragmented. The many denials which sustain that coherence break down
under the impact of his daughter's violent death. His idealism is suddenly
juxtaposed with a pragmatism that has darkened towards criminality. He has
betrayed more than a daughter. He has betrayed his own youthful self. The
echo of that self remains, in a reluctant liberalism, but it co-exists with actions
which, if confronted, would threaten his own carefully sustained self-image.

Which way is he to turn? Is compromise the essence of living, denial the
necessary price of sanity? For Miller, he finds his way back to something
he thought lost. The play, he insists, 'ends in his affirmation; in her catastrophe he has rediscovered himself and glimpsed the tragic collapse of values
that he finally cannot bring himself to renounce' (T.591). If this is so it is a tentative affirmation. Just before offering the name of the likely killer, he reprises
his experiences with the black soldiers, as though retrieving a moment which
he now, once again, wishes to be the defining moment in his life. However, he
is left bereft, staring into space, proud of his daughter's convictions but aware
of the price she paid for the convictions he had himself betrayed. 'Here's a

man', Miller insists, 'who inadvertently taught his daughter to be a heroine. Inadvertently he reached his apotheosis through her.'[11]

This is not, though, a play about one man. To Miller, he was 'bringing onto the stage a slice of our historical experience over the past decades since World War II' (T.59). Like Kroll, the detective 'used to have a lot of understanding' but 'gave up on it'. The violence he witnesses has eroded his idealism and his faith. 'I used to have a lot of questions about life', he remarks, 'but in these last years I'm down to two – what did the guy do, and can I prove it?' (44). For him, images of the concentration camps had convinced him that all values had died and that the only way to function was to reduce his life to the simplest terms, to strike before he is struck (perhaps a reference to Israel, whose policies increasingly disturbed Miller). For his part, Kroll, confronted with his daughter's murderous lover, had sought to argue her out of her naive faith, his own instinctive values having been accommodated to a new, apparently more violent, less forgiving world.

In a sense, one of Miller's central themes has been a concern with how to sustain values in the face of accumulating evidence of their betrayal. The camps constituted a fundamental challenge, but so did the corruption of Marxism and of the American dream. Writing in the 1980s, a time in which self-interest was presented as a value and individual competition a primary virtue, a time when idealism could be presented as naive, in both *I Can't Remember Anything* and *Clara* he sought to explore the basis on which life could constitute something more than a sanctification of greed or an ironic submission to absurdity. The answer, tentative though it is, lies in part in the past, in a confrontation of the denials and betrayals that had come to seem the necessary price for continuance. As the detective remarks, 'What you can't chase you'd better face or it'll start chasing you' (34).

— ✳ —

In 1983, Tennessee Williams died, a man whose reputation Miller felt had been destroyed by the critics, a fact he increasingly felt true of himself. Later that year he left for China for a production of *Death of a Salesman* with himself as director. His wife, Inge, had learned the language but he had to content himself with working through an interpreter and listening to the rhythms of his language buried within another. It was while he, his wife and daughter were in Beijing that his house in Connecticut, planned and built during his marriage to Marilyn Monroe, was partly burned down. Many of his books were burned but his manuscripts survived, being stored in the nearby barn.

The following year's production of *Death of a Salesman*, with Dustin Hoffman, John Malkovich and Kate Reid, put him back at the centre of attention, though he noted that this was still for a work first produced thirty-five years earlier. It was now sixteen years since his last Broadway success. Meanwhile, he had other projects. He started work on a play which fourteen years later would be produced as *Mr Peters' Connections*. He had also begun to write his autobiography, which would appear in 1987.

In 1985, he and Harold Pinter visited Turkey to make enquiries about the fate of writers under the military regime. At a reception thrown for them by the American Embassy, they found themselves involved in an argument with the Ambassador when he took exception to their remarks about torture and American complicity. They were effectively thrown out, only to be embraced by the French Ambassador who hurried them to his embassy for champagne.

Elsewhere in Europe a number of his plays were scheduled to open, including *The Archbishop's Ceiling*, *The Crucible*, *The American Clock* and *The Man Who Had All the Luck* (forty years on from its failure on Broadway) in England, and *Death of a Salesman* in Paris.

Following a visit to London, where he was impressed by both *The Archbishop's Ceiling* and *The American Clock*, the first at the Royal Shakespeare Company's London headquarters at the Barbican, and the latter at the Royal National Theatre, he went to the Soviet Union, where he and other writers had a surprise meeting with Mikhail Gorbachev. It was a meeting which convinced him that the Soviet Union was genuinely changing. Back home, however, he found little interest in his report. The American media, it seemed, were not ready to acknowledge that change was possible.

His next play had been in the making for more than a decade. In 1991, he decided to open it not in New York but London and not at one of the major subsidised companies but in the West End. *The Ride Down Mount Morgan* had been through many drafts and would change again before its New York opening. That, however, would be delayed until 1998. Astonishingly, one of America's major dramatists would have to wait for most of a decade before his new play reached the Great White Way.

✳

24

'The Ride Down Mount Morgan'

The Ride Down Mount Morgan was, in part, a response to Reagan's America. It was Miller's Spenglerian vision of a world in which if not precisely money then the imperial self became triumphant. It was in some ways a play about a man who believed he could have everything and not pay the price, in a decade in which that presumption seemed to have become an article of faith. Yet it is also a play about a man who determines to abandon compromise, to commit himself to his feelings, to relinquish fear, resist death. He is, it seems, simultaneously a hypocrite and an honest man.

At its centre is Lyman Felt, a bigamist suddenly exposed when, following a car crash, he is visited by both wives who discover, for the first time, the extent of his deceptions. Momentarily stilled as he lies in a hospital bed, he is brought into confrontation not only with his wives but also with his life. As Miller has observed, in effect he 'falls into his life'.[1] Indeed, Lyman himself speculates that his accident might not have been so accidental, that he might have reached a point at which it had become psychologically necessary to understand himself and a world that suddenly seems to be slipping away from him.

'The point of the exercise', Miller insists, 'is to investigate some of the qualities and meanings of truthfulness and deception.' Lyman Felt is

> a man of high integrity but no values . . . He is intent on not suppressing his instinctual life, on living fully in every way possible. That is his integrity. He will confront the worst about himself and proceed from there. The question is, what about other people? As he says in the play, what we all know is that a man can be faithful to himself or to other people, but not both. This is the dilemma of the play. He manages to convince himself, and I believe some part of the audience, that there is a higher value than other people and that value is the psychic survival of the individual. That is the dilemma. The play has no solution to it.[2]

It is in that sense that *The Ride Down Mount Morgan* concerns itself with a contemporary dilemma, while engaging issues which transcend the moment. The 'me decade' of the seventies had given way to a period in which the political orthodoxy absolved individuals of responsibility to and for society. Lyman tests that proposition, prompted simultaneously by a growing fear of death (he has reached the age at which his own father had died) and by a sudden surge of desire. No Blanche Dubois, he nonetheless sees desire as an antidote to death but beyond that as the legitimate source of meaning. In the past his idealism has been directed outwards, into the creation of a business that acknowledges a social responsibility, promoting racial minorities to positions as salesmen. For nine years, however – that being the time from his bigamous marriage to the present in which he finds himself called to account for his actions – he has directed his energies onto an inward path, seeing his life as an experiment in living to the full.

As Miller explained,

> it is an attempt to investigate the immense contradictions of the human animal. It is also an attempt to look at man's limitless capacity for self-deception and for integrity. This character is terrible, he is ghastly, but he does create, for example, a very socially responsible corporation. He works himself up from nothing to chief executive of an immense insurance company, which has very progressive liberal policies towards minorities. He has a lot of terrific qualities. He has also got an immense appetite for life, for women, for everything. So he is a kind of Faustian character and, like our civilisation, he is capable of enormous construction and destruction.[3]

The play's first production was not entirely satisfactory. Lyman Felt the protagonist, and indeed the play itself, walks a difficult edge between a sometimes whimsical, sometimes ironic humour and genuine introspection and seriousness. It is a fable. Stylistically, it moves from scenes in which the characters are products of Felt's imagination, to others in which they seem to have a degree of autonomy. In part these characters, the two wives in particular, act out his fears, obligingly stage his anxieties, as though performing a psychotherapeutic function. They become actors in the drama he has constructed (as he, too, is an actor), playing the roles into which he has forced them, even, on occasion, speaking the lines he has devised for them.

In part they are expressions of the dialectic of the age, focussing social and moral concerns, and in part they are what they appear to be, people struggling to come to terms with who they are and what has happened to them, for they, too, have effected their compromises, negotiated the terms on which they are prepared to settle.

Miller has spoken of critics' fondness for such terms as 'poetic', 'lyrical', 'non-linear', 'dream-like' and 'surreal', as they struggle to account for divergences from a presumed baseline realism. To him, the only question worth asking is not the extent to which a play is dream-like or non-linear but its efficiency in conveying 'a playwright's vision of life'. This, he suggests, in turn raises questions about the suitability of style to subject and the nature of the language the writer uses. This, of course, might seem to beg a number of questions. A playwright's vision is a nebulous concept until earthed in the specifics of the play and that, presumably, is in essence what he means. With *A Ride Down Mount Morgan* the challenge is, indeed, one of style and he was, eventually, not entirely satisfied with his own solutions. A few years later he revised the play and it is that version, finally completed for the 1998 production at the Joseph Papp Public Theatre, which he now offers as the definitive text.

It is a play that seems to Miller to have a 'tragic tide' but that is also 'very idiotic at times and almost farcical'.[4] It was that style, that alternating rhythm, that was difficult to capture, not least because at different moments in the play it moves from ostensibly realistic scenes to memories, to fantasies, each sliding over one another as Lyman lapses into semi-consciousness, recalls an actual past or animates other people quite as if they were indeed no more than performers in his personal play.

Behind Miller's concern with realism was a deeper concern, namely the nature of the real which it offered to capture. That, in essence, had lain behind his work of the 1980s, *Two Way Mirror* and *Danger, Memory!* In *The Ride Down Mount Morgan* he explores a man who is precisely concerned with creating his own reality. He is a man who lives experimentally, doubling himself through doubling his wives. He creates a doppelgänger, an alter ego, a shadow self, seeing the world differently depending on where he stands, resisting mortality by refusing to be defined. He is Protean, a confidence man, a trickster, but deception is not his game, merely his method. He wishes to be various, to be real without being defined.

Thus, Lyman Felt is a published poet who turns into an insurance executive, a man afraid of flying who becomes a pilot, a man fearful of speed who buys and drives a Ferrari. For one of his wives it is impossible to imagine him depressed; for his best friend it is easily imaginable. He is part Jewish, part Albanian ('In the Jewish heart is a lawyer and a judge, in the Albanian a bandit defying the government with a knife'[5]). He is part rationalist, part romantic. He is a life-lover who perhaps attempts suicide and certainly risks that life. One of his wives is Jewish, the other not. He is exploring 'all the different ways there are to try to be real' (30). The risk is that thereby he becomes nothing.

As a published poet and short-story writer, Lyman reveals, 'the first thing I bought was a successful blue suit to impress my father how real I was even though a writer' (30), an echo, perhaps, of Miller's own desire to convince his father that writing was a route to success which, for that father, was a measure of the real. Beyond this reality, however, lies another. As a writer and as an insurance man Lyman struggles to make his mark, to leave a trace of his passing: 'You're buying immortality', he suggests, with an insurance policy, while 'nobody lusts after the immortal like a writer' (29). Afraid, like so many other Miller characters, that he is 'going to vanish without a trace' (32), he takes steps to guarantee his survival in one form or another. Two children, by two wives, double his chances of genetic survival, beating death. He lives the American promise of possibility, of becoming anything and anyone, pursuing immediate satisfaction and deferred meaning. Loman, the loser salesman of

Death of a Salesman, has become Lyman, the salesman who believes he has found a way to win.

Tom, his friend and his wife Theodora's lawyer, suggests that perhaps 'he just wanted to change his life; become a completely different person' (36), as Leah, his second wife, had asked, 'Can he be two people? Is that possible?' (16) (in the first version the question was 'Can he be insane?').[6] In fact, he is not about the business of substituting one self for another but of pluralising himself, refusing to be contained or restrained, to be defined. As he explains, 'a man is a fourteen-room house; in the bedroom he's asleep with his intelligent wife, in his living room he's rolling around with some bare-assed girl, in the library he's paying his taxes, in the yard he's raising tomatoes, and in the cellar he's making a bomb to blow it all up' (44).

If he is a different person to different people, however, is there a stable self at the centre, unaffected by the changing polarity of his emotional and physical life? For Patrick Stewart (in the 1998 Broadway production), faced with playing a man of apparently contradictory impulses, there was a continuity. Sometimes, he explained,

> I found it necessary to talk about Lyman in the same terms that one would talk about a child, because his needs are often child-like. A child will develop interests, enthusiasms, fears, passions, very much based on the messages he is getting from his parents and those around him. And that is what made two different, completely contrasting sides of his life, straightforward to me in that in his relationship with Theo what she brought to that marriage, and her particular influences on her husband, was what made him fearful about so many things, so doubting, though ambitious, of course, and certainly enjoying the life of a sophisticated East Sider. But men on whom women's impact is particularly important really do come under the influence of those women. Theo imposed herself on Lyman and the end result was a man who did not like driving fast, for whom anything risky or dangerous was not comfortable.
>
> Then he meets Leah, who has a completely different view of the world, and as a result he becomes something he could never have been with the other wife. That's why he is such a mess. He cannot cut a furrow which is entirely his. He is a weak man who seeks out the company of strong women. It is when he met Theo that he abandoned his earlier life as a writer and enlightened businessman.[7]

The use of the word 'insane' in the first version of the play recalls the multiple personalities of *Some Kind of Love Story*. It suggests, too, the dangerous line Lyman treads and, evidently, one night, on Mount Morgan, his foot went over the line. But even here there are two possibilities. Did the man who removed the safety barrier preventing people from descending the icy road do so to commit suicide or to provoke the confrontation that now ensues in the hospital? Did he wish to reveal the multiplicity of his life which he now thinks of at times as betrayal and at times as redemption? Has he brought down anarchy ('Feeling is chaos' (17), he insists, even while suggesting that 'any decent thing I've ever done was out of feeling' (17)), or has he energised the life of everyone he has touched? Aware that to 'live according to your desires' is to end up 'looking like a shit', he nonetheless insists that it is necessary to 'Believe in your feelings' (21), since love is 'the only reality' (23). The challenge with which he ultimately presents his wives is whether they can deny the truth of this merely because he had shared his love with two of them. Did he even drive down Mount Morgan, as he suggests he may have done, to see his first wife and shock her with the reality of his feelings? To Stewart, it seems clear. He has precipitated the crisis in which he now finds himself:

> I was absolutely clear about that. Lyman got out of that room where he was going crazy. Fortunately I had had an experience like that myself once and I could closely identify with the panic, the terror, the desire not to be here but somewhere else, regardless of what it costs trying to get there. I was always convinced that he got into the car, drove out into the night and removed the barrier. I think he desperately wanted Leah because in that room at last all of the things he had managed to keep suppressed were visiting him, all of his fears, terrors, all of his guilt was overwhelming him and the only thing he could think to do was be in her arms and he drove far too fast. He was pushing things right to the edge. This man needed something to happen in his life. He needed a crisis. He precipitated it, unconsciously, but he precipitated it.

When he launched his bigamous plans, Lyman Felt insisted to his friend Tom that 'deception has become like my Nazi, my worst horror', and that 'I want nothing now but to wear my own face on my face every day till the day I die' (20). He aspired, he insisted, to 'honesty'. Since he is at that very moment planning deception and untruth, is this simply more evidence of his casuistry, or is it possible that truth lies in multiple selves, that deception is a product of stasis, habit, stability and that the true face changes with the light? Certainly, his dedication to truth, seemingly paradoxically, echoes throughout the play as he tries to rationalise and explain why he has done as he has. At times, indeed, he seems reminiscent of Eugene O'Neill's Hickey, a self-deceiving salesman for truth, a huckster for reality trapped in self-created illusion. 'I have lost my guilt', he announces, only to be overcome by such a moment later. Like Hickey, he insists he is opting for life, having just killed something in those he affects to love.

Who is he? Nobody can be sure. Like Gatsby, he is his own Platonic invention. His first name is a shortened version of his mother's; his last name was borrowed from that of the judge who officiated at his father's citizenship hearing. Leah, his second wife, having just been told that the husband who is terrified of speed races down mountainsides, likens him to a frog, because, 'you never know when you look at a frog . . . it's the same one you just saw or a different one' (35). But, then, as Lyman asks, 'You ever have the feeling you never *really* got to know anybody?' (32). He is merely the logical extension of the unknowability of the other.

Like Gatsby, he began with nothing, creating over four thousand jobs. He is rich and famous, but such things fail to touch his life, fail to prove his reality. His father is no longer the one who can validate his existence. Now he has to validate himself and he sets out to do so by following his instincts, releasing his energies, transcending guilt and social obligations.

In one sense this is the portrait of a man experiencing a midlife crisis, suddenly aware of death as a defining boundary and asking himself what his life might have amounted to. His achievements no longer seem enough. His marriage appears to identify the limits of his possibility. He is aware of something beyond a domestic tedium which is in danger of defining his limits. It is as though it signified his willing acquiescence in his own irrelevance. The roles of husband and father are no longer adequate. He refuses to accept that he 'has lived somebody else's life' (43), and that his function is to acknowledge the justice of that. After all, as he insists, the relationship with his first wife was the product of pure contingency, a serendipitous meeting. Is this to be allowed to contain him? Can such contingency really be the source of meaning?

As a consequence, he decides against self-denial. When he insists on truth, what he evidently means is that he will refuse to deny the truth of his desires. As he says, 'A man can be faithful to himself or to other people – but not to both. At least not happily . . . the first law of life is betrayal' (42). However, he convinces himself, and now tries to convince his wives, that such betrayal has redeemed not only him but them, since his new happiness has embraced them as well.

Neither woman can claim to have been unhappy as a result of his decision to free himself of guilt. Quite the contrary. Indeed, he is inclined to see himself as a martyr to others' happiness, protecting them, as he has, from a knowledge of the fragility of that happiness at cost to himself. For if he feels liberated he also bears the responsibility of sustaining the life-lies he offers (and Ibsen is, perhaps, not quite as remote as he might seem).

The key moment is one in which, in a scene reminiscent of Saul Bellow's *Henderson the Rain King*, he confronts a lion during an African safari (and Miller had been on such a safari when he interviewed Nelson Mandela for BBC television). Having engaged in a debate about monogamy, having given the reasons he might choose to settle for what he has got, what he has made of his life to date, he finds himself facing a charging lion. Rather than retreat like his wife and daughter, he stands his ground and shouts out the terms of his new reality. Face to face with the death he fears, he announces that he will not 'sacrifice one day to things I don't believe in – including monogamy', that 'I love my life, I am not guilty!'

He dares the lion to eat him. It is a moment of epiphany, albeit a suspect one. When he survives he feels sanctioned in his decision to pursue his happiness, an American injunction whose ambiguities he no longer feels obliged to address. He is, he believes, free of guilt, justified in the action he is about to take. This is the moment he decided on bigamy, on a double life that would be his defence against unmeaning. He refuses to 'stand still for death' (55), but revels in his 'anachronistic energy' (56). Like the lion, he believes, he now accepts what he takes to be his nature, his appetites and hungers. He feels liberated from guilt, like Bellow's Henderson no longer striving.

For Stewart, what interested him about the scene was its emotional range.

> It begins with a man seemingly in a deep depression. He is with one woman but wishes to be with another. He is in agony. The lion has appetite and nothing else. Lyman has not been able to satisfy his appetite without feeling the guilt that goes with it. He has never been utterly free. The encounter with the lion frees him from his guilt.

In playing the scene, Stewart drew on his experience of scuba diving in the Sea of Cortez during which he had come face to face with a giant sea lion:

> I was nose to nose with him and he was in his own environment. We looked into one another's eyes, lying there at the bottom of the ocean. I felt a thrill run through me because I knew there was a risk in it. I remember when it was over a terrific sense of elation and invincibility because of being face to face with this wild creature. There was some talk of cutting the lion scene. It is difficult to stage, but audiences loved it and absolutely got it. It also drop-kicked us into the last part of the play.

Lyman lacks the courage, or even the necessity, to divorce Theodora, though, like O'Neill's Hickey, he resents her caring for him. And, indeed, beneath his self-justifying insistence that he is selflessly working for the happiness of others, lies the egotism that had been at the heart of O'Neill's character. He was, he confesses, 'risking everything to find myself' (58). That is the reason for his confronting the lion. It is also the reason he takes Leah to see Theodora through the window of their apartment. It is why he challenges her to go in and why, when she has returned to their hotel, he himself goes in, makes love to Theodora and then telephones Leah as his wife listens. By living dangerously, he convinces himself that he lives more fully, more completely.

Meaning, indeed, he seems to assume, will precipitate out on the boundary between one life and another, one wife and another. The danger he seeks in driving fast cars, in hunting and flying, is precisely his route to reality. Beyond that, he believes he has 'beaten guilt forever' (59), liberated himself from the meaningless constraints of society, the assumed rules of the tribe.

Yet, as the wives recognise, there is a powerful egotism behind his new vision and more than a touch of megalomania. This is hardly diminished by the question he asks of Theo: 'has there ever been a god who was guilty?' (60). There is a self-mocking irony to the question yet, at the same time, he has been acting as a god in manipulating the lives of those around him. He offers Polonius's advice to his son, urging him to be true to himself, only to have Theo ask, 'Even if he has to betray the whole world to do it?' (62). And that is the essence of the tainted nostrum he offers, the redemption he wishes to claim. His truth begins, if it does not end, with the self, to which everything else is subordinate. It is born out of fear and resentment. As he insists at the end, 'I still don't see why I am condemned' (69). Condemned to what? To death and hence, retrospectively, to unmeaning? He follows the path Camus's Caligula takes when confronted with absurdity, though without the extremes of cruelty. He piles experience on experience, refuses prohibitions, rejects restrictions, follows his desires, believing that this is to create the meaning he pursues.

To Patrick Stewart, there is no doubting his hypocrisy: 'He creates devastation. I remember sitting in a coffee shop on the Upper East Side and two women came over to me, very angry. I had to assure them that I was only acting the role. Lyman is a dangerous individual. He has a devastating effect on at least three lives.'

In the original version of the play Miller suggests that the path Lyman has chosen is a product of his gender: 'It's just two worlds, see? – Women want it safe, but it's dangerous. Just is. Can't help it. It's terrible. And it's okay.'[8] Men find meaning, proof of their reality, in risk, women in security. Meanwhile, the latter offer 'warmth', which, in the first version is 'the last sacredness' and in the final version 'the last magic'.

The play ends with a conversation between Lyman and his nurse, who seems to be offered as a symbol of acceptance, of the extraordinary contained within the banal, as she describes her family sitting on the ice and fishing while discussing shoes. Perhaps that Whitmanesque insight is what he has been moving towards. At least Lyman now comes to feel 'What a miracle everything is! Absolutely everything!' The first version ends with him weeping. In the final version, however, he dries his tears and concludes with his announcement that 'You have found Lyman at last!' (70), though the truth is that he now has to 'learn loneliness', that being the final condition.

In a sense, this is a play about separateness, about the limits to love and reason, the intransitive nature of experience. It is in part about the difficulty of reading the world, of understanding, of constituting a reality that can become the basis of meaningful action. If the self is unstable, what is to be made of the relationships which seem to offer some stability, some consolation, some hope?

There comes a moment when all the major characters are suddenly transfixed by the contradictions of life, its pain and its transcendences. Theo's daughter Bessie bursts into tears, precipitating a more general wave of weeping. In a stage direction/character note, which is also an interpretative observation, Miller indicates that at this point, 'All strategies collapse . . . The four of them are helplessly covering their faces. It is a veritable mass keening, a funerary explosion of grief, each for his or her own condition, for love's frustration and for all their capacity to reason' (67). Yet at this very moment, Tom, whose head has been bent in prayer, and who has insisted on his immunity to sexual temptation, finds himself staring at Theo's bare leg and the mood is broken.

The contradictions, it seems, are simultaneously both the mark of absurdity and of a redeeming and irrepressible vitality. And that, in part, explains a play in which serious concerns rub shoulders with vulgarity, in which pain and humour co-exist. The differences that breed despair are equally those that energise, that charge the world with possibility.

Lyman and his wives are both drawn to and repelled by one another, just as he is the selfless employer of minorities and the selfish exploiter of other people's emotions. He is a symbol of his age, justifying his own pleasures with a trickle-down theory of emotional wealth. If he finds satisfaction in the arrangements he makes, do his wives not also benefit, he asks. Yet he is also something more than this. He is aware, as the others are not, or do not permit themselves to be, of the unreality of unexamined lives, the fragility of identity, the ease with which habit becomes a defining boundary.

He is an agent of change, the source of a trauma that sends the other characters back to their own lives injured but forced to inspect the basis of their identities and the nature of their existence. The simple question which confronts the two women in the waiting room – who is Mrs Felt? – has resonances beyond the mere embarrassment of the moment. Lyman is the source of anarchy, pursuing his own agenda, anxious to rationalise his behaviour, but he is also, perhaps, a catalyst, provoking a reaction, generating a new, if temporary, reality.

In a play so concerned with the nature of the real, and in which the central character sets himself to create it, reality is problematic at the level of stage representation. As in Death of a Salesman, After the Fall and The American Clock, we see characters, at least for part of the time, through the mind and imagination of the central character. It is he who, from time to time, invokes, invents, manipulates the other characters, giving them lines to speak and actions to perform. As Lyman remarks of those he brings on to the stage of his imagination, 'What strong, admirable women they are! What definite characters!' (12). He, himself, lies in a hospital bed throughout the play and yet leaves that bed, in mind if not in fact, to replay scenes from the past as he seeks to justify to himself, as much as others, a life of apparent dubiety.

The first confrontation between the two women is imagined rather than experienced. He suffers, Miller tells us in a stage note, 'a catastrophic vision' (9). As a perhaps over-directive clue to the audience, Lyman remarks early on,

'Thank God I'm only imagining this' (12), an intensification of his observation in the earlier version, 'Oh, I can just see it.'[9]

In that early version Miller specifies that Lyman is to slip out of a body-cast at moments, leaving the cast behind, almost the shell of a man in search of himself. In the later version he leaves the process more vague but includes a production note that defines the nature of the play's style. The play, he explains,

> follows Lyman's mind through scenes in real time as well as in memory and dream. The set must therefore be an open one to allow scenes to move fluidly without pause as noted in the text. Lyman can leave and enter the hospital bed without having to change in and out of costumes; simply by drawing covers up near his chin, even though dressed, it is sufficient to suggest him in a hospital gown. (5)

Not only is the stage effect of the body cast removed but so, too, are some of the scene divides of the first version.

The Theodora of the first version is more fully described by Miller. She is turning fifty when we first see her in the hospital, idealistic and intellectually forceful, a believer in the American way and convinced that everything ultimately fits together. Marriage is part of the order in which she believes. Leah, by contrast, is thirty, sensuous, a powerful businesswoman, quite prepared either to abort her child or raise it outside of marriage. Yet the clarity of these portraits is compromised by the degree to which their compliance is in part a projection of Lyman's desires.

At one stage they appear on elevated platforms, as Miller suggests, 'like two stone deities' (39). Both are wearing kitchen aprons and sporting ribbons in their hair. They engage in a mock combat via competitive culinary skills. A moment later they strip off their domestic costumes and appear in black body stockings and high heels before beginning a lesbian tryst, interrupted only by a murderous assault on the sleeping Lyman who has been staging the fantasy in his mind. Yet, in a sense, of course, they are merely rehearsing the roles conventionally ascribed to women, recalling the extent to which character is a projection of other people's fantasies and presumptions. They are what Lyman wishes to make them, minor characters in the drama that is his life.

At the conclusion of Act 1, the two women and Tom are set moving by Lyman, 'criss-crossing, serpentine paths, just missing one another, spreading further and further across the stage until one by one they disappear'. They do so as an externalisation of his sudden realisation of 'how quickly it's all going by', his conviction that 'you never *really* got to know anybody', his fear that he is going 'to vanish without a trace' (32).

This moment, indeed, is, in essence, an externalisation of the fear that provoked his ride down Mount Morgan and hence the drama that he, and Miller, stages. For he has come to feel that

> with all the analysis and the novels and the Freuds we're still as opaque and
> unknowable as some line of statues in a church wall . . . We're all in a cave . . .
> where we entered to make love or money or fame. It's dark in here, as dark as
> sleep, and each one moves blindly, searching for another; to touch, hoping
> to touch and afraid; and hoping, and afraid.
>
> (32)

This is not the drama of a man who has found certainty. The bright-eyed
assurances he offers about his actions founder on an awareness that the other
side of his decision to follow his desires is precisely an isolating egotism, that
betrayal is the first law of life. Why else, Lyman asks, 'did those rabbis pick Cain
and Abel to open the Bible?' (42). 'We're all ego . . . plus an occasional heartfelt
prayer', he insists (43). The New Testament message of self-denial holds no
truth for him.

The play, as Miller has admitted, offers no solution. Like a number of Bellow's
novels, it presents a character, in this case part Jewish, who worries about the
extent of his responsibilities, who is intimidated by the fact of death, unsure
of the boundaries of his identity, uncertain of the nature of the contract he
has with the women he loves but betrays. Like the protagonist of *Henderson
the Rain King*, he wants to shock himself into reality, burst out of his egotism;
like Bellow's Herzog, he conducts a debate with himself through a debate with
the world. Rather than sending letters out into that world, however, he works
through dreams and fantasies, improvising himself and others. He resists a
sense of absurdity, born in part out of an existence with no evident purpose, a
journey with no destination beyond the grave, and in part out of habit which
offers itself as consolation but becomes a Sisyphean irony.

He is left, ultimately, with the paradoxes with which he began, except that
passion can be said to have been vindicated while he has glimpsed, at least, a
redemption in the simple domesticity he feared. In the end he cannot tolerate
the struggle to sustain two separate stories. Like Fitzgerald's Dick Diver, he can
no longer reconstruct the world to suit his needs and, as he supposes, those of
others. Danger, as such, has surely not rendered his life into his hands. There
is no immunity to the logic of mortality that he fears. But there is a reborn
sense of wonder. 'What a miracle everything is', he remarks, in the concluding
speech, 'Absolutely everything!' And if there is a potentially reductive irony to
his final words – 'cheer up!' (70) – there is also, perhaps, an acceptance that the
meaning that he sought is closer to hand than he had imagined.

However, the much rewritten ending (audiences at the Public Theatre,
Stewart confessed, had felt dissatisfied with the original one) includes Lyman's
statement, addressed to himself, that, 'You have found Lyman at last!' (70).
How much weight did Stewart place on this?

> We were rehearsing this speech when Arthur slapped his knee and said,
> 'I've got it! I've got it! He's at the foot of the right mountain! All his life

Lyman has been climbing a mountain. It was the wrong mountain.' I don't think Lyman fully understands but he knows something he had not known before. For a man whose life has been unimaginably complex, the black nurse's story of a simple happiness and contentment is a revelation. It is like the ending of A Christmas Carol. When Scrooge leaves the Cratchits, he says, they were not a handsome family, they were not rich . . . but they were happy, pleased with one another and contented with the time. It has a huge impact on Scrooge. I think Arthur and I talked about that. It is a revelation, too, for Lyman. The vision is not complete but he has been given something that he can use as a tool to start again.

The problem of the first production lay, to some large degree, in the casting of the central character. Tom Conti, an accomplished actor, nonetheless seemed to have considerable difficulty in bridging the different aspects of Lyman Felt's admittedly quixotic character. He settled for charm as a character note, but charm is only one part of a complex figure. Indeed, the action begins at the point at which Felt finally realises that this can no longer carry him through a life whose inner contradictions have begun to expose themselves. He is, after all, an actor, simulating his life while trying to convince himself of his authenticity. He is appearing in two different dramas, rather like an actor in an Ayckbourn play, stepping from one set into another, yet in his case deliberately rehearsing contrasting roles, as if trying to define the spectrum of possibilities.

For nine years he has convinced himself of the integrity of his motives, believed that he has served something more than his own self-interest. Now, as a consequence of serendipity or his own psychological need to resolve this breach in his sensibility, these roles are revealed for what they are. A confidence man who has deceived himself, a salesman who has sold himself a suspect proposition, he is now pressed to the point of confrontation as fantasy, self-deceit and, perhaps, a genuine desire to discover a way of living without definition and yet with integrity collide in a crisis which he both wills and resists. It is this complexity that was resolved in the first production in the direction of nothing much more than amused irony.

Rehearsals were difficult and the play's opening delayed. Reviews, however, were respectable, and the production had many strengths, not least in the shape of Gemma Jones and Clare Higgins who played the two wives, but it was not until Scott Elliott's production in Williamstown, Massachusetts, in 1996, that Miller felt moved to return to the play, producing a revised text for the 1998 production, directed by David Esbjornson at the Joseph Papp Public Theater/New York Shakespeare Festival, and starring Patrick Stewart as Lyman. At this point he was finally satisfied and reviews reflected the success of a production that managed to sustain a tension between the humourous and the tragic, the vulgar and profound.

He had said of the original work that it was designedly 'fluid', moving in and out of the protagonist's memory. It deployed past and present and involved a fluid use of the stage. That fluidity was increased in the final shortened version. Out went a somewhat gnomic figure, that of Lyman's dead father, who had drifted through the action, an accusing presence before whom Lyman had felt the need to justify himself or against whom he had revolted, at one stage urinating into his panama hat. But beyond being an embodiment of reproach, the father represents the threatened death that had set Lyman on his experiment in living. Lyman, in the original version, is forty-seven years old, the age at which his father had died, a father who trails behind him a length of dark cloth, representing Lyman's fear of an approaching death. In the final version he is fifty-four when he contracts his bigamous marriage and sixty-three in the present. It is tempting to see in this character a version of Miller's own reproachful father. Even the length of cloth he carries seems a reminder of the cloak-maker who had worked to hold onto the son who had been so determined to escape.

In the original version this figure proved somewhat mystifying and though his death, and Lyman's sense of what he fears may be his own, gives a clear motivation for Lyman's actions, Miller decided to remove the character entirely. He also removed a reference, in an early draft, to his appearing before a congressional committee, and an incident in the past in which Lyman had turned informer against a colleague in his business, thus provoking suspicion that he might have offered him up in order to protect himself, a curious echo of *All My Sons* and *After the Fall* and, perhaps, even of the notorious womaniser Elia Kazan who did, of course, inform, and whose unashamed behaviour, on both counts, had transfixed and intrigued Miller. Never really an organic part of the play, the incident disappears as a distraction but it is tempting to feel that Kazan provided something of the inspiration for the play.

Gone, too, is a reference to Lyman having an earlier affair that had resulted in a child, a child he had encountered many years later without acknowledging. In this case, such a back story had potentially vitiated the significance of the affair with Leah though it had, perhaps, explained why guilt might have led him to embrace rather than abandon this mother and child. Nonetheless, the reference was potentially obscuring and Miller removed it. The effect of these excisions is a leaner text, one which has greater momentum, focusing more completely on Lyman and the women he deceives and perhaps liberates.

In some ways *The Ride Down Mount Morgan* revisits the territory in part explored in *After the Fall*, but for the anguished self-exploration of Quentin he substitutes the exuberant, wilful hucksterism of Lyman. Both edge towards an acceptance of a flawed humanity, both resist the absurdist implications which confront them, but in the later play the mood has changed. The comedy is a value. Memory and imagination are the source of something more than self-accusation.

Lyman is a figure of his age, breathing in the world as if he had presumptive rights to everything. He has, in Miller's words, 'ridden on his personality'. He wishes to believe that beneath the material is the spiritual, while fearing that there is 'a fall into nothingness'.[10] He has a hunger for meaning but looks for it in walking the edge as if there were an existential truth to be discovered there. He sees his double-dealing as a form of integrity. Seeing guilt as constraint, he comes to regard himself as free simply by purging himself of it. He is also, however, a juggler, a magician, a poet, alert to the excitements as well as the contradictions of experience.

He is anything but indifferent, indeed why else is he in this place, why else does this drama take place, his plunge down the mountainside being an ambiguous gesture? The man who has everything now faces the possibility of having nothing, exploring what that transformation might mean.

For Miller, this is a play about the biology of morals, the absurdity of aspects of the male–female relationship. Incompatible strategies and objectives meet as they themselves never fully do. Beyond that, however, it is a play that addresses a deeper failure. Deception – of the other, of the self – becomes a defining feature of experience, as does denial, a failure to distinguish what is fundamental from what is not. As Miller has remarked, 'what we've got going now are an infinitely greater number of ways of satisfying appetites of all kinds, of avoiding looking in the mirror. You can buy a car, change your house, your family. A lot of people don't need to confront themselves because of the fact that there are so many escapes in the commodity civilisation.'[11]

The Ride Down Mount Morgan is a study of denial. It is also a study of hypocrisy but, perhaps, also of the fiction-making skills necessary to give form to mere experience. 'I have to consent to him', Miller has said,

> and condemn him. He is telling a truth. There is a reptillian mind in us that predates all morality. It is the force of nature . . . And that is immune to education. It's what we rely on for a creative act but which has to be disciplined or we will destroy each other. It is both holy and dangerous. Moral systems are there to discipline that force . . . But you need the artist, the chaos maker. That transaction is tragic.

Here it is less tragic than comic and, indeed, he confesses that 'comedy is the closest to what we are now'.[12] But note that the artist brings both discipline and chaos. And that is perhaps what attracts Miller to Lyman, poet turned business-man, fiction-maker and, under pressure, truth-teller. In that sense, perhaps, *The Ride Down Mount Morgan* is a study of the writer, who lives multiple lives, tells lies in the name of truth, creates a factitious world whose shape, nonetheless, appeals because it hints at a creativity without which the world never rises above a series of contingent events. Just as in *The Price* the qualities of both brothers were necessary – the one self-serving but imaginatively forceful, the other moral but oddly ineffective and perhaps even self-deceiving – so, here, the two identities of Lyman Felt, brothers in spirit, constitute something more than contrasting possibilities. They are both necessary. And that recapitulates something basic to Miller and his drama. As he remarked in 1997,

> Like everybody else, I think I believe certain things, and I think I believe others, but when you try to write a play about them, you find out that you believe a little of what you disbelieve and you disbelieve a lot of what you think you believe. The dramatic form, at least as I understand it, is a kind of proof. It's a sort of court proceeding where the less-than-true gets cast away and what's left is the kernel of what one really stands for and believes.[13]

Given the nature of Lyman, his last words – 'so ... cheer up!' (70) can hardly be seen as unambiguous. After all, he had convinced himself of this once before, when confronting the lion. Yet there does seem to be a reconciliation in that Miller himself recognises something more than the hunger for meaning that drives Lyman. The wild and irresponsible inventiveness, the dangerous and even immoral exploration of alternatives, the desire, uncontrolled by precept, uncontained by social edict, are as compelling and, perhaps, ultimately necessary as the loyalty, responsibility, ordered sensibility and honesty without which those other qualities become nothing more than a random and unfocused energy, destructive because serving nothing beyond themselves. And those contrasting qualities are reflected in some ways in the writer, whose imaginative freedoms, surges of invention, amoral explorations have to be contained and shaped if they are to speak a complex truth.

— ✳ —

Following the London production of *The Ride Down Mount Morgan*, which had a respectable run and respectful reviews, there were successful German productions in Dresden and Frankfurt.

The following year, 1992, saw a revival of *The Price*, nearly a quarter of a century after Miller's last great success, and the publication of a novella, *Homely Girl*. Negotiations were meanwhile under way for a screen version of *The Crucible*. Kenneth Branagh was one of several to consider directing it. In July Miller began to write what he was then calling the 'Gellburg' play, later renamed *Broken Glass*. He finished a first draft two months later. In July, too, there was a first reading of *The Last Yankee* at the Manhattan Theatre Club. It opened in America and Britain in 1993 to contrasting reviews. The London production, at the Young Vic, was celebrated; the American production was largely, though not wholly, dismissed. By now, this was no more than Miller expected.

✳

25

'The Last Yankee'

Arthur Miller has said that a central theme of American writing has been an argument with the American dream, and it has certainly been a central theme of his work. The tension between materialism and a sense of transcendence, of the poetic, has lain at the heart of many of his plays. The poet and the businessman, the visionary and the materialist, have done battle, sometimes within a single sensibility – Willy Loman, Quentin – sometimes spun off into separate and opposing selves: Arnold and Ben in *No Villain*, Chris and Joe Keller in *All My Sons*, Biff and Happy in *Death of a Salesman*, Victor and Walter in *The Price*. In the early 1990s, he returned to this dichotomy in a play in which a businessman debates with a craftsman and that craftsman with his wife.

At issue is an interpretation of experience, a clash of values. It expresses a sense of individuals and a society divided as to the purpose of their lives and the function of that society. It is a play, too, shadowed by history. It acknowledges that the debate goes back to the very beginnings of the Republic. It invokes if not a framer of the Constitution then one of those who argued over what this new democracy was to be, whether it was to favour the material over the spiritual, the rich over the poor.

The Last Yankee (1993) is a play in which, as Miller has explained, he wished to make plain his sense of the life of a man 'swinging a hammer through a lifetime' and a 'woman waiting forever for her ship to come in';[1] the man wishes to shape the world with his hands while the woman has eyes only for the dream of success that brought her family to an America that offered transformations. The tension he identifies there is not contained by the lives of these people. It is, as the frequency with which he has returned to this subject suggests, a tension that exists in the culture at large.

One other echo apparent in the play is the figure of a woman whose psyche is under pressure. This, too, is a recurring motif: Maggie in *After the Fall*, Angela in *Some Kind of Love Story*, Sylvia in *Broken Glass* and, here, Patricia in *The Last Yankee*. It is tempting, if none too profitable, to trace this figure back to Monroe, and Miller's experience of trying to sustain someone broken by internal and external pressures. He himself is prone to identify a more general sense of crisis. At the London press conference to launch *The Last Yankee*, he invoked the prevalence of women in mental hospitals, a disproportionate number of whom suffer from depression, as an explanation and justification for the figures of Patricia and Karen in the new play. He might, of course, justifiably have drawn attention to the number of male characters in his work similarly psychologically pressured: Willy Loman, Eddie Carbone, Phillip Gellburg. In fact men and women alike register the tensions in their society and their conflicting needs as individuals struggling to make sense of a world that fails to offer what they believe themselves to need.

The Last Yankee was first staged, in June 1991, by the Ensemble Studio Theatre in New York as part of the Marathon Annual Festival of One-Act Plays. It consisted of the first of what would become two acts in the version that opened at the Young Vic in London eighteen months later. It presented a conversation between two men visiting a state mental hospital to see their respective wives. In the extended version, we meet those wives and explore the nature of the desperation that has driven them to this retreat from the world.

The two men are sharply contrastive. Frick is a businessman, sixty years old, conservative, vaguely resentful at finding himself in this place. Leroy Hamilton, forty-eight, is a carpenter but, ironically, also a descendant of Alexander Hamilton, the federalist politician who had been conservative, distrustful of the common people, a believer in the legitimate power of the wealthy. As they wait to go through to their wives, they engage at first in a stilted conversation, passing the time, offering banal comments. By degrees, however, they begin to reveal more of themselves and their circumstances than, perhaps, either intends. In particular, we learn something of the women who, in the one-act version, we never meet.

Frick is vaguely racist and deeply materialist, admiring of those who make it and baffled by those who seemingly opt out of the competition to succeed. Leroy emerges as a craftsman, more interested in what he creates than maximising his income. Indeed, despite his subdued Ivy League jacket and slacks, his shined brogue (which confuse Frick, who expects appearance to match his assumptions), he is plainly not well off, perhaps because of his seven children. Frick has no children.

This is Frick's first visit. His wife has been in the hospital for around a week. By contrast, this is the third time in two years that Hamilton's wife has been hospitalised. Indeed, she has suffered for twenty years. Both women are diagnosed with depression, both are, in Hamilton's words, 'frightened', unwilling to leave the house, though neither can understand why. The men try to find some common cause but their experiences are so dissimilar that none immediately manifests itself. The women simply stare into the future and apparently see nothing there.

There are hints, though, about their private lives which might seem to offer a clue to their dilemma. Frick explains his frustration that his wife should not have welcomed discussion of his real estate deals or the state of the stock market, that she feels as she does despite their 'wonderful home'. He uses a state facility rather than the private one eighty miles away because 'what are we paying our taxes for?' At the same time he revealingly confesses of that private hospital that

'It's one of the top places in the country. Some very rich people go there.'[2] When he learns that Leroy's relatives have offered to pay for his wife's treatment there he insists that, 'it's absolutely first-class, much better than this place. You should take them up on it' (10). It would seem, therefore, that he has knowingly settled for second-best for his own wife.

He emerges as a man of contradictions, resenting the hourly rates of plumbers ('Seventeen dollars an hour!' (10)) while praising Leroy for charging the same ('Good for you . . . if they'll pay it, grab it' (11)). He denounces the fact that 'Everybody's got the gimmes, it's destroying the country' (10), while maximising his own income. Meanwhile, he is bewildered that a descendant of Alexander Hamilton should be reduced to being a carpenter, despite acknowledging his skill and praising the work he has produced.

Under the weight of this condescension Leroy momentarily breaks, angry at an attitude that demeans his life, an attitude that extends beyond the man who now confronts him. They revert to silence and a concluding banality: 'It's one hell of a parking lot, you have to say', remarks Frick. And there the play ended until it was opened up by allowing access to the stories of the women. In the original one-act version, however, it is a subtle character study, a two-hander in which we discover the fragility of two men who are supposedly balanced and secure, in contrast to their wives.

In the extended version we move into the hospital and into Patricia Hamilton's room. In one bed a woman lies, motionless, and remains such throughout the play (though in the American production, unwisely, she was permitted to rise from time to time). Intriguingly, in the Young Vic production a movement coach assisted the actress playing the role. The play begins with the sounds of table tennis. Patricia enters to retrieve the ball and then returns with Karen Frick, a woman in her sixties, thin, with wispy hair.

Karen's speech is full of non sequiturs. Her memory is faulty but beyond that she is plainly in a state of tension, not least because she knows that her husband is waiting and 'he doesn't like being kept waiting'.[3] Patricia, too, is nervous but in her case because she is trying to decide whether to leave or not. With a history of failure, she is unsure, but for the first time has taken herself off her medication: 'the longest I've been clean in fifteen years' (13). On the other hand, there is something disturbing about her attachment to a minister from the Marble Baptist Church (though, confusingly, she was raised a Lutheran and regards herself as Methodist), who has convinced her that she is 'almost continually talking to the Lord' (14). There is something disturbing, too, about her belief that if Leroy had been 'a Jew or Italian or even Irish' (14) he would be suing her doctors, still willing, it seems, to deflect responsibility on to others.

Resentment and love do battle. A one-time beauty-contest winner, a daughter of immigrants, she had expected so much of her life and of America that she is baffled by a man who shows no interest in success, no commitment to the culture's animating myths. After years together they have built a family but seemingly little more. Like Willy Loman, she looks for validation and expects to find it in the success which once lured her family across the ocean. One of her reasons for admiring the minister seems to be that his previous congregation had bought him a Pontiac Grand Am. Their own car, meanwhile, a nine-year-old second-hand Chevrolet, is in a state of near collapse. Again like Willy Loman, she has failed to understand that success in human terms – the love of her husband and children – was always to hand.

Speaking of the play, Miller has said that he wished to write of the confusion of those who are 'bedrock, aspiring not to greatness but to other gratifications – successful parenthood, decent children and a decent house and a decent car and an occasional nice evening with family or friends, and above all, of course, some financial security. Needless to say', he added, 'they are people who can be inspired to great and noble sacrifice, but also to bitter hatreds. As the world goes I suppose they are the luckiest people, but some of them – a great many, in fact – have grown ill with what would once have been called a sickness of the soul.'[4]

It is that sickness which infects Patricia, precisely because she cannot settle for what is within her grasp. As Miller explains, she is in 'the grip . . . of a success mythology which is both naive and brutal, and which, to her misfortune, she has made her own. And opposing it, quite simply, is her husband Leroy's incredibly enduring love for her, for nature and the world.'[5]

Patricia is bemused that her husband refuses to pursue the main chance, that he would rather take banjo lessons than chase success, donate his tools to a museum rather than sell them on the open market. Karen, on the other hand, finds no meaning in her wealth, wishing instead that she and her husband could raise vegetables together. But Frick is an accumulator, a businessman for whom such an ambition is merely evidence of sickness. It is almost as if they have married the wrong husbands. Karen likes banjos while Leroy does grow vegetables.

Patricia not merely has to find her way back to health, she has to relinquish the destructive dream that has destroyed her happiness. She recalls her family, blond, good-looking, poised to become what America promised its citizens they could be. Not only had she won a beauty contest, her two brothers had, respectively, won the All New England golf tournament and, almost, but not quite, the Olympic gold medal for pole-vaulting. But that was the peak of their achievement. Both men committed suicide, while she ended up in a mental hospital, because of their sense of disappointment: 'We were all brought up expecting to be wonderful, and . . . just wasn't' (21).

When Leroy enters he notices a difference about his wife. She is 'connected', one of Miller's favourite words indicating, as it does, a sense of inner coherence as well as partnership in the joint stock company of society. But there is still a barrier between them. Disappointment, blame, guilt still inhibit a true connection. These are two people with different interpretations of the world, different senses of the real, different priorities, who are nonetheless intent to reach out to one another. An expected kiss is not delivered, a greeting too easily turns into accusation. A history of failure and resentment has yet to be fully overcome, though the will to do so survives. A daughter, Leroy feels, has learned to condescend to him, and why else than because she has learned this from her mother. He remains baffled by Patricia's illness and understandably suspicious of her new sense of possibility, not least because of past disappointments.

Yet there are signs of compromise. Under her pressure, he has begun to ask for adequate payment for his work. For her part, she has determined to abandon regret in favour of hope, though no longer that distant hope which had rendered her life ironic. He is aware that his optimism irritates her, she that her pessimism has undermined their relationship.

Nor is it the women alone who are depressed and bewildered. Frick is bemused that he can have understood his wife so little, while Leroy is so independent that he distrusts those around him. He is as full of contradictions as his wife. Having resisted Frick's assumption that his forebears should determine his present behaviour, he denounces a man he thinks may have stolen one of his tools because 'he's a Chapman . . . they've had generals in that family, secretaries of state' (26). Then, having confessed to his own lack of trust, he insists to his wife that 'if you could only find two ounces of trust I know we could still have a life' (27).

She accuses him of denying his lack of ambition; he accuses her of denying the illusions that had destroyed her own family. He accuses her of living in the past; she him of failing to acknowledge the urgencies of the moment and blindness with respect to the future. She wants him to compete; he insists that the only one worth competing with is himself, that he is in a one-man line. Anger flares and subsides. Yet for all this, they are held together by love even as they are thrust apart by their differing values. They move towards a sense of acceptance, of one another, of their lives.

As Leroy observes, 'we're getting old! This is just about as rich and handsome as I'm ever going to be and as good as you're ever going to look' (31). They have, without knowing it, shared disappointment, differently defined, differently conceived but jointly experienced. Ironically, it is, in part, what now brings them together, that, and the glimpse of meaning that they separately conceive, she in a religious yearning, he in 'whatever makes me forget myself and feel happy to be alive. Like even a well-sharpened saw, or a perfect compound joint' (32). Given Miller's own background, it is hard not to feel that this is a statement that carries the weight of his own convictions. Certainly Leroy's assertion that 'you just have to love this world' (32) recalls *After the Fall*, in which the acceptance of imperfection becomes the natural route to an understanding of existence and the restoration of relationship.

But Patricia, too, released from her medication, has already taken a step along this road, rejuvenating Karen by a 'positive' attitude that surprises and gratifies Leroy, for whom this is precisely the promise of fundamental change. Her comment to Frick, still bemused by his wife's behaviour but aware of a transformation, that he should not 'all the time be disappointed in her' (34) is directed less at Frick than Leroy, who now learns, to his own astonishment, that she is the source of the 'optimism' that has so changed Karen.

'Who knows what's normal?' (35) asks Patricia, when Frick complains at his wife tap dancing at two in the morning, and, indeed, that question lies behind a play in which fractured relationships and damaged psyches can be traced to expectations about the norms of behaviour, the legitimacy of desires and the nature of existence. It is the misalignment of ambition with achievements, of needs with fulfilments that generates destructive anxieties.

Yet Frick, for all his apparent and actual impatience with the needs of others, is still sufficiently dedicated to his wife's recovery to allow himself to look ridiculous by singing Swanee River, as his aging and seemingly absurd wife tap dances. Short-tempered, abrupt and, finally, unable to extend his sympathy sufficiently to embrace her, he nonetheless shows some evidence of the care which may eventually redeem her.

For the moment, though, he can tolerate no more than a minute or so before his temper flares. Karen, vulnerable, close to collapse, falters and stops. Her escape from the hospital is problematic, depending, as it does, not only on her husband's return but his transformation. For Patricia, though, it does seem possible and she and her husband manage to come together, after so many years of tension and doubt. Though Karen and the catatonic woman stay behind, Leroy and Patricia leave. The stage direction, however, indicates that the play ends not with their departure – though audiences wish to applaud this as their preferred ending – but with a stage dominated by the woman who has shown not only no signs of recovery but no consciousness of the world around her: '*The* PATIENT *on the bed remains motionless. A stillness envelops the whole stage, immobility seems eternal*' (38).

In his essay 'About Theater Language', which appeared in the Penguin edition of *The Last Yankee*, and was reprinted in his collected *Theater Essays*, Miller speaks of *Waiting for Godot*, a play 'stripped clean of plot and even incident', and whose theme is stasis, a 'vaudeville at the edge of a cliff'. It is, he suggests, a play about 'humanity's endlessly repetitious paralysis before the need to act and change'.[6] He is talking in the context of a discussion of dramatic language but what is most striking is the degree to which everything he says of *Godot* could be said with equal force of *The Last Yankee*. It, too, is stripped clean of plot and incident. It is precisely concerned with repetition and paralysis and with the absolute necessity to change.

And what better description not only of Karen's performance, on the very edge of despair and collapse, but of Patricia and Leroy, dancing around a truth they have so much difficulty in facing, than a 'vaudeville at the edge of a cliff'. The difference is that for Beckett the irony was inescapable, that repetition is of the essence for his characters. They perform their lives with subtle variations, yet are afraid of difference for fear that it will only serve to intensify the irony.

In Miller's play we are offered the range of possibilities. The woman on the bed is a pure Beckett gesture, defeating absurdity only by succumbing to it, becoming inert, living a life without irony because a life without consciousness. Karen, meanwhile, rehearses for a life she cannot yet claim, readying herself for another performance against the possibility of one day escaping such repetition, an escape that can only come with a change which must be born in her husband's life no less than her own. Patricia and Leroy are Miller gestures, acknowledging imperfection, understanding what they have permitted history to do to them because it is in large part their own invention. They, too, dance at the edge, but the removal of drugs is the first step towards stripping off illusions which are not bred only in themselves. Their needs are in part shaped by the social world which they in turn must shape.

There are no certainties here, except that irony is not allowed final authority, beyond Miller's decision to end the play not with their hopeful exit but with the one who stays behind. But, then, this decision is not evidence of a new sensibility, a shift of emphasis. How, after all, did *All My Sons* end except with a man weighed down by the irony of his own idealism? How did *Death of a Salesman* end except with a baffled woman shouting out the word 'Free' while trapped in an isolation from which there seems no escape? *The Crucible*, *A View from the Bridge*, *Incident at Vichy*, *The Price*, all end equivocally. In the first, change is possible; meaning can be snatched from unmeaning. So, too, in *Incident at Vichy*. Not so, in *A View from the Bridge*. All the same, there is a resistant force here, a sense if not of balance then of transcendence. In Beckett's work that transcendence, or the longing for it, is the source of the irony, the humour, the vaudeville of human existence.

The theme of *The Last Yankee*, Miller has said, is hope, but 'hope is tentative always'. It is never possible to be sure that depression is entirely and permanently held at bay or that meaning has been grasped in its totality. The play thus 'simply sets the boundaries of the possible'.[7] Besides, a resounding climax would be out of keeping with New Englanders such as these for whom repression is a cultural inheritance. They live inwardly. That is both their strength and their weakness. But they inhabit a society in which externals are constantly paraded as the most immediate means of judging success or failure. And it is this cultural imperative that has sent the two women in the play into this retreat from the world: 'the endless advertising-encouraged self-comparisons with others who are more successful than they', hence 'the repeated references to ambition, to success and failure, to wealth and poverty, to economic survival, to the kind of car one drives and the suit one wears'.[8]

In his introduction, Miller comments on the significance of the forces that bear on the characters in *The Last Yankee*: 'the moral and social myths feeding the disease' from which they suffer. For him, the discussion of the size of the parking lot is something more than an attempt at phatic communion by a nervous Frick (incidentally, unlike all the other characters, always referred to by Miller in the speech indicators by his last name, he being the least intimately open, the most alienated and alienating). It is a 'direct blow' aimed at the 'thematic center', stressing, as it does, the sheer scale of the hospital and hence of the problem which otherwise we view only in microcosm. The vision of the play, he suggests, 'is intended to be both close up and wide, psychological and social, subjective and objective, and manifestly so',[9] and in that respect no different from the rest of his plays which exist precisely at this boundary, in this liminal zone.

There was a real Last Yankee. He lived just over the hill from Arthur Miller. Eventually, he heard that he had been turned into a character in a play and asked Miller if he could see it. Unfortunately, there was no production at the time. He is dead now and never did see what a playwright had made of his life. Of course, he was the inspiration rather than the subject of the play, which was far from being simply the portrait of a man and his wife in rural Connecticut. Yet there was something in this honest man wrestling with the contradictions of life that made him seem exemplary as he struggled to reconcile what he was with what he would be, the dreams of a culture with those of a man who sought contentment outside the parameters of national myths.

— ✳ —

Following the British opening of *The Ride Down Mount Morgan* plans were already in hand for an American production. To that end, Miller watched Patrick Stewart, who was appearing in *A Christmas Carol*. Stewart would indeed play Lyman Felt, but not for several more years. Meanwhile, however, another new play was in preparation.

The first reading of what Miller was still calling the 'Gellburg' play took place in March 1993. He had been working on it for some time. It had gone through many changes and would be changed again in rehearsal and even in previews. It was to open in both Britain and the United States and there were negotiations as to which would have priority. It was a play, he has explained, which looked over the edge of an abyss, an abyss which had suddenly become clear in 1938 and whose relevance had hardly disappeared with time.

In the end the play had its first performance at the Long Wharf, in New Haven, before moving to New York. In London, it opened at the Royal National Theatre. By now it scarcely came as a surprise that it was received with muted praise in his home country while winning the Laurence Olivier Award for Best Play in Britain. The British director David Thacker, responsible for the National Theatre production, subsequently went on to direct a film version.

✳

26

'Broken Glass'

Broken Glass concerns a woman, Sylvia Gellburg, who has suddenly lost the use of her legs. There is apparently no physical reason for this. Nonetheless, the effects are undeniable. If the cause is psychological, however, what can its source be? Admittedly, she is obsessed by the news from Germany. In particular, she is transfixed by a newspaper photograph of elderly Jews forced to scrub the sidewalks with toothbrushes. But these events are taking place thousands of miles away. She herself is, ostensibly, safe. Why, then, can she not get the images out of her head? And why is she curiously happy unless because, as Miller has said, 'it is as though something has settled now. She is a cripple. There is nothing she can do.'[1]

Sylvia is located at the point where the private and the psychological inter-leave with the public and the social. Her own life had been in a state of suspended animation long before the traumatic events of 1938. She is married to a man ill-at-ease with himself and others. He is proud to be the only Jew in a WASP company, seemingly unaware of the condescension that is the price to be paid for being transformed from a man into a symbol. His employer refers to him and his fellow Jews as 'you people'.[2] A prize-winning yachtsman, he 'had me aboard twice . . . The only Jew ever set foot on that deck' (11). By the same token, Gellburg celebrates his son's success in the military less for its own sake than for its significance as a sign of acceptance. He has entered the military precisely because his father 'wanted people to see that a Jew doesn't have to be a lawyer or a doctor or a businessman' (19). He is terrified of the stereotype.

Yet, at the same time, Gellburg is desperate to distance himself from his own Jewishness, constantly correcting those who mistakenly refer to him as Goldberg, determined to create a space between himself and what he takes to be a more obviously Jewish name. Suspected by his employer of collaborating with other Jews, possibly to the disadvantage of the company, he is anxious to deny it while performing functions that he suspects are given to him because of his race. And he pays a price for trying to inhabit this spiritual no-man's-land, for his profound unease about his identity and role. His relationship with his wife decays to the point at which their life together becomes a performance, a show in which they act out an intimacy that is no longer real. In particular, they have no sexual contact.

He lives, in short, a life of denial and *Broken Glass* is essentially a play about denial, on the personal and national level. Gellburg is a snob who has internalised the values of those who, for the most part, either despise or ignore him. It is, Miller has said, 'his defence against the feeling of emptiness he has'. And, indeed, these are characters who seem to lack inner resources precisely because they have evacuated everything from their lives which might provoke change and growth. Rather than question the world, they accommodate themselves to it. Rather than confront pain, they find a way to dull it with routine, lies, the self-abdicating strategies which leave them seemingly content with the status quo. As Miller has remarked of Gellburg, 'He is denying everything. He is denying his ethnicity, his Jewishness, and he is denying his wife's love as well.'

Why have they stayed together? It is the Depression. When others are without jobs, he is a provider. At some level, too, she knows he worships her, or the idea of her. It is a paradox she lacks the will to resolve. And besides, what else is on offer, except a sense of failure and shame. They have not had sexual relations for some twenty years, a good cause for divorce. But how was this truth to be uttered without herself attracting accusations? The answer, Miller says, is 'just stop the organism. Psychologically speaking, it goes into a state of arrest . . . just pulsing, not moving any more.'[3] Besides, she lived at a time when divorce was rare, an admission of failure, a sign of pathology. There were, Miller has said, many living out their years in Brooklyn unwilling and seemingly unable to act on the logic of their position.

There is a connection between *The Last Yankee* and *Broken Glass* in that in both works a woman retreats into mental anguish and, indeed, a form of paralysis, in one case emotional in the other literal, in the face of the failure of experience to come into line with expectation, hope, human necessities. In both works, the dramatic drive comes from the need to reconstruct lives that have stalled. These are characters who feel betrayed but are also agents of their own betrayal. The process of both plays is one by which they come to an understanding that they are principals and not agents, that they are active participants in their own fate.

Miller has said that

> what intrigued me in *Broken Glass* is the human animal's capacity to create a fantasy – based on reality to be sure – so powerful as to paralyse an otherwise physically sound woman. She has made war against herself, and the trigger is what she reads in a newspaper, something she can't possibly believe . . . In this play they are struggling with resignation all the time. Everybody in the play, including Gellburg. Gellburg is trying to find the way out of it, too.[4]

But the change of title – from *Man in Black* to *Gellburg* to *Broken Glass* (the last title offered by its British director, David Thacker, who urged that the play should, in Miller's words, 'spill over into its generalised application') – suggests the degree to which the emphasis changed. It is certainly Sylvia who finds her way back to an understanding which is painful but necessary, who becomes a teacher, an exemplary force, albeit when her husband is on the brink of death.

It is her dilemma, after all, that drives the action and focuses the private and public issues.

The wider society, meanwhile, beyond these two, and an employer whose lofty self-concern is merely another form of denial, is constituted by Sylvia's sister, Harriet, and her doctor, Harry Hyman, along with his wife. They 'bring the neighbourhood into the play'. They are 'a kind of secret chorus'. The women in particular offer a sense of normality. 'They are upholding the system, emotionally.' They are, Miller insists, 'real people'. Yet they are not immune to denial themselves. They have simply found ways to integrate their secret fears and temptations into a productive life. Problems, for the most part, remained unspoken. 'In 1938', he explained, 'we didn't talk about certain things. You don't talk about sexual problems openly. You do not embarrass your husband. You do not expose personal, family matters. You're Jewish. There is a need to keep it under the table. You do not draw attention to yourself.'

By way of illustration, he invoked the story of his first mother-in-law, an Irish–German Catholic who lived in Cleveland. Reading a report in the newspaper of a particularly gruesome crime she had said, ' "I hope he's not Catholic." And I can hear my mother, reading the same story, saying, "I hope he's not Jewish." It's a function of a minority, or of people who feel that they are.' Then, with obvious relevance to the play, but with a gesture characteristic of his drama as a whole, he broadened his remark from the personal to the political, 'I was in Cambodia, and the Vietnamese used to go around with this load because they were known as the Jews of Cambodia. They did all the business. And, indeed, two weeks after we left, some two hundred thousand of them were slaughtered in one night by Cambodian people. There was a pogrom. Right through the night. The Mekong River was red with blood.'[5]

The repressions which have generated not only Sylvia's condition but the broken relationship between her and her husband and, indeed, between her and her life, plainly has its deeply personal origins, but it is also, we slowly discover, a product, too, of her situation as what she later, proudly, and to her husband, shockingly, declares to be a 'Jewish woman'.

The doctor, meanwhile, has his own repressions, his own ambiguities. He is an idealist, 'in the sense' Miller explained in rehearsals, 'that a man of tremendous energy always is'. 'He's a little bit like Dr Stockmann, in *An Enemy of the People* – life-loving. He has a good taste of fresh bread in his approach.'[6] But he is also a womaniser though, for his wife, this seems to add a curious frisson to their relationship. An early version of the play left the nature of this relationship somewhat vague. In subsequent drafts subtle changes were made and a new scene written, Miller's work method often being not only to make changes as he goes along but also to wait until the read-through to get a sense of what might be missing. Hence, he added a scene after the first day's read-through for the American production, and another, between the three women characters as Gellburg lies dying, at the request of his British director, before the British production.

The changes with respect to Dr Hyman and his wife were firstly to push back the date of his last affair, and, then, to write a brilliantly witty scene, the end of the current scene 1. In this it becomes clear that Hyman's wife is in part drawn to him because of his wit, his ability to embrace her within a story of his own imagining, as well as by the very sexuality which makes him attractive to others. He is a Dick Diver figure with the ability to create sustaining fictions. He is, Miller stresses, 'a lover of life'. Between treating patients he rides his horse along the bridle path which runs along Ocean Parkway, heading for Coney Island.

The effect of these changes was somewhat to moderate the sexual charge which seems to leap between doctor and patient as Sylvia responds to a man who appears to care enough about her to address her needs without thinking of himself. It is a key moment because in part she is jolted from the stasis into which she is lapsing not only by the external shock of the news she reads but also by the reanimation of an aspect of her life that she had thought dead. Her sexual reawakening, albeit not fulfilled, sends a charge through her, sufficient, at one moment, to persuade her that she might indeed be able to walk once more. She gets to her feet and walks a few stumbling paces, a scene, incidentally, which poses actors and director a major difficulty in that the play ends with her rising to her feet and it is necessary that this should not prove anti-climactic or overly melodramatic.

The play opens with the sound of a lone cellist, in the American production recorded, in the British, live and on stage. Gellburg has come to consult Dr Harry Hyman. Gellburg is dressed in a black suit and with a black tie. When he offers to buy his wife a car, it is a Dodge: 'aren't they all black?' (20), asks his wife. It is an echo of the opening lines of Chekhov's *The Seagull*. 'Why do you always wear black?' asks the schoolmaster Medviedenko of the young woman Masha. 'I'm in mourning for my life', she replies, a line itself derived from Maupassant's *Bel-Ami*. It is a remark Miller is fond of quoting, applying it once to the 'sad sack' Lee J. Cobb. Here it would seem to have an immediate application to a man whose life is as much on hold as is his wife's.

The scene is in part expository, immediately establishing the fact of Sylvia's paralysis, but, in a characteristically humorous opening, it deftly establishes the nature of the characters. Margaret, Hyman's wife, is an insatiable talker, indiscreet in her curiosity about her husband's patients, intellectually alert. She is also disappointed, however, in the sense that Patricia had been in *The Last Yankee*: 'By rights he ought to be on Park Avenue if he only had the ambition, but he always wanted a neighbourhood practice.' By the same token, Gellburg says of Sylvia that she 'could have run the Federal Reserve' if she 'was a man' (7). Like Miller's own mother, then, Sylvia is a woman whose possibilities have been closed down in a world which offers no role for a woman other than living vicariously through her husband. As she says, 'if I'd had a chance to go to college, I'd have had a whole different life' (17).

Though she had secured a good job, as head bookkeeper in a large corporation, she allowed herself to be persuaded to abandon it by her husband. There is, in other words, another kind of paralysis at work here as women are socially immobilised, denied the right to act. She is, as Hyman tells her, cut off from herself. The effect of the paralysis, indeed, as of the mental illness in *The Last Yankee*, is briefly to reverse gender roles, the husbands in both instances listing the domestic chores that have now devolved on them, thereby underscoring the gendered nature of their world.

Gellburg, meanwhile, is impatient with her chatter, humourless, inward, a Republican in the age of Roosevelt and the New Deal. His values, it transpires, are close to those of his employer. When Hyman appears, he is described as 'conventionally handsome . . . a determined scientific idealist'. He is plainly socially aware, conscious of the plight of the poor, aware of the situation in Germany, not least because his new patient, Sylvia, is obsessed with it, though he is no less naive with respect to it than anyone else. Having qualified as a doctor in Germany, driven from America by the quotas applied to Jews in American medical schools, he cannot reconcile his own experiences there – 'We had a marvellous student choral group' (6) – with the Anschluss and the threatened invasions of Czechoslovakia and Poland. He detects, however, that this situation is not only the root of her problem but also the occasion for disagreement between Gellburg and his wife. Where she is anguished by what she reads, her husband is inclined to withhold his sympathy: 'It's no excuse for what's happening over there but German Jews can be pretty . . . you know . . . (*Pushes up his nose with his forefinger.*) Not that they're pushy like the ones from Poland or Russia . . .' (5).

In this first encounter between the doctor and Gellburg, Hyman probes dangerous territory. As the director of the American production John Tillinger observed to Ron Rifkin, playing the part of Gellburg, 'he talks about sex, the major taboo. It comes close to everything that's dangerous in your life. And the Nazis. He confronts every issue that is a disaster in your psyche.' And if it seems strange that a doctor should seem to enter the province of a psychoanalyst, Miller pointed out that 'in those days, doctors, MDs, confronted psychological problems all the time. It was an age when you never thought of going to a mental doctor unless you were climbing up the wall. A GP in those days took everything. He was part of the neighbourhood.' But this doctor is not without problems of his own. His compassion and his sexuality are connected. In that sense it is, perhaps, not surprising that he should turn so quickly to this area as a possible key to his patient's problem.

This is a man prone to enter his surgery wearing his riding clothes, exuding a sexual charge of which his wife is all too aware. Indeed we are offered a hint, even this early in the play, that his wife suspects his motives in becoming involved in a case which he should perhaps refer to a psychiatric specialist. And, indeed, he does call in a second opinion but cannot let go of the case, intellectually challenged, as he is, but also drawn to a woman whose needs are manifest if as yet unfocused.

As the play progresses, indeed, Gellburg's association, at least in Sylvia's mind, with the forces at large in a remote Germany, begin to pull the private and the public stories together. Margaret's observation, as he leaves the surgery, that 'He's a dictator, you know', resonates later as we discover more about a man whose inner conflicts lead him to violence. When Ron Silver, who played Hyman in the American production, observed in rehearsals that Gellburg has an anti-Semitic streak, and that Sylvia has 'her own personal Nazi who made her into a passive, fearful victim, paralysed, incapable of doing anything on her own to change her position or save herself', Miller immediately endorsed his interpretation. He also endorsed Tillinger's remark that, 'if the Nazi thing had not happened I think she would have gone to her grave accepting that this is the way I am supposed to have lived. But witnessing their passivity somehow changes her, gives her a catalyst.'

Later in the play we learn that Gellburg has struck his wife. In rehearsals there was a debate as to the extent to which there should have been a record of such violence. Miller recalled his grandfather throwing clocks at his mother, and missing. In the play it is a piece of steak. The idea, though, was not that he should seem simply to be a brutaliser of women but that there should be tensions within him that could lead to such actions. The fact that the weapon should be steak was a means whereby the violence could be invoked and at the same time, if not mitigated, then, through ironic humour, drained of too great a centrality.

At the same time, Sylvia's later remark that 'Phillip can hit, you know' (55), together with her sister's recalling of an event in which he had dragged his wife upstairs, accidentally hitting her head as they went, makes a connection between the violence in Europe and that closer to home which serves to put the two elements together in Sylvia's mind, a link which she later makes in recounting a dream to Hyman.

Sylvia, when we first encounter her, is described as 'buxom, capable and warm', but also 'intense' and with an 'almost haunted interest' in the newspapers that she scans for the news from Europe which appals and fascinates her in equal degree. But the conversation with her husband which follows deals not simply with events in Germany, but with the long-suppressed truth of their relationship. At first obliquely, and then more directly, Gellburg admits to her, as he must, what he cannot admit to the doctor. On first marrying her he had felt no love and soon developed an impotence from which he has never recovered. In his eyes, moreover, she had betrayed him by mentioning it to her father, who in turn referred them to a rabbi, a fact which, incidentally, says something about her relationship with her mother who, in the American rehearsals, Miller admits, might have been a more likely confidante. Indeed, the mother, who 'worships Phillip' (26), had to be protected from the truth. Thus,

Sylvia has stayed in the marriage 'for my mother's sake, and Jerome's sake and everybody's sake except mine' (23). This is that other paralysis from which she has suffered for twenty years.

Sylvia centres her hope on Dr Hyman, responding to a sensuality which is almost instinctive on his part. This is a man with a reputation from his youth. Sylvia's cousin still remembers him from a brief relationship twenty-five years before, though to him she was simply one among many. He comes to examine Sylvia and in the process comments on her 'beautiful legs' and 'strong beautiful body'. When she sits up he begins to cup her face in his hand, 'but stands and moves abruptly away' (33), suddenly aware, as it seems, of what he may be doing, the logic of his own response. Even so, he tells her that she is 'a very attractive woman' and that he has not 'been this moved by a woman in a very long time' (33). As Miller observed in the American rehearsals: 'It's the conflict we want, between him and himself. That's his domain. Where the dialectic stops we've got to back up and keep the dialectic going. If he seems to have solved it by saying "I'm going to screw her", that's out. Wherever it overflows the part we can lower the temperature.'

The fact is, though, that Hyman, too, has his demon. His power is also his weakness. When she impulsively kisses his hand, he retreats from her but still finds himself saying, 'Your body strength must be marvellous. The depth of your flesh must be wonderful' (36). His techniques, indeed, are deeply suspect. Trying to elicit information from her he says, 'I want you to imagine that we've made love . . . And you begin to tell me some secret things' (37). He kisses her on the cheek: 'he'd love to do that', Miller explained to the London cast, 'but he's not going to. She'd love him to, but it's not going to happen. That's life!'

When Gellburg next meets Hyman, for the first time he admits that he and Sylvia have not had a sexual relationship for many years but insists that they have now renewed that relationship. He simultaneously wishes to reveal the truth and cover it up. He is, in that sense, paralysed emotionally and sexually. The result is a bizarre story in which he alleges that they have made love but that she, being asleep, had subsequently denied it. He is caught in his own contradictions, protecting himself against her likely denial while himself wishing to deny the profound anxiety and self-doubt he comes close to confessing.

Describing the scene in the American rehearsals, Miller says of Hyman that he assumes that Phillip had made love and that 'this forces Phillip to agree'. We feel the 'repressed nature of the man – the torture. It's got to be the outcry of a man who is terribly contained.' He was, he explains, very insecure with Sylvia. 'She is a beauty. The slightest suggestion that he would not be able to dominate her had made him insecure. He lives in a world of appearance, of documents, of total control. He tries that with the doctor.'

For his part, Hyman is sensitive that Sylvia may have hinted something of his own behaviour, a sensitivity which signals the extent to which his motives may, indeed, be confused. When Gellburg leaves, Hyman's wife Margaret immediately registers this: 'You don't realize how transparent you are. You're a pane of glass' (45). The windows of Jewish shops and houses are not the only broken glass in a play in which the shattering of social contracts is at issue. The irony is that Sylvia's concern for what is happening thousands of miles away is the best evidence for the survival of a sense of social obligation otherwise denied by her society and others. As Hyman observes, 'It's like she's connected to some . . . some wire that goes half around the world, some truth that other people are blind to' (46). Connection, as ever, is a key word to Miller. Sylvia's problem is that she is aware, in a confused way, of her connection to distant events but has lost the connection with her own life.

When Hyman next visits Sylvia she is wearing perfume and her hair has been done. It is as if she had prepared herself for the visit of a lover. For the first time she grants him access to her dreams, in particular to a dream in which she is pursued by Germans and brutalised by a man with Phillip's face. It is simultaneously an account of a dream and an act of betrayal as she exposes her fears about her husband to a man whom, on one level, she seems to regard as her symbolic or potential lover. Commenting on this episode during the British rehearsals, Miller remarked to Margot Leicester, playing the part of Sylvia, that,

> dreams somehow make us seem important and she is dying to tell it. She has finally got someone to tell it to. It has surrealistic elements to it and at first she can't quite place Phillip in it. It's a mixture of the pleasure of telling it and the suppression of it that you've got to find the balance for. By pleasure, I mean relief. This play is largely about denial and this is one moment when she is confronting denial. In recounting the dream, she turns Phillip around before her own eyes and ours.

Impulsively she draws Hyman to her and kisses him. As Miller observed in the American rehearsals,

> She is suddenly totally alone and if she draws him down and kisses him, gratefully, that he is there and that he is sympathetic, that's what's involved. And that action is more scary than anything they've said. She is scared to have done that. She is scared she is going to lose him. This is the first time she has been able to talk about this with anybody. It's not as if it were a twice-told tale. And so there is a freshness to her interest in this whole thing. She could never talk about it with her sister and she certainly couldn't talk about it with her mother because her mother loves Phillip.

There is a freshness about her discovery of all this, and a gratitude to him that he is equally capable of listening to her, spending time with her.

For Miller, the image he associates with Sylvia is that of suspended animation.

> It is as though she has something in her and she can't bring it out, she can't give it birth. There's something alive in there that's trying to get out. The reason Hyman is important to her is that she feels she is being judged all the

time. She is being judged by her mother, if she says she can't make it with Phillip. She is being judged by the rabbi who says, look, you are just going to have to get in there and be a wife. No matter which way she turns there is going to be a judgement upon her. And he is the first one who comes into her life who manifestly isn't judging her. And she knows that there is a welcome for anything that she wants to say or could say now, because she is judging herself.

Amy Irving, who played Sylvia in the American production, chose an allied metaphor. For her, 'it is as if the baby's been born but the soul hasn't been put in yet'.

It is precisely because of her dependence on Hyman, however, that she is especially shocked to be asked to confirm or deny Phillip's story of their making love. The very thought that this man, on whom she has pinned her hopes (romantic and sentimental no less than medical), should have believed her husband is a blow. Perversely, it is as if this man, too, has betrayed her, as if he is impotent to help her and thus becomes like her husband, more especially when, like her husband, he seems to minimise the crisis she sees as happening in Germany. The two principal anxieties in her life come together and she feels suddenly vulnerable. If in Germany they 'pick Jews off the street' (56), Hyman, in suggesting that she should be seen by a psychiatrist, seems to want 'to put me away somewhere!' (56). Hysterical with fear, she climbs out of bed to reach Hyman, and though the stage direction merely indicates that she collapses on the floor she herself indicates to her husband that she 'almost started walking' (58). In production, this is a difficult scene to get right. It has to convey a sense of possibility without detracting from the final moments of the play. It is a crescendo within a larger crescendo. In the London rehearsals, Miller offered the following suggestion to Margot Leicester: 'when you get off the bed to go to him, if you could possibly take one step towards him so that she looks as though she might be walking, though needless to say it's nothing she's thinking about. She needs to be at the height of her anxiety so that she doesn't think about it.' He then offered an apparent non sequitur by way of explanation, a remark, however, which ties the action into the play's central theme.

It's fear and the feeling we get that we've learned to suppress it, as with this Ruandan thing [the genocidal attack by the Hutus on the Tutsis in 1994] with half a million people down the sluice. And some of these people had been there for six generations. You go to Africa, it's the Indians who are the businessmen. And you think, well, why doesn't someone do something about this? It's the helpless feeling of observing this thing happen, but of course in this instance they are her people. The point of my remark is that if she can throw one foot out and then go down on that, we should, for an instant, think that she is going to do it. For one split second. When you get up we could feel your astonishment that you are on your feet.

It is a physical sign of the struggle to reclaim her rights to her own life, to overcome the inertia that she has allowed to define her.

When Phillip appears, he senses the intimacy between the two and is anxious to replace Hyman as Sylvia's doctor but she has begun to feel more than the return of physical strength. To his surprise, she resists his decision with what she tellingly calls 'a Jewish woman's tone of voice' (58), having begun the process of reclaiming her identity. After years of quiet acquiescence, she is now prepared to confront him: 'I'm going to say anything I want to' (59). She laments: 'What I did with my life! Out of ignorance. Out of not wanting to shame you in front of other people. A whole life . . . I took better care of my shoes' (59). As Miller explained to Amy Irving, 'it's the reassertion of the trap that she's in. I did what I did and now I'm back to square one. But it only lasts for a moment. It has to flip back and forth. Passivity and then activity.'

At last Phillip, too, feels able to address the subject he has been suppressing. He had become impotent, he explains, desperate suddenly to explain and therefore justify himself, because he felt her resentment at his asking her to leave work. In that resentment he felt a challenge to himself and his manhood, amplified by her refusal to have another child. 'She had apparently been the kind of woman he wanted', Miller explains, 'she wouldn't menace him. She resembled her father, a kindly sweet man who would have died without bothering anyone.' But her resentment had unmanned him. Now, however, rather than respond to his confession, she refuses to share a bed with him. The tears Phillip sheds are less those of anger than defeat, though even now Miller retains a rhythm of acceptance and rejection as Sylvia reaches out a consoling hand, which nonetheless never quite touches him. 'She is moved', he remarked in the British rehearsals, 'by the fact that his front has broken, that he is helpless. And that is very hopeful. It is moving because she is moved.' He has, in effect, to be broken in order to have any chance of reconstructing himself.

And rhythm is central to Miller's concerns. In the British rehearsals he clapped his hands to indicate the rhythm of a speech. But just as important to him is the emotional rhythm of the play, with its fluctuating moods, its pulse of revelation and concealment, hope and despair. The notes he offers to the actors are frequently to do with the need to modulate emotional intensity, to withhold when necessary, to look for the humour interlaced with seriousness. As he remarked to the British cast early in rehearsals,

> the irony of the play has to come out more. My presence probably makes it seem more of a serious play than it is. There's enough seriousness in this play. We don't have to do it every minute. Whenever there's a chance to lighten it, do so. First, because it makes it more real. We can't stay serious all the time. You're always looking for an outlet for your human emotions. It shouldn't get lugubrious.

To explain the blend, he told a joke about two people burying their friend. As they looked in the casket one remarked, 'He looks good in there', to which the other replied, 'Why wouldn't he? He's just back from two weeks in Florida.'

The crisis now deepens as Gellburg, in confronting his employer, has a heart attack ('He has a heart attack', Miller explained, 'because it's turned inward. He can't make it.') This is followed by a scene added at the request of the British director, David Thacker, who wanted to see the women together before the concluding confrontation between the men. It is a scene in which Sylvia at last feels able to tell others about herself and the history of her relationship with Phillip: 'I was stronger than him. But what can you do? You swallow it and make believe you're weaker. And after a while you can't find a true word to put in your mouth' (64). Her sister, providing the wider context of such passivity and denial, adds, 'How can people start saying what they know? – there wouldn't be two marriages left in Brooklyn' (65). For Margaret Hyman, there is a simple fatalism: 'You draw your cards face down, you turn them over and do your best with the hand you got. What else is there, my dear? What else can there be?' (65). The 'what else' is the subject of the play.

The ending was always the most problematic part of the play, changed several times in the writing and in rehearsals. The question centred around the final moments, rather than Phillip's sudden understanding. It is as though the heart attack has shocked him into a realisation of what he has made of his life and what he has allowed others to make of him. He understands, or permits himself to understand, for the first time, the role in which his employer has cast him – 'You got some lousy rotten job to do, get Gellburg, send in the Yid' (67). As he lies in his bed he tries to confess to the burden he felt as a Jew, a subject which has obsessed him but, ironically, about which he knows so little, surprised that Hyman should so readily have married outside the faith, that Jews ride horses, that there are Chinese Jews.

His fear, it seems, had led him to deny those aspects of himself that left him deeply anxious and insecure, including his identity as a Jew; it has led him to self-hatred. In the same way, Sylvia's fear has led to her blotting out her own personality, to her paralysis. Nonetheless, despite the significance of the scene, Miller's advice to the British cast was to 'enjoy it as much as you can because guys like this can last another twenty years or die in the next three minutes' and 'it's in Hyman's nature to find humour in everything'.

The ending itself changed considerably between the various drafts. In 1992, when it was still called *Gellburg*, Phillip collapses on the floor. Hyman calls for an oxygen mask, unable to reach it himself since he is busy giving artificial respiration. Sylvia rises from her wheelchair, walks the few steps to it, and hands it to him. Phillip dies. The play ends with Hyman's ambiguous question to Sylvia: 'Do you have some feeling?' This remained the ending in the August 1993 version, now called *Broken Glass*. By February 1994, however, it had been changed so that as they await the arrival of an ambulance Sylvia calls out, 'I'm all right! Can you hear me? I'm all right, Phillip! Can you hear me!' By April 1994, the ending was further modified as Phillip seemingly dies at the moment Sylvia struggles to her feet.

The version that went into rehearsal in America called for oxygen cylinders and involved debate about resuscitation techniques, including the plunging of a needle into Phillip's chest. It was also a version whose ending caused some anxiety among the actors, who, in Miller's absence, nerved themselves to raise their worries with him. There were concerns that it could seem melodramatic or 'operatic'. Ron Silver, playing Hyman, 'didn't want the feeling of the black widow, able to stand up because he is dead'. And, indeed, that was a problem inherent in the ending in that Sylvia needs to find her own way to abandon her paralysis and not have that gifted to her by her husband who, after all, has effectively controlled her life to this point.

By this stage, however, Miller himself was modifying the ending. The press night was deferred and new material added, so that the play ends not with the death of Phillip and a final comment from Hyman, but with Sylvia, rising from her wheelchair. As he explained,

> I don't want him to die, though he might later. On the other hand, he might not. The reason is that when a dead body is on stage everybody knows he's not dead. Aside from that, I think it's much better that it be open. They could very well end up together again. This thing need not be ending here. So we've got it both ways. I don't know what would happen because I can't predict people in that way. He could come out of this and she could say, 'I'm happy you're better, but I can't stand it any more. I'm going to leave.' She could also say, 'I think we understand each other somehow,' and certainly he would know more than he did at the beginning of the play about how she was and what she was going through. He would be a much more informed and mature man than he was at the start. Given the conventions at the time you would have to lean toward them not being divorced. People just didn't do it. So, I'm not going to say one way or the other. I really don't know. He may not be dead. That's not the issue – whether he lives or dies. The issue is their possible relationship, or not, or what has been gained or learned from all this. That's the issue.

Dead or not, Gellburg has reclaimed his Jewishness, understood, finally, what he has denied. Sylvia has recovered more than the use of her legs. She at least has the potential to take her life in her hands at last. Meanwhile, beyond these two people in Brooklyn, struggling to rediscover their identities and hence their ability to act, is the story of a society unwilling to engage political and moral realities and a world stunned into inaction. Historically, isolationism would end. Hitler would eventually be confronted though only, it has to be said, because of Pearl Harbor and Hitler's historic mistake in declaring war on America. The price of inaction, however, would prove profound, then and later, as, on a personal level, it did for Sylvia and Philip Gellburg who came so close to destroying themselves and one another.

In *Broken Glass*, as in so many other Miller plays, the need is to acknowledge responsibility for one's own life and thereby for the common life that is society. We are, he insists, the makers of History, as of our private histories. Unthinking acquiescence is a threat not only to identity but to the survival of a moral sense, and perhaps to survival at all.

— ✳ —

Broken Glass ran for ten weeks on Broadway. At the end of 1994, Miller went to Prague where there was a staged reading of *The Archbishop's Ceiling*. Five years on from the fall of the Berlin Wall, the play was being performed in the city where it had been set.

In 1995, he spent time at Oxford University, worked on the script of the film version of *The Crucible* and attended and participated in a gala performance at Britain's Royal National Theatre to mark his eightieth birthday. He also attended a gala dinner hosted by the Arthur Miller Centre at the University of East Anglia. The two principal speakers were David Thacker and Salman Rushdie. By the end of November he had twenty-seven productions in Germany alone.

He had suspected that *Broken Glass* might prove his last play. He was wide of the mark. In 1995, less than a year after that play had closed, he began writing a play he was calling 'The Club'. He was, as yet, unsure as to its direction or theme. After a few months he had changed its title to 'The Powder Room', reflecting the women characters he had begun to introduce. Then it became 'Digressions'. It was, he thought, about a dying man who was 'suffering from a severe case of life'. After several more title changes, including 'Subject', the play finally became *Mr Peters' Connections* and opened, in 1998, as part of the special Signature Theatre season of Miller's plays, with Peter Falk as Mr Peters. It opened in London, at the Almeida Theatre, two years later.

✳

27

'Mr Peters' Connections'

In the plays of the 1980s and 90s, Miller's characters seem to come under increasing pressure. They spiral down into depression, fragment into competing personalities, lose their grasp on the past, base their ethical systems on nothing but their own desires elevated to moral principle. The external world becomes a kind of theatre in which they play roles as though performance were itself a value, while the internal world seems to lose definition. His increasing distaste for a society that seemed to offer little by way of community and nothing in terms of transcendence, led him to write plays in which the very structure of meaning seemed insecure. These were plays in which characters struggle to make sense of themselves and a world bereft of certainties. His next two plays, indeed, were mordant comedies about a society seemingly in decline, an existence apparently without direction or purpose.

In 1998, came a play, *Mr Peters' Connections*, which seemed appropriate to a playwright in his eighty-third year, writing as a decade, a century and a millennium slowly wound down. It was, he suggested, 'a crazy comedy' in which 'a man is confronting his own death and wrestling with the inconsequential nature of what he conceives his life to have been, because he can't find a meaning for the whole affair'.[1] As he said at the time of the British production in July 2000, 'It's tough to be near death and have to think that there's no definition to your life.'[2]

Mr Peters has outlived his passions and feels abandoned by the retreating tide, the victim of an irony without redress: 'Look at the veins in the back of my hand – shall these warped fingers stroke a breast, cup an ass . . . ? And you call life fair?'[3] As his guide to this world of memory and regret observes, 'life is one to a customer and no returns if you're not satisfied' (23).

Yet the concern out of which the play was born was not just a product of age, of a sense of the slow closing down of options and a slackening grasp on the real. In 1962 he had lamented the fact that 'People no longer seem to know why they are alive; existence', he suggested, 'is still a string of near experiences marked off by periods of stupefying spiritual and psychological stasis and the good life is basically an amused one.' Such stasis, such 'standing around with nothing coming up is as close to dying as you can get'.[4]

The action of the play, he has explained, 'is the procession of Mr Peters' moods, each of them summoning up the next, all of them strung upon the line of his anxiety, his fear, if you will, that he has not found the secret, the pulsing centre of energy – what he calls the subject – that will make his life cohere.'[5] As he explained, 'This play doesn't proceed in a narrative manner, but one emotion breeds another . . . I think we are driven more by feeling than objective reality anyway.' How else, he asked, 'could you elect Reagan?'[6]

It is a play that laments the loss of youth, the stilling of urgencies, the dulling of intensity, as love, ambition, utopian dreams devolve into little more than habit and routine. It is a play about loss, the loss of those connections that seemed so self-evident as moment led to moment, as relationships gave birth to their own meaning, as the contingent event shaped itself into coherent plot, as the fact of the journey implied a purposeful direction and a desirable desti-nation. It is about a deracinated man who has lost his connections to the past, to other people, to a sense of himself. It is a contemplation of life itself whose intensity and coherence slowly fade, whose paradox can never be resolved, as it is also a confrontation with death.

In 1995, when he was just sixty-five pages into what he was now calling *The Powder Room*, it seemed to Miller essentially a play about life's incoherence. The daily details of living stripped away, the essential nature of experience seems to stand exposed. The past may have seemed secure but with death approaching seeming is no longer enough. Peters's once apparently secure grasp on life, its shape and purpose, has loosened but in the process he comes to feel that such confidence may have been illusory.

The play's central character, Mr Peters, is in a kind of reverie, somewhere between wakefulness and sleep, 'when the mind, still close to consciousness and self-awareness, is free to roam from real memories to conjectures, from trivialities to tragic insights, from terror of death to glorifying in one's being alive'.[7]

As in *Death of a Salesman* and *After the Fall*, we are inside the head of the central character. Where Quentin had sought to reconcile himself with his life, its betrayals and fallibilities, before moving on, Mr Peters is looking for some structure of meaning that can justify having lived at all. He summons up fragments of his own past – people, places, events. These had once seemed so vivid but now appear no more than dissociated moments, shards of a past that no longer relate to any greater purpose. They are remnants of experience that fail to offer the grace of order or the illusion of coherence. He is a man who can 'hear the shovel biting a hole into the earth', feel the threat of 'utter darkness' (18). Yet he cannot convince himself that he has lived to a purpose or that the world manifests a sense which can offer him the sanction of meaning.

A one-time pilot for Pan American Airways, he seems to be approaching a final landing. 'If you planted an apple tree when I was born', he says, 'you'd be cutting it down for firewood by now', a reminder of another airman, in *All My Sons*, whose death was marked by the planting of an apple tree. Aware that he is 'in the long glide down to the wrong side of the grass' (25), he discovers that 'the sweetness' has gone without a compensatory gift of wisdom. In the grandstand at last, he can make no sense of what he sees, feel no connection with what goes on around him.

One by one he summons those with whom he has shared his life, but he encounters them first as strangers, as if they had already passed beyond the sphere in which he exists. Asked why he fails to recognise them, Miller replied, 'I am not quite sure why that is, to tell you the truth, excepting that relatives, friends he has known, are strangers, the equivalent of strangers, and it is only through the course of the play that they become his relatives again, become his people. He meets them as unnamed human beings before they become members of his family.'[8] A one-time lover, a brother, a daughter, they appear and disappear but he can never quite recall what they were to him or he to them. Yet he knows they must hold a clue to the meaning of his existence. The question is, what did he derive from them? What was important? What was the subject?

For Willy Loman, meaning always lay in the future. Meanwhile, he felt merely temporary. In *Mr Peters' Connections* meaning lies not in the future but the past, in memories that even now are dulling like the embers of a once-bright fire. It lies in the lives of those others who, in dying, had taken with them pieces of the jigsaw, fragments of the world whose clarity of outline had been a product of shared assumptions, mutual apprehensions.

What happens, he implicitly asks himself, to our sense of ourselves and the world when one by one his fellow witnesses withdraw their corroboration. As they die and withdraw from the stage, lovers, friends, relatives take incremental elements of meaning with them, gradually thin his sense of the real to transparency. And what of his own former self, with its passions, convictions, necessities? What connection does he have with that, what continuities can be said to imply a plot to his life, a subject to the drama he performs?

The word "connections" refers not only to his links with other people, particularly those once closest to him, but also to his desire to discover the relationship between past and present, simple event and the meaning of that event, act and consequence, between what he was and what he has become. In other words, he is in search of a coherence that will justify life to itself. In facing the impending fact of his death, he is forced to ask himself what life has meant, what has been its subject. The simplest of questions remains the most necessary of questions: 'What is it all for?'

Like so many other Miller protagonists, Mr Peters wants to convince himself that he has left a thumbprint on the world, but to do so has to believe not only that his life has amounted to something but that there is a solid surface on which that thumbprint may be left. He is not so much raging against the dying of the light, as desperate to believe that the light was real and illuminating, that his life and its existence went beyond mere contingency. He wants to believe that the light which once flooded it is not yet extinguished. Recalling his time as a pilot, he observes that 'When you've flown into hundreds of gorgeous sunsets, you want them to go on forever and ever . . . and hold off the darkness' (37).

Mr Peters' Connections is a play in which a man struggles to make sense of his own life, his times, his broken memories, somehow dislocated from their context, drained of their animating power. The 'broken structure' which is the set is a projection of the broken structure which is his life, a performance drained of inner logic. He even speaks like a playwright, or, perhaps, a member of the audience, observing his life as an audience observes a play: 'conflict is not my game anymore; or suspense; I really don't like trying to figure out what's going on' (4).

But that is what he is trying to do. As Miller remarks, he is looking for the 'pinion which connects' the events that he recalls. In his search for a connecting principle, indeed, he discovers a fluency which has plainly deserted him in his waking state, or why should he repeatedly remark upon it? So, in his conscious state spaces have begun to open up in his language, as in his memory. He is left trying to construct a whole from a handful of fragments, to infer a coherent picture from no more than a few seemingly random pieces of jigsaw. Indeed, silence seems to have become his more usual response: 'I'm known for not saying anything for eight hours at a time' (6).

Mr Peters's guide is Calvin, whom he vaguely recognises, as he should since he is his dead brother, who now acts as an escort not to the underworld but the subconscious. Once again, then, as in his early work, this is a play that has at its centre two brothers, except that the dialogue in this play is essentially with the self.

The play begins with what looks like a one-time nightclub, though oddly the three chairs grouped around a dusty piano still have instruments propped up against them – a bass, trumpet and drums, seemingly abandoned by musicians who simply walked away (details omitted from the British production). Equally discordant is the figure of a black bag-lady, Adele. She, Miller has said, 'is like the dust in the air. She is part of the city that he is always aware of, but nobody pays any attention to her. She makes remarks and nobody listens. They go right past her, through her. Occasionally, she takes the stage, but nobody is particularly listening, and that is really the way it is.'[9] She is 'neither dead nor alive, but simply Peters' construct, the to-him incomprehensible black presence on the dim borders of his city life'[10]. She is seated on the floor amid her bags, sipping from a bottle of wine, from time to time examining her face in a mirror and reading *Vogue* magazine. The scene, fittingly enough, is like a surrealist painting.

On to the stage come the figures of Calvin and Mr Peters, the latter slowly looking around himself before becoming still, as though trying to make sense of what he sees, as though in suspended animation. A man who confesses to having everything, he seems unsure what that everything might be, beyond an accumulated past which refuses to render up the meaning he seeks. After a moment, he absent-mindedly plays a few bars of 'September Song', with its invocation of passing time, but the music continues when he lifts his hands from the keyboard, a further surreal gesture, suggesting the nature of the world into which we are being inducted (in the British production at the Almeida Theatre, in July 2000, a player piano was used). And, indeed, laced through the play are songs from another age, redolent of old passions, stained with emotional memories ('This Can't Be Love', 'Just One of Those Things'). Peters seems to have the power to summon them up by doing no more than touch the keys of the piano or run his fingers over the strings of the bass.

Back from the past, too, comes an outmoded language, once the evidence of contemporaneity and now stale, hollowed-out, of antiquarian quaintness. An attractive woman becomes 'juicy. A prime sirloin. A rich pomegranate. A Spanish blood orange. An accordion-pleated fuck' (16). Even obscenities, once so current, so of the moment, so satisfyingly with-it, are no more than curiosities, drained alike of their fashionable, colloquial smartness and their seductive threat. By the same token, he struggles to make sense of the language around him. When told by another character that she eats bananas because she needs 'trace elements for the knees', he comments, 'you see, this is what I mean; when I was young no human being, from one end of the United States to the other, would have uttered that sentence' (34).

Language, social habits, values, politics, no longer make any sense to him. Age leaves gaps in his mind. He can now only observe a life he once lived. He has reached that stage in his life when names and memories slide away, turning life into a series of minor humiliations, humiliations that in part derive from what he once was when life could still thrill.

Suddenly, he has a vision of Cathy-May, a young woman, seated, naked but for a red veil. She is, it transpires, dead, and yet here she is vibrantly alive, as once she was, still with the power to animate him, if, simultaneously, to remind him of the irony of his present situation. He later imagines her as she might be now, since memory and imagination are organically related. Accordingly, as he imagines that middle-aged woman into existence, so the actress dons a wig, a middle-aged woman's coat and glasses. 'Would it be a little less angry between us now that she's complete and her fires banked?' (17) he wonders, only for them to dance together to a Cole Porter song as if that reconciliation were fact rather than imagined event.

There is a level on which he knows that some of those he encounters are dead. Thus Cathy-May suddenly becomes lifeless so that he struggles to infuse her with life. Later, he acknowledges Calvin's dead eyes and remembers his death by drowning. At the same time, however, they are alive in his memory, as the dead return in dreams, dulling the pain of loss.

His problem is that he now inhabits a supposedly real world in which reality is so absurd that it challenges the imagination. He has outlived those he loved, the career that once seemed to gift his life a shape and meaning. All that was stable has slipped away. Governments have fallen, friends are no longer reassuringly at the other end of the telephone line as he dials numbers which are, anyway, now defunct. For Miller, *Mr Peters' Connections* is a mixture of a social history, on the one hand, and a personal quest for some kind of redemption by the protagonist on the other. In other words, there is something more than sentimental lament about Peters's restless shuffling of experiences.

Nor is he, like Beckett's Krapp, simply running his fingers down the razor-blade ironies generated by a sudden collapse of the space between past and present. Nearly fifty years earlier, Willy Loman had searched through his life looking for the moment when hope became despair, when the logic of his life was broken. Later, Quentin, in *After the Fall*, had pressed the search key, looking for repeated evidence of betrayal, in hope, finally, of redemption. Mr Peters is less calculated, less in control, less sure of why his mind suddenly fills with such disparate moments. Yet he, too, is not finally content to submit to irony. Conscious that some connecting thread has seemingly broken, he nonetheless struggles to discover what it might be.

The play appears to take place in a kind of limbo. The building has served many other functions in the past, including that of a library, a restaurant and a bank. It contains its own history, as Peters does his. This is that New York that builds itself up only to pull itself down. And that changing cityscape contains long-dead stories whose traces are faintly visible. There are echoes and shadows here, too, to match those of this man who has lived to see the world change around him, its certainties dissolving along with social habits, national priorities, the values which had once seemed to pin it in place, guarantees of permanency.

His mind moves restlessly. At one moment the nude girl, Cathy-May, returns, now clothed, and he tries to reanimate her, breathing life into the corpse of the past. A moment later he is thinking of the war, when there had appeared to be a structure of meaning, a clear reason for living. That had been a morality play in which it was possible to play a role with confidence. Now, and throughout the play, though, he is aware of the spaces that have opened up – between him and other people, between the past and his baffled present, between events separated in time. 'What is the subject?' he repeatedly asks, desperate to find some spine to existence, to recapture the confidence of youth, the self-justifying certainties of sexuality, the collective effort for a purpose that was war. Slivers of that past return because, as the bag-lady remarks, 'something you forgot hasn't forgotten you' (10).

One thing that returns is his memory of working for Pan American Airways, evidently something more than a job. It was an avocation: 'Pan Am was not an airline, it was a calling, a knighthood' (11). It was also an institution that has disappeared, another sign of permanency and coherence turned to dust. Mr Peters is a man who has lived to see all the signs of his youth erased, the certainties dismantled, the clear paths to meaning occluded. Suddenly, there is no map to his life. He is lost. He is left with no more than a broken text, a cipher to which he lacks the key. He looks for the connections 'between his own experience and his demand for some meaning in his life'.[11]

He recalls a time when banks, 'built like fortresses' (18), were solid, resistant, seemingly a moral foundation stone even in their intimidating sense of exclusiveness. He invokes the robber barons who, out of religious fear if nothing else, bequeathed libraries and museums, monuments to fixity, confident gestures projected into a certain future. At the other extreme he invokes the force of revolutionary politics – 'science, hope, reason, equality' – as Calvin recalls 'Philosophical Marxist discussions going through the night' (22). This, it seems, was one of many promises on which history seems to have reneged, leaving, as Calvin suggests, 'Vacillation, indecision, self-satisfaction' (23).

Even the small change of life, that seemed to hold the world together – The Eagle Cafeteria, blueberry pie for ten cents – has disappeared: 'Remember banana splits; four balls of ice cream on a sliced banana, covered with hand-whipped cream, chocolate sauce and a maraschino cherry on top . . . for twenty-five cents? That, my friend, was a country, huh? I mean *that was a country!* – and whoever had a key to their front door?' (25).

Peters finds himself living in a world in which history is no longer common ground. Now, as a professor, he is confronted by students to whom the past is a mystery to which they feel no connection so that he ends up 'having to explain to a Princeton class which war you were in . . . behind our propellers we were saving the world! And now! which war . . .' (25).

The present moment seems all and the present is as mysterious to him as the past is to the students. It appears to be a world without values. The magazines are full of advertisements for breast or penile enhancement which cost the same as his family home had once done. The air is full of noise which does anything but give delight: 'Turn on the radio, turn on the television, what is it – just talking! It can sink the ship' (26).

Nor does public life offer a sense of moral fixity. Written at the time when President Clinton's sexual delinquencies were headline news, the play suggests that the institutions of the state can no longer even pretend to offer a defining structure: 'The President of the United States was above all morally righteous, you see, rather than just entertaining' (38). It is true that adultery in office was itself something of a national institution, providing a dubious sense of continuity, but it somehow managed not to displace the idea of virtue, in part precisely because it never became material for prime-time television, transformed, thereby, into soap opera serving nothing but ratings. As Calvin remarks, while the belief that 'A man who betrays his wife will betray his country' is no more than a vacuous slogan from another age, 'Morals count . . . even if you just say them' (32).

There is no longer a hierarchy of values. As a character says, accusingly, 'you are trying to pick and choose what is important' (40). In fact, Mr Peters is having a hard time hanging on to values of any kind, not least because everything on which he had based his life has dissolved. Miller himself has admitted to the naivety of some of his own earlier convictions, or at the very least the sense of unreality that comes with the disappearance of what had once seemed such solid ground. A one-time defender of Soviet Russia, who was later to speak out for those imprisoned there, an isolationist who tried to enlist, an enthusiast for America's wartime use of nuclear weapons who would later appear on anti-nuclear platforms, he was fully alive to the problem of sustaining a sense of oneself and of the world in the face of private and public change. As Mr Peters confesses, 'what's begun to haunt me is that next to nothing I have believed has turned out to be true. Russia, China, and very often America. People keep joining together to sweep back the ocean with a broom and call it a philosophy of life. Or a tribe or a country . . .' (43).

In a conversation with Vaclav Havel, Miller himself remarked, 'I am a deeply political person; I became that way because of the time I grew up in, which was the Fascist period . . . I thought . . . that Hitler . . . might well dominate Europe, and maybe even have a tremendous effect on America, and I couldn't imagine having an audience in the theater for two hours and not trying to enlist them in some spiritual resistance to this awful thing.'[12] Today, like Mr Peters, he is no longer so sure of an easy redemption, alive as he is to the transformation of a world he once believed himself to know in its fixities.

Ideologies, nationalisms, creeds, suddenly seem nothing more than structuring devices. They are expressions of fear, compensations for a sense of helplessness. And it is surely not irrelevant that this play should be written at a time when capitalism was triumphant, and in a world menaced by fundamentalisms. On the one hand, materialism, in which the self is seen as the ultimate value; on the other, a spiritualism which subordinates the self in the name of competing absolutes. On the one hand, a system that trades transcendence for immediate satisfaction and untrammelled freedom; on the other, a system that trades freedom for transcendent meaning. And between the two, a vacuum in which Mr Peters finds himself.

He is joined, suddenly, by a young couple, Leonard and Rose, she pregnant, though by whom is never clear, that no longer being a question with any social force. The connections between people, it seems, like everything else, lack permanence. Rose, we later learn, is his daughter, but, once again, in this dream world he encounters her as a stranger, as representative of a younger generation, more evidence of a broken continuity than anything else, though it is continuity he seeks. As he explains, 'I think what I'm trying to . . . to . . . find my connection with is . . . what's the word . . . *continuity* . . . yes, with the past, perhaps . . . in the hope of finding a . . . yes, a subject. That's the idea, I think' (36).

The enemy is in part fear and in part indifference, boredom, which is a form of dying. But if an unexamined life is not worth living, is an examined one? Is the broken connection a function of individual life, of social decline, or is the loss of energy he detects more profound? Is it a world which, in losing God, lost, too, a reason for existing: 'Washington, Jefferson . . . believed that God had wound up the world like a clock and then disappeared' (47). Seen thus, time is simply a process of that clock running down and individual lives merely echoes of that more general entropy: 'things have been getting worse since Eden' (46). God is 'precisely what is not there when you need him' (47). Some sanction has been removed from the world, some ultimate redemption, and this is in a play whose principal subject is a man's search for redemption, for some reason for living that will charge if not each day then each life with significance.

Marriage, is perhaps one such principle. There was a time when everything else faded away and that had seemed the essence of his existence. Now, though, among the names that slip away from him is his wife's. Indeed, he has trouble even recalling what she looks like until she enters the stage of his mind. It is not, he insists, anything as simple as Alzheimer's, merely that in his current state everything presents itself as part of a greater mystery.

That wife, Charlotte, however, herself fantasises, at least as she is improvised by his imagination and memory. Her needs generate realities, a reminder, like the play itself, that the real is in part a product of need.

As Peters tracks through his life looking for the single pathway that will unfold a redeeming logic, a central subject other than himself that will, nonetheless, reveal that self, he has a constant reminder that he has lived variously. Everyone is a tangent to everyone else's centre. His question to Calvin – 'if you forget me . . . who the hell am I?' – lies at the heart of his fear, not least because at some level he understands that the redemption he seeks lies through others. 'God, if no one remembers what I remember . . .' says Peters (59), never finishing the sentence because it comes too close to the heart of his deepest anxiety.

He recalls dreaming of a planet of great beauty, inhabited by people 'full of affection and respect,' whose defective inhabitants are flung off into space. Full of 'avarice and greed . . . they broke into thousands of pieces and fell to earth, and it is from their seed that we all descend' (59). The smashed connections, in other words, are no more than a product of self-concern. It is a theme he had developed many times before – in *After the Fall, The Price, The Creation of the World and other Business.*

Cathy-May now re-enters, with her husband, Larry. He is 'Peters' conjecture as to the kind of man she might have married, given her nature as he knew it when they were lovers.'[13] She is provocative, like Marilyn Monroe refusing to wear underwear, thus creating a sense of humiliation and anger in her husband. In turn, she wears a dog-collar and is humiliated by Larry as he insists on his ownership of her. Love and cruelty co-exist, as, incidentally, they had in the relationship between Monroe and Dimaggio. Egotism, greed, possessiveness cut a vector across potentially redeeming relationships, as they do across those other connections which are presumed to offer the context for social meaning. Mr Peters covers his eyes in horror, a horror born not just of a flawed human nature but of the isolation which turns death into mere absurdity: 'Footsteps. And darkness. Oh, how terrible to go into that darkness alone!' (64).

Yet this is not a play without redemption. Mr Peters invites himself and the audience to 'think of the subject. While breath still comes blessedly clear' (64). As Miller has said, with no a priori meaning the individual has to create it, and that is what essentially he sees not only Mr Peters as doing. It is, after all, what most of his characters do. And if Mr Peters's life is coming to an end, his daughter still lives, declaring her love for him. His last line, however – 'I wonder . . . could that be the subject', – is perhaps less an encomium to love, whose fragility has already been displayed, than a recognition that the continuing story contains its own validation, that a line has not yet been drawn across the ledger. 'As crazy as it sounds', Miller has insisted, this 'is a play about life . . . in confronting his end all his livingness erupts in him and it is necessary for him to confront death with his life intact . . . armed with his life.'[14]

As the play's references to history and pre-history make clear, this dilemma is hardly a product of the end of the century or millennium. However, he has insisted that it presents itself with a special intensity at a time when there is a sense of moral and experiential chaos, when everything is possible and consequently nothing is necessary.

However, if Peters is deracinated this comes in part from his perception that 'everything is made up and nothing is rooted'. The world the individual enters seems fixed and coherent. Life, however, slowly reveals the contingency which appears its governing principle. Farms have become suburbs, which in turn have become cities. Buildings have been torn down, friends lost, relationships attenuated. He feels a stranger in something more than the neighbourhood in which he suddenly finds himself. Knowledge no longer seems relevant; the real is not what he had once taken it to be.

At the time of the British premiere, Miller confessed that 'a play with both living and dead characters interacting may justifiably ask for a word or two of explanation',[15] and, indeed, the greatest difficulty in rehearsal was, as Miller has explained of rehearsals for the American production, the actors' need 'to consider what level of consciousness they were in'. His protagonist, after all, is speaking to the dead but, as he insisted, 'one does that in a dream' and, besides, 'nobody ever dies in the human mind'.[16] Beyond that, the play is a comedy, a form which has increasingly attracted him, and 'comedy is tougher'. Chekhov sub-titled The Cherry Orchard a 'comedy', and there is something of Chekhov here, something of his ironies. That play ends with a man on his own in a room, the meaning of his life on the verge of dissolving. Mr Peters's connections are similarly disappearing, his connections to others, to himself, to a deeper structure of meaning. Yet, at the end, there is, perhaps, a moment of understanding, a glimpse of what survives the collapse of so much else and which, at what seems possibly the moment of his death, offers him the subject for which he has been searching.

There is an associational logic to the appearance of figures from Mr Peters's past, a dream-like quality to the world he peoples with his memories. As in *Death of a Salesman*, time dissolves as characters transmute from youth to age; as in *After the Fall*, the dead return; as in *The Ride Down Mount Morgan*, desire generates fantasy. Yet there is only one tense, a present compacted with the past. There is only one reality, that constructed by memory and imagination.

As in those earlier plays, a man struggles to render his life into his own hands. He, like the protagonists of those earlier plays, attempts to locate himself, to retrieve what seems at risk of being lost. Willy Loman never understands the vital connections that might redeem him. Quentin, in *After the Fall*, accepts those connections which link him in one direction to betrayal and in another to a transcending love. Lyman Felt is left ambiguously balanced between an overweening egotism and what seems to him the purity of his desires. For Mr Peters, a pregnant daughter is the only assurance of connection. But perhaps that is enough. Love may be the force which creates that coherence, love or simply a commitment to a continuing interrogation of life in the hope, if not the expectation, of meaning.

Reviewers of the British production tended to stress what they saw as the autobiographical nature of the play. The name Cathy-May seemed reminiscent of Norma-Jean, the more especially since the director, Michael Blakemore, chose to dress her in a blond wig. Her character, too, seemed to match that of a star, responsive, as here, to applause, yet vulnerable to abuse by men.

The two brothers, who continue 'the competition between them', is reminiscent of other brothers in other Miller plays, and perhaps not remote from his unstated competition with his own brother, or more accurately, perhaps, the other way around. Miller himself concedes its autobiographical thrust: 'Sure. I think it is very autobiographical.' But he adds, 'I hope it's autobiographical for a lot of people.'[17]

As he has said,

> I suppose that to me a play is the way I sum up where I am at any particular moment in my life. I am not conscious of that when I'm working, but when I look back at what I've written, it's quite clear to me that that's what I'm doing, trying to find out what I really think about life.[18]

It was also, however, a work that looked back over a century that had moved beyond ideology without, seemingly, finding any purpose, any master story that offered the grace of meaning beyond self-aggrandisement. *Mr Peters' Connections* is not so much Miller's attempts to rethread the beads on a broken necklace as an acknowledgement that time robs us all of certainties, that entropy is a governing principle. Passion, he confesses, dies, memory falters, patterns dissolve. Yet pitched against that is a redemptive humour which never deepens into annihilating irony, a will to understand never quite defeated by the refusal of experience to hint at ultimate meaning. It proposes a love of life embodied in the love of others that makes even Mr Peters wish to resist the idea of defeat and dissolution.

'We live', Miller insists, 'in an era of signs and hints rather than themes.' You hear the notes but not the tune. The play is about the loss of a sense of harmony, an inner structure to experience. Undoubtedly, Mr Peters's nostalgia for a time of conviction and idealism, or simply coherence, echoes Miller's own, as does his bafflement at a society and an existence that seems to serve nothing beyond its own processes. Mr Peters has everything he could want except a reason for having it. He has lost a sense of necessity. The overwhelming feeling is one of loss. In the war 'we knew we were good and the Japs were evil, so the whole thing was necessary ... Whereas now', he admits, 'I just cannot find the subject' (10). That, of course, is the subject, and one to which Miller has repeatedly returned, except that, as in *Death of a Salesman*, his protagonist has looked past the real answer to his desire for justification, purpose and direction. Close to hand is a love that generates its own logic. It is this that enables him to imagine a future no longer characterised simply by the fading of the light.

There is, of course, a potential banality about the idea that all you need is love, and at least one critic suggested as much.[19] Yet that it should seem a banality is itself evidence for the play's central thesis, that meaning is sought everywhere than where it might be said to exist. In a world in which so little is permanent, in which ambition, career, desire are taken as the route to meaning, it becomes necessary to retrieve what is so easily lost. The daughter, at least as he recalls her to mind, is herself bewildered, trying to find a purchase on experience, yet there is an instinctive level at which contact is still made and something more than blank incomprehension passed from generation to generation.

Mr Peters' Connections requires its audience to replicate its own procedures as they struggle to piece together a whole from seemingly random parts. Indeed, the very processes of theatre redeem that lack of communication that Peters himself regrets. If the media offer no more than a flow of words, then the theatre recalls the surviving possibility of community. Thus, in remarks addressed to the audience at the Almeida in July 2000, Miller said of modern communication that rather than opening channels between people it was 'cutting off confrontation with other people'. By contrast, 'You go to the theatre, you hear others laugh and you know it's funny. It's hard to laugh at television, sitting by yourself.' As he explained, 'I do all the acting, then the director does it all, then the actors, then the audience and there's something magical about that that can't be rationalised.'[20]

For Miller, the 1990s proved more productive than any decade for the previous fifty years. Besides *The Ride Down Mount Morgan*, there were premieres of *The Last Yankee* (1993) and *Broken Glass* (1994), together with the publication of his novella *Homely Girl* (1992). With the turn of the millennium came first *Mr Peters' Connections*.

And though it was the British productions of both *The Last Yankee* and *Broken Glass* which were commercial and critical successes (the latter not only winning the Laurence Olivier Award but running to 97 per cent audiences at the country's leading theatre), there was a sense that America was, after three decades of critical disparagement, rediscovering its principal playwright, prompted largely by the success of the fiftieth anniversary production of *Death of a Salesman*, one of the season's most sought-after tickets, which won four Tony Awards and a lifetime-achievement award for Miller himself. The momentum created by that production was sustained when an outstanding Broadway revival of *The Crucible*, directed by Britain's Richard Eyre, was staged on Broadway, on the other side of the millennium, with Liam Neeson as John Proctor.

Miller also remained an active citizen in another respect, firing off pieces to the *New York Times* on matters of national significance and publishing a challenging essay called '*The Crucible* in History', in 2000, and another 'On Politics and the Art of Acting', his trenchant Thomas Jefferson Lecture for the National Endowment for the Arts, in 2001. Though he lived in rural Connecticut there was never any sense that he had withdrawn from the world, either in his art or his active engagement with day-to-day politics and social issues. The man who had written to the President of the United States in 1938 protesting against the government's attitude to the Spanish Civil War continued to protest about aspects of his society that seemed to him to be denials of its principles.

More productions of Miller's plays have been staged by the Royal National Theatre than of any other playwright's, with the single exception of Shakespeare. There is never a moment when a Miller play is not being staged somewhere in the world. Somehow, the most American of playwrights, engaging with American values and myths, has proved the most international of playwrights, as that international playwright has finally been reclaimed by America as its own.

The reasons for his continuing popularity are not hard to find. The immediate social, political and moral issues which might have sparked his plays may seemingly have grown less urgent with time (though it is hard to think so), but those issues are engaged through the lives of his characters. As he has said, 'My plays are involved with society, but I'm writing about people, too, and it's clear over the years that audiences understand them and care about them. The political landscape changes, the issues change, but the people are still there. People don't really change that much.'[21]

Though both as a citizen and a writer he has been concerned with the public world, the public and the private have never seemed separable to him. We make the world we inhabit. We are not merely its products. The political is an expression of individual acts of commission and omission. In Miller's work there is no separate peace. Yet what has engaged him, through a career that has stretched from the Depression through the century's end and on, has fundamentally been the nature of man, capable of slaughtering so many of his kind in a century stained with blood, but capable also of a selflessness which leaves Miller astonished at a capacity for love.

Miller is an atheist nostalgic for faith. He is a non-practising Jew who constantly returns to the Bible. God is not irrelevant for him. He exists because we will him into existence both to account for our need and to explain our capacity to address it. All of his characters fall short of who or what they would be. They shout their names into the wind only for the wind to snatch those names away. And yet, to him, the writer's task is to memorialise, to celebrate, to understand. 'When I want to state clearly what I believe', he has said, 'I write an essay. If I'm exploring a human dilemma, I write a play.'[22]

That is, indeed, the nature of his theatre. He is not, and never has been, a writer of 'problem plays'. He is not a realist, straining to generate a consensus as to the nature of the real or imitate the cadences of speech in such a way as to provoke a sympathy reliant on the merely familiar. As he has said,

> It is necessary to employ the artificial in order to arrive at the real. More than one actor in my plays has told me that it is surprisingly difficult to memorize their dialogue. The speeches sound like real, almost reported talk when in fact they are intensely composed, compressed into a sequential inevitability that seems natural but isn't. But all this, important though it may be, is slightly to one side of the point. Experimental or traditional, the real question to ask of a work is whether it brings news, something truly felt by its author, an invention on his part or an echo.[23]

In the Church of the Holy Trinity in Straford-upon-Avon, there is a description which I especially like. On the tombstone marking the burial place of William Shakespeare are the words, 'William Shakespeare Poet'. This is not because he was the author of poetry, which of course he was, or because he wrote in that most basic rhythm of the English language, iambics, but because his was an art whose language, whose characters, whose metaphoric allusiveness lifted present fact into universal significance. I also take that inscription to be a reminder of the origins of drama, born out of the rib of poetry, to be an indication of the metaphoric force of the theatre. I also warm to the implication that in Shakespeare's age the title 'poet' was not only a badge of honour but the mark of a man seen as a chronicler of the age.

Arthur Miller has confessed that in America a poet is seen as being like a barber trying to erect a skyscraper, but this is a man, too, who has spoken of Willy Loman as being 'a figure in a poem'. That poem is not simply the language he or the other characters speak, though this is shaped, charged with a muted eloquence of a kind he has said was not uncommon in their class half a century or more ago. Nor is it purely a product of the stage metaphors which, like Tennessee Williams's, he presents as correlatives of the actions he elaborates. The poem is the play itself and hence the language, the *mise en scène*, the characters who glimpse the lyricism of a life too easily ensnared in the prosaic, a life which aspires to metaphoric force.

He has never forgotten the power of the Greek plays he learned about at university, writing a number of his plays in verse before transforming them into prose. In a way that was no more than a means of practising condensation. Beyond that, however, he is concerned to see in the particular, the universal.

What is the poem in a play such as *Mr Peters' Connections*? It is Mr Peters's life, as it is the play itself which mimics, symbolises, offers a metaphor for that search for coherence and meaning that is equally the purpose of art and the essence of life.

Meaning, for Miller, is not something that will one day cohere. It is not an ultimate revelation. It is not contained within the sensibility of an isolated self. It lies in the connections between people, between actions and their consequences, between then and now. The true poetry is that which springs into being as individuals acknowledge responsibility not for themselves alone but for the world they conspire in creating and for those with whom they share past and present.

In October 2000 Miller was eighty-five. He might only have received a single Pulitzer Prize but he had slowly accumulated a daunting number of awards, several of which were scattered carelessly about his Connecticut home. His wife, Inge Morath, was similarly honoured in Spain. She continued to roam the world, taking photographs for an increasing number of books and overseeing exhibitions of her work. For his part, Miller continued to write. He jotted down poems in his notebooks and wrote essays and stories for magazines and newspapers. He also worked on two plays that would be premiered in 2002 and 2004 respectively.

One of these, *Resurrection Blues*, was a satirical response to an American society with which he continued to argue, as he had in his first plays, despite the fact that it is set in South America and owed its origin to his visit to Colombia twenty years earlier. The other, *Finishing the Picture*, first sketched out twenty-five years earlier, revisits the traumatic time of the collapse of his relationship with Marilyn Monroe on the set of *The Misfits*. A brief novella, 'The Turpentine Still,' set in Haiti had also first been sketched out two decades earlier.

There had, in short, been no diminution in his energy. He remained as engaged with his society as ever, as committed to writing as he was when he first returned from university at Michigan determined to break through on to Broadway. While one play was being prepared for production, another was in development and the ideas for still others were being worked out in his notebooks. And as *Resurrection Blues* shows, he was as acutely attuned to the language and assumptions of his culture as he was when he staged the last twenty-four hours of a travelling salesman determined to leave his mark on the world and struggling to get by on a smile and a shoeshine.

*

28

'Resurrection Blues'

By the time Miller came to write *Resurrection Blues*[1] in 2002, something had changed. The old master stories that once offered to give a spine to existence could no longer be told. Marxism was dead and capitalism in embarrassing disarray, major corporations emerging as the corrupt dreams of corrupt men. The American century had ended; the turn of the millennium was fast disappearing in the rear-view mirror. What idea, what value, what purpose drove us now? What could be said to justify life to itself?

Very few of Arthur Miller's plays are without humour. That is, in part, the source of their authenticity. Even the most serious are laced, if not with wit, since few of his characters are conscious jokers, then with the kind of humour that comes from character, from misunderstandings, the discrepancy between thought and deed. As noted earlier, often his tactic seems to be to start his plays – as he does *All My Sons* and *Death of a Salesman*, *The Price* and *Broken Glass* – on a humorous note, the more effectively to create the growing feeling of desolation when that fades away. In *The Creation of the World and Other Business* and *The American Clock*, there is an alternating current of comedy and moral seriousness, and much the same could be said of *Resurrection Blues*, his first play of the new century. Now, though, that language is more determinedly satiric, more drawn to parody, perhaps an apt form from a postmodern age in which the real is seen as problematic and performance stands in place of being.

In 1992, concerned at what seemed to be America's growing enthusiasm for the death penalty, Miller wrote an article for the *New York Times* in which he called for the institution of public executions before paying audiences. It was a modest proposal in which he identified Shea Stadium as a likely venue, with ringside seats ranging from $200 to $300 and the bleachers going for a bargain $25. The whole affair would be run by private companies, with the proceeds being split between the prisoner's family, the prison and rehabilitation schemes.

Nor was the context without its advantages; indeed, in many ways, he suggested, the sporting analogy might seem appropriate. The electric chair could be set on a platform around second base while the execution itself would be preceded by a soprano singing 'The Star-Spangled Banner'. Meanwhile a catalogue of the prisoner's previous crimes, together with a listing of his failed appeals, would be read out. The condemned would then appear to a trumpet fanfare, or incidental music provided by a police or army band, unless it was thought to offend against good taste, which risk he was clearly anxious to avoid. A priest would then invoke God's blessing. The whole event would not only be good box-office, he suggested, but an exemplary act suitable for children, who would be simultaneously inducted into the evils of crime and the virtues of capitalism.

He conceded that some people might be so entranced by the idea that they would commit murder merely in order to become stars of the show, but thought this a price worth paying for such an innovation in the criminal code.

The real risk, however, lay, he thought, in the fact that repetition might lead to falling interest, which in turn might lead to a questioning of the value of executions themselves, more especially since an increase in executions to date had seemed merely to lead to an increase in the murder rate. Indeed, there was always the possibility that enthusiasm for executions could actually be explained by the fact that most people had never witnessed one. It was, then, a high-risk strategy but one, nonetheless, worth trying.

It was a Swiftian intervention that predictably had no effect. Executions proved ever more popular, especially in election years, and despite the fact that the United States found itself one of very few countries with pretensions to civilised values that persisted with such a practice. Others, somewhat embarrassingly, included Communist China, Saudi Arabia and Libya.

In the ensuing years, indeed, death as spectacle became a standard feature of public life, though not as yet in the form of public executions in sports arenas. In fact, it was no longer necessary to risk venturing out to take advantage of death as entertainment. High-tech wars in the Gulf and the former Yugoslavia now made it possible, thanks to on-board cameras, to watch the impact of missiles and so-called smart bombs on their targets, intended and not. News programmes displayed images of public shelters, trains, individuals, shortly before they were eliminated in a sudden rush of static as camera and targets exploded into pixels, before the grace of a commercial offered the balm of an 'important message'.

These became a common feature of press briefings designed to underline the extent to which war, once an art, was now a science, with precision tools seemingly capable of eliminating bloodshed and random violence through the use of so-called 'surgical' strikes. Such a moment, in the form of a televised death, is at the heart of a play which is in part about our ability to abstract ourselves from responsibility for our own actions or the actions of those we elect to express our will.

There was a synchronicity, a symbiosis, between the needs of the military and those of the media. War became a voyeuristic entertainment in which questions of morality or, indeed, taste, deferred to the fascination of a technology which had always been capable of showing the urgent rise of missiles, thrusting into the night sky, but which previously had denied its audience the pleasure of witnessing the orgasmic epiphany.

But television itself was changing. H. L. Menken might have suggested that nobody ever lost a dime by under-estimating the intelligence of the American public, but it became ever more apparent that the word 'taste' could easily be substituted for the word 'intelligence'. Now programmes were transmitted that enabled the citizenry to enjoy 'real' car crashes, genuine medical emergencies. Shootings, sieges, riots were all beamed directly into the home from helicopters hovering a hundred feet above the action.

Vicarious pleasure was available in complete safety and with the press of a button on a remote control, remote, too, from the reality of the event thus instantaneously translated into fragmented images and sound bites. Rodney King was repeatedly beaten not only by police officers but also by the television stations which, like the attorneys later defending the accused, replayed the scene so many times that it ultimately seemed to be drained not only of pain but also of any sense of the real. After a time the action became balletic, a choreography to be deconstructed by lawyers who thus became critics, as ethics turned into aesthetics.

Television, meanwhile, sought to present the presumed reality of private anguish by bringing together those in psychological pain, exhibitionists, betrayed wives, the sexually confused, to provide entertainment for the masses. And, lest this should begin to pall, producers encouraged physical assaults which slowly became as formularised as any of those movie scripts prepared to the precise prescriptions of highly paid media advisors. 'Reality TV' purported to present truth, as people performed their lives for our entertainment.

Life, it appeared, existed as raw material for the media. As satellite and cable increasingly competed to bring extreme sports, pornography and uncensored violence to the screen, so mainstream broadcasters dropped pebbles into the wishing well of bad taste in the hope there would prove to be no bottom to it. The Fox network reached some kind of temporary nadir when it offered to marry a woman, live, on screen, to a millionaire she had never met before, a man who, incidentally, turned out to have a criminal record. There were a bewildering number of volunteers, drawn, no doubt, largely by the money, but also by that paradoxical sense of hyper-reality that is a special gift of television. It began to seem that events lacked reality until processed by the camera, which now became the ultimate proof of authenticity. Today, we are all potential voyeurs, not so much living ourselves as watching others who simulate life having grown tired of the thing itself, or viewing newsfilm of deaths that hardly seem like deaths because the images come from the same source and deploy the same aesthetics as television soaps.

Meanwhile, presidents, as Miller pointed out in his barbed National Endowment for the Arts Jefferson Lecture, have turned actors, not only reading other people's words, but practising their gestures, faking sincerity the better to secure our support. Indeed, in ancient Rome actors were banned from moving into politics precisely because it was thought they would have an unfair advantage.

When the Oklahoma bomber Timothy McVeigh was executed, bids were submitted to carry his execution live on the internet (if this is not a contradiction in terms), quite as if news of *Resurrection Blues* had already leaked out, for the first draft was already complete at that moment. As Miller's Henry Schultz says in an early draft, there is 'no one left to call anything unreal'. And there, of course, is the challenge for a writer. Even America's involvement in the Vietnam War, as one of the play's characters suggests in that same draft, was prompted by an event (the Gulf of Tonkin incident) which never occurred, as the weapons of mass destruction in the second Gulf War, which followed the production of *Resurrection Blues*, were believed in because they seemed to justify decisions already made. Cynicism aside, we find what we so desperately seek, make real what we urgently need to believe in. *The Crucible* is not so distant.

In *Mr Peters' Connection*, as we have noted, the protagonist had been baffled by the media. Unlike Caliban, for whom the air was full of noises that delight and hurt not, he heard no more than the white noise of voices with nothing in particular to say about anything. The world as he saw it seemed to have lost the plot. His was a life, a society, an existence, without a subject, entertaining itself, meanwhile, with a jumble of disconnected images. That spirit seems evident in *Resurrection Blues*, by turns impassioned, bitterly ironic, satirical, and, perhaps, despairing. Even faith betrayed, however, as it is here, may imply a surviving instinct for transcendence and redemption, no matter how completely they appear to have been evacuated from the modern, or perhaps the postmodern experience. It was a play that took the millennium as a point of reference not merely to the extent that that milestone seemed to invite summaries, cool assessments of history, of human nature, but in that it necessarily recalled a moment in which the world had once supposedly been redeemed from its corrupt values and failure of love.

Resurrection Blues takes as its premise the idea that had been expressed in Miller's *New York Times* article eight years before. What, he asks, if there were public executions? But a further eight years' experience left him less inclined to settle for what did, indeed, by now, seem a modest proposal. Accordingly, he gives the screw another turn in a play about a world not only with no sense of values but in which there is no sense of the real.

In the hyper-reality of the twenty-first century, fittingly at the turn of the Christian millennium, the Son of God returns, or so it seems. He does so only to find himself a hot property, not only the subject of a planned crucifixion, but also, eventually, invited to share the advantages of living in an age in which no one need be a loser if he or she should only be willing to accept the logic of a triumphant capitalism. Compromise is, after all, a small price to pay for effectiveness. Who would not pay that price to find themselves charged with a significance that, finally, seems only the gift of global technology? And which owner of global technology would not rush to invest in an event that could rival the Superbowl, the World Series and the Masters rolled into one?

The problem for what the characters tend to call the 'Original' Son of God was that he had predated the technology that would have granted him instant access to the collective soul. He preached to a few hundred in a remote part of the world, not the most effective way to spread the good news. The action of *Resurrection Blues* takes place in an equally insignificant country but now global participation is guaranteed. The world waits to consume whatever is on offer. Christ was taken to a high place by the Devil and offered the world. In *Resurrection Blues* the offer is effectively renewed. The question, however, remains that which Christ himself asked, a question, incidentally, that Eugene O'Neill had seen as central to his own concerns: 'What shall it profit a man if he inherit the whole world, and lose his soul?'

The play is reassuringly set somewhere else, in what appears to be a Central American country, with extremes of poverty and wealth. But Miller is no less concerned than he had ever been with what America has made of itself. And if this seemed a curious moment to be questioning a country threatened by those who saw its vices and none of its virtues (though the play was finished before September 11), what better time to ask what the values of this country might be beyond a flutter of flags and a super-patriotism which offered a reactive unity but scarcely an answer?

Resurrection Blues takes place in a country in which the wealthy own large estates and seek their pleasures, and medical attention, abroad. The impoverished are riddled with disease and despair. Drugs and violence prevail. A revolution has failed, some of its former leaders having made the compromises necessary to secure their personal comfort and success. The CIA obligingly sweeps government buildings on a regular basis, a reminder of where power actually resides. The churches have turned into bingo halls.

Of course, America, too, like this invented country, is a post-revolutionary culture, with the crackle of gunfire in the night and drugs a prominent feature. It, too, is a society of extremes, in which religion has negotiated a profitable relationship with Mammon. In the country of *Resurrection Blues*, 2 per cent of the population owns 96 per cent of the wealth. In America, in 2000, 1 per cent owned 40 per cent and 10 per cent, 73 per cent. Whether or not this Latin American country is a displaced version of the United States, America remains a point of reference, its values, or lack of them, infiltrating those of a society in which some prosper and others suffer, a society now about to have conferred on it the dubious benefit of a media blessing.

Miller's stress on inequality and deprivation does not betoken a rekindled Marxism, which foundered, as in this play, in authoritarianism and brute indifference, but a concern for our ability to filter out disturbing truths because we have no idea what to do with them, how they bear on our own necessities, which take primacy now as perhaps they always have.

There is, however, it appears, a new source of hope, news of a charismatic figure whose followers see him as something more than a man. But he is already under arrest, awaiting execution. The play, in other words, begins as though it were to be a political drama, a debate about injustice and the necessity for action. And that element is clearly central. But if this is a play that engages serious moral concerns, it is also a satire, a Swiftean comedy, and it is the braiding together of those two elements that represents the fundamental challenge for director and actors.

The two central figures are Felix Barriaux, Chief of State, and his cousin Henri Schultz. Henri is a former revolutionary turned landowner and successful industrialist. More recently, though, he has been a lecturer in philosophy at Munich where his new enthusiasm is for Immanuel Kant, as once it was for other philosophers and, indeed, for Buddhism. He is, in other words, a man in search of the truth but also something of an intellectual and moral butterfly, flitting from idea to idea.

Felix, also radical in his youth, has long since accommodated himself to the necessities of power, blind to the literal blindness of his disease-riddled citizens, concerned only to consolidate his own position. According to his cousin, he has been 'dousing the flames of revolution'. Certainly the marks of revolution have been removed. The once-damaged airport is now functioning and Felix's residence restored. He himself, however, is not so functional, undergoing psychoanalysis for impotence. Nonetheless, the rebels, he insists, are now coming down from the hills, like his brother, and going into business. Ideology is dead. 'We are the future', he declares. Yet, of course, ideology is not dead, since one survives: capitalism. Self-interest, whether enlightened or not, remains in place.

Henri has also given up his hopes for revolution and substituted a dream of avarice, though not without a sense of regret for abandoned values and not without a continuing sensitivity about the needs of the poor, not least because his daughter, Jeanine, had followed in his footsteps. She, too, however, has abandoned the cause, in despair, but, not so easily reconciled to the collapse of hope, has turned to drugs and walked through a third-floor window to fracture her spine on the ground below. She is now in a wheelchair, as was Sylvia in *Broken Glass*, an image of the paralysis that seems to infect both her and her society. Her plight, though, seems to have resensitised her father to the horrors around him, though his response is to plan a move to Europe for both of them.

Henri is married to a countess, a concert pianist, and is owner of a Mercedes, albeit one he can no longer drive for fear of being attacked on the streets. He is caught in his own contradictions, feeling empathy for those he fears. He finds himself living in a world menaced by the threat of imminent collapse. The elegance, the beauty, the balance of the past, as embodied in his house, is at risk, as water from a leaking aqueduct undermines the property and the 'whole lovely eighteenth-century neighborhood' is slowly destroyed by termites.

Felix is a rationalist, an empiricist, a pragmatist. There are no values except those validated in action. There are no principles except those which serve his practical purposes. Henri is drawn to less rational interpretations of experience.

He wears a cap because 'most of the body's heat escapes through the scalp'. He claims it has cured him of a number of illnesses, a mystery that 'keeps reminding me that our planet is not spinning in the clear and lucid center of the universe but far, far out at the dark edge where practically nothing at all is comprehensible'. The irrational, he suspects, may yet prove the only real source of redemption. Certainly, he is struck by the fact that 'utility' and 'futility' are separated by no more than a letter, a sophomoric observation but one that suggests the despair deepening to cynicism that he feels on seeing a dead baby abandoned on a sewer grating and his own daughter turned from revolutionary to addict to cripple.

So far, so apparently serious, though even in the opening section there is a dark comedy in the exchanges between the two men, a comedy rooted in character but generated from the gap which has opened up not simply between the two of them but between what they were and what they have become. The pieces are in place for an impassioned drama of betrayed values and broken lives, in which the dissolution of public morality reflects the collapse of private values, in which the failure of ideology leaves nothing in place but the self. This, however, is a play that changes direction and it is that change of direction that is crucial to its style and, ultimately, its concerns. Miller now spins on a dime as political morality play, laced with wit, becomes comic satire.

The play begins as Henri visits Felix, whose military uniform is a symbol of the discipline he would enforce, though, since 70 per cent of the killings in the country are carried out by men in uniform, such discipline hardly serves the cause of justice. He has come because he feels that 'something terrible, ultimate and final is gathering itself . . . trembling under the ground'. He wishes, he explains, to found a new university 'to learn what is real', as it happens a timely proposal since his sense of the real is about to suffer a major blow.

He has, he explains, heard a rumour that the the new rebel leader is seen as the returned Messiah. The man, about whom little is known, has already chased Bingo players from a church as Christ expelled the money lenders from the Temple. There is talk of miracles and he, himself, has seen what seems to him to be evidence of such. However, he has also heard not only that his cousin plans to crucify the man as a warning to revolutionaries, but that an American advertising company has offered fifteen million dollars to televise it, with CNN entering a counter-bid. And it is at this point that the play moves in a different direction.

In an early draft, the advertising agency is named as Batten, Barton, Durstine and Osborne, of Madison Avenue. This is not an invented company. It was the company for which he had written his radio plays in the 1940s. When it was formed by merger, in 1928, it was the fourth largest and best-known agency in America, with US Steel, General Electric and Lever Brothers as clients. The most significant of the partners, however, was Bruce Barton whose achievements included not only the creation of 'Betty Crocker' but also success in cleaning up the image of Andrew Carnegie following the violence he unleashed in the steel strike of 1919. His slogan was 'He came to a land of wooden towns and left a nation of steel.' However, Barton managed to combine his support for corporate violence with charitable work, even devising a motto for the Salvation Army: 'A man may be down, but he is never out.' And, indeed, his right-wing politics and admiration for the Robber Barons were not inimical to his commitment to Christian values.

He is best known, though, for a series of inspirational books, including *The Man Nobody Knows* (1926), a study of Jesus Christ in which he described Christ as the greatest advertiser of his day and the world's greatest salesman. It was on the *New York Times* bestseller list for two years and stayed in print for forty. A life-long Republican, he returned to Congress in 1937 from New York's wealthy, so-called 'Silk Stocking', Seventeenth District. He was a fierce opponent of Roosevelt's New Deal and devised yet another slogan: 'Repeal one useless law a week.' He was ridiculed by Roosevelt, along with fellow congressmen Joseph W. Martin and Hamilton Fish, as a member of the mythical company, Martin, Barton and Fish.

For Miller, Roosevelt devotee, scarcely an admirer of the Robber Barons, and contemptuous of the nexus between religion and boosterism, the company was a natural choice, more especially since Barton's book, while selling millions, was widely regarded as a monument to bad taste and hence greatly admired both by those who could not tell the difference and by those who could and took perverse pleasure in it. In a later draft Miller seems to have been overcome by a sudden, and uncharacteristic, sense of discretion and the name is dropped. Or perhaps he hardly needed to keep the reference since he had invented his own emissaries from Madison Avenue who, for the most part, have long since made their peace with a profession which can require a certain accommodation with moral equivocation.

Miller's ear for a self-validating language is acute, as is his sense for the absurdity of words used less to describe or engage reality than to deny it. The world of *Resurrection Blues* is one in which everything has a moral equivalency. A commercial product recalls a natural wonder; the feeding of a cat is interfolded with a debate about being accomplices to murder.

These are people who insist that they are agents and not principals, and thus not responsible for their actions. But in that they are scarcely distinct from those of us who merely observe the world as though it were a movie whose unfolding drama we are powerless to deflect; those of us who live unexamined lives aware only of our own desires, never questioning what life might be for or how our own identities must necessarily be intimately related to the fate of others.

Miller's parodistic skills are unleashed by Felix's agreement to the globally televised crucifixion of a man who might be Christ reborn. Thus, Henri sees the advertisers as likely to seize the occasion to sell products relevant to a man nailed to a cross – remedies for underarm sweat, runny stool, anal swelling,

RESURRECTION BLUES' 429

nasal blockage – since 'there is not one hole in the human anatomy they can't make a dollar on', and 'with a crucifixion the sky's the limit'. Far from blunting Felix's interest, however, Henri's predictions whet it. With potentially a hundred million at stake, he suggests, it would prove possible to irrigate half the country, put shoes on the feet of policemen, educate the prostitutes and install sewers to enable 'decent people' (read, the rich) to build their homes on more desirable land. The rapid and bathetic decline from the worthy to the self-interested is an indication of the speed with which he is seduced by the idea, as it is of the nexus between idealism and pragmatism in the mind of this one-time radical turned avatar of the status quo.

What follows is, briefly, almost a vaudeville routine with Felix pointing out of his intended victim that 'the son of a bitch is not even Jewish' while Henri warns that since people will interpret the crucifixion as the end of the world: 'It'll turn California into a madhouse!' Felix offers to substitute a Stalinist so as not to offend anyone's religious sensibilities and rejects Henri's suggestion that he will be despised for his actions, by invoking the ghost of Richard Nixon: 'Five years after they kicked Richard Nixon out of the White House he had the biggest funeral since George Washington. Believe me, Henri, in politics there is only one sacred rule – nobody clearly remembers anything.'

Indeed, briefly, America, and not this Latin American republic, seems to become the subject when Felix claims both that the most important characteristic of a leader is that he should be prepared to kill, and that his models are Roosevelt, Truman and Lincoln: 'those three killed more people than any other Presidents. Johnson did pretty well in Vietnam but no comparison with Roosevelt and Lincoln. Greatness lives on murder. Imagine if Roosevelt or Lincoln had refused to fight, or Truman refused to drop the bomb! They'd've gone down in history as ridiculous clowns.' Perhaps Miller had President Bush and the Gulf War in mind, though the principle clearly extended beyond the United States. He certainly wrote it as Vladimir Putin reduced Chechnya to ruins on his way to success in the Russian elections of 2000. Miller's central difficulty would seem to lie in the fact that reality has long since outstripped the satirist.

By this point, the tone is wholly different. It is almost as if Felix and Henri were a conscious double act, feeding one another lines. Asked what his achievements to date have been, Felix lists air-conditioning the army barracks, installing six new flush toilets at the airport and issuing every soldier with a poncho and a toothbrush. Anxious, briefly, to ship the trouble-maker out of the country rather than deal with the complexities of the situation he is about to enter, Felix proposes to seek out the man's parents and offer them indoor plumbing and a Honda Civic 'or equivalent' if they will encourage him to disappear. In short, 'he leaves the country or he's nailed'.

They even debate whether they could go ahead with the crucifixion but stop short of actually killing him, only to reject this as being unacceptable to likely sponsors. The first scene ends as they open the door to the prisoner's room, only to see a blinding light pour out. Far from this persuading Felix to abandon his plans, however, it stimulates a call to the vice-president of the advertising agency. After all, how much more compelling will the television coverage be if they are dealing with the real Son of God.

In the second scene the parody becomes broader, as into this world, carrying cameras and cellphones, come representatives of Madison Avenue for whom the world is so much product. We are on a mountain, towards dawn, and in the presence of Skip Cheeseboro (Vice-President, originally, of Batten, Barton, Durstine and Osborne) and Emily Shapiro, director of commercials and of the proposed television special. The spectacular view recalls others they have shared, but what comes to mind is less the beauty than the products they were selling at the time: 'remember the road to Cali for Jeep Wrangler? That view of the Himalayas for Alka Seltzer'. This is the world of Nathanael West's *The Day of the Locust* in which, from the perspective of the characters, nature apparently modelled itself on the movies rather than the other way about.

Emily has qualms about the project, not least, as she explains, because, as a director of commercials she has 'never shot anything like . . . real . . . it's comfortably fake'. To Skip Cheeseboro, though, 'This is a door to possibly Hollywood.' He offers to 'parse it out' for her, suggesting that she has no responsibility for what will happen but that, on the contrary, in bringing it to the world she could perhaps end such practices for ever. 'If I were moralistic', says the wholly amoral Cheeseboro, 'I'd even go so far as to say you have a *duty* to shoot this.' They are, he insists, not 'doing' anything, merely photographing it. It is, he suggests, by way of being a documentary. Accordingly, he points to the beauty of the mountains as a perfect backdrop, a tasteful framing device for a crucifixion.

Her doubts flicker briefly. 'Do not use ordinary beseeching language to me', she insists, before placing a telephone call to her mother which prompts a brilliant aria in which the welfare of cats, her probable pregnancy, her cleaning woman and her aversion to marriage all rank above her concern for filming a crucifixion. She is, she explains, waiting to 'see how disgusting I'm willing to be', though a female colleague insists that women are as capable of filming crucifixions as men. This is to be an equal opportunities Second Coming.

There follows a debate about whether the suspected Son of God can be permitted any kind of pain relief as he is crucified, without his appearing to be drunk and thus offending those in a dry state such as Kansas. Skip suggests aspirin, 'Tylenol if he's allergic', while rejecting the idea that he should be carried to the cross since this would prove 'blasphemy in the United States!' In the end they decide to rely on the good taste of their subject by appealing to him not to scream.

They remain worried, however, that a residual association of the messiah with the Jews could be offensive, not only in America's Bible Belt but also in the Muslim world, where it will already prove a marketing challenge to sell a programme featuring a Christian, let alone a Jew: 'You know it and I know it', says Cheeseboro, 'but what's the point of going worldwide with it at this particular time?' The proceedings are now momentarily interrupted when the prisoner escapes, quite possibly by walking through the prison walls, thus disrupting Felix's planned visit to Miami for his regular psychoanalysis.

The play then shifts into another mode, parody largely giving way to a serious debate about values, as Henri visits his daughter with Emily, who has decided that she cannot go ahead with the project. It is almost as if another play was bursting through in the way that Twain has *Huckleberry Finn* move from farce to moral seriousness and back again. Indeed, when he first saw designs for the Guthrie Theatre production in 2002, Miller suddenly realised that the raising of a giant cross in the middle of the comic interplay between those preparing to film the crucifixion might already have changed the tone:

> I don't know at this point what the ramifications might be. Some people may be filled with awe, others with resentment, amusement, I don't know what. But it's certainly going to count, because it's a great big cross, and it will be interesting to see what happens. But, then, it's built into that play. The sublime and the ridiculous are cheek by jowl.[2]

For Jeanine, meanwhile, her father has turned his back on the possibility of change, become a 'philosophical shopper', content to interpret experience rather than change it. In America, she implies, pain is real enough but the shopping is more literal: 'you live in New York, you know the blues. But here you can't shop them away. It's not bitterness you're strange to, you just don't dare lick it with your tongue as we do here.' The French expression for window shopping is 'lèche-vitrines', licking the plate glass, and that, it seems, is what the Americans are accused of substituting for tasting the pain at large in the world.

Later, Jeanine seems miraculously cured, following a visit from the possible messiah, a man who changes his name constantly so as not to be defined. Despite her injuries, she rises from her wheelchair and we seem close to that scene in *Broken Glass* in which Sylvia Gellburg does likewise. Broken in body and spirit, she rises not because she has found the will to stand on her own feet, but because a miracle seems to suggest the possibility of redemption. That redemption, though, is ambiguous, rooted, as it is, in a man whose status as charlatan or messiah is uncertain. To be sure, unlike Sylvia, her paralysis is the result of a broken spine, but she was already narcotised by drugs, having retreated from commitment like her father, who now manufactures drugs. As he himself confesses, 'a man who has outlived his convictions is not a very inspiring sight'.

His daughter's restoration, however, shocks him into a new consciousness as he realises that 'this whole crazy worship of money' has to stop. But there is, as his daughter suggests, still a gap between understanding and action, a sense of resignation which leaves him as much a victim as those he fails to aid. And, indeed, as in *Broken Glass*, it is that resignation, that retreat from commitment, that is, in part, the subject of Miller's fable. For Henri, 'The world will never again be changed by heroes ... people cannot change, they are oak and plantain and wheat.' They are, in other words, what they were made, separate creations. 'One must learn to live in the prison of one's self', he insists, a statement, of course, at odds with the assumption that has driven Miller's work from his very first play and that was implicit in the title of his first success, *All My Sons*.

Only a miracle, Henri suggests, can change anything, but the miracle he looks for is external to the self, a projection of the action he and others lack the will to undertake and which they all eventually reject as too disruptive of their personal needs. The reality of existence is, it seems, too painful to be confronted or even named. As Henri asks, 'Who would ever have believed that a country can reach a point of such pain and corruption that everyone in it goes mad, and there is no one left to call anything unreal?'

The play moves towards its end with a possible compromise. Felix discusses the idea of absorbing the rebel–messiah into his government, while the man himself, who we never see, increasingly doubtful about his own status, but seduced by the social advantages that might accrue from the televised crucifixion ('property prices ... tour buses ten miles long ... a whole new tax base, new schools, roads, swimming pools'), offers to submit himself to crucifixion, in part to resolve his own confused identity. In the end, though, and for differing reasons, they all come together to beg him not to return. The Second Coming, real or not, is declined. The world is not ready for redemption.

In 2000, before a rewrite of the play the following year, Miller noted that, unconsciously, he had shadowed the story of Christ, with Barriaux as Pilate, Shapiro as Magdelene and Cheesboro as a Jewish priest. It was a play, he felt, beyond its satire, in part concerned with the fact that religion is a worship of death as the only source of coherence, making life itself mere appearance and shadow. Seen in this way, the ending becomes ambiguous as the characters reject the putative Christ out of fear, self-interest and moral equivocation but also, in the process, become their own potential redemption.

Beneath the humour, the comic exaggerations, the vaudeville, in *Resurrection Blues*, is a genuine lament over the decay of principles, the tainted utopianism of a generation trading social concern for narcosis or self-interest. Inequity and suffering are met not with an engaged conscience but anarchic violence or complacency. Radical change, once a moral imperative, now seems no more than a chimera. On the one hand is the rebel, trying to jump the rails of history with random violence, worn down slowly by the absurdity in which he collaborates; on the other are those paralysed by self-doubt, distracting themselves with immediate pleasures or dreams of avarice, immured in their own egotism. The real, meanwhile, is reprocessed as entertainment, life transformed into lifestyle, pain aestheticised, suffering rendered as designer product.

As Miller finished the play, Benetton ran an advertising campaign in which photographs of condemned killers on America's death row were used to sell sweatshirts in a gesture that virtually defies analysis, as social conscience is accommodated to the imperatives of worldwide capitalism. At the same time there were those who became famous by installing cameras in every part of their houses and apartments and allowing people to access them at any time through the World Wide Web. In various European countries the same principle was applied by network television. Somewhere along the line the real dissolved. In this context, the idea of televised executions, with product placements, sponsorship and discreet logos, is not, perhaps, as Swiftian as at first it appears.

Despite the jokes, the straightfaced comic dialogue, the self-deflating moral casuistries, the revelling in bad taste repackaged as the morally exemplary, *Resurrection Blues* is a serious play. Below the satire, the precise rendition of a language evacuated of sense and moral force alike, the humour of self-serving hypocrisy, lies a genuinely felt lament, an anger wedded to regret. It is simply that its comic grotesques, like Nathanael West's would-be actors in *The Day of the Locust*, convince themselves that the meretricious is of profound significance and that the ethically perverse is a necessary function of the art they serve.

If *Mr Peters' Connections* was a retrospective search for meaning, *Resurrection Blues* is a glimpse into a future in which transcendence and redemption are not simply absent but rejected. In both plays the past exists only as postmodern quotation, so many museum pieces crumbling away along with the culture they reflect. In both plays, youthful assurance seems to dissipate in a swirl of indeterminacy, as reality thins to transparency. But on one side of the millennial divide it still seemed possible to find some justification for living in the mere processes of life. On the other side, it appears, something has finally snapped. Only a miracle can turn aside the logic of self-concern, and miracles are too randomly scattered, too deeply suspect to serve as evidence of true purpose and meaning. Religion has anyway either become an aspect of capitalist enterprise or an expression of a merely arbitrary grace.

There is, however, another battle going on here beyond that waged between resignation and commitment, the real and its representation. It is that between reason and romanticism, neither of which has seemingly proved adequate to human need. Reason has hardly rendered the world into our hands, ended poverty, secured justice, while romanticism has engendered only the rebel dying into existence. Henri turns his back on reason, pure and not so pure, and tries his hand at mysticism, but seems to have ended up with nothing more than regret codified into cynicism. The Age of Faith, the Age of Reason, the Age of Revolution seem all to have collapsed into nothing more admirable than self-interest.

Resurrection Blues is not only about America, or a distant country spiralling down from civil war to military dictatorship and drug-fuelled crime. Like any blues it is a lament over suffering. It speaks of pain, private and public, and it speaks of loss. For all its humour, it presents broken relationships, casual betrayals, a denatured language, greed disguised as principle, a vacuity at the heart of affairs. The question it raises is what transcendent idea makes us welcome each dawn, or have we consigned the very idea of transcendence to a history in which we no longer believe? Would we rather not be embarrassed by the thought that we serve something beyond our own desires, exist to do something more than insulate ourselves from the reality we fear?

The play is also, though, a fable, a mordant satire, an all too accurate parody of a society bereft of values and unable to distinguish the real. This is a world no longer animated by belief, deeply materialistic, in recoil from failed utopias, refusing commitment, content with distraction. Wyndham Lewis's term for distraction was the 'moronic inferno', a phrase picked up by Saul Bellow, for whom it seemed an apt description of a world losing touch with essentials. Much the same spirit is observable in *Resurrection Blues*. The question is whether anything can survive in a world in which everything is possible and nothing, it seems, necessary, a world in which there appears to be no reason why the sacred and the profane should not merge, why all experience should not be seen as a transaction priced for its utility. Is redemption, in other words, any longer available and if available, embraced?

Miller himself has said that, 'I suppose in some ways, however unacknowledged and even perverse, the play touches on a kind of longing for deliverance from this bleak frustration in which all of us live, the promised *real* revolution and its apocalypse having died aborning after World War and the victory over Fascism.'[3] In other words, he is still, even in this play set at the beginning of the twenty-first century, haunted by the collapse of an idealism that had once seemed to promise a secular salvation, an idealism whose betrayal seemed to leave nothing in its place but a cynicism which infected human relationships, social organisation and, indeed, art itself.

As he wrote the play, capitalism was undeniably triumphant and capitalism is the ultimate pragmatism. Validation comes not from God or the enlightened proletariat but from the market, a new Darwinism, a natural selection in which ideas, values, principles are tested only for their utility. And since the market is worldwide the image dominates. This is a new dark and distorted romanticism, an age of sensation. It is a time of wonder not in the face of the unknown but of the fully revealed, a world in which there are no secrets, no intimacies, no profundities not to be probed, exposed, redeemed for cash. Today, even our genetic codes are broken in order to be owned, controlled, traded on the stock market, the final, absolute, apocalyptic triumph of capitalism. The question is no longer why but why not?

There is something almost Spenglerian about a situation in which money and power become the primary desiderata, this, for Spengler, being the final stage of a civilisation. The whole world is become Carthage. Yet, for Miller, a modern Cato, there is still hope, even given, or perhaps especially given, the collapse of attempts to rally believers to another fraudulent cause. Speaking of the Second World War, which so significantly failed to usher in a new idealism, he has said, still in the context of *Resurrection Blues*, that it is

> Interesting how often the idea pops up of that having been 'the good war', which somehow we failed again and again to replicate. The most murderous such inflationary attempt of course was Vietnam, which they tried to spiritually pump up to crusade size, but it leaked and collapsed and the scar of its fraudulence is definitely still upon us. Which should be encouraging news when you think about it – the spirit, apparently, like the proverbial horse that can be led to water but declines to drink, so in some incomprehensible way Truth is still alive and discerning in the world.[4]

There is, then, to his mind, still evidence of a surviving desire for moral discrimination, transcendence and redemption, qualities supposedly destroyed in the camps of the Second World War, denied by the absurdist writer and finally declared irrelevant in a world attentive only to the immediate satisfactions paraded as ultimate values by a triumphal marketplace. Indeed if such a desire did not exist, *Resurrection Blues* would be a realist drama and not a satire. That it comes so close to being the former is a mark of how tenuous is the faith it sees in such jeopardy.

Arthur Miller was raised in an ideological age. He finds himself living in an age in which ideologies carry little conviction and religion seems no more than the source of violence. Speaking in 2002, he observed:

> I often think that the last remnants of religion have been flattened out. Some acid has been dropped on the thing and dissolved it. It's gone. If you pick up a nineteenth-century novel, whether it's Dostoevsky or a French or British novel, in the distance you hear the Bible somewhere, the spirit of the transcendent spirit. All we get now is the spirit of decay, the threat of dissolution, the feeling that this is imminent. It's on the horizon.[5]

As we edge uneasily into the second Christian millennium, religion increasingly seems the handmaiden of reaction or the agent of terror. Is there, though, yet redemption and if so where is the new messiah? Do we have to invent a god in order to believe in the justice he represents? Or would we rather dispense with an idea that would reforge the link between act and consequence, uneasy guilt and a necessary responsibility? The poor get poorer and the rich get richer quite as if that were the missing certainty that gives coherence to our existence, and yet where are we if that is the only order in which we can believe?

In *Resurrection Blues* lifestyle has replaced life. Conviction is seen as suspect. The axle has come off the cart. Money, drugs, ambition, pragmatism prevail. Religion is either compromised or appropriated to serve other causes than the spirit. Indeed, this reductiveness extends to art, which is itself in the service of a spirit no longer respected.

It's a reductionist attitude. Things are nothing but . . . x. You no sooner put
out a work of fiction than flies start swarming around it, digging in to find
out where it comes from, did this happen to you. In other words they are
trying to eviscerate the writer, whereas in ancient times he was part of some
zeitgeist. He was the voice of some mysterious spirit. Now, it's directly the
opposite. They reduce everything.[6]

The mysterious figure in *Resurrection Blues* is a bright light into which no
one wishes to stare. He is a sense of mystery – in experience, in art – to be
evacuated from a contemporary sense of the real, to be denied in the name of
nothing more profound than self-concern.

In Saul Bellow's *Ravelstein*, the protagonist is wont to ask his students, 'With
what, in this modern democracy, will you meet the demands of your soul?'[7]
He would talk to them, the narrator adds, about their souls, 'already thin and
sinking fast – faster and faster' (20). It is increasingly Miller's question and
Miller's conviction.

Ravelstein is prone to invoke Plato's story of the cave and so, though not
literally, is Miller, in that he has become increasingly concerned with how we
may distinguish the real from the images projected on the psyche by those who
process experience without understanding it. What is true, what is real, is no
longer addressed. How much more comfortable it is to accept the grace offered
by fantasy, to allow ourselves to be chained in place watching images play on
the cave wall than face the truth that lies in wait if we choose to release ourselves
from imprisonment in our seemingly protective world?

Preparing for new productions in 2003, Miller made some small changes to
the ending. The characters still wave the potential Christ away but his closest
disciple indicates that he at least will await his return. Whether that is a last
flickering candle in a world seemingly opting for a darkness of the soul or
a failure of nerve by a man still dependent on an external meaning is left
instructively unclear.

29

'Finishing the Picture'

Finishing the Picture,[1] which Arthur Miller had first sketched out in 1977–8, is something more than a dramatisation of a struggle to finish a film, of the competing necessities, ambitions, psychological compulsions of a group of people who come together to serve art and commerce. It is a study of power and the price of creativity. It is an account of individual lives and a culture at risk of losing a sense of purpose and direction. It is a dramatisation of a life balanced between performance and being. What, after all, is real in a context of those who come together to construct a fiction, which nonetheless is designed to capture truth? As a character observes, 'Life isn't real to movie people.' Yet at the same time, as is said of Kitty, the damaged movie star at the centre of the play, 'she's more real than people like us who live in the sunlight'.

Beyond the immediate action, which centres on whether a film can continue, over budget and with a star seemingly slipping into a private world, in an election year in which politicians are arguing over the future of the country and the sky is lit by flames, there is more than a hint of apocalypse. There are decisions to be made not only here on the location of a film but also in a society poised between its own utopian myths and the pragmatics of the material world. As Nixon and Kennedy debate on television (we are back in 1960), being judged in large part by their appearance, it seems clear that life is no more real beyond the world of movies.

Finishing the Picture is also about what F. Scott Fitzgerald, in another context, called a 'Crack Up', and as with Fitzgerald's essay, in which he saw a connection between his own mental collapse and the Crash, that threatened dissolution occurs both at a private and a public level. For Fitzgerald, the culture seemed to resonate to his own sense of psychological collapse. In Miller's case it is quite other. He has always seen the private and the public as implicated in one another, not least because social and political values are the product of individual decisions. We are constructors of the world, whose contradictions are therefore rooted in a flawed, a contradictory or perhaps simply a protean humanity. Art offers form to contingency, yet its creation is not untouched by chaos or uninfected by what it would seek to challenge. There is, in other words, a paradox in art which Matthew Arnold saw as pitched against anarchy, but which in itself may be the product of what it would deny.

Finishing the Picture is set in the west and opens on the veranda of a penthouse hotel apartment. It is dawn and the sky is aflame, though not with the rising sun.

There is a distant forest fire. Beyond the confines of a group of people brought together to create a film there is a suggestion of impending catastrophe.

Phillip Ochsner, of Bedlam Pictures, has flown in to assess the problems affecting the shooting of the film. He has evidently still found time, however, to sleep with Edna Meyers, a woman in her forties, who is to be his secretary and who is assistant to the film's troubled star. Both are stunned by what has happened. His own wife has died and he had, in his own words, 'cemented myself in a wall', condemned, as he assumed, to loneliness. Instead, the reminder of death has made him sensitive to the necessities of living. The encounter has not been untouched by absurdity – her toothache somehow commingling with her passion – but it seems that something has been lit between them, though she is anxious that nobody should know: 'There's so much gossip on location like this.' It is striking, though, that a play which seems concerned with personal and social entropy should begin and end with the possibility of renewal, albeit hedged around with an ambiguity which seems inescapable in human affairs.

So, we enter *Finishing the Picture* not with the problems of an actress seemingly in decline and facing personal terrors, nor with a fragmenting marriage (she is married to the screenwriter), but with what seems, potentially at least, a mutually vivifying experience for two people who thought that life had passed them by. It is the first of a series of seeming contradictions in a play apparently concerned with the co-existing possibility of apocalypse and redemption.

For Ochsner, the distant fires are evidence that 'there's not a single rotten thing that human beings aren't capable of doing'. Yet at the same time he reveals a sensitivity which suggests that he is himself a man of contradiction. He is a successful businessman, making his money in trucking before entering the movie industry. Yet he is a long way from being a caricature money man. His apparent one-night stand with Edna is, it seems, something more than the casual sex which passes for small change in Hollywood. His ambivalence, indeed, is in some ways an echo of that to be found in Miller's earlier plays, particularly *The Price* and *The Ride Down Mount Morgan*, in which he seemed to suggest the necessity for a combination of idealism and practicality both in the individual and in society. As Miller has remarked of Ochsner, 'he's got to make it happen'.[2] Money and art have always been related, as in this society the dream of possibility has always wedded the spiritual to the material.

Ochsner is there 'to get this picture finished, preferably without stepping on too many toes'. Ironically, in a memo to the director, it is not primarily the difficulties with the star that concern him but, having seen a rough-cut of the first seventy minutes, the film's 'coldness'. It strikes him as 'remote'. It is, he insists, not sentiment he is looking for but 'feeling', a distinction which says something about him as a man of divided responsibilities and passions. The film is five weeks behind schedule and ten million dollars over budget. He is there to close it down or give it a brief reprieve. His first concern, though, is for an absence at its centre, an absence that has equally characterised his own life but which may now be on the verge of being filled.

Nonetheless, it is primarily Kitty who has brought him to this place and his conversation is now interrupted as the star wanders, naked, though off-stage, past his door. In an early draft she is to be heard asking, 'Where is this?' Later, Miller decided that she would be silent throughout, from the perspective of the audience, though heard by the characters whose conversations with her thus have the feel of monologues. Each person who addresses her does so for immediate personal reasons, sees her as something different.

Kitty, in the view of the director Derek Clemson, is suffering from 'Pills . . . and a bad life'. For Flora, ostensibly her drama coach, but in fact a self-serving and self-important woman whose significance depends entirely on the influence she is assumed to wield with Kitty, she is a lunch ticket. And not Kitty alone. She lays claim to those other actors who have passed through her husband's hands in his drama studio, 'our people', as she describes them.

Flora is something of a comic grotesque. Like Paula Strasberg, on whom she is patently based, she is dressed in black, despite the heat. She wears five watches, all set to different times in order to remind her when her husband's star pupils are to appear on stage or film at various places around the world. The quality of the pictures scarcely seems to bother her. Thus, one actress is to appear as a female Mounted Policeman in an unlikely remake of *Nanook of the North*, a film not renowned for its mounted policemen or women. Yet, despite the comedy, there is a dark side to this woman. As Kitty slides dangerously close to psychosis, Flora's primary concern is for her own status. For her, evidence for things falling apart on the project lies in the fact that she has been assigned a double room rather than a suite in the hotel and that she lacks a car and chauffeur. It is, she insists, a matter of 'principles', this from a woman who seems to lack them.

Beyond the question of Flora's hypocrisy, this character is a focus for one of the play's central themes. The creation of the film depends upon an essential mutuality, but this seems to break on the rocks of self-interest and ambition. There is a delicate balancing act if this joint stock company – in some ways a mirror of the society beyond – is to function. There comes a moment, though, when self-absorption threatens the whole enterprise.

Kitty is in some ways a tragically exemplary figure. She is a deeply flawed but talented actress. The black-robed Flora is altogether more sinister and not entirely unlike the figure of Richard Nixon, briefly invoked, a man who also chose to cloak ambition with principle and who likewise had a corrosive impact on the mutuality which he invoked but betrayed. As Paul, the screenwriter and husband to Kitty, remarks, 'There's something perversely beautiful in the perfection of any type. Her consistency is flawless . . . if there is the slightest choice between the truth and a lie she will always choose to tell a lie.' The observation could apply with equal accuracy to Nixon.

Flora is an intermediary between Kitty and the director, seeing herself as an agent for her absent husband. In the process she has plainly exacerbated a bad situation, destroying the necessary intimacy and trust required between director and actress. The result, as that director, Derek, points out, is that 'as a consequence the girl lies gasping for life like a stranded salmon'. And that is the point. At stake is far more than the finishing of a picture, far more than the completion of a commercial venture, the furthering of individual careers. The marriage between Kitty and her writer husband, Paul, is winding down, while Kitty herself is plainly in crisis, having reached a point at which her sanity and even her life are potentially at risk.

Kitty, indeed, lies at the heart of the play, seen but not heard by the audience, apparently traumatised. She is an actress who exists in and through her performance but has ceased to believe in herself. For Derek, hers is 'a case of terminal disappointment. With herself, her husband, the movies, the United States, the world'. When Ochsner replies, 'That sounds like most of us', he is effectively underscoring the wider implications of a play that is not merely concerned with the plight of an individual actress or a movie, which may or may not be completed. When Ochsner insists that she 'must be the envy of ninety per cent of humanity', Derek replies, 'So is the United States – why are *we* so unhappy?' The movie star and the City on the Hill, it seems, share something. Idealised image and daily reality move apart while, as Miller had suggested in *The Man Who Had All the Luck*, success itself raises questions of its own. This had, indeed, been the American century. The American dream has gifted many the success they sought. What it seems not to have gifted is contentment, not least because the dream builds discontent into itself.

The answer, in Kitty's case, is, at least in part, that she wishes to believe she deserves what she has, that she wants to be loved independently of the power she feels constrained to exert, a power which is less an expression of strength than weakness. As to America, the answer is perhaps much the same. It maintains a version of itself, a dream which it insists is reality. Its power, recklessly used, can also destroy its own legitimacy, and perhaps it is worth noting that Miller went back to this play, which he had first worked on twenty-five years earlier, as America launched a war on Iraq which he believed illegitimate. It was a time, too, when the question sparked by the events of 9:11 was, 'Why don't people love us?' It is not only Willy Loman who has the need to be 'well liked'.

Kitty is damaged and has been for much of her life. As Derek observes, 'she's been stepping on broken glass since she could walk'. To close the picture would not only end her career; it would potentially end her life. She has, as Derek notes, 'ghosts sitting on her chest; ghosts of things she's done, or been done to her'. Nonetheless, somewhere in her is 'a sense of honor'. Being human, she is 'unpredictable'. There is also a sense in which her confusions, imperfections, sufferings are what has made her the actress she is. As the film's cinematographer remarks of the fire, which burns in the distant Sierra Nevada, but with an obvious relevance to Kitty, 'Fire invigorates the seed buried in the soil. Some seed won't sprout without fire.' Her art is in some senses a product of her life.

In desperation they send for Jerome, the distant guru, urging him to fly in, albeit at considerable expense, and despite the fact that he 'does not board sinking ships'. The question is, however, whether Kitty is disabled by drugs or whether she is simply being wilful. The delays she causes are the evidence of her power. For so long used to ingratiating herself, she is aware that the tables have turned. Now she confuses power with significance.

For Edna, though, the problem is simply that Kitty 'doesn't think she is wonderful anymore', an echo of a line from *The Last Yankee*, in which another woman was disabled by despair at the failure of the world to match her expectations, the failure of love to redeem her. Kitty has lost belief in herself. What was once natural has become artificial. She has been made self-conscious, and that self-consciousness has come close to paralysing her as an actress and a person. She is afraid. Knowing how much she is needed, she fears she is no longer loved, and that is what she primarily needs, what she had mistaken adulation to mean.

The first act ends as news comes that the power supply to the hotel may be cut because of the encroaching fire. One match has potentially stopped everything, as one actress had halted the picture.

The second act begins with the arrival of Jerome, a mock-heroic figure dressed as a cowboy and supremely conscious of his own importance, while determined to accept no responsibility for Kitty. Informed that Kitty's husband had told her 'to stop blaming people and look at herself', he replies, 'That can be destructive', a significant remark from a man himself busy denying responsibility. When Ochsner comes into the room he fails to rise to his feet, receiving him like a potentate, a fact not lost on the man who is paying his per diem.

A succession of people now enter Kitty's bedroom and speak to her. We hear only one side of this dialogue and hence have to infer not only what Kitty says but also her mood. With Edna it is bantering, amused. With Derek it is cautious. With both, however, she raises questions about her husband, as if at one moment she wants to enrol them in her private battle while at another she seeks assurance that she has been loved.

When Ochsner enters he tries to tune in to her by speaking of his own problems. Not only had his wife died but, he explains, his son had committed suicide, using pills. As for himself, he had been a militant Marxist, then a union organiser and subsequently a millionaire. He confesses to having no understanding of how things fell so easily into his hands 'Am I so brilliant? Do I have such a good smell? Or is it luck . . .?' We are, in part, back in the world of *The Man Who Had All the Luck*.

He feels a connection with Kitty, who, he believes, is as bewildered by her life as he is with his. He urges her not to 'wrestle too long with your fate'. What she needs, he insists, is 'Acceptance . . . A person can't jump up and down on the board forever, you've finally got to jump.' She is, he plainly thinks, paralysed by her own self-doubts. She is waiting, though for what is never clear, except, perhaps, for her life to begin, as though her fate lay in the hands of others to whom she has abdicated responsibility for it.

Jerome and Flora are now ushered into her presence. He is plainly not only at a loss at what to do but something of a charlatan. He launches into a confused and confusing account of Eleanora Duse, seemingly oblivious to what he is saying or to its effect on Kitty. When she begins to cry and is handed a handkerchief he advises, 'Don't blow too hard, it's bad for the brain.' The man who was supposed to fill her with a new energy and persuade her to resume her work has managed to reduce her to something approaching hysteria. When her husband enters the room she simply screams.

What follows is a three-way conversation with Kitty silent. Paul demands to know who is responsible for her. It is a rhetorical question since the director has a production to run, Jerome is plainly unwilling to intervene for fear he may become associated with failure, while Paul and his wife can barely communicate. The answer, Paul insists, is that Kitty should assume responsibility for her own life.

Jerome's diagnosis is that Kitty is 'not surrounded by culture or by love but exploitation, by people digging out pieces of your flesh! So you are left trying to sing intimately in a roaring wind, a gale, a typhoon of greed and insensitivity', which is plausible enough except that he is primary proof of that exploitation. Desperate for the credit which accrues from his relationship with her, he is equally determined not to associate himself with any possible failure. He cannot, he tells her, publicly take responsibility for her because 'if god forbid let's say the worst happens and you can't get yourself back to work it'll be all over the papers and who are they going to blame. Me! . . . I have to think of my school and my students . . . I know it seems impossible to you but there are people who hate me.'

When Kitty seemingly agrees to appear for the day's shooting, his response is 'it would be fantastic for me too'. When she evidently thanks him for his help, he modestly insists that 'All I did was come and remind you of who you are and what you are and forge the link between you and the whole cultural history of your art!' This is a man not only lacking in modesty but seemingly devoid of irony.

Kitty appears to recover and ready herself. When Paul appears, Edna tries to persuade him to leave but Derek, the director, insists they should 'all resolve to end this humiliation, hers and ours . . . we can only help her by being ourselves and not the dream creatures her desperation sometimes turns us into . . . reality has to intervene sooner or later'. It is a plea for honesty but even now, and in this place, it has an ironic ring. They are, after all, gathered together to make a film, create a fiction.

Kitty collapses. She is to be hospitalised for a week. As she sleeps so Paul and Edna speak to one another. With Kitty asleep there are certain truths that can be faced. Though Edna thinks the marriage might be saved, Paul confesses that it is at an end because 'I didn't save her, I didn't bring the miracle! . . . and she didn't save me.'

The phone rings with news that the external danger has passed. The fires that had lit the sky are out and the sky is blue again. The emergency is over. Kitty is to be prepared to leave for the hospital, like Blanche Dubois, though not on the arm of a stranger. Edna, meanwhile, prepares for a dinner with Phillip Ochsner. She is forty-five. She looks at herself in the mirror and sighs 'at the sight of her tired self'. She 'gives her hair a few brushes, then leaves off, and plucks at her cheeks to bring color into them . . . Then she stares ahead.'

The play ends on an ambiguous note. The story is incomplete. A marriage is broken. A fragile romance has barely started. A picture is as yet unfinished. It remains to be seen whether life will be born out of the burned-over land.

Nor, as far as the culture is concerned, has the smell of burning dissipated. The real is still traded for performance; a society that has everything is still uncertain that it has earned its luck or justified the power by which it is nonetheless seduced. The sense of dereliction that seems to lie behind the arson has invaded human affairs. A number of the key characters are in flight from responsibility. The making of a film relies on a mutuality but that is precisely what is threatened by the self-concern and self-interest which seems to accompany it.

At the heart of the play is both the specific dilemma generated by the seemingly inescapable relationship between art and commerce, a contest for power, a clash between two interpretations of reality, and also the ironic gap between desire and fulfilment which characterises more than this group of people struggling to create what was never there before. For Miller, speaking in 2003, 'what is really involved there is the terrible impact of power upon creativity. There are moments when they are all sitting there baffled as to how to get this thing to move.' It is a portrait of 'the human predicament where everybody wants the same thing but nobody can get it. It just won't move.'[3]

30

Fiction

When Arthur Miller returned to New York from the University of Michigan in 1938 he was determined to be a writer. Despite his success as a fledgling playwright, drama was by no means his only option. Indeed he quickly wrote a series of stories and sent them to the major magazines of the day. He was nothing if not confident. The stories came back but at least two of them were considerably more effective than their swift rejection suggests. They were turned down, in all probability, because one was a modernist, stream-of-consciousness piece, in many ways brilliant but difficult to see in the context of popular magazines, while another, also impressive, was much more sexually frank than would have been acceptable. He had not researched his market. In 1940 he also wrote a novel, again surprisingly accomplished, set on a freighter whose crew are deeply racist. It was a novel that featured two black characters, struggling to survive. Though the book was never finished it still stands not only as sign of his social commitments but of a talent which might have turned in another direction. Prose fiction, then, drew him in the late 1930s and early 1940s and would continue to do so, if infrequently, throughout his career.

Miller has confessed to thumbing through novels in search of dialogue as though there were a special authenticity and authority associated with the spoken word, as if characters were freed of the authorial voice at that moment and allowed to speak their lives. He saw in his response evidence of the playwright in him, before playwriting had become his avocation. Yet at the same time he felt that the writer stood more completely revealed in stories and novels than in the ventriloquism of characters on the stage, the latter offering a potential means of evasion, a way of concealing the self.

He felt closer to Chekhov, he confessed, when reading his stories than he did in his plays in which language was declarative, dialectical, as characters engaged one another and the public gaze encouraged strategies of avoidance. The short stories he felt even more revealing than the novels in that they offered less cover, fewer mechanisms for concealment. So, it was the Hemingway of the stories rather than the novels that seemed to him revealing, just as it was 'The Cossacks' or 'The Death of Ivan Ilyitch' that he preferred to *War and Peace*.

Playwriting he thought aggressive, immodest. The playwright was in essence a performer, striding the stage he would people. Of its nature drama foregrounded action, a conflict which only seemed generative of truth. 'The object, the place, weather', he insisted, 'the look of a person's shift of posture – these things can have but secondary importance on the stage . . . in life, however, and in the story, place itself and things seen, the mood of the moment, the errant flight of apprehension which leads nowhere, can all register and weigh.'[1]

Perhaps for this reason, he confessed to finding it more difficult to write dialogue in a story than a play, despite his riffling through novels in search of the spoken word. His own explanation was that in part he was struck by the redundancy of preparing speech for actors who would never be auditioned and cast, and in part he was aware of the absurdity of staging as conversations what was better rendered in some other form. Speech was too emphatic and definite, he suggested, too disruptive of what surrounded it, too determinedly dialectical to locate in a story without deforming everything around it. It was, he explained, as though a friend, speaking of an incident, were suddenly to stand up and imitate the voices of those who had participated in it. It was the formality of this, what he called the 'immanence of the actor' (xii), that disturbed and inhibited him. And yet, for all these comments in his introduction to the collection of stories, *I Don't Need You Any More*, one story, 'The Prophecy', is rendered largely through dialogue while another, 'Gimpse of a Jockey', is a monologue, or one side of a conversation, rather like O'Neill's *Hughie*. The truth is that, unsurprisingly, each story generates its own necessities

There is, Miller suggests, an intimacy to the short story. It closes the space between writer and reader. It is generally of a length that can be read at a single sitting. It is like an anecdote, a shared confidence, intimate, potentially confessional. Its scale gives a special weight to each detail. It invites concision and in that sense shares something of the playwright's economy without the public resonance which is a product and precondition of the theatre. As he confessed, 'I have found . . . that from time to time there is an urge not to speed up and condense events and character development, which is what one does in a play, but to hold them frozen and to see things isolated in stillness, which I think is the great strength of a good short story' (x). The oblique, the ironic, the understated perhaps play a greater role in a story.

The weakness of his unpublished novel version of *The Man Who Had All the Luck* lay not only in its anxious inclusiveness, in the tumble of stories which constituted the master story, but in its over-elaboration of motive and event. In *Focus* there was greater economy, a clearer sense of the way in which each incident was a further elucidation of character, germane to an unfolding central plot. But in the best of his stories his prose is honed down, oblique. In such stories, the influence, if such there is, seems to be Hemingway or, perhaps, Chekhov, since Hemingway himself acknowledged him as one of the sources of his own prose style.

In Chekhov's work very little seems to happen. He deliberately eschews dramatic events. He advised that writers should keep their titles simple, a pre-scription Miller seems to follow, and avoid the use of modifiers. 'When you read your proofs', he suggested, 'strike out where you can the qualifications of nouns and verbs.' He urged simplicity: 'colour and expressiveness in descriptions of nature', he suggested, 'are only achieved by simplicity, by such simple phrases as "The sun set", "It grew dark", "It rained."'[2] Miller's 'Monte Sant'Angelo', in which he seems to strive for precisely this simplicity, ends with the uninflected 'setting of the sun'. Selective details, for Chekhov, and subsequently, for Hemingway, were keys to emotional effect.

Yet, at the same time, he called for an awareness of 'the human mass out of which' his characters 'had come' (208), precisely the connection that Miller's character struggles to make in that story as he sees a stranger 'trudging down the mountain, across the plains, on routes marked out for him by generations of men, a nameless traveler' (69). In like manner, in 'I Don't Need You Any More', a young boy slowly works his way towards an understanding of his place in a larger story, as he comes to appreciate more of his relationship to others in the present:

> For the first time in his life he had the hard, imperishable awareness of descent, and with it the powers of one who knows he is being watched over and so receives a trust he must never lay down. In his mind's eye there rushed past the image of his angry father, and behind Papa was Grandpa and then other men, all grave and bearded, watching over him and somehow expecting and being gratified at the renewal of their righteousness and bravery in him.
>
> (47–8)

In both cases, what is at stake is a sense of Jewish identity in a world in which history seems necessarily truncated, a society in which rebirth and renewal are imperatives with roots in an alien religious tradition. In each story, the central character discovers the present through discovering the past and finds himself at the confluence of these two streams. They are American stories and they are Jewish stories simultaneously.

A number of his stories, indeed, seem to spring out of his concern for a Jewish identity, as though they offered a more private space than the theatre to engage such a question. They reflect what appears to be an anxiety about a past to which his characters have an ambiguous relationship, simultaneously within and without, drawn to a secret world of shared symbols, common griefs, but reaching out to a wider world.

The price of such ambiguity, however, seems to be guilt at what might seem to be denial, a crisis of identity which may also be a crisis of faith. What, after all, is the son and grandson of immigrants to claim as his heritage? Is it a past from which he is severed by new experiences, a past, indeed, constantly under assault to the point of near annihilation, or is it the heritage of his new home inviting his assimilation as if such were no more than a gift to be gratefully accepted?

Two stories from the 1950s are an interrogation of his Jewishness. The first, 'Monte Sant'Angelo', published in 1951, is an account of a visit by two Americans – Vinny Appello and Bernstein (we never know his first name) – to a small Italian town. Appello has spent his time in Italy looking for evidence of his ancestors, an obsession which seemingly baffles his companion who feels 'left out and somehow deficient' (55). As their trip continues so Bernstein comes to feel that Appello is constructing a history which will leave him 'less dead' when the time comes for him to die.

For his part, Bernstein feels his path to the past blocked. 'I have no relatives that I know of in Europe . . . And if I had they'd have all been wiped out by now' (55). So, the Holocaust enters the story as a shadow. Bernstein's denial of interest in his past, it seems, is something more than an immigrant's desire to inhabit the present, though, for him, his European origins are associated with shame. They were what had made flight necessary. They were the reason for a journey away from origins. Indeed, it slowly becomes apparent that his Jewish identity is precisely what he himself has fled. The distance between himself and his origins has in some way become important to him, the source if not of pride then of seeming contentment. But something has been lost in this process and this is a story which identifies something of what that might be. It is a story of rediscovered identity.

When a man enters a restaurant in which they are having lunch, Bernstein suddenly feels a seemingly irrational sense of intimacy with him. He is a sales-man, it transpires, selling cloth to the locals. Bernstein watches him with a growing sense that he and the old man share something. It seems to him that he must be Jewish. There is something in the way he ties the knot of his bundle that seems familiar: 'There's a Jewish man tying a bundle' (64). The man's name is Mauro di Benedetto, 'Morris of the Blessed. Moses', as Appello translates. The man denies any such identity but leaves them because he needs to return home, with his loaf of fresh bread, by sundown, a habit, he explains, though one for which he has no explanation beyond the fact that his father had always returned home before sundown on Fridays.

For Bernstein this is proof of his Jewish identity. Why else does he feel the need to return home on what is the eve of the Sabbath, carrying bread? The man continues to deny being Jewish, indeed is unsure what Jews might be, beyond, perhaps, some sect within the Catholic Church, but this no longer matters to Bernstein. He suddenly feels at home. Beyond that, he feels a sense of pride. Here, after all, is not only a link to his own past, no matter how indirect, but here is a Jew who has survived. Here is 'a proof as mute as stones, that a past lived. A past for me, Bernstein thought, astounded by its importance for him, when in fact he had never had a religion or even, he realized now, a history' (68).

Here, he feels, is an end to a shame he has never confronted as he embraces what he has shunned. In a small Italian town, lifted high above the surrounding plain, he rediscovers what was lost, a history and hence a present and an identity.

He is an American but he is also, he now realises, something else. It is not that America is not his home but that his had been a life constructed on denial so that he had never felt at home in the world.

This is a story told by indirection. There are echoes here of Hemingway, not only in that indirection but also in Bernstein's mock British usage. People are 'awfully frightened', a driver is a 'Princeton chap'. The influence is clear but the story surely grows directly out of Miller's own sense, then and later, of ambivalence about his own Jewish identity. Like Bernstein, he was not a practising Jew. At the time of writing the story the Holocaust was a shapeless fact not susceptible of direct confrontation. When, on his own visit to Italy in 1947, he had seen survivors of the camps, stark, gaunt figures waiting out time before travelling, as they hoped, to Israel, they had hardly impacted on him. They were a product of peripheral vision. But what he did not confront directly he plainly registered and the pressure of that occasion is clear here, if only in the unexamined significance, to Bernstein, of the fact of survival. Yet Miller was a believer in the significance of the past. The nature and composition of identity would prove central to many of his plays. Bernstein's denial and Bernstein's affirmation are both part of Miller's sensibility and this tightly controlled story explores that tension.

He returned to this self-examination in another 1950s story, 'I Don't Need You Any More', which dates from 1959. In this, he revisits his own youth. Here, surely, are his parents, the father illiterate, the mother frustrated at denied possibilities. Here, too, is his brother Kermit and here a portrait of himself, at the age of five, struggling to make sense of the world, of himself and of his relationships. Here, too, is the family's summer home at Rockaway in 1920, when all was well with the world and the economic crash that would ruin the family was still nine years away.

At the heart of the story is Martin, feeling his way through a world which makes no clear sense to him. It is September. The seasons are on the change as, in a sense, is he, though without understanding what that change might be. Everything is a mystery: his parents, his brother, the religion that seems to shape their behaviour. He wants simultaneously to be included, to be part of adult experience, and to be separate, his own person, independent.

He is aware of religious rituals but neither understands nor is a part of them. There are injunctions and restrictions but these seem not to extend to him. He has been granted immunity, as though excluded from something vital.

His mother appears to retreat into her own privacies. The intimacy between them is threatened, not least when she meets a man on the street and later confesses to a shocked and bewildered son that she might have married him, had her father not disapproved. While not fully understanding what he is told, Martin senses some treachery. The man is a rival to his father but so, too, to himself. She has a history, it seems, which goes back beyond him, loyalties to something other than the family.

He struggles to draw attention to himself, embroidering the truth in order to put himself back into the central position he used to inhabit. And when this ceases to work, in his frustration and anger he strikes out at his mother and shouts: 'I don't need you any more', less a declaration of independence than a confession of bewilderment. She seemed not to need him; why, then, should he need her?

Among the things he fails to understand, however, is that his mother is pregnant, though this is never stated, just as we learn of the frustrations of her marriage only by indirection. It is this that explains her volatile mood, this that underlines a change coming towards him as he is about to be displaced by someone else who will become the centre of attention.

Yet for all his confusion, his misreading of a world which still seems alien to him, he can detect what he has yet to understand. His father and mother are, as he begins to sense, separate people, in some ways at odds in their needs no less than their talents. He is aware both of his strength and his weakness, knowing, seemingly instinctively, how to wound, how to command the attention he craves.

Tomorrow the holiday will be over and school will begin. Tomorrow he will become something different. At first accompanied by his brother, he is already looking to the time when he will go alone. This, too, accounts for the sense in the house that this is a special occasion. It is so in religious terms, as they celebrate a festival that means nothing to him. It is so, too, in that soon he will be inducted into mysteries of all kinds, secular and religious. Soon, a new child will be born and he will no longer be the vulnerable one, staring uncomprehendingly around him as though in an alien place.

In 1960 Miller wrote a story which came directly out of his relationship with Marilyn Monroe. It is a story with echoes of Hemingway's 'The Cat in the Rain'. 'Please Don't Kill Anything', is about a husband and wife watching as fish are brought to shore. Those of little value are tossed on to the sand where they writhe and twitch. It is clear that to the woman this is near to unbearable. They are living creatures, which must be saved. Her husband dutifully, but clearly with embarrassment, tosses a number back into the sea, leaving two, seemingly dead, as a token to those who watch that she is not the fanatic she appears, but also to get her to accept the fact of death and to break the connection which she clearly feels between her own situation and that of the fish.

He acts, it seems, out of love, as she acts out of a human sympathy for living things. But it becomes clear both that that love is under strain and that her sensitivities cut far deeper than a concern for a handful of fish on a seashore. She identifies with these creatures, sees in their fate her own. And just as her husband cannot, finally, rescue the fish, so he cannot rescue her.

She urges him to throw the two remaining fish back, thereby refusing the lesson he had tried to offer, but when he does so a dog bounds into the

sea and retrieves one of them, doing so again when the man throws it back.
There is, it seems, no escape. A minnow slides from the mouth of the now-
dead fish, a Darwinian lesson that again the woman refuses to accept. And
though eventually the fish is thrown back it is clear that she is fighting a losing
battle.

As the two of them stroll from the beach, holding hands, we are told that
he 'felt a great happiness opening in him' (75). She seems a combination of
child and woman. What follows are a Hemingwayesque conversation and a
Hemingwayesque ending:

> 'But some of them might live now till they're old.'
> 'And then they die,' he said.
> 'But at least they'll live as long as they can.' And she laughed with the
> woman part of her that knew of absurdities.
> 'That's right,' he said, 'they'll live to a ripe old age and grow prosperous
> and dignified . . .'
> She burst out laughing. 'And see their children grow up!'
> He kissed her on the lips, blessing her and her wish. 'Oh, how I love
> you,' she said with tears in her eyes. Then they walked home
>
> (75–6)

What appears to be a love story is, it seems, a story about the end of love.
This could be the end of *The Sun Also Rises*, with its dying fall. The woman
is clearly on the edge of breakdown, neuraesthenically sensitive. The husband,
equally clearly, is aware of her fragility and of his own inability, finally, to save
her. What we are left with as they hold hands is the space between them. This
is the end of something, the more remarkable for the fact that the story was
written before Miller had finally accepted that his relationship with Monroe
had run its course, that he could neither rescue her nor save his marriage. There
is a control in the prose that is no longer there in the relationship, and it is from
the tension between those facts that the story's power derives.

The biographical elements, of course, are largely irrelevant. The power
of the story derives from its indirection, from what is not said. The ironies
of the relationship are not explored or, indeed, even stated. They emerge from
the differing sensibilities of two people who have convinced themselves of a
mutuality whose imperfection is increasingly clear, if not yet to them. Something is dying, and it is not only the fish gasping for air on the edge of the
surf.

'Glimpse of a Jockey' stands at the other extreme from the nearly fifty-page
'I Don't Need You Any More'. Published two years earlier, it is barely three
pages long and consists of a an entirely one-sided conversation. It is a character
sketch of a jockey, broken, it seems, in body and perhaps in mind. He has been

successful. He has the money but now he sits drinking in a bar. The language flows relentlessly, one idea giving birth to another. He needs no reply and none comes. The language is covering something and that something emerges only obliquely. He never knew his father, he explains, until he wrote to a television station for which his father had briefly worked. A reunion came to nothing. The relationship, it turned out, meant nothing to the old man, who had walked out on the family when his son was one, and who cares nothing for him now, except, perhaps, as a source of financial help.

The jockey son buys him a power mower, but its roar inhibits their conversation, denies him the consolation of relationship for which he had been looking. Indeed, this story is as much about identity as 'Monte Sant'Angelo' and 'I Don't Need You Any More': 'What did I come for?' asks the jockey, a question, like the rest of the monologue masquerading as a conversation, addressed not to another but himself. 'Who is he? Who am I if he's my father . . . I'm the son of my father. I knew it even if I was a total stranger . . . I was ready to lay down my life for him . . . Who knows the inside from the outside?' (116).

This is the key to a man who explains in passing that he has seen an analyst and that he loves his wife 'married eighteen years, and my kids', but, oddly, adds the thought that 'you draw a line somewhere, someplace' (115). He is now a long way from wife and children, in a bar, eyeing up two women who, like the German women in Hemingway's story 'Soldier's Home', are unattractive: 'What's the difference what they look like, they're all the same, I love 'em all' (117).

Below his accounts of success is a counter-current. He recalls failed rides, broken-down horses, accidents in which he had broken multiple bones. The jaunty tone, the stream of language, the broken-backed sentences, fractured syntax, suggest something fundamentally wrong. As he confesses, 'Nobody knows any more where he begins or ends, it's like they pied the maps and put Chicago in Latvia . . . What the hell do I know . . .' (115). He is like the father who refused to turn the motor off 'so we could talk quietly' (117). So long as he sings his tainted aria there is no opportunity for his listener to question, reproach, despise, engage. 'Glimpse of a Jockey' is a character sketch which works by slow accretion. Like O'Neill's figure in *Hughie*, what he primarily seems to fear is dying without ever discovering the meaning of living. He is as self-deceiving as Hickey in *The Iceman Cometh*: 'I admit it, the whole scam is pistils and stamens, all right I surrender. But Jesus, give me room, let me die laughing if I'm goin' to die. I'm ready. If I slide off a snowbank under a cab outside there I'll cheer death' (115).

Unlike most of Miller's other stories, it is possible to conceive of this as a brief play. The man who tries so hard to conceal himself, in fact slowly reveals the drama of his life which has been the slow loss of meaning, the sacrifice of value to ambition, of love to obsession.

Miller has said that

> It is only very rarely that I can feel in a short story that I am right on top
> of something, as I feel when I write for the stage. I am then in the ultimate
> place of vision – you can't back me up any further. Everything is inevitable
> down to the last comma. In a short story, or any kind of prose, I still can't
> escape the feeling of a certain arbitrary quality. Mistakes go by – people
> consent to them more – more than mistakes do on the stage . . . To me the
> great thing is to write a good play, and when I'm writing a short story it's as
> though I were saying to myself, 'Well, I'm only doing this because I'm not
> writing a play at the moment.' There's guilt connected with it. Naturally I
> do enjoy writing a short story, it is a form that has a certain strictness.[3]

'The Prophecy' has a certain flaccidness while 'I Don't Need You Any More'
could perhaps have been tightened somewhat. But 'Monte Sant'Angelo' and
'Glimpse of a Jockey' seem to be 'inevitable to the last comma', and to benefit
from the strictness of the form, in the latter case perhaps because of its close
affinity to drama.

'Fame' (1966) is an ironic story about a successful playwright who encounters
an old high-school companion in a bar. He fails to recognise him but assumes
that his own fame has motivated the man to approach him. In fact, this figure
from the past has not connected the name of a famous writer and his schoolyard
friend and, accordingly, boasts of his own success. When he realises who he is
speaking to, he and his wife withdraw, humiliated.

Miller relates just such an incident in his autobiography, published some
twenty years later, and subsequently transformed the story into a brief play.
The story is little more than an anecdote, but it captures his own ambiguous
feelings about fame. It is something he both welcomes and resists. He is afraid
of being recognised and afraid of not being recognised. To have his name in the
papers and above theatres opened up certain avenues and closed down others.
The pleasure of success carried with it the threat of isolation, as it coloured
relationships which could never quite be the same again. There is, in other
words, a kind of guilt which accompanies fame as there is damage done to
relationships, which potentially lose their spontaneity and honesty. 'Fame' was
an anecdote transformed into a fable.

Miller has always sunk his roots down into his own experience, finding inspiration in those he encounters, as in his own life. From time to time, indeed, he has
deliberately set himself to look outside himself almost as if there were something illegitimate about the process of putting friends and acquaintances into
his work. That was the impulse between his setting sail on a freighter in 1940,
two weeks after his first marriage, in search of raw material. In the end, though,
he came to realise that the process of invention is a complex one. Imagination

and experience are the warp and woof of fiction. Understandably, he resents those who seek to decode his work purely in terms of autobiography, as if it were no more than an elaborate subterfuge, a cover for confession. What matters, he insists, is the work. Some of his stories do find their inspiration in his own life. Their achievement, however, as he insists, lies elsewhere, in characters raised to exemplary status, in stories which work by indirection.

'A Search for a Future' (1966) concerns a Jewish actor who one day, staring into the mirror as he does his make-up, 'felt that I had never done anything but make myself up for a part I never got to make' (220). The reason for this, he tells himself, is that he has been 'waiting to hear that my father has died' (221). He is not the only Miller protagonist to have lived a temporary life. Like the character in Henry James's 'The Beast in the Jungle', he is waiting for something to happen while everything he has done, or failed to do, ensures that this will seemingly never come about.

He has never married. Several engagements have come to nothing. Each time it was to a gentile girl and he has convinced himself that to go through with the marriage would have broken his mother's heart. He is not a man ready to make commitments. He is not a man with certainties. He has been told that he is too attached to his mother but does not 'feel sure about that', or anything else, it seems. Marriage anyway, he tells himself, 'was not absolutely necessary'. In a curious phrase he says to himself that it 'gave me a false heart' (221).

Son of an immigrant Jew, he affects to like the idea of arranged marriages. They, at least, require nothing so definite as a decision, or passion. 'I miss a wife and children I never had', he says to himself, nostalgic for a life he never lived because he could not bring himself to make anything as definite as a choice, could never commit himself to someone else, commitment seemingly being beyond his power.

He has, however, and uncharacteristically, agreed to attend an anti-war meeting, 'Broadway for Peace', effectively coerced into it, though, he confesses, 'I do not know who is right about this war' (222). In what sense, then, can he protest? He is sure, anyway, that in five years no one will remember it, any more than he can remember the details of his own career in which he has done little more than watch the days pass. There was no doubt an ideal at stake in the protest rally, as there had no doubt been in the case of his acting, but he can no longer recall with any clarity what kind of actor he had wished to be, except that it 'wasn't this kind is all I know' (222). In other words, just as he is vaguely nostalgic for the family he never had, so he is for the career that never was, quite as if he has not been an agent in his own life, never the principal in his personal drama.

Miller is drawing a portrait of an invisible man who seemingly exists only in the parts he plays, parts which themselves seem to lack any significance. On this night he is playing the role of 'a loud farmer' (220). He had, he insists, always respected those with convictions, 'Leftists and so on'. The 'and so on' is indicative of the fact that he sees commitment as in some way independent of any particular cause. What strikes him is less what sends people into battle over their beliefs than the 'wonderful friendships between them', quite as if they had been looking for a social club, as if their politics stood justified by its unintended consequences.

Friendships, however, seem not to be something he quite understands, simply envies in a quiet and uncommitted way. Friendship is what he lacks as he sits alone inspecting his life for its absences. Certainly he has never put his own name on 'anything political', convinced that it could make no difference, that, indeed, it might threaten his equanimity or even his career, such as it has been. Why, after all, would this man of no substance send out any ripples and, if not, then why venture out where demands may be made of him? The world and he do not interact. He observes it with no more than a kind of detached interest.

His reverie is interrupted by a young man who has come to remind him of the imminent meeting. For a moment, he thinks his father must have died and he had forgotten and was to be summoned to a midnight ceremony, a curious displacement of anxieties. Then he recalls that he had agreed to sit on the platform for the event, not exactly a statement but a presence. The young man, he realises, believes that he is trying to stop the world from ending, but that is because 'it wasn't all the same to him', as it patently is for this man who watches, removed, not ironic but simply remote, unaffected.

He sees a sense of expectation, hope, belief in the young man, while aware that these are not emotions and reactions he shares: 'I cannot imagine anything I would sit and wait for', he tells himself, 'and I wished I had something like that. I ended up a little glad that I was going to be at the meeting' (223). It is a small enough enthusiasm, almost neutralising itself in its expression.

That night he fancies he acts better than usual, though there is hardly any evidence for this as a man walks out in the middle of the play. It strikes him suddenly that in a way everyone is an actor, even the man who walks out, performing as though forgetting that 'some of us very soon are actually going to die' (223). It is an absurdity which momentarily fascinates him. Everyone, he realises, presidents included, costumes themselves for their performance, but he is aware that they do something more. Reverting to his earlier thought, he observes that 'I, instead of actually marrying, stop short at the last moment every time.' In truth, it seems that he stops short of everything, including living, because he acknowledges that 'it would make my life real' (241), and patently reality disturbs him.

He now visits his father, caged, as it seems to him, in a nursing home, having suffered from a stroke. The world has become strange for this man who no longer seems so very much older than himself. Everyone here is waiting for the end. He suddenly remembers the previous night when, at the meeting, and to his dismay, he had been summoned to the microphone and stuttered out a few words, some meaningless. His wish that the war might end, however, had sparked applause and suddenly, irrationally, in the middle of this peace rally, he wishes that he had married. He is aware of having missed something, some company, some assurance of his existence.

His father is damaged, but still seems to be driven from within: 'there is some kind of force lying in pieces inside of him, the force of a man who at least has not all settled for this kind of room and this kind of life. For him, as for me and everybody else, it all seems some kind of mistake. He has a future' (228). The irony of this, the essential contradiction, seems not to strike him.

On a whim, and stirred by his meeting with his father, he catches a bus to Harlem where, like Miller himself, he had been born. Everything has changed. He can no longer see himself here, no longer locate himself in the past or the present.

That night his father walks out of the nursing home in the rain, being found the following morning. He, too, had returned to Harlem, trying to go home, though home is no longer there. Something about his drive, even in his befuddled state, seems a reproach and a spur. 'I have a terrific desire to live differently', the now aging actor says to himself. He wishes to put his soul back into his body. Just for moments, he confesses, 'it makes me feel as I used to when I started, when I thought that to be a great actor was like a making some kind of a gift to the people' (236).

It is not clear whether some change is possible. He has, perhaps, been nudged if not into commitment then into something more than a self-cancelling introspection. The phrase 'terrific desire' would not have come to his mind earlier. He has recalled what he had earlier forgotten, namely what it was that once drove him as an actor. On the other hand, he still seems to stare out at the world from the fastness of a self which has never entirely come into focus. His father, even in his confusions, had struck him as being real, whereas for him reality had always been something to hold at arm's length for fear of the demands that might follow.

The very style of the story, distant, understated, seemingly impersonal even as it articulates the thoughts of this non-committal man, suggests the gap which has opened up between him and the life he observes, the life he regrets never having lived. The story is something of minor masterpiece, the style as controlled and clinical as the man who has excluded so much from his life that nothing is left but regret, while even that is held up to catch the light as though he were entranced by the dull lustre of his own insignificance.

One of Miller's skills has always been his ability to capture the mood of his times, to read his society and question its values. His stories, however, frequently take an inside track. They are, as he implied, more intimate. They focus more directly on the small gesture, the momentary insight, the sudden irony, the self-revealing remark. At the same time, he was aware that such apparent privacies have a cultural force, that the personal may be a mechanism of evasion, and a story that he first published in 1961, 'The Prophecy', explores the truth of this. It is a story, seemingly about a woman tempted into an adulterous relationship, which, in effect, is a judgement on a decade.

It is true that the 1950s could scarcely be said to be non-political, and Miller was more aware of this than many others, having found himself the victim of right-wing zealots. This, after all, was the decade of the Korean War and the beginnings of the Civil Rights movement. Yet an imposed orthodoxy, capable of intimidating even a president, did press the individual back into the supposed securities of private life and 'The Prophecy' is, in part, about a society seemingly content to embrace materialism, substitute mysticism for religion and sexual and psychological game-playing for an engaged life.

Set in a small community in Pennsylvania, the story centres on the relation-ship between Stowey Rummel, an internationally successful artist–architect, and his wife, Cleota. He has seemingly reached a stage in his career when every-thing he does is well received and hence he has no stimulus to innovate. His wife, too, appears content with what they have. They have settled for routine, an emotional life as unchanging as the winter weather: 'day after day and week after week, the same monotonous wind sucks the heat out of the house' (118). Something has equally been sucked out of their lives. For almost thirty years, we are told, he has lived in the same farmhouse with the same wife, rising at the same time each day and performing the same domestic rituals. He is not bored. Indeed he regards himself as 'a fortunate man' (121). Yet, as the story progresses, it becomes apparent that his equanimity is something less than secure and that the wife, who has become part of his routine, feels a sense of incompletion, though she is not as yet fully aware of this.

Stowey leaves for Florida to supervise an exhibition of his work, while his wife prepares for a dinner party at which she is joined by her sister-in-law, a close neighbour who is the source of an undefined irritation. Cleota is a woman who has never felt the need to make judgements, to exercise discriminations, moral or otherwise. The world is as it is. At best, she 'often appeared to verge on moral indignation', though usually because she sees in public events a reflection of her own resistance to being imposed upon. Even then it was 'not indignation she felt so much as bewilderment' (129). For a brief moment, however, this equanimity is disturbed.

Her guests at the dinner party include a friend, Lucretia, Madame Lhevine, a fortune-teller, and John Trudeau, a schoolteacher and would-be poet who arrives with a young girl, who calls herself Eve Saint Bleu, on his arm. As the evening progresses so Cleota feels increasingly disturbed. The fact of Trudeau's lover erodes something of her feelings about the permanency of relationships. Indeed, she comes to realise that her friend Lucretia has also separated from her husband and that at some level she had known how fragile that relationship had been without acknowledging it to herself. In other words, there is a level of her own sensibility that she has denied. Her life seems to unravel as the dinner party progresses. She confesses that 'when one gets to a certain point, and there's more behind than ahead, it just somehow . . . doesn't seem to have been quite worth it . . . you wonder if it wasn't all a little too . . . small' (141–2).

Madam Lhevine, whether sage or charlatan, like the practised fortune-teller she seems to be, then offers this perception back to her as evidence of her own insight when she observes that there comes a moment in people's lives when 'one sees there will be no ecstacy . . . we see the future too clearly, and we see that it is a plain, an endless plain, and not what we had thought – a mountain with a glory at the top' (142). Offered external validation for her own thoughts, Cleota realises that she is, indeed, at just such a moment. Madame Lhevine then prophesies that Cleota's husband will die before his sister, and she has a vision of her husband dead and herself, after thirty years of marriage, with 'nothing to show' (144). She is, what one of her guests assumes, an unhappy woman unaware of her unhappiness.

The party is then joined by a young Jewish writer called Joseph, a neighbour and friend of the family and ten years younger than Cleota. It is tempting to see elements of the young Arthur Miller in this figure. This is not simply because both tell anecdotes about aunts who had read their palms and predicted failure at university, but because there is a similarity between the description of Joseph's moral qualms at involving himself with Cleota and Miller's later accounts in *Timebends* of his own temptations and rationalisations as a young man.

Thus, the young writer, though drawn to her, feels that he cannot succumb to such feelings unless 'he should strike out toward another sort of life and character for himself, a life, as he visualized it, of truthful relations of a confessional sort' (146). He shies away out of decency, 'For the true terror of living in a false position was that the love of others became attached to it and so would be betrayed if one were to strike for the truth. And treason to others . . . was the ultimate destruction, worse even than treason to himself, living with a wife he could not love' (146).

Meanwhile, he finds himself criticised by Madame Lhevine and Lucretia for writing works which are over-constructed, works in which characters learn from their experiences rather than submitting to inevitabilities, a criticism with which Miller himself was familiar. He is attacked for believing in the need for social change, having been expelled from university for refusing to disavow his left-wing youth. Cleota intervenes, offering an emollient comment that both sides of the argument could be right, precisely the bland withdrawal of commitment most calculated to irritate Joseph. To him, these are people who had 'simply lived in an oblong hum' (151).

When the others leave, Joseph stays and Cleota confesses to her confusion. The world around her seems to be falling apart, relationships breaking, a certain insanity beginning to characterise everything. Like Mr Peters nearly forty years later, she laments that there no longer appears to be a 'subject . . . Any other *thing*' (155). Joseph momentarily acknowledges the truth of this, conceding that 'there is no larger aim in life any more. Everything has become personal relations and nothing more' (156), while feeling that the fight for justice and the oppressed is the something more they are not addressing. In a society that has seemingly given up on animating ideas, that 'no longer knows its aims' (156), sexuality is a retreat from engagement.

Apparently ignoring his remarks, she tries to seduce him and, though he breaks away and leaves, when she visits him to apologise the next day, he is tempted.

The action then moves forwards. The prophecy about the death of Cleota's husband is proved false when his sister dies first. Joseph's marriage has by now broken down and he returns to settle affairs, only to encounter Cleota and her husband happily together as if nothing had happened, their equanimity recovered, their existence apparently what it had been before the dinner party had momentarily disturbed her.

Speaking of the story five years later, Miller remarked that it 'was written under the pall of the Fifties' but that

> there's been a terrific politicalization of the people these past four or five years. Not in the old sense, but in the sense that it is no longer *gauche* or stupid to be interested in the fate of society and in injustice and in race problems and the rest of it. It now becomes esthetic material once again. In the Fifties it was out to mention this. It meant you were not really an artist . . . it has been an era of personal relations . . . This intense personal relations concentration of the Fifties seem now to have been joined to a political consciousness, which is terrific.[4]

Fifties theatre, apart from his own, he characterised as 'piddling private conversations'.[5] 'The Prophecy' is his portrait of a decade which was not devoid of political and social issues but which, for the most part, prompted a destructive privatism, a withdrawal into self-concern and the empty routines of a life ostensibly lived for no purpose.

'Fitter's Night' (1966) looks back to Miller's war work in the Brooklyn Navy Yard, when he had served as a shipfitter. It tells the story of a man trapped into marriage by his own greed, who takes pleasure in the vengeance he wreaks by withdrawing all contact with his wife. Promised by his immigrant grandfather that he will inherit the money he has brought with him from Italy, he had fallen in with his family's plans for his marriage and even had a child. The collapse of the exchange rate, however, had turned the promised fortune into pocket money, leaving him no one to punish but the innocent wife.

His work at the Navy Yard, meanwhile, is merely a means of getting by. He feels no connection with it. He takes pride in his strategies for avoiding work while appalled by the waste he sees around him. His life is, effectively, on hold. Then, resentfully, he is pressured into effecting repairs to a destroyer waiting to join a wartime convoy. The job is dangerous and he does everything he can to avoid it. When he succeeds in accomplishing it, however, he discovers a sudden sense of pride and an unexpected sense of solidarity with the Captain of the ship and those who are about to risk their lives at sea. Briefly, he discovers a missing purpose to his existence, acknowledging a sense of connection between himself and the world. Until then a man with no plot to his life, he glimpses those missing connections that have left him adrift and undefined.

Not the most impressive of the stories in his 1967 collection, 'Fitter's Night' nonetheless embodies a familiar Miller theme. It is concerned with the need to discover personal meaning in and through the link between individual actions and social action. As in *A View from the Bridge*, he is dealing with a character who cannot fully articulate his own feelings, who acts instinctively, though his passions, unlike those of Eddie Carbone, seem oddly marginal to him, displaced from his sense of himself. His mistress is no more than a convenience, another way of filling a blank life. However, the reader is permitted access to his thought processes, as audiences are not in *A View from the Bridge*, and the effect of this is in some senses reductive.

There is no authorial condescension in Miller's presentation of Eddie Carbone; there is, at times, with respect to Tony Calabrese. Eddie is a complex man whose denials are necessary to his survival. Tony is disturbingly simple and direct, like a figure from a naturalistic novel, the victim of circumstance and fate. He feels trapped in what he thinks of as 'The Story', the plot offered to him in the form of supposed good fortune from the Old World. Until what amounts to his existential act, he seems no more than the sum of the influences exerted on him. His discovery of purpose, therefore, though effectively presented, seems somewhat arbitrary. In effect it becomes his new 'Story', the new animating idea that dominates his limited imagination and seems likely to sustain him, though without redeeming a life that appears no less empty than before, merely more ironic from the potential it briefly revealed.

Miller has written short stories throughout his career, not all of which are covered here. He was still writing them in the twenty-first century. 'The Performance', published in 2002, is discussed later. He followed this, in 2003, with a striking work called 'Presence'.[6] It concerns an encounter on a beach which becomes the focus for thoughts of a distant and immediate past, the occasion of a minor epiphany as a man, fresh from an argument with his wife, witnesses a couple making love on the foreshore.

Back comes a memory of his youth. The woman he now encounters recalls another, long dead, as it stirs not so much a sexual excitement as a simultaneous feeling of loss and joy. The sea, meanwhile, the backdrop to this seemingly minor drama, seems to shadow equally his sense of life and a vague sense of menace. The couple leave and he finds himself both dismayed and exulted. The beach is now empty but a presence remains, a sense of immanent meaning. The story begins in the present tense, then flows into the past but, then, this is a piece about a moment that seems to take place outside of time, much as the sea, whose rhythms echo those of the lovers, was mute witness to a long-ago moment of love and is again now. In 'Presence' prose is pressed in the direction of poetry, as language carries the idea of fact elevated into myth.

In 1992, Miller returned to the 1930s and 40s for a novella called *Homely Girl* [7] (*Plain Girl* in the United Kingdom). Its sub-title is 'A Life', quite as if this were to be a biography, as, in a sense, it is, except that this fifty-two-page story is a spiritual autobiography in that it is an account of a woman's discovery of herself.

Janice Sessions is the daughter of Jewish immigrants. The story begins when she is in her sixties and alone but with a sense that 'after all her life had amounted to a little something' (4), quite as if it might not have done. Why that should be so becomes the real subject of the story.

As the title implies, Janice is plain, without being unattractive. She had decided to get by on style and irony. Born to money, she had thrown herself into 'doing good' during the 1930s, even marrying someone below her in the social scale in part as a gesture that was of a piece with her support for the Loyalists in Spain or the National Maritime Union. Her solidarity was not only with the poor but with the future, almost as if her parents were embodiments of the past as well as of the reactionary forces which she saw herself as fighting. Her parents were, in some senses perforce, assimilationists, owing their Anglicised name to the ignorance of immigration officials. They were also deniers of history, refusing to believe that the Germans would submit to Hitler.

In marrying Sam Fink she was thus wedding herself to someone whose name reflected an honest embrace of his race, and a representative of the revolutionary class, or the closest she was likely to get to it. Love and pity seem to have fused together. Where her father seemingly accepted injustice in the world, she set herself to confront it, her marriage being a skirmish in this war, though, it is implied, there was more to her father than she could see at the time.

When he dies and is cremated Janice inadvertently leaves his ashes in a bar, an irony which simultaneously underscores and breaks her connection with the past. Meanwhile, her husband's, and her own, commitment to the cause – of communism, social justice, anti-fascism – means that they tend to live externally. Social justice, political change, seem to lie ahead, but so, too, does the meaning of her life. It is as if everyone were living provisionally: 'It was like the Depression itself – everybody kept waiting for it to lift and forgot how to live in the meantime' (12).

Sam is no better-looking than Janice, perhaps another, though unacknowl-edged, reason for marrying him. His commitment to the cause seems somehow related to his commitment to her, while he stands for that rejection of the mate-rial world, of the past, which, for a while, seemed to hold the meaning of her

life. Yet, for him, everything is to be seen in terms of the political life. Art is to
be explained by class origins or commitments. His willing submersion of his
own personality in the cause seems, for a while, to reassure her about her own
abnegations and denials. They are united not by love but an apparently shared
set of beliefs.

Sam is a bookseller, with an encyclopaedic knowledge of his trade and even
of the content of the books, while affecting to dismiss them in favour of political
urgencies. Her own discontent, meanwhile, is swallowed up in what she takes
to be the importance of the cause which he serves, and in whose redeeming
shadow she lives her life. The future blots out their present.

When the Hitler–Stalin pact is signed, it might have released them, but Sam
is one of those radicals who continued to believe, who found pragmatic reasons
to sustain idealism which once was sufficient to sustain itself. It is not that Miller
is mocking such naiveties, or even writing a story to explain his own youthful
idealism, swept away by history, the cause only of a sentimental regret (he,
after all, also swallowed the Hitler–Stalin pact). Indeed, the story momentarily
flashes forward as Janice talks to the man who eventually replaces Sam and who
refuses to allow her to indict herself for past failings. As he remarks, 'A lot of
the past is always embarrassing – if you have any sensitivity . . . memories of
one's naivety are always painful. But so what? Would you rather have had no
beliefs at all?' (18).

The observation echoes Miller's own response to the enthusiasms of the
thirties which he shared, the wrong allegiances, the false utopias. It was legitimate enough to regret belief in false gods, but not to regret belief itself. Asked
before the House Un-American Activities Committee to disavow the past, he
was happy to acknowledge wrong decisions, even a false consciousness, but not
the fact of his commitment to social justice, his judgement of a system which
had itself failed in essential human ways.

In the same way, *Homely Girl* is not a sentimental account of lost dreams, the
cooling of passion, but a celebration of the survival of passions which could so
easily have been transmuted into cynicism. It is the account of a woman who
discovers her real beauty, which has nothing to do with good looks, and her real
avocation, which is to transform the world not with rhetoric or public actions
but a transfiguring imagination.

Sam goes to war, his faith in the Soviet Union restored, if it had ever been
dented. Janice stays behind, waiting for the miracle that will flood her life with
meaning, waiting for the redemption that she despairs of discovering. Once
again, she lives provisionally. If the Depression had been about waiting for the
end so, too, was the war. On the other side, seemingly, awaited the justification
for living which she had until now looked for in the external world. She tries
a brief affair, which awakens her sexually but in no other way. She meets a
professor of art history, who inducts her into an existentialism which seems
little more than a justification for self-concern, more especially since it is a

prelude to seduction. Nonetheless, she is aware, as she had not previously been, that she had not until then chosen the life she lives.

These experiences serve to snap some final connection with her husband, a relationship finally smashed on his return when he proudly recounts his rape of a German woman, as though she will take pleasure in this evidence of his revenge on fascism and of a sexuality of which he had previously shown so little evidence. She walks out, ready, in effect, to begin her life again.

Boom times return and she is invited by her brother to join him in benefiting from them, but by then she is searching for something more than comfort and success. What she is looking for now manifests itself in terms of a chance encounter with a blind man, who is unaware of her plain appearance and responds to her neither as a potential sexual conquest nor a fellow ideologue. They live together for fourteen years but that relationship occupies barely half a dozen pages. The story then jumps to after his death.

The hotel where they had first met is being demolished. She watches from across the street, recalling their life together and the moment when her homeliness ended as a blind man detected her inner beauty. The causes in which she had once believed and which, in turn, she believed would give her life purpose and direction, have long since faded into memory, though she still works for a Civil Rights organisation. It is simply that she no longer believes that this is the essence of her life. At sixty-one, she is content, fulfilled and now, in her own eyes, because in his, beautiful.

There is something familiar in this contemplation not so much of lost causes as of commitments which once seemed to offer redemption in and of themselves. Miller, no less than the protagonist of *Homely Girl*, has lived on beyond the moment when he believed he had the power to shape the world. For her, and certainly for her first husband, private life seemed secondary to public events and ideological convictions. They were surfing the future and in the meantime failing, in effect, to live at all. A blind man brings her not so much an *égotisme à deux*, a validation for withdrawal from the world, as insight into the value of relationships, the virtue of passion and the true value of love.

As with *Broken Glass*, Miller flirts with cliché. The crippled woman stands, the homely woman becomes beautiful, redeemed, like Patricia in *The Last Yankee*, by love. Sentimentality is a breath away. What for the most part holds it at bay is an awareness of sheer contingency, of the fragility of lives for so long immobilised by a failure of will and understanding. Of these three works, however, *Homely Girl* is the one which ends most confidently. The protagonist may be alone but it seems clear that she can never now lose what she has gained.

Homely Girl would not be Miller's last story to engage with lost passion and recovered purpose. 'The Turpentine Still' begins in the early 1950s.[8] Mark Levin, thirty-nine, had once been on the left, believing in the possibility of changing

the world. And though the tides of that passion have long been on the ebb
he had still been sufficiently out of step with a new orthodoxy to resign from
his newspaper job rather than become a cheerleader for Cold War simplicities.
Now, he tells himself, he is content with his music and with literature. His
politics are still of the left but he is happy for this to be no more than a gentle
background noise to a life whose point now lies elsewhere. His former passion
is muted.

By contrast, his friend Jimmy is or was a 'sentimental communist', something
absorbed from his father who had disappeared into Bolivia in the cause of
the revolution. His politics aside, however, he has a disproportionate respect
for those with talent, as if they command some mystery from which he was
excluded.

It is winter when the story starts, and in more ways than one. The Cold
War is freezing attitudes, making public life uncomfortable for those unwilling
to make the necessary adjustments. This, after all, is a period in which it is
unwise to appear committed to social justice, indeed to appear committed at
all. But the literal temperature in wintertime New York has also plummeted
so that when Jimmy returns from Haiti with news of a new democratic spirit
and an artistic renaissance, Levin and his wife Adele decide to go, though they
know little of the island beyond a jumble of images. In their minds it is exotic,
vaguely menacing, with a history of violence and the dark threat of voodoo.
The reformist candidate in the previous elections has been hacked to death,
along with his family. Rather than put them off, though, this seems to attract
them.

The Levins, we are told, are 'serious people', a description freighted with
judgement, implying as it does a kind of doubtful self-consciousness. They
are passionate but their passion is seemingly reserved for foreign films, French
and Italian. They are accomplished musicians and plainly still alert to liberal
causes. Levin may tell himself that he has moved away from the naive politics
of his youth and withdrawn into an untroubled private existence, but in fact
'they could be naive enough to be swept up, at least at a discreet distance, in
one another's scheme for social improvement'. The 'naive enough' and 'at a
discreet distance', however, denote a somewhat self-deprecating sense of irony
and a level of calculation, a careful disposition of priorities which is almost
self-cancelling in its claim for commitment.

He still reads the *New Republic* and gave 'an occasional dutiful glance at
the *New Masses*'. Again, the word 'dutiful' seems to negate the meaning of the
radicalism which he seems to embrace partly out of nostalgia and partly out of
respect for what he had been. A distance has clearly opened between what he
was and what he is, one that he has convinced himself he does not regret. There
is an implied sense of balance to this life which might seem close to inertia
were he to inspect that life, which he is not inclined to do until his balance is
overthrown.

The narrative voice of 'The Turpentine Still' is detached, ironic, and Levin and his wife are in some ways likewise. They are presented to us as two people who maintain a strict distance between themselves and the views they seemingly hold. They are, we are told, 'guarded'. This, after all, is not a bad time to be such. His resignation from the newspaper had been a public gesture but he no longer feels any obligation to be in contention with a world whose priorities are not his own. He runs the family business and embraces the arts. His favourite book is Proust's *The Remembrance of Things Past*, itself an ironic title for a man who is no longer what he was. For the fact is that somewhere passion is leaching away, from his marriage no less than the rest of his life. He thinks he has no regrets for this but is about to discover otherwise, from the most unlikely of sources.

He and his wife now fly to Haiti 'fending off the likelihood that the trip was likely to be one more bead on the string of their mistakes'. In other words, they seem to concede past errors without quite knowing how to address them. And that is in part what the story is about.

Their hostess in Port au Prince is Mrs Pat O'Dwyer, mother to *New York Post* columnist Lilly O'Dwyer. She presides over a kind of salon. Her walls are hung with expensive art, including a scattering of indigenous paintings now fast accumulating value. She abhors the witch-hunts back in America, something she shares with the Levins. Once a social worker who distributed condoms to the poor, she had become wealthy by establishing a factory to manufacture them. She has abandoned Catholicism for Christian Science, which in her mind, we are told, combines self-reliance with a kind of soft socialism. She is certainly wealthy enough not to inspect such contradictions and, an ex-patriate, far enough removed from America to feel no need for reticence in her political opinions.

Her house provides a kind of air-lock through which the Levins can pass into the real Haiti, supposing such a thing to exist, as they soon have reason to doubt as they solicit information about a country seemingly uncertain of its own identity and direction. For this is a country in which it is possible seriously to debate whether the dead truly walk the streets.

Among the other guests are the Commander of an American cruiser, at anchor in the harbour, and a Bishop on the island in search of converts but not blind to the world as it is, sheltering the odd revolutionary from those who present themselves at his door with guns. The Commander dissents from his hostess's politics but refrains from challenging her, not least because her hospitality is not likely to be matched elsewhere.

There is only one Haitian present, a huge man who distances himself from talk of voodoo as, for other reasons, does a black Jamaican and head of the UN agency for aforestation, a job which, it transpires, brings him into direct conflict with those who even now are beginning to strip the island of its resources, trading the future for a present which seems to have little to recommend it.

Each of the people in the room has his or her Haiti. All but one come from elsewhere and bring with them their own versions of what this place might be. Bishop, Commander, UN official, ex-patriate, visitor, like Melville's Pip in *Moby-Dick* each sees something different. The Levins are unsure what they flee or what they seek. They are drifting, anxious for experiences, for a world elsewhere. After a week, however, Mark begins to feel the lack of that sharp tension which he finds in business and which evidently is what gives a spine to his life.

But there is a sub-text to this journey. He and his wife have been married for seven years and somehow they have begun to drift in their personal life as they have in their public existence. So it is that 'he resolved to begin trying to get to know Adele', an odd remark so far into a marriage. They have, he concedes, 'lost a lot of curiosity. He had', he tells himself, 'to stop hiding himself. Time was flying. He had to start listening again.' The zombies who wander the streets are not, it seems, the only ones awaiting animation. Zombies are those who have had their spirit withdrawn. There is a sense in which Levin, personally, politically, suspects that the same may be true of him. The journey to Haiti is thus in part an attempt to rediscover lost passions of one kind or another. Their pose of detached irony has, it seems, had a price.

With Vincent, Levin sets out for the interior, through a tumble of stores and down a street lined with telephone poles from which broken lines hang down. Only the bank appears spotless and functional, money being the one unassailable reality. In Vincent's words, it is a country 'waiting to start existing', as Willa Cather had spoken of a land that was not so much a country as material out of which a country might be made. For now, this seems a nation of fixers, repairers, improvisers. The government is corrupt. The depredations of the natural world, meanwhile, seem to suggest that this society has begun to unwind itself, revert back to some pre-civilised existence. Something is lacking, someone to imagine it into existence. Levin feels something stir in himself but is overcome by the absurdity of the idea that he could intervene, this man who had once felt that he could change the world. The fact seems to be that with maturity and common sense had come, too, a sense of paralysis, a failure of the imagination. What, after all, is to be done? What it needs, it seems, is some kind of holy fool, and that is essentially what he finds.

They come across a log bungalow, bleak, dishevelled. It is home to Douglas who at one time had worked for BBD & O (the Madison Avenue advertising company for which Miller had written his radio plays in the 1940s), but who had abandoned it to cruise with his family on a surplus Navy boat, showing films to people on the islands. It was an absurd idea, the islanders lacking the money to pay. Now he has a new venture, seemingly even more absurd. Discovering a gigantic metal tank near the dock, he decides to use it to distil sap from the pine trees into turpentine, used throughout the island. Accordingly, he has the tank cut up, dragged inland and welded back together. Nothing about the venture seems to make sense. The trees are not the right kind. He has no engineering skills. Every tool and nail has to be brought from the coast. The tank, which has to sustain high pressures, seems likely to explode. Meanwhile, his children run wild, with no schooling, and his wife has broken her arm unloading fifty-five gallon drums. Inside the house there are no tables or chairs and only a handful of books.

There is something of Paul Theroux's *The Mosquito Coast* about the story. There the product was ice; here it is turpentine. In both cases the protagonist subordinates everything to an animating idea, building a suspect construction deep in the country and sacrificing his family and virtually everything else to his project. In Miller's story, though, the focus is not primarily on the seemingly absurd figure, apparently blind to difficulties, but on those around him. His imagination and commitment, even the sacrifice he is prepared to make, compel attention. Vincent, who had set out to stop him, finds himself acquiescing. For the fact is that Douglas had seen the island before it began to slide into corruption and irrelevance. He may be blind to the needs of his wife – who is plainly torn between love and fear – but not to the needs of the country. He loves them both, but the country needs saving and he is offering himself as saviour. In contrast to everyone else he not only wants to do something, he acts. It is his passion that compels attention.

He wants above all to create something. In the advertising agency, with its creative department, he created nothing. Here he is building something that never existed before. In a sense he is an artist and buried in this story is a defence of the imagination and of the products of the imagination. Douglas's identity is implicated in what he does. He wants to be of service but above all, like a writer, wants to create.

For the first time Levin feels a tug of envy. He is himself childless and has convinced himself that both he and his wife are happy with this situation. Now he is conscious that he will be leaving no mark.

And that may be another motivation for Douglas. For the fact is that he is dying of cancer. This is the reason for his urgency. He wants to leave his thumb-print on the world.

Levin returns to the coast. Do either he or Vincent believe in the project? The most they can offer is what the writer demands, a willing suspension of disbelief. And at that moment Proust comes to mind, but not the Proust he had known before. Now it is Proust as the creator of fantasies, detailed in their apparent facticity but nonetheless pure inventions. A connection is forged between the writer and this desperate believer on a Haitian hillside creating something from his imagination.

At this point there is a caesura in the story. We move forward thirty-three years. Mark Levin is now nearing seventy and obsessed by time, not least because he is manifestly running out of it. It moves fast; he moves slowly. His wife is now six years dead. He has ceased to play the piano. His evenings are empty. He is a free man and has nothing of worth on which to exercise his freedom. There is a much younger woman, but he dare not presume to believe that he can offer love, or if love then not marriage. He has no obligations, but the loss of obligations cannot be seen as pure gain. He watches the sun set and moves with shortening steps to the sea shore. Suitably, it seems, the season is the fall. Suddenly, thirty and more years after he met him, he thinks of Douglas.

No sooner does he do so than he resolves to travel back to Haiti to see how the story ended, the story of Douglas and his still and the story of Haiti itself. Beyond that, though, is another question, a question to do with the meaning of those events and their relevance to him. He is aware that Douglas may be dead, but there is a sense in which he suspects that Douglas may, paradoxically, have kept him alive, if only because he has left unfinished business, a mystery not yet solved.

Even now he begins to see something of the significance of that story. The turpentine still, he thinks, 'must have been his work of art'. He had sacrificed everything 'to the creation of a vision of some beauty in his mind'. In that moment Levin sees the connection with himself who had never imagined anything into existence but who had once imagined that he could. 'What matters', he realises, 'was creation, the creation of what has not yet been.' The very realisation sends a surge of energy through him. 'How glorious to be here standing upright on the earth! To be free to think! To ride one's imagining!' It is as though he had suddenly broken the cipher. He immediately plans his return to the island.

When he arrives, no one remembers the incident, or Douglas. But Levin is now driven by necessity. Rediscovering the still will be his act of invention. He enrols Lilly O'Dwyer's son Peter, and once again sets out for the interior.

Everyone he knew is dead, here as in New York, but now he feels something more than loneliness and his enthusiasm spills over on to Peter as Douglas's had spilled over on to Vincent and himself those years before. He has rediscovered his own passion in trying to account for someone else's.

The land that was once covered with trees is now bare. As Levin observes, 'It's like they ate the country and shat it out.' Whatever Douglas may or may not have done he had not, it seems, redeemed the country he wished to save. But the anger in Levin's voice echoes that of the man who had cared enough to travel this same path. The man who had once abandoned his faith that he could change the world has begun to understand that there is more than one kind of transformation.

On their way up the hillside they come across a broken Land Rover and Peter repairs it without asking for a reward in an echo of a moment, three decades before, when others had repaired the vehicle in which Levin and Vincent had been travelling. The trip begins to assume the nature of a pilgrimage, with repeated gestures, recurring events.

As though miraculously, they now find Douglas's bungalow looking as it had before, with everything seemingly in place. More miraculously, they find the still, and even a man who had worked it and to whom Douglas had left it on his death. The still, then, had worked. He had even given turpentine free to those who could not afford it. The quality, however, had been poor and the bank – that neat, clean bank he had passed on his first visit – would lend no money. Douglas had died and the still was abandoned. Was it then without purpose and Douglas's work without meaning?

There is a moment when Levin recalls his wife as she had been that first time, thirty years before: 'I guess I'm looking for what was lost, he thought, and the idea, coming to him so suddenly seemed to freshly illuminate his having returned to this place. The idea made him smile – "then it's her I'm looking for?" he almost said aloud.' It is not, though, all he has been looking for.

Douglas had left a note for the man to whom he bequeathed the still: 'If the idea goes, let it go, but if you can keep it, do so and it will surely lift you up one day.' It was of a piece with the man who had, Levin thought, slid into oblivion 'all that life and all that caring, and all that hope as incoherent as it was'. Yet, of course, he has not slid into oblivion because this old man remembers and was changed by his encounter, as was Levin and as, now, is Peter: 'Well, he passed it on', the young man observes.

Levin and his wife had come together that night after his encounter with Douglas and do again now in his memory. Not for nothing is *Remembrance of Things Past* the book he clings to. What Douglas had done had seemed absurd but now Levin feels that he 'may have touched something sacred, having wanted to make a Madison Avenue life mean something and not knowing how except to do something so absurd'.

In retrospect, Levin, too, had once devoted himself to something absurd, to 'some kind of socialism', undone by the 'camps and the backwardness' and undermined by 'American prosperity'. Now it seems all gone, as Peter despairs of the island, undone not by communism but by greed. Yet the surviving turpentine still stands as a kind of emblem, an emblem of hope, a unique creation with its own integrity. 'In some sense', thinks Levin, it is 'like a work of art that transcended the pettiness of its maker, even his egotism and foolishness.' Beyond that it was a symbol of his imagination, a refusal to accept the given that had once driven Levin himself and the writing he admired and which even now gifts him a sense of life and the value of living.

There is a moment when Levin imagines the idea of 'a national holiday . . . when people could visit their dead convictions . . . What was more dispiriting than the waste of devotion that leaves behind the vanishing footsteps of the people it misled? Or was there some point in striving, he wondered?' It is a question his experience with Douglas has answered. Douglas was driven by hope and a commitment to life. The absurdity of a project is not, finally, proof of its insignificance. Those who value their detachment, who substitute irony for commitment, who observe a world they hesitate to transform, become no more than witnesses to their own lives. It takes Levin thirty years to learn this but it is knowledge that even now transforms him.

— ✳ —

Arthur Miller is to American drama what Saul Bellow has been to the American novel. Politically at odds, they are alike in many other ways, not least as Jewish writers who have set their faces against the absurd, though less in the name of religious faith than a humanism born out of an American experience. Wry and humorous, both have staged the confusions of those struggling to make sense of themselves and the world. They write in the American grain and against the American grain, simultaneously celebrating a natural democracy of spirit yet challenging a culture too often seduced by its own rhetoric or demeaned by a confusion between spirit and material values.

Saul Bellow is a precise contemporary of Miller and it is perhaps hardly surprising that their experiences and attitudes are so alike. Bellow was an immigrant son of Russian Jews, Miller the son of a Polish Jew. Both grew up in the Depression, were involved in Roosevelt's Works Progress Administration, were radicalised and later witnessed the collapse of the ideology to which they had been drawn and which had structured their way of seeing the world. Bellow's observation, in the mid 1970s, that with 'increasing frequency I dismiss as "merely respectable" opinions I have long held – or thought I held – and try to discern what I have really lived by and what others really live by',[9] was mirrored by Miller's own sense of commitments outstripped by time.

Bellow speaks of the 'true impressions' that Proust and Tolstoy thought of themselves as offering in their attempt to convey the 'essence of our real condition, the complexity, the confusion, the pain of it', and insists that the value of literature lies precisely in such intermittent 'true impressions'. For him, a novel 'moves back and forth between the world of objects, of actions, of appearances, and that other world, from which these "true impressions" come and which moves us to believe that the good we hang on to so tenaciously – in the face of evil, so obstinately – is no illusion' (97).

Miller's conception of the function of drama is no different. That same negotiation between the poles of human experience is observable in his work, that same commitment to the idea of character in art that animates Bellow and which leads him to claim kinship with the nineteenth-century authors both men admire. 'Can anything as vivid as the characters in their books be dead?' Bellow asks, and with a logic that Miller would share, 'Can it really be that human beings are at an end? Is individuality really so dependent on historical and cultural conditions?' (91).

Bellow readily acknowledges a contemporary sense of crisis:

> In private life, disorder or near panic. In families – for husbands, wives, parents, children – confusion; in civic behavior, in personal loyalties, in sexual practices . . . further confusion. It is with this private disorder and

public bewilderment that we try to live. We stand open to all anxieties. The
decline and fall of everything is our daily dread; we are agitated in private
life and tormented by public questions.

(92)

But, he insists, 'When complications increase, the desire for essentials increases
too', a desire for 'certain desirable human goods – truth, for instance; freedom;
wisdom'. It is that desire which Miller serves.

Bellow has responded to what he sees as Proust's insistence that without 'an
art that shirks no personal or collective horrors . . . we do not know ourselves
or anyone else', and that only 'art penetrates what pride, passion, intelligence,
and habit erect on all sides – the seeming realities of this world' (93). There is,
he insists, 'another reality, the genuine one, which we lose sight of' (93), and it
is art that makes it visible. It is that reality which concerns Arthur Miller.

His Willy Loman takes the world at face value. He deals in appearance,
takes the tangible world as evidence of nothing more substantial than desire
sanctioned as national myth. He believes that the images society projects to
itself are real. Miller is concerned to identify those truths which exist beyond
the disorder, confusions and seeming realities which distract and baffle his
characters. When Bellow says that art attempts to discover 'what is fundamental,
enduring, essential', he could equally well be describing Miller's objectives.

Bellow and Miller alike took the war at first as no more than another imperialist conflict. Despite the evidence of Kristallnacht, it seemed an argument over
colonial territories. It took the fall of France to change Bellow's views and the
invasion of the Soviet Union to change Miller's. Bellow was rejected for military
service because of a hernia; Miller because of a knee injury. The former went
into the Merchant Marine; the latter worked in the Brooklyn Navy Yard. Bellow
later confessed to failing to register the enormity of the Holocaust, as Miller
has similarly described its delayed impact on him. It was, Bellow admits, the
American rather than the Jewish experience that commanded his imagination.
And that was certainly what he saw in looking back on *The Adventures of Augie
March*. Jewish criticism, he felt, had been harsh on him for focusing on the
American portion of his life. He was accused of being an assimilationist. Miller
would face a similar charge, in that despite his engagement with Jewish issues
he, too, was concerned with American values, myths and identities. *The Victim* and *Focus*, however, are evidence to the contrary, while the Holocaust left
its shadow on both men. It finally came home with full force to Bellow when
he visited Auschwitz in 1959 and to Miller, as we have seen, when he visited
Mauthausen shortly afterwards, in 1962.

Surely, Miller's attempts to revivify the idea of tragedy had its roots in a desire
to retrieve values most clearly threatened in the camps of Europe. But there
was another problem for those newly sensitised to particularities of genocide.
The narrator of Bellow's *Ravelstein* remarks that 'I had a Jewish life to lead

in the American language, and that's not a language that's helpful with dark thoughts.'[10] American nihilism was nihilism without the void. And if as a result it resisted the absurd, so it did the tragic. That, indeed, was to be Miller's problem.

Edith Wharton had expressed doubts as to whether a play with a sad ending and a negative hero could ever gain a hearing from American audiences, as William Dean Howells had observed that what the American audience wanted above all was tragedy with a happy ending. It was certainly perceived as a fundamental problem by Eugene O'Neill, who felt increasingly alienated from American audiences, turning to Europe where tragedy seemed to him to have roots in history and everyday experience.

There is, though, a sense of obligation that seems reflected in the world of both Bellow and Miller. As Bellow's character observes in *Ravelstein*, 'Jews . . . were historically witnesses to the absence of redemption' (179). For both writers, this fact laid a special responsibility on those who survived, an obligation not simply to bear witness but to reconstitute the redemption thus denied. Both had seen their faith in redemption dented, yet for Arthur Miller, in particular, the struggle has been to justify life, to rescue the individual from a wilful collusion either with despair or the false epiphanies of a material life.

✳

31

Arthur Miller as a Jewish writer

This has been the story of Arthur Miller, whose people came from a world where to be Jewish was to draw down the lightning. He was born into a community which wrapped itself in mysteries for protection, and because buried at the heart of those mysteries was a vivifying hope. Later, there would be those who accused him of turning away not so much from a faith, which he did indeed abandon, as from an identity. His characters, it was suggested, were either studiously non-Jewish or denied roots revealed only in the language they deployed. He was, in short, a Jewish writer who hesitated to confess to his origins or address the major traumas of what he forbore to acknowledge as his people. It is a view which has such currency and which is so far from the truth that before ending our journey through his work it is worth pausing and asking how far the story of Arthur Miller is not only one of the making of a playwright but the making, more specifically, of a Jewish playwright?

Miller, like Delmore Schwartz, Alfred Kazin and Saul Bellow, came from a home where Yiddish was spoken, a reminder of another world, and other loyalties. America offered a promise of transformation, of reinvention. That promise was embraced by his parents, who first claimed and were then betrayed by the American dream. Miller himself had a double consciousness and that fact would be evident in the plays he wrote over seventy years.

He grew up to articulate America, to offer, through his own imaginative inventions, the story of its continued struggle to come into being, to recon-cile its utopian impulses with the flawed individuals who wished to realise its possibilities. He was and is an American. Like Schwartz, Kazin and Bellow, he has interpreted that culture to itself to the point at which he and they became synonymous with it. De Tocqueville was theirs, as was *Huckleberry Finn*. They claimed the language and they changed that language until what once had been distinctively Jewish became simply American. And yet, was there not always another identity, another history never, finally, relinquished in the desire to debate with, dissent from, embrace a society and a culture from which they nonetheless remained crucially detached?

'They are a people, and they lack the props of a people. They are a disembodied ghost.' Chaim Weizmann, giving evidence before the United Nations Special Committee on Palestine in July 1947, had a special reason for stressing the rootlessness of the Jewish people. 'We ask today', he said, 'What are the Poles?

What are the French? What are the Swiss? When that is asked, everyone points to a country, to certain institutions, to parliamentary institutions, and the man in the street will know exactly what it is . . . If you ask what a Jew is – well, he is a man who has to offer a long explanation for his existence, and any person who has to offer an explanation as to what he is, is always suspect.'[1]

The Jews of Russia, of Poland, had such an explanation, had a story to tell which was not that of those alongside whom they lived. They inhabited these countries but were not fully of them, no matter how loyal they were to national values and presumptions. They looked to another place, spoke another language, insisted on a separate history, declared themselves chosen and were accorded the special status they claimed, though not always in the way they wished. Their grasp on their native land was always insecure, no matter how long they had lived there. They set themselves apart and were set apart. And every now and then, in a seismic spasm, they would be assaulted, murdered, driven out.

As Miller remarked, 'pogroms and tales of pogroms were woven into the sky overhead' (T.26). And when they moved on, such memories left a stain. Something was to be passed down, no matter by what subterranean channels. As Diana Trilling remarked of herself, 'On the surface, there may have been little in my childhood to create Jewish memories but apparently there was enough to be crucial. I think that it chiefly derived from my father and from his memory of himself as a child in the Polish ghetto.'[2] Miller's father, and still more his grand-father, carried such memories from Poland. They slid into his consciousness, too, though there were reminders of a threat rather closer to home.

In 1945, at the age of thirty and in the concluding year of a war that had seen a systematic attempt to eradicate the Jews, Arthur Miller published a novel that expressed his alarm that the same disease infected America. The casual racism of his own country had, he suggested, the capacity to recreate the conditions that so many had fled in Europe. As a character observes in Focus,

> You know as well as me that everybody, pretty near, has no use for the Jews . . . A depression comes, there's people out on the street, an organization comes along that can get them going and it's the end of the Hebrews . . . one year after there is one big organization in this country there won't be a Jew standing up in America.[3]

In 1946, a year after the war, the American Jewish Committee conducted a poll in which gentiles were asked if there were 'any nationality, religious or racial groups in this country that are a threat to America'. Eighteen per cent cited the Jews.[4]

Son and grandson of Jewish immigrants, Miller has never lost his sense of possible catastrophe, of imminent apocalypse. More than fifty years on from Focus, in the first year of a new millennium, he confessed that, 'I think in the back of the mind is the possibility of anarchy, of collapse, of the laws not working, of the trains stopping and not starting again. I think that civilisation is about one sixteenth of an inch thick and underneath we're the old human being who is capable of just about anything.'[5] And who knows this better than the Jews? Figuratively and literally, they kept their bags packed.

In a review of Amos Elon's *Herzl* (the Vienna-based proponent of a Palestinian state for the Jews), Miller pointed out that it was 'the story of a man with a premonition, unbelievable at the time, that an inch below the Strauss waltzes, the stolid bourgeois orderliness, the noble civilization of a much-loved city, was a burgeoning monster preparing to devour the Jewish people and with them civilization itself. Beyond the application to the Jews', he insisted, 'Herzl's paranoia calls up our own, our sense of existing on the thin film of security below which is a seething volcano of wild fury which nothing can assuage.'[6] Interestingly, the pronouns simultaneously claim and abandon the inclusiveness once demanded of him but in many ways that is the essence of Miller's stance. The Jewish experience of implacable vulnerability contains a social, political and, ultimately, metaphysical relevance to all.

That vulnerability, however, demands a refusal of the role of victim. In all his plays the individual is held responsible, history is seen as a product of human choice, apocalypse is shunned as a dangerous flirtation with the idea of annihilation, a wilful submission to exquisite irony. That is why for many years he would resist what he read as Samuel Beckett's merciless account of humankind born to suffer from the evidence of his humanity, hope become a Sisyphean torture. For Miller, Kafka was the paradigm, the Jew who knew 'there was no bottom, that everything was permitted'. It was this conviction, implied by Herzl, proposed by Kafka, which explains a fundamental precept of Miller's work as he painfully reconstructs a moral world seemingly denied by history, reconnects past and present like a surgeon re-establishing the neural pathways so that stimulus and response are once again related. God may be dead in Miller's work, but he has to be reinvented in order to accuse and confess.

Miller is not a religious Jew, though as he explained in 1948, and significantly in an article published in a magazine called *Jewish Life* (a product of the Jewish section of the Communist Party of the United States), an article called 'Concerning Jews Who Write', 'during my first 15 years I was brought up in a religious home, my grandfather was the president of his synagogue, and I read enough Hebrew to understand about 20 per cent of what I read'. He recalled 'the order of the Sabbath ceremony on Friday night'.[7] Though memories of this would later be the source of reassurance, it was not an experience that implied true faith, at least not beyond his teenage years. He would later admit that 'in my most private reveries I was no sallow Talmud reader but Frank Merriwell or Tom Swift' (*T*.62). Jewishness had thus seemingly been shuffled off.

In that 1948 article, however, he made a distinction between religious conviction and cultural responsibility. In his thirty-third year he saw an urgency to such a commitment:

To my mind the Hebrew religion is a matter of option to the Jewish writer as to all Jews, but Jewish culture is his to defend whether he is Jewish or not. For if he does not defend it he may die of its destruction. In the last analysis, the minimum of what we mean by culture today, and in this present world context, is simply the right to have been descended from Jews. Jewish culture is the sum and total of what history has made us. It is what the enemy wishes to burn. It is us, expressed in any form.[8]

The sheer pressure of anti-Semitism, in the early years of his career, left him acutely aware of personal threat but also of the danger of provoking the anarchy he feared. Today, Miller does not participate in the rituals of the shul, and has not for seventy years. He is not a believer in the tenets of the faith. In political terms, and quite separate, of course, from a Jewish identity, he is not a Zionist, not to be found raising funds for Israel. But his Jewish upbringing, ambiguous as it was, remains crucial.

It in part explains his fascination with the notion of a problematic identity, with the need to sustain the idea of a moral world, with the acknowledgement of community, the sheer contingency of experience and the imminent threat of dissolution. It goes to the heart of his debate over an individual's responsibility for his or her own life, his sense of the central importance of history, of the need for the individual to intervene in his or her own fate. Of course, none of these concerns is unique to the Jewish experience. There is at their heart a kind of liberalism widely shared by others, though in an American context liberalism has itself taken on a certain Jewish flavour. Nonetheless, taken together, they do suggest the extent to which his Jewish background has proved crucial, laying down the parameters of his writing and in part determining the nature of his thematic concerns, concerns often seemingly at odds with those of the culture of which he otherwise seems such a direct expression.

If there was an element of denial in his father's and his own attitude towards a Jewish identity or, perhaps more precisely, their special vulnerability, history was ready with a corrective.

As it turned out, we were building a fortress of denial that would take two massive onslaughts to crack – the Depression and Hitler's war. Nor was it only a question of Jews denying the world's reality, as events would show, but also a failure in practice of the most sacred claims of our democracy itself to a more perfect decency and sensitivity toward injustice.

(T.62–3)

It is, perhaps, not surprising that those two events should resonate throughout his work, both in their way evidence that the sky could fall, that what seemed to be solid foundations were in fact deeply suspect. And the Jew was likely to be more acutely aware of this than those whose myths celebrated progress and the pursuit of happiness. As he remarked in 2003, the Jew was like the canary taken down the mineshaft. Even America offered evidence of threat. In his 1948 article he wrote, 'today I am no longer innocent. I have been insulted, I have been scorned, I have been threatened. I have heard of violence against Jews, and I have seen it. I have seen insanity in the streets and I have heard it dropping from the mouths of people I had thought were decent people.'[9]

To a greater extent than critics have supposed, to a greater extent than perhaps he would himself once have acknowledged, the story of Arthur Miller is that of a Jewish writer. It is his default setting. Alfred Kazin once remarked, 'The Jews are my unconscious.'[10] They are Miller's, too, though he was born into a society in which denial of such could be the acknowledged price of entry. The American might be the product of other identities, other histories, but these were now to be disregarded in the name of a redeeming future. As Philip Roth has remarked of the Jewish immigrants, they displayed a wilful amnesia: 'They'd left because life was awful, so awful, in fact, so menacing, so impoverished or hopelessly obstructed, that it was best forgotten.'[11] On the other hand, as Alfred Kazin observed, 'Never before had so numerous a mass of Jews been free citizens of the country in which they lived, and so close to the national life.'[12]

Instead of a forgotten or discarded past they placed their faith in an imagined future, projecting themselves along the line of need energised by hope. Even one generation on, when, soon after the war, Arthur Miller decided to visit France and Italy, his father was astonished that he should have chosen to move against history, to go back to a Europe that father and both sets of grandparents had chosen to leave. And, indeed, Miller himself found little more than poverty: ruined, subsistence societies that seemed to justify his family's desire to forget, that and the broken remnants of the Holocaust haunting their former countries like the projections of a bad conscience, shadows among the shadows. There would be those, however, who regarded such forgetfulness, such absolute rejection of a particular past, as a form of treachery, not least because something more than place was being forgotten. The words inscribed at the Yad Vashem, the Holocaust memorial in Jerusalem, read, 'Forgetfulness is the way to exile. Remembrance is the way to redemption.'

He could make little of the survivors of the concentration camps he saw on his trip to Italy, however. They seemed to come out of another world in a literal and psychological sense. There would come a time, though, when that experience would catch up with him and he would write a number of plays in which that experience became emblematic. There would come a time, indeed, as we have seen, when he would describe one of the functions of the writer to be 'a rememberer'. As he would write in the speech with which he marked the award to him of the Jerusalem Prize in 2003, 'it may be that as a Jew of a certain generation I was unable to forget the silence of the Thirties and Forties when fascism began its destruction of our people, which for so long met with the indifference of the world.'[13]

Early in his relationship with Inge Morath, whom he was to marry in 1962, he had been taken by her to Mauthausen concentration camp. She had personal demons to confront, demons summoned forth again by marriage to a Jew, though she had herself suffered at the hands of the Nazis, climbing on to the parapet of a bridge in the chaos of wartime Germany in order to end her life. She survived, and survival became a fundamental theme of the playwright she now married, a man who had witnessed from afar and whom she now accompanied, weeping, into the place where, had his forebears not enacted their own exodus, they and their descendants would almost certainly have perished. Suddenly, in the solid and substantial buildings of that place, plainly constructed as a long-term venture, he began to see the connection between its horrors and those other personal and public betrayals that concerned him. He had known of the camps, of course, felt, intellectually, though at a remove, their threat to any system of order or justice. Now, though, there was a face to the abstract terror, a geography, a topography to sadism. Now the nature of the task of reinventing God, or the moral sanction which had been denied, seemed clearer than before.

Albert Speer had visited Mauthausen in 1943 and purported to understand nothing of its function. Simon Wiesenthal was there as a prisoner and would one day search out those who sought to escape the consequences of their crimes, and in doing so force attention on what had been forgotten. Later denials, erasures, suppressions, perhaps, had less self-interested motives. The enormity of the events themselves could stun the mind. As the Dutch theologian W. A. Visser 't Hooft remarked, 'People cannot find a place in their imagination (or allow themselves to remember) unimaginable horror. It is possible to live in a twilight between knowing and not knowing.'[14] Miller plainly knew but, like so many others, camp survivors included, it took time for meaning to emerge out of unmeaning and this seems to have been the moment.

In terms of his writing, there is a sense in which Miller was a Jew from the beginning, He wrote about a Jewish family in his first play, *No Villain* (rejected by Broadway in a revised form as 'too Jewish'), and in *The Golden Years* addressed the stunned paralysis that he saw evidenced by European powers confronted with Hitler. At the age of seventeen, he wrote a story about a Jewish salesman and then another a few years later. He wrote a play that featured a Jewish refugee in one unproduced play, *The Half-Bridge*, and a harassed Jewish piano-tuner turned air-raid warden in another, *Boro Hall Nocturne*, before exposing American anti-Semitism in *Focus*, all this by 1945, before the plays for which he is celebrated. In his 2003 biography, Martin Gottfried saw him as turning to Jewish characters and issues (*Focus* aside) only in the early 1960s. He was wide of the truth. Ahead, meanwhile, lay *After the Fall, Incident at Vichy, Playing for Time, Broken Glass, Homely Girl* and a series of short stories which placed Jewishness at their heart. For a Jewish writer who supposedly evaded his Jewishness he certainly seems to have written a remarkable number of works which addressed it, either directly or indirectly.

To Miller, the essence of the treatment of the Jews is not that they are so often tested, like Job, to discover the ultimate extent of faith by seeking to confront it with evidence of its futility (and the figure of Job haunts his first Broadway play, *The Man Who Had All the Luck*), that they are the purest expression of absurdity in being made to suffer for the sin of existence. He is scornful of such a notion, itself, perhaps, a dark reflection of the Jewish assumption of particularity, of being singled out, chosen, set apart. For him, this is not a divine fate, as if suffering were the evidence of a unique status; it is the product of human agency and that fact leads him to explore history as it does to engage ontology.

George Steiner's suggestion, that potential nuclear warfare added to the actual Holocaust had seemed to justify metaphysical despair, was one that Miller could not endorse. It is, perhaps, the Jew in Miller that makes such irony unacceptable as method or conclusion, as it was the Jew in Steiner that made him acknowledge less irony than paradox in Jewish respect for the very German tradition of secular enquiry that would betray his father and a generation of fathers: 'By virtue of what was to become an unbearable paradox, the Judaism of secular hope looked to German philosophy, literature, scholarship and music for its talesmanic guarantees', observed Steiner. It looked to 'German metaphysics and cultural criticism, from Kant to Schopenhauer and Nietsche, the classics of German-language poetry and drama, the master-historians such as Ranke, Mommsen and Gregorovius.'[15]

Miller's parents and grandparents lacked the Steiners' library and his parents' breadth of intellectual reference. They came from a different stratum of society, lived deeper into Austro-Hungary where language and action seemed less nuanced, more direct, but they shared that respect for German culture and civility. It was one reason why denial sunk its roots so deep, why it took so long to believe the unbelievable. Betrayal piled on betrayal. But to Miller the conclusion was not accumulating evidence for the absurd but grounds for a growing urgency, a compulsion to inhabit a despised history and insist on the possibility of reinventing a discredited God.

Sensitised to the fact of a winnowing violence, he tracks it back beyond history into an explanatory mythology, his territory what else but the Bible and the Old Testament of his ancestral faith, a Bible which he continues to read for the power of its stories, its exemplary tales of innocence and bone-deep guilt. The impulse begins and ends with a flawed Eden and even more with Cain, the lodestone who draws him back, the brother who invented murder, having no model beyond himself and no impulses which did not originate with him. It was Cain, to Miller, who set history in motion as he envisaged a future he could attain only on the other side of a death that his parents, Adam and Eve, could not imagine, any more than they could the future, itself a product of sin. And in that moment Cain created the concept of victim, seemingly thereby establishing the polarities of human nature.

The brothers of so many of Miller's plays in part reflect his own condition, one of two, different in their ambitions, but also his sense of contending possibilities, a centripetal force spinning human qualities to extremes. Those primal brothers, Cain and Abel, are the evidence of a fractured unity, mankind divided against itself, while there, on the dividing line, the Jew, transformed in the post-war world from stateless alien to resurgent nationalist, is recombined only in that he now embodies victim and oppressor in the same moment. For ahead lay a new country, where victims could gather, forged into one polity by a refusal to submit, even if the price be the submission of others. As he remarked in his Jerusalem Prize speech:

> I was invited to the Waldorf dinner in 1949 to celebrate the Soviet Union's recognition of the State of Israel . . . The very idea of a nation of Jews existing in modern times was hard to imagine then. It was almost as though a scene out of the Bible were being re-enacted, but this time with real people smoking cigarettes. Imagine! Jewish bus drivers, Jewish cops, Jewish street sweepers, Jewish judges and the criminals they judged, Jewish prostitutes and movies stars, Jewish plumbers and carpenters and bankers, a Jewish president and parliament and a Jewish secretary of state. All this was something so new on the earth that it never dawned on me – or, I think, on most people – that the new Israel, as a state governed by human beings, would behave the same as any state through history – defending its existence by all means thought necessary and even expanding its borders when possible.

There was, he noticed, a denial of this process, especially in America, and it was a denial of which he himself felt guilty: 'I was not a Zionist but I certainly participated, however unwittingly, in this kind of denial.' Certainly with the assassination of Rabin, but, in fact, far earlier, he saw that country apparently abandon Enlightenment values. A country which had represented 'a righting of the scales of justice' and a 'refusal of death' had seemingly lost its moral integrity and 'needed to reclaim its own history'.

As Miller would say in 1998, in a poem marking the fiftieth anniversary of the establishment of the state of Israel:

> I quickly understand the Jewish dead,
> Know their shock at departing alone;
> See Jewish women at the blast
> Glancing back across the centuries
> As laughter of Goyim cracks the air;
> All this I see at the gunshot.

Yet his was a journey towards unfaith, for no sooner did 'the pieces of the Jew / Combine' than brother fought brother as Israelis and Palestinians battled for land, both absolute and hence irreconcilable in their separate truths:

> . . . . From this very sand
> Where the brotherhood of man was first
> proposed . . .

is born, he suggests, a familiar theatre,

> The one where everyone is right
> And all must share the wrong

And in this theatre the audience check their watches, aware, suddenly, that what was to have been a new beginning is a familiar melodrama, and the chosen people, 'A nation no different than all the rest'. As he observed,

> I have been trying these eighty years
> to become an atheist, and with the help
> of Orthodoxy have at last come really
> close to succeeding. I salute the Jews,
> the Christians, the Muslims, Iranians,
> the Hindus – all their absolutists in our
> dear world – and thank them for having
> settled the question of whether god can
> possibly exist, and leaving me in peace.[16]

Atheism – and he is an atheist – thus stands justified, though he has always been conscious of the space left vacant by that absent faith and filled, perhaps, by his art. He thus places enormous weight on art as mediator between man and his need for a validating principle. It stands in place of the faith whose absence he feels 'like a never-ending ache'. Chekhov had once declared that he would join any monastery that would take unbelievers, but Miller's atheism is less a kind of inverted faith than a regret to be balanced by a need to reconstitute the values seemingly lost with such a profound abandonment.

First had come the camps and then the echoic violence of those who had suffered there, or those so determined that genocide would never be repeated that the gun seemed necessary evidence of a new will, a resistance of a kind that could not be marshalled to defend the six million or, more disturbingly, had not been. In 1988 he was tempted to write to PEN protesting about Israeli violence. It was, he felt, the Holocaust that made compromise seem impossible. It was also, he felt sure, his refusal to line up to offer Israel the conventional support that accounted for a hostility to his work among certain Jewish critics.

An acknowledgement of sheer contingency, a resistant spirit, a concern for survival, and the price to be paid for survival, run through much of his work, work which is so often an argument with despair as he locates himself simultaneously inside and outside the tradition from which he came and the tradition to which his parents had laid claim in travelling to America.

Whether practising Jew or not, however, he is of the Book, aware of the mythic potency of archetypes. The Old Testament, whose rhythms he once chanted in a language whose own structures carried a history, sounds through his work. The music of faith itself creates a rhythm not easily forgotten because recalled in the consolidated pathway of neurons, the pattern which poetry wears in the subconscious, a rhythm inherited from another time and place from which he imagines himself liberated but which still beats in his blood.

In his poem, a Teacher wanders in the desert waiting to be summoned, a Teacher who holds the secret of Justice, which is 'in another's humiliation learn to see his own'. But who, he asks, 'will open the gate to the Teacher'? Who is the Teacher but the author, who seeks understanding through inhabiting the mind and sensibility of the other, staging a theatre which sees all lives as exemplary, creating characters who are themselves the conduit to self-knowledge, precisely because in their differences they are the same? Who is the Teacher but art itself, whose promise is precisely to discover in the particular, the universal, in the other, the self? Miller's own appeal lies, surely, in the fact that in his case the teacher in him shadows the writer. The word 'rabbi' means teacher and there is, though he would recoil from the thought, and perhaps in horror, something rabbinical about Miller.

For him, the text can never be self-limiting, reflexive. It relates to the world beyond. It bears a responsibility. It is not discontinuous with the speeches he has made against the Vietnam War, racism, torture, censorship, and in favour of social commitment. His is not a polemical drama but it is one in which the action is archetypal, private gestures extend out into the world where they become exemplary. Drama is, in its very essence, social, as is the language it deploys (itself an embodiment of the past whose integrity he insists upon and whose causalities he sees as the backbone of a moral existence).

Indeed, he is perplexed by a country that seeks to deny history, since the very language of rejection carries the history it would reject. But the breakdown he in part addresses occurs at the level of language, as the rhetoric of community is denied by the fact of alienation and anomie, as moral abstractions are invoked in a culture whose values seem to negate them.

His characters may seem stubbornly alone in their dilemmas. Who can help Joe Keller, Willy Loman, John Proctor, Eddie Carbone, Phillip Gellburg, encysted, as they are, in their own dilemmas, driven back on to a self that can hardly bear the burden of decision? Even so, their final act is performed in the name of something more than themselves. His plays lean out into the world; his characters edge towards an understanding of a responsibility to serve something other than what they take to be their own self-limiting necessities. And where they deny, they do so the better for him to affirm.

Few of his characters grasp how incomplete is their understanding of themselves or the world they inhabit. What they share is a need to make sense of their existence, to leave a mark, to affirm their names, to survive. In the case of some of them, of the protagonist of 'Monte Sant'Angelo,' for example, of Phillip Gellburg in *Broken Glass*, it is their Jewishness, but the principle is wider than that.

For a while, after the Second World War, the Jewish writer, whose characters' sense of alienation and anomie yet desire for inclusion, whose problematic identity and ironic take on a society en route to nowhere in particular, seemed in tune with the popular mood. Bellow, Mailer, Roth, Malamud became defining figures; but there were also others, some creative writers, others critics, sociologists, observers of and participants in the emerging dramas of a post-war America not entirely free of the debates that had defined a pre-war America. Alfred Kazin identified some of them – Lionel Trilling, Philip Rahv, Delmore Schwartz, Harold Rosenberg, Paul Goodman, Irving Howe, Daniel Bell, Sidney Hook, Lionel Abel, Leslie Fiedler.

He offered, too, a reason for their prominence: 'The sudden emergence of Jews as literary figures was certainly due to their improved status in an economy liberated by the war and catapulted by war into domination of the "free world".[17] It is less than convincing. What united them, as he also suggested, was a fierce commitment to ideas and to European modernism. To a degree, too, perhaps, it was the very fact of the European attempt to silence the Jew that gave to the voice of the Jew a special significance. Was Miller, then, one of those Jewish writers who felt a pressure to tell his own story as exemplary of the Jewish story, a narrative of threatened dispossession, identity sustained in the face of a resistant culture, denial as the price of survival? In part, perhaps. Certainly all those elements are there, as is the necessity to stare into the blank face of genocide in an effort to distinguish its hidden features. But that story is also, in part, an American story, the story of immigrant anxiety, of those grasping at new myths, struggling to create an identity in tune with a culture not so much contemptuous of the past as insisting on its irrelevance.

He came from those whose identity had once seemed clear, defined by their own messianic destiny or by those who drew a circle around their possibilities, identifying themselves in part through their exclusions. Now they found themselves in a country in which change was a virtue and an ideology, and identity provisional precisely because it was charged with an existential need to link the self to action.

The result was in part an ambivalence. In Clifford Odets it found a writer whose Jewishness was evident but who was now in the service of an ideology which offered to subsume tribal and national identities, albeit one whose origins carried a Jewish shadow – Marxism. At the other extreme was Nathanael West, born Weinstein, whose sense of a cruel and oppressive world, ending in apocalypse, simultaneously offered a recuperated history of oppression and a prophetic grasp of impending disaster, but did so in the guise of an analysis of American eschatology. In the 1940s, Jewish and American anxieties were often recast as the comedies of an over-heated consciousness, dialogues with the self which became ironic dialogues with the world. For Saul Bellow, Philip Roth, Joseph Heller, irony and exuberance co-existed, as though one might cancel the other out. But behind this lay a revealed truth not easily assimilable or expressible.

Though the Holocaust appeared so particular, an event of colossal scale and importance that nonetheless seemed for a while a private anguish, too ambivalent in its echoing meanings to be shared, it could nonethless be seen as grounding the Jewish experience in the fundamental experience of all: the ineluctable power of contingency, the idea of total vulnerability, the casual extinction of the self. The issue of human nature was squarely on the table. Such an appropriation of the Holocaust as memory was the source of shock and revulsion to some, but it is clear that a general readership began to respond to a literature of anomie, angst, alienation, laced, nonetheless, with a humour which seemed to negate the absurdism with which it appeared to flirt. It caught the national mood.

And Miller addressed the Holocaust to an extent that no other American dramatist would do. He addressed it in its particularities and risked the anger of those who thought those particularities excluded its use as metaphor. How, then, could he be accused of evading Jewish characters, a Jewish trauma?

The irony is that what had once seemed defining characteristics of Jewish writers now made them seem representative figures, in a society itself made suddenly aware of vulnerability and increasingly concerned with questions to do with identity, social coherence and alienation. This was a generation that deployed the language of familiar myths and values but doubted their efficacy or, indeed, substance, in a world transformed by nuclear threat and social divisiveness. That very doubt, however, became definitional. As Clement Greenberg observed, 'the position of the Jew becomes like every other plight today, a version of the alienation of man under capitalism; all plights merge, and that of the Jew has become less particular because it all turns more and more into an intensified expression of a general one'.[18] For Delmore Schwartz, too, Jewishness became a symbol of alienation.

As Alfred Kazin pointed out, the Jewish intellectual, as guide, philosopher and moral conscience, had arrived in terms of literature, sociology and psychoanalysis. In some ways, perhaps, it was the Jewish stance – simultaneously part of the culture and apart from it – that gifted him this role. And, as he has confessed, that was undoubtedly Arthur Miller's role.

These were creative writers who, often in contradistinction to their immigrant fathers and grandfathers, revelled in the English language, listened acutely to its differing accents and rhythms, often shot through with Jewish idioms and constructions, almost as if they were deploying first their gifts for mimicry (and Miller was a gifted mimic as a child, performing on street corners for his friends) and then their power to bend the language to reflect their own needs. Where their parents could point to material possessions as evidence that they had been accepted, if not assimilated, thus justifying their decision to abandon one home, and sometimes religion, for a new one, this new generation could point to their infiltration of the language with which America chose to describe itself and through which it sought to define its shifting realities and fictions.

The tone of many of these writers – and it is a tone to be heard in Miller – was frequently a blend of the tragic and the comic. There is in their work – for all their manifest and manifold differences – a sense of the absurd redeemed by the assertion of moral certainties, or if not certainties then a wager that from chaos order can form. They are often jokers, as Miller is both in person and in his work. That Martin Gottfried, in his biography, insists that Miller has no talent for comedy reveals not only how little he knows the man but how little attention he must have paid to the plays he reviewed, few of which are without a humour which at times carries the very values he seeks to endorse.

Yet Miller, whose characters seemed, to some, at times, to avoid any particular ethnic or religious identity, was somehow seldom identified as part of this group, even by its members in their many autobiographies and cultural histories, or, indeed, listed among those Jewish writers who quickly formed the basis for university courses, and this despite *Focus* taking anti-Semitism as its central theme. The 'New York Intellectuals' were a self-defining group. Joseph Heller, among others, certainly never felt he was part of them and nor did Miller. Beyond that, they never showed much interest in drama and American drama could not then, and did not later, win the place on the syllabus claimed by poetry and the novel, and later by critical theory, that sometimes gnomic and self-referring language of academe so opaque beyond the confines of the campus and, to many writers, so alien to the essence of their endeavours.

The fact is that in some respects Miller appears to resist his Jewishness. And yet at a certain level so did many of them. The trick, as Kazin observed, was to 'be a Jew and yet not Jewish; to be of course a liberal, yet to see everything that was wrong with the "imagination of liberalism"; to be Freudian and a master of propriety; academic and yet intellectually avant-garde'.[19] Miller was neither academic nor intellectually avant-garde, but he did live and work within a number of the tensions identified by Kazin.

He remains Jewish in his regard for history, his concern with guilt, his faith in the connection between the individual and the group, his belief in reason modified by passion. On the other hand, he resents appeals for unthinking acquiecence in the policies of a distant state, loyalty to an idea transformed into *realpolitik*. He casually neglects Jewish ceremonies and rites, accepts no limiting precepts. Yet, at the level of theme, his work bears the imprint of a past that has shaped him, a past that reaches further back than Brooklyn or Manhattan, to a rural world in which time itself seemed to stretch and breathe, as in America it rushed forward fuelled by the energy of ambition. It was, however, a world in which need and fear had led his family to move on, as Jews had always moved on.

From time to time he would lament the loss of an identity that was a product of a faith he could no longer embrace. But such anxiety, occasionally breaking surface, suggests nothing so much as a yearning for connection and yet a simul-taneous suspicion of an unquestioning embrace of the tribe. His art might be social but his instincts as a writer are to withdraw, to stand back, to be solitary.

Despite his unwillingness to address or speak out of a particular group, he continued to reveal a sensibility shaped by those with whom he maintained an ambiguous relationship. Jews, in some senses like Americans, are separate from and yet part of him. He may not have wished to address only his own kind, but the paradox was resolved by the fact that the Jewish experience was simultaneously narrowly focused and outward. The ultimate irony, of course, is that for most of the world Arthur Miller is the embodiment of the America from which he feels displaced.

The axiom that cosmopolitanism is Jewish parochialism neatly suggests the simultaneous legacy of internationalism and privileged detachment that sometimes defines the Jewish perspective. Certainly, Miller, who grew up with a German-speaking grandfather and a Polish-born father, was amenable to an internationalist perspective. He was inspired by Dickens and read Dostoevsky. Marx and Freud entered his bloodstream with relatively little resistance. In the mid-1930s, Spain would matter as much to him as strikes in Detroit. At the same time the internationalism that was, perhaps, a legacy of Judaism convinced him that Judaism was itself limited in its concerns, representative of outmoded ways of thought.

Perhaps internationalism was a way of breaking with another kind of provincialism. It was to lay claim to loyalties beyond the tribe. Marrying a Catholic, as he did, was not an ecumenical gesture but was perhaps offered, to himself at least, as an aggressive sign of disregard for what he then saw as an outmoded tradition, his wife seeing her own Catholicism in the same light. Yet that tradition remained a part of him. His roots, like those of so many Americans, lay outside the country, but more specifically they lay in a Jewish experience that was, in fact, never quite to leave him, at the level of imagination, moral commitment, ontological concern. Ironically, when his daughter Rebecca became a Catholic in her teenage years, he became angry though she was betraying a faith he no longer embraced. Meaning, it seems, so often exists in the tension between mind and instincts.

There is one last aspect of his Jewishness that is worth remarking upon. Alfred Kazin has observed of his mother that she would 'never accomplish anything except us'.[20] The real drama behind most Jewish novels and plays, he suggests, is the contrast between what he calls the hysterical tenderness of the Oedipal relation and the world; Jews may not believe in original sin, but they do believe in the love they first knew in the kitchen, in the Jewish household. Moving out into the world, therefore, becoming a writer, is thus an ambiguous adventure, both a fulfilment and a denial.

There was, indeed, something remarkably similar in Kazin's experiences and Miller's. Here is Kazin, acutely conscious 'of my father's powerlessness . . . I used to think of him', he remarks, 'as "the orphan" . . . I felt myself engulfed in my parents' marriage; trapped in their loneliness with each other . . . I was attentive to every minute shade of feeling and temperament in everyone around me . . . was full of my commanding, endlessly resourceful work slave of a mother, my reclusive, ungiving father.'[21] There was, Miller has said, an element of the orphan about his father, abandoned for a while by his family. His parents' marriage, too, turned into a trap, with his father retreating into naps, shutting out the truth of his situation, and his mother working to keep the family solvent. Both sons left their families to become writers, the justification of their parents' efforts and yet in some sense betraying them by leaving.

Admittedly, Kazin's comments on Jewish writing and its connection to the Jewish family drift close to stereotype, but to read Miller's diaries and public remarks is to be reminded how inclined he is to revert to his family relationships as a clue to his own psyche and to his work. His readings of Freud alerted him to such tensions. On the other hand, his own exposure to Greek drama, the source for Freud's metaphors, had already done as much. The battles he would observe in his family home, battles in which he felt himself manoeuvred into taking sides, left him acutely aware that the idea of patricide tended to surface in his work and that the incestuous pull, a mother love charged with something more, also threaded through his drama. His leaving home had the feel of treachery, his very linguistic fluency an implicit challenge to his illiterate father. His mother's love, meanwhile, he knew was contaminated with her increasing scorn for her husband. The result was a drama in which the family becomes the site of moral and psychological battles, with guilt the price for leaving or for staying. In later years he would lament his failure fully to mourn his mother, whose love had been both sustaining and tainted, unsure, as he was, of her motives and hence uncertain of his own, though never doubting the crucial nature of that relationship.

His mother features in three of his plays – *No Villain, After the Fall* and *The American Clock* – his father, either directly or by inference in these and, as an absent force, in *The Price* and perhaps an early version of *The Ride Down Mount Morgan*. What there is not, though, is the feeling that some comfort has been lost, that the world can be gained only by losing a familial paradise. But that is seldom there in other Jewish novels or plays. The step into the world is fraught with dangers, but the family, even when offered a retrospective grace, is itself profoundly ambiguous.

For Irving Howe, however, that step was something more than the natural process whereby a child moves out into the world or a family loses the coherence it once had: 'it was the ferocious loyalty of Jews to the idea of the family as they knew it, the family as the locus of experience and as the fulfillment of their obligation to perpetuate their line, that enabled them to survive'.[22] Beyond that, to leave the family is to recreate that initial step in which an earlier generation had turned away from the country of their birth and sought redemption in an alien world, which had to be transformed in order to become inhabitable. Perhaps that is a defining quality of the Jewish writer, or, indeed, the immigrant writer: a sense of a world elsewhere, whether an abandoned family, a country relinquished to make the act of invention more possible, or a faith renegotiated to make assimilation less a betrayal than a legitimate action.

Yet, in the end, what seems so Jewish, as Freud suggested, had its own deep structure. It was an archetypal experience and that, perhaps, is why so many were to interpret Miller's specificities in terms of their own experience. Willy Loman was to be seen as everyone's father. The disappointed and frustrated mother from *After the Fall* and *The American Clock* reverberated in the minds of generations who had seen their own mothers sacrifice themselves for their sons and daughters and thereby leave them with a love forever entwined with guilt and potential resentment. Chris Keller in *All My Sons*, Biff Loman in *Death of a Salesman*, have, in effect to abandon their parents, and even commit an act of patricide, in order to become themselves. That theme, which Kazin saw as quintessentially Jewish, was familiar enough to allow Miller's work to slide effortlessly between cultures, to make his experience as the son and grandson of Jewish immigrants speak to those whose knowledge of the world was different but whose experience of the ambivalences of love and the tension between home and the world was the same.

There was a time, in the 1950s, when he was accused of being insufficiently attentive to the growing evidence of Soviet anti-Semitism. Old loyalties, it seemed, were simply not susceptible of contrary evidence. If it was so he would more than make amends as he took up the cause of Soviet writers, often Jews, persecuted and imprisoned. In 1964, before his first trip to Russia, he wrote a careful article in which he confessed to the limits of his knowledge and yet levelled a tentative accusation. Yevtushenko's poem 'Babi Yar' had been condemned, Jewish food was banned, criminals identified as Jews. In formulating a complaint he staked out his own territory. 'I am not religious. I do not believe in Jehovah . . . I believe, nonetheless, that I am a Jew . . . What is at stake here for me, therefore, is not a religion but the good name of a people, a people that has in fact suffered beyond all measure of its possible failings.' He spoke not only of but for a people, a people that he plainly acknowledged as his own. At the same time he has insisted that, 'I had already been programmed to choose something other than pride in my origins' (*T.*24).

He has spoken of one day listening to Gershwin's Piano Concerto on the radio, tears streaming down his face, partly from sheer pleasure but partly for the 'Jewish heart of it', a Jewish heart to which he responded not out of a shared faith but a shared history. In 1994, he set his play *Broken Glass* in the Brooklyn to which his parents had brought him when their dreams began to dissolve. It addressed the threatened destruction of the Jewish race. Their faith was not his, but their anxieties and hopes were. He was an American, but he was also, in spirit, a Jew, for whom forgetting the past was a sin against identity itself. As he said of the Old Testament, the more he lives, the more he believes that somewhere it poured into his ear. Indeed, it was something more than the Old Testament: 'my skin had been absorbing some 2000 years of Jewish history' (*T*.24).

In 2002, at the age of eighty-six, he published a story set in 1936 called 'The Performance',[23] in which a Jewish performer comes face to face with Adolf Hitler, the embodiment, the acme of centuries of fear. Two stories come into confrontation, two narratives, two dreams. One story was to prove deadly, unwinding a history back to its beginnings. The other contained a mystery, never quite resolved. The Jew is seduced by the sheer intensity of the attention offered to him, rather as Montezuma had been mesmerised by Cortes in *The Golden Years*, written some sixty years earlier. In Hitler, there is a man who cares enough to kill the Jew if he recognises him for what he is. Such implacability is a mystery not to be understood then or, it seems, later, except perhaps through revisiting that time in story in the hope that meaning will precipitate out. The Jew in his story escapes to tell his exemplary tale. Miller, himself, never quite of them, never quite apart, has also used story to explore and explain the nature of identity, his own and that of those who, like him, have a heritage which reaches back beyond the seeming confidence of a City on the Hill. He, too, has escaped and hence feels a special responsibility to tell his story, though not a story of Jews alone. It is the story of a flawed humanity and the necessity not merely to survive but survive with meaning.

Miller has said that 'in every man there is one thing he cannot give up and still remain himself – a core, an identity, a thing that is summed up for him by the sound of his own name on his own ears'.[24] It is tempting to feel that that 'one thing' might be his Jewishness. More truthfully, though, it is his writing, his one true religion, though that in turn serves something else: his belief in the capacity of a flawed humanity to construct meaning, and the necessity for the individual to acknowledge responsibility for his own fate and the state of his society.

NOTES

1 THE MICHIGAN PLAYS

1. All quotations are from the unpublished text held at the University of Michigan.
2. These papers are held at the University of Michigan.
3. All quotations are from the unpublished text held at the University of Michigan.
4. All quotations are from the copy of the unpublished text held at the Billy Rose Theatre Collection, Library of the Performing Arts, Lincoln Center.
5. All quotations are from the unpublished text held at the Harry Ransom Humanities Research Center, University of Texas at Austin.
6. Unpublished text held at the University of Michigan.
7. Unpublished text held at the University of Michigan.
8. Interview with the author, 2003.

2 'THE GOLDEN YEARS', 'THE HALF-BRIDGE', 'BORO HALL NOCTURNE'

1. Arthur Miller, Introduction, *'The Golden Years' and 'The Man Who Had All the Luck'* (London, 1989), p. 5.
2. Howard Blue, *Words at War* (Lanham, 2002), p. 82.
3. Miller, *'The Golden Years'*, p. 53.
4. *Ibid.*, p. 76.
5. *Ibid.*, p. 78.
6. *Ibid.*, p. 93.
7. *Ibid.*, p. 107.
8. Miller, 'Introduction', *'The Golden Years'*, pp. 7–8.
9. Miller, *'The Golden Years'*, p. 106.
10. All quotations are from the unpublished text held at the Harry Ransom Humanities Research Center, University of Texas at Austin.
11. Unpublished text held at the Harry Ransom Center, University of Texas at Austin.
12. Interview with the author, 2003.

3 THE RADIO PLAYS

1. In Erik Barnouw, *Radio Drama in Action: Twenty-Five Plays of a Changing World* (New York, 1945), p. 268.
2. Alfred Kazin, *New York Jew* (New York, 1978), p. 5.
3. Unattributed quotations from Miller's radio plays in this chapter are taken from programme recordings in the author's possession.
4. Typescript held at the Harry Ransom Center, University of Texas at Austin.
5. Arthur Miller, *Glider Doctor*, transmitted 20 June 1944. Typescript held at the Harry Ransom Center, University of Texas at Austin.
6. Arthur Miller, *The Doctor Fights*, programme 4, transmitted June 27, 1944. A typescript of the programme is held at the Harry Ransom Center of the University of Texas at Austin.
7. Interview with the author, May, 2002.
8. Interview with the author 4 October 2003.
9. David Mamet, *Writing in Restaurants* (New York, 1986), pp. 14–15.
10. Arthur Miller, *Situation Normal* (New York, 1944), p. 5. Further page references appear in parenthesis in the text.

4 'THE MAN WHO HAD ALL THE LUCK'

1. There are a few copies of this novel, at various stages. These references are to a copy given to me by Arthur Miller. Since page numbering is erratic and the typescript is not in the public domain I have omitted page numbers.
2. Arthur Miller, *'The Golden Years' and 'The Man Who Had All the Luck'* (London, 1989), p. 124.
3. *The Best Plays of 1944-H5*, ed. Burns Mantle (New York, 1946), p. 8.
4. Bristol Old Vic programme, June 1988.
5. *Ibid.*
6. Miller, *'The Golden Years'*, p. 231.
7. Quoted in Mel Gussow, 'Life, He Thought, Meant Waiting for One Bad Thing', *New York Times*, 28 April 2002, Arts, p. 9.
8. Arthur Miller, *Focus* (New York, 1945), p. 131.
9. George Steiner, *No Passion Spent: Essays 1978–1996* (London, 1996), p. 340. Further page references appear in parenthesis in the text.

5 'FOCUS'

1. David Reisman, *The Lonely Crowd* (London, 1961), p. 23.
2. *Ibid.*
3. Arthur Miller, *Focus* (New York, 1945), pp. 94, 132. Further page references appear in parenthesis in the text.

4. Irving Malin, ed., *Saul Bellow and the Critics* (London, 1967), p. 3.
5. Bruno Bettelheim, *Recollections and Reflections* (London, 1990), p. 251.
6. *Ibid.*
7. *Ibid.*, p. 252.
8. *Ibid.*, p. 261.
9. *Ibid.*, p. 269.
10. Saul Bellow, *The Victim* (London, 1965), p. 185.
11. *Ibid.*, p. 186.

6 'ALL MY SONS'

1. Arthur Miller, *Echoes Down the Corridor: Collected Essays, 1944–2000*, ed. Steven R. Centola (London, 2000), p. 32.
2. Arthur Miller, *Situation Normal* (New York, 1944), p. 33. Further page references appear in parenthesis in the text.
3. Arthur Miller, 'Ibsen and the Drama of Today', in *The Cambridge Companion to Ibsen*, ed. James McFarlane (Cambridge, 1994), p. 227.
4. Arthur Miller, '*A View from the Bridge*' *and* '*All My Sons*' (Harmondsworth, 1961), p. 104. Further page references appear in parenthesis in the text.
5. Arthur Miller, *The Theater Essays of Arthur Miller*, ed. Robert A. Martin and Steven R. Centola (New York, 1996), p. 129.
6. Matthew Roudané, *Conversations with Arthur Miller* (Jackson, 1987), p. 129.
7. Martin and Centola, eds., *Theater Essays*, p. 128.
8. *Ibid.*, p. 130.
9. Edvard Beyer, *Ibsen: The Man and his Work*, trans. Marie Wells (London, 1978), p. 138.
10. *Miller Shorts*, a series of four brief television programmes for BBC Education, 1999.
11. *Ibid.*
12. Roudané, *Conversations with Arthur Miller*, p. 101.
13. *Ibid.*
14. Christopher Bigsby, ed., *Miller and Company* (London, 1989), p. 50.
15. Roudané, *Conversations with Arthur Miller*, p. 101.
16. *Miller Shorts.*
17. *Ibid.*
18. *Ibid.*
19. *Ibid.*
20. Steven R. Centola, *The Achievement of Arthur Miller: New Essays* (Dallas, 1995), p. 20.
21. Roudané, *Conversations With Arthur Miller*, pp. 362–3.
22. Typescripts are held at the Harry Ransom Center, University of Texas at Austin.
23. Martin and Centola, eds., *Theater Essays*, p. 551.

7 'DEATH OF A SALESMAN'

1. Arthur Miller, *The Theater Essays of Arthur Miller*, ed. Robert A. Martin and Steven R. Centola (New York, 1996), p. 419.
2. *Ibid.*, p. 136.
3. *Ibid.*, p. 420.
4. Matthew Roudané, *Conversations with Arthur Miller* (London, 1987), p. 17.
5. Martin and Centola, eds., *Theater Essays*, p. 423.
6. Arthur Miller, *'Salesman' in Beijing* (London, 1984), p. 49.
7. *Death of a Salesman* notebook held at the Harry Ransom Center, University of Texas at Austin.
8. Miller, *'Salesman' in Beijing*, p. 79.
9. Martin and Centola, eds., *Theater Essays*, p. 423.
10. Roudané, *Conversations with Arthur Miller*, p. 17.
11. Miller, *'Salesman' in Beijing*, p. 14.
12. *Ibid.*, p. 22.
13. *Ibid.*, p. 50.
14. Earl Shorris, *A Nation of Salesmen: The Tyranny of the Market and the Subversion of Culture* (New York, 1994), pp. 10–11.
15. *Ibid.*, p. 331.
16. Miller, *'Salesman' in Beijing*, p. 90.
17. *Ibid.*, p. 130.
18. *Ibid.*
19. Arthur Miller, *Death of a Salesman* (New York, 1998), pp. 59–61.
20. *Ibid.*, p. 106.
21. *Ibid.*, p. 105.
22. Timothy B. Spears, *100 Years on the Road* (New Haven, 1995), p. 219.
23. Miller, *'Salesman' in Beijing*, p. 151.
24. *Ibid.*, p. 151.
25. Miller, *Death of a Salesman*, p. 91.
26. Miller, *'Salesman' in Beijing*, p. 152.
27. Miller, *Death of a Salesman*, p. 75.
28. Quoted in Spears, *100 Years on the Road*, pp. 424–429.
29. Erich Fromm, *Fear of Freedom* (London, 1942), p. 226.
30. Erich Fromm, *The Art of Loving* (London, 1957), p. 74.
31. *Ibid.*, p. 86
32. Miller, *'Salesman' in Beijing*, p. 78.
33. Letter to Stephen Marino.
34. *Ibid.*
35. Miller, *'Salesman' in Beijing*, p. 49.
36. *Ibid.*
37. Arthur Miller, Letter to 'George', 6 June 1975, in Arthur Miller's private papers.

38. F. Scott Fitzgerald, *The Great Gatsby* (Harmondsworth, 1950), p. 188.
39. Arthur Miller, *New York Times*, 5 February 1950.

8 ARTHUR MILLER: TIME-TRAVELLER

1. Arthur Miller, 'On Broadway: Notes on the Past and Future of the American Theatre', *Harper's Magazine*, March 1999, p. 38.
2. Quoted in Amy Lippman, 'Rhythm and Truths', *American Theatre*, April 1984, p. 11.
3. Arthur Miller, 'Preface', *Death of a Salesman* (New York, 1999), p. ix.
4. Quoted in Jonathan Morse, *Word by Word: The Language of Memory* (Ithaca, 1990), pp. 28–9.
5. *Ibid.*, p. 69.
6. Nathaniel Hawthorne, *The Scarlet Letter* (London, 1992), p. 173.
7. Arthur Miller, *The Theater Essays of Arthur Miller*, ed. Robert A. Martin and Steven R. Centola (New York, 1996), p. 180.
8. T. S. Eliot, *The Selected Prose of T. S. Eliot* (London, 1975), p. 32. Further page references appear in parenthesis in the text.
9. William Faulkner, *Requiem for a Nun* (Harmondsworth, 1960), p. 81.
10. L. P. Hartley, *The Go-Between* (London, 1953).
11. John Fowles, *Wormholes* (London, 1998), p. xii.
12. Interview with the author, 3 January 1999.
13. Miller, '*Salesman* at Fifty', in *Death of a Salesman*, p. xii.
14. *Ibid.*
15. Martin and Centola, eds., *Theater Essays*, p. 427.
16. *Death of a Salesman* notebook held at the Harry Ransom Center, University of Texas at Austin.
17. Interview with the author, 3 January 1999.
18. Studs Terkel, *Hard Times: An Oral History of the Great Depression* (New York, 1970), p. 93.
19. Fania Fenelon, *Playing for Time*, trans. Judith Landry (London, 1977).
20. Martin and Centola, eds., *Theater Essays*, p. 422.
21. Arthur Miller, 'Ibsen and the Drama of Today', in *The Cambridge Companion to Ibsen*, ed. James McFarlane (Cambridge, 1994), pp. 229–30.
22. Quoted in Richard Gray, *Writing the South* (Cambridge, 1986), p. 272.
23. Arthur Miller, *Death of a Salesman* (New York, 1998), p. 74.
24. Quoted in Alan J. Parkin, *Memory, Phenomena, Experiment, and Theory* (Oxford, 1993), p. 2.
25. See Ernow Haigen's analysis, 'Ibsen as Fellow Traveler', in *Scandinavian Studies*, 51, 1979, 345–53.
26. Benjamin Nelson, *Arthur Miller: Portrait of a Playwright* (London, 1970).

9 'AN ENEMY OF THE PEOPLE'

1. Arthur Miller, *The Theater Essays of Arthur Miller*, ed. Robert A. Martin and Steven R. Centola (New York, 1996), p. 399.

2. Henrik Ibsen, *Speeches and New Letters*, trans. Arne Kildal (New York, 1972), pp. 53–4.
3. *Ibid.*, p. 98.
4. Henrik Ibsen, *'The Pillars of Society' and Other Plays by Henrik Ibsen* (London, 1890), p. 249.
5. *Ibid.*, pp. 284–5.
6. *Ibid.*, pp. 287–8.
7. Arthur Miller, *'An Enemy of the People' by Henrik Ibsen* (New York, 1951), p. 58.
8. Ibsen, *'The Pillars of Society' and Other Plays*, p. 304.
9. Robert Brustein, *The Theatre of Revolt* (London, 1965), p. 72.
10. *Ibid.*, p. 71.
11. Ibsen, *'The Pillars of Society' and Other Plays*, p. 315.
12. Miller, *'An Enemy of the People' by Henrik Ibsen*, p. 77.
13. *Ibid.*, p. 62.
14. Ibsen, *'The Pillars of Society' and Other Plays*, p. 294.

10 'THE CRUCIBLE'

1. *The Crucible* notebook held at the Harry Ransom Center, University of Texas at Austin.
2. Christopher Bigsby, ed., *Arthur Miller and Company* (London, 1990), p. 81.
3. Marion L. Starkey, *The Devil in Massachusetts: A Modern Enquiry into the Salem Witch Trials* (New York, 1969).
4. Arthur Miller, *The Crucible* (Harmondsworth, 2000), p. 57. Further page references appear in parenthesis in the text.
5. All quotations from the original screenplay are from a typescript in the author's possession.
6. John and Alice Griffin, 'Arthur Miller Discusses *The Crucible*', *Theatre Arts*, vol. 37, October 1953, pp. 53–4.
7. Bigsby, ed., *Arthur Miller and Company*, p. 95.
8. Gerald Weales, ed., *The Crucible: Text and Criticism* (New York, 1971), p. 422.
9. *Ibid.*
10. Arthur Miller, 'Brewed in the Crucible', *New York Times*, 9 March 1958, II, p. 3
11. Sheila Huftel, *The Burning Glass* (New York, 1965), p. 146.
12. *Ibid.*, p. 147.
13. Weales, ed., *The Crucible: Text and Criticism*, p. 240.
14. *Ibid.*, p. 241.
15. Bigsby, ed., *Arthur Miller and Company*, pp. 90–92.
16. Griffin and Griffin, 'Arthur Miller Discusses *The Crucible*', pp. 33–4.
17. Starkey, *The Devil in Massachusetts*, p. 227.
18. Henry Hewes, 'Arthur Miller and How He Went to the Devil', *Saturday Review*, 36, 31 January 1953, p. 225.
19. Arthur Miller, *'The Crucible in History' and Other Essays* (London, 2000), p. 3.
20. *Ibid.*

21. *Ibid.*, pp. 26–8.
22. *Ibid.*, pp. 34–5.
23. Larry Gregg, *The Salem Witch Crisis* (Westgate, 1992), p. 50.
24. Miller, 'The Crucible in History', p. 55.
25. Starkey, *The Devil in Massachusetts*, p. 230.
26. Griffin and Griffin, 'Arthur Miller Discusses *The Crucible*', p. 33.
27. *Ibid.*, pp. 33–4.
28. *Ibid.*, p. 34.
29. Arthur Miller, 'Author's Note', *The Crucible: A Screenplay* (London, 1996), p. vii.
30. *Ibid.*
31. 'Director's Foreword', *The Crucible: A Screenplay*, p. ix.
32. *Ibid.*, p. x.
33. *Ibid.*, p. ix.
34. *Ibid.*, p. x.
35. *Ibid.*, p. xi.
36. *Ibid.*, p. xiii.
37. Gregg, *The Salem Witch Crisis*, p. 129.

12 'A VIEW FROM THE BRIDGE'

1. Arthur Miller, *The Theater Essays of Arthur Miller*, ed. Robert A. Martin and Steven R. Centola (New York, 1996), p. 426.
2. *Ibid.*, p. 66.
3. *Ibid.*, p. 220.
4. *Ibid.*, p. 67.
5. *Ibid.*, p. 220.
6. Arthur Miller, 'A Memory of Two Mondays' and 'A View from the Bridge' (New York, 1955), p. 158.
7. Martin and Centola, eds., *Theatre Essays*, p. 68.
8. Christopher Bigsby, ed., *Arthur Miller and Company* (London, 1990), p. 116.
9. Martin and Centola, eds., *Theater Essays*, p. 426.
10. *Ibid.*, p. 427.
11. Miller, 'A Memory of Two Mondays' and 'A View from the Bridge', p. 85.
12. Arthur Miller, 'A View from the Bridge' and 'All My Sons' (Harmondsworth, 1961), p. 11. Further references in the text are to this edition.
13. *Ibid.*, p. 62.
14. *Ibid.*, p. 83.
15. Miller, 'A Memory of Two Mondays' and 'A View from the Bridge', pp. 159–60.
16. Miller, *A View from the Bridge*, p. 85.
17. Martin and Centola, eds., *Theater Essays*, p. 221.
18. Bigsby, ed., *Arthur Miller and Company*, p. 111.
19. *Ibid.*

20. Miller, *A View from the Bridge*, p. 21.
21. Interview with the author, 2000.
22. *Ibid.*
23. *Ibid.*
24. *Ibid.*
25. Bigsby, ed., *Arthur Miller and Company*, p. 113.

13 TRAGEDY

1. In P. E. Easterling, ed., *The Cambridge Companion to Greek Tragedy* (Cambridge, 1997).
2. Quoted in Raymond Williams, *Modern Tragedy* (London, 1969), p. 33.
3. *Ibid.*, p. lv.
4. *Ibid.*, p. lvi.
5. George Steiner, *No Passion Spent: Essays 1978–1996* (London, 1996), p. 134.
6. *Ibid.*, p. 134.
7. *Ibid.*, p. 135.
8. *Ibid.*, p. 37.
9. *Ibid.*
10. *Ibid.*, p. 40.
11. Arthur Miller, *The Theater Essays of Arthur Miller*, ed. Robert A. Martin and Steven R. Centola (New York, 1996), p. lvii.
12. *Ibid.*, p. 4.
13. Williams, *Modern Tragedy*, p. 87.
14. *Ibid.*, p. 103.
15. *Ibid.*, p. 100.
16. *Ibid.*, p. 104.
17. *Ibid.*, p. 104.
18. *Ibid.*, p. 105.
19. *Ibid.*
20. Karl Jaspers, *Tragedy Is Not Enough* (New York, 1969), p. 11.
21. *Ibid.*, p. 12.
22. Martin and Centola, eds., *Theater Essays*, pp. 4, 5.
23. *Ibid.*, p. 5.
24. *Ibid.*, p. 7.
25. *Ibid.*, pp. 5–6.
26. *Ibid.*, p. 97.
27. *Ibid.*, p. 7.
28. Jaspers, *Tragedy Is Not Enough*, p. 41.
29. *Ibid.*, p. 52.
30. *Ibid.*, pp. 55–6.
31. Christopher Bigsby, ed., *Arthur Miller and Company* (London, 1990), p. 110.
32. Martin and Centola, eds., *Theater Essays*, p. 11.

33. Bigsby, ed., *Arthur Miller and Company*, p. 55.
34. Arthur Miller, 'Ibsen and the Drama of Today', in *The Cambridge Companion to Ibsen*, ed. James McFarlane (Cambridge, 1994), p. 231.
35. *Death of a Salesman* notebook held at the Harry Ransom Center, University of Texas at Austin.

14 'THE MISFITS'

1. James Goode *The Story of 'The Misfits'* (New York, 1963), p. 44.
2. *Ibid.*, pp. 67–8.
3. Arthur Miller, *The Misfits* (Harmondsworth, 1961), p. 7. Further page references appear in parenthesis in the text.
4. Goode, *The Story of 'The Misfits'*, p. 45.
5. *Ibid.*, p. 73.
6. *Ibid.*, p. 74.
7. *Ibid.*, p. 75.
8. *Ibid.*, p. 76.
9. *Ibid.*
10. *Ibid.*, p. 78.
11. W. J. Weatherby, *Conversations with Marilyn* (New York, 1992), p. 49.
12. Goode, *The Story of 'The Misfits'*, pp. 205–6.
13. *Ibid.*, p. 247.

15 'AFTER THE FALL'

1. Christopher Bigsby, ed., *Arthur Miller and Company* (London, 1990), p. 140.
2. Arthur Miller, *After the Fall* (London, 1965), p. 78.
3. *Ibid.*, p. 87.
4. Arthur Miller, 'After the Fall', *Saturday Evening Post*, February 1964, p. 32.
5. *Ibid.*
6. Miller, *After the Fall*, p. 21–2. Further page references appear in parenthesis in the text.
7. Elia Kazan, *A Life* (New York, 1989), p. 715.
8. Albert Camus, *The Fall*, trans. Stuart Gilbert (Harmondsworth, 1963), p. 80. Further page references appear in parenthesis in the text.
9. Typescript held at the Harry Ransom Center, University of Texas at Austin.

16 'INCIDENT AT VICHY'

1. Arthur Miller, *Echoes Down the Corridor: Collected Essays, 1944–2000*, ed. Steven R. Centola (London, 2000), pp. 67–8.
2. *Ibid.*, p. 70.

3. Christopher Bigsby, ed., *Arthur Miller and Company* (London, 1990), pp. 139–40.
4. Arthur Miller, *Plays Two* (London, 1986), p. 285. Further page references appear in parenthesis in the text.
5. Leslie Epstein, 'The Unhappiness of Arthur Miller', *Triquarterly*, Summer 1965, p. 172.
6. Harold Clurman, 'Director's Notes: *Incident at Vichy*', *Tulane Drama Review*, vol. 9, Summer 1965, p. 78.
7. Arthur Miller, *The Theater Essays of Arthur Miller*, ed. Robert A. Martin and Steven R. Centola (New York, 1996), p. 432.
8. Matthew Roudané, *Conversations with Arthur Miller* (London, 1987), p. 80.
9. *Ibid.*, p. 145.
10. *Ibid.*, p. 146.
11. Clurman, 'Director's Notes', p. 83.
12. Roudané, *Conversations with Arthur Miller*, p. 339.
13. Erich Fromm, *The Fear of Freedom* (London, 1942), pp. 231–2.
14. Miller, *Echoes Down the Corridor*, p. 70.
15. *Ibid.*
16. *Ibid.*, p. 71
17. *Ibid.*, p. 74.
18. *Ibid.*, p. 66.
19. *Ibid.*, p. 75.
20. *Ibid.*, p. 73.
21. Epstein, 'The Unhappiness of Arthur Miller', p. 172.
22. Albert Camus, *The Fall*, trans. Stuart Gilbert (Harmondsworth, 1963), p. 60.
23. *Ibid.*
24. Clurman, 'Director's Notes', p. 80.
25. Albert Camus, *Carnets 1942–1951*, trans. Philip Thody (London, 1966), p. 103.
26. Barbara Gel, 'Am I My Brother's Keeper?' *New York Times*, 29 November 1964.
27. Philip Rahv, *Literature and the Sixth Sense* (London, 1970), p. 385. Further page references appear in parenthesis in the text.
28. Fromm, *The Fear of Freedom*, p. 180. Further page references appear in parenthesis in the text.
29. Robert Brustein, *Seasons of Discontent: Dramatic Opinions 1959–1965* (London, 1966), pp. 259–69. Further page references appear in parenthesis in the text.

17 'THE PRICE'

1. Arthur Miller, 'The Crucible in History' and Other Essays* (London, 2000), p. 60.
2. Arthur Miller, *The Price* (London, 1968), p. 4. Further page references appear in parenthesis in the text.
3. Matthew Roudané, *Conversations with Arthur Miller* (London, 1987), p. 316.

4. *Ibid.*, p. 329.
5. *Ibid.*, p. 340.
6. *Ibid.*, p. 188.
7. Arthur Miller, *Echoes Down the Corridor: Collected Essays, 1944–2000,* ed. Steven R. Centola (London, 2000), p. 297.
8. *Ibid.*, p. 298.
9. Roudané, *Conversations With Arthur Miller*, p. 340.
10. *Ibid.*, p. 341.

18 'THE CREATION OF THE WORLD AND OTHER BUSINESS'

1. David Rosenberg, ed., *Genesis* (San Francisco, 1996), pp. 36–7.
2. Matthew Roudané, *Conversations with Arthur Miller* (London, 1987), p. 281.
3. Rosenberg, ed., *Genesis*, p. 39.
4. June Schleuter and James K. Flanagan, *Arthur Miller* (New York, 1987), p. 124.
5. Roudané, *Conversations with Arthur Miller*, p. 252.
6. Rosenberg, ed., *Genesis*, p. 39.
7. Roudané, *Conversations with Arthur Miller*, p. 377.

19 'THE ARCHBISHOP'S CEILING'

1. Arthur Miller, *In Russia* (New York, 1969), p. 46.
2. See Arthur Miller, *Echoes Down the Corridor: Collected Essays, 1944–2000,* ed. Steven R. Centola (London, 2000).
3. Mel Gussow, *Conversations with Arthur Miller* (London, 2002), p. 35.
4. Arthur Miller, *Plays 3* (London, 1990), p. 131. Further page references appear in parenthesis in the text.
5. Christopher Bigsby, ed., *Arthur Miller and Company* (London, 1990), p. 172.
6. Miller, *In Russia*, p. 26.
7. *Ibid.*, p. 77.
8. Arthur Miller, 'Introduction: Conditions of Freedom: Two Plays of the Seventies', *The American Clock and The Archbishop's Ceiling* (New York, 1989), p. x.
9. Bigsby, ed., *Arthur Miller and Company*, p. 163.
10. *Ibid.*, p. 164.
11. *Ibid.*, pp. 167–8.

20 'PLAYING FOR TIME'

1. Fania Fenelon, *Playing for Time*, trans. Judith Landry (London, 1977).
2. Arthur Miller, *Playing For Time* (New York, 1981), p. 2 (screenplay). Further page references appear in parenthesis in the text.

3. Arthur Miller, *The Portable Arthur Miller*, ed. Christopher Bigsby (New York, 1995), p. 566.
4. Arthur Miller, *Playing For Time* (New York, 1985), p. 91 (stage version). Further page references appear in parenthesis in the text.
5. Arthur Miller, *Plays Two* (London, 1986), p. 2.
6. *Ibid.*

21 THE SHEARING POINT

1. Jonathan Morse, *Word by Word: The Language of Memory* (Ithaca, 1990), p. 234.
2. George Steiner, *Language and Silence* (London, 1967), p. 201.
3. Lionel Trilling, *The Liberal Imagination* (New York, 1953), p. 256.
4. In Lawrence L. Langer, *The Holocaust and the Literary Imagination* (New Haven, 1975), p. 1.
5. Quoted in Steiner, *Language and Silence*, p. 144.
6. Primo Levi, *The Drowned and the Saved*, trans. Raymond Rosenthal (New York, 1988), pp. 34–5.
7. Quoted in Langer, *The Holocaust and the Literary Imagination*, p. 1.
8. Quoted in Shoshana Felman and Dori Laub, *Testimony: Crises of Witnessing in Literature, Psychoanalysis, and History* (New York, 1992), p. 204.
9. Bruno Bettelheim, *'Surviving' and Other Essays* (London, 1979), p. 97.
10. Langer, *The Holocaust and the Literary Imagination*, p. 30.
11. In Robert Alter, *After the Tradition: Essays on Modern Jewish Writing* (New York, 1971), p. 46.
12. *Ibid.*, p. 50.
13. Felman and Laub, *Testimony*, p. 184.
14. Felman and Laub, *Testimony*, p. xi.
15. Quoted in Howard Blue, *Words at War* (Lanham, 2002), p. 316.
16. Interview with the author, January 1999.
17. Bettelheim, *'Surviving'*, p. 96.
18. Matthew Roudané, *Conversations with Arthur Miller* (London, 1987), p. 80.
19. *Ibid.*, p. 108.
20. Arthur Miller, *Danger: Memory!* (New York, 1986), pp. 59–60.
21. Quoted in Joyce Antler, 'The Americanization of the Holocaust', *American Theatre*, February 1995, p. 69.
22. Bettelheim, *'Surviving'*, p. 104.
23. Arthur Miller, *After the Fall* (London, 1965), p. 127.
24. Roudané, *Conversations with Arthur Miller*, pp. 203–5.
25. *Ibid.*, pp. 185–6.
26. Interview with the author, January 1999.
27. Christopher Bigsby, ed., *Arthur Miller and Company* (London, 1990), p. 233.

28. Quoted in Alan J. Parkin, *Memory, Phenomena, Experiment, and Theory* (Oxford, 1993), p. 1.

22 'THE AMERICAN CLOCK'

1. Matthew Roudané, *Conversations with Arthur Miller* (London, 1987), p. 307–8.
2. Arthur Miller, *The Theater Essays of Arthur Miller*, ed. Robert A. Martin and Steven R. Centola (New York, 1996), p. 479.
3. Interview with the author, 3 January 1999.
4. *Ibid.*
5. *Ibid.*
6. *Ibid.*
7. *Ibid.*
8. *Ibid.*
9. *Ibid.*
10. Arthur Miller, *Plays 3* (London, 1990), p. 5. Further page references appear in parenthesis in the text.
11. Richard Eyre, 'Nothing Will Come of Nothing', *News from the Royal Society of Literature* (1999), p. 21.
12. Interview with the author, 3 January 1999.
13. Roudané, *Conversations with Arthur Miller*, p. 314.
14. *Ibid.*, p. 309.
15. *Ibid.*, p. 313.
16. Martin and Centola, eds., *Theater Essays*, p. 479.
17. Interview with the author, 3 January 1999.
18. *Ibid.*
19. Martin and Centola, eds., *Theater Essays*, p. 483.

23 THE ONE-ACT PLAYS: 'TWO-WAY MIRROR' AND 'DANGER: MEMORY!'

1. Arthur Miller, *Two-Way Mirror* (London, 1984), p. 1. Further page references appear in parenthesis in the text.
2. Arthur Miller, *The Theater Essays of Arthur Miller*, ed. Robert A. Martin and Steven R. Centola (New York, 1996), p. 427.
3. *Ibid.*
4. Author's Note, *Two-Way Mirror*.
5. Arthur Miller, *Plays: Five* (London, 1995), p. 135.
6. Arthur Miller, 'On Screenwriting and Language,' preface to *Everybody Wins* (London, 1990), p. vi. Further page references appear in parenthesis in the text.
7. Miller, *Plays: Five*, p. 140.
8. Mel Gussow, *Conversations with Arthur Miller* (New York, 2002), p. 156.
9. *Ibid.*, p. 133.

10. Arthur Miller, *Danger: Memory!* (New York, 1986), p. 9. Further page references appear in parenthesis in the text.
11. Gussow, *Conversations with Arthur Miller*, p. 133.

24 'THE RIDE DOWN MOUNT MORGAN'

1. Interview with the author, 1991.
2. *Ibid.*
3. *Ibid.*
4. *Ibid.*
5. Arthur Miller, *The Ride Down Mount Morgan* (final acting version) (New York, 1999), p. 31. Further page references appear in parenthesis in the text.
6. Arthur Miller, *The Ride Down Mount Morgan* (London, 1991), p. 13.
7. Interview with the author, September 2001. Further quotations from Patrick Stewart are taken from this interview.
8. Miller, *The Ride Down Mount Morgan* (1991), p. 87.
9. *Ibid.*, p. 5.
10. London Weekend Television, *The South Bank Show*, 1991.
11. *Ibid.*
12. *Ibid.*
13. Address at the Guthrie Theater Global Voices, Forums on Art and Life, 23 March 1997.

25 'THE LAST YANKEE'

1. Arthur Miller, *The Theater Essays of Arthur Miller*, ed. Robert A. Martin and Steven R. Centola (New York, 1996), p. 539.
2. Arthur Miller, *The Last Yankee* (New York, 1991), p. 9. Further page references appear in parenthesis in the text.
3. Arthur Miller, *The Last Yankee* (London, 1993), p. 12. Further page references appear in parenthesis in the text.
4. Martin and Centola, eds., *Theater Essays*, p. 539.
5. *Ibid.*, p. 539.
6. *Ibid.*, pp. 537, 538, 537.
7. *Ibid.*, p. 541.
8. *Ibid.*
9. *Ibid.* p. 540.

26 'BROKEN GLASS'

1. Interview with the author, 1994.
2. Arthur Miller, *Broken Glass* (London, 1994), p. 30. Further page references appear in parenthesis in the text.

3. Interview with the author.
4. *Ibid.*
5. *Ibid.*
6. *Ibid.*

27 'MR PETERS' CONNECTIONS'

1. Interview with the author.
2. *Ibid.*
3. Arthur Miller, *Mr Peters' Connections* (London, 1999), p. 12. Further page references appear in parenthesis in the text.
4. Arthur Miller, *Echoes Down the Corridor: Collected Essays, 1944–2000,* ed. Steven R. Centola (London, 2000), p. 54.
5. Programme note, Almeida Theatre.
6. Interview with the author.
7. Programme note, Almeida Theatre.
8. Interview with the author.
9. *Ibid.*
10. *Ibid.*
11. *Ibid.*
12. Statement made in conversation with Vaclav Havel at the Second International Festival, 'Theatre '94', held at Plzen in Czechoslovakia in 1994.
13. Programme note, Almeida Theatre.
14. Interview with the author.
15. Programme note, Almeida Theatre.
16. Interview with the author.
17. Interview with the author, Theatre Royal, Norwich, October 2000.
18. Arthur Miller, 'Address at the Guthrie Theater Global Voices, Forums on Art and Life', 23 March 1997.
19. Nicholas de Jongh in the *Evening Standard*, 27 July 2000.
20. Quoted in Heather Neill. 'A Playwright Calls', *Independent on Sunday*, 30 July, 2000.
21. Quoted in Dan Hulbert, 'Arthur Miller: a Dramatist for the Ages', *The Atlanta Journal-Constitution*, January 2000.
22. Quoted in 'So Tragic, You Have to Laugh', *New York Times*, 28 July 2002.
23. Miller, *Echoes Down the Corridor*, p. 311.

28 'RESURRECTION BLUES'

1. At the time of writing the play had not been published. References are to a typescript supplied by Arthur Miller.
2. Interview with the author, May 2002.
3. *Ibid.*

4. *Ibid.*
5. *Ibid.*
6. *Ibid.*
7. Saul Bellow, *Ravelstein* (New York, 2000), p. 18.

29 'FINISHING THE PICTURE'

1. This chapter draws on a typescript provided by Arthur Miller in 2003. He continued to revise it through 2003–4.
2. Interview with the author, 4 October 2003.
3. *Ibid.*

30 FICTION

1. Arthur Miller, *I Don't Need You Any More* (London, 1967), p. x. Further page references appear in parenthesis in the text.
2. Ronald Hingley, *Chekhov* (London, 1950), p. 205.
3. Matthew Roudané, *Conversations with Arthur Miller* (London, 1987), p. 87.
4. *Ibid.*, p. 100.
5. *Ibid.*
6. Arthur Miller, 'Presence', *Esquire*, July 2003, pp. 108–9.
7. Arthur Miller, *Homely Girl* (New York, 1992). Further page references appear in parenthesis in the text.
8. At the time of writing, this story had not been published. References are to a typescript provided by Arthur Miller.
9. Saul Bellow, *It All Adds Up: A Non-Fiction Collection* (London, 1994), p. 96. Further page references appear in parenthesis in the text.
10. Bellow, *Ravelstein*, p. 167. Further page references appear in parenthesis in the text.

31 ARTHUR MILLER AS A JEWISH WRITER

1. In Linda Grant, *When I Lived in Modern Times* (London, 2000), n.p.
2. Diana Trilling, *The Beginning of the Journey: The Marriage of Diana and Lionel Trilling* (New York, 1993), pp. 43–4.
3. Arthur Miller, *Focus* (London, 1964), pp. 116–17.
4. Peter Novick, *The Holocaust and Collective Memory: The American Experience* (London, 1999), p. 113.
5. Arthur Miller, speech at his eighty-fifth birthday, University of East Anglia, October 2000.
6. Typescript in Arthur Miller's private papers.

7. Arthur Miller, 'Concerning Jews Who Write', *Jewish Life*, vol. 12, no. 5, March 1948, p. 8. I am indebted to Nathan Abrams for drawing my attention to this article.

8. *Ibid.*, p. 9.

9. *Ibid.*

10. Alfred Kazin, *New York Jew* (New York, 1978), p. 9.

11. Philip Roth, *The Facts* (New York, 1988), pp. 122–3.

12. Alfred Kazin, 'The Jew as Modern Writer', in Peter Rose, ed., *The Ghetto and Beyond* (New York, 1969), p. 423.

13. Arthur Miller, 'Israel: You Will Never Know Peace Until You Rediscover Justice', *The Times*, 3 July 2003, T2, p. 5.

14. In Gitta Sereny, *Albert Speer: His Battle with Truth*, quoted in David Edgar, *Albert Speer* (London, 2000), p. 89.

15. George Steiner, *Errata* (London, 1997), pp. 9–10.

16. Arthur Miller, 'Waiting for the Teacher', *Harper's*, July 1998.

17. Kazin, *New York Jew*, p. 44.

18. 'Under Forty: a Symposium on American Literature and the Younger Generation of American Jews', *Contemporary Jewish Record*, 7, 1944, pp. 32–4.

19. Kazin, *New York Jew*, pp. 44–5.

20. *Ibid.*, p. 16.

21. *Ibid.*, p. 12.

22. Irving Howe, *The World of Our Father* (New York, 1978), p. 124.

23. Arthur Miller, 'The Performance', *New Yorker*, 22–9 April 2002, pp. 176–88.

24. Ira Wolfert, 'Arthur Miller, Playwright in Search of His Identity', *New York Herald Tribune*, 25 January, 1953, IV, 3.

INDEX